PROFESSIONAL PRACTICE FOR

Interior Designers

PROFESSIONAL PRACTICE FOR

Interior Designers

Fourth Edition

Christine M. Piotrowski, FASID, IIDA

John Wiley & Sons, Inc.

For my parents, Martha and Casmer:
I am sorry you are not here to share this with me.

Published by John Wiley & Sons, Inc., Hoboken, New Jersey
Published simultaneously in Canada

Limit of Liability/Disclaimer of Warranty: While the publisher and the author have used their
best efforts in preparing this book, they make no representations or warranties with respect to
the accuracy or completeness of the contents of this book and specifically disclaim any implied
warranties of merchantability or fitness for a particular purpose. No warranty may be created or
extended by sales representatives or written sales materials. The advice and strategies contained
herein may not be suitable for your situation. You should consult with a professional where
appropriate. Neither the publisher nor the author shall be liable for any loss of profit or any
other commercial damages, including but not limited to special, incidental, consequential, or
other damages.

For general information about our other products and services, please contact our Customer
Care Department within the United States at (800) 762-2974, outside the United States
at (317) 572-3993 or fax (317) 572-4002.

Wiley also publishes its books in a variety of electronic formats. Some content that appears in
print may not be available in electronic books. For more information about Wiley products,
visit our web site at www.wiley.com.

Anniversary Logo Design: Richard J. Pacifico

Library of Congress Cataloging-in-Publication Data:

Piotrowski, Christine M., 1947–
    Professional practice for interior designers/Christine Piotrowski.—4th ed.
        p. cm.
    Includes bibliographical references and index.
    ISBN: 978-0-471-76086-3 (cloth)
    1. Interior decoration firms—United States—Management. 2. Design services—
United States—Marketing. 3. Interior decoration—Practice. I. Title.
    NK2116.2.P57 2007
    747.068—dc22   2007032148

Printed in the United States of America

10 9 8 7 6 5 4 3

CONTENTS

The profession of interior design is challenging and competitive. Being a professional interior designer, however, is more than creating exciting interior spaces. Those within the profession must willingly accept the legal, ethical, social, and business responsibilities that go with being a professional interior designer in the twenty-first century. Clients expect excellence not only in creative work but in conduct as well. Ethics complaints and legal challenges have increased, indicating that clients demand more from interior designers in today's profession.

Part of the education of an interior designer rests in learning about the business practices of the profession and how these practices impact the creative side of interior design. Regardless of the size of firm or design specialty, professional interior designers must understand and conduct themselves as businesspeople. Today, clients are more inclined to question a designer's decisions and hold interior designers responsible, resulting in an ever-increasing need for comprehensive knowledge of business. This knowledge contributes to the welfare of the client by saving money and creating value in design decisions.

Since its first publication in 1990, this book has become the leading choice of educators for use in teaching an interior design business practices course. This book is also embraced by professionals who tell me they continually refer to the topics within this book as they work for others or start their own practices. This new edition adds a wealth of answers to practical questions about the practice itself for the already engaged professional.

As the practice of interior design continues to be transformed through the challenges of legislation, sustainable design, aging in place, advancing electronic technologies, and generational changes in the workplace, so has the professional practice of interior design. Information and ideas on revisions for the fourth edition were obtained from working professionals, educators, and industry associations. A large body of business topics literature was reviewed to ascertain current information on business in general and interior design business in particular.

In addition, this book has been thoroughly reviewed to bring additional clarity to the content. Some sections have been relocated to improve the logical arrangement of topics. New material has been added to every chapter, whether through updated information, new examples, revised methods of practice, or topics that have evolved since the previous edition.

The text remains easy to read, with many new examples added to help explain some of the more difficult topics. In this edition, each chapter now begins with a list of key terms and concepts, as well as a list of critical issues. Also added to each chapter are brief case studies or scenarios called "What Would You Do?" describing situations that present, for the most part, ethical questions. These scenarios will no doubt encourage discussion and debate whether by students or professionals.

Practitioners will continue to find this book to be a thorough discussion of every aspect of planning and maintaining the business tasks of interior design. Several new discussions have been added that focus on topics more attuned to the professional. Many topics have been expanded and new items included so that this book continues to be a comprehensive text on interior design business practices.

Let me share with you highlights of the changes and additions to the fourth edition of this book.

Part I and Part II provide a comprehensive overview of the profession. The chapters in Part I offer a foundation for professional practice. Topics include defining a profession, why the study of business practices is important, the NCIDQ examination, professional association requirements, the importance of licensing, pursuing continuing education, and giving back to the profession. Because it was strongly suggested that one should not be discussed without the other, Chapters 3 and 4 in Part I bring together critical ethics and legal responsibilities issues. The chapters in Part II focus on goals and career options. This combination was suggested by educators to show students that there is more to the profession than working in either "residential" or "commercial" design.

A major restructuring of Part III brings more clarity and order to the topics about establishing an interior design practice. The reader is led through the process of examining motivations and risks, as well as decisions concerning the structure and legal formation. Part III then culminates with the preparation of a business plan. Students and practitioners will learn that starting a business is certainly a goal worth achieving, but not one to be taken on lightly.

Part IV has been reorganized as well, with a focus on topics needed to help grow a practice. An expanded discussion on strategic planning should be of particular importance to any practitioner with the goals of expanding and enriching his or her practice. The chapters on business organization, personnel management, and business finances have been updated as well.

Educators and professionals suggested that the discussion of marketing and business development be next in the sequence. Part V on marketing and business development has been revised to include information on branding and buyer behavior. The promotional tools chapters have also been reorganized, bringing current practices such as creating and utilizing Web sites into proper focus. In addition, business etiquette is now more succinctly discussed in this part of the book.

Parts VI and VII are thought by many to be the heart of the discussion of professional practice. Part VI focuses on compensation and fees, contracts for interior design services, product pricing explanations, the Uniform Commercial Code, and warranties and products liability. The updated material in Part VII discusses project management trade sources, contract documents, and all facets of contract administration.

Finally, Part VIII places the spotlight on getting a job and settling into a first or next job in interior design. Chapter 33 discusses the job search, portfolios, and resumés. A consolidated section on electronic job-hunting topics has been created for this chapter. The last chapter highlights the interview and the transition from student to professional. A discussion of career change issues for professionals concludes the text.

New to this edition is the listing of Internet Web sites that are included in the References at the back of the book that the reader may wish to search for additional information. These Web sites include listings for professional associations and affiliated associations or organizations that are important to the study of professional practice and the interior design profession. Also included in the References are magazines, journals, and other print media. The glossary has been expanded to include all the new terms that have been introduced in this edition of the text. The long version definition of interior design from the NCIDQ is provided in the Appendix.

For the first time, a companion CD-ROM disc is included with this book. The compact disc contains many additional short articles that supplement the main theme of the chapter as well as copies of business forms included in the text. Some business forms proprietary to a design firm might not be included due to a design firm's request; however, a similar form has been added to the compact disc. A special section on the CD-ROM includes numerous references from older resources that were previously listed in the text. For educators, a revised *Instructor's Manual*, located on the Instructor Companion Web site, can be accessed by contacting the publisher.

This edition also includes a 210-day trial of the Standard edition of Design Manager, a software program for project management and accounting used by many interior design practitioners. This trial version allows students and other readers to experience creating documents and performing accounting procedures by entering information themselves possibly as part of class projects. The author and publisher do not recommend this program over other software programs that are on the market. However, since Design Manager has been widely accepted this trial version offers real world practice with an advanced system. Many designers find general software programs such as Quickbooks to also be of use in their practices. The reader should try out several systems and become proficient in those that are likely to be used in practice.

Thoughtful criticism and suggestions from students, educators, and professionals alike have helped to improve the fourth edition, and I am grateful for their suggestions. It is an honor that this book has been embraced by so many educators who teach the business side of interior design and has been chosen by professionals to assist them with their practices. Thank you to all and I wish you continued success in your professional practices.

A project of this magnitude cannot ever be accomplished without the advice and assistance of many others. First, I want to thank the educators and reviewers who provided suggestions of what to improve and what to leave as is for this edition. Although the reviewers selected by the publisher are anonymous, I want to thank them and also thank Carl Clark from Northern Arizona University, Dr. Carol Morrow from the Art Institute of Phoenix, Robin Wagner from Marymount University, Tom Witt from Arizona State University, and Bob Krikac from Washington State University for their suggestions. I would also like to thank the many professionals who informally provided ideas for items to include or change in the text.

I would like to acknowledge a few individuals who have been so very supportive of this effort over the years, namely, Dave Petroff, IIDA; Fred Messner, IIDA; Jain Malkin, CID; and educators and students too numerous to mention specifically. I also want to give a special thank-you to my good friend Greta Guelich, ASID, for her contributions to this edition.

It is especially important to acknowledge the authors and publishers who have graciously granted permission to use their materials. I would like to thank the American Society of Interior Designers, the National Council for Interior Design Qualification, the International Interior Design Association, the Interior Design Educators Council, the Interior Designers of Canada, and the Council for Interior Design Accreditation for allowing me to reproduce information from their organizations.

A special thank-you is due to those designers who graciously provided their thoughts about the interior design profession as it enters the twenty-first century for the Part Opener pages. I am very greatful to Rosalyn Cama, FASID; Susan Coleman, FIIDA, FIDEC, CID; Marilyn Farrow, FIIDA; Beth Harmon-Vaughn, FIIDA; Charles D. Gandy, FAISD, FIIDA; Jain Malkin, CID; Linda E. Smith, FASID; and Lisa M. Whited, IIDA, ASID, for allowing me to include their thoughts as part of this textbook.

I am indebted to all the firms that have allowed me to reproduce their proprietary materials in this edition. Thank you to Greta Guelich, ASID, Robin Wagner, Kathleen Chaffee, Hickory Business Furniture, and Leonard Alverado of Contract Office Group, along with the many other firms and designers who provided material for previous editions and displayed again in this edition. These numerous designers have been listed in a special acknowledgment on the companion CD-ROM disc.

Finally, I would like to give a special thank-you to Paul Drougas, my editor and good friend. Thank you, Paul, for your patience, support, and understanding. I also want to thank several others at John Wiley & Sons; Amanda Miller my friend and previous editor who saw me through earlier editions of this book; Lauren LaFrance for her assistance with the compact disc, Raheli Millman, and the many others for their help in completing this edition of the book.

Christine Piotrowski

*I*n order to prepare students to compete in the global workplace, we must focus on teaching students how to learn. The most valuable skill that we can teach our students is how to access, analyze, and apply information to the "real world" of design practice. Teachers must become the facilitators of learning. As we move from the industrial age to the age of technology, we must equip students with the skills to become lifelong learners.

Susan Coleman, FIIDA, FIDEC, CID retired after 31 years as a design educator at Orange Coast College. She continues to work as a consultant for Education 4 Work writing grants, developing career development materials, conducting workshops for faculty, and writes a bi-weekly newsletter. In addition, Susan consults with design firms and architects on learning resource projects. Coleman has served in leadership positions with Interior Design Educators Council, International Interior Design Association and California Council for Interior Design Certification. Traveling continues to be a passion with Susan as she takes groups around the globe to study Architecture, Design, Textiles, and Crafts.

The Profession of Interior Design

1. Interior Design as a Profession

What Is Interior Design?
Why Study Professional Practice?
Defining the Profession
History of the Profession
Interior Design Specialties

2. Professional Preparation

Educational Preparation
NCIDQ Examination
The STEP Program
Licensing and Registration
Professional Associations
Continuing Education
Giving Back

3. Ethics and Professional Responsibility

Ethics in the Business Environment
Professional Conduct
Disciplinary Procedures
What Would You Do

4. Legal Responsibilities

The Legal Environment of Interior Design Practice
Criminal versus Tort Law
Negligence
Intentional Torts
Code Compliance
Plan Review Boards

CHAPTER 1

Interior Design as a Profession

Key Terms and Concepts

These terms and concepts are important to material in this chapter. Many of the terms will be utilized in other chapters as well. Be sure you understand these items as you read this chapter.

Terms and Concepts

Interior design

Profession

The six characteristics of a profession

Stakeholders

Ensembliers

Ateliers

Society decorator

Vignette

Residential interior design

Commercial interior design

Contract design

Names

Elsie de Wolfe

Dorothy Draper

William R. Moore

Charles Gelber

Florence Knoll

Quickborner Team

Louis Tregre

Norman de Haan

Organizations

American Institute of Interior Decorators (AIID)

American Institute of Decorators (AID)

National Society of Interior Designers (NSID)

American Institute of Interior Designers (AID)

National Office Products Association (NOPA)

American Society of Interior Designers (ASID)

National Council for Interior Design Qualification (NCIDQ)

Interior Design Educators Council (IDEC)

Council for Interior Design Accreditation (formerly FIDER)

Institute of Business Designers (IBD)

International Society of Interior Designers (ISID)

International Interior Design Association (IIDA)

Unification Task Force

Critical Issues

After completing this chapter you should be able to:

- Discuss why the study of professional practices is important to any entry-level designer.
- Identify the characteristics of a profession.
- Explain how these characteristics relate to the practice of interior design.
- Explain how interior design is different from decorating as if you were talking to a client.
- Discuss some issues as to why it was difficult for professional associations to represent practitioners in the first half of the twentieth century.
- Name the organizations that are now the American Society of Interior Designers and International Interior Design Association.
- Explain why it is important for the National Council for Interior Design Qualification to be an independent organization.
- Compare the practice of residential interior design to commercial interior design.

As a student of interior design or a practitioner, you no doubt already know that the interior design profession is much more than the selection of materials and colors to create a pleasing environment. The design process to solve the problems of a client and meet their needs is complex and always challenging. The body of knowledge and skills needed by professionals today is extensive, and the work of the interior designer—regardless of specialty—is demanding as well as exciting.

The professional interior designer must gain knowledge and proficiency in a wide range of subjects and skills combining elements of architecture, aesthetics, psychology, the use of space, sustainable design, functional planning, safety issues—and business practices. The individuals who design interiors today must be sure that the design meets building, fire safety, and accessibility codes. Their solutions have to meet functional needs of the client, as well as exhibit a pleasing environment. Specifications and planning might well be impacted by sustainable design criteria to limit or eliminate environmental hazards for the occupants.

A designer must be willing to accept the legal and ethical consequences of his or her actions in practice as they relate to the general public and local laws, clients, the profession in general, and other practitioners. The profession of interior design is also a business, and the management and efficient operations of a business are part and parcel to the successful, ongoing life of an interior design practice.

Individuals embark in the interior design profession for many reasons. Some find the challenge of creating exciting spaces like a hotel or restaurant a blend of creative work and functional design. Many designers enjoy developing home environments that enhance spaces and even enrich lives. There are probably as many reasons to enter this exciting and challenging profession as there are those who are involved in the profession.

Designing interiors is not only an enjoyable way to make a living but also an awesome responsibility. Part of that responsibility lies in being professional and businesslike about what we do as a professional. This chapter sets the stage for the study of the professional practice of interior design by defining interior design and discussing why the study of professional business practices is important to the preparation of anyone about to enter the profession. It further provides a historical overview of the profession and concludes with a brief discussion about the design specialties.

WHAT IS INTERIOR DESIGN?

Did you realize that the use of the term *interior design* did not appear in general usage until after World War II? Interior design is a young profession, as you will learn in detail later in this chapter. Individuals and organizations involved in the interior design profession work tirelessly to help the profession gain recognition in the minds of the public, as well as among practitioners and allied professionals.

What constitutes interior design has been debated and nurtured for many decades. Much of the public believes that "People who decorate interiors are interior decorators." They often do not understand that there is a difference. In an article by Charlotte S. Jensen, FASID, then president of the National Council for Interior Design Qualification (NCIDQ) board, "Interior design is not the same as decoration . . . Decoration is the furnishing or adorning a space with fashionable or beautiful things. Decoration, although a valuable and important element of an interior, is not solely concerned with human interaction or human behavior. Interior design is all about human behavior and human interaction."[1] And much more, as many would say.

Here are a few other thoughts on what defines interior design. According to the U.S. Department of Labor, Bureau of Labor Statistics, interior designers "plan, design and furnish interiors of residential, commercial or industrial buildings. Formulate design which is practical, aesthetic, and conducive to intended purposes, such as raising productivity, selling merchandise, or improving life style."[2] On a new Web site providing information on careers in interior design jointly created by several professional associations, this collaborative effort answers the question "what is an interior designer?" by stating, "Interior designers are creative, imaginative and artistic. They also need to be disciplined, organized and skilled business people. Combining knowledge with aesthetic vision, interior designers work with clients and other design professionals to develop design solutions that are safe, functional, attractive, and meet the needs of the people using the space."[3]

The most commonly quoted and utilized definition of interior design comes from the NCIDQ. This definition, offered in part with the complete version presented in the appendix, has been acknowledged and supported by the interior design professional associations.

"Interior design is a multifaceted profession in which creative and technical solutions are applied within a structure to achieve a built interior environment. These solutions are functional, enhance the quality of life and culture of the occupants, and are aesthetically attractive. Designs are created in response to and coordinated with the building shell, and acknowledge the physical location and social context of the project. Designs must adhere to code and regulatory requirements, and encourage the principles of environmental sustainability. The interior design process follows a systematic and coordinated methodology, including research, analysis and integration of knowledge into the creative process, whereby the needs and resources of the client are satisfied to produce an interior space that fulfills the project goals."[4]

WHY STUDY PROFESSIONAL PRACTICE?

The profession of interior design is incredibly fascinating. Practitioners have the opportunity to design the interiors of multimillion-dollar houses or help any family have a more pleasing and nurturing home environment. Practitioners also have the opportunity to assist small businesses or huge business complexes of all kinds provide an interior environment to employees and customers that can help the business achieve greater functionality and success.

The profession of interior design is also a business. If the firm is not successful as a business, it makes no difference how creative the owner and other designers might be. Knowledge and application of business practice concepts is essential to the overall professional practice of interior design. These skills are critical whether the interior designer works for someone else or ventures into ownership. It is also of critical importance to students getting ready to enter into this exciting profession.

When teaching or lecturing to students, I have repeatedly commented that an interior design business practices class is probably one of the two most important classes they will take in their course of study. Maybe it's not the most important, but not having grounding in business as it applies to interior design could mean the difference between success and failure in the profession. Why? Because being professional in both the creative and business side of interior design is part of representing to the public that interior design is a profession. It is not a hobby; it is not the quick, do-it-yourself situation as portrayed on cable TV. It is a creative endeavor that must adhere to codes and laws that exist within the jurisdiction where the firm operates. It is an endeavor that must recognize the importance of ethical conduct. The professional practice of interior design involves standing by the promises made in design contracts with clients and suppliers, as well as many other business issues.

It is easy to understand that an interior design firm must make a profit—or at least hopes to consistently make a profit. But how is that profit obtained? Studying and applying business practices helps the owner of the firm have a greater chance of achieving a profit. It does not happen simply because the individual or group of designers happens to be very creative. The effective management by the owner or managers is important for any firm to achieve a profit. Likewise, the effective work of an employee is necessary for that firm to achieve a profit. If the company wastes funds because of poor business practices, that means there is less for raises or bonuses. It can also mean the business will not last. A poorly operated practice can quickly become a workplace that is no longer enjoyable.

Designers who are not good businesspeople have a harder time doing their job. Clients might argue and second-guess their decisions. Clients file ethics complaints and lawsuits against designers who are not using good practice procedures. *Stakeholders*—all the parties to a project who have a vested interest in the completion of the project—might eventually not trust the designer's decisions.

Employees are accountable and play many roles in the ongoing success of an interior design firm. They have a responsibility to work productively and bill hours or otherwise professionally and effectively complete their job tasks. They need to have some awareness of the expense it takes to operate a practice so that they are not wasteful of company resources. Employees can and should share in obtaining new clients for the firm—even if the new client ends up working with some other employee. And the owner should be willing to include employees in the future planning of the company, thus showing the employee that he or she is part of a team, not just a hired hand.

If you are a designer planning to open a studio or office or someone that now owns a firm, it is important for you to understand all the aspects of professional practice to allow your company to grow to the extent you would like it to grow. That means understanding and engaging in planning for your future, developing an effective marketing plan to continually find new clients, and fine-tuning your skills and standing in the profession through licensing and credentialing by examination so that you can obtain new and different work. These are only a few of the critical practice skills among the other business skills that are discussed in this text.

Students must master many skills and learn many facts, theories, and concepts in order to graduate from an interior design curriculum and begin their work experience. Although a business practices class may come late in the curriculum, that does not make it unimportant. It may not seem to be the most important; however, you must keep in mind that operating in an ineffective and unprofessional way will cause serious problems for any practitioner.

DEFINING THE PROFESSION

In each edition of this text, it has always been important to include a brief section that discusses what defines a profession. This has been done in particular because the profession is quite young in comparison to many others allied with interior design. It is also provided because the issue of defining a profession often comes up in discussions with state legislatures when any type of regulation of interior design or use of the title "interior designer" takes place. There is another reason to continue to include this section: Discussing the broad range of topics involved in the professional practice of interior design without discussing the profession itself would do it an injustice.

Let us begin with a few definitions of the term *profession*. According to one dictionary, a profession is "a paid occupation, especially one that involves prolonged training and a formal qualification."[5] Johnson writes, "As defined by sociologists, a profession is an occupation that is based on theoretical and practical knowledge and training in a particular field. . . . Professions tend to be credentialed and regulated in relation to certain standards of performance and ethics, which makes them more autonomous and independent than other occupations."[6]

A profession is defined by sociologists as existing when a specific set of characteristics can be associated with it. According to Nicholas Abercrombie, they are as follows:

1. The use of skills based on theoretical knowledge
2. Education and training in these skills
3. The competence of professionals ensured by examination
4. A code of conduct to ensure professional integrity
5. Performance of a service that is for the public good
6. A professional association that organizes members[7]

Gordon Marshall writes, "A profession includes some central regulatory body to ensure the standard of performance of individual members; a code of conduct; careful management of knowledge in relation to the expertise which constitutes the basis of the profession's activities; and lastly, control of number, selection, and training of new entrants."[8]

The profession of interior design, as we know it today, is guided by all of the points noted by both of these authors and as further clarified by the definitions. Whether interior design is a profession can no doubt be argued by some. However, if the measure of a profession involves the criteria offered by the material presented in the preceding paragraph, then interior design is a profession that has evolved and continues to evolve.

A professional does not emerge merely as a consequence of learning the technical principles needed in the profession. Becoming a professional also requires an attitude of dedicated commitment to the work one does and to the advancement of the profession. In addition, he or she must have some understanding of the history of the profession and the issues that are important to maintaining the vitality of the profession. Understanding what it takes to organize and maintain an interior design practice follows understanding the roots and contemporary concerns of the profession. Being a professional also involves keeping oneself informed about the latest advances in the design specialty in which one chooses to work. It also means learning to have a professional attitude in one's dealings with others in the industry and in operating or working in a design firm as a knowledgeable businessperson. A short article on interior designers' responsibility in a changing world is provided on the CD as Item 1-3.

What Would You Do?

Elizabeth graduated from an accredited four-year program in interior design and has been working in the industry for three years at an office furnishings dealership. She has been in one of the professional associations since being a student and has recently taken the NCIDQ examination. Through a relative, Elizabeth had the opportunity to meet one of the state legislators who will be on the committee to review her state coalition's proposed interior design legislative proposal. This legislator expressed to Elizabeth her skepticism about the necessity for legislation of "decorating." If you were Elizabeth, frame a response to this legislator on why interior design legislation is necessary to protect the public.

HISTORY OF THE PROFESSION

There have always been interiors of one sort of another, from caves to palaces. There has not always been a profession of interior design. From the previous section, you can readily see how the profession of interior design is actually quite young. In fact, it was not called interior design until nearly the mid-twentieth century.

Nevertheless, it can be argued that similar work to that of today's interior designer dates from the earliest times. The ancient Greeks were some of the first civilizations to put on theatrical performances in specialized spaces, referred to as theaters. Monasteries provided some of the earliest settings for health-care facilities and were among the most important early school settings. Religious facilities have always existed in one form or another. The hospitality industry dates back many, many centuries, beginning with taverns and inns that sheltered travelers. Perhaps you recall seeing the market stalls of the seventeenth century—the forerunners of today's malls—in recent, popular movies. During the Renaissance, the aristocracy began collecting antiquities and displaying them, creating, in effect, early museums. And, of course, homes have progressed from caves and dugouts to a variety of residential spaces. The "interior design" of all these different types of early architecture and consequent interiors came into being out of necessity at first. Interior design evolved as technology, skills, and education improved.

Before the twentieth century, interior decoration was the responsibility of architects and artisans, such as Michelangelo, the Adam brothers, Antonio Gaudi, and William Morris, to mention a woefully small number. No matter what their "profession" was in the arts, they clearly served as interior decorators. Early architects, painters, sculptors, and other artisans were considered artists or craftsmen. Those who designed and produced the fabrics, carpets, and furniture items were considered shopkeepers. Called *ensembliers* or *ateliers* in Europe, the shopkeepers and shops did not deal with interior decoration as a profession, but, rather, they were suppliers.

Charles Percier (1764–1838) and Pierre-François-Léonard Fontaine (1762–1853) are thought by many to be the first professional interior designers. "Percier and Fontaine conceived of interior spaces developed under their full control in the manner of modern interior designers."[9] Further, according to John Pile, most other work before and until the twentieth century was done as a collaborative effort of architects and artisans. In these early years, the terms "interior decorator" and "interior decoration" were the standard references to the profession.

It continued for many years that interiors were not accomplished by people who might be called professionals at solving interiors problems. Elsie de Wolfe (1865–1950) was among the first individuals who brought the concept of professionalism to interior decoration at the end of the nineteenth century. It was approximately during her career that the term *interior decoration* began to be used. Born in New York City and a member of the upper class, de Wolfe began her career as a professional interior decorator in 1904, when she was 39 years old. Her first commission, in 1905, was for the design of the Colony Club in New York City. Her use of white and pastels was a decided change from the dark colors that were popular in the Victorian period. Among de Wolfe's clients were such notable figures as Henry C. Frick and Anne Pierpont Morgan. Because these early decorators often had wealthy clientele, the term *society decorator* was often associated with them.

De Wolfe also wrote one of the earliest books about interior decoration, *The House in Good Taste* (1913; recently republished), in which she related her philosophy of decoration for homes. She also is credited with being responsible for another milestone in the profession, when she received a fee for her design services rather than a commission on the sale of furniture.[10]

De Wolfe's success inspired other women to enter the profession. Ruby Ross Wood (1880–1950) was an assistant of de Wolfe and later started her own business. It was, after all, one of the few acceptable professions for women at the turn of the century. Formal training, however, was difficult for them to obtain. It was not until 1904 that courses in interior decoration became available. The New York School of Applied and Fine Arts, founded as the Chase School and now known as Parsons, The New School for Design, was one of the first to offer such courses. Those who could not afford such courses or were unable to avail themselves of formal courses would learn from magazines of the time, such as *House Beautiful* or *House & Garden*.

Formal educational preparation in interior design began approximately in 1904 when what is now Parsons, the New School for Design began offering a specific program. Informal preparation in this career came from a few courses that were offered in art or home economics. Of course, architecture programs were in existence prior to the beginning of the twentieth century, but these offered few classes in interior decorating. Throughout the twentieth century, educational programs developed all across the country. Curriculums varied for many years, resulting in uneven preparation. Although programs such as that at Parsons existed for many years, educational standards and the number of programs offered grew as the numbers of decorators increased after World War II.

This profession seems to always be at the mercy and whim of the economy. After World War I, postwar prosperity became more widespread, allowing an increased interest in, and employment of, the interior decoration professional. As the profession grew, this led to an increasing number of professionals with specialized knowledge in different types of interiors. Department stores, with their displays of home furnishings, flourished as women had more time to shop. Furniture manufacturing centers grew in places such as Grand Rapids, Michigan, and High Point, North Carolina. At first, most of these manufacturers produced inexpensive imitations of period pieces that were popular in the United States at that time. By the 1920s, furniture manufacturers were producing finer-quality furniture. However, the society decorators were still traveling to Europe to purchase antiques. Magazines continued to be used by the masses of consumers to appreciate quality interior decoration primarily available by professionals only to the wealthy.

In the 1920s, the Art Deco style had an important impact on the interior design of houses and offices. Department stores such as Macy's, Wanamaker's, and Marshall Fields constructed vignettes to display the new style. *Vignette*, as used in the interior design profession, means a display of furniture and furnishings that simulates an actual room. Furniture manufacturers increasingly created "suites" of furniture from one period that could allow consumers to utilize better-quality design in their homes.[11]

The Art Deco style revolutionized the interior and exterior design of office buildings and other commercial structures. At that time, most interior design in commercial structures was done by men. Dorothy Draper (1889–1969) is credited with being the first woman interior decorator who specialized in commercial interiors.[12] Other educational programs of interior decoration were being established in New York and other cities in the United States in the 1920s. In 1924, Eleanor McMillen opened McMillen Inc., claiming to be the first full-service interior decorating firm in the United States.[13]

By the late 1920s, many local Decorators Clubs had been started in various parts of the country. The Decorators' Club located in New York is credited with being one of the first, if not the first, such organization.[14] Design education strengthened as an increasing number of formal college courses and programs in interior decoration became available. The profession was becoming more formalized and began to change its image from that of the untrained decorator to that of the trained professional.

Grand Rapids, Michigan, bears mention, as it was the site of one of the earliest and largest to-the-trade-only semiannual furniture markets. The Grand Rapids Furniture Exposition, as it was officially called, was first held in December 1878.[15] The market was held in January and June for 87 years. Local manufacturers displayed their products, educational programs were held, and manufacturers from other locations rented storefronts to show their goods.

The economic depression of the 1930s was having a profound effect on the furniture industry—much of it centered in Grand Rapids at the time. The Great Depression had a disastrous effect on the ability of the middle class to purchase furniture produced in the United States and Europe. Many furniture manufacturing centers were on the brink of closing. The leading society decorators remained relatively unaffected by the depression, since their wealthy clients could still purchase goods. However, most of these decorators were still purchasing goods from Europe rather than using American-made goods.

The leaders of the Grand Rapids manufacturing center conceived of an idea that would bring the decorators to Grand Rapids. They would hold a larger furniture market than they had ever held before in an attempt to attract the decorators to see American-made furniture. With William R. Moore of Chicago, they put together a conference to organize a national professional organization. The conference was held during July 1931, in Grand Rapids, and speakers such as Frank Lloyd Wright were scheduled to appear in order to entice decorators to the conference. The manufacturers provided the money—and furnishings—for the decorators so that they could design model-room displays. And, of course, the decorators were invited to the various manufacturing plants and showrooms to see the furniture firsthand.

By the end of the conference, the American Institute of Interior Decorators (AIID) had been founded, with William R. Moore as its first national president. Standards for membership as an active (professional) and associate member were developed even though the national board actually approved members. "In its early years it is little more than a social club, with far to go before becoming a real professional society."[16] In 1936, the organization moved its headquarters from Chicago to New York City and changed its name to the American Institute of Decorators (AID). Over the years, education and work experience requirements changed and became more stringent. However, for many years, there was no formal testing for competency.

From the 1930s on, the modernism of the Bauhaus school had a great effect on the design of buildings and interiors in the United States. The industrialism of post-World War II also led to new manufacturing techniques that changed furniture and design styles. For example, molded plywood and molded fiberglass designs, such as those by Charles Eames, revolutionized seating design. It was during the 1940s that the term *decorator* began to lose favor in the industry; however, that term remains in use to some degree even today.

After World War II, nonresidential design became an increasingly important aspect of the profession. Florence Knoll established the Knoll Planning Group in the 1940s. This design company's focus was on commercial interior design.[17] The evolution of giant corporations was one factor. Curtain wall construction, suspended ceilings, and changes in construction to allow for vast, open interior spaces in office buildings impacted architecture, interior design, and the role of the decorator/designer. In the 1940s and 1950s, more stringent educational opportunities meant that the decorators of the post-World War II era would have to rely on educational preparation rather than on just having "good taste" in order to obtain jobs and commissions.

The furniture and furnishings industry, inexorably tied to the interior design profession, forced further changes in the profession. Trade shows, first held at manufacturing centers like Grand Rapids and, later, at metropolitan market centers like the Merchandise Mart in Chicago, became a popular way for manufacturers to present their new products to decorators, designers, and other tradespeople. The Herman Miller Furniture Company, originally a residential furniture manufacturer in Grand Rapids, Michigan, moved to the production of modern office furniture designed by George Nelson (1908–1986) and others, including Charles Eames.

Changes in the philosophy of the workplace created new furniture concepts, such as that of the "office landscape." The office landscape concept was first introduced in Germany in the early 1950s by the Quickborner Team für Planung often referred to as the Quickborner Team. Office landscape, as practiced in Germany, produced offices without walls, utilizing plants, bookcases, and file cabinets as "screens" while creating wide-open floor plans. As companies embraced this planning philosophy, new specialists in space planning, lighting design, acoustics, and so forth became part of the profession. These new design concepts and other issues created tension and arguments over admission and educational requirements for interior designers. A renewed debate ensued over the words "decorator" versus "designer."

In 1957, a group belonging to the New York branch of AID broke off and formed the National Society for Interior Designers (NSID). For many years, deep-seated disagreements over qualifications, testing, and terminology continued between the two organizations. In 1961, the American Institute of Decorators became the American Institute of Interior Designers (AID). Finally, in 1975, the American Institute of Interior Designers and the National Society for Interior Designers overcame their differences and merged into one national organization, the American Society of Interior Designers (ASID). Norman de Haan, FASID, took office as the first national president. Today there are nearly 40,000 members of ASID in chapters in the United States and Canada.

All through the 1960s, there existed discussions regarding educational training and testing procedures for qualification. NSID likewise favored licensing to restrict practicing to qualified professionals. According to Olga Gueft, the Southern California chapter of AID was fighting for licensing as early as 1951, whereas some chapters of NSID were lobbying for licensing in the 1960s. AID favored creation of a qualifying examination. An examination was devised, and in the 1960s and early 1970s, prospective members of AID had to pass the examination for professional membership. Because of philosophical differences, NSID designed and utilized its own qualifying exam. In 1974, the National Council for Interior Design Qualification (NCIDQ) was formed to develop an examination that both organizations could use. The examination developed by Louis Tregre in the1960s for AID became the basis of the exam later devised and administered by NCIDQ. Tregre was elected the first president of the NCIDQ board in 1974 and remained at the post for 12 years.

As interest in the profession grew, the numbers of programs in colleges, universities, and professional schools increased, as did the number of faculty involved in education. Since most of these educators considered teaching as their full-time occupation, many limited their practice of interior design. Needing an organization to keep abreast of the profession as well as of advances in educational goals, they formed the Interior Design Educators Council (IDEC) in 1963.[18] Today, IDEC publishes the only scholarly journal of the profession, the *Journal of Interior Design Education and Research*.

As concerns about educational programs evolved, AID, NSID, and IDEC worked together to encourage the creation of the Foundation for Interior Design Education Research (FIDER) in 1970 in order to deal with the accreditation of educational programs. In 2006 the FIDER board voted to rename the organization the Council for Interior Design Accreditation. It remains the agency charged with evaluating interior design education programs and determining which ones meet the standards established for formal accreditation. This organization yearly publishes a list of the schools that provide accredited undergraduate interior design programs in the United States. That list can be found on the council's Web site.

In the late 1960s, a new professional organization, the Institute of Business Designers (IBD) was incorporated to meet the needs of the commercial/contract designer. IBD was conceived in 1963 by members of the National Office Furnishings Association (NOFA), who were concerned about the importance of interior design service in office furnishings dealerships. In 1963, NOFA-d (NOFA designers) was formed to accommodate interior designers who were working for office furnishings dealers. In 1967, NOFA was renamed NOPA (the National Office Products Association) after it merged with stationery and office supply dealers. NOPA-d for interior designers became an independent organization in 1969 and was renamed the Institute of Business Designers (IBD). Charles Gelber was elected the first president in 1970.

Along with the incorporation of IBD in 1969, that year saw the first NeoCon (National Exposition of Contract Furnishings) market in Chicago. Today, Neo-Con Chicago is the largest contract furniture exposition in the country and is attended by thousands of interior designers, architects, planners, and end users. After the formation of IBD, NSID established in 1971 a council to accommodate members specializing in commercial interiors. Many special-interest professional associations, such as the International Society of Interior Designers (ISID) and the Institute of Store Planners (ISP), were established during the 1970s and 1980s.

Beginning in 1989, discussions were once again held by the associations concerning the creation of one umbrella organization. Called the Unification Task Force, representatives from ASID, IBD, ISID, ISP, Interior Designers of Canada (IDC), and IDEC formed the task force to discuss if an umbrella organization could address the needs of all aspects of the interior design profession. With NCIDQ, FIDER and the Council for Federal Interior Designers (CFID), the Unification Task Force worked to develop a unified professional association. During 1993 the leadership of IDC and ASID voted to withdraw from the unification discussions, although the concept was supported. The IDC board felt that it would be in the best interests of IDC to withdraw from the talks. The ASID board voted against continuing discussions based on a membership response that was not in favor of unification. During the early part of 1994, members of the remaining organizations debated unification. In the end, members of IDEC and ISP decided to remain separate from the new group under discussion. Members of IBD, ISID, and CFID approved the merger in 1994 and formed the International Interior Design Association (IIDA). Those designers who were members of IBD are now members of the International Interior Design Association (IIDA).

A proliferation of new pressures and responsibilities began to be imposed on the interior design profession in the 1970s. Table 1-1 lists some of those that have been keys to the changes in the profession. Let us not forget that, while all these challenges were having a dramatic impact on commercial interior designers, those who chose to work in residential design were also seeing changes in their professional area. The changing makeup of the family has required renewed considerations about how the family and its members use their home environment. Issues of the "green" environment have become even more important in homes, as the various volatile odors and gases released by the increasing numbers of products that are being made from hydrocarbons have affected the lives of residential clients. Design styles, color trends, new product development, and bigger interior spaces also have challenged the residential interior designer.

At the turn of the twenty-first century, one of the biggest challenges to the residential interior designer will be to find appropriate ways to design and remodel homes for an aging population. With huge numbers of baby boomers (those born between 1945 and 1964) already approaching their senior years, homes and assisted-living facilities are needed to satisfy their changing lifestyles.

This short history provides a context for the development of the interior design profession. It is meant to give readers an appreciation of the roots of the profession called *interior design*. Table 1-2 summarizes its chronological development. Interior design has seen many changes in its brief history and will continue to see changes as efforts such as licensing and certification increase and as outside influences continue to affect professional practice. This table is also include on the CD as Item 1-1.

TABLE 1-1.

Design Challenges

The following lists a small number of changes that have challenged how interior designers work.

- Stringent fire codes were imposed to make commercial facilities safer.
- The increased cost of electricity created the need to find new ways to provide better lighting at low cost.
- Space-efficient furniture products for open office design help rapidly growing businesses save money and create new challenges in space planning.
- Formalized legislative efforts for interior design licensing became a reality in 1982, when Alabama passed the first legislation for title registration of interior design.
- The Americans with Disabilities Act (ADA) requires public spaces to be accessible to those with disabilities as of 1992.
- Personal computers impact the design of all types of interiors to handle technology in businesses and later the home.
- Computers require changes in commercial design to prevent glare, carpel tunnel syndrome, and other health problems.
- Design work changed with use of computer-aided design and drafting software.
- Sustainable design and the "greening" of interiors moves to the forefront of concern for designers and manufacturers.
- Aging-in-place concepts changes the design of residences for older individuals and families.
- Some suppliers formerly opened to the trade only open showrooms to the public.
- Rapid communication via e-mail impacts the speed that designers can transfer information and graphics to and from their clients on the World Wide Web.
- Design–build concepts speeds the construction of commercial facilities.

The profession thrives during economic booms and, like every industry, redefines itself when the economy is slow. Regardless of the impact of the economy, interior design professionals and students will be faced continuously with changes in the profession. Finding one's way in the profession by gaining the education, experience, and competency to work as a professional interior designer in the twenty-first century includes achieving knowledge and skills in professional practice.

INTERIOR DESIGN SPECIALTIES

Since the mid-twentieth century when some interior designers began to focus on commercial interior design rather than on residences, there have been two divisions of the profession. That line has always been a bit blurry, as many of those who think of themselves as residential designers occasionally do some small offices or other types of commercial spaces. Of course, those that are commercial designers also occasionally design a client's residence.

The line between residential and commercial interior design as "divisions" of the profession has begun to blur even more in this century because of the changes in lifestyle and work style throughout the world.[19] Increasing numbers of workers are given offices at home, outfitted by their employers. Other workers have no office per se, telemarketing via wireless laptop computers, cell phones, and handheld computers and organizers. A huge number of entrepreneurial businesses operate out of the home office. Residences in resort towns became bed-and-breakfast locations. A residence becomes a gift shop, and a church

TABLE 1-2.

Highlighted Chronology of the Growth of the Interior Design Profession

1878	First of its kind semiannual furniture market. Held in Grand Rapids, Michigan.
1904	First real use of term "interior decoration." First courses in interior decoration offered at the New York School of Applied and Fine Arts.
1905	Elsie de Wolfe obtains her first commission as an interior decorator. She is credited as being the first interior decorator.
1913	Elsie de Wolfe publishes the first true book on interior decoration, *The House in Good Taste*.
1920s	Greater effort is made by department stores to market home furnishings.
	Manufacturing centers of home furnishings begin to develop.
	Art Deco period creates greater interest in interior decoration of homes and offices.
	Dorothy Draper credited as being the first woman interior decorator to specialize in commercial interiors.
	Decorator clubs begin forming in larger cities.
	Design education strengthened in many parts of the country.
1931	Grand Rapids furniture show. Meeting to create a national professional organization.
	In July, American Institute of Interior Decorators (AIID) is founded.
	William R. Moore elected first national president of AIID.
1936	AIID's name changed to American Institute of Decorators (AID).
1940s	Post-World War II industrialism encourages new technologies in furniture manufacturing.
	Industrialism produces increased need for, and importance of, nonresidential interior design.
1950s	Development of open landscape planning concept in Germany by Quickborner Team.
1951	First time a state considers legislation to license interior design.
1957	National Society for Interior Designers (NSID) founded from a splinter group of the New York AID chapter.
1961	AID changes its name to American Institute of Interior Designers (AID).
1963	National Office Furnishings Association (NOFA) creates NOFA-d (NOFA-designers), a professional group for interior designers who work for office furnishings dealers.
	Interior Design Educators Council (IDEC) founded to advance the needs of educators of interior design.
1967	NOFA and NOFA-d change names to NOPA and NOPA-d, respectively, when NOFA merges with stationery and supplies dealers to form National Office Products Association.
1968	Introduction of "Action Office," designed by Robert Probst for Herman Miller, Inc. First true open-office furniture product.
1969	Institute of Business Designers (IBD) incorporated. NOPA-d is parent organization.
1970	Charles Gelber elected first national President of IBD.
	Foundation for Interior Design Education Research (FIDER) is founded. Is responsible for reviewing and accrediting undergraduate and graduate interior design programs.
1974	National Council for Interior Design Qualification (NCIDQ) incorporated. Charged with the development and administration of a common qualification examination.
	Louis Tregre, FAID, serves as first president of NCIDQ.
1975	American Society of Interior Designers (ASID) formed from the merger of AID and NSID. Norman de Haan is first national ASID president.
1976	The first Canadian Provincial associations—Interior Designers of Ontario and the Interior Designers of British Columbia—were admitted as members of NCIDQ.
1982	Alabama becomes first state with title registration legislation for interior design.
1988	First major discussion of 1995 Hypotheses, the document that begins a discussion of unification of interior design professional associations.
1992	Passage of Americans with Disabilities Act (ADA), which provides accessibility standards for all public buildings.
1993	U.S. Green Building Council (USGBC) formed to promote sustainable design.
1994	Unification of IBD, ISID, and CFID to form International Interior Design Association (IIDA).
	The existing code councils form the International Code Council (ICC) to develop a new universal standard of building codes.
1995	First International Code from the ICC was published.
1996	Federal government officially recognizes interior design as a profession.
1990s	Numerous states pass title, practice, or certification legislation.
2000	ASID and IIDA leadership begins discussions concerning potential merger. Talks discontinued in 2002.
2002	ASID and the Government Services Administration (GSA) sign an agreement to promote interior design excellence in federal buildings.
2003	InformDesign® is initiated as a Web site to locate and make available research on interior design practices.

becomes a residence. In many cities, people continue to move into urban high-rise condominiums and mixed-use high-rise buildings. These obvious examples evidence the blurring of the use of spaces.

Many in the profession question whether there really are two classic divisions in the interior design profession. Members of this profession have always thought that there were "residential" interior designers and "commercial" interior designers. Residential designers focus exclusively on the interiors of private residences, especially single-family dwellings, as well as other types of dwellings such as a condominium, a townhouse, a mobile home, or an apartment. Commercial interior designers focus on one or more types of spaces used for business and government such as offices, stores, hotels, restaurants, schools, airports, hospitals, and so on.

Some refer to commercial interior design as nonresidential or contract interior design. The term *contract design* comes from the fact that many years ago commercial projects more frequently were executed based on contracts for services. Of course, both residential and commercial projects are undertaken after a contract for services has been executed. In this book, I have labeled anyone who works with public spaces as a commercial interior designer.

It can no doubt be argued that the biggest change in the responsibilities and scope of work in the "divisions" would be for those in residential interior design. The practice of residential interior design must include the study and application of many technical areas that were less critical just 20 or so years ago. Building and fire codes today are now critical concerns for residences in a high-rise condominium. Home owners need a fourth bedroom for a home office accommodating computer equipment or other technology. Even the entertainment needs of a family today often requires consultation with specialists to plan special wiring panels to accommodate cable television along with Internet access in any room in the house.

Commercial interior designers see the blurring as well. Perhaps their challenge is to convert a commercial space into a different type of commercial space. They are often asked to design a client's residence. Those in commercial interior design are also challenged to keep up to date on codes, life safety, and technical issues such as security design and sustainable design.

Perhaps it remains easier to think of the interior design profession as the design of residences versus commercial spaces and retain that concept of two divisions. Perhaps it is time to consider that regardless of the type of space, the process of design follows the same path. To put it very simply, information must be gathered concerning the client's needs (programming); ideas must be generated to potentially solve those concerns (schematic design); those ideas are further developed into drawings or documents that are detailed and accurate (design development); additional drawings and documents are needed to ensure the project is constructed and installed properly (construction documents); specifications for the goods and materials needed are processed and managed, as well as the installation or finishing of all those interior goods (construction administration); and numerous business practice issues must be managed and practiced.

In this edition, to consolidate the discussion of the design specialties, the chapter on career options has been moved to a new part of the book. It is joined with the chapter on professional goals in Part II, "Getting Started." As a prelude to career choices, you may wish to complete Item 1-2, "Early Career Assessment" on the CD.

Perhaps it is not so important to define a division as to define the profession. The definition of interior design accepted by the professional associations, educators, and others involved in the practice of the profession does not differentiate any particular number or types of divisions of interior design. Perhaps it is time to consider that neither one is less or more important.

SUMMARY

Society tends to grant professionals higher status, money, and respect. Yet these do not come only with accomplishing the educational criteria required of the profession. They come to the individual who has the attitude of service, commitment, and knowledge that is expected of the professional. This is no less true for an interior design professional than any of the "traditional" professions.

Practicing interior design today requires educational training that encompasses a very large body of knowledge. It also requires legal and ethical practice and behavior that many never thought much about when interior decoration began in the early twentieth century. Contracts and promises made to clients must be fulfilled, or a legal consequence can occur. Incorrectly specifying products, allowing substandard work to be performed, or not following applicable codes can lead to serious problems, even lawsuits. The professional practice of interior design requires attention to business procedures, strategies, and protocols that any business must apply for the business to be successful, profitable, and long lasting.

This chapter, to use a design metaphor, is a foundation of information important to the overall study of the profession and how it functions as a business. It has presented information that defines interior design as a profession and why the study of professional practice is important. The chapter also provides a brief history of the profession. Having an understanding of what the roots and issues of a profession are is an important part of being a member of that profession. Knowing what it is all about is crucial to making the time spent in the career a meaningful commitment of one's time and effort rather than an ordinary "job."

REFERENCES

1. Jensen, September 2001, p. 91.
2. U.S. Department of Labor, Bureau of Labor Statistics Web site, www.bls.gov
3. www.careersininteriordesign.com, July 2006.
4. NCIDQ, July 2004.
5. *Concise Oxford American Dictionary*, 2006, p. 706.
6. Johnson, 1995, p. 216.
7. Abercrombie, Hill, and Turner, 2000, p. 279.
8. Marshall, 1998, p. 527.
9. Pile, 2005, p. 180.
10. Campbell and Seebohm, 1992, p. 70.
11. Pile, 2005, p. 317.
12. Tate and Smith, 1986, p. 322.
13. Abercrombie, December 1999, p. 148.
14. Abercrombie, December 1999, p. 146.
15. Carron, 1998, p. 72.
16. ASID, "History," 2005, p. 11.
17. Russell, 1992, p. 11
18. IDEC Web site, 2000.
19. Martin & Guerin, 2006, p. 90.

CHAPTER 2

Professional Preparation

Key Terms and Concepts

These key terms and concepts are important to material in this chapter. Many of the terms will be utilized in other chapters as well. Be sure you understand these items as you read this chapter.

Terms and Concepts

The three Es

Accreditation

Interior Design Experience Program (IDEP)

Self-Testing Exercises for Preprofessionals (STEP)

Health, safety, and welfare (HSW)

Licensing

Registration

Certification

Title acts

Practice acts

Professional member

Allied or Associate member

Continuing-Education unit (CEU)

Organizations

Council for Interior Design Accreditation

Foundation for Interior Design Education Research (FIDER)

National Council for Interior Design Qualification (NCIDQ)

American Society of Interior Designers (ASID)

International Interior Design Association (IIDA)

Interior Design Educators Council (IDEC)

Interior Designers of Canada (IDC)

Critical Issues

After completing this chapter you should be able to:

▨ Explain the three Es and how they relate to the interior design profession.
▨ Discuss how the interior design profession protects the health, life safety, and welfare (HSW) of clients and the general public.
▨ Explain the responsibility of NCIDQ and why you believe (or don't believe) this examination is important to the profession.
▨ Identify the criteria for qualification to sit for the NCIDQ examination.
▨ Compare a practice act to a title act on a practitioner's qualifications and impact on the public.
▨ Explain the responsibility of the interior design professional associations to its members and the general public.
▨ Discuss pros and cons of affiliating with a design professional association.
▨ Explain why continuing education is important for all interior designers.
▨ Name three ways how you will give back to the profession after you begin practice.

A professional, as defined in the previous chapter, must attain certain standards as acknowledged by those in the profession. Professionals and educators often talk about the "three Es" as a necessary part of the practice of interior design: education, experience, and examination.

A professional interior designer in the twenty-first century requires educational preparation in a wide variety of courses specifically within the body of knowledge for interior design. Educational standards have become progressively more stringent over the years, with advances in technology, regulations, and safety of clients and the users of spaces moving to the forefront of the body of knowledge. Individuals in interior design must realize that education preparation does not end at graduation. It should continue with professional seminars and workshops for updating and expansion of the professional practitioner's knowledge and skills.

Experience in the actual practice of interior design benefits clients and users of interiors. Experienced professionals have gained valuable on-the-job familiarity in working with clients and the industry. They have also enhanced an important knowledge base that will aid in effective solutions that meet client needs and adhere to local laws. Work experience is part of the requirements for eligibility to sit for the NCIDQ examination—to be discussed in detail later in the chapter—and to gain registration or licensing within state and provincial jurisdictions. For students, that experience begins with an internship during the period of formal studies and might expand with a part-time job in some aspect of the industry. Practitioners gain experience on the job in a wide variety of office and studio settings in design specialties that are of interest to the individual.

Professions seek to further qualify their members by expecting or requiring an examination that tests their basic competency. An examination after completion of formal education and some period of work experience seeks to test a practitioner's knowledge and skills of the body of knowledge recognized as necessary for the practice of the profession.

Of course, not everyone who has something to do with the planning and design of an interior has received formal education and training and has been certified by examination. That's still an option for many individuals. However, that option is disappearing as the knowledge base, skills, and regulations applicable to the interior design profession continue to grow in complexity.

Chapter 2 focuses on the elements of the profession that relate to the credentials of a professional interior designer. A brief discussion of the major professional associations will help the reader appreciate the breadth of design specialties within the profession. The chapter also reviews the qualifying examination that has been established as the benchmark for licensing and for professional-level association membership, which provides evidence of competence. The chapter examines licensing and title registration issues, as well as continuing education.

There is a new section in this chapter called "Giving Back". This topic was suggested by several interior designers and educators who felt it was important to discuss that a professional also has a responsibility to contribute expertise and skills back to the design community and the community in which the professional lives.

EDUCATIONAL PREPARATION

Seeking formal educational preparation in interior design before entering any aspect of the profession should not be a question in the twenty-first century. Regardless of whether someone wishes to design residences or become involved in designing any type of commercial interior space, educational preparation should be considered mandatory. Owners and users of interior spaces who hire professional help expect that the interior designer that they retain has the knowledge to perform the required work with more in mind than aesthetics. Technical knowledge is required to understand how a building is built and the codes and regulations that are necessary to meet to plan a safe interior environment. Not all materials work in all situations, and learning the performance characteristics of products used in interiors is therefore essential. The interior environment is more than a nice-looking place, as it is a background for healthy living and working. Clients hold professionals to business standards, and gaining an understanding of these business standards is part of the educational process.

The traditional roots of interior design education are in the fine arts, home economics (today referred to as human ecology), and architecture. Current interior design programs at universities, colleges, community colleges, and professional schools generally assign interior design academic programs within a school or department of interior design or one of these other three areas. In some schools they may be found in other departments or divisions. Interior design programs are interdisciplinary, drawing from the arts, architecture, and human ecology, as well as from the supporting areas of business and the liberal arts. Depending on the location of the program, the professional and technical course work will have a slightly different focus.

Programs range from two years to as long as seven years. Two-year programs are primarily offered in community colleges and some professional schools. In many situations, students begin at one of these two-year programs and transfer into a four-year (or longer) program in order to obtain a bachelor's degree. Other students are satisfied with a two-year associate degree in interior design and move on to employment. Most of these graduates work in small interior design studios or retail stores. Graduates of four-year (or more) programs generally accept initial employment with larger-sized interior design firms or architectural firms. Programs that last more than five years lead to a master's or other post-graduate degree.

A very important part of educational preparation in interior design is an internship. An internship is a supervised work experience within an interior design firm or other appropriate company within the industry. Internships are generally a part of the required curriculum. It is an intensive work experience where the student is expected to meet the general policies of the design firm. Although most internships are with interior design and architectural firms, the interests of some students may find valuable internship experiences at other options such as contractors and vendors. An internship should include as many tasks and activities as possible that mimic the actual work environment. However, the actual experience will vary for each company and student. Internships are often arranged by faculty members, although students are welcomed to suggest companies at which they would like to work.

Interior design academic programs have a different emphasis because of the mission of the institution and department, and the focus of the faculty. A program housed in fine arts will have a different focus than one in another department. It is up to the individual student and his or her family to investigate carefully the academic programs of all the institutions in which the student has an interest. Prospective students should talk to academic advisors, program alumni, and design businesses in the area that may have knowledge of the preparation given at a particular school.

Many professionals seek an advanced degree. The master's degree level of preparation is for those designers who are seeking advanced studies or research work in interior design. Master's degree work commonly requires a minimum of 30 semester credit hours, with actual degree requirements being left up to the institution. A graduate student's work culminates in a graphic or written thesis, depending on his or her academic focus and the requirements of the institution. Studies might be research based in some area of interior design, or toward specialized studies like business management, gerontology, architecture, or numerous other areas of study. Individuals particularly interested in teaching at the college or university level might seek a doctorate. This advanced degree requires extensive additional directed course work and a dissertation reporting primary research in an area of interest to the individual.

Regardless of the level of degree sought, professional, educational training in interior design must provide the student with the theory and skills of the profession as well as with the general education that is required in the twenty-first century. The focus of that training must also meet the interests, abilities, and career goals of the student.

Curriculum Accreditation

An accredited program indicates to the student that the curriculum meets the educational standards that are accepted and supported by the profession of interior design. Voluntary accreditation of interior design programs was not available until the creation of the Foundation for Interior Design Education Research (FIDER), which was established in 1970 by the organizations at the time—AID and NSID—now the American Society of Interior Designers (ASID). FIDER was renamed in 2006 as the *Council for Interior Design Accreditation*. This nonprofit organization, recognized by the Council on Higher Education Accreditation, is considered the reliable authority on the quality of postsecondary interior design education in North America.

The mission of the Council for Interior Design Accreditation is that it "provides the foundation for future excellence in the interior design profession by setting standards for education and accrediting academic programs that meet those standards."[1] The council continues to develop and evaluate educational

TABLE 2-1.

Council for Interior Design Accreditation (Formerly FIDER) Professional Standards 2006

1. Curriculum Structure
   The curriculum is structured to facilitate and advance student learning.

2. Professional Values
   The program leads students to develop the attitudes, traits, and values of professional responsibility, accountability, and effectiveness.

3. Design Fundamentals
   Students have a foundation in the fundamentals of art and design, theories of design, green design, and human behavior, and discipline-related history.

4. Interior Design
   Students understand and apply the knowledge, skills, processes, and theories of interior design.

5. Communication
   Students communicate effectively.

6. Building Systems and Interior Materials
   Students design within the context of building systems. Students use appropriate materials and products.

7. Regulations
   Students apply the laws, codes, regulations, standards, and practices that protect the health, safety, and welfare of the public.

8. Business and Professional Practice
   Students have a foundation in business and professional practice.

9. Faculty
   Faculty members and other instructional personnel are qualified and adequate in number to implement program objectives.

10. Facilities
    Program facilities and resources provide an environment to stimulate thought, motivate students, and promote the exchange of ideas.

11. Administration
    The administration of the program is clearly defined, provides appropriate program leadership, and supports the program. The program demonstrates accountability to the public through its published documents.

12. Assessment
    Systematic and comprehensive assessment methods contribute to the program's ongoing development and improvement.

standards in interior design programs as a means to granting accreditation. These standards are reviewed from time to time, and updated standards are available on their Web site, www. accredit-id.org. An abbreviated statement of the standards is presented in Table 2-1. The complete statement of standards is available on their Web site.

Research studies in the 1980s revealed distinct differences in educational programs throughout the United States and Canada. The length of the programs varied from two years to as much as seven years. The number of credit hours of interior design classes varied considerably as well. With the research study information, the Council for Interior Design Accreditation, with assistance from NCIDQ and additional ongoing research, has worked with the Interior Design Educators Council (IDEC) to define a common body of knowledge and skills that are needed by competent professional interior designers. This study of the common body of knowledge in interior design was reviewed in 2005 and has identified numerous elements of the common body of knowledge in interior design. The basic knowledge areas are human environment needs; interior construction, codes, and regulations; design; products and materials; professional practice; and communication. The complete listing of the subcategories of these basic elements of the body of knowledge is available on the IDEC Web site. There is a brief summary of the body of knowledge report contained in CD as Item 2-1.

Currently, the Council for Interior Design Accreditation accredits a single program of interior design education: the professional level. As of January 1, 2004, the program must result in a minimum of a bachelor's degree. Some programs that are less than a bachelor's degree are accredited prior to that date. Such programs must comply with the bachelor's degree requirements by January 1, 2010, to retain accreditation.

Accreditation by an interior design program is a voluntary process of self-study and measurement of the curriculum against the common body of knowledge and the program standards established by the council. This self-study investigates the quality of programs as meeting the needs of professionals in the current market. After the self-study, a group of site visitors conducts reviews of materials and discussions with faculty, students, and administrators. Accreditation is not "forever," and a program must be reevaluated every six years.

Additional information about accreditation can also be found at their Web site.

NCIDQ EXAMINATION

As we saw in Chapter 1, a professional competency examination is one of the criteria of a profession. In the interior design profession, the examination that is accepted as that professional competency examination by the major professional associations in the United States and Canada, as well as IDEC, and the Council for Interior Design Accreditation is the examination administered by the National Council for Interior Design Qualification (NCIDQ). It is also the qualifying examination for professional-level membership in ASID, IIDA, IDC, and IDEC. The NCIDQ examination is also the primary examination in those U.S. states and Canadian provinces that have licensing, certification, or other registration statutes.

The NCIDQ was organized in 1972 and became an independent corporation in 1974. It is concerned with maintaining standards of practice through the testing of members of the profession and the establishment of requirements for legal qualifications for licensing and title registration. "The core purpose of NCIDQ is to protect the health, life safety and welfare of the public by establishing standards of competence in the practice of interior design. The National Council for Interior Design Qualification serves to identify to the public those interior designers who have met the minimum standards for professional practice by passing the NCIDQ Examination."[2]

It is not a professional association in the same way as ASID or IIDA. No individual memberships exist within NCIDQ. Membership resides with state and provincial member boards representing jurisdictions that regulate the interior design profession. Individuals are certificate holders, meaning that they have successfully completed all the requirements of the examination. Certificate holders are not allowed to place the NCIDQ acronym on their business cards or other marketing materials like they would an appellation. Each certificate holder receives a unique number, and they may place this number along with NCIDQ on their marketing materials. For example, "NCIDQ Certificate number 12345."

Ongoing research is conducted by NCIDQ to evaluate and analyze candidate performance, educational and professional practice skill, and knowledge requirements, along with methods to promote public protection by the interior design profession. Major research studies began in 1998 to gather the most up-to-date information about the practice of interior design in order to revise the NCIDQ examination. A similar study is conducted approximately every five years to ensure that the content of the examination parallels the body of knowledge and skills currently required in the profession.

The NCIDQ examination is given twice during the year—usually in April and October—at examination centers throughout the United States and Canada. When a designer has achieved the minimum combination of education and work experience, the designer contacts the NCIDQ office for application materials. In some states, such as in Texas, candidates must apply to the state regulatory board in order to take the examination.

Eligibility requirements involve a combination of years of education in interior design and a minimum period of work experience. An individual who has graduated from a four- or five-year degree in interior design or equivalent educational credit would need approximately two years or 3500 hours of professional experience. Work experience can be full- or part-time. NCIDQ recommends that the work experience be under the direct supervision of an NCIDQ Certificate holder, a registered interior designer, or an architect who offers interior design services. The information on the Interior Design Experience Program (IDEP) is very important related to work experience. Individuals without a baccalaureate degree would be required to have a larger number of hours of work experience. All candidates must have a minimum of a two-year certificate or equivalent credits in interior design for their educational requirement consisting of 40 semester credits or 60 quarter credits of interior-design-related courses. Recommendations and academic transcripts are also required of all candidates.

The Interior Design Experience Program

A work experience program established by NCIDQ called the Interior Design Experience Program provides structured, diversified, and monitored experience in interior design after graduation. It is not the same thing as an internship. According to NCIDQ, "IDEP provides a complete and balanced 'curriculum' for the first years of work after graduation. It targets critical experience areas for the professional interior designer in any specialty area."* This is a voluntary program in most jurisdictions. However, a state or provincial board may require enrollment in IDEP for work experience requirements for licensing/registration. Participants gain valuable experience that is often helpful to them in passing the NCIDQ examination.

Very briefly, here is how the IDEP program works. After finding a job in interior design, a participant secures a supervisor at that place of employment who is an NCIDQ certificate holder or licensed/registered interior designer or architect. The supervisor supports the entry-level professional by assessing skills and promoting development of the individual's experience in the scope of work expected at the firm. Participants are also required to have a mentor who also is an NCIDQ certificate holder or is a licensed/registered interior designer or architect. This mentor might be in the same firm or work for some other firm. The mentor is someone who does not supervise the individual (if the mentor is within the firm) and can provide career advice during the IDEP experience. Participants are required to track their structured work experiences with a log book provided by NCIDQ. The participant, supervisor, and mentor review and check off progress on the requirements. NCIDQ recognizes that an individual participant may have more than one supervisor, place of employment, or mentor during the time frame of approximately two or three years (or 3520 hours if the participant has a baccalaureate degree in interior design).

Additional information on the IDEP program can be obtained from NCIDQ. Visit their Web site listed in the Internet Resources appendix.

*National Council for Interior Design Qualification, IDEP program brochure, November, 2004.

Beginning in 2008, the work experience requirement was changed. It now must be completed under the supervision of an NCIDQ certificate holder or a registered interior designer or architect who provides interior design services. Previously, individuals who had their own business could count that work experience toward their qualifications. Now that work experience must be supervised. That does not mean that someone starting a sole practitioner practice cannot gain work experience credit. All work experience, regardless of where the candidate works, must be supervised through a reporting program set up by NCIDQ. Questions about this program should be directed to the NCIDQ Web site or office.

The Examination

As of the fall of 2006, the examination is given over two consecutive days—usually Friday and Saturday. It is divided into three sections, with two sections given on Friday and the third on Saturday. A candidate may take all three sections of the exam at one time or may elect to take individual sections or combinations of sections at different times. Only sections of the examination that are not passed must be taken again. Unless a professional association or a state statute has different requirements, there is no time limit within which a candidate must pass the examination.

The first two sections given on Friday only are two multiple-choice, computer-graded tests. The third section given on Saturday only is the practicum section. The exams are based on six performance domains that are characterized within the work of interior design: (1) programming, (2) schematic design, (3) design development, (4) contract documents, (5) contract administration, and (6) professional practice. Many questions incorporate drawings, pictures, symbols, and textual formats that are typical in the interior design profession, requiring candidates to recall, apply, and analyze information. A discussion of the project activities that occurs within these domains is presented in Chapter 28, "The Project Management Process." Descriptions of these performance domains are also on the NCIDQ Web site. A brief description of the three exam sections follows.

Section I, "Principles and Practices of Interior Design." This is a multiple-choice test consisting of 150 questions. It addresses the domains of programming, schematic design, and design development.

Section II, "Contract Development and Administration." This 150 question multiple-choice test addresses the domains of contract documents, contract administration, and professional practice. Questions focus on practice situations, knowledge, and activities associated with the domains.

Section III, "Schematics and Design Development." This is the practicum section of the exam. It requires that candidates produce a design solution. Design skills will be tested in programming, schematic design, design development, and contract documents. Candidates are required to plan a multifunctional facility with at least three of seven specialized areas of design included. All candidates at any one testing session are given the same problem. Besides being required to interpret a design program and to provide a design solution, all candidates are required to apply principles of universal design to their solutions and meet applicable codes.

An examination guide is available from NCIDQ. This guide provides the candidate with an overview of the three sections of the examination, a bibliography of source information, sample multiple-choice questions, and a sample practicum exam. It provides valuable general information about the examination, the rules for the exam, the schedule, and other important information.

THE STEP PROGRAM

Recognizing the importance of the NCIDQ examination in the profession, ASID devised a special study program to help candidates prepare for the exam in 1979. Though sponsored by ASID, any candidate for the NCIDQ exam may participate. This Self-Testing Exercises for Preprofessionals (STEP) program helps applicants review and experience what will be expected of a candidate to pass the examinations. STEP program leaders point out that the program is not a crash course in design; rather, it is a means to help preprofessionals and candidates gain an understanding of what areas they may need to review or brush up on concerning knowledge areas (for the multiple-choice sections) and design skills (for the practicum sections) that will likely be tested.

The 20-hour STEP workshop, given over two and a half days, is conducted by educators and professionals who are specially trained by ASID. The program provides a review of applicable material and study skills for the examination. Practice tests for both the multiple-choice and practicum sections are included and reviewed during the workshop. Workshop activities take candidates through various exercises, which help them assess where they need additional work prior to taking the examination.

The STEP workshop is primarily sponsored by local ASID chapters around the United States and at the ASID National Meeting. Registration fees are slightly higher for non-ASID members. There is a recommendation to participate in the STEP program a minimum of four months before the scheduled exam date in order to have time to review and prepare for the exam. Registration information can be obtained from local ASID chapter offices or the ASID Web site.

LICENSING AND REGISTRATION

Professions and professionals within a profession are in some way licensed or registered by a state or provincial regulatory body. Licensing or registration is done to recognize the minimum standards and qualifications of those who wish to engage in the interior design profession within a jurisdiction. The terms *licensing*, *practice acts*, *title acts*, *legal recognition*, *certification*, and *self-certification* are all associated with licensing and registration status in the interior design profession. Each term is defined within this section.

Licensing and registration efforts have been a part of the profession's activities since 1951, when the Southern California chapter of AID attempted to get a bill passed in the state legislature. They failed. NSID formed a licensing committee in the 1960s. Professionals, with the assistance of local licensing coalitions and the ASID and IIDA national organizations, continue to pursue and obtain licensing on a state-by-state basis.

The term *licensing* is most frequently associated with a state or province whose legislation defines who may practice interior design—much like a state law defines who may practice medicine. The term *registration* or *certification* is most frequently associated with legislation that defines who may use a certain title such as "registered interior designer." In a few cases, a state may have a combination of this terminology, since a state with a licensing law will also protect a certain title.

Licensing and registration standards are established by state and provincial legislation. The purpose of such legislation is to ensure the *health, life safety, and welfare* (HSW) of the public who hires interior designers as well as the general public that uses interiors designed by a professional interior designer. Licensing and registration laws help the general public determine what level of professional is appropriate for their needs. For example, not all projects require the preparation of working drawings, and thus the client may not need a licensed professional to do the work.

These laws are enacted to establish minimum standards of competency of any individual who wishes to practice or engage in interior design activities as defined by the legislation within the jurisdiction. Legislation does not regulate the creative activity of interior design. An added tool of enforcement and redress exists for clients when licensing legislation exists. Since legislation seeks to ensure that only competent practitioners offer design services or call themselves by a regulated title such as "interior designer," if something goes wrong, the client can ask the jurisdiction's board of registration to investigate and even fine and/or discipline the designer.

The two most common types of legislation are title acts and practice acts. *Title acts* are concerned with limiting the use of certain professional titles, such as *interior designer, registered interior designer,* or *certified interior designer.* Only individuals who meet agreed-upon qualifications and who have registered with a state board may use the regulated title. In states with title legislation, individuals can engage in activities that are considered "interior design" but cannot use the regulated title.

Practice acts are a type of licensing in which guidelines are established concerning what an individual can or cannot do in the practice of a profession in a particular state. If a state has a practice act, individuals cannot engage in any of the activities defined by the act unless they are licensed. Individuals who wish to engage in the work defined by the practice act must meet the qualifications and with a state board. Those working under the supervision of a licensed interior designer in a jurisdiction with a practice act do not themselves need to be licensed. However, when a designer decides to work for themselves or have their own business, then they must become licensed. In some states, those who only design residences are exempt from having to be licensed.

At present there are also two special types of legislation. One is called *self-certification*. This legislation exists in California and is a type of title act that regulates the use of the title *certified interior designer*. What makes it different from other title act legislation is that California did not establish a governing board to oversee who may call themselves a certified interior designer. States generally have a board of technical registration or state board of registration—or some other titled group operated by the state—to oversee professional registration of any kind. In California there is an independent agency that is not accountable to the state called the California Council for Interior Design Certification that is involved in who may use the title.

The other special type of legislation is in Colorado and is referred to as a *permitting statute*. In that state at this time there is no state board to oversee qualifications and no title that is regulated. Interior designers who meet education, experience, and examination requirements can submit plans for a building permit. This regulation is an amendment to the architecture statute.

To differing degrees, licensing and title acts, in some respects, serve to limit who can practice a profession. A title act does very little to limit who can practice the activities of interior design, whereas practice acts do a great deal. The intent of legislation, however, is to indicate to the consumer which individuals have met the specific criteria that are related to education and work experience, indicating that they have acquired professional competence in the field. Licensing or title registration legislation also provides a definitive measure of experience and educational preparation for those who practice interior design. Licensing serves to protect the consumer from unregulated practice by those who do not have proper educational background, training, and experience in the profession of interior design.

Title acts only restrict the use of the title *interior designer* (or other designated title) to those who meet the qualifications of the state title act. Interior designers who meet these qualifications must also register with a state agency or board. An individual who does not meet the qualifications of the title act may not use the title of *interior designer* in any of his or her business dealings. With title registration, the title of *interior designer* connotes to the public that the individual has met the highest standards of the profession and can thereby provide the most competent service to the consumer. These standards are related to education, experience, abiding by a code of conduct, and passing a qualifying examination.

Practice acts are commonly legislated for those professions that deal with the health and safety of the public employing individuals in those professions. Lawyers, doctors, architects, and engineers have had to meet state practice act regulations for many years. Practice acts definitely limit who may practice a profession, since they usually require that individuals meet very stringent qualification criteria. When a person enters into a contractual relationship with an unlicensed professional, the contract may or may not be enforceable, depending on the statutes in the individual states.

An important part of the practice of interior design to many individuals is the right to stamp their drawings with a stamp or a seal and signature, showing that the drawings have been prepared by a professional and submit drawings to building departments to receive a permit for construction. Permitting status is on a state-by-state basis whether the jurisdiction has a title act or practice act. Work executed by a nonregistered or nonlicensed designer would not have this stamp.

Interior designers need to understand how legislation can impact their practice. Various factions in the design–build industry in various states have been known to try to limit the practice of interior design by trying to legislate certain activities that are common to the interior designer. Not having legal recognition of the profession through some type of legislation can mean that interior designers might be prevented from providing all of the services normally considered part of the interior design process. As mentioned, many designers feel that a normal part of their project responsibilities can involve preparing working drawings and documents to building departments to obtain a building permit. Lacking legislation to define the work of an interior designer can prevent this part of the work offerings of a designer. This "protectionism" by others results in loss of work of interior designers even though they do have NCIDQ certification, education, and experience to do the work normally defined as interior design.

Those who have been actively engaged in bringing licensing legislation to their states would all agree that it has not been an easy task. Nor will it be in the future. Despite the frustration of many years of struggling with legislators and those who would rather that interior design not be licensed, many states have obtained some type of interior design legislation. In 1982, Alabama became the first state to pass a title registration act. In 2001, Alabama successfully converted its title act to a practice act to become the sixth jurisdiction (at the time of this writing) to have a practice act. Table 2-2 lists the jurisdictions and the type of legislation that exists in that state or province. Many other states are working on legislation for either title registration or practice acts.

Readers may wish to contact their state coalition or the Government and Public Affairs Department of ASID, the Legislative Issues Committee of IIDA, or the national offices of other professional associations for information on legislation within the reader's jurisdiction.

TABLE 2-2.

States with Interior Design Registration Laws as of 2006

State	Type of Law	Total Education Plus Experience Required	Registered Title
Alabama	Title/practice	6 years	Interior Designer/Registered Interior Designer
Arkansas	Title	6 years	Registered Interior Designer
California	Self-certification	6–8 years depending on education	Certified Interior Designer
Colorado	Permitting statute	6 years	(Interior Design Permitting)
Connecticut	Title	Follows NCIDQ	Interior Designer
Florida	Title/practice	6 years	Interior Designer
Georgia	Title	4 years—no experience specified	Registered Interior Designer
Illinois	Title	6 years	Interior Designer/Registered Interior Designer
Iowa	Title	6 years	Registered Interior Designer
Kentucky	Title	Follows NCIDQ	Certified Interior Designer
Louisiana	Title/practice	6 years	Registered Interior Designer
Maine	Title	6 years	Certified Interior Designer
Maryland	Title	6 years	Certified Interior Designer
Minnesota	Title	6 years	Certified Interior Designer
Missouri	Title	6 years	Registered Interior Designer
Nevada	Title/practice	6 years	Registered Interior Designer
New Jersey	Title	6 years	Certified Interior Designer
New Mexico	Title	6 years	Interior Designer
New York	Title	7 years	Certified Interior Designer
Oklahoma	Title	6 years	Interior Designer
Puerto Rico	Title/practice	2 years—no experience specified	Interior Designer/Interior Decorator
Tennessee	Title	6 years	Registered Interior Designer
Texas	Title	6 years	Interior Designer
Virginia	Title	6 years	Certified Interior Designer
Washington, D.C.	Title/practice	6 years	Interior Designer
Wisconsin	Title	6 years	Wisconsin Registered Interior Designer

Legislation was pending in seven additional states at the time of the writing of this table. The reader can check with the government affairs offices of ASID or IIDA for information on new states with title or practice legislation. The information above is provided courtesy of ASID and is available from the American Society of Interior Designers Web site, www.asid.org.

What Would You Do?

Jones Interior Design has been designing hospitality spaces in the Midwest for three years. One of those clients has decided to open a restaurant in a suburb of Las Vegas. The restaurant will be over 50,000 square feet, and the owner wants to include a small casino area off the lobby. The owner is looking for a design concept that is reminiscent of the Old West casinos, and so he has hired an architect from Colorado to do the structural design. The client wants Jones Interior Design to do the interior planning and specification.

Carl Jones is not registered in the state where his business is located. He has told the client that he really would like to be involved in the project in Nevada, but he isn't licensed to do work there. The client is insisting that Carl's company do the interior and said he doesn't understand why Carl is reluctant.

Whether one works toward licensing through title registration or practice acts, interior design professionals and students must be prepared to accept the ethical and legal responsibilities that such recognition brings. The next chapter discusses the ethics and codes of conduct, and Chapter 4 discusses many legal responsibilities that one must face.

PROFESSIONAL ASSOCIATIONS

There are many reasons one might decide to become a member of one of the professional associations. In fact, some professionals belong to more than one association, as each can bring different benefits or professional advantages to a member.

A large number of professionals feel that the greatest tangible benefit of professional association membership is the privilege to place ASID, IIDA, IDC, or other association appellations after a member's name. It is not the primary benefit; it is only one benefit. Although the tangible benefits are important, sometimes the intangible ones bring the greatest satisfaction and growth to members. Some of the intangible benefits most noted by members are as follows:

Interaction with colleagues. Friendships established with colleagues within the chapter and around the country or the globe are enriching personally and professionally. There are thousands of individuals who are affiliated with associations, and yet the profession is small enough so that many professionals meet and become friends with colleagues at national and regional meetings.

Educational opportunities. It is vital in this age of technology and regulations that designers continually update their skills and knowledge in their field. Professional associations at the national and chapter levels provide continuing education seminars and workshops to assist members in advancing their knowledge in all areas of the profession. Associations provide other opportunities for educational upgrading through chapter meetings, newsletters, national conferences, research studies, and online discussion groups of issues and concerns.

Important friendships. Professional colleagues are competitors at times, but many consider each other as friends as well. Through an association, designers get to know their competitors, not only as great designers or good businesspeople but also simply as people. Designers are proud of the professional and personal friendships that they have made through association activities.

Pride in accomplishment. It is important to have a sense of pride in having achieved the educational, experience, and testing milestones that indicate that one has achieved the highest level in one's profession.

Recognition. Consumers and allied professionals recognize the dedication and credentials of the interior designer who is affiliated with professional associations. To many others, peer recognition as a member of an association is gratifying. In addition, association chapters offer competitions for all levels of members so that the highest-quality design can be recognized on the local level.

These are just some of the intangible benefits of membership. You may think of others that are just as important.

TABLE 2-3.

Tangible Member Benefits of Interior Design Professional Associations

- *Association leadership.* Membership offers an opportunity to be involved in the growth of the profession through positions as chapter and national officers.
- *Leadership training.* Association chapter and national board members and officers receive training to assist them in accomplishing their association responsibilities. Much of this training can be directly applied to an individual's work experience as well.
- *Chapter participation and networking.* By participating in chapter committees and events, members meet colleagues for opportunities for leadership growth, friendships, and collaborative work.
- *Mailings.* Associations provide mailings to members that keep them informed of the associations' activities as well as of external influences on the profession. Mailings might take the form of member magazines, supplemental newsletters and news bulletins, chapter newsletters, and conference reports.
- *Practice aids.* A number of associations provide sample contracts, business forms, marketing tools, reference books, and other useful aids for members to use in their practice in order to become better professionals.
- *Government affairs.* The associations maintain contact with federal, state, and/or provincial government agencies that may have an effect on the right to practice. Members are kept informed of any pending legislation that might affect design practice.
- *Group insurance.* It is possible for members to take advantage of low group insurance rates for a variety of personal and business insurance needs.
- *Business services.* Discounts and special pricing are available from some associations for car rentals, telephone service, express shipping, credit cards, and other similar business services.
- *Magazine subscriptions.* Members receive a limited number of complimentary subscriptions to trade magazines.
- *Design competitions.* Professional prestige can be achieved through juried national competitions for projects, research, and writing.
- *Industry liaison.* Members receive technical information from industry suppliers.
- *Continuing education.* Members can find out where continuing education sessions are being held throughout the country via their association's Web site.
- *World Wide Web.* Members can obtain information from association national offices, be informed of association business and issues affecting the members, and even carry on online chats with the national office or with other members. Chapters may also offer marketing programs in which a member may link his or her Web site to the chapter's Web site.

Members of associations are pleased to discover and take advantage of numerous tangible benefits. For example, attending a chapter meeting might be a social opportunity for the sole practitioner or, more likely, an educational opportunity with a speaker. Many other tangible benefits are available, although they vary by the organization. Those shown in Table 2-3 are the most common that are available to the largest of the interior design professional associations.

Becoming an active member of a professional association can bring many personal and professional rewards. I have always encouraged students and professionals to find the associations that best meets their needs and to become involved by participating on chapter committees and programs. The activities and benefits offered by a chapter and the national associations take place only with the voluntary contributions by members. In one way or another, a volunteer always gets more out of the activity than the time represented that goes into it.

There is no lack of reasons for becoming affiliated with an association that is appropriate to the interior designer's interests and needs. The remainder of this section briefly describes the major professional associations. The reader can obtain a great deal of information about membership, benefits, and activities from association Web sites—including online membership application. Of course, you can also contact the national or provincial offices (listed in the Internet

TABLE 2-4.
Other Professional Organizations

There are several other professional organizations that might be of interest to interior designers based on their professional interests. Complete information regarding the qualification and application procedures of these associations can be obtained from these organizations' national office or Web sites.

American Institute of Architects (AIA). The professional organization for architects. Interior designers may be eligible for affiliated membership.

Building Office and Management Association (BOMA). Members are owners and managers of office buildings. Interior designers who design large corporate office facilities often are members.

National Association of Home Builders (NAHB). NAHB represents members of the building industry concerning public policy on a wide variety of home construction issues.

Certified Aging-in-Place Specialist (CAPS). Individuals who have achieved additional technical business and customer service skills necessary for working in the aging-in-place segment of the industry.

Construction Specifications Institute (CSI). Members are those involved in creating and building any type of building structure.

International Facility Management Association (IFMA). This organization is for those who are actively engaged in corporate facility management and planning.

The Institute of Store Planners (ISP). The ISP is for professionals specializing in the design of retail stores and shopping centers.

National Kitchen and Bath Association (NKBA). This organization is for those who are interested in specializing in kitchen or bath design.

U.S. Green Building Council (USGBC). This organization represents designers and others in the built-environment industry that design and promote buildings that are environmentally healthy.

Many other organizations are listed in the Internet Resources appendix.

Resources) for more specific details about the association. Brief information on several other professional associations is also included in Table 2-4.

Before reviewing specific information on the professional associations, you might find the article on Interior Design and the Economy, Item 2-2 on the CD, of interest.

American Society of Interior Designers (ASID)

The largest of the interior design professional associations, with nearly 40,000 members, is ASID. Members are engaged in both residential and commercial interior design, and include students and industry partners. "ASID is a community of people—designers, industry representatives, educators and students—committed to interior design. Through education, knowledge sharing, advocacy, community building and outreach, the Society strives to advance the interior design profession and, in the process, to demonstrate and celebrate the power of design to positively change people's lives."[3]

ASID provides many membership benefits, including meetings and activities held at 48 chapters throughout the United States and Canada, and a membership magazine called *ASID ICON.* In addition its national conference held in the spring offers numerous continuing-education classes and seminars; an e-newsletter, *newsflash,* that arrives biweekly; extensive online interface; legislative support for states that are seeking licensing; and many other programs, documents, and activities for the support of the association, its members, and the profession. The members-only link to the association's Web site provides focused information for members on a continually updated basis.

There are seven membership categories in ASID as of 2007: (1) professional, (2) allied, (3) educator (professional), (4) educator (allied), (5) international, (6) student, and (7)industry partner. Each category has different requirements and benefits. However, such benefits as the *newsflash* e-newsletter, *ASID ICON* magazine, and access to members-only Web information are universal benefits. All members are invited to chapter meetings and events.

The highest level of membership is *professional*. Members in this category have satisfied rigorous standards of education, work experience, and testing in order to qualify as professional-level members. The minimum requirements for professional-level membership are (1) graduation from a recognized college, university, or design school with a major in interior design or a related field; (2) a minimum of two years of full-time employment in interior design; and (3) successful completion of the NCIDQ examination. The educational requirement for ASID is a minimum of a two-year certificate in interior design for all levels of membership. Individuals who have had no formal accredited educational preparation in interior design or a related field might not qualify for professional-level membership in ASID, since they will not have met NCIDQ's qualification standards. The educational program must include a minimum of 45 semester credit hours or 67 quarter hours in interior-design-related courses at a school that is accredited by a recognized accrediting agency. Only professional-level members may use the appellation *ASID* after their names and in advertising.

The second level of membership is *allied*. Allied members are practicing interior designers and must meet the same general membership requirements as for professional membership. However, an allied member has not as yet satisfactorily completed the NCIDQ exam. An allied practitioner member must have a four- or five-year interior design or architecture degree; or a two- or three-year degree or certificate in interior design. Allied member status is no longer allowed based on experience only. Allied members are able to use the appellation *Allied Member, ASID* after their names.

As of January 1, 2008, professional and allied practitioner members of ASID are required to complete 6 contact hours (equal to 0.6 CEUs) every two years. This is a self-reporting requirement. Failure to comply with the CEU requirement will mean the member is subject to a termination of Society membership.

There are two categories of membership for *educators*. Educators who are teaching or working as full-time administrators in postsecondary programs of interior design and who have passed the NCIDQ examination may obtain educator (professional) member status. An educator that has not passed the NCIDQ examination would be granted educator (allied) member status in the association.

The *international member* category recognizes that ASID members reside in many foreign countries. They must meet membership criteria as any other practitioner-type member. If they have passed the NCIDQ examination, they are considered professional-level members. If they have not yet completed the examination, they are granted allied member status.

Students who are enrolled in interior design programs may become *student* members of an ASID chapter at their school, if the school has one. If the school does not have an ASID chapter but they are enrolled in a program requiring at least 40 credit hours of design related class work, they may be independent student members. Students receive mailings from the national office and have the opportunity to participate in the local professional chapter. Student members who are in good standing through graduation may apply for allied membership immediately upon graduation. Student members may use the membership appellation *Student Member, ASID* after their names.

Industry partner (IP) members are those who work for suppliers to the interior design industry. For the most part, these members are wholesalers and suppliers. Many representatives of the manufacturers and suppliers, trade showrooms, and market centers become IP members in order to interact with the membership. Industry partner members also have generously provided financial backing to the profession through sponsorship of continuing-education classes, chapter activities, and design competitions.

It is important to note that when an individual applies for any level of membership, by signing the application, he or she agrees to abide by the association's bylaws and code of ethics. Incorrect use of the appellation on business cards and in advertising is one considered issue in the code of ethics. Of course, there are many other serious issues, and ethics will be discussed in detail in the next chapter. Detailed information on membership qualifications and benefits can be obtained from the association Web site or contacting the national office listed in the Internet Resources appendix.

International Interior Design Association (IIDA)

The IIDA "works to advance the value of the interior design and its practitioners as well as to cultivate leadership within the profession."[4] There are over 10,000 members in 30 chapters around the world working in all areas of residential and commercial interior design. Members are able to be involved in two of eight specialty forums that bring special benefits and targeted information to the forum groups. The eight forums are corporate, residential, healthcare, hospitality, retail, facility planning and design, government, and education and research.

Membership benefits include chapter meetings and activities; a national conference held in conjunction with NeoCon, a major professional trade show held in Chicago, and a national news magazine called *perspective*. The national office also provides educational programs, industry liaison, design competitions, job postings, and many other programs and activities. The IIDA Web site provides a communication avenue to and from its national office to members around the world. An e-mailed newsletter, *Design Matters*, helps keep members informed of the latest news and events of the association. The members-only section of the Web site provides specialized information for IIDA members.

Membership categories provide special benefits and participation to a wide range of individuals in the industry. There are eight categories of membership as of 2006 in IIDA: (1) professional, (2) associate, (3) affiliate, (4) student, (5) international, (6) industry representatives, (7) international design school members, and (8) educator.

Professional membership is the highest category of membership in IIDA. It is reserved for those members whose work experience, educational background, and successful completion of the NCIDQ examination permits them to apply for this membership category. To obtain professional membership level, the member must be either a practicing interior designer or architect. The interior design professional must meet one of these standards: (1) the educational and experience requirements of the NCIDQ in order to take the examination or (2) proof of satisfactory completion of the NCIDQ examination or the National Council for Architectural Registration Board (NCARB) examination. Architects must also show six years of experience in interior design. Only professional members who hold voting privileges may use the appellation *IIDA* after their names without a suffix qualifier. IIDA also requires that professional members complete 1.0 continuing-education units (CEUs), or ten hours, every two years. CEUs are discussed later in this chapter.

The second level of membership in IIDA is called *associate* membership. Associate members are actively engaged in the profession of interior design similarly to allied members of ASID. Associate members meet the same educational requirements of professional members but have not completed the NCIDQ examination. Associate members are also required to complete 1.0 CEUs every two years. These members may use the appellation *Associate IIDA* after their names for marketing purposes.

The third membership category is called *affiliate* membership. These members are individuals who are involving in an area related to interior design, such as graphic design, lighting design, or landscape architecture, but do not qualify for professional membership.

Student memberships at a national level are available to students who are enrolled in a recognized design school or college program. A special newsletter for students called *Custom* provides information helpful to students concerning academics, the job market, and other topics in the industry. Student members are also able to elect joining two forums and receive the *perspective* magazine as well as the *Custom* newsletter. Students who maintain their student membership in good standing through graduation may apply for allied membership immediately upon graduation.

Industry members are individuals who are interested and supportive of interior design but who are not practicing designers. These members include manufacturers, individual representatives, design centers, and schools.

The *educator* membership category is for full-time educators. There are professional-level educators who also meet the qualifications as a professional member as a practitioner or architect and the associate-level educator who meet the same qualifications as the practitioner associate-level member. Educator members are also required to complete the 1.0 CEU credits or ten hours of continuing education every two years and may elect two specialty forums.

A new program started by the IIDA is International Design School Membership. "The International Design School Membership is a pilot program to support the exchange of information within the global design community. IIDA does not endorse any interior design program."[5] For more information on this program, visit the IIDA Web site.

As with ASID, by signing the application for any level of membership, the individual agrees to abide by IIDA's bylaws and code of ethics. Additional detailed information on membership qualifications and benefits can be obtained from the association national office listed in the Appendix or the Web site listed in the Internet Resources.

Interior Design Educators Council (IDEC)

Individuals who are actively engaged in teaching interior design often choose to become members of the Interior Design Educators Council. Many IDEC members are also professional or educator members of ASID, IIDA, and other associations. IDEC is "dedicated to the advancement of education and research in interior design. IDEC fosters exchange of information, improvement of educational standards, and development of the body of knowledge relative to the quality of life and human performance in the interior environment. IDEC concentrates on the establishment and strengthening of lines of communication among individual educators, practitioners, educational institutions, and organizations concerned with interior design education."[6]

Two of the most important benefits to educators are the annual and regional conferences and the publication of the only academic journal for the interior design profession. Speakers, seminars, and workshops are provided for the presentation of research and for the exchange of ideas at the national and regional conferences. The publication of the *Journal of Interior Design Education and Research*, a refereed journal, provides a mechanism for research materials to be widely distributed to educators and interested professionals. The *IDEC RECORD* has become a Web-based member newsletter. Many other programs, reference materials, and activities to assist members in improving the teaching of interior design are also available. The IDEC Web site contains information for the general public and has a members-only link that gives members access to a large body of interior design information specifically for use in teaching.

Full-time interior design educators who also have received appropriate interior design education and have professional work experience may become *professional* members, the highest membership level. Qualifications for professional member status are a diploma, a bachelor's degree or master's degree in interior design or a related field, and two years of full-time teaching experience in interior design. If a professional member also practices professionally in interior design, he or she also must complete the NCIDQ examination or be a professional member of an association.

Members who teach interior design courses sometimes do not qualify for professional membership and join as an *associate* member. Associate members may advance to professional membership when they meet the qualifications. Associate members who practice professionally in interior design also are required to pass the NCIDQ examination or to be a professional member of an association.

Graduate student level membership is available for those who are enrolled in postgraduate degree programs in interior design or other programs deemed acceptable by IDEC. Graduate student members can attend most IDEC meetings and functions, receive publications and mailings, and are encouraged to participate in committees.

Interior Designers of Canada (IDC)

The Interior Designers of Canada (IDC), founded in 1972, is the national professional association in Canada. IDC works in coordination with seven provincial associations:

- Interior Designers Institute of British Columbia
- Registered Interior Designers of Alberta
- Interior Designers Association of Saskatchewan
- Professional Interior Designers Institute of Manitoba
- Association of Registered Interior Designers of Ontario
- Association of Registered Interior Designers of New Brunswick
- Association of Interior Designers of Nova Scotia

The IDC is "a national association of provincial interior design associations. It works with its seven provincial association members to advance the interior design profession and to promote high quality in education and practice from coast to coast"[7] Its members work in all specialties of interior design and design education throughout the provinces of Canada. Members of IDC must hold the highest level of membership in their provincial association and must pass the international NCIDQ qualification examination.

IDC offers its members conferences, a newsletter entitled *Communique*, and education and learning opportunities through continuing education classes and programs. It supports quality education through affiliation with the Council for Interior Design Accreditation. IDC also serves as the primary representative of the Canadian interior design profession to the Canadian federal government. It supports forums related to government relations, the environment, and cross-disciplinary collaboration and offers assistance to members who are working in the global market.

The seven provincial associations have individual membership categories and requirements. The reader should contact the appropriate provincial association for information. There is a direct link to those associations at the IDC Web site.

CONTINUING EDUCATION

Formal educational preparation provides the foundation for the knowledge and skills needed to function in the interior design profession. One should not decide that learning in the profession ends upon graduation. Whether one desires technical updating, wants access to focused topics related to a specific design specialty area, or has a general interest in some area of interior design, like all other professionals, interior designers should seek out continuing-education venues. Courses that provide *continuing-education units* (CEU) furnish short-term course work in a wide variety of topical interest. CEU classes provide a means for professional interior designers to remain current in the practice of interior design.

Continuing education is also very important because several states that have passed licensing or title registration acts require continuing education for maintaining registration. The exact requirements are the responsibility of the licensing board in each state. It is the individual's responsibility to inform state boards of any CEU activity.

Many designers seek postgraduate education in interior design, architecture, and business, to name just a few broad areas. Sometimes designers obtain additional education in order to increase their technical skills and to allow themselves an opportunity to advance within the firm in which they work. Sometimes they seek additional education in order to retrain for a new area of expertise, such as lighting design or CAD, or to move into management. Not all professionals have the time to seek college credit, however. And many professionals do not really desire the depth of study that is required when taking college courses.

There are now many hundreds of seminars, workshops, lectures, correspondence courses, online seminars, and intensive professional studies to meet individual needs. These continuing-education offerings are available in almost every topic and area of the profession. The subject matter topics of theory and creativity, interior design, interior design education, design specialties, technical knowledge, codes and standards, communications systems, business and professional practice, and history and culture do not do justice to the range of topics available but do provide a context of content.

Courses are also evaluated as to whether they can be categorized as health, safety, or welfare or of general content. This is very important, as many states that have regulated interior design practice require their interior designers to complete a certain number of continuing-education hours specifically in health, safety, and welfare topics. A topic that would receive a "health safety" (HS) designation must have more than 75 percent of the content cover topics such as codes, regulations, and performance standards of materials, as well as mechanical systems concerning protecting the public and the environment. A course designated as "welfare" (W) must have 75 percent or more of content covering social, psychological, financial, and physical well-being of users and the environment. Certain topics in business practices, ethics, budgeting, and construction administration would fall under this designation. General content classes encompass any continuing-education sessions that do not meet either of the two above content criteria.[8]

Unlike formal academic settings with courses that last several weeks, continuing-education courses last anywhere from one hour to a few days; most common are all-day courses. The course length and level of difficulty are primary factors in determining the number of CEU credits available for the class. One-tenth of an hour of credit (0.1) is given for each hour of the class. Most CEU classes are under 1.0 total credits or 10 hours of involvement.

Continuing-education courses are taught by educators, interior design practitioners, and other experts in many fields. All CEU courses are rigorously reviewed by a voluntary committee of members representing ASID, IIDA, IDEC, and IDC. Courses are also reviewed by participants after each session, ensuring the content meets the content proposed by the instructor and reviewed by the Interior Design Continuing Education Council, which grants the approval of the course.

Each association provides a number of CEU classes each year, most often sponsored at the local chapter level or as part of a national conference. In addition, numerous CEU classes of various credit amounts are offered at the professional association national and regional conferences. CEU classes are also offered at major market shows, such as NeoCon.

It is important to note that reciprocity exists between many of the professional associations. It is possible for an ASID member, for example, to take a class sponsored by IIDA, IFMA, or another association. The member should check with his or her association to determine if a course offered by a different professional association will be applicable to his or her association. In some cases, the member may need to send a formal request to his or her association to determine if the course will be accepted.

Once a class is completed, the CEU credits are registered with NCIDQ through submission of a form and a nominal fee. This registration is maintained whether or not the individual is an NCIDQ certificate holder. It is up to the individual interior designer to keep track of his or her CEU credits. If the designer's association requires CEU credits to maintain membership, the member must request that transcripts be sent to the association's office. Some states require additional proof of completion of courses. The group offering the class should provide documentation to participants so that the interior designer can submit required proof to his or her registration board. The NCIDQ does not automatically inform the professional association or state registration boards of a professional's CEU course work each year.

Today's technological, litigious society makes it incumbent upon interior design professionals to keep current regarding the many technical, legal, and business skills and concepts of the profession. Whether or not one's professional association or state requires continuing education, all professionals should seek out appropriate seminars for updating, as well as for challenging one's thinking.

GIVING BACK

Accomplishing the course work to attain a degree in interior design in not an easy road—nor should it be. Taking that first step provides the grounding in subjects necessary for the professional in the twenty-first century. Experience on the job site with clients and colleagues is the second step to understanding what the profession is really all about and achieving a place in the profession. Attainment of certification through testing and licensing are further actions critical of professionals in the twenty-first century. Whether or not one works in a jurisdiction that has licensing or a title act, taking the NCIDQ examination should be a goal for all professionals today. Many professionals find involvement with a professional association gratifying, and continuing education should be another professional involvement that all interior designers accept as a necessary part of staying up-to-date in the profession. Maintaining ethical standards—whether or not one chooses to become a part of an association—is another critical part of professionalism.

All of these measures and tasks of becoming and maintaining professionalism are, of course, important. However, there is one more responsibility that interior design professionals should consider a critical part of their career. That responsibility is to give something back to the profession.

Giving back to the profession can be done in many ways. Giving back to students can be accomplished by volunteering to critique class projects. This might take only a few hours out of the professional's schedule once or twice a year. Professionals can fill a need for students while helping themselves by agreeing to be internship sites or serve as IDEP supervisors and mentors. Professional association chapters often have student design competitions, and volunteering to jury this competition is another way of giving back. There are many other ways of supporting education and students. Professionals need only contact liaisons at the interior design programs in their area to find out how they can give back.

Naturally, the professional may wish to become a member of one of the associations, and while membership may have its marketing rewards, greater rewards come from active involvement in the local chapter. Chapters have numerous activities run by committees of volunteers. There are never enough volunteers to help put on those activities and meetings for the members. Involvement in the chapter might result in chapter leadership, where the professional can make a greater impact on the activities of the chapter while learning many new skills and meeting other professionals. Chapter leadership is often the way to become involved on the national level, creating another way to give back to the profession.

Design professionals can also give back by contributing design expertise to community service organizations and activities. Local chapters often have some type of community service activity where members can provide design skills or monetary contributions to one or more selected community programs. Of course, the professional can also become involved in community service on his or her own, directing service or contributions back to the community.

Time is precious to many practitioners, and for some, giving back can't be accomplished by being actively involved in the schools or associations. Thus, giving back can take a monetary form through gifts, grants, trusts, special awards, and other methods of financial support of the profession. Association foundations accept many forms of financial support to help further the profession. Some of these include supporting students and design education and research through grants and awards for professional contributions.

These are just some of the ways that a professional can give back to the profession. The satisfaction of being involved in interior design can often be quite great. That satisfaction grows immensely when one gives something back.

SUMMARY

Being a professional interior designer means commitment to one's colleagues, clients, allied professionals, and students. Professionalism begins with educational preparation that meets the needs of the profession as well as the individual interests of the practitioner. However, in the twenty-first century, education preparation cannot come from reading magazines alone. It requires serious application of effort to a formal program—whether that is a four- or five-year bachelor's degree or a supplemental two-year degree.

This chapter also has explained the importance of examination and certification through the NCIDQ examination. The exam seeks to identify practitioners with baseline knowledge in the broad body of knowledge that impacts interior design profession. In my opinion, it should not be a matter of "should I take the exam?" but rather "I will."

Being a professional means being involved in an appropriate association, not just becoming a member. Being a professional means having sufficient pride in one's profession to fight for the profession throughout ethical performance and legislation. And being a professional recognizes the importance of continuing education to supplement and improve one's knowledge of the practice and skill sets of interior design. All these concepts and more demonstrate what a professional interior designer can attain as the profession continues to grow in complexity, stature, and, well, professionalism.

REFERENCES

1. Council for Interior Design Accreditation, 2006, *Accreditation Manual*, p. 1-1.

2. NCIDQ Web site, 2006, www.ncidq.org

3. ASID Web site, 2006, www.asid.org

4. IIDA Web site 2006, www.iida.org

5. IIDA 2006 Web site, www.iida.org

6. IDEC, 2006 Web site, www.idec.org

7. IDC Web site, 2006, www.interiordesigncanada.org

8. *IDCEC 2006 Presenter's Manual*, p. 11.

CHAPTER 3

Ethics and Professional Responsibility

Key Terms and Concepts

These key terms and concepts are important to material in this chapter. Many of the terms will be utilized in other chapters as well. Be sure you understand these items as you read this chapter.

Terms and Concepts

Ethics	Kickback
Conflict of interest	Ethical standards
Fiduciary duties	Codes of conduct
Proprietary information	Disciplinary procedures
Commissions	

Critical Issues

After completing this chapter you should be able to:

- Explain a conflict of interest that might exist between yourself and your client or between you and a colleague.
- Discuss at least two fiduciary duties you have to your employer and your client.
- Differentiate and explain an example of proprietary and nonproprietary employer information.
- Explain how someone's unethical behavior can impact others working in your market location.
- Discuss why ethical behavior is important for anyone working in the interior design profession regardless of association affiliation.
- Explain the purpose of ethical standards and codes of conduct in this profession.
- Name the three specific reasons discussed in the text why people behave unethically. Discuss how these actions negatively impact dealing with clients.

Don was very excited that the primary home magazine in his city was interested in publishing photos and a story about a large residential project Don had completed a few months ago for a high-profile celebrity. Before the photo shoot by the magazine, a reporter interviewed Don about the project and what it was like to work with the client. Don had never been published before and was very energized during the interview, giving the reporter all kinds of interesting information about the project and the client. The reporter—uncharacteristically—asked if Don was a member of ASID and Don said yes, though he did not clarify that he was in fact an Allied member. When the photographer and the editor arrived to shoot the house, the client indicated that although Don had "been involved," the client's designer from another city had actually been the primary designer. The client also was now a little uncomfortable with a photographer taking pictures of the interior. He did not realize that a photographer was going to be coming to the house. The client thought that the photos would come from the designer in the other city who had already had photos taken of the house.

The news headlines continually give us a lesson in ethical behavior—or, rather, the lack of it. Politicians, business leaders, corporations, sports figures, and practitioners in almost every walk of life test how far ethical behavior can be stretched before someone would notice and take action. Unfortunately, this also holds for interior designers. As a result, the teaching of ethics in all professional education programs has increased in importance. Although the unethical behavior of an interior designer is very unlikely to garner headlines in one's local newspaper or to be discussed on MSNBC, ethical standards are just as important in the interior design profession.

Interior designers on occasion will come to an ethics crossroad: down one path leads to behavior that is expected of a professional; down the other path leads to behavior that is contrary to one or more ethical standards. Perhaps the stumble down those ethical paths comes from omission rather than outright commission, yet the unethical behavior occurs. The decision has consequences for the individual, his or her company and client, and the profession as a whole.

The expectations and demands for ethical professional behavior in interior design increase as our world continues to become more complex. If we expect other professionals who affect our lives to behave ethically, interior designers can demand no less. Thus, it is imperative that ethical behavior be treated as more than just a brief discussion in class while the class anticipates getting into subjects that are "more important."

This chapter presents an overview of ethical concepts and issues as they relate to the professional practice of interior design. A few additional changes have also been made in this edition. The first you may have already noticed. A case that emphasizes an ethical situation has been added to each chapter in a box called "What Would You Do?" The chapter on legal responsibilities has also been moved to follow this chapter, since it is quite clear that many of the issues that involve ethical responsibility often involve legal responsibility.

This chapter is only a beginning, and I hope that the reader—whether a student or a professional—will seek additional information and guidance related to this important topic from an association chapter or an organization. Questions are raised through examples so that the reader will think about and discuss ethical solutions to the examples. It is hoped that, in this way, the reader will begin to connect the code of ethics to situations that might occur in the profession.

ETHICS IN THE BUSINESS ENVIRONMENT

Marty is the design director for an interior design firm who specializes in healthcare, medical office suites, and also other nonmedical office facilities. His firm is considering responding to a request for proposal (RFP) for the redesign of the emergency services and outpatient services areas of a major hospital. Marty's wife, Jane, is on the selection committee who will review RFPs from firms responding, as well as make the recommendation for which design firm to hire. Marty's employer knows this and wants to proceed with the RFP.

Ethics Definitions

Following are a few definitions of ethics from a variety of sources.

Ethics are "moral principles that govern a person's or group's behavior; the moral correctness of specified conduct."[*]

"Ethical standards are not the standards of the law. In fact, they are a higher standard. Sometimes referred to as normative standards in philosophy, ethical standards are the generally accepted rules of conduct that govern society. . . . Ethics consists of those unwritten rules we have developed for our interactions with each other."[**]

"Ethics in a business context; a consensus of what constitutes right or wrong behavior in the world of business and the application of moral principles to situations that arise in a business setting."[***]

[*]*Oxford American College Dictionary*, 2002, p. 463.
[**]Jennings, 2006, p. 3.
[***]Miller, Jentz, 2006, p. 47.

Making ethical decisions in the general business environment often comes down to making choices that have something to do with such areas as competition, conflict of interest, misuse of proprietary information, and employee theft.[1] Of course, other problems can also cause ethical dilemmas. These four are discussed because they represent major ethical issues in business and also can affect the interior designer as an individual or the individual's design business.

The free-market system creates rivalry between businesses—in other words, competition. When there are many businesses that offer the same or similar services or products, the competition can be intense. Sometimes competition becomes intense because of the state of the economy. In slow economic times, competition can become very intense. When competition becomes intense, business owners, managers, and some employees may stretch ethical boundaries in order to win customers. Maybe a designer asks for a special discount (without passing it on to the client) from the manufacturer in order to specify one product over another and ensure the winning of a project. On the other hand, what if the vendor offers a special discount (on the side) in order to have his or her product specified? Perhaps the designer makes an offer to the client during negotiations that is very good because the designer desperately needs the revenue to pay outstanding bills of the firm.

Many interior designers feel that there really is no problem with competition in interior design. However, this is not really true. All design firms are in competition with each other, in one way or another. Architectural firms, retail stores, and vendors who sell directly to the client are also competitors of interior designers. In a practical sense, they are not likely to be pursuing the exact same clients, but some are. And when the economy is slow, even more designers are competing for the same clients. Regardless of the size of the interior design firm and how well the local economy is doing, plenty of competition exists among interior design firms.

An ethical crossroad concerning a competitive market can be met from another direction. Rather than designers bending competitive ethics, clients can put designers into a position that can test the interior designer's ethics. Some clients shop around for a designer's ideas and prices, which in some ways is fine. Sometimes a client, however, who has a contract with designer A takes drawings prepared by designer A to designer B in order to get a lower price on merchandise specified for the project. What is designer B to do?

These examples also deal with conflict of interest. According to Bryan Garner, editor-in-chief of *Black's Law Dictionary, conflict of interest* is "a real or seemingly incompatibility between one's private interests and one's public or fiduciary duties.[2]" *Fiduciary duties*, by the way, means that one person acts in a position of trust or confidence for someone else. For example, when a supplier offers a *personal* advantage to a designer for specifying a certain product, the designer, if he or she accepts it, acts in a manner that is a conflict of interest. Putting personal gain above the good of the person or the organization that the designer is supposed to represent is an example of unethical behavior.

Another issue that has an impact on ethics in business is the misuse of propriety information. *Proprietary information* comprises a wide variety of data or information, graphics, or designs that belong to a particular person or business. Employers own all sorts of propriety information, such as financial data, client lists, discounting policies, and many others. Clients also can own proprietary information, such as trade secrets about a product or unique information about the operations of the business. Whether the proprietary information belongs to the design firm or a client, the owner of the proprietary information would not want an interior designer, or anyone else, to divulge the information to competitors or to the public. For example, a designer leaves a company, taking and using proprietary information on that company's bidding strategies, and goes to work for a competitor. If the employee shares that information with the new employer, he or she could be sued by the original employer. This behavior can also result in an ethics complaint against the designer. Firms try to combat this issue by having employees sign nondisclosure agreements, which means that the employee is not allowed to take proprietary information upon termination or voluntary separation.

Here is another situation. Gerald Smith is under contract to design the research and development offices for Netscape. Shortly after receiving the contract, his firm is contacted to provide design services for the same type of department at Microsoft. The Microsoft project is a much larger project and is therefore more lucrative than the Netscape project. Would it be a conflict of interest for Gerald Smith's company to contract with Microsoft at the same time that he is working on the project for Netscape?

Employee theft is another common problem in the general business environment that can also affect interior design firms. Technically, taking home office supplies that are provided by the employer for personal use is employee theft. It is rare indeed for any employer to press charges against an employee for taking a few pens home. But employees have taken money, goods from the sales floor or warehouse, or even office equipment—all of which are of greater value to the company. Perhaps a designer "borrows" a lamp for his home, and "forgets" to sign it out on approval. Or, a designer makes a copy of a software specification template so that she can use it for a personal business. Theft by employees does occur, although hopefully it is not a great problem in interior design offices. What would you do if you knew that a colleague had borrowed a copy of some software to use while he was moonlighting in his spare time?

Why do some people behave unethically? According to Brown and Sukys, it is because people (1) are motivated by self-interest, (2) are careless, and (3) see no harm in the behavior.[3] When someone places his or her own interests before others', he or she may be behaving unethically. Consider the case of a design student who shows work to an employer that has been done by someone else in her portfolio and represents it as her own. Since in reality she cannot do that quality of work, she has put self-interest first. The employer at some point will figure out that something is not right.

People become careless about ethical behavior when they get into a habit of being unethical. Perhaps a designer has gotten away with overbilling clients for services. Maybe a designer consistently over-orders upholstery fabrics by a few yards and charges the extra yardage to the client, not to ensure that the amount will be enough for the project but to warehouse the extra fabric in order to use it to make throw pillows for other clients.

The "But everybody does it" and "I see no harm . . ." excuses are another reason why people behave unethically. For instance, the statement, "Everybody uses down payments from one client to pay for orders for another client," could be made by many designers. This practice is unethical and can be illegal if the state that designer works in requires that those down payments be held in escrow and used only for the client who made the down payment (see Chapter 25 for a further discussion of this). Just because "everybody does it" does not make it right. Harm is caused by this kind of thinking.

Related to this issue is the practice of accepting commissions. Interior designers receive a commission from some vendors when the client purchases products directly from the vendor. These commissions constitute additional revenue to the interior designer. This type of commission is not usually very large and is only paid to the designer if the client actually orders from the vendor. However, these commissions raise ethical debates and ethical problems. Is the interior designer required to tell the client about these commissions? According to the codes of ethics from both ASID and IIDA, it is necessary to disclose all forms of compensation to the client. Some interior designers debate whether their colleagues should accept these commissions at all.

A clear conflict of interest and unethical situation occurs when a designer receives a kickback. According to the Cornell Law School Web site, *kickbacks* "entail the return of a certain amount of money from seller to buyer as a result of a collusive agreement."[4] Kickbacks are clearly improper and are not the same as the commissions described in the previous paragraph. An example of a kickback is when a vendor gives a special discount to one designer for specifying or bidding on a project but not to other designers who are also bidding on the job. Another example of a kickback is when someone gives a payment of some kind as a very special inducement to favor the specification of one product over another. It is important to note that the discounts or commissions that vendors regularly give to interior designers are not illegal or unethical. It becomes unethical when the special price is given for special treatment, such as the preceding examples.

In commercial interior design, a practice that might be considered unethical but can also be an appropriate business practice is buying a job. Some firms lower their price drastically on services or bids on goods in order to obtain a project. *Buying a job* refers to the practice of pricing the goods or fees at an unusually low level in order to make the sale. Some feel it is unethical because it sets a price with which other firms cannot compete. Others argue that setting a very low price is merely a marketing and business tool to enter a market, to obtain a specific type of work, or for other reasons that are legal and essentially ethical.

However, how would you feel if you owned a firm and discovered three recent projects were lost to a firm that did not charge a design fee and offered to sell the merchandise to the client at a very substantial discount?

These issues provide a background for looking more closely at professional conduct and ethical behavior in the interior design profession. Ethical behavior does not affect only interior designers who have joined one of the professional associations. Ethical behavior should be practiced by anyone involved in this profession and in business in general. It is important to note that conducting oneself according to an ethical compass affects those in jurisdictions with practice or title act legislation. The legislation defining the practice, title, or certification parameters almost uniformly include an ethics portion of the statute.

PROFESSIONAL CONDUCT

Professional conduct and performance includes the concept that a professional is expected to provide competent services in a manner considered customary by those in the profession. In addition, professional conduct means that those entering the profession must abide by standards accepted by others in the profession. A point of fact is that when a designer at any level signs the application for membership in the professional associations, the applicant is agreeing to abide by the association's code of ethics.

Ethical behavior is not a new interest brought to the fore because of the ethical lapses of others showcased in the media in recent years. It has always been a concern of the interior design professional associations. Adherence to the "Code of Ethics and Professional Practice" was expected of members of the AID in its earliest years.[5] In fact, the "AID Code of Ethics and Professional Practice" was published in a professional practice manual at least as early as 1961.[6] As discussed in the first chapter, one of the characteristics of a true profession is that the profession and its members are guided by a set of *ethical standards*. These ethical standards define what is right and wrong in relation to the professional behavior of the members and even the practice of the profession.

The teaching and discussion of ethics and an enforceable code of ethics that comes from professional associations provides definable and enforceable standards for this profession. However, a code of ethics cannot by itself produce ethical behavior. Ethical behavior must come from individual designers themselves in their daily dealings with clients, peers, the public, and allied professionals.

The codes of ethics of the professional associations deal with enforceable ethical standards of practice and provide philosophical comments concerning the professional conduct of its members. The discussion of codes of conduct and codes of ethics utilize those from ASID and IIDA, since these two organizations represent the majority of professional association memberships in interior design. The ASID Code of Ethics and Professional Conduct (see Figure 3-1) reviewed annually and recently revised, contains standards related to five areas of responsibility: (1) to the public, (2) to the client, (3) to other interior designers and colleagues, (4) to the profession, and (5) to the employer. The IIDA Code of Ethics (see Figure 3-2) is also reviewed annually. It consists of four sections: (1) the designer's responsibility to the public, (2) the designer's responsibility to the client, (3) the designer's responsibility to other designers and colleagues, (4) the designer's responsibility to the association and interior design profession. Of course, the other associations also have their own code of ethics or conduct. Readers interested in the code of ethics from other associations should contact them directly.

ASID Code of Ethics and Professional Conduct

1.0   PREAMBLE

Members of the American Society of Interior Designers are required to conduct their professional practice in a manner that will inspire the respect of clients, suppliers of goods and services to the profession and fellow professional designers, as well as the general public. It is the individual responsibility of every member of ASID to uphold this code and bylaws of the Society.

2.0   RESPONSIBILITY TO THE PUBLIC

2.1   Members shall comply with all existing laws, regulations and codes governing business procedures and the practice of interior design as established by the state or other jurisdiction in which they practice.

2.2   Members shall not seal or sign drawings, specifications or other interior design documents except where the member or the member's firm has prepared, supervised or professionally reviewed and approved such documents, as allowed by applicable laws, rules and regulations.

2.3   Members shall at all times consider the health, safety and welfare of the public in spaces they design. Members agree, whenever possible, to notify property managers, landlords, and/or public officials of conditions within a built environment that endanger the health, safety and/or welfare of occupants. If, during the course of a project, a Member becomes aware of an action to be taken by, or on behalf of the Member's client, which in the Member's reasonable opinion is likely to result in a material adverse effect on the health, safety and welfare of persons occupying or using the space, the Member shall refuse to consent to, or participate in that action, and if required by law and/or under circumstances the Member deems reasonably prudent to do so, the Member shall report such action to the governmental agency having jurisdiction over the project.

2.4   Members shall not engage in any form of false or misleading advertising or promotional activities.

2.5   Members shall neither offer, nor make any payments or gifts to any public official, nor take any other action, with the intent of unduly influencing the official's judgment in connection with an existing or prospective project in which the members are interested.

2.6   Members shall not assist or abet improper or illegal conduct of anyone in connection with any project.

FIGURE 3-1.

ASID Code of Ethics. (Reprinted with permission, American Society of Interior Designers, Government and Public Affairs, Washington, DC)

3.0   RESPONSIBILITY TO THE CLIENT

3.1   Members' contracts with clients shall clearly set forth the scope and nature of the projects involved, the services to be performed and the methods of compensation for those services.

3.2   Members shall not undertake any professional responsibility unless they are, by training and experience, competent to adequately perform the work required.

3.3   Members shall fully disclose to a client all compensation that the member shall receive in connection with the project and shall not accept any form of undisclosed compensation from any person or firm with whom the member deals in connection with the project.

3.4   Members shall not divulge any confidential information about the client or the client's project, or utilize photographs of the client's project, without the permission of the client.

3.5   Members shall be candid and truthful in all their professional communications.

3.6   Members shall act with fiscal responsibility in the best interest of their clients and shall maintain sound business relationships with suppliers, industry and trades.

4.0   RESPONSIBILITY TO OTHER INTERIOR DESIGNERS AND COLLEAGUES

4.1   Members shall not interfere with the performance of another interior designer's contractual or professional relationship with a client.

4.2   Members shall not initiate, or participate in, any discussion or activity which might result in an unjust injury to another interior designer's reputation or business relationships.

4.3   Members may, when requested and it does not present a conflict of interest, render a second opinion to a client or serve as an expert witness in a judicial or arbitration proceeding.

4.4   Members shall not endorse the application for ASID membership and/or certification, registration or licensing of an individual known to be unqualified with respect to education, training, experience or character, nor shall a member knowingly misrepresent the experience, professional expertise of that individual.

4.5   Members shall only take credit for work that has actually been created by that member or the member's firm, and under the member's supervision.

4.6   Members should respect the confidentiality of sensitive information obtained in the course of their professional activities.

5.0   RESPONSIBILITY TO THE PROFESSION

Continued

5.1   Members agree to maintain standards of professional and personal conduct that will reflect in a responsible manner on the Society and the profession.

5.2   Members shall seek to continually upgrade their professional knowledge and competency with respect to the interior design profession.

5.3   Members agree, whenever possible, to encourage and contribute to the sharing of knowledge and information between interior designers and other allied professional disciplines, industry and the public.

6.0   RESPONSIBILITY TO THE EMPLOYER

6.1   Members leaving an employer's service shall not take drawings, designs, data, reports, notes, client lists or other materials relating to work performed in the employer's service except with permission of the employer.

6.2   A member shall not unreasonably withhold permission from departing employees to take copies of material relating to their work while employed at the member's firm, which are not proprietary and confidential in nature.

6.3   Members shall not divulge any confidential information obtained during the course of their employment about the client or the client's project or utilize photographs of the project, without the permission of both client and employer.

7.0   ENFORCEMENT

7.1   The Society shall follow standard procedures for the enforcement of this code as approved by the ASID Board of Directors.

7.2   Members having a reasonable belief, based upon substantial information, that another member has acted in violation of this code, shall report such information in accordance with accepted procedures.

7.3   Any violation of this code, or any action taken by a member which is detrimental to the Society and the profession as a whole, shall be deemed unprofessional conduct subject to discipline by the ASID Board of Directors.

7.4   If the Disciplinary Committee decides the concerned Member did not violate the Society's Code of Ethics and Professional Conduct, it shall dismiss the complaint and at the concerned Member's request, a notice of exoneration from the complaint shall be made public. If the Disciplinary Committee decides that the concerned Member violated one or more provisions of the Society's Code of Ethics and Professional Conduct, it shall discipline the concerned Member by reprimand, censure, suspension or termination of membership. The Disciplinary Committee may, in its discretion, make public its decision and the penalty imposed. The Disciplinary Committee does not impose any other form of penalty. The Disciplinary Committee cannot require payment of any monies or mandate certain action to be taken by the concerned Member.

FIGURE 3-1.

Continued

Policy D.8:	Code of Ethics and Professional Conduct
Purpose:	To establish minimum standards of behavior and conduct for Professional and Associate Members of the Association
Intent:	To provide the public, legislators, and the profession of Interior Design with standards of conduct and behavior for Professional Interior Designers

1.0 PREAMBLE

Professional and Associate Members of the International Interior Design Association shall conduct their interior design practice in a manner that will encourage the respect of clients, fellow interior designers, the interior design industry and the general public. It is the individual responsibility of every Professional and Associate Member of IIDA to abide by the Code of Professional Ethics and Conduct, Bylaws, Policies and Position Statements of the Association.

2.0 DEFINITIONS

The terms used in this Code shall be defined in the same manner in which they are defined in the Bylaws, Policies and Position Statements of the Association.

3.0 RESPONSIBILITY TO THE PUBLIC

3.1   In performing professional services, Professional and Associate Members shall exercise reasonable care and competence, and shall conform to existing laws, regulations and codes governing the profession of interior design as established by the state or other jurisdiction in which they conduct business.

3.2   In performing professional services, Professional and Associate Members shall at all times consider the health, safety, and welfare of the public.

3.3   In performing professional services, Professional and Associate Members shall not knowingly violate the law, or counsel or assist clients in conduct they know, or reasonably should know, is illegal.

3.4   Professional and Associate Members shall not permit their name or signature to be used in conjunction with a design or project for which interior design services are not to be, or were not, performed under their immediate direction and control.

3.5   Professional and Associate Members shall not engage in any form of false or misleading advertising or promotional activities and shall not imply, through advertising or other means, that staff members or employees of their firms are Professional or Associate Member unless such is the fact.

3.6   Professional and Associate Members shall not make misleading, deceptive or false statements or claims about their professional qualifications, experience, or performance.

3.7   Professional and Associate Members shall not, by affirmative act or failure to act, engage in any conduct involving fraud, deceit, misrepresentation or dishonesty in professional or business activity.

3.8   In performing professional services, Professional and Associate Members shall refuse to consent to any decision by their clients or employers which violates any applicable law or regulation, and which, in the Professional and Associates Members' judgment, will create a significant risk to public health and safety.

FIGURE 3-2.

IIDA Code of Ethics. (Reprinted with permission, International Interior Design Association, Chicago, IL)

3.9   Professional and Associate Members shall not attempt to obtain a contract to provide interior design services through any unlawful means.

3.10   Professional and Associate Members shall not assist any person seeking to obtain a contract to provide interior design services through any unlawful means.

4.0   RESPONSIBILITY TO THE CLIENT

4.1   Professional and Associate Members shall undertake to perform professional services only when they, together with their consultants, are qualified by education, training or experience to perform the services required.

4.2   Before accepting an assignment, Professional and Associate Members shall reasonably inform the client of the scope and nature of the project involved, the interior design services to be performed, and the method of remuneration for those services. Professional and Associate Members shall not materially change the scope of a project without the client's consent.

4.3   Prior to an engagement, Professional and Associate Members shall disclose, in writing, to an employer or client, any direct or indirect financial interest that they may have that could affect their impartiality in specifying project-related goods or services, and shall not knowingly assume or accept any position in which their personal interests conflict with their professional duty. If the employer or client objects to such financial or other interest, Professional and Associate Members shall either terminate such interest, or withdraw from such engagement.

4.4   Professional and Associate Members shall not reveal any information about a client, a client's intention(s), or a client's production method(s) which they have been asked to maintain in confidence, or which they should reasonably recognize as likely, if disclosed, to affect the interests of their client adversely. Notwithstanding the above, however, Professional and Associate Members may reveal such information to the extent they reasonably believe is necessary (1) to stop any act which creates a significant risk to public health and safety and which the Professional or Associate Member is unable to prevent in any other manner; or (2) to prevent any violation of applicable law.

5.0   RESPONSIBILITY TO OTHER INTERIOR DESIGNERS AND COLLEAGUES

5.1   Professional and Associate Members shall pursue their professional activities with honesty, integrity and fairness, and with respect for other designers' or colleagues' contractual and professional relationships.

5.2   Professional and Associate Members shall not accept instruction from their clients which knowingly involves plagiarism, nor shall they consciously plagiarize another's work.

5.3   Professional and Associate Members shall not endorse the application for membership in the Association of an individual known to be unqualified with respect to education, training or experience; nor shall they knowingly misrepresent the experience, professional expertise, or moral character of that individual.

5.4   Professional and Associate Members shall only take credit for work that has actually been created by the Member or the Member's firm or under the Member's immediate direction and control.

6.0   RESPONSIBILITY TO THE ASSOCIATION AND INTERIOR DESIGN PROFESSION

6.1   Professional and Associate Members agree to maintain standards of professional and personal conduct that will reflect in a responsible manner on the profession.

6.2   Professional and Associate Members shall seek to continually upgrade their professional knowledge and competency with respect to the interior design profession.

FIGURE 3-2.

Continued

6.3 Professional and Associate Members shall, wherever possible, encourage and contribute to the sharing of knowledge and information among interior designers, the interior design industry, and the general public.

6.4 Professional and Associate Members shall offer support, encouragement, and information to students of interior design.

6.5 Professional and Associate Members shall, when representing the interior design profession, act in a manner that is in the best interest of the profession.

6.6 Professional and Associate Members may only use the IIDA appellation in accordance with current Association policy.

6.7 Professional and Associate Members shall not knowingly make false statements or fail to disclose any material fact requested in connection with their applications for membership in the Association.

03/01

FIGURE 3-2.

Continued

These rules of conduct exist for members of the organizations. They have no actual impact on interior designers who are not members of one of the organizations. Members must keep them in mind and use them when they deal with other designers, whether or not the other designers are members of one of the organizations, their clients, others in the industry, and the public in general. Just because someone who is practicing interior design or interior decoration is not a member of one of the associations does not mean that the individual can behave unethically. However, an ethical charge cannot be made against an unaffiliated designer. It is important for anyone in this profession to behave within ethical and moral standards. To not do so is not only harmful to that individual but also to the entire profession.

The examples that I have mentioned in this chapter pose serious ethical problems. However, they do not encompass the most common ethical problems that have found their way into the national associations' ethics committees for disciplinary hearings according to the interior design professional associations. Some broad examples of ethics complaints filed with the ASID national office are shown in Table 3-1. It is important to note that according to ASID staff,

TABLE 3-1.

Some of the Most Typical Complaints Heard by ASID in 1999 (Provided by ASID, Washington, DC)

- Withholding merchandise that is already paid in full
- Undisclosed methods of compensation
- Overbilling, double-billing
- Failure to disclose all business practices and compensation methods
- Purposely avoiding or not returning phone calls, faxes, letters, and other forms of communication
- Designer not qualified by professional history and experience to do the job
- Merchandise ordered of a poor or unacceptable nature
- Failure to pay suppliers after deposits or full payment has already been made
- Failure to adhere to budget, unless discussed and approved by client first
- Unclear or nonspecific contract
- Contract alteration as the job progresses without prior client approval
- Not performing in best interest of client
- Unprofessional or improper business relationships

the list does not contain all the issues reported to ASID in a year. The largest number of complaints deal with financial or compensation questions and miscommunication.

Professional conduct and professional responsibility are interwoven in the overall practice of interior design. Designers do not necessarily give conscious thought as to whether a daily activity that is part of working on a project for a client is done ethically or in a manner prescribed by the profession. But sometimes a designer comes to an ethical crossroads where a choice is made to behave in a manner that is in contradiction to a code of ethics or even the person's personal moral compass. When this happens, it hurts the individual to be sure—tomorrow if not today. And it impacts everyone else and the profession in general.

A thought-provoking contract and exercise concerning an ethical situation has been included on the CD as Item 3-1a and 3-1b. The exercise questions in Item 3-1b will challenge your understanding of professional code of conduct in interior design.

DISCIPLINARY PROCEDURES

Ethics complaints received by the professional associations have increased over the years. Fortunately, most designers have little if any idea of what happens when a client, or someone else, feels that the interior designer has conducted themselves in an unethical manner since a grivance may not be field. This section briefly describes what happens when someone—a client or another designer—feels that a member of an association has violated professional conduct. Note that disciplinary procedures may vary slightly from the information provided in this section with each association.

The individual against whom a complaint is made must be a member of one of the professional associations. The complainant—let us say a client—must file the complaint in writing, explaining the details and facts of the situation. The letter is sent to the national or chapter office of the appropriate association. The complainant should include supplemental information with this originating letter. Sometimes clients who are unfamiliar with the process may be asked to supply supplemental documentation if they wish once the initial contact is made to the association.

Upon receipt of the information from the complainant, the information may be reviewed by an appropriate party, such as an attorney or a chapter ethics committee, in order to make an initial determination of whether a violation has actually occurred. This is done because disputes concerning design features— the client is upset because the design is not what the client expected—generally do not constitute a violation of ethical conduct.

If a determination has been made that a more detailed review and consideration are warranted, the member is notified. A copy of the complaint is sent to the designer, and the designer is given an opportunity to respond within a specified period of time. All the materials from the complainant and the designer are then sent to the association's ethics committee. The makeup of the ethics committee varies by association, but it generally consists of three or more professional level members. Sometimes the ethics committee may request additional information from one or both parties.

When the ethics committee determines that a violation may very well have occurred, the complaint may be reviewed by another committee—although this step varies by association—before going to the association's disciplinary committee. If the complaint is forwarded to a disciplinary committee, each party to the complaint is permitted to provide testimony, bring witnesses, and/or provide additional documentation before the disciplinary committee. If additional materials are provided by either party, that submitting party must also send a copy of these supplements to the other party prior to the hearing. At the time of the disciplinary committee hearing, the parties may also have legal counsel present. The disciplinary committee then determines if the facts provided by each party truly indicate that the designer charged by the complainant has violated the association's code of ethics. The committee may take several courses of action, from dismissing the case to terminating the designer's membership in the association.

Disciplinary hearings are not "courts of law" and have no legal bearing on either party. A client, however, may also decide that the designer's actions are legally actionable and may file a civil claim (see the next chapter). Thus, a disciplinary committee functions to investigate allegations of unethical behavior by members of the association. It has no authority over nonmembers who may behave unethically.

Actions taken to the disciplinary committee are no light matter. ASID publishes, in the *ICON*, the names of those members whose membership have been revoked by the disciplinary committee. Although this may be personally embarrassing to the member whose name appears in print, it also serves to advise all members that the code of ethics will be enforced by the association.

WHAT WOULD YOU DO?

Discussions concerning professional responsibility and ethical conduct are an important, even mandatory, part of the education of students and ongoing reference for professionals. As mentioned earlier, throughout this book you will find sidebars called What Would You Do?, which give the reader an opportunity to think through common situations in interior design practice and consider the ethical implications of the case.

This chapter concludes with several situations that may or may not involve ethical behavior and choices. These ethical situations are posed as case situations that the reader can, individually or in groups, discuss whether the situation is an example of unethical behavior. As you read these examples and the others in the chapters, consider these questions, as well as which—if any—item in the code of ethics from ASID or IIDA apply to the situation. If you were the designer in each case, what would you do to avoid ethical complaints? What would you do if you were a coworker? What would you do if you were a designer at another firm and heard about any of these situations? Which specific ethics item in the ASID and/or the IIDA codes might apply to each situation?

- John has been running radio ads in his community, which give the impression that he and all his staff are professional-level members of one of the associations. John and half of his staff are not professional members of the associations mentioned in the ads.
- Marsha has a strongly held belief that abortions are wrong, but she has always kept these feelings to herself. The design firm she works for has recently obtained a contract for the remodeling and design of several offices for Planned Parenthood. Marsha was assigned the role as lead designer and project manager for this client.
- Samantha goes to the home of a new client. The client shows Samantha boards and plans that obviously were not prepared by the client. The designer would really like to do this project, because the client is quite a well-known celebrity.

- Katie has been working for a design firm for five years, having gained much experience in a design specialty area. She became a bit disgruntled because she did not receive a raise and promotion recently. Katie has been approached by other design firms in the past year. Deciding to finally look for another job, without permission, she takes plans of projects she has been involved in and includes them in her portfolio for the job interviews.

- It came to the attention of Phyllis that her boss was considering hiring a designer—Jane Doe. Phyllis knew Jane because they worked together at a different design firm a few years ago. Phyllis knew that Jane had been fired because the other employer discovered Jane had been falsifying several types of client documents in connection with projects.

- During her initial marketing presentation, Mary makes it clear to the client that she is experienced in handling a complex restaurant design. Her marketing materials show photos of restaurants in other cities. In fact, Mary has no experience in this area. Mary was awarded the project and now numerous errors have already been made in the floor plans.

- Gray designed a doctor's suite providing space-planning services, finish specifications throughout the suite, and specifications of furniture items for the waiting room and the offices. The client approved samples and furniture items from a sample board. Gray only charged the client for design services and the furniture items. He did not sell the client the architectural finishes, nor was he responsible for the construction work. The project is now at the stage of installation of the finishes. The client is upset that the colors and materials for the walls and floors do not look like what he expected and is also upset that the whole project is six weeks behind schedule.

- Roberta owns a design studio and specializes in the design of high-end residential projects. She recently has lost two projects to a competitor. One of those projects was for a former client, who is building a very large penthouse in Manhattan. Roberta plans to ask vendors about her former competitor.

- A designer has learned that a colleague in another design firm always orders extra rolls of some wall coverings, billing the product to the clients whose project needed the wall covering. Rather than giving that extra material to the client paying the bill, the designer donates it to charities, taking a tax deduction on his income taxes.

- Richard works at GBS Interiors. He has been hinting to some vendors that he is responsible for three or four major model home designs, but that his boss is taking all the credit. Richard feels that because all the boss did was meet with the client to show ideas that Richard had developed, the projects are really his own.

SUMMARY

Some feel that it is not possible to teach ethics once an individual has become an adult. It is argued that we learn our values and morals as we grow up and that our ethics spring from those years of learning. Value systems and moral conduct start with what parents and other relatives teach us or show us, say philosophers. Ethics and values also come from others with whom we come in contact, such as clergy, teachers, coaches, and friends.

Whether it is possible to teach ethics or not is not the point of this chapter. Rather, the discussion of ethics is offered to encourage further discussion of ethical behavior in the interior design field. Perhaps you are someone who would never overcharge a client or do work for which you are not capable and qualified or any number of other things that some others carry out. Unprofessional, unethical behavior by anyone hurts everyone and the profession in general.

It really does not matter if a practitioner has chosen to be a member of a professional association or chooses to be unaffiliated. If one chooses membership in an association, ethical behavior is expected in order to remain in good standing in that organization. If one does not choose to join an association, ethical behavior should still be practiced and is expected.

As was stated in an early version of the IBD Code of Ethics, "To be a professional involves the acceptance of responsibility to the public. . . . Ethical conduct is more than merely abiding by the letter of explicit prohibitions. Rather, it requires unswerving commitment to honorable behavior, even at the sacrifice of personal advantage."[7]

REFERENCES

1. Ivancevich et al., 1994, p. 97.

2. Reprinted from page 295 in *Black's Law Dictionary*, 7th ed., by Bryan A. Garner, ed., 1999, with permission of the West Group.

3. Brown and Sukys, 1997, p. 8.

4. Cornell Law School Web site, Wex—definitions.

5. Allwork, 1961, p. 13.

6. Allwork, 1961, p. 13.

7. *Code of Ethics*. Reprinted with permission from the Institute of Business Designers, 1980, p. 3.

CHAPTER 4

Legal Responsibilities

Terms and Concepts

These terms and concepts are important to material in this chapter. Many of the terms will be utilized in other chapters as well. Be sure you understand these items as you read this chapter.

Constitutional law	Intentional torts
Statutory law	False imprisonment
Administrative law	Spam
Case law	Defamation
Electronic law	Slander
Ordinances	Libel
Uniform laws	Fraud
Crime	Misrepresentation
Statutes	Puffing
Tort law	Assault
Negligence	Battery
Professional negligence	Conversion
Duty of reasonable care	Codes
Causation	Building codes
Breach of contract	Fire safety codes
Legal injury or harm	Barrier-free regulations
Assumption of risk	Plan review boards (PRB)
Contributory negligence	Red-lined
Proximate cause	

Critical Issues

After completing this chapter you should be able to:

- Identify where the laws that govern business and personal behavior originate.
- Explain how an interior design business meets its legal obligations in the business environment, citing specific examples.
- Compare the differences (in a general sense) between criminal and tort law.

- Explain the issues that must be proved to show an interior designer was negligent.
- Analyze a situation and determine if the interior designer was negligent.
- Explain the concept of assumption of risk as it applies to an interior design project.
- Discuss how a client might contribute to an event that the client later claims was professional negligence by the interior designer.
- Compare statements that are misrepresentation versus statements that are considered salesperson's puffing.
- Explain the difference between the unintentional and intentional torts discussed in the chapter.
- Compare the intent of the building code, fire safety code and barrier-free regulations.

We generally do not read about or even hear about interior designers being sued by a client over some dispute or harm that might have occurred as a result of the work of an interior designer. Yet lawsuits do occur in this profession. A lawsuit might involve a designer being sued because he did not complete the project according to the provisions of state law—specifically, a state home improvement act. Or perhaps someone breaks an arm after tripping and falling over an unsecured area rug. Or the wrong-size draperies are made because the measurements were not taken correctly by the supplier or checked by the interior designer.

This chapter now follows the chapter on ethics because so many legal issues are also ethical concerns. Not holding a proper license to hire a tile installer who does a substandard job of installing tile in a bathroom not only can result in a lawsuit concerning the work, but in a fine from the state and an ethics hearing should the client complain to the professional association. One designer saying strong negative comments to a prospective client about a designer at another firm that costs the second designer the project and other work is both a legal and ethical dilemma for the first designer.

Interior designers are legally liable for the work they or members of their staff do and, as such, can be sued. This exposure includes the planning, specification, and execution of the design and design documents. Even the smallest design project involves activities and responsibilities that can lead to potential legal actions against the designer. Legal responsibility is not a matter of choice in the twenty-first century; it is a fact of professional life.

The recognition and acceptance of legal responsibilities continues to increase. Perhaps only a small amount of disputes and problems that occur in the interior design profession actually make it to a court. That should not matter. Interior design students and practitioners must be aware that lawsuits can negatively affect their practice. Issues of malpractice and negligence can ruin a designer's reputation and severely affect them financially. It is the responsibility of the professional designer to be aware of the legal responsibilities that affect his or her practice. It is not necessary to become a lawyer, but it is necessary to understand all the ramifications of engaging in a professional practice so as to avoid legal problems.

This chapter provides an overview of legal responsibilities that can affect the practice of interior design. The chapter begins with an overview of the legal environment in interior design practice and continues with a focus on tort law issues of negligence. As has been presented in earlier editions of this text, legal issues related to other specific areas of management and practice are discussed in the context of those chapters for clarity.

The examples given in this chapter are simple illustrations that help clarify the legal concepts discussed in the chapter. In reality, a great many factors are involved in the determination of the actual guilt or innocence of persons in situations that are similar to the examples given in this chapter. These chapters do not constitute legal advice. The information provided should not substitute for any discussion with an attorney.

THE LEGAL ENVIRONMENT OF INTERIOR DESIGN PRACTICE

Legal responsibility in interior design practice is woven into every aspect of practice. It is also intertwined with ethical conduct. As you read this chapter and the others that include information about legal responsibilities, you will see clearly how this is true. That was a critical reason why the chapter on legal responsibilities follows the chapter on ethics. Many legal issues are discussed throughout this text. This brief section provides an overview of the legal environment of interior design professional practice.

Laws that govern business and personal behavior come from several sources. The highest level of law in the United States is *constitutional law* as expressed in the U.S. Constitution. Each state and commonwealth also has a constitution that must not supersede U.S. constitutional law. Another source of our laws is *statutory law*. This type of law is created by governmental entities such as the U.S. Congress and state legislatures. Local governments can also create *ordinances*, such as those for zoning, building codes, and traffic issues. A state statute only applies to that state, an ordinance only applies to that municipality or county, and a federal statute applies to all states. Of course, numerous states and municipalities often have similar statutes and ordinances.

Another source of law in the United States is called *administrative law*. This source of law relates to rules and decisions of agencies of federal, state, and local governments. An example is the Department of Justice, which enforces rules concerning accessibility, and a state health department enforces rules and codes related to many issues in the design of facilities such as hospitals and restaurants. The local building department will enforce the building codes in a municipality. One additional source of our laws is *case law*, also called *common law*. When a case is decided in court, that ruling enforces or adds to case law. Case law is what directs areas of law not regulated by statute or administrative law.

There are also laws called *uniform laws* that try to bring consistency to the numerous versions of similar laws passed by individual states. A group called the National Conference of Commissioners on Uniform State Laws (NCCUSL) has been responsible for writing many of these uniform laws. An important law for businesses is the Uniform Commercial Code, which consists of statutes governing commercial transactions. It is discussed in detail as it relates to sales law in Chapter 26.

A relatively new area of law that affects businesses including interior design practice is that of *electronic*, or computer *law*. This area of law is also called cyber law by some. Specific discussions on electronic law appear in other chapters. A brief introduction about cyber law is found in Item 4-1 on the CD.

There are a diverse and large number of statutes and rulings that impact businesses. State statutes requiring a resale license for businesses that sell merchandise is one example. Federal laws concerning what can and cannot be asked on job applications and during interviews is another example. Disputes that occur between the client and the designer are affected not only by what is in the contract, but by the statutes within the jurisdiction. What obligations a designer might have should a product that he or she specifies for a project fail is defined in the uniform laws. Ownership of items of intellectual property such as the drawings the designer creates for the project fall under federal laws. These are only a few examples of the abundant ways laws affect business.

Business practice accountability does not suddenly heighten when licensing or registration legislation is enacted in a jurisdiction. Any size or type of practice has to meet its obligations in the business environment from the time someone begins the business and continues until the owner decides to close or sell the firm. However, business owners are not the only parties who must adhere to legal precepts. Legal responsibility holds employers and employees responsible for their actions and interactions with clients, vendors, and others.

Let us start at the beginning of a business. A new practice must be created in accordance with laws existing in the jurisdiction. This means filing forms with state and local government agencies. Obtaining a resale tax license for firms planning on selling merchandise to clients is one example. Meeting regulations concerning the practice of interior design is another, as is obtaining a contractor's license in order to sell and supervise the installation or construction of interior finishes. Information concerning these areas of legal responsibility is discussed in Chapters 9 and 10.

Interior design professionals enter into many kinds of contracts in the course of operating the practice. The contract that most comes to mind is with the client that describes the services to be performed for a project. A second type of contract is for the sale of goods to clients. Some employers use employment contracts to define the responsibilities of employees. When a firm purchases goods for a client, the firm enters into a contract each time a purchase order for a goods or service in the name of the client is created. The design firm also enters into contracts for various marketing activities such as advertising, Web site hosting, and photographing projects. The primary discussion of contracts is in Chapters 24, 25, and 26.

Employers own a duty and responsibility to employees to treat them fairly and to provide them with a safe work environment free from harassment and discrimination. The employee also has duties and responsibilities to the employer. An employer's responsibility begins with the hiring process in knowing that certain types of questions are not permitted during the interview or on employment applications. It continues throughout the working association, encompassing wages, benefits, promotions, and recommendations, as well as discharge when the employee's services are no longer required by the firm. An employee is expected to follow the legal direction of the employer to accomplish the tasks that the employee has been hired to perform. Issues of employment law are included in Chapters 14, 15, and 34.

By far, the most common kinds of cases that involve interior designers are related to tort law—specifically, negligence and breach of contract. *Negligence liability*, often referred to as *professional negligence*, legally means that the designer has failed to use due care in carrying out his or her design responsibilities normally expected by a professional. *Breach-of-contract liability* refers to the failure of the designer to complete the requirements of a contract. Breach of contract is discussed in Chapter 24, while negligence is a major portion of the discussion of this chapter. The tort of strict liability refers to liability regardless of who is at fault. Under strict liability, people are responsible for their acts, regardless of their intent or use of reasonable care. For example, a painter who has been hired to paint the exterior of a home uses reasonable care when he is using spray-painting equipment. However, the next-door neighbor goes out to inspect her house and finds overspray of the blue paint on the side of her white house. The painter is liable under strict liability.

Although strict liability issues can be raised concerning an interior designer's performance, like the painter in the example, to an interior designer, this tort is most related to product liability and product specification. It is discussed in detail in Chapter 27 on warranties.

I hope that this brief overview helps the reader recognize that interior design practice is more than creative problem solving and creation of aesthetic and functional interiors. Students beginning their pursuit of a career must realize that their design efforts—whether in residential or commercial design or in the specification of products or the drafting of floor plans—place them in a position of responsibility to their clients that goes beyond designing an aesthetic environment. As practitioners, it also involves many areas of legal responsibility to clients, colleagues, employees, the profession, and many others with whom the designer will come into contact.

CRIMINAL VERSUS TORT LAW

Our laws are also classified into criminal laws and tort laws. A criminal offense, referred to as a *crime*, is an offense that is regulated by *statutes* that are created to protect the public at large and are considered wrongs against all of society. The punishment for the criminal act is imprisonment and/or a fine. We are all familiar with the concept that an individual person can commit and be punished for a crime. A legal entity can also commit a crime. Corporations are legal entities, and thus the business and its officers can be accused and tried for crimes. If someone within the corporation falsifies public records or alters legal documents, he or she is committing the crime of forgery. For example, executives from corporations have been tried and found guilty of insider trading, bank fraud, embezzlement—taking of another person's property or money by the one entrusted with it—obstruction of justice, and many other widely publicized activities.

The legal problems that might ensnarl interior designers rarely involve criminal law issues. Most legal problems that interior designers experience involve some aspect of tort law. *Tort law* involves acts when a person commits a wrong against another and causes injury to the other, who is considered the harmed party. Torts are not legislated by statute and thus are considered civil matters. A tort issue might be unintentional, which is commonly thought of as negligence. There are many kinds of intentional torts where the wrong is committed consciously or deliberately.

Since the act is against one person (or entity) by another, a tort is a civil action, in which the person harmed sues, in a civil court, the person who has done the harm. When we think of "harm," we normally think of someone suffering a physical injury. In tort law, harm can be to property, to a person's reputation, to a person's physical being, or even to a person's business. The injured person may seek various remedies for the damages caused. A remedy might be monetary, performance of the task at issue, or even stopping performance, to cite a few types. For example, a client might sue an interior designer to provide the complete set of drawings that were agreed to in a contract. Some torts, such as assault and battery, are also criminal acts if there are statutes that define them as such.

NEGLIGENCE

Alice was the project interior designer for an assisted-living facility. The project involved reselection of all the architectural finishes for common and public areas, as well as setting up a program of finishes that the residents could choose for their apartments. Alice marketed herself as an experienced residential designer and talked about some of the homes and apartments she had done for seniors. About six months after the installation was completed, the staff noticed an increase in the number of residents who were stumbling and a few falling while walking down the corridors and in the dining room. A doctor thought it was due to the pattern and style of the carpeting. It was a medium-sized pattern that was slightly sculpted. Could Alice and her design firm be liable in any way for this sudden number of falls?

It is far too easy for an interior designer by omission or commission to become involved in a tort that could result in a lawsuit. *Negligence* is an unintentional tort that can occur because of omission or commission in the activities and responsibilities of a person engaged in—for our purposes in this text—interior design.

"Negligence is the failure to exercise the standard of care that a reasonable person would exercise in similar circumstances."[1] Incorrectly specifying which fabric goes on which furniture item on your purchase order to the upholsterer is an example of a commission. Forgetting to order the fabric at all is an example of omission. These examples, however, in themselves are not negligence.

The negligent act must be the cause of the harm and harm must actually occur to a person or his or her property. Negligence is unintentional because the designer did not think that any wrongful consequences of an act would occur and did not want them to occur. The person accused of negligence creates a risk, and that risk created the environment for the tort of negligence. This risk is such that a reasonable person can anticipate it and prevent it. If there is no creation of risk, there cannot be negligence.

To prove negligence, the harmed party must prove several things: first, that the defendant owed a duty—most commonly, "reasonable care"—to the plaintiff; second, that there was a breach of that duty either intentionally or unintentionally; third, that the act was the proximate cause or more simply the causation of the harm; and fourth, that there were damages or harm to persons or property. For example, inadvertently switching numbers on a purchase order, which results in the wrong wallpaper being hung in the client's home, is negligence. Selling and installing a carpet that the designer knows does not meet fire codes is negligence. An improper specification of textiles that has been proven to contribute to a fire is negligence.

Anyone can be involved in a situation that results in negligence. Not stopping for a stop sign and running into another vehicle could also be considered negligence. Professional negligence indicates that the designer in some way was negligent in his or her conduct while executing a project. All the elements of negligence apply to professional negligence. Some examples of professional negligence, pointed out in Justin Sweet's *Legal Aspects of Architecture, Engineering, and the Construction Process*, are worth repeating here:

- Specifying material that did not comply with building codes
- Failing to inform client of potential risks of using certain materials
- Drafting ambiguous sketches, causing extra work
- Designing closets not large enough for the clothing to be contained in them
- Designing a project that greatly exceeded the client's budget
- Failing to engage and check with a consultant[2]

Interior designers plan interiors and specify products and materials that, when not planned or selected carefully, can cause injury or harm to the client or the business. A dresser drawer pulled out causes the drawer to fall on a child. Specification budgets for the interior furnishings of a second home are 45 percent over budget. Custom furniture items do not fit into alcove seating locations, resulting in a restaurant not opening on time.

As can be seen by these examples, there are a large number of relatively unintentional acts related to everyday responsibility that can be considered professional negligence. Let us look specifically at the factors that must be proven in order to show negligence and how they relate to an interior design practice. If these factors do not exist, then it is most likely that the courts would say that negligence has not occurred.

Duty of Care

Everyone has a duty to use reasonable care in his or her interactions with others. For a professional, that duty also extends into using reasonable care in his or her dealings and actions as a professional working for others and in the interests of clients. Following are a few additional examples to clarify the concept of duty of care and negligence.

Specifying residential grade carpet in most commercial interiors would give inadequate performance and would be negligent. Another common issue is the correct preparation of working drawings. Incorrectly labeling dimensions for a custom cabinet is a mistake, but it is also negligence if it results in the wrong size cabinet being constructed. A designer cannot allow defective work to be done on the job site. For example, if a designer who is visiting a job site sees that the carpet installer is using a non-quick-release glue to affix carpet tiles when a quick-release glue was specified, the designer has a duty to the client to stop the work and have it corrected. Staying within the budget stated by the client is another duty, and thus designing and writing specifications that are in excess of the budget also constitutes negligence.

Breach of Duty

Other criteria of whether negligence has actually occurred concerns whether a breach of duty owed to others really took place. A breach of duty results when a designer fails to act in a way that is considered reasonable for the professional designer. The reasonable-person standard in terms of interior design practice would mean that the actions considered a breach are things that others in the profession would not have done. The breach may be an act, such as knowingly specifying the wrong carpet for the client (intentional), or an omission, such as not stopping the work when the designer sees that the carpet being installed is incorrect (carelessness). The benchmark of "reasonable" is sometimes hard to define, so expert witnesses are often used to help the court determine what is reasonable for an interior designer concerning the case in question.

Causation

Another important criterion that must be proved to show negligence is that the action causes the injury or harm. The causation might be the *proximate cause* of the harm, which means the "connection between the unreasonable conduct and the resulting harm"[3] is strong enough to justify the person's liability. In other words, if the injury occurs exclusively because of the designer's act, then there is proximate cause. For example, a designer knows that a certain manufacturer requires 5/8-inch drywall to support its wall strips and knows that the client already has installed 1/2-inch drywall. If the designer has the wall strips hung anyway, there is causation in fact. Often the "but for" test is used to determine causation in fact: "But for the wrongful act, the injury would not have occurred."

"The question is whether the connection between an act and an injury is strong enough to justify imposing liability.[4] If the consequences of the act that does harm are unforeseeable, there is no proximate cause. For example, if the wall strips pull out from the wall and, as a result, the falling books hit a lamp, which shatters and starts a fire that then burns down the house, there would probably be proximate cause if it were shown that the lamp would have created a fire if it had broken in such a manner. How foreseeable one act is over another is determined by the courts and is not easy to establish. For the designer to be held liable, actual cause between the act and the harm created must be present.

Injury or Harm

A tort of negligence does not exist unless there is some legally recognizable loss, harm, wrong, or invasion to a plaintiff. Injury must occur in order for the plaintiff to recover compensation. There does not have to be an injury to a person for this element to exist. The delay in delivery of furniture for a business to operate can be considered an injury if the delay is the fault of the designer. Remember, plaintiffs in tort cases seek compensation for damages from the defendant; they usually do not seek to imprison the defendant. Courts more often find in favor of the plaintiff when personal injury, rather than property or economic damage, occurs.

Principal Defenses for Negligence

For an act to be considered negligent, the four criteria just discussed must all be proven. Beyond proving that one or more of these criteria did not happen or were not the responsibility of the defendant, there are some additional defenses for negligence. The first is called assumption of risk. In *assumption of risk*, the plaintiff who knowingly and willingly enters into a risky situation cannot recover damages if harm or injury occurs. If a client agrees to purchase a residential-grade carpet, knowing it will not provide the wear required in his or her commercial installation, the designer is absolved of negligence.

Another defense to negligence is *contributory negligence*. In this defense it must be shown that both sides have been negligent and that injury has resulted. This comes from the idea that everyone should look out for his or her own interests and safety. Many states, however, have modified this defense to a defense called comparative negligence. In this instance, it is recognized that both parties are in some way at fault, and thus their level of negligence is compared and determined. The courts determine the degree of fault by both sides and grant damages related to it. Comparative negligence often softens the effects of contributory negligence.

What Would You Do?

Your firm prepared design drawings to explain to a client what an outdoor gazebo at a restaurant would look like. There were no notations on the drawings that they were for design only and not for construction. The client gave those drawings to a carpenter who was doing work on the interior of this new restaurant. The carpenter constructed the gazebo using only those design drawings. At an opening-night party, a large number of people gathered within the gazebo, and someone was injured when one of the railings gave way. The injured person and the client named you in a lawsuit, since you designed the gazebo.

INTENTIONAL TORTS

Negligent acts are considered unintentional torts. There are several kinds of torts that are considered intentional, meaning that they have occurred by a plaintiff on purpose and with knowledge that they were wrongful. Some of these acts occur against a person and others against property. Assault, battery, false imprisonment, defamation, invasion of privacy, and misrepresentation (fraud) are some of the torts included in the area of intentional torts against persons. Intentional torts against property are less likely to impact the practice of interior designers but are discussed briefly as well. Trespass, conversion, and nuisance are the most common types of intentional torts against property.

Against a Person

Intentional torts against a person must show intent; that is, the person must have consciously performed the act and must have known or have been substantially certain that the act would harm another person. The tort of false imprisonment (or false arrest) is of particular importance to designers who are engaged in retail selling and have a showroom or store. *False imprisonment* is the intentional confinement of a person for an appreciable duration of time without justification. This most often occurs in this profession when a store owner believes a customer has tried to shoplift something that belongs to the company. A business owner must be reasonably certain that a customer has shoplifted in order to detain that customer or the customer can sue for false imprisonment. In many jurisdictions, shoplifting has not occurred until the person has walked out the door of the business with goods that have not been properly paid for.

No one would argue that their good name is important to him or her. Harming that good name is very stressful and even painful to people. *Defamation* is the wrongful harming of a person's good reputation. If the defamation is in writing, it is called *libel*; if it is oral, it is *slander*. To be defamatory, statements must be made to, or read or heard by, a third party. It is not necessary for the defamed party to hear or read the defamation. Again, some harm must result from the statements made in order for them to be considered to be defamation by a court. Making derogatory comments about competitors could be harmful to that competitor. Interior designers must be careful about what they say or write concerning their competitors or competitors' products. For example, telling a client that Jones Interiors "did a lousy job" on their last three residential commissions would be defamation by slander if Jones Interiors lost work because of the comments. Jones Interiors could sue the offending designer.

The Constitution of the United States grants us all an absolute right to privacy and freedom from "prying eyes." The tort of invasion of privacy protects everyone's right to freedom from others' prying eyes. Say, for example, a designer named Ralph photographed a client's home after completion of the project. The client later found out that Ralph had placed those photos on his Web site. The client never gave Ralph permission in any way to use the photos in that context. It is important to obtain written permission to photograph an installation. This is especially important if the photograph becomes part of an advertisement or a printed promotional tool of any kind.

Permission should be obtained even if the designer does not intend to cite the location in the promotional piece or display. In addition, a release must also be signed by any people who are seen in the photograph, even if permission has been given to photograph the interior by the employer.

Disclosure of personal information about clients can also be found to be an invasion of privacy. For example, Karen's credit check on her client uncovered a questionable credit rating. She decided not to work with the client. At a meeting she discussed this client's credit rating with another designer. Care must be taken when obtaining information concerning a person's or a business's affairs. Obtaining credit information about a potential client should be done with permission, because to do so without permission could be invasion of privacy. Information about a project, especially any private, personal, and financial information about the client, must be kept confidential by the designer and must not be distributed intentionally or unintentionally

Fraud (also thought of as *misrepresentation*) is another intentional tort against a person. When a designer intentionally misrepresents facts to deceive a client in order to receive personal gain, fraud has been committed. The common test in this situation is misrepresenting facts. A misstatement of facts, not opinions, unless the person expressing the opinion is considered an expert in the subject matter, is what is considered to be fraud. Perhaps a designer tells the client that a specific upholstery fabric does meet code requirements for seating in a theater. If the fabric does not meet code requirements, the designer has misrepresented the facts. These "untrue facts" must be made with the intent that the client will rely on them. The deceived party must have justifiably relied upon the information, and the reliance must have caused damages to occur.

It is not unusual for designers or salespersons to use language that might exaggerate a service or a product. If a designer's or salesperson's statements are not misrepresenting facts, then those statements are likely to be considered seller's talk or "puffing." The use of puffing, or offering personal opinions about intangible qualifiers of a product or a service, is not usually considered fraud unless the seller represents as fact something that he or she knows is not true. To say that your design firm is the "best interior design office in town" is not fraud, since the word "best" is subjective. To say that your design firm is the only firm in town that can do the work when it is clearly not true is misrepresentation if, in fact, your firm is not the only firm in town that can do the work. Factual deception in order to obtain personal gain is a form of misrepresentation.

Two additional torts that are probably more often considered crimes are assault and battery. *Assault* occurs when a person intentionally performs an act so that another person has a feeling of apprehension or fear of harm or physical injury. Actual contact or physical harm is not necessary for an assault to occur; causing another to be apprehensive is enough. *Battery* occurs when there is intentional touching or other physical contact by one person upon another without the person's consent or without any justification.

There is another type of tort that involves wrongful interference with a business relationship and/or contract. Quite often this type of tort is also a violation of ethical conduct. A business can engage in any lawful activity to obtain clients. Interfering with a business relationship between one designer and his or her client to obtain business is not considered lawful. This is especially true and significant if a contract exists between the designer and his or her client.

Paula has developed the drawings, specifications, and sample boards for a client's vacation home, but no orders have been placed. A contract exists between the client and Paula and the client has given Paula a $5000 deposit for purchases plus additional funds for the design fees. The client took these documents to Fred, a designer at a furniture store in a neighboring city. Fred offered to complete the project as shown on the documents for 20 percent less than the prices quoted by Paula. Even though a client certainly has a right to shop around for the best price, it is likely to be determined that Fred wrongfully interfered with Paula's business relationship unless it can be shown that the agreement between Paula and the client had been terminated prior to the client going to talk to Fred. If the contract had not been terminated before the client shopped Paula's price, Fred also should not try to entice the client into canceling the contract with Paula. Review the codes of conduct and see where this action is also an ethical issue.

Against Property

The three torts against property are conversion, trespass to land and personal property, and nuisance. Although each may be a problem to the interior designer, the torts of conversion and trespass to personal property are potentially the most damaging.

The most common form of trespass of personal property is conversion. The tort of *conversion* occurs when the rightful property of one person is taken by another. In criminal law, this is commonly called stealing or theft. For instance, Grant asked his interior designer to let him take an office chair on approval. Grant had the chair for nine weeks and the designer e-mailed, called, and finally wrote Grant a letter asking for the chair back. Grant has yet to return the chair or even acknowledge the correspondence from the designer. This can be considered conversion because Grant apparently refuses to pay for or return the chair. In another example, an employee uses a company-supplied laptop computer for a design project she is doing "on the side" when it was clear that this type of personal use was not permitted.

Trespass to land occurs when a person enters onto or causes something to happen to land that does not belong to him or her. Trespass to personal property occurs when a person either injures the personal property of another or interferes with the owner's right to exclusive possession or use of the personal property. Let us say that in order to construct an addition to a client's house, a contractor's truck must drive over the neighbor's property and the weight of the truck will damage the landscaping. To do this without permission and consideration would be trespass.

A suit for nuisance can also be brought against an interior designer. "A nuisance is an improper activity that interferes with another's enjoyment or use of his or her property."[5] For the designer, this could mean that the designer and the client can be sued by a neighbor if the noise and dust from a remodeling project has interfered with the neighbor's enjoyment of his or her home. Designers should always work with the client and the neighbor's when major construction work is going to occur on a project in order to avoid any type of lawsuit of this nature.

CODE COMPLIANCE

It does not matter what type of design specialty a practitioner focuses upon; compliance with codes is a professional responsibility that is very important to all interior designers. *Codes* are systematic bodies of law created by federal, state, and local jurisdictions to ensure safety. For the most part, codes originate from independent agencies and are adopted and modified by federal, state, and local jurisdictions. During the course of a project, the interior designer's work may need to be judged against building codes, life safety or fire codes, and barrier-free (handicapped access) codes. Other codes might need to be applied as well. These include electrical, other mechanical, health department, and zoning laws.

No interior designer today can ignore code compliance. Codes affect many aspects of the work of the commercial designer. However, residential designers hired to design spaces in high-rise buildings and high-rise condominiums must also meet many of the same codes as an interior designer in commercial specializations.

It is important for the designer and firm to have access to many code references, since code requirements can vary by cities within the same general area. The code that applies to a specific project is the code that is in effect within the community where the project is being built or remodeled, not the location of the interior design firm. For example, an interior design firm located in Phoenix, Arizona, is preparing design drawings for a hospitality project in Tempe, Arizona (adjoining Phoenix), and Santa Barbara, California. The designer must meet the code requirements within Tempe and Santa Barbara, not those in Phoenix. Requirements might be similar, but the designer must research and make sure that the codes relevant to the specific project location are met in all aspects of the design.

Code compliance is not an option; it is a legal necessity. Information can be obtained from local fire marshals, planning and building departments, and state and federal agencies responsible for specific types of structures. It is possible to purchase the necessary code books from the local planning and building department, bookstores, or online. Noncompliance with codes can result in work being stopped, torn out, and/or redone, generally at the expense of the interior designer.

This section provides a brief overview of key codes. Numerous reference guides have been published recently to assist the designer in complying with the law. An excellent reference for the interior designer on the various codes is *The Code Guidebook for Interiors* by Sharon Koomen Harmon and Katherine E. Kennon.

Building Codes

Building codes primarily regulate structural and mechanical features of buildings. They define minimum standards for the design, construction, and quality of materials, based on the use, type, and occupancy of the building. Public safety is a key purpose in the code requirements of the building code. Issues of egress, accessibility, and some architectural finishes are also included.

The International Building Codes (IBC) is a set of model building codes first approved in 2000 by a joint commission. As all model codes, these are reviewed and revised every two to three years by the International Code Commission (ICC). A new version of the IBC will be published in 2006. In 2006 the majority of states had adopted the International Building Code, the International Residential Code, and/or the International Fire Code. However, not all jurisdictions have adopted all these model codes in all locations. A few jurisdictions might not have adopted the International Codes at all and may still be using a former model code such as the Uniform Building Code (UBC).

Jurisdictions have the option to adopt the Building Construction and Safety Code®, also referred to as the NFPA 5000®. This code was first published in 2003 and is updated every two to three years. It deals with building, planning and construction issues, as does the IBC. The reader should check to determine if his or her state has adopted any of the NFPA 5000 building code.

Not all jurisdictions change to the new code each time it is revised. Thus, it is possible that a jurisdiction retains use of a model code dated 2000 rather than one dated 2006. In addition, local building conditions may require additional code requirements. Designers who work in metropolitan areas or who design work in several different cities also need to be sure that they are using the right version of the building code for each jurisdiction. Two cities next to each other in an urban area may have slightly different requirements. The local planning or building department can advise the designer on the applicable code.

Residential interior designers should note that there are separate building codes for residences. The International Residential Code (IRC) from the ICC covers code issues in construction of single-family and duplex residences and townhouses. If the residential structure is over three stories—such as a high-rise condominium—the design would then have to meet the IBC codes.

Fire Safety Codes

Fire safety codes and regulations exist to provide a reasonable measure of safety in a building from fire, explosions, or other comparable emergencies. It is used along with the building code in most jurisdictions. The intent of these codes is to prevent a fire whenever possible. However, since all fires cannot be prevented, the codes also focus on fire control. Fire prevention is facilitated by the regulation of hazards and such things as controls on the kinds of materials—both construction and furnishings—that can be used in buildings. Fire safety control is facilitated by the requirement of fire sprinklers, fire doors, and the like.

The International Fire Code (IFC) from the ICC and the Uniform Fire Code (UFC) from the NFPA are code standards that may be adopted in any jurisdiction. Fire codes provide additional requirements that are applicable to specific situations than just the building code. In addition, there are code restrictions concerning furnishings in the fire codes.

The Life Safety Code—also called NFPA 101— concentrates on fire safety and attempts to lessen the danger to life from fire, smoke, and hazardous fumes and gases. It is also updated every two to three years. It does not focus as much attention on construction of a building as it does on fire safety and evacuation issues. The Life Safety Code is used by many jurisdictions.

The building and fire codes deal with regulations concerning architectural finishes. Fire regulations related to furniture items, furniture construction, and fabrics or finishes are more a matter of federal, state, and local regulations. Standards and test benchmarks are often used to classify finishes and furniture fabrics. The reader should become familiar with tests such as the Steiner Tunnel Test, the Pill Test, and the Upholstered Seating Test, since these standards are likely to be mentioned as minimum requirements in many occupancies.

Codes developed by the New York Port Authority, the Boston Fire Department, and the California State Fire Marshall's Office, to name a few, have been adopted by many of the states in order to regulate furniture construction and the fabrics or finishes of furniture. The most far-reaching fire code related to furnishings is California TB 133. The ASTM E1537 Standard Test Method of Fire Testing of Upholstered Furniture and the UL 1056 Standard for Safety for Fire Test of Upholstered Furniture are two of the other new tests that are similar to the California TB 133.

These tests require that the whole of the upholstered seating piece be tested and meet standards related to smoldering and ignition. The frame, stuffing, and padding, as well as the upholstery itself, must meet the standards. This is a very stringent standard for furniture and applies to certain types of commercial installations as required by the jurisdiction. The designer is again cautioned to check with local or appropriate fire marshals or building departments to clarify which fire safety standards are applicable in the firm's working area.

Barrier-Free Regulations

Building codes have worked to make public buildings more accessible to the handicapped and thus *barrier-free*. However, the accessibility requirements in the building codes do not detail all the barrier-free issues. In January of 1992, the Americans with Disabilities Act (ADA) opened the door, literally and figuratively, to making all buildings—public and private—accessible to those who are handicapped in the United States. The ADA itself is civil rights legislation, not a building code. Until a state or a local jurisdiction creates statutes of enforcement or incorporates the ADA regulations into its building code, a complainant would have to file a civil rights action in federal court. ADA regulations do not apply in the Canadian provinces or other nations. However, the international community has adopted many types of accessibility standards to meet their needs.

The ADA legislation deals with four distinct areas: employment, public service and transportation, public accommodations and commercial facilities (businesses that are not open to the public), and telecommunication services. This means that the legislation is a comprehensive package of requirements that denies discrimination against disabled individuals in many areas of their life. The ADA affects every public and private building and type of business, with few exceptions. Private residences are excluded, as are commercial facilities. Commercial facilities are defined in the ADA as nonresidential buildings used by a private entity and that only employees of the entity are given access to. Commercial facilities may have to make reasonable, readily achievable accommodations for employees, based on Title I of the ADA. There are special application requirements for restaurants and cafeterias, medical care facilities, business and mercantile buildings, libraries, transient lodging, and transportation facilities.

Applicable to our discussion in this section are the items concerning the design guidelines referred to as the ADA Accessibility Guidelines (ADAAG) prepared by the Architectural and Transportation Barriers Compliance Board (ATBCB). These accessibility guidelines deal specifically with such issues as public bathrooms, accessible travel routes, alarm systems, signage, and communications devices. The reader should be aware that the ADAAG guidelines have been revised and are under review as of 2006. Many aspects of the revised guidelines will help make them easier to reference and apply to designs of public buildings and others covered by the ADAAG. Adoption will again occur on a jurisdiction-by-jurisdiction basis after the review period and final adoption.

The intent of design guidelines is to provide access for a disabled person that is equal to that of the general public. New construction must be designed and built to meet the new design criteria called for in Title III. Existing buildings may have to make what are called "readily achievable" accommodations and changes to meet the criteria. If an existing building is going to be remodeled, it has to include all reasonable design changes. If an existing building is not undergoing any remodeling, the owners have to make the readily achievable changes if it is economically feasible to do so. Building code accessibility standards also influence these same issues and may, in some jurisdictions or types of occupancies, supersede the ADAAG. The designer, as always, must be sure which accessibility standards are required for the space being designed in jurisdictional location.

Having had a disabled parent for nearly 30 years, I understand and appreciate the importance of this landmark legislation, and I hope that designers will not view the ADA—or any code or regulation, for that matter—as infringement upon design creativity but rather as part of making all interior environments enjoyable to all individuals.

PLAN REVIEW BOARDS

The section on licensing and registration in Chapter 2 briefly discussed permitting status as part of legislation. New construction, most major remodeling projects, and projects involving a change in occupancy require a building permit be obtained from the local jurisdiction. Construction documents are evaluated by *plan review boards* (PRB) or design review boards (DRB), whose responsibility it is to ensure that the plans meet codes and standard construction methodology required in the jurisdiction. This evaluation must be done prior to issuance of building permits.

Depending on the contract responsibility, the type of project, and jurisdiction laws, the owner, architect, or interior designer submits copies of plans and specifications to the plan review board. Interior designers can only submit the construction drawings under their name and seal for a building permit if the interior designer is licensed or registered. A permit application and fee is part of the process.

The plans are first reviewed by a member of the building department. Large projects and especially commercial projects will also be reviewed by the fire marshal. These individuals look for any omission or discrepancy in design as regulated by building, mechanical, fire, and accessibility codes and regulations, as well as compliance with all other local building and construction standards. Plans get *red lined* or are marked in red to show where problems exist. If too many red marks occur, the plans are rejected and must be redrawn, and perhaps, if necessary, redesigned. If only a few red marks appear on the plans, these are usually worked out among the owner, architect, designer, contractor, and the building department prior to or during construction. Many projects also are reviewed by the engineering department, planning and zoning department, state health department, or other groups that are looking specifically for compliance with regulations and codes within their jurisdictions.

Since meetings of the plan review board are subject to open meeting laws, anyone can sit in on the meeting. Designers who have never been "under the fire" of a PRB meeting should sit in on one sometime. If nothing else, it will make the designer more careful about the production of plans and specifications for all future projects!

SUMMARY

Today's interior designers are held accountable for their activities in design and must accept professional responsibilities and liabilities in all areas of their practice. Interior designers must gain awareness of their legal responsibilities in designing interiors as well as in their everyday professional practice. Laws change frequently as state legislatures, municipalities, and the federal government create new laws and statutes to meet what they interpret to be needs to protect citizens.

Ignorance of the laws in effect in one's business jurisdiction can and do adversely affect how a business operates. It also keeps attorneys busy mitigating disputes and problems between their interior designer clients and those who seek some remedy from that designer. The designer is responsible for being familiar, if not thoroughly cognizant of, the many regulations and legislation that affect the interior design and related professions.

This chapter has provided a brief overview of the legal environment of business related to interior design practice. It included a discussion of the differences between criminal and tort law. It also discussed many of the common tort classifications that can result in a civil lawsuit being brought against an interior designer. Chief among these are negligence and the concept of professional negligence, and the chapter emphasized the discussion of negligence in relation to interior design practice. Legal responsibility also impacts many design decisions, and thus a short review of issues concerning the building codes, fire safety codes, and barrier-free regulations was included in the chapter. Finally, an overview of the design review process was provided.

Designers must gain awareness of their legal responsibilities in designing interiors as well as in their everyday professional practice. Today's interior designer is held accountable for his or her activities in design. The information in this chapter is provided to help the designer gain some understanding of that accountability so as to avoid legal problems. The reader may also wish to review items in the references, obtain copies of the applicable regulations, or take CEU classes for familiarization.

REFERENCES

1. Miller, Jentz, 2006, p. 123.
2. Sweet, 1985, pp. 329–330.
3. Brown and Sukys, 1997, p. 80
4. Clarkson et al., 1983, p. 53. Copyright West Publishing Co
5. Jentz et al., 1987, p. 55. Copyright West Publishing Co.

*N*CIDQ—for some intersior designers these letters spell "dread." For others, it is a challenge they cannot wait to trakle. I believe that the NCIDQ (National Council for Interior Design Qualification) must become an experience for designers to embrace rather than reject—it is here to make sure we have the knowledge and experience to call ourselves professional interior designers. The NCIDQ exam is simply the starting point to becoming a professional. The years spent after the exam—working with clients, contractors, architects, and engineers—will refine, shape, and sharpen an interior designer's skills. The NCIDQ acronym means "begin," not "dread!"

Lisa M. Whited, IIDA, ASID, was President of a commercial design firm in Portland, Maine, for 14 years, and has served as president of the National Council for Interior Design Qualification (NCIDQ). She believes that collaboration between the architectural and interior design professions will strengthen the public perception of good desing, and has taken a leadership role in bridging the respective professions. In her ongoing efforts to enhance the credibility and value of professional interior designers, Ms. Whited served as head of the interior design department within an architectual college, serves as an educator to several New England design schools, and has created and presented seminars, written articles, and spoken to groups across the country.

Photographer—Abbie Sewall

Photographer—Maine Audio Visual Services

Maine State House, Senate Chamber, Augusta, ME

Certified Interior Designer: Lisa Whited

Registered Architect: Weinrich & Burt

Contractor: Granger Northern

Getting Started

CHAPTER 5

Personal Goals

Key Terms and Concepts

These key terms and concepts are important to material in this chapter. Many of the terms will be utilized in other chapters as well. Be sure you understand these items as you read this chapter.

Terms and Concepts

Goals

Personal goals

Professional goals

Personal mission statement

Critical Issues

After completing this chapter you should be able to:

- Explain why it is important to set goals.
- Discuss factors that make goal setting difficult for some people.
- Define and explain what a personal mission statement is and why it is a helpful tool for students and professionals.
- Complete the personal goals exercise and the professional goals exercise.

The interior design profession offers students and professionals numerous options and directions for career opportunities. For many, the direction in the profession seems very logical and direct. "I intend to design residential interiors," say many. "My goal is to be involved in the design of restaurants and hotels," say others. And clearly, this latter sentiment could mean any number of commercial specialties. Our world certainly has grown more complex, challenging, and stressful since the first edition of this text was published. It is also filled with almost unlimited opportunity for anyone who is willing to seek and achieve success in the interior design profession.

Deciding on which opportunity and direction to seek at the beginning of one's career is somewhat daunting. At first, the goal is to obtain employment in a good firm doing the kind of work one most desires. As one gains experience in the field, goals become refined and maybe even changed completely from one type of design to another. Many students and professionals have a goal of going out on their own, having their own studio. Work experience is gained in order to eventually reach that goal. Maybe one's goal is to have a project published or win an award. For some, the goal might be to become involved in a professional association chapter. Of course, there are many other kinds of career and professional achievements to set as goals. Yet for many, these goals are never reached.

Goals are, of course, achieved through hard work, determination, and planning. Sometimes family, friends, children—all of these and others—may enter the picture and delay or prevent an individual from reaching personal and professional goals. But in most cases, the inability to achieve a goal or a dream is not due to other individuals or job responsibilities; rather, it is usually due to a lack of planning and of setting goals—or maybe setting the wrong goals.

Although businesses spend a lot of time and energy on determining and setting goals for the coming year, individuals often ignore their own goals for the future. In this chapter, we will look at personal goal setting.

WHAT ARE GOALS?

Certainly, hundreds of books have been written about setting goals, with new ones appearing every year. To know where you are going can sometimes be very difficult. In these various books, authors discuss how individuals with the greatest success have set goals all through their careers. Without some kind of direction, your personal and professional life can be very frustrating and unfulfilling.

Several years ago, I was visiting a friend in San Diego, California. Because she had not lived there for long, I admired her intuitive ability to find her way around a strange city. We never checked a map. Her intuition was uncanny. Many people approach all aspects of their lives in the same way. Flying by the seat of their pants, purely on intuition, they seek out educational preparation, make career decisions, move to other cities, or invest in stocks, experiencing life with little planning. For a few lucky people, this method works fine. Unfortunately, for the majority of us, living life purely on intuition leaves us somewhere other than where we want to be.

There is nothing wrong with using your intuition. There is also nothing wrong with just experiencing life—letting it happen. However, according to Brian Tracy, "Success is goals, and all else is commentary. All successful people are intensely goal oriented."[1] Whatever your concept of success is, it will be far easier to achieve it if you have a "destination" with goals to help you reach the success you desire. Always consider that goals are concrete ideas requiring effort and commitment for their achievement.

Most people have dreams, but many have no goals. There is a difference. Dreams are imaginary hopes, whereas, to many, goals are concrete ideas that represent something that a person wants to achieve. Philosophically, goals are brief stops along the way of life that mark achievement in an individual's personal and professional life. Owning your own studio someday is not an end in itself, even though it may have been the goal. Now you must be ready to create new goals related to the success and growth of the studio. "A goal is the ongoing pursuit of a worthy objective until accomplished."[2]

Whether an individual is a professional who has been actively practicing in interior design for several years or a student who is still negotiating his or her way through design classes, personal and professional goal setting is important. The professional who may feel unfulfilled needs to take stock of what he or she has accomplished and the skills that he or she possesses. When tighter job markets limit choices, students must have a clearer idea of the type of job they are interested in pursuing while remaining open to any reasonable opportunity.

Even though you may have some general idea about what you want out of your personal and professional life, without some kind of concrete plan, you will find yourself reacting to what happens to you rather than having some control over events in your life. Taking control can and does make a big difference. The most successful people are those who create and develop a vision of what they want their career and personal life to be. They establish goals and strategies that help accomplish that vision. And they continually evaluate possibilities that are presented to them to determine how those possibilities positively or negatively will affect their career and personal life. Those who do not do this may find themselves saying, like the cartoon character Pogo, "We have met the enemy and he is us!"

RISKS IN GOAL SETTING

Setting a goal requires commitment of time, energy, and mental processes. Some people do not wish to really make a commitment of any kind beyond their immediate physiological needs. In setting goals, a person runs the risk of failure, that is, of not achieving the goal. But not achieving the goal does not automatically mean failure. The goal may be unattainable at the present time for one reason or another.

Mark made a point of setting and reviewing his goals every three months. He even took a day during a weekend to go through the effort. Yet Mark felt like he was not getting anywhere. He finally took a long look at what he was doing and his goals and discovered that he started many things to get toward goals but never seemed to finish up what was needed to reach the accomplishment phase.

There are risks in setting goals. A big risk for many is that not accomplishing the goal might feel like failure. Not accomplishing a goal should never be thought of as failure because there can be many reasons that the goal was not accomplished. The chief among these is that the goal may have been set so high that it was unattainable in some reasonable length of time. For example, Jack, a recent graduate, wanted to design high-end residential projects where the house was valued at over $2 million within a year. However, Jack lived in a smaller city where the number of projects of that size was limited. Jack had set himself up for "failure," since the chances of him obtaining that type of project one year out of school was very slim.

People do not set goals because of the risk of feeling the pain of failure. It is emotionally difficult to admit that you have not achieved some goal that you would like to have accomplished. Of course, it is painful to "fail," but not trying is also emotionally painful. Everyone fails occasionally, and learning from the failure and resolving to fix the issue or try harder or whatever is needed to succeed the next time is very important for successful people.

Here are a few important thoughts to keep in mind when setting goals. The first is particularly important for students: Set goals that satisfy you—not parents, a boyfriend or girlfriend, a spouse, or peers. If you are setting a goal to please someone else, then you will probably never achieve it. And if you do achieve it, it may never bring you satisfaction.

Second, clarify your purpose. You have to know what you want more than anything else in order to determine the smaller goals and directions on how to get there. "What do you want to do when you grow up?" is a question we have all been asked. As you set out establishing career goals, try your best to determine what is most important to you. If it is to make a lot of money, that is okay. If it is to be a published and award-winning designer, that is okay. Getting to that kind of clarity is something that many never seem to achieve.

A third consideration is that some goals are unattainable without the proper experience. Certain goals take time to achieve. Becoming a design director at a major interior design or architectural firm or increasing a practitioner's income by 100 percent in one year does not happen overnight. It takes time to gain the experience to have such opportunities. The attainment of such goals happens in only the most extraordinary situations.

Fourth, be sure you are honest with yourself in setting goals. Sometimes our temperament, habits, or behavior interfere with achieving goals. The casual, even sloppy, dress that is okay as a student does not translate into the professional world. Being argumentative with clients does not endear them to a practitioner regardless of the number of years he or she has worked. Continually not returning phone messages and e-mails can cost even the most creative designer success. If any of these types of conduct are part of you, the ability to achieve many goals will be diminished.

A fifth important consideration is to not be afraid to change goals or change direction. Life is not perfect, and reality usually does not match fantasy. Be flexible in goal setting. Whatever first brought you into the interior design profession will probably change somewhat as your opportunities and experiences change. I have talked to numerous practitioners over the years, and few have traveled a straight path from school to their current position 10, 15, or more years later. All of your career and life challenges will affect your potential ability to accomplish the goals that you set in college or after you have worked a few years in the interior design profession. Unexpected circumstances and a lack of understanding of career requirements are just a few things that can affect reaching your goals.

There is one indisputable fact about life: Life will change. For most, change means growth. So don't be afraid to grow. Being open to a change of plans may offer you an opportunity for personal and professional growth that you have not even considered. For example, Jim has a goal of becoming a design director at a major firm. One day, he was offered a two-year position as a designer in Hawaii. He did not look at the possibilities that the opportunity provided and refused the position, and continued working in a medium-sized city in the Northwest. Several years later, he still was not in a position to be a design director, and he looked back longingly at that lost opportunity. Do not be afraid to consider or even embark upon different paths when they arise.

What Would You Do?

A good friend of yours works for another interior design firm in the area. You know that she applied for membership in one of the professional associations because you both applied at the same time. Your application is still pending, and you know hers is as well. At a meeting, you noticed that her card had the appellation "ASID" after her name. This is puzzling to you because you also know that she has not passed the NCIDQ examination as of yet. In fact, she is not even eligible, since you both graduated only six months ago.

A PERSONAL MISSION STATEMENT

Many readers have heard of Steven Covey and his very popular book *The Seven Habits of Highly Effective People*. To Covey, a personal mission statement helps a person set a direction for what that person wants to do in his or her personal and professional life. Much like a business mission statement, "it focuses on what you want to be (character) and to do (contributions and achievements) and on the values or principles upon which being and doing are based."[3]

Once you develop a personal mission statement, it will help you with many life decisions as you travel through personal and professional relationships and activities. It will help you define your focus, which, in turn, will help you determine on what you most wish to spend your emotional, psychological, and financial resources. According to Covey, a personal mission statement will help you more effectively handle the changes that will constantly affect your life.

Creating a personal mission statement starts with allowing your innermost self to make you aware of what you most want in life—not just today, but in the future. It starts by determining the end you most desire: to own a successful design practice, to be the principal project designer at one of the top five design firms in the country, to have a highly respected international reputation in design, to have both a satisfying family and professional life, or anything else you can imagine.

Here is a brief example of a personal mission statement:

To believe in myself and allow myself to try, to experiment, to experience, thus to learn.

To strive each day to be willing to pay the price to achieve greater happiness, confidence, and spiritual growth.

To do some work that benefits others and that is enjoyable to me.

To treat others based on the principles that I hold as important.

Perhaps you would like to write a personal mission statement before you continue reading this chapter. Think of what you want to be known for at the end of your career, or even your life. Consider the roles that you now play within your family, in your career (or potential career), with friends, and in the community at large. Are you satisfied with those roles? Reflect on the principles that mean the most to you. Determine your values—what makes you the person that you are. Make notes about the things, words, places, and activities that inspire or excite you. Then take some time away from the hustle and bustle of your daily life to write down a personal mission statement. It doesn't have to be structured like the example. Any format or length will do. You can use Item 5-1 on the CD to help develop a personal mission statement.

SETTING GOALS

Whether you write a personal mission statement or not, the best way to set goals is to try to look at yourself in terms of the future. Steven Covey calls it "beginning with the end in mind." In many ways, a similar approach is to write your own obituary today—a rather jarring thought at the age of 21 or at any age. This exercise in goal setting was required by an instructor whom I had in college. The idea was to focus on long-range goal setting. Occasionally, we all need to look at what we want to be remembered for—what we hope we will be able to accomplish by the time we pass away. Writing that obituary or at least beginning with the end in mind has helped many to more clearly see a focus for future actions.

Understandably, writing your own obituary is an unsettling thing to do. It may be easier to start thinking about what you want to accomplish by the time you are 30, 40, 50, and at retirement age. And, if you find *that* too difficult to do, just try to figure out where you want to be in your professional and personal life during the next five years. Be sure that you include considerations for your personal life as well as professional life. Let me be one of the first to tell you that your professional life should not *be* your life.

Personal Goals Exercise

> The purpose of this exercise is to analyze your skills, interests, and abilities in relation to the kind of job opportunities you will be seeking in interior design. Completing this exercise will make you more aware of what you have to offer your present or future employers. It will also help you discover goals that you need to work on in the next year or so.
>
> 1. What is your number one interest in interior design?
> 2. What or who influenced your interest in this profession (family, teacher, mentor, the media, work experience, etc.)?
> 3. What kind of skills in interior design do you have right now?
> 4. What special skill(s) do you have to offer your present employer or another employer?
> 5. If you were going to a job interview tomorrow, what specific career goal would you share with the interviewer?
> 6. What could you do right now to improve the chances of getting the job you most want?
> 7. List three of your biggest successes.
> 8. List five goals you wish to accomplish during the next calendar year.
> 9. List three goals you hope to accomplish by the time you are 30 years old.
> 10. List three goals you hope to accomplish by the time you are 50 years old.
> 11. Assuming it were possible for you to achieve any goal in interior design, what would it be?
> 12. List ten mini-goals needed to support the goal stated in number 11.

If you are unsure of what you want to accomplish, it might help if you use Tables 5.1 and 5.2 to get started. Find a quiet place where you can think undisturbed. Be brutally honest with yourself as you answer the questions in these two tables. Worksheets for Table 5-1 and 5-2 have been included on the CD as Item 5-2 and Item 5-3.

Once you have some idea of where you want to be, you can start looking at goals in terms of the concrete things that need to be accomplished in order to achieve them. In the business methodology of strategic planning (discussed in Chapter 13), the activities and tasks that must be done in order to achieve the higher-level goals are referred to as strategies. Strategies are specific actions that are needed to achieve goals. For example, Beth has a goal of owning her own studio by the time she is 35. Assuming Beth is a 23-year-old student about to graduate, what strategies might she need to plan out to achieve that goal? For example, what kinds of work experience will be needed to meet that goal? Where could she get the finances to open the doors? And so on. Being your own boss sounds good to many students and practitioners. Business ownership, as you will see in Part III, also means a certain amount of sacrifice of family and personal time to keep the studio in operation. Some of the strategies and tactics related to achieving this goal might be the following:

Work with a residential firm for five years to gain experience in residential practice.

Work with a commercial firm for five years to gain experience with a type of commercial client that interests the designer.

Become a senior designer or design manager with either a residential or a commercial firm to gain business and management experience.

If necessary, take additional business classes at a community college or enter an MBA program to gain the business knowledge to own a studio.

Find a mentor that can help suggest ways to achieve strategies and discuss various professional and perhaps personal growth issues.

TABLE 5-2.

Professional Goals Questionnaire

In these questions, you are asked to look at a variety of issues concerning your professional and personal life. Combined with the questions in Table 5.1 these questions provide you an opportunity to look at some additional issues that can help clarify your professional and personal goals.

1. List at least three things that drew you into a career in interior design. Write several comments about each of these items.
2. List any three people you most admire. Write down a few words or sentences that explain why you admire them.
3. List three or four companies (or types of firms) that provide the kinds of design work you wish to do.
4. Which of the following is most important to you in your career: money, recognition, self-satisfaction, or creative expression?
5. If you had the means to do so, what would you most like to do—personally and professionally? Remember, no restrictions.
6. What do you think you need to change to make yourself happier in your professional and personal life?
7. What frustrates you most about your professional and personal life?
8. What do you like most about work in interior design? What do you like least?
9. When are you at your best and most secure (professionally and personally)?
10. Do you prefer to work independently or with a group?
11. Write a paragraph that would sum up what you most want to be remembered for in your professional (and/or personal) life.
12. On a sheet of paper, make two columns. On the top of one column, write the word *problem*, and on the other, the word *solution*. Then write in the "problem" column those things that you feel are holding you back or are problems in your professional and/or personal life. In the "solution" column, write down potential solutions to each problem. In some cases, you may find that you are really writing down thoughts rather than true solutions, but those thoughts will help you find solutions to the problems.

These are all examples of concrete strategies that Beth (or you) would need to accomplish in order to bring about the larger goal of owning a studio. Once the opportunity of opening a studio occurs, new goals must be decided upon, related to the business and the next "stop" on the road.

The process, in some ways, is never ending and is the same for any goal. New opportunities occur all the time if they are recognized and acted upon. Unexpected problems and challenges might derail you momentarily or even forever. Although staying on track to accomplish goals in the shorter term are always a good idea, keeping oneself open to opportunities that might have long-term implications is important. But isn't that part of the fun?

SUMMARY

Goals provide direction in our lives. Professional goals help make choices that occur during our careers easier to navigate. Personal goals help to balance professional activity for a fuller life. Setting goals is risky and takes commitment, but if the goals we set are goals that interest us, they likely will be fulfilled. Goals take time to reach. Just as Rome was not built in a day, obtaining the credentials to create designs that are purchased by custom furniture manufacturers, or presented awards by magazines and associations, or perhaps work for a major manufacturer does not come overnight.

Achieving a goal may or may not be within our control. Remember that some goals take a certain kind of expertise or maybe a credential like an M.B.A. Without the expertise or credential, accomplishing the goal may be unlikely.

Always keep in mind that life changes either by actions that we take ourselves or by actions that have an effect upon us. Do not be afraid of those changes, and do not be afraid of making changes if new opportunities look interesting.

REFERENCES

1. Tracy, 2003. p. 7.
2. Canfield et al., 2000, p. 61.
3. Covey, 1989, p. 106.

CHAPTER 6

Professional Options

Key Terms and Concepts

These key terms and concepts are important to material in this chapter. Many of the terms will be utilized in other chapters as well. Be sure you understand these items as you read this chapter.

Terms and Concepts

Commercial interior design	LEED
Contract interior design	Wayfinding
Residential interior design	On the boards
Sales reps	Dealer

Do you know what type of interior design work you plan to do when you graduate? Creating the interiors in mansions located in Florida, Beverly Hills, perhaps a penthouse in Manhattan sure sounds exciting to many students. Perhaps you are more interested in being part of the team that designs luxury boxes in the new stadium for the New York Yankees or a resort in the Caribbean. Remodeling the assisted-living facility your relative had to stay in might give you satisfaction. Then again, perhaps working in sales, traveling to visit members of the architecture and design (A&D) community as a representative for a major manufacturer is more your interest.

There are so many different ways to work in the interior design field and so many ways in which an individual can find the right path that will match his or her talents and interests. Regardless of where you start in the profession, 5, 10, 15 years later, you might find yourself doing something totally different in the field. And to many designers, this is just one more exciting aspect of this profession.

The interior design field encompasses substantially more than designing homes. Commercial interior design has taken on increasing importance over the past 50 years with the planning and design of hotels, restaurants, medical facilities, and offices of every kind, creating career paths for many interior designers. It is important for the student to realize that the variety of career options that are open to an interior designer goes far beyond designing residential or commercial interiors.

It is very common for interior designers to work in both residential and commercial design at the same time, although focusing on one or the other.

There are also those who enter one specialty and remain in that specialty essentially their whole career. Some start in one specialty area and switch to the other. I had a student who was emphatic about doing residential interiors after graduating. Two years later, she was back asking if I knew any openings in commercial studios.

This chapter has been moved near the beginning of this book for this edition based on the recommendations of many educators who say they discuss this topic early in the semester. They say it helps them set the stage for professional practice topics and career topics that students must face. Blending it with the chapter on personal goal setting creates an effective beginning to getting started in the study of professional practice for interior designers.

This chapter begins with some basic concepts about making a career choice in interior design and then follows with a discussion of numerous career paths within the interior design profession and industry. This topic is followed by a discussion of several career options that often require specialized education or experience. A section on practice settings will help the reader understand where jobs are. Chapter material on the job-hunting process including resumés and interviews is retained at the end of the book on recommendation by many educators.

CAREER DECISIONS

Your first real job in the interior design profession is a significant milestone. For everyone it is the first step on a journey that can lead to a rewarding and successful future in a career full of challenges and excitement, and it is enjoyable more than not. That first position can also chart a direction toward a goal for the future. Quite honestly, for some, that first position ends up being a misdirection requiring reevaluation of professional and personal goals.

Few designers remain with the same company for decades as your parents or grandparents once did. Many sources report that graduates in general in this century might have up to ten different jobs before they retire. Certainly within the interior design industry, you will probably have at least three or more different jobs as you move up in responsibility and experience. Don't be concerned about that because it is important to keep yourself open to new opportunities—especially after you have gained some on-the-job experience.

Regardless of what type of design or size and kind of office or studio, the entry-level designer will likely start with low-level work at the beginning of employment. Despite the new employee's training and talent, the interior design firm will want to train and observe the employee for some period of time before giving him or her substantial project responsibility. This is called "paying one's dues," and although no one likes it, paying one's dues is part of making the transition from student to professional. The IDEP program briefly described in Chapter 2 can help speed this transition, since it encourages employers to involve entry-level designers broadly into the whole of the design process.

There is nothing wrong, however, in maintaining the library, gathering materials for presentations, calling for pricing, and organizing sample boards. All of these tasks are part of the design process and are undertaken by the most experienced professional as well as the beginner. Attending meetings between senior designers and clients helps one learn how interactions between the designer and client happen and see firsthand how presentations are made by designers. As the design director or owner and staff become comfortable with, and confident about, the ability of the new designer, he or she will be given more responsibility.

Working in a small firm, the new employee has the opportunity to work on a variety of projects and have a variety of experiences fairly quickly. Small firms need people to contribute, so the expectations will be high for a new employee to assist the more experienced designers in many ways. In some cases, the entry-level designer in a smaller company will be given project responsibility more quickly. This, of course, depends on the talents and attitudes of the employee.

In a larger firm, it is not unusual for the entry-level designer to progress a bit more slowly. The old joke of entry-level architects drafting bathroom partitions for a year is matched by the old joke of entry-level interior designers taking care of the library or inputting sketches for a year. Fortunately, this has changed—in most firms. This less critical involvement notwithstanding, an important advantage is that larger firms give an entry-level designer the opportunity to see how a variety of bigger projects are handled.

The selection of a first job can be impacted by the compensation that will be paid to the employee. Sometimes working for a firm at a lower salary is a good idea because of the experiences that the new designer can have with that firm. Maybe one firm has better benefits than another or benefits that appeal to the designer. Location is another issue. Wanting to live in a major city like New York City has many advantages, but the cost of living is quite high. The new designer will need to be sure that the salary and benefits pay the rent and other living expenses.

Even though it most likely will take an entry-level designer up to two years to move up in a design firm to the next job level, this varies from firm to firm. And it is another issue for the new designer to consider when he or she is thinking about options. Ambition is a good thing, but sometimes the expectations and ambitions of entry-level designers exceed their competence levels and the actual career path that is offered at a particular design firm. A certain amount of patience is necessary in this profession, since the employer wants to feel comfortable that an individual can work successfully with clients and others in the industry. Remember that as an employee you represent the company you work for as well as yourself. Creating problems due to lack of experience not only can hurt your professional life but the employer's reputation as well.

Interests in specific kinds of design work obviously influence career options. Outside interests or experiences from a previous career can move you toward a particular specialty. If for some reason you have skipped the previous chapter on personal and professional goals, you are encouraged to return to that chapter, read the material, and complete the exercises. Understanding who you are and what your interests are will help you make the decision as to which area to go into in interior design. You might want to look at some of the books recommended in that chapter and this as well, because when you do what you think you will enjoy, your progression in the profession will be rewarding. This *is* a challenging, exciting—sometimes frustrating—profession. But it is also a great way to make a living!

As you decide about a career specialty, it is important to have a grounding in what work is like in the "real world". Item 6-1 on the CD provides important information about the real world of work.

DESIGN CAREER SPECIALTIES

There are many specialty areas in which to practice interior design. An interest in the profession is the spark one needs to begin a path of acquiring a knowledge base and learning skills needed by and associated with the interior design profession. With so many potential career options, the reader may be unsure which direction to go in this exciting and varied profession. This section directs attention to numerous opportunities for the professional and student.

In interior design, there are two recognized branches of the profession. The one with which most readers are familiar is residential interior design or the design of houses and private living spaces. The other is commercial interior design or the design of many kinds of public businesses and private or government facilities. Within each of these branches are many specialties that become career options in themselves, such as the design of kitchens and baths, home offices, retail stores, and restaurants.

There are many other career options within the interior design profession and built-environment industry that someone with an interest and education in interior design may enjoy. These specialty career areas might focus on a narrower or even an additional range of knowledge and skills suitable for the specialty, such as lighting designers, barrier-free design consultants, and interior design management. This section in this edition continues to explain many of these career options in order for the reader to get an idea of the work of the specialty. It is not all-inclusive, because one could argue that a focus on any one type of space or service also creates a specialty. To gain further understanding about preparing for a design specialty, be sure and read the information in the following box.

Preparing for Career Specialization

An interior designer who is a generalist feels that he or she is able to design any kind of space whether it is a residence or a commercial facility of some kind. The heyday of the generalist has definitely gone by the wayside. Clients expect interior designers to have broad knowledge about design, but specific knowledge about types of interiors. A client who hires someone to design a private residence wants that designer to understand the needs of residential design. A client who hires someone to design a store or medical office wants to know that the interior designer is familiar with that client's business and design needs.

The first choice in specialization is determining if one's interests focuses on residences or commercial spaces. Many interior design specialties require additional education or job experience. Students and practitioners need to keep this in mind when they are considering career interests or changes in their career path. But how can one find out what experience or education is required of any specific career option in interior design?

Researching the specialty is one way of understanding a specialty. Reading textbooks and design books on the specialty is one easy way to learn about it. Libraries often have copies of trade publications and journals that can help provide an overview of many commercial businesses. Interior design and architecture trade magazines provide impressions of what it is like to design all types of interiors.

Another way to prepare for career specialization is to interview designers who already work in that segment of the design field. Interior designers are like most people—they love to talk about what they do and are flattered to find out that others are interested in their work. Appointments can be set up with experienced designers so that the prospective designer can ask a short series of well-considered questions about their work in the specialty. It is suggested that the individual ask for no more than 30 minutes of the designer's time; this shows respect for their professional responsibilities.

Personal experience can be another way to learn about a specialty. Some students become interested in health-care design because of a family member's health problems. Those who work in retail stores in order to work their way through college often become interested in visual merchandising or retail design. A career in hospitality design may blossom as a result of working in a restaurant. Family members and family friends certainly influence a career direction and may also influence a specialty. For example, perhaps an uncle is a veterinarian and might talk about the importance of the interior for keeping animals calm during office visits. An injured relative needing to be admitted to a special-care facility can influence an interest in the design of senior housing or specialty health-care facilities. These are only a very few examples.

Once a decision is made concerning a specialty, it might be advisable or necessary to seek additional course work that would provide general background information about that specialization. For example, someone who wishes to specialize in hospitality design should take some introductory classes in the hospitality industry. Those who wish to work in retail design would be wise to take merchandising and visual merchandising classes. Residential designers could take classes on salesmanship or human behavior. This type of introduction to a specialty will provide valuable help to the student as he or she seeks to understand the unique functional problems of the specialty.

Students should also recognize that many specialized interior design firms may not hire an entry-level designer. I have heard from numerous specialized firm principals over the years that they simply do not hire entry-level designers. In general, the reason is that the lack of actual work experience prevents an entry-level designer from working at the pace and intensity that are needed in their firms. "We need designers who can hit the ground running," commented one such principal. "Entry-level designers, regardless of the quality of their talent, cannot do this," the principal continued. Their advice is for students to get good-quality actual work experience and learn what it is really like to work in design before they apply for a job in a highly specialized design firm. Of course, there is no reason a student could not apply anyway. Being in the right place at the right time has gotten many designers their first job!

Commercial Interior Design

As we saw in Chapter 1, commercial interior design involves the design and specification of public spaces, such as offices, hotels, hospitals, restaurants, and so on. There are many kinds of public spaces, and it is normal for a commercial designer to focus his or her practice on only one area or perhaps on a few types of related public spaces. Depending on the size of a design firm, a firm might offer expertise in multiple specialties. The list in Table 6-1 gives a partial list of the specialties that exist within commercial interior design.

An important skill of today's commercial interior designer is to have knowledge and appreciation of the client's business. This knowledge helps the designer ask better questions about the needs and goals of the client during the extensive programming that is often necessary. The designer also realizes that clients are different even when they are in similar business categories. Space requirements for an office in a privately owned company may be quite a bit different than those for government offices. Therefore, the designer needs to understand the business of the business in order to make appropriate design decisions. It is also important to realize that the client who has contracted with the designer is often only one user that must be satisfied. The satisfaction of employees and the public or the clientele of the business impacts the success of the design and future business. For example, a restaurant interior that pleases the owner but does not attract the public may be a beautifully designed interior but may cause the business to fail.

Commercial interior designers commonly work in teams and must know how to contribute and work in a team environment. Individuals who have a hard time collaborating or do not feel comfortable with work assignments that

TABLE 6-1.

A Partial List of Commercial Interior Design Specialties

Almost any kind of commercial or business facility can become a specialty in interior design. Choosing too narrow a specialty, however, can limit the amount of business the interior designer will be able to obtain.

General offices

Facility planning

Corporate executive offices

LEED specialist

Professional offices

Law

Advertising/public relations

Accounting

Stockbrokers and investment brokers

Real estate and real estate development

Financial institutions: banks, credit unions, and trading centers

Architecture, engineering, and interior design

Consultants of various kinds

Healthcare

Hospitals and health maintenance groups facilities

Medical specialty office suites

Nursing homes and assisted-living facilities

Medical and dental office suites

Outpatient laboratories

Psychiatric facilities

Rehabilitation facilities

Medical laboratories

Veterinary clinics

Hospitality and recreation

Hotel, motels, and resorts

Restaurants, coffee shops, etc.

Commercial kitchens

Recreational facilities

Health clubs and spas

Country clubs

National and state park facilities

Amusement park facilities

Sports complexes

Auditoriums and theaters

Museums

Convention centers

Casinos

Set design: movies and television

Retail facilities/merchandising

Malls and shopping centers

Department stores

Specialized retail stores

Gift shops in hotels, airports, and other facilities

Store visual merchandising

Displays for trade shows

Showrooms

Galleries

Boutiques

Educational and institutional

Colleges, universities, and community colleges

Secondary and elementary schools

Day-care centers and nursery schools

Private schools

Churches and other religious facilities

Financial institutions

Government offices (federal, state, and local)

Courthouses and courtrooms

Prisons

Industrial facilities

Corporate offices

Manufacturing facilities

Training facilities

Employee service areas, such as lunchrooms and fitness centers

Transportation

Airports, bus terminals, train depots, etc.

Tour ship design

Custom and commercial airplane interiors

Boats and ships

Recreational vehicles

Adaptive use

Restoration of historic commercial sites

Commercial products design

seem "trivial" will have a difficult time adjusting to today's commercial design firm. Entry-level commercial interior designers must have experience with computer-aided drafting and design (CAD). CAD is a prerequisite skill for any designer who wishes a career in any but the smallest commercial design firms. Experience in other types of computer software that are used for presentations, scheduling, database record keeping, and project management are often recommended, if not required. It might take two or more years for an entry-level designer in any of these specialties to be promoted and achieve greater project responsibility. Commercial interior design firms primarily pay their designers a salary, since they are less likely to be involved in the selling of merchandise.

Facility Planners

Many corporations and institutional organizations realize the economic benefit of having their own planning and design team. Facility planners are part of the facility management department, which is responsible for the physical plant (the building and its systems). The facility management department ensures that everything involved in the business—building, equipment, and people—are organized and provided to best function together to meet the management's goals.

Generally speaking, facility planners are responsible for space planning for a corporation. This work is most frequently done for corporations that extensively use open-office systems products, though a facility planner can work for any type of business. Facility planners are required to have experience with CAD software and to understand workplace functionality, workspace strategies, and change management. Specialized degrees in facility planning are available, but many facility planners are interior designers or architects. If they are designing solely for a corporation, facility planners often find traveling among the various plants and office buildings a necessity. These individuals are paid a salary.

The job of facility manager, sometimes in the same department as a facility planner, is a more specialized career and requires additional training in psychology, physical plant management, and engineering.

Residential Interior Design

Residential interior design deals with private living spaces, most frequently the freestanding, single-family home, as well as many other types of private residences. Designers might also specialize on functional areas within the umbrella of a residence, such as those listed in Table 6-2. Residential interior designers sometimes describe their job as helping the home owner express the personality and lifestyle of the family through the design of the interior. Others say the

TABLE 6-2.

A Partial List of Residential Interior Design Specialties

Single-family homes	Model homes and apartments
Townhouses	Dormitories
Condominiums	Sustainable design
Patio homes	Senior housing
Apartments	Apartments in assisted-living facilities
Manufactured housing units	Color consultation
Vacation homes	Historical restoration/renovation
Residential restoration	Custom closets
Kitchen and/or bathroom design	Residential children's spaces
Home offices	Renovation for the physically challenged
Home theater design	Private yachts and houseboats

challenge is to create a functional environment that will be comfortable for the family. Interpreting client feelings and translating them into an environment that the client will be comfortable with and will enjoy is a key element of the work of residential designers.

An important characteristic of residential interior design is the personal relationship that usually develops between the client and the designer. The ability to get along with people and develop sensitivity for questioning the client to uncover client needs and wants is very important. Residential clients are much more particular about what they buy and how their home reflects their image. Tact and diplomacy are a must in order to show the client the realities of good and bad design ideas and to translate expressed desires into a design concept with which the client can live.

The design process for a residential project is the same as any commercial project. Programming is critical to determining client needs and wants. The skill to prepare sketches, detailed floor plans, working drawings, shop drawings, and other project documents is also required.

The professional residential interior designer is frequently hired not only to consult with the client but also to assist the client in communicating changes and needs to the architect and contractor. Understanding the construction process, therefore, is very important. Extensive product knowledge helps the designer provide design recommendations to satisfy even the most discerning client.

The entry-level residential interior designer often begins as an assistant to an experienced designer at a retail store or an interior design studio. Pulling and organizing samples, drafting plans and completing sketches, and obtaining pricing are all common activities for assistants. CAD and other computer skills are necessary in residential interior design. That is not to say that free-hand sketching, manual drafting, and manual rendering skills are passé in many studios.

Once assistants are given an opportunity to work independently with clients, they often start with projects involving single rooms or even consultations regarding individual items within a room. With experience, they will become involved in the design of an entire home. As in a commercial specialty, it might take entry-level professionals in residential design specialties a minimum of two years to be promoted to a position where they are given full responsibility for their own clients. Since many residential studios and stores sell merchandise as well as provide design services, compensation for the employee might be a salary, or the employee might be paid on some sort of commission basis.

What Would You Do?

Marilyn had been working very hard for the past nine weeks with a very difficult client, Mr. Norton, owner and developer of a facility for Alzheimer patients. He constantly challenged her suggestions and had already caused four major changes in the specifications of products and three changes in the equipment plans for the common areas for the facility her firm was designing for his company. His primary argument was that she was overspecifying materials, using "expensive" products when cheaper ones would do—at least as far as he was concerned.

"You have not even come close to staying within the budget we discussed at the beginning of this project. I insist that you find something besides that expensive cubical curtain and drapery fabric and find me a cheaper chair for the dining room," voiced Mr. Norton. "It's not that the cubical curtain and drapery fabric is expensive, but it must meet a certain level of code compliance, which this one does. Less expensive chairs will not hold up to the special needs of the residents who need an armchair," responded Marilyn. "I don't care about that!" exploded Mr. Norton.

Lighting Designers

Although all designers learn lighting concepts and lighting design as some part of their curriculum, lighting interiors to create special environments involves skills and experience that the average interior designer does not achieve. Designers can specialize in lighting design, continually learning about new products but also about all the intricacies of lighting science and design application. There are firms that specialize in providing consulting to other designers as well as to clients in the lighting design of all types of spaces, both residential and commercial in context.

Sales Representatives

Sales representatives, also called *sales reps*, can work in retail furniture and furnishings stores and dealerships, manufacturer's showrooms, and as outside sales reps for manufacturers. Sales reps in retail stores might be referred to as sales associates. A sales associate is not always an interior designer, but someone who is skilled in sales techniques. Many retail stores and office furnishings dealers hire interior designers to be sales associates. Sales associates in retail stores are most commonly paid a straight commission or a small salary plus a commission.

Some representatives who work in the wholesale trade rather than the retail trade are called independent reps, while others are considered to be factory representatives. An independent rep works for himself or herself, while representing many products from a variety of manufacturers. A factory rep works for one manufacturer as an employee. He or she handles all or part of the product line of that manufacturer in a specified territory of the country. Some factory reps also have specific obligations to dealers in their territory. A dealer might have an exclusive right to sell a product in a specific city or area of the country.

Sales representatives call on the interior design and architectural firms that might specify products. The rep is compensated with a commission whenever a product has been sold in his or her territory, whether or not the rep has had anything directly to do with that sale. In addition, the factory representative is paid a commission on all goods sold in his or her territory, whether or not the rep has had anything to do with that sale. Both kinds of reps may have large territories and must travel extensively. In most cases, individuals must have proven sales experience to obtain a position as a manufacturer's representative.

CAD Specialist

CAD specialists, sometimes called CAD technicians, rarely are responsible for design decisions. They input into the computer sketches from designers and architects, and produce the drawings that are required to finish a job. Design firms might utilize a CAD specialist who may or may not hold a degree in interior design, and the firm might also expect its interior designers to have CAD skills. CAD specialists most likely are salaried employees.

Outsourcing CAD services has become a way that designers who wish to have their own business can offer a limited amount of services. These outsourced services by experienced designers are of particular benefit to the small interior design practice that does not have in-house CAD capability. Of course, it is also becoming common for CAD services to be outsourced out of the United States. The Internet allows for work to be done almost anywhere in the world.

Other Computer Specialists

It is unusual in today's market to find any size or type of interior design firm that does not utilize the computer. In large firms, individuals who have a strong interest in the computer might choose to work using one or more types of programs, or add the "tech" responsibility to their other office responsibilities. Specification writing and preparation of bid documents and complicated equipment lists for open-office systems projects are just a few examples of how computers can aid the office and create specialty work areas. The use of the computer has become a required skill in the everyday responsibilities of the interior designer, regardless of the size of the design firm.

Barrier-Free or Universal Design

Although compliance with accessibility standards is required for new construction, many owners of public buildings that were built prior to adoption of accessibility standards are unsure of what must be done to comply with the standards. A career option for some designers experienced with barrier-free design concepts is consulting to businesses to help them comply with standards when a lawsuit is filed. Perhaps the prime designer might not be knowledgeable about barrier-free requirements and will engage a consulting designer to review plans for new or remodeled facilities to be sure that the plans will meet the law prior to submittal for building permits.

Sustainable Design

Many in the built-environment industry including interior designers choose to focus their design approaches and specialties into sustainable design. Designers who focus on sustainable design assist an increasing number of home owners and various types of commercial facilities. Their practice focuses on the use of products and methodologies to lessen the impact on the natural environment and improve the interior environment.

Helping to provide standards in this area is the LEED (Leadership in Energy and Environmental Design) program from the U.S. Green Building Council (USGBC). The program has established standards for sustainable designed buildings and a professional accreditation program qualifying designers to more successfully design sustainable projects. LEED-accredited designers might work for any type or size interior design or architectural firm.

Professional Renderers

Many in design feel that rendering is becoming a lost art. However, clients and other designers continue to utilize renderings to express design concepts to clients and for clients to use to market properties. The professional renderer is very skilled in perspective and various rendering media including the use of 2-D and 3-D CAD. He or she may be employed by a large interior design or architectural firm, or may be self-employed as a freelance renderer.

Model Builders

Allied to the professional renderer are model builders. These individuals may also be professional renderers, or they may only produce architectural and interior models. Multidisciplinary firms might have model builders on staff, although there are many model building companies or freelance model builders.

Model building requires that the individual have an excellent sense of scale, knowledge of the kinds of material that can be used to produce a scale model, a concern for detail, and patience to do the work required in model building.

Product Designers

Interior designers who have gained a strong reputation in the field and experience in the custom designing of products may supplement or modify their practice with product design. Designers can start their own company to produce their designs or license their designs to a manufacturer. Product designers working directly for a manufacturer may need to have an industrial design background.

Interior Design Management

A position in interior design management requires extensive experience in the field or experience in general management. Most design directors are former designers. It is important for the design director to have knowledge of interior design and a good general business knowledge or experience related to the management of personnel, marketing, and general business principles. A position in design management might involve being the director of the design department, in which the individual has almost sole responsibility for marketing the firm, or any combination of these areas. Design management personnel most often are paid a salary, with some bonus or commission structure supplementing the salary.

Marketing Specialists

Large interior design firms frequently utilize a marketing specialist to prospect and market for new clients. This person may be an interior designer who has a special ability to market or who is a business major with an emphasis in marketing. The marketing specialist is expected to locate new clients and to respond to inquiries from potential clients. He or she assists the firm's PR consultant in the development of any promotional materials, such as brochures, Web site materials, and other collateral materials. Depending on the size and the needs of the firm, the marketing specialist may have other responsibilities. As with other design management staff, the marketing specialist is paid a salary.

Teaching

A very satisfying way to "give back" to the profession is to join the faculty of an interior design program. The minimal educational requirement for a full-time faculty position is a master's degree in addition to some professional experience. Most programs regardless of size and type of institution expect that faculty members will continue their education beyond a master's degree, engage in academic research and publishing, and/or remain active in the design profession. Interior design programs also hire practitioners as adjunct or visiting instructors to teach part-time.

Graphics and Wayfinding

The development of graphic and signage design is another career option for many designers. Graphic design work is often included in many projects and can be part of the design firm's services or obtained from a graphic design specialist. Some large interior design firms have affiliated graphics companies that seek out any type of graphic design or desktop publishing work.

Wayfinding involves creating graphics and signs that will help individuals locate themselves within a large facility, such as a hospital, and easily find their direction around the building. This is an important, even critical, service in very large commercial facilities or campuses, such as hospitals, mega hotels, and conference centers.

Additional training in graphic design and desktop computer graphics is especially useful in this specialty. Compensation is generally by salary.

Architectural Photographers

An architectural photographer today is usually someone who has trained to be a professional photographer. These individuals specialize in the photography of exteriors and interiors, and are hired by the interior designer, the architect, or the owner of the building. It is rare that an architectural photographer is working on staff of an architectural or interiors firm. Those who work for an architectural photographer are paid a salary. Those who own their own business compensate themselves as any business owner would.

Museum Work

Interior designers with experience or additional training in museum, restoration, or curatorial areas can work for one of the many historic site museums that exist. This can be very rewarding work for those individuals who have a keen interest in history and restoration. Most of these job opportunities require advanced degree work in such areas as art history, history, and archaeology. This is not the same career opportunity as those designers who specialize in historical restoration, renovation, or adaptive use of residential and/or commercial facilities.

Journalism

A journalism career is possible for interior designers who are very good writers or who have had training in journalism. The positions might be with a large city newspaper or a trade or shelter magazine. Some designers who find their way into full-time journalism positions might also serve as design critics.

Designers who write well but who do not wish to work full-time in this specialty can submit articles to various trade, shelter, and general print media. As discussed in Chapter 20, this can be used as an excellent marketing tool.

Merchandising and Exhibit Design

Many of the skills that an interior designer learns can be applied to visual merchandising, display, and exhibit presentation. Department stores, retail specialty shops, mall management corporations, galleries, and trade show coordinators require merchandise displays. Department stores have in-house visual merchandising departments to constantly change merchandise displays. Others work for exhibit companies that specialize in the coordination and setup of trade show and convention displays. In addition, others freelance display work to retail specialty shops and boutiques. This can be very interesting and challenging work for an interior designer.

This section has provided just a glimpse at the wide variety of opportunities in the interior design industry. Many of these career options are possible with a degree major in interior design, while some require at least several years of experience in the field. Some also require additional education, training, or advanced degrees for eligibility. Additional specialties that might be of interest to the reader are listed in Table 6-3.

TABLE 6-3.

Additional Career Options Related to the Interior Design Profession

Acoustic design	Real estate
Lighting design	Tenant improvement planning
Art consulting	Installation supervisors
Client representative/facilitator	Contract administrators
Feng shui	Wayfinding
Expert witness	Feasibility studies
Codes consultant	Behavioral factors design
Universal design specialist	Security design
CAD specialist	Specification writer
Graphic design	

PRACTICE SETTINGS

This section provides a brief overview of the places where interior designers commonly obtain employment, not the design specialty. These descriptions are very general in nature, and actual experiences and settings will vary based on such things as size of firm, geographic location, design specialty, and business philosophy of ownership.

"On the Boards"

The term *on the boards* is an old one used by many interior designers to refer to those people who are essentially doing pure interior design. They are involved in all phases of a design project; they prepare the plans and specifications and are, for all intents and purposes, responsible for all the other documents that are needed to design a project of any type space. This designer can be involved in any of the specialty areas of design commonly thought of as residential or commercial.

In today's profession, an on-the-boards designer is more likely to be working for a firm with a focus on commercial interior design. Commercial interior designers must be well versed in the building, accessibility, and fire safety codes that are extremely important in commercial design. (Of course, a residential specialist also has many code responsibilities.)

This essential interior designer might not sell furniture to clients, depending on the exact practice setting. Another term for this type of specialty is *designer/specifier*, since this term also refers to those interior designers who prepare all the design elements of a project and specify the needed products, but rarely sell merchandise. In either case, these designers are paid a salary.

Retail Furniture Store—Residential

Entry-level designers who begin their careers in a residential retail furniture store generally do so as an assistant to one of the senior designers. Assistants learn the business and gain experience with clients as they help senior designers with product specifications, drafting, sample boards, specifications, along with many other activities. Direct client interaction only occurs as the assistant gains experience and confidence.

The experienced designer works with the client in either the store or the client's home. Projects might involve designing a single space or designing and specifying items for an entire home. The designer is encouraged to sell what the store inventories but is rarely limited to selling just those items. Most often, the design service is free or is nominal, since the expense of the designer's service is covered through the sale of goods at retail. Designers are often required to meet sales quotas and most often are paid on a commission basis rather than a salary. Entry-level individuals are more often paid a salary and might receive a small commission. Depending on the philosophy of the store's management, it might take an entry-level person from two to four years before promotion from an assistant's position.

Retail Department Store

Department stores often have interior design staff. The size and complexity of the design studio is impacted by the size of the store. Working for a department store is very similar to working for a retail furniture store. A designer might sell one item or a range of products for a house. Often, however, the designer is limited to selling what the department store carries. Department stores can have a studio that focuses on commercial projects as well as residential. There are also department stores that offer a limited range of design services through the drapery or floorings departments. In this situation, it is less likely that the designer also sells furniture, since this is often handled by furniture salespeople. Generally, design services are offered free to the client. The designer is generally paid only a commission on sales.

Retail Specialty Store

A specialty store is a retail store selling a particular type of product other than furniture to the end user. Design services, if offered, are complementary. Specialty stores are excellent opportunities for the entry-level designer to gain sales experience and product knowledge. Depending on the product, the staff will receive training related to the products. However, some specialty stores such as art galleries or antique stores may require staff to have specialized knowledge prior to hiring. Designers are commonly paid a small salary plus a commission.

Office Furnishings Dealer

An office furnishings *dealer* is, in a sense, a retail showroom for commercial furniture products. As the name implies, office furnishings dealers primarily design various office complexes. However, some also design other kinds of commercial interiors. The company has showroom space and an inventory of furniture to back up what is displayed. Many office furnishings dealers have certain exclusive products that they expect designers to specify most often.

An office furnishings dealer rarely sells products at suggested retail. More often products are sold at a discount from suggested retail or a markup on cost. Outside salespeople are largely responsible for selling furniture products, while the design staff provides planning services. Design services are billed to clients similarly to many other types of design studios.

The design employee might be part of an in-house design department or may work in a subsidiary design company that is owned by the dealership. Designers who work in these organizations are often required to have substantial space-planning skills and to be experienced with CAD. It often takes at least two years to advance to a position of project responsibility. The pay is usually a salary for the designers who might also be eligible for commission on certain items.

Becoming a member of the sales staff at an office furnishings dealership is another option for interior designers. Salespeople have the primary responsibility to sell furniture and other products. They are usually not required to be designers, although many were at one time, and are generally not required to do any interior design planning. Sales staff must generate new business and are paid a commission on the furniture products they sell.

Architectural Office

Many architectural offices have interior design groups, providing another setting for the interior designer. These designers work primarily on projects in partnership with the architects. The work might involve residential or commercial projects, or both, depending on the nature of the architectural practice.

Interior designers work as part of a team with the architects and others in the firm. Very good space-planning and technical skills, design creativity, skill with the production of construction drawings and documents, and the use of CAD are all critical to this practice setting. Interior designers are compensated by a salary.

Independent Design Firm

An independent design firm is one that has no affiliation with a particular product and may not have any products displayed for sale in its office or studio. However, independent design firms may have a limited amount of showroom space. Because such a firm is independent, it may specify any products for clients that are available in the marketplace. The firm may specialize in some type of interior or design a combination of types of spaces. The projects obtained by independent design firms frequently requires that the designer travel extensively, since the firm's work comes from all over the country, if not the world. This is especially true for the very specialized firm.

It may be a one-person design studio or a large firm that has dozens of employees. Many independent design firms design and specify but do not sell products to their clients. Unless the firm also sells products, income is generated through design fees. Design employees are paid a salary and possibly a commission or bonus for product sales.

Manufacturer

An individual may work for a manufacturer in several ways. A designer might work in a manufacturer's showrooms. In this case, a designer might assist the interior designers and other allied professionals who come to the showroom. A few manufacturers have staff designers at a factory location to aid other designers and architects in planning and specifying the company's products. Usually, the designer is in a sales position and is paid a small salary and/or a commission. An interior designer with a minimum of three years' experience in the business might be hired as part of the sales representative group. Sales reps are almost always paid a commission rather than a salary. These individuals call on design firms and large clients who are considering the use of the company's products. Becoming part of the product design staff is a less frequent but possible option. Depending on the product, the company may require that the designer have an industrial design background rather than an interior design background.

When a designer is working for a manufacturer, there is often the opportunity to travel throughout the United States and to possibly work outside the country. Many of the major manufacturers have showrooms in foreign countries. Those designers who do design layout work as an employee of a manufacturer also have an opportunity to travel within the United States. Compensation depends on the actual job. Showroom sales positions and sales reps are commission based; designers are paid a salary.

Corporations

Many large corporations have in-house interior designers or facility planners. Corporate designers might be in charge of the complete design process for departments and facilities or work with outside designers in the design of corporate facilities. Responsibility might involve designing the chief executive officer's office as well as any group of offices or spaces within the facility.

Hotel chains, for example, have in-house designers who work with architects and franchise owners in the design or remodeling of their facility. Interior designers can also be employees of many other kinds of commercial spaces, such as hospitals, restaurants, and retail stores. In some situations, the designers might travel to various company locations. Designers who work in a corporate environment are paid a salary or possibly an hourly wage.

Developers

Interior designers sometimes find interesting positions with developers and construction companies. One of the most common is the designer working for a residential developer. The designer assists new home buyers with finish selections. The common job title for this position is "colorizer." Although the home builder has a group of standard materials that are calculated into the purchase price, the buyer may upgrade to more expensive materials. These designers earn a commission when the buyer upgrades any of the materials.

Other designers might be hired as construction project managers or as marketing specialists. Positions are also available for designers who help create the basic floor plans of a new development, prepare renderings of the various models, and perhaps design the model homes.

Federal Government

The federal government's General Services Administration (GSA) is responsible for employing interior designers. These designers prepare space plans, design office facilities and court facilities, and perform many other kinds of government agency interior design work. The designer is commonly limited to designing with the products currently on the GSA purchasing schedule, although some projects allow additional flexibility in product specification. The GSA designer designs spaces in a certain geographic area of the country. He or she will be working on projects throughout that area, which may require some traveling away from the main office. The salary, which is based on the individual's "GS" rating, is sometimes a bit higher than an entry-level salary in the private sector, and the government, of course, offers excellent benefits.

State and City Governments

Some state and city government agencies have salaried interior designers and architects. These professionals function in much the same way as designers who work for the federal government. Not all state governments have design employees, since many states have laws forbidding state agencies from performing work that competes with work from the private sector. Compensation is salary based. States and cities also have very good benefits packages.

Independent Organizations

There are numerous independent organizations that employ individuals as interior designers or who utilize the skills acquired in an interior design career for other management or administrative work in the agency. A very few examples include the USGBC, Construction Specifications Institute (CSI), National Association of Home Builders (NAHB), and professional associations such as ASID, IIDA, IFMA, and NCIDQ.

Universities and Colleges

Most universities, colleges, and community colleges—whether private or public—have a facilities planning office. This office works with architects, interior designers, and the school staff to develop new building designs and to remodel existing structures. Educational design work is challenging, since most projects must be designed as economically as possible while still providing interesting and functional environments. Compensation is by salary and the employee benefits are also very good.

At some point in an interior designer's career, another career option might become of interest: to own one's own design firm independently or to join forces with others. The next section of this text is focused on the processes and decisions that are necessary to developing that business. However, this information is also valuable to any employee. Understanding professional business practice in interior design makes a designer a more valuable employee.

SUMMARY

One of the fascinating aspects of the interior design profession is the variety of ways in which an individual can work in the field. This chapter has reviewed many areas of interior design that an individual might find exciting and rewarding. Although some areas do require training or experience beyond the undergraduate level or the normal interior design degree, many offer positions that the trained interior designer can achieve with work experience in the field. This section shows that it is not absolutely necessary for everyone to be highly creative, a great salesperson, a great artist, or a space planner in order to find a niche in interior design.

This chapter concludes what can be called the introductory chapters concerning the interior design profession and practice. These six chapters are offered to create a foundation concerning the profession and why the study of professional practice is important to all students and practitioners.

W hen the time came for me to open my own business, I knew that in order to succeed, it would be best for me to "focus." I deal with very determined couples and individuals who respect my skills and allow me to guide them into making the best decisions for their particular situation. I have budgets and projects that allow my creativity to be exploited in ways that I didn't realize were possible. I feel honored and privileged to be a "residential" designer.

Charles D. Gandy, FASID, FIIDA is President of Charles Gandy, Inc., an award-winning Atlanta design firm, which specializes in both residential and commercial interiors. An accomplished lecturer, Gandy has also written countless articles on the business of design. He has held numerous national and international academic positions, and recently collaborated with the Smithsonian Institution on a series of seminars about interior design. His latest book, *Beautiful Interiors: An Expert's Guide to a More Liveable Home,* is based on a collection of weekly columns entitled "Design 101" written for *The Atlanta Journal-Constitution.*

Establishing an Interior Design Practice

11. Preparing the Business Plan

What's Your Mission?
The Business Plan
Start-up Costs
Business Location
Equipping the Office/Studio
Design Library
Inventory Issues

CHAPTER 7

Creating a New Interior Design Practice

Key Terms and Concepts

These key terms and concepts are important to material in this chapter. Many of these terms will be utilized in other chapters as well. Be sure you understand these items as you read this chapter.

Terms and Concepts

Entrepreneur	Dealer
Sole practitioner	Office furnishings dealer
Independent interior design practice	Architectural firms
Residential retail stores	

Critical Issues

After completing this chapter you should be able to:

- Describe the common characteristics of an entrepreneur.
- Evaluate your motivations of business ownership by using Table 7-1.
- Discuss at least three advantages and disadvantages of business ownership.
- Explain why it is important to obtain experience in the profession before starting a practice.
- Compare basic differences between at least three practice settings.

Are you considering starting an interior design practice? Maybe this year? Maybe in a few years? It is exciting to make that decision. It is also scary for many. When the economy is good—as it is in many markets today—starting a business seems like a no-brainer. "There are plenty of clients to go around" is the comment made by many budding entrepreneurs. "At last I can be my own boss and produce design work the way I want to do it!"

Reality needs to set in with the excitement of becoming part of the nearly 600,000 new businesses started in 2004.[1] By the way, this number does not include

TABLE 7-1.

Personal Motivations and Attitudes about Starting a New Design Practice

These sample questions should be used to evaluate your motivations and attitudes toward starting your own business. If you are seriously thinking of starting your own business in the near future, use these questions only as a starting point to determine your interest and sincerity.

1. Why do you want to own your own business?
2. Are you dissatisfied with your present job? Why?
3. Are you prepared for the sacrifices of your personal time and energy that you will have to make?
4. How do your present skills and abilities prepare you for business ownership?
5. Do you have finances available to commit to the business venture, or must you obtain outside start-up financing?
6. Are you willing and able to survive financially without a regular salary or paycheck?
7. Do you have sufficient experience in the interior design industry to operate and maintain a design practice?
8. Do you have clients who will switch to your business if you leave your current employer?
9. Are you a self-starter, or do you need direction in your present work situation?
10. Are you willing to work the extra hours that are often required of a business owner?
11. Are you good at performing many tasks at the same time, or are you better when you only have to do one thing at a time?
12. What skills and abilities do you have that you can offer your potential clients?
13. Why would a customer desire your services more than those of other interior designers?
14. Have you done any evaluation of potential competitors?
15. Are you prepared to handle the difficulties of operating your own business during the start-up year and beyond?
16. Can you work without others around, or do you need others to help keep you motivated?
17. What kinds of business skills or experiences do you have to operate a business?
18. Are you a good organizer?
19. Do you have a lot of self-confidence?
20. Is the financial risk involved in having your own business acceptable?
21. Is your financial condition at present in a satisfactory state for you to start a business?
22. Are family members prepared to accept your long hours and lack of attention as you start and operate your own business?
23. If your business is to be located at home, do you have sufficient space and privacy to perform your work activities?
24. Can you define the kind of design firm you want in only three sentences?

the number of businesses created without any employees, which is often the case for a new interior design business. This means the number of new businesses (of all kinds that are non-farm) started in a year can be well over 1 million.

What do I mean by reality setting in? This means that anyone who might consider starting a design practice needs to do serious research, thinking, and planning. Wanting to be free to set one's own time and work the way "you want to" are not all that needs to be determined. The potential business owner needs to research his or her own business skills and experience. In addition, the potential business owner must also evaluate his or her motivation for starting a design practice.

Planning formalizes the decisions and ideas surrounding the creation of a new business. It helps the potential business owner see if the idea is feasible and what will be required to make it work. It provides an operational tool for the owner to handle potential problems with thought rather than by pure gut reaction. A plan helps the budding business owner to clearly consider the business idea. Such things as which design services will be offered, how many customers might potentially be interested in those services, and the amount of financial resources that will be necessary until revenue starts coming in must be thought through before "opening the doors." It might seem like boring work. However, it is very important to clarify the business idea and purpose in order to provide a better chance for it to survive through the first year or two when clients are probably less likely to be banging down the doors.

Part III of this text focuses on information design professionals need concerning the decision to organize a new interior design practice. This chapter serves as an introduction to the idea of establishing an interior design practice. It sets the stage for the information offered throughout the remainder of the text concerning professional business practice. Practitioners ready to begin will find a wealth of information to help them make decisions as they plan and organize their practice. Students will gain an understanding that the decision to start a practice is not to be taken lightly, nor without experience in the field no matter how tempting it might be to open a business right after graduation.

WHAT IS AN ENTREPRENEUR?

An *entrepreneur* is someone who is willing to take a risk by starting and managing his or her own business. Many business experts say that entrepreneurs are also visionaries or innovators. They want to do things differently because they feel they have a better way to provide services, to manage an office, or to sell products. Someone who starts a small business, like many interior design practitioners, is not necessarily an entrepreneur in the true sense of the word. However, most people regard anyone who starts a business as an "entrepreneur."

It should not matter whether an interior design business is truly different and visionary. Perhaps you will have a very unique idea on how to offer services or in some way create a business that is "visionary." Given enough thought and planning, a potential business owner can develop an interior design business idea that is cutting-edge for its area and in contrast to all the other design firms in the market, even if it is not truly unique.

Is there any specific characteristics of an entrepreneur that "guarantees" the individual and his or her business idea will be a success? Not really. An entrepreneur does need experience in the industry. Obtaining experience in the business world helps the individual understand that having a business means hard work and long hours. Entrepreneurs are also ambitious, are independent, have a lot of self-confidence, are passionate about their business, and are committed to making it work. They understand that it is common to put in long days, not thinking about punching in at 8 A.M. and out at 5 P.M. An entrepreneur—or should we say a new business owner—often takes work home as well, if not in terms of actual paperwork or design work, then in terms of thinking about existing problems that must be resolved. Many do not see a salary for many years, preferring to retain any profits in the business to help it grow and become financially stable.

For someone considering starting an interior design practice of any kind, there are some skills and traits that are most beneficial. These are suggested in part because of licensing and registration requirements that are becoming more universally accepted throughout North America. Performing design services properly in today's markets requires a new interior design business owner to have technical design expertise gained through education and work experience. Most have worked for someone else, providing an opportunity to gain experience and perhaps help manage a business. Business owners are highly self-motivated people who do not need to be prodded into working. Designers who find it difficult to work on their own without direction and supervision will find it difficult to put in the time and effort necessary to operate a business.

Being the boss is fun. It is also risky and a lot of hard work. Knowing what it is that you are trying to accomplish with a design practice and how you are going to go about accomplishing that purpose is critical to its success.

UNDERSTANDING MOTIVATIONS AND RISKS

The desire to have one's own business is very common within the interior design industry. Desire will take the budding entrepreneur a long way. However, success will be more feasible with planning. Unfortunately, too many interior designers begin an interior design practice without carefully thinking through why they want their own business and the scope of the business concept. Understanding your motivations for having a business is important. Running a professional interior design practice is a lot of hard work beyond the hard work necessary to design projects for clients.

The decision to start a new design practice must involve careful evaluation of many items. One of the first things to consider is personal motivation. Maybe your motivation comes from a desire to work only with clients who really want to buy your creative design ideas rather than the need to meet the demands of an employer. You may be motivated by the idea of making more money or working for yourself rather than for someone else. Or you may be motivated by a feeling that you can somehow "do it better"' than other designers in the marketplace.

Whatever motivations you have for wanting to have your own design practice, the important point is to know and recognize what they are. Although the motivations noted previously may appear to be positive, they can also result in negative issues. Many designers start out picking and choosing clients but find that, in leaner economic times, they cannot do this. Besides, it will not take the new business owner long to realize that the client most often is not buying a designer's creative ideas as much as solutions to his or her problems. The motivation of making more money may be only a dream for many years, as the number of projects, low margins, and costs of operating the business reduce the profits of all small businesses. Numerous questions that will help the potential business owner evaluate his or her motivations and attitudes concerning starting a new design practice are highlighted in Table 7-1. This exercise is very important and should not be taken lightly. A worksheet of this questionnaire has been provided on the CD as Item 7-1.

Starting a business also involves financial risk. Financial risk changes depending on many factors. It can take several thousands of dollars, if not tens of thousands of dollars, to start up a design practice and to survive during the first year. In addition, the entrepreneur must consider how he or she will pay personal expenses while waiting for revenues to be realized. Banks are reluctant to loan money to many small businesses for start-up funding. Besides, banks will not loan funds to a budding entrepreneur for living expenses, regardless of how great the business idea.

An evaluation of the personal financial risk entailed in starting a new design practice begins by determining the amount of funds that are needed each month to pay living expenses. Figure 7-1 is a simple form that will help you determine personal living expenses. Please note that this form is not all-inclusive. You may have personal living expenses that are not shown on this form. Be sure you include them in your calculations. A worksheet of this figure has been included on the CD as Item 7-2.

It is generally suggested that the entrepreneur set aside at least one year's living expenses before starting a small business, since it may take that long for the business to be able to pay the entrepreneur a salary. Note that many small-business practitioners never take a salary, keeping profits in the company. Thus, it is very important to set aside funds to cover personal living expenses.

The entire business concept has an impact on personal financial risk. The more ambitious the plans are for the business, the greater the risk. A practice that involves even a small showroom as part of the business concept

Personal Expenses		
Item	**Monthly Amount**	**Annual**
Housing (Rent):		
Home Owners Association		
Insurance		
Yard Maintenance		
Property Taxes		
Utilities:		
Electricity/Gas		
Telephone		
TV (Cable)		
Internet		
Water/Sewer		
Food		
Automobile:		
Payment		
Insurance		
Gas and Maintenance		
Personal Prop. Tax on Autos		
Health Insurance		
Medical and Dental *Not* Insured		
Credit Cards		
Other Loans		
Clothing & Laundry		
Child Care		
Dues and Subscriptions*		
Nonreimbursed Business Expenses		
Savings/Investments		
Entertainment		
Gifts & Charities		
Miscellaneous		
TOTAL:		

*Those that are not business expenses.

FIGURE 7-1.

Personal expenses can be calculated on this form. It is helpful in budgeting for a new business venture.

will require a larger amount of start-up funds than many other arrangements. Any design practice with a high overhead will put more strain on the designer's ability to meet personal financial obligations. Willingness to live on less while the business gets on its feet may be an important consideration while funds to pay personal bills are limited. Careful evaluation, savings, and planning of personal financial responsibilities are very important parts of planning a new design practice.

There are also legal risks in starting a business. If you live in a jurisdiction with licensing or registration laws regarding interior design work, you will need to meet those requirements. There can be legal consequences to starting a business in your home. Many home owners associations have very strict prohibitions on operating a business from a residence. Most jurisdictions also prohibit a business in the home if employees are hired. These are just two examples. Clients may take legal action against you if you are negligent in performing the required services. Becoming involved in design work for which you are experienced and capable should help lessen the potential for negligent performance. In other words, careful research and planning will help the entrepreneur understand any limitations and requirements on the business concept.

Starting any kind of interior design practice takes thought in order to organize a professional practice. Success starts with what the entrepreneur is willing to put into the business on the "front end"—gaining education and experience in the profession and planning the concept carefully. The other chapters in this section provide a great deal of information that will be helpful in planning the business.

By the way, many practitioners and educators I have talked to have said to be sure and caution students about thinking of starting a design company too soon after graduation. It is quite common for students to be given an assignment in a business practices class to plan a design practice. However, receiving an "A" on that assignment does not guarantee success if an interior design practice is started soon after graduation. Regardless of one's previous experience, age, or financial situation, starting a practice without experience in the field rarely leads to success for recent design program graduates.

What Would You Do?

George took his client to a furniture trade showroom to look at living room and bedroom items. A few days later, the client goes back to the showroom alone. Unbeknownst to George, the client had previously obtained a resale tax license, planning to use it to buy furniture directly from suppliers. The client meets the representative of a furniture company without George present. The sales representative tells the client details about the discount and commission program that the furniture company has offered to George and is willing to offer to the client as well, since the client has a resale license.

ADVANTAGES AND DISADVANTAGES OF BUSINESS OWNERSHIP

As with any risk, there are good things and bad things about owning a business. Being the decision maker, independence, working with clients one chooses, and achieving greater financial rewards are common reasons given by designers when asked why they decided to start their own interior design firm. Naturally, there are disadvantages, and at times these seem to outweigh the advantages. Part of the decision-making process in owning your own business is to look at both the advantages and the disadvantages—especially the disadvantages—of ownership to be sure that you are prepared to accept these constraints. Some of these are as follows.

Advantages

- Having the opportunity to perform the kind of design work the individual most enjoys.
- Independence. As the boss, the owner makes the decisions. For some, of course, this becomes a disadvantage.
- Personal satisfaction in achieving success.
- Making a potentially higher income drawn from the business's profits.
- Job security. The job exists as long as the business succeeds and the owner wishes to remain in the business.
- Developing and marketing a creative style. Designers working for others often must design in the style of the owner of the firm.
- Greater opportunity for personal recognition.
- Increased contact with clients, suppliers, and other industry members. The owner makes more client contacts, deals directly with suppliers, and has the opportunity to meet others in many aspects of the design industry.
- Depending on the business formation selected, there may be tax benefits.

Disadvantages

- Financial risk. Business assets and possibly personal assets are at risk.
- Legal liability. Owners are liable for their own actions, as well as for those of their employees.
- Longer hours. Typically, owners work 12-hour days, sometimes even seven days a week, with little time off for vacations or for a personal or social life. This is especially true in the first few years of the life of the business.
- Greater stress. The owner is concerned about bringing in enough business to meet all the bills and to prevent any kind of bad publicity or poor customer service. He or she also must worry that the employees are all doing their jobs properly and legally, and must worry about many other problems and constraints that affect the business.
- Job security. The owner's job is only secure if the business remains active and solvent.
- Income is minimal, even nonexistent, during the first year or more. Profits for a new business are traditionally low and are often plowed back into the business, either to pay expenses or to expand the business.
- No employment benefits for owner. Benefits such as workers' compensation and unemployment insurance do not exist for owners in most cases. Health insurance costs are also totally paid by the owner.
- Greater tax burdens. Depending on the business formation, the owner pays both the employer and employee portion of Social Security tax on income as self-employment tax.
- Need to satisfy customers. Even though a business owner is the boss, he or she is now controlled by the wishes of the client.

- Greater management responsibility. Business and employee management is the owner's responsibility. Many designers who start their own practice lack management skills.
- Less design input. As the business grows, the design owner often finds that he or she is spending less time on design and more time on managing the business.
- Less flexibility. It is not easy to quit if the business owner finds that he or she does not enjoy ownership or otherwise no longer wishes to remain in business. A financial loss might result from closing down. It can also be difficult to even take a vacation.

It is an unfortunate reality that the disadvantages often outnumber the advantages when it comes to business ownership. This reality should not discourage anyone from starting his or her own business; on the contrary. The intention in pointing out these issues is to be sure that the potential business owner realizes the risks involved and contemplates the business venture thoroughly before starting the new design practice.

TYPES OF PRACTICE ORGANIZATIONS

An interior design practice can take many forms. The exact nature of the business is as varied as the desires of owners and their business concept. There are, of course, primary forms of business organizations that are found in the interior design profession. The purpose of this section is to describe the different ways in which a practice can be organized. These brief descriptions do not represent all the types of business organizations in which an interior designer may practice. Many of the career options discussed in Chapter 6 can also be a type of business organization.

Sole Practitioner Interior Design Firm

It is very common for interior designers to start their business working alone with no full-time employees. Individuals who work alone are called *sole practitioners*. There is no accurate way to know how many interior design firms are sole practitioners working alone or with occasional part-time assistance. It is a quite common means for many to venture into owning a business, however. It seems that the majority of sole practitioners are involved in residential interior design rather than commercial. It is not uncommon for a sole practitioner to sell merchandise to supplement revenue from providing design services.

Working Alone

Free to work when you want and how you want. It has a lot of advantage, and it is a big reason many start an interior design practice. Working alone can also mean having the freedom to do interior design work in the way you really want to do it, without constraints being placed on you by a boss. It means that all the profits stay with the owner—you. However, "Free isn't easy. It means risks. It means responsibility. It means hard work."[*]

Working alone also has disadvantages and "traps" that can keep you from realizing the freedom that you imagined as well as from realizing the profits from the business that you expected. Maintaining discipline to keep to the task at hand is a big problem for many people working alone. Some find that they are procrastinators, putting unpleasant things off, like record keeping. Then again, there is the possibility that the designer may become a workaholic, not taking time off to pursue personal interests. Understand that the sole practitioner must do all the paperwork and business development as well as the creative work.

Sometimes the realization of how alone "alone" can be is pretty hard to take. It is not easy for many who enjoy the social interaction that comes with working with other designers to make the transition to being the only one to answer the phone, do all the work, and maintain the discipline to work. The silence of an empty home office can be unnerving and lonely. For many, it is a big test of one's will.

Too many designers start a business without understanding the risks involved. As a sole practitioner, it is up to you to develop business. Those clients do not appear out of thin air. They must be prospected for, cultivated, and finally encouraged to sign contracts with you. Working from a home office results in lower overhead expenses. However, you will still have expenses that are needed to operate the practice, taxes to pay on income earned, and bills to pay to suppliers. You are responsible for raising all those funds. If you make a mistake that causes physical or business harm, you are responsible for the consequences and perhaps even legal judgments. All of this and more comes with starting a business and working alone.

Here are some guidelines that you can follow that will help to make working alone a positive experience:

- Determine that what you want to offer in the way of interior design services is readily needed by clients in your area.
- Understand that the probability of making a lot of money during the first year—even the first three years—is an illusion.
- Think about how much making money means success for you and whether money is the reason you have decided to go it alone.
- Keep yourself charged up. Become involved in your professional association chapter, network with clients at their associations, or start a network group of like-minded designers who could also use some camaraderie.
- Set goals that are challenging yet attainable. Do not undermine your confidence by setting goals that are impossible to meet.
- Give yourself a break. Take that mini-vacation. Attend a trade show or a conference. Have lunch with old friends. Look out the window and remember to smell the roses!

Owning one's own business and being able to work alone is an exciting challenge as well as a scary proposition. It takes courage to start any new business. Carefully considering what you are trying to achieve and why, planning how to go about achieving those results, and then having the determination to do it will likely give you a great deal of pleasure and enjoyment!

[*]Fisher, 1995, p. 14.

Sole practitioners working alone face issues that have less an impact on work performance and business success than other forms of business. A sole practitioner must have a strong sense of discipline. For some the isolation of working alone can actually be quite hard. Designers who have a lot of energy when they are working with others may not have the same energy as a sole practitioner. Finding the time to get all the necessary tasks done can be a struggle at times. The sole practitioner must manage the time necessary to continually develop business, meet with existing clients, prepare design documents needed for projects, and perform all the other work of maintaining a business.

Of course, there must be something positive about the sole practitioner experience for so many interior designers to begin business ownership in this way! The independence to work with the types of clients the designer seeks most is a big reason. The other advantages listed previously also positively impact the sole practitioner. These business owners must make sure they understand their creative and business abilities as an interior designer. Sole practitioners must also examine their ambitions to be sure that they have the determination to keep going, even in the face of adversity. It is not enough to be creative.

Independent Interior Design Firms

Of course, a sole practitioner is also a form of *independent interior design practice*. The term "independent" means that the firm is free to specify any type of product for the projects they are engaged to design. In some other forms of business, this is not always the case.

There are many variations on the independent interior design firm. Independent interior design practices may or may not sell furnishings or have a retail showroom. The majority of their revenue can come from fees for services or include selling product. The company might have a few employees or dozens. In a small firm, client contact, contract development, design, and project management are all part of what each designer in the firm is expected to do. Most likely, the owner is also doing a lot of project work in addition to managing.

The larger firms will have various management and staff levels. Client contact is usually the responsibility of the owner, the senior designers, or possibly a design marketing manager. Senior designers are primarily responsible for managing projects, and they often supervise a team of designers and support personnel during the completion of the project. In some firms, there are also individuals who have many specialized job functions, such as specification writers and renderers, who can free the project designers from such activities.

Residential Retail Stores

An interior designer whose residential design practice involves selling goods to the client might increase that service to the point of having a retail store while maintaining interior design services. Other individuals begin a business as a retail store selling some type of furnishings to the consumer. A retail store in the interiors industry can sell many kinds of products or specialize in products like lighting fixtures or flooring. This business type requires a large financial investment and risk.

A retail furniture store will almost always have interior designers as part of the staff. Clients who require the services of an interior designer are referred to the design staff. The interior designer is responsible for finding out what the client needs in the way of products and services, for discussing contracts (if the company charges a fee for design service), and for all the design work that needs to be done. In some situations, the designer may have an assistant (an entry-level interior designer) who will help him or her gather information, find appropriate products, and prepare necessary documents. However, the experienced interior designer is the primary person who deals with the client.

A second group has a group of individuals who are strictly floor salespeople. These individuals work in the store and sell merchandise to clients who do not really need an interior designer's services. These clients are often just looking for one or two items to supplement or replace something in their homes or offices. If the retail store is large enough, these in-house salespeople may specialize in areas such as furniture, wall coverings, and floor treatments. In-house salespeople may or may not be trained as interior designers.

Note that some residential furniture stores are actually factory-owned or independently owned franchise stores that focus sales on a single manufacturer's products. These stores have interior designers on the staff and work with clients to sell a complete project or individual items for the home. An example of this type of retail store is Ethan Allan, Inc.

Office Furnishings Dealers

Another type of business involving interior design services is the *office furnishings dealer.* The term *dealer* means that the company has a special buying relationship with one or more manufacturers. The focus of this type of business is on selling furniture, and design services are provided to augment sales and assist the client. Dealerships require a large infusion of funds to start, since they must inventory a great deal of furniture items. Note that there are also residential retail furniture stores that could also be called dealers, since they also have special buying relationships with one or more manufacturers.

Office furnishings dealers are retail establishments even though they often sell furniture at less than retail prices. Outside salespeople are responsible for selling products. It is not unusual for an outside sales person to formally have worked as an interior designer.

A major portion of the interior design work done by the company is often initially obtained by the outside sales force. The interior design department manager and staff make other presentations and develop design contracts for services. The design director either visits with the client face-to-face or assigns one of the senior designers to the task. He or she administers the design department and assigns design staff to projects. Although many projects are assigned to a single designer, many are based on a team concept. Designers are assigned to work with specific sales personnel or for a specific project manager most of the time. These team members work and coordinate their efforts to program, plan, and ultimately sell the project to the client.

Architectural Firms

Many architectural firms incorporate design services by interior designers with the architectural services. Interior designers typically work on the projects obtained by the firm, though they may also obtain projects independent of the architectural firm. This is especially true of larger firms. Interior designers may be responsible to an architectural services project manager or a senior architect. In larger firms, there may be a sufficient number of designers so that a design director or an interiors managing partner is required to supervise the interiors staff.

In many ways, the organization of an architectural firm is similar to the independent interior design firm. For the most part, these firms do not sell merchandise to clients, although some firms find that this is a way to generate additional revenues. Most focus on design and specification activities instead.

Buying an Existing Business

The challenges of starting up a new interior design practice scare many away from ever taking a chance being an entrepreneur. One alternative for those who wish to have a practice without the problems of starting from scratch is buying an existing business. There are many practitioners who look forward to the day when they are in a position to sell their established business. They may reach this decision because of retirement or a feeling that withdrawal from the business at that time is an appropriate idea. Buying a business—especially for someone who could also start a sole proprietorship—is often more expensive than starting from scratch and should be undertaken cautiously and with good research.

There are many reasons why buying an existing business is a good idea. The new owner begins with an established client list who will potentially work with the new owner. There may be employees willing to stay on and help the new owner keep the business going. The challenges and problems of setting up the business are lessened, since an existing business is already organized. Initial start-up costs to run the business may be lower. (Of course, there will be costs involved in purchasing the business.) There is also less risk for the first year, as the existing client base and reputation of the company will help bring in new customers.

Naturally there are some disadvantages as well. The prospective buyer will want to investigate the reputation of an existing business that is for sale to be sure it is in good standing. Research needs to discover a bad credit rating or poor relationships with vendors. Since there are so many potential vendors involved, it is not always easy to determine the financial good standing with vendors. The location or target market client might not suit your interests, making it difficult to pursue the types of design work you most wish to have. Any inventory that is part of the purchase might be items that are difficult to sell to your future clients. Equipment—especially computers and other office machines—might be out-of-date and expensive to replace.

Before making an offer to purchase an existing business, the prospective owner should at least do these key tasks:

- Be sure you clearly understand why the business is for sale. Although it may simply be because the owner wishes to retire, it might also be for sale because of legal or financial problems.

- Talk to your accountant to see if the asking price is in line with other service businesses. Although your accountant might not have any reference points locally, he or she may have contacts with accounting colleagues who can give comparison pricing information in other cities or states.

- Carefully investigate the company's financial records for the past five years. A long financial history review will give you a better idea of how successful the firm and its name will be in the future. Of course, your accountant will be very involved in this review. Make sure you are seeing profit and loss statements, balance sheets, and income tax forms for those five years.

- Beware of exaggerated profit claims or extensive client lists that do not seem logical.

- Have your attorney determine if the company has ever been sued or has any judgments pending. You should also check other agencies like the Registrar of Contractors, Better Business Bureau, and professional associations to which the owner belongs to be sure there are no pending problems in the company's name that could be harmful to you in the future.

- Remember that you are not only buying equipment, inventory, and library materials. You are buying the company name. Make sure that the name is well regarded. Investigate the business by talking to vendors, past customers if possible, credit rating services, and other sources that can tell you something about a company.

This is only a brief glimpse at what is involved in deciding to buy a business. In-depth details on this decision as well as a look at valuing a business the reader might wish to purchase are beyond the scope of this book. A few of the books listed in the references will provide additional guidance in this matter.

SUMMARY

The recognition of the desire to have one's own business or to start an interior design firm with a partner is the first part of planning for that new practice. Success requires more than desire, experience, and skills in this highly attractive and competitive industry. Understanding one's motivations for wanting an interior design practice is certainly a part of developing a road map to increase the chances for success and personal satisfaction as a business owner.

Of course, an interior design firm's operational organization comes from comprehensive planning and careful decision making. Numerous questions about the focus of services, customers that will be sought, pricing, and many other issues should be well thought out before the stationery is printed. The stakes can be too high when this type of thought and planning is not done. No one wants to suffer financial loss, loss of reputation in the field, or even litigation by unhappy clients or vendors. If the prospective owner is not willing to put forth the effort needed to consider the ramifications and then develop plans to move the business forward, he or she may not be ready to own or operate a practice.

This chapter provided an overview of business ownership. It defined the term *entrepreneur* and provided guidance for potential business owners to help them clarify their motivations in venturing into business ownership. The chapter also presented some of the advantages and disadvantages of business ownership. Finally, a review of some of the different types of interior design businesses was presented. The next chapter will discuss the role of advisors the prospective owner may wish to meet with to discuss his or her business idea.

REFERENCE

1. Small Business Administration, November 2005, www.sba.gov/faqs.

CHAPTER 8

Advice and Counsel

Key Terms and Concepts

These key terms and concepts are important to material in this chapter. Many of these terms will be utilized in other chapters as well. Be sure you understand these items as you read this chapter.

Terms and Concepts

Income statement

Profit and loss statement

Operating funds

Revenue

Expenses

Profit

Balance sheet

Accounts

Banker

Bookkeeper

Accountant

Certified public accountant (CPA)

Professional tax preparer

Operating funds

Collateral

Debt capital

Long-term loans

Short-term loans

Line of credit

Secured loan

Unsecured loan

Equity capital

Venture capital

Angel investor

Affiliated angel investor

Pro forma credit

Trade credit

Credit Green Book

Lyon Red Book

Independent insurance agent

Exclusive agent

Insurance broker

Business owner's policy

Property damage insurance

Professional liability insurance

Malpractice insurance

Errors and omissions (E&O)

Liability insurance

Personal injury insurance

Business income insurance

Automobile insurance

Workers' compensation insurance

Accounts receivable insurance

Business Organizations

U.S. Small Business Administration (SBA)

Service Corp of Retired Executives (SCORE)

Dun & Bradstreet (D&B)

Allied Board of Trade

Lyon Furniture Mercantile Agency

Critical Issues

After reading this chapter you should be able to:

- Explain the different roles in which an attorney can advise a practice owner.
- Understand the differences between an accountant, CPA, and certified tax preparer.
- Discuss how a banker advises a practice owner.
- Compare debt capital and investment capital.
- Name and define the types of information a creditor would require for a business loan application.
- Discuss some ways that a business would establish business credit with vendors.
- Identify the types of insurance that a sole practitioner operating out of his or her home will want to obtain.
- Identify the types of insurance that a partnership operating from a studio located in a shopping center will require.
- Explain malpractice and errors and omissions insurance.
- Discuss ways in which technical consultants might need to be used in a residential and commercial design practice.

Business owners need several professional advisers and counselors. Seeking advice from business experts is a natural and important step in the evolution of bringing a business idea to reality. Topics in this chapter are also of benefit to the practitioner who has had a business for a few years and may be contemplating taking the business in a new direction. Since very few people have expertise in all areas of business, the prospective business owner should find the best advisers possible to help establish and maintain an interior design practice.

In this chapter, we will discuss the most important advisers one should consider engaging when starting or operating an interior design practice. Those advisers are an attorney, who renders assistance in many legal areas; an accountant, who provides information concerning financial matters; a banker, who may help obtain the financing needed to operate the interior design practice; insurance advisers, who help obtain proper insurance protection; and technical consultants, who are the many allied professionals who help the interior designer with specialized design problems.

This chapter also includes information on other key topics related to these advisors. A discussion on sources of capital and establishing business credit follows the section on the importance of a banker as a business consultant. Additional information on many types of business insurance is also included.

ATTORNEY

An *attorney* provides legal advice and counsel to business owners and individuals. All interior design firms will at some time seek the advice of an attorney. Hopefully, it is only to review contracts and leases and not due to legal entanglements with clients. Attorneys do specialize in areas of legal practice. The entrepreneur should look for an attorney that has a strong background in business law and contracts.

For the interior designer contemplating a new practice, an attorney can help determine which business formation is best. An attorney will not be required if the firm forms as a sole proprietorship with a single owner. His or her advice is still valuable for a sole proprietorship. If a new design firm is considering using a partnership or corporation formation (discussed in the next chapter), an attorney will be a helpful consultant and advisor. Depending on the jurisdiction, an attorney may be required to draw up business formation papers, articles of incorporation, or other documents. Attorneys can assist the new owner in understanding the numerous legal questions in starting a business.

An interior design business may have other incidents and dealings that require the attention of an attorney throughout the life of the business. It might occasionally need legal advice with the questions concerning liability, employee firing, clients not paying bills, tax issues, as well as others. The interior design firm owner should not wait until a problem occurs before finding an attorney for part of the business's "team" of advisors. Of course, the main reason for having an attorney as part of the team is to help the firm avoid potential problems.

A business's attorney should be familiar with contract law, negotiation and arbitration, copyright, and other business issues of the kind that might occur in an interior design practice. Sometimes colleagues in a professional association will recommend their attorney. The local bar association may be able to refer you to one or more prospective attorneys. Obviously, an attorney familiar with the interior design, architecture, and building industry is highly desirable over one that does not deal with this industry. You might want to read the information on the CD in Item 8-1 on hiring an attorney to help in your search.

Here are some additional services that can be provided by an attorney on behalf of an interior design firm:

- Review design contract formats and clauses.
- Review leases, purchase agreements, purchase orders, and other business forms.
- Advise the owner who is considering a change in legal formation.
- Provide counsel on how to avoid a potential lawsuit and represent the firm if it is sued.
- Provide counsel concerning required licenses and permits.
- Assist with intellectual property issues such as copyright.
- Resolve employee rights, safety, and compensation questions.
- Assist with questions concerning estate planning.
- Assist with collection problems.

The design firm owner has to constantly be looking out for his or her best interests in a legal and ethical manner. Always using design contracts that spell out what the firm is going to do and how they are going to charge is one very important step. Keeping good documentation on all the work done on the client's behalf is another absolute necessity. Of course, there are many other tasks and responsibilities that the owner of any size interior design practice must perform to avoid the need of an attorney in a liability issue. Avoiding problems is less expensive than retaining an attorney when the client claims the interior designer did not do what was expected.

ACCOUNTANT

Keeping accurate daily financial records is very critical for any size interior design firm. Daily *bookkeeping* reports are the means for the owner to keep track of income and expenses. Bookkeeping is done to make record keeping for required reports such as monthly sales tax reports and internal reports such as a monthly profit and loss statement easy to prepare. A profit and loss statement summarizes the firm's net income or loss for a period of time. Table 8-1 defines a few of the terms and reports concerning accounting that are discussed in this chapter. These items are discussed more thoroughly in Chapter 16 with other basic accounting information. Good record keeping is also necessary to make income tax reporting for the business accurate and easy. An accountant will help a new firm determine what accounts to set up for that record keeping as well as suggest a methodology for financial record keeping.

Most new firms and sole practitioner practices will probably do their own record keeping or hire a bookkeeper. A *bookkeeper* is an individual who can do the various day-to-day posting, calculating, and verifying of financial records of the firm. An *accountant* usually has more expertise in the preparation and analysis of financial reports such as the balance sheet and profit and loss statement. Only the larger design firms hire an accountant as an employee. A large, existing firm may have one or more bookkeepers or accountants on their staff and may retain an outside accounting firm to do special reports.

Accountants also provide financial advice to a business owner. A *certified public accountant (CPA)* is an individual who has met educational and testing requirements established by the jurisdiction. A CPA holds a different license to practice accounting than a bookkeeper or noncertified accountant. Another type of accountant is a professional tax preparer. A *professional tax preparer* will have the training and experience to interpret tax laws in relationship to the owner's actual business operations. A professional tax preparer is not

---

TABLE 8-1.

Accounting Terms and Reports

Accounts. Financial entries with different names for clarification to show additions (increases) and subtractions (decreases) to the account.

Balance sheet. An accounting form that shows the financial position of a firm at a particular moment in time, including a statement of its assets and liabilities; sometimes called a statement of financial position.

Expenses. The amount of outflows of resources of a firm as a consequence of the efforts made by the firm to earn revenues.

Income statement. An accounting report that formally reports all the revenues and expenses of a firm for a stated period of time. The result shows the net income (or loss) for the firm during the period; also called a profit and loss statement.

Net profit. The amount of funds left during an accounting period after all expenses are paid and any retained earnings are determined and funded.

Operating funds. The amount of funds that are required every month to operate and keep the business open for the month.

Revenue. The amount of inflows from the sale of goods or rendering of services during an accounting period.

Additional detailed accounting terms are provided in Chapter 16.

necessarily a CPA. This type of accountant will also be able to provide other accounting services.

The accountant's job is to help the business owner decide what kinds of operational reports are going to be needed. With today's accounting software programs, many reports can be generated with financial data to help the business owner understand the financial health of his or her firm. Some of these reports might also be needed to obtain loans. Accountants can provide guidance on what software program might be most appropriate for the business and how to use this software effectively. They can also prepare those reports with data from the design firm and assist the owner in interpreting these reports. This information is discussed more thoroughly in Chapter 16. An accountant also prepares quarterly income tax statements for the business and possibly annual financial audits that are required for a corporation. It is important, even for the sole practitioner, to utilize the expertise of an accountant to prepare income tax statements. Tax laws change every year, and interpretation of those laws can become quite involved. A professional tax preparer or CPA will be able to provide this guidance.

Accountants can do many things for a design firm besides prepare income tax returns and formal accounting reports. Some additional services include the following:

- Help the small-business owner organize office management procedures.
- Help the owner to prepare records that may be needed to obtain loans.
- Provide investment counseling.
- Advise on the sales tax liabilities the firm has to various jurisdictions. City, county and state, or provincial jurisdictions have different regulations concerning sales taxes on goods and services sold to the consumer.
- Recommend operational changes that can help the firm reduce income taxes.
- Depending on the license of the accountant, serve as a representative of the design practice to the Internal Revenue Service concerning tax questions.
- Suggest changes in business operations and procedures as the design practice grows.

An accountant familiar with interior design or architecture services is the ideal candidate for the interior design firm. All accountants can provide the many services that the design practice will need, of course. Regardless of the accountant's experience with other interior design firms, it is important that the accountant be someone who will talk plainly and will answer questions about the design firm's financial situation. Many small-business owners become intimidated by their accountant and never understand the actual financial condition of their company. The information provided on the CD in Item 8-2, Hiring an Accountant, will be helpful information for the prospective business owner.

BANKER

An important advisor for any size interior design firm is a commercial banker. A *banker* can provide many services and counsel to new business owners. An ongoing relationship with a banker is needed as a firm grows. Working with someone who is familiar with the firm helps make it easier to obtain needed loans for various business needs.

A banker familiar with working with small businesses is ideal. The prospective business owner should be sure that the loan officer and others with whom he or she is working always will be willing to explain how things work. They should readily answer questions about how the loan process is structured so that the owner does not get any surprises. And they should clarify the charges for commercial checking accounts, as these often have charges the personal checking account does not have. If this does not happen, the business owner should ask to work with another person or go to another bank.

The business will need a commercial checking account, a savings account, and perhaps a payroll account. A sole proprietorship—a common business formation in interior design—should have a commercial checking account if the company name is a fictitious name (see Chapter 10). Otherwise, a checking account (and other accounts) separate from the owner's personal checking account should be obtained to keep business funds separated from personal funds.

Here are some additional services useful to an interior design firm:

- Offer credit card services so clients can purchase on credit.
- Make available payroll services when the firm has several employees.
- Issue credit cards for business purchases.
- Provide the designer with help in checking credit references of clients.
- Offer assistance with cash management.
- Provide information on investors who may wish to invest in, or loan money to, the firm.
- Provide investment services such as money market accounts, individual retirement accounts (IRA) and self-employed IRAs, and 401K retirement plans.

SOURCES OF CAPITAL

A new interior design business requires funds for basic start-up items such as computers and stationery and many other kinds of start-up expenses. Obtaining funding for the business, regardless of the needs, can come from a variety of sources. This section explains important financial terminology related to sources of outside capital financing and briefly describes important information about establishing business credit.

It is not unusual for a small interior design practice to be initially funded by personal funds. Once a budget is established (refer to Chapters 7 and 11), personal resources are accumulated to begin the firm. Some designers obtain additional start-up funds from family members. At some point, every business needs outside financing beyond what can be obtained with personal credit, personal funds, and friends and family.

Banks are reluctant to finance a new business, especially a service-oriented business, if the owner has little or no collateral. They generally shy away from making loans to small businesses until the business has shown for several years that it is successful. Business loans are a major funding source for design practices, although they are not the only source of capital used by interior design firms. A banker, along with the firm's accountant, can advise the entrepreneur on the pros and cons of various alternative funding sources based on the entrepreneur's personal situation.

It is important to discuss the basic terminology associated with business financing. Funds that come from creditors as loans are called *debt capital*. Debt capital always must be secured with some sort of collateral or asset that can be used to repay the loan if the person taking out the loan cannot make payments. Creditors expect the debt capital to be repaid with interest. For example, Allyson received a $10,000 loan from a bank for her business. She will pay monthly interest on the loan, along with gradual repayment of the $10,000 principle amount. Her *collateral*, which is an asset pledged to repay a loan if the borrower cannot actually pay back (defaults) on the loan, is her home, which has an equity value exceeding the $10,000 loan. Allyson has received debt capital.

Private lenders, such as commercial banks and finance companies, offer long-term and short-term loans. *Long-term loans* are for more than one year and are usually granted to purchase capital items, like office equipment and delivery trucks, or an office location. The items being purchased with long-term loans are usually the security for the loans. Long-term loans for simple, daily operating expenses, like stationery, are generally not available.

Short-term loans last for one year or less. A common short-term loan used by many interior designers is called a *line of credit*. This type of short-term loan helps cover purchasing inventory and credit purchases from suppliers. It usually cannot be used to buy equipment like a computer. These loans are used to satisfy a temporary need for cash rather than long-term needs. Monthly interest is charged on the amount of the credit extended until the principal amount is repaid. In many cases, these loans are also called *unsecured loans*, meaning that collateral is not required. If collateral is required as protection against nonpayment, the loan is considered a *secured loan*. Unsecured loans are made on the basis of a business owner's ability to repay it. In addition, unsecured loans generally carry a higher interest rate than secured loans. As a business performs positively, the owner will be able to obtain larger lines of credit. New businesses and businesses with poor credit histories have to function on a cash basis for many purchases.

Equity capital represents funds obtained from investors. They are gambling that they will receive a return on their investment and know if the business fails, they may not even get their investment back. *Venture capital* is a common name associated with equity capital funds that come from investors. Venture capital for small interior design businesses is hard to obtain, however. Venture capitalists usually only invest large sums in businesses with a very high potential for a return on the investment.

Another type of investor term that has cropped up in the last several years is *angel investor*. An angel investor is more likely to invest in small entrepreneurial businesses like interior design practices, since they generally have less money to invest. Angel investors are often entrepreneurs themselves who want to see someone else succeed.

Someone who knows the interior designer but is not necessarily a relative is called an *affiliated angel investor*. For example, Sally's neighbor has agreed to invest $25,000 in Sally's business. The agreement he has worked out with Sally is that he will obtain 10 percent of net profits. He will patiently wait for a return on his investment. Someone who is not connected with the designer and does not know him or her is called a *nonaffiliated angel investor*.

If the business is a corporation, investment funds will often be obtained through selling stock in the company. Even a small interior design practice can be organized as a corporation (see Chapter 6). Stock can be sold to anyone with a willingness to earn a small return on his or her stock purchase investment.

Loans for a small business can also be obtained by applying through the loan guarantee program with the U.S. Small Business Administration (SBA). The SBA does not give loans. It guarantees loans provided by an SBA agent-lending institution. Most new interior design firms do not need large sums, and many banks are unwilling to make small loans for this type of business. The loan guarantees from the SBA are more frequently for small amounts. Information on the SBA loan program can be obtained by checking the SBA Web site, listed in the Internet Resources appendix.

ESTABLISHING BUSINESS CREDIT

Naturally, establishing business credit is very important to any interior design firm. It is even more important for a firm that wishes to sell merchandise along with providing design services. Anyone who has tried to buy a car or a house or even to obtain a credit card has dealt with establishing credit. For most proprietorships and partnerships, business credit starts with a personal credit history of the individuals involved. If the business owners have good personal credit, the business will have an easier time obtaining credit. New corporations, since they are legal entities themselves, must establish credit, just like an individual.

Small-business owners often obtain business or "corporate" credit cards from the bank where they have their commercial account. These credit cards can be used for travel expenses, items that alternatively might be paid for with petty cash, or any number of other small expense items for the business. However, these cards should be used cautiously, as monthly payments and interest charges could become a problem. The high interest rates on credit cards should discourage entrepreneurs from using these cards for large-dollar-value purchases.

In a similar vein, many entrepreneurs have used personal credit cards as a source of start-up capital for a new business. This convenient source of capital, however, is very expensive as well, with its high interest rates, making it far too easy for the new owner to go deeply into debt quickly, which possibly could pose problems concerning future personal credit needs. This source of capital should be used very cautiously. If a personal credit card is used for business purposes (the firm's accountant will advise as to the opportunity to do this), it should not be used for any personal expenses so that personal and business expenses are not mixed.

If the company plans to sell merchandise to clients, at some point it will need to obtain a credit line from a bank to help make those purchases. Interior design firms that resell products work to establish credit with suppliers. It is vital for the practice to have good practices established in obtaining up-front payments from clients to order merchandise for a client. Funds received in advance of completing the work or delivering merchandise will have to be returned if the project is terminated or in many cases if the orders for the goods can be canceled.

When a designer begins to order from a supplier, it is necessary for the designer to pay the full price for the goods in advance of the shipment. This requirement is sometimes referred to as *pro forma credit*, which means the supplier must be paid in advance. Note that *pro forma* is a term that can mean in advance or hypothetical. A pro forma income statement is an example of a hypothetical version of an income statement that is often included in a business plan for a new business. This is why designers ask for a down payment or deposit from customers. The down payment or deposit becomes the prepayment required by suppliers from whom the designer cannot order on credit.

As a designer establishes credit with a supplier, the designer is working with the supplier's money, or what is called *trade credit*. Suppliers may extend some customers 30, 60, or even 90 days of credit without charging interest. Trade credit is harder to obtain for new buyers and new design firms. The designer establishes credit with a supplier by first filling out a credit application provided by the supplier. This information is verified, along with further checks on the designer's general credit rating through credit reporting organizations. The supplier then determines the credit limit and conditions for the designer so that he or she can order without making down payments.

When the designer pays bills promptly, his or her credit rating goes up with those suppliers. With small suppliers and tradespeople, this information is sometimes shared, so, for example, a good credit history with a wallpaper hanger may help get custom cabinets built on credit.

A bad credit rating can cause serious problems for a business. Late payment of any bill from a supplier or other entity that the business owes money impacts the business's credit rating. This in turn can mean the design firm cannot purchase from a supplier without paying in full for any items required. As the reader can imagine, that can be a substantial outlay of funds. Paying bills on time or even earlier than the due date creates a positive credit rating with more potential allowances from suppliers and others for credit.

For businesses, credit reporting agencies serve as clearinghouses on the credit soundness of a business. Manufacturers and other suppliers the firm may use look for these credit listings before extending credit to the firm. In turn, the design firm may check the credit rating of business clients before extending the business client credit. This is discussed is Chapter 31. See the box on the credit agencies most related to the interior design industry.

Credit Agencies for the Interior Design Industry

A national credit agency that gathers information on thousands of businesses, big and small, is Dun & Bradstreet (D&B). It obtains information on a business's operations, legal structure, financial condition, and payment history. It also reviews and makes available to a business owner who requests it information on a creditor's banking records, financial records such as income statement, the D&B credit rating, and whether legal proceedings against the business have occurred or are in process. The design firm should seek to have a good credit rating with D&B and can use the D&B reporting service to obtain information on the credit rating of potential business clients. Of course, the design firm will also check with Dun & Bradstreet to review the credit history of a commercial client.

The Allied Board of Trade (ABT) is a credit agency specific to the interior design industry. Designers register with ABT in order to show to trade sources that they and/or the design firm are a member of the design community. An ABT membership will speed purchasing opportunities with many vendors in the home furnishings and commercial interior design industry. A listing with the ABT is only accomplished after the design firm completes an application process that reports a sales tax number and previous trade relations with suppliers as well as meeting academic training and practical experience standards. The *Credit Green Book* references thousands of registered designers and is used both by interior designers to find trade sources and by suppliers to clarify credit information on designers.

Another credit reporting agency important in the interior design industry is the Lyon Mercantile Group, Ltd. corporate group for the Lyon Furniture Mercantile Agency. Founded in 1876, Lyon began by providing credit information and collection services for the furniture industry.[*] Of importance to the interior design industry today is the Lyon Red Book which is a credit rating reference book for the home furnishings industry. The Lyon Red Book is also available on CD-ROM. Information in the Red Book includes a firm's financial statements, credit activity, pay trends, and other information.

[*]www.lyoncredit.com/merc/history (November 22, 2005).

Laws allow individuals and businesses to find out the status of their credit rating. In some cases, these reports are free, while other credit agencies charge a fee. Knowing the interior design firm's credit rating is very important to the owner of the firm whether that owner operates a sole proprietorship from a home office or a large firm in a commercial office or studio. If there are errors, it is necessary for you and/or the business to protest the errors and see that your credit history is correct.

Financing a design firm's operations is an ongoing activity. Few firms use profits to continually finance the daily operations of the company. Investors expect a return, and some portion of the profits is paid to investors. No matter how small or large the design firm is, obtaining funds and maintaining credit with suppliers is very important.

INSURANCE ADVISORS

Regardless of the type or size of the interior design firm, it will be necessary to obtain certain types of insurance. Owning a business comes with inherent risk. Insurance is a necessity to minimize the financial risk of the firm in the course of the business day. Risk to the financial stability of a firm can come from the actions of the owners or employees. Theft, natural disasters, accidents, and other unforeseen events create the need for insurance so that a business and its employees will be protected. The firm with part-time or full-time employees also is required by law to have certain kinds of insurance for employee protection. Design firms cannot afford the risk of operating without appropriate business insurance. Of course, it is best to operate so as to avoid risk rather than depend on insurance policies and an attorney to limit liability.

An *independent insurance agent* commonly works for him- or herself and can represent more than one insurance company. An *exclusive agent* works for a particular company and only writes (sells) insurance policies from that one company. A *broker* also represents multiple companies. The difference between an independent agent and broker is that brokers most often only write commercial insurance, not personal. Regardless of what the agent is called, the business should consult with an insurance agent familiar with commercial business insurance issues. Not all companies can provide the combination of business insurance an interior designer or firm might need. Professional associations or sometimes an association chapter sponsors certain types of insurance for its members.

The self-employed business owner requires insurance similar to any other type of business formation. Professional liability and errors and omissions insurance are musts for any business owner. Insurance to protect the self-employed business owner from personal liability claims, interruptions in business, and the other situations and types of insurance discussed are crucial for the self-employed interior designer. The remainder of this section provides a brief overview of the typical types of insurance that are often required or suggested for an interior design practice.

Professional Liability Insurance

Jim was designing a gift shop located in a strip shopping center. During the course of the project, he convinced the owner to use custom-made display cabinets and fixtures throughout the store rather than using items from a display products vendor. He assured the owner that the cabinets would be ready on time. Three weeks before the store was scheduled to open, the cabinet fabricator's business closed for reasons unknown to Jim. The most important cabinets for the store had not been delivered to the store site, and the opening—planned around an important grand-opening party—cannot occur as scheduled.

One of the most important types of insurance all practicing interior designers need to obtain is professional liability insurance. By commission or omission, there are many ways that an interior designer can have a situation occur that will require professional liability insurance. Called *malpractice insurance* by many, *professional liability insurance* protects the design professional in the event an action causes acts, errors, or omissions in the course of working on the design project. One example is incorrect spatial layouts on design documents that delay the project or cause harm to the client's property. Recall that "harm" in legal terms does not only relate to physical injury. Another is actual financial loss to the client because the project was not finished on time. Errors in the design plans that resulted in plans failing to comply with building codes is yet another example that can easily occur. This insurance also covers the interior designer should bodily injury or property damage occur as a result of the professional negligence of the designer. Has Jim's selection of the custom-cabinet shop resulted in professional negligence on Jim's part?

Interior designers also can be held responsible for errors or omissions for work performed or advice given to a client. This type of insurance is called *errors and omissions coverage* (E&O). E&O coverage provides protection should the interior designer or his or her employees make a mistake, which would be an error, or forget or not do something that was required, which is considered an omission. An example of an error is specifying a non-code-compliant material as a wall covering in the corridors of a hotel. Another example of an error is specifying the wrong wood veneer stain on cabinets for a kitchen remodeling. One example of an omission is forgetting to include smoke detectors in a remodeling of a residence. Another example of an omission is failing to make sure the type of recess-mounted lighting fixtures specified could be properly shielded from the ceiling insulation. The designer technically has committed an act in these examples that could result in legal proceedings being filed by the client. This insurance provides coverage for claims should judgments against the designer occur. See Chapter 8 for additional discussion on professional liability.

Property Damage, Liability, and Personal Injury Insurance

A group of insurance coverage referred to as property damage, liability, and personal injury insurance is very important for any size of interior design firm regardless of business formation. Insurance policies that cover these areas of business are not all the same. The business owner can purchase combination policies or a policy for each type of coverage. When a combination policy is purchased, the owner needs to be very clear about what is and is not covered. For example, "property coverage" insurance might not include coverage for furniture and equipment used in the business unless it is specifically mentioned. If the interior design firm sells merchandise, property insurance should also cover display items and inventory.

A *business owner's policy* is a combination policy that is particularly important for any interior design firm that owns a studio, store, or warehouse. It is a package offered by many companies and includes various levels of property damage, liability, and personal injury insurance and often includes business interruption insurance. Designers who rent space can obtain variations on this package to take care of their needs. Some insurance might be part of the lease, so be sure you understand what is covered. However, most insurance included in a lease is to protect the building owner's interest, not the tenants. Additional insurance to cover your property within the leased

TABLE 8-2.

Filing Business Insurance Claims

When the business suffers a loss of any kind, it is necessary to file a claim with the firm's insurance agent immediately. These tips on filing insurance claims will help process a claim faster and, hopefully, efficiently!

- Keep records of all equipment and other resources you purchase to operate your business. Have copies of receipts for purchase that show price paid for an item such as a computer or even a reference book needed for the practice.
- Contact the appropriate agent promptly after the event or loss.
- Read your policies—have them handy on file—so that you know what your coverage and responsibilities are.
- Contact the police in the case of theft or other events that might be deemed a crime.
- If damage has occurred, take photographs as quickly as possible before anything is moved.
- Unless directed otherwise by your insurance agent, get two bids on any repairs or to the property.
- Protect the damaged property as best you can by making temporary repairs such as having plywood installed over broken windows.
- Determine if there are any witnesses to the event, and get statements of what they saw.
- If someone falls in your office, get a written statement and release from the injured party. This is especially important if the person leaves saying he or she is all right. Of course, if they are injured, you may also need to call 911.

space will be necessary. Table 8-2 provides an overview of the process for filing a claim.

Property damage insurance generally protects the building and its contents from loss due to fire, theft, windstorms, lightning strikes, and other types of loss detailed in the policy. Not all policies cover all potential types of loss, so the business owner may need an additional policy for some potential situations. Supplemental coverage can be obtained for businesses that are in areas that are prone to events like floods or earthquakes. Remember that the contents of the building—furniture, accessories, reference books, and office equipment—are considered personal property. Accounting records are generally not covered by the property damage insurance portion.

Liability insurance protects the business should the business be sued by a third party for injury or property damage due to negligence, product failure, or other claims of that kind. Note that the business can be sued for the acts of the owners, employees, agents, and suppliers. For example, one of your clients, Mrs. Smith, trips on a small area rug in the resource library of your studio. She fell and broke her wrist. Liability insurance would cover the business in this case. In addition, if a carpet installer hired by the designer breaks a lamp at a client's home, the designer is potentially as liable as the installer.

Another type of liability insurance that is important for interior designers is *product liability insurance*. This insurance covers injuries caused by products that are designed, sold, or specified by the interior designer. For example, should one of the chairs sold for a doctor's medical suite break causing injury to a patient, the interior designer could be sued. If you sell products from a vendor, the vendor will be more liable than you. If you design custom furniture, you will have more liability.[1] However, it is very common that the interior designer who has been involved in the design and specification of a project is also included in the lawsuit whether or not the designer has custom-created a furniture item.

Personal injury insurance is part of liability coverage and provides insurance in case of slander, libel, defamation, false arrest, and other personal injury torts. These personal injury torts are discussed in Chapter 4.

Other Important Types of Insurance

There are several other important types of business insurance that might be needed. Some of these items are needed by firms with employees, and others might be recommended by the design firm's insurance agent.

Commercial *automobile insurance* is necessary for the vehicles owned by a business. Auto insurance on a personal vehicle used by the business, a small van used for deliveries, for example, might not be covered if the vehicle is used primarily for business purposes.

The interior design firm must also verify that employees have proper insurance for their jurisdiction on their personal vehicles that are used for business purposes. When an employee uses his or her car for business purposes, if he or she has an accident, the business could be liable. The employee's vehicle is covered by the design firm only if the firm has purchased employer's nonowned liability coverage policy. Personal insurance is the primary insurance on employee vehicles generally. Design firms that hire tradespeople should be sure that the tradesperson has auto insurance so that the designer is not sued if the tradesperson has an accident while on a job for the designer.

Workers' compensation insurance is required by the jurisdiction when employees are added to the firm. Most jurisdictions require that the employer provide this insurance in order to protect the employee in case of work-related injuries whether the injury happens in the office or at a job site. Workers' compensation insurance is not available to sole proprietors, but for their employees. Partners and officers of other types of business formations may have the option, depending on state law.

Business income insurance (also called business interruption insurance) pays for the loss of net profit and for operating expenses in case a fire or other specifically covered event prevents the business from operating. The loss of business suffered by many companies after catastrophic earthquakes, hurricanes, terrorist attacks, and other events has been the end of many businesses. The business owner must be sure the policy covers events that might occur in the location of the business. It is not a "blanket" policy, and the events covered must be specified in the policy.

Even with the use of computers, records of what clients owe to the firm can be easily lost due to fire or other events. *Accounts receivable insurance* covers the loss of accounts receivable records due to fire or other specific events. Of course, prevention also is important by backing up files and storing backup files in safe places.

Crime insurance protects the firm in case of theft of money or property. Depending on the policy, it covers the company regarding theft by employees or by individuals other than employees. Not all policies cover both groups. Interior design businesses with showroom space must be concerned about shoplifting of small items. Someone breaking in and stealing the office computer can have a devastating effect on the business if the data on that computer is not backed up on CDs or other media. Be aware that the use of a personal laptop computer, not owned by the business, but left at the business location and stolen is not likely to be covered by the business property insurance.

Owners and officers should make sure that they have some sort of personal *health and disability* insurance. It is also important that business partners agree that all partners have health and disability insurance. A death, serious illness, or injury to one partner could devastate a business if a partner has no health or disability insurance. *Disability income insurance* provides continuing income if certain covered injuries or illnesses occur that prevent the business owner from working. The insurance provides benefits to help pay personal and business expenses. The employer may also wish to provide *health insurance* to employees as a benefit of working for the company.

What Would You Do?

Arne needed to visit the purchasing manager for a long-standing client. He needed to drop off a revised floor plan for another section of the office complex. He didn't make an appointment, since he had already discussed the changes in the plan. Arne also was bringing some alternate fabric samples for conference room chairs.

The purchasing manager was in his office and as soon as Arne said "hello," the client began to berate Arne for his recommendation of vendors for the furniture that was being installed that week. "Those guys are idiots!" screamed the client. "They have totally disrupted the office and now I understand they have damaged the carpet in the CEO's office! How could you recommend such incompetent fools!" said the purchasing manager.

Interior designers working from home should purchase a separate rider for the equipment (such as computers) that they use at home but are for primarily business purposes. Most straight home owner's policies do not cover equipment used primarily for business purposes. There may also be other exclusions related to liability and injury on the residential property to clients or others doing business with the home-based design practitioner. This exclusion also can apply to the designer's personal automobile, if it is used for business.

There are many other specialized types of insurance that may be important for an interior design business based on the nature of the practice and business formation. Consultation with the firm's attorney, accountant, and insurance advisor is indispensable in order to determine if other types of insurance are also necessary.

TECHNICAL CONSULTANTS

Various technical consultants and allied professionals are needed from time to time by almost every interior design firm. Technical consultants may be hired to obtain advice or to explain how part of a project will be accomplished. For example, a codes consultant may be retained to discuss code requirements for a particularly large, complex project. Some are engaged by the interior design firm to work on parts of the project scope that the interior designer might not be legally allowed to design. An example is for securing the input and design specifications by an architect or engineer for the design of a multistory residence to be located on sloped property.

Interior design firms will establish a working relationship with technical professionals and will hire them on a per-job basis, just as a client would hire an interior designer. Of course, larger firms often have one or more of these allied professionals on staff. The owner of an interior design firm should not be afraid to admit the need for these professionals. Interior designers who prepare documents without the proper license and expertise can easily be sued by the client.

The interior designer must understand the laws within his or her jurisdiction regarding what the interior design firm can do concerning technical construction and mechanical systems design and when a technical consultant is needed. Jurisdictions do not allow a professional such as an architect to affix the architect's stamp to drawings that have been prepared by an interior designer who is not an employee of the firm and who thus is outside the supervision of the technical consultant. In a similar vein, a registered interior designer cannot affix his or her stamp to drawings produced by a nonregistered interior designer. The interior designer must include fees for the consultant—if called for by the scope of services of the project—in the fees to the client.

TABLE 8-3.

Common Technical Consultants

Many of these consultants might be needed by the interior designer depending on the project requirements and responsibilities of the designer.

Architects. They are needed to prepare and review plans that require an architect's stamp. An architect's stamp is usually required on plans for residences over 3000 square feet and commercial spaces that will have more than 20 employees. Both these criteria vary with the local ordinances. Check with the building department of the project jurisdiction.

Electrical engineers. They provide advice and assistance on planning questions for electrical components for projects. Electrical engineers also may be needed to prepare and stamp electrical plans in order for the owner to obtain a building permit.

General contractors. General contractors will oversee all tradespersons needed for a project's build-out. Note that the term *build-out* is industry jargon for the construction process.

Specialty contractors or subcontractors. These contractors provide advice on ways to build or specify interior design concepts. A cabinetmaker can advise the designer on how to detail drawings for a custom conference wall that might include storage, plumbing, and audiovisual equipment.

Lighting designers. They can provide assistance or can provide the design and planning of specialized lighting concepts.

Commercial kitchen designers. These designers provide plans for commercial kitchens in restaurants, hotel foodservice areas, health-care foodservice areas, and so forth.

Acoustical engineers. Consultants who can advise the interior designer on materials and finishes for architectural surfaces, and locations of acoustical treatments to solve noise problems.

Landscape architects, interior plantscapers, and florists. These specialists can advise the designer on the proper selection and positioning of plants in the interior. They can also provide the designer with maintenance instructions.

Health-care facility specialists. Individuals who have worked in health care may be hired by designers to consult with them on the design of health-care professional offices. Designers often hire nursing professionals as consultants.

Other consultants. The design business owner may wish to retain other specialty consultants from time to time. Examples include public relations, advertising and marketing agencies, employment agencies, management consultants, computer consultants, Web page designers, and communications consultants.

A technical consultant might be called upon to perform such duties as:

- Meet with the client to determine needs related to his or her specialty.
- Prepare drawings to be used to obtain needed permits.
- Provide expertise not resident within the interior design firm.
- Provide on-site supervision during the construction and/or installation of the project.
- Work as a directly paid subconsultant or subcontractor to the design firm or the client.

A listing of a few of these specialists and how they can help the interior designer is provided in Table 8-3.

SOURCES OF INFORMATION AND ASSISTANCE

Whether the firm is a small proprietorship operating out of a home office or a large multi-employee firm offering services in several specialties, the business will require advice and assistance from time to time beyond those previously discussed in the chapter.. There are many private organizations and government agencies that provide consultation or reference materials to the business owner—far too many to list in this text. Information on many helpful organizations is provided in the Internet References.

Private Organizations

Local chapters of the chamber of commerce are business lobbying groups for all sizes and types of businesses. The chamber of commerce does not necessarily provide direct assistance to businesses. However, members can network at chamber meetings, attend programs on a variety of topics, and obtain useful information about the business community. The chamber also provides information to consumers on businesses in the local area and work for the benefit of all businesses in the community.

Professional organizations such as the American Bar Association can provide assistance to business owners who are seeking an attorney. Other professional organizations can help the business owner select a consultant as well. Check the yellow pages for the phone number or address of a professional organization's local chapter. To find the name and address of a specific trade association, check the *Encyclopedia of Associations*. This book is available at libraries. Information on lists of associations can also be found by searching the Internet.

Local chapters of the interior design professional associations may have information on business advisors within the chapter area. However, it might be necessary to be a member of the association to obtain this type of contact information.

Universities and community colleges often have a small-business development center or small-business institutes in conjunction with the SBA. These groups provide seminars and one-on-one counseling to the small-business owner.

Private outside consultants and business coaches are also an option for the new entrepreneur and the small-business practitioner seeking advice or assistance for his or her business. These consultants can be found in the yellow pages or possibly through interior design professional associations as well as through a search on the Internet.

Government Agencies

A great source of information for designers to obtain information on local regulations is from their state's department of commerce and department of revenue. Much information, including forms to apply for licenses and business formation documents specific to the jurisdiction, can be obtained from the Internet. Although the address may change by state, generally a Web site such as www.*<state>*.gov will direct you to the state department of commerce link. State income tax information for businesses is also available from the state department of revenue. State forms for applying for such things as business formation, business names, and resale licenses may also be available online through the state department of commerce or department of revenue.

Many cities have small-business development centers or economic development offices. These offices can provide pamphlets, seminars, and one-on-one consulting services. They can be located through the government section of the telephone white pages or the local government Web page. A small-business resource center is frequently available at the local public library.

The Small Business Administration is a federal agency that provides many kinds of assistance to the small-business owner. Assistance may come in the form of informational pamphlets and books, seminars, clinics, and one-on-one counseling. SCORE is the Service Corps of Retired Executives, a SBA group of volunteers providing consulting to small-business owners. SCORE volunteers can be contacted through the local SBA office. Numerous SBA publications are now available online as PDF documents. In addition, the SBA may be able to provide financial assistance for qualified small businesses through its program of guaranteeing loans provided by member banks. The main address for the SBA is listed in the Internet References. Local offices may be found in the U.S. government section of the white pages in the local phone book.

The Internal Revenue Service has business tax kits for different business operations. Publication Number 334, "Tax Guide for Small Business," is especially useful to the owner of a sole proprietorship. Addresses for local IRS offices are in the U.S. government section of the white pages. Some additional tax forms are available online at the IRS Web site shown in the Internet References.

SUMMARY

There are many very important advisers with whom the owner of an interior design firm should consult. This is true of both the potential entrepreneur interested in having one's own studio or a business that has lasted for many years and experienced much growth. No one designer, or even group of design professionals, will have the educational or job experience to have all the answers. Business advisers are engaged to help the firm remain professionally competent, to stay out of legal problems, and most important, to remain a viable business. Advisers such as attorneys, accountants, bankers, and insurance agents can help with specialized business questions. Allied professionals offer advice on technical matters that the staff of the design firm may not be familiar with or legally qualified to handle.

Ways in which businesses can obtain funding and establish credit, different kinds of business insurance, and sources of information were also discussed in the context of the appropriate business advisor. If the reader is a professional seeking to start a new practice, the information in this chapter should be read in conjunction with the other chapters in Part II.

REFERENCE

1. Steingold, 2005, p. 12/9.

CHAPTER 9

Business Formations

Key Terms and Concepts

These key terms and concepts are important to material in this chapter. Many of these terms will be utilized in other chapters as well. Be sure you understand these items as you read this chapter.

Terms and Concepts

Sole proprietorship	Incorporation
Partnership	Private corporation
General partner	Public corporation
Limited partner	Close corporation
Partnership agreement	Domestic corporation
Uniform Partnership Act (UPA)	Foreign corporation
Limited liability company (LLC)	Articles of incorporation
LLC members	S corporation
Corporation	Professional corporation
Incorporate	Joint venture

Critical Issues

After completing this chapter you should be able to:

- Compare and contrast the different forms of business organization.
- Discuss at least three advantages and disadvantages of the different business organizations.
- Compare the general partnership from the LLC.
- Discuss the differences in the legal responsibility for the owner of a sole proprietorship, general partnership, LLC, and corporation.
- Compare the LLC and regular corporation form as they relate to interior design businesses.
- Explain the benefits of a joint venture when a project you want to try to obtain is too large for just your design firm.
- Name the stakeholder owners of a sole proprietorship, general and limited partnership, LLC, and joint venture.

As you might imagine, numerous decisions must be made when you are starting a new interior design practice. A very important decision is the legal formation elected. The legal business formation impacts management structure, taxes, liability, financing, and investment potential.

This chapter offers an overview of this topic, discussing the sole proprietorship, general and limited partnerships, the corporation, the limited liability company, and some specialized formations. These specialized formations are the S corporation, the professional corporation, and the joint venture. Each type has its advantages and disadvantages suitable to the business plan.

As discussed in the previous chapter, it is important for the interior designer to consult with an attorney and an accountant to be sure he or she is making the right choices. An attorney is not required to help set up all these choices, but the advice of an attorney is always prudent. The prospective business owner should discuss the merits of the different business formations with his or her accountant as well, since the formation chosen has direct income tax implications for the owners and the business.

It is appropriate for the student to study these formations as a way of understanding the responsibilities of the owner. Many students look forward to having their own design firm some time in the future. Recognize that many businesses change legal formations sometime during the life of the business. This is a perfectly acceptable business practice. For example, many sole practitioners change to a different legal form as their business grows.

Table 9-1 provides a summary of the key characteristics of each business formation. Many books are available concerning detailed specifics of each of the legal formations for a business, and many are listed in the References which will supplement the information on the topic provided in this chapter. The next chapter provides details on licenses and filings required by the government.

In this chapter you will meet Margaret, Alex, Peter, Robert, Barbara, and Jane. All of these individuals are planning to create an interior design practice using different legal formations.

SOLE PROPRIETORSHIP

The simplest and least expensive form of business ownership is the *sole proprietorship*. Generally, all that is necessary is to establish a location, obtain any required licenses, and begin operation. Fees for business licenses, resale licenses, and registering the business name are minimal. These fees may be under $500, depending on the jurisdictions. Some of these fees are annual fees. It is advisable to open a bank account in the firm's name, obtain business stationery, and begin to establish credit with trade sources. A transaction sales tax (resale license) is required if the company plans to sell merchandise to clients. Table 9-2 highlights important advantages and disadvantages of this type of business formation.

James has worked for a residential furniture store for eight years and has developed a loyal following of clients who regularly refer their friends to him. A change in ownership of the store has prompted James to decide it is time to start his own company, which he will call James Jones Interiors. He might need an assistant, since he knows he will have some instant business from clients once he leaves the store. He will be selling products and offering design services to high-end residential clients. Is the sole proprietorship right for James?

In this form of business ownership, the company and the owner are one and the same. Since there is only one owner, that individual makes all the decisions as to how to organize and operate the business. Often the business name is the owner's name (e.g., Madelyn Smith Interior Design) but may also be conducted

TABLE 9-1.

Chart Showing the Key Characteristics of Business Formations

	Owners	Personal Liability of Owners	Who May Legally Obligate Business	Continuity	Organizational Paperwork	Business Profits Taxed
Sole Proprietorship	Sole proprietor	Unlimited personal liability	Sole proprietor	Ends when proprietor wishes; might be able to sell it	Minimal	Individual rates of proprietor
General Partnership	General partners	Unlimited personal liability	General partner	Ends with death of a partner; may be transferred with consent of all partners	Minimal; partnership agreement recommended	Supplement to Form 1040
Limited Partnership	General and limited partners	General partner has unlimited liability; limited partner up to limit of investment	General partner only	Same as general partnership; limited partners can sell their share	Start-up filing required; partnership agreement recommended	Individual tax of general and limited partners
Corporation	Stockholders	Stockholders have no personal liability; officers and directors have liability	Board of directors and officers	Continues unless corporation ends by decisions of board or reason of law; stock transferred without needed consent	Articles of incorporation; bylaws; annual meeting of stockholders	Corporation pays taxes on profits; stockholders, on personal taxes
S Corporation	Same as corporation	Same as corporation	Same as corporation	Same as corporation	Same as corporation	Taxed as partnership
Limited Liability Company	Members	Member is limited to amount invested	Members or manager/ member	May have to dissolve, depending on state	Start-up filing; operations agreement recommended	Varies depending on number of members
Professional Corporation	"Partners"	Similar to corporation	"Partners"	Same as corporation	Same as corporation	Same as corporation

under a company trade name (e.g., Creative Retail Interiors). When the owner uses a name for the business other than his or her own name, a fictitious business name statement is required. Chapter 9 discusses this registration form.

A sole proprietorship flourishes because of the involvement and reputation of the owner. Thus, being a sole owner has a special disadvantage in that income generation is stopped or slowed when a sole proprietor takes vacations, since usually there is no one to take over in the absence of the owner. In addition, the company has no existence if the owner quits operating the business because of illness or death. Sole proprietorships are harder to sell to others because of the tight connection with the owner. If it is sold, the value relates to the assets of the business and possible goodwill based on previous clients. However, clients may not stick with the business if it is sold to someone else.

TABLE 9-2.

Advantages and Disadvantages of the Sole Proprietorship

Advantages

- It is simple to start.
- There is great freedom in management.
- All profits (and losses) go to the proprietor. Profits and losses are not shared with others.
- There are minimal special fees and minimal formal actions to create the proprietorship.
- There are no required filings with the federal government to begin the business, unless employees are hired.
- Depending upon the location of the business, it is not required that the owner pay unemployment tax for any income.
- Profits are taxed as income on the sole proprietor's regular income tax statement. Similarly, the deductions of the business also can affect the individual income tax due.

Disadvantages

- Owner has personal liability for all debts and taxes.
- The owner could experience tax problems, since too often a sole proprietor mixes business and personal income. (This should not be done!)
- It is more difficult to obtain business loans from banks.
- Suppliers often require substantial down payments or payments in full prior to shipping until credit is established.
- A sole proprietorship that also operates in other states may need to obtain licenses or prepare other types of registrations in order to do business in those other states.
- The sole proprietor cannot collect unemployment benefits if the business closes its doors.
- In states with community property laws, if a couple divorces, the sole proprietor may be forced to sell or close the business in order to divide the proceeds of the business.

Financing the sole proprietorship frequently comes from personal savings or other personal assets. Business funds should be deposited in a business account so that personal funds and business funds are not mixed. This can be a very difficult problem if the individual is ever audited by the taxing authorities. From time to time, the business may require additional funds from banks. It is more difficult for a sole proprietorship to obtain these loans even when the individual has substantial personal savings and a good credit rating. Banks do not often view a proprietor's personal assets or an excellent personal credit rating as proof of the credit rating of a business.

Sole proprietors must be especially careful in the operation of their business, since the owner has personal responsibility for legal and financial liability of the business. If a sole proprietor is sued by a client, the damages due the plaintiff can be collected from the firm's assets and, if necessary, from the owner's personal assets. The sole proprietor is also personally responsible for all the business's debts. Money owed to a vendor might have to come out of personal savings accounts if the business's account is insufficient. The owner must pay self-employment taxes (Social Security and Medicare contributions) on business income even when a "salary" is not drawn. Income taxes on the business are filed as part of the personal income tax reports. These types of financing, liability, and management issues are a challenge for sole proprietors. Having a good business coach or advisor is very important for these practitioners.

PARTNERSHIPS

Many interior design firms begin when two designers decide to join forces. They could start up their business for many reasons. A common one occurs when one has some strength that the other does not. When two or more individuals agree to start a business, it can be formed as a *partnership*. States generally do not require that a formal written agreement be prepared to form a partnership. However, it is widely recommended that a partnership agreement be prepared. If a partnership agreement has not been written, most states refer to the Uniform Partnership Act (UPA) for the terms of the partnership.

Partners are co-owners, unless some other agreement about the level of ownership has been made. Partners also act in each other's behalf and, depending on the type of partnership formed, are each able to bind the company to agreements. There are two types of partnerships that can be created: the general partnership and the limited partnership.

General Partnership

A general partnership is a common business formation in the interior design profession. The essential definition of a *general partnership* is this: When two or more people join for the purpose of forming a business and these people alone share in the profits and risks of the business, a general partnership is formed. Two or more interior designers often start a business as a general partnership (1) because it brings more design talent (perhaps some skill or experience that one partner lacks) to the company, (2) because of the assets and credit rating of the partners, and (3) because the responsibilities of the company can be shared.

Alex and Peter have been working in commercial interior design for a combined 14 years, with Alex having two more years of experience than Peter. They now feel it is time to join their talents and start their own design firm specializing in hospitality spaces and offices. Alex and Peter can each contribute the same amount of money as start-up capital. They agree that they will share equally in the profits and management of the company; thus, they have decided to legally form their business as a general partnership.

It is relatively easy to legally form a partnership. In many ways, it is very similar to a sole proprietorship except that there are two or more owners. A written *partnership agreement* is not required to form a general partnership, though it is recommended. The following are among the most common questions that must be answered when two or more people are developing a partnership agreement. An attorney may suggest additional items, depending on the nature of the business:

- What will be the name and address of the business location?
- Where will the partnership be located?
- What is the purpose of the partnership?
- What are the names and addresses of the partners?
- What are the responsibilities of each partner?
- How much capital will each partner contribute?
- How will business profits be distributed?
- How will business holdings be divided in the event of the dissolution of the partnership?
- How will each partner's drawings (salary) be distributed?
- How will the partnership be dissolved in the event of a partner's disabling illness, death, retirement, or other reason?
- How can ownership be transferred to another partner?

- How will any other changes in the management or other agreements be made?
- Which partners have fiduciary responsibility?
- How will disputes be resolved?

A worksheet for developing the parts of a partnership agreement has been included on the CD as Item 9-1.

If a written agreement is not prepared, these same items should still be discussed by the partners. Some states may require registration of the partnership with the secretary of state. As with a sole proprietorship, general partnerships need to register the company name, whether they use a trade name, like Creative Interior Designs or ID Associates, or a name consisting of the partners' names, such as Brown and Williams Associates.

Any change in the relationship of the partnership can dissolve the business. For example, if Alex wishes to withdraw from the partnership for any reason, the original partnership is usually dissolved. Depending on many factors, the remaining partner (Peter in this case) may vote in new partners, and the business can continue with adjustments to the partnership agreement. Should one of the partners die or become physically incapacitated so as not to be able to perform agreed-upon duties, the partnership is likewise dissolved.

Financing most often comes from the partner's investment into the company. A partnership may have an easier time obtaining capital and establishing credit, because more than one person is involved in the business. General partners are equally responsible for debts of the company (unless some condition exists in the agreement). Thus, there is unlimited financial liability for any losses or debts that the partnership incurs. Liability goes beyond the initial investment of the partners. If assets of the partnership are insufficient to satisfy debts, personal assets (up to the limitations established in each state) of the partners are vulnerable.

As with a sole proprietorship, partners are personally liable for lawsuits. Because a partnership does not protect the personal assets of the partners from the penalties of litigation, a lawsuit could result in the plaintiff being awarded business assets as well as personal assets of both partners. This is an important reason to be very careful about selecting a partner, since the bad acts of one partner impact the other. The firm and each partner of the firm are responsible for the actions of all the other partners. Any wrongdoing by one partner or any promises made by one partner are also the responsibility and obligation of the other partners. Table 9-3 highlights other advantages and disadvantages of the partnership formation.

Limited Partnership

A variation on the general partnership is the *limited partnership*. Let us say that in addition to Alex and Peter, Peter's parents have provided an asset in the form of office space in a building Peter's parents own. For this investment, Peter's parents will receive 10 percent of the yearly earnings rather than charging them monthly rent. In this situation, a limited partnership has been formed rather than a general partnership.

A limited partnership is formed according to statutory requirements, with a limited partnership agreement filed with the state in which it was formed. Because of this requirement, it is more expensive to start up than a general partnership. If the limited partnership operates in other states, it may be necessary for the partners to file an agreement in those other states.

TABLE 9-3.

Advantages and Disadvantages of a General Partnership

Advantages

- It is easy and inexpensive to start, similar to a sole proprietorship.
- There is the benefit of having two or more people involved in the affairs of the business.
- The tax responsibility on profits is paid on each partner's individual taxes. However, partnership profits must be reported on Schedule E of Form 1040. Other filings are required, however, for the partnership itself (see Chapter 10).
- Partners do not have to pay unemployment taxes on partners' income.

Disadvantages

- Disagreement between partners as to how to manage the partnership may create difficulties.
- Profits are split, as determined by the partnership agreement (or equally, if no written agreement has been prepared).
- Partnerships are required to file many more forms with the federal and state tax authorities than for a sole proprietorship (see Chapter 10).
- A partnership doing business in other states may need to obtain licenses or file other registrations in order to do business in those other states.

If a design practice decides to form as a limited partnership, it must have at least one general partner, with other partners who invest in the design practice designated as limited partners. The general partners have responsibility for the management of the firm, while the limited partner cannot. The role of a limited partner is restricted to that of investor, contributing assets toward the operation of the partnership. For this investment, they receive a portion of the profits. The limited partners have financial responsibility for only the losses and debts of the partnership to the amount of each limited partner's investment in the firm.

The general partners in a limited partnership have the same legal responsibilities as members of a general partnership. A limited partner is only liable up to his or her investment. Should any one of the limited partners become involved in the management of the design firm, he or she is no longer a limited partner but is, rather, a general partner. When this happens, the former limited partner now shares in the liability of the firm, as do the general partners. If any of the partners (limited or general) withdraw from the business, the business may need to cease operations.

The limited partnership is a less attractive alternative today since all states now allow for a business formation called a limited liability company (LLC) discussed in the next section.

What Would You Do?

Jonathan and Henry have worked in interior design for several years, each working for a different commercial firm. Jonathan specialized in medical facilities and Henry was mostly involved in offices and some hospitality projects. They met when they were elected to the board of directors of their local professional association. Jonathan suggested at a post-meeting dinner that they team up and start their own design firm. They elected the partnership form of business and created a brief, loose agreement with the focus on the dollars each contributed to the firm.

A year later, Henry was accused by a client of overbilling and other activities that the client said was fraudulent practices. Jonathan stepped in to try to resolve the problems and understand what was going on, but the client refused to speak to him. Three weeks later, the client sent a letter to the firm informing them that he was planning to speak to an attorney and was also filing an ethics complaint against both of them.

LIMITED LIABILITY COMPANY

Robert is considering going out on his own after working for several years in commercial interior design—specifically, small retail specialty shops. He plans to work by himself for at least a year and then hire an assistant. Robert's design solutions often include custom furniture pieces as well as items purchased from many vendors. His wife also works, but not in the interior design industry. He is considering the limited liability company as his legal business formation.

The *limited liability company* (LLC) is a hybrid of the general partnership or sole proprietorship and the corporation. This type of formation has only been available to the business community since the 1980s. Interior design firms are finding this to be an advantageous business formation to begin an interior design practice. However, the prospective business owner should discuss the pros and cons of this business formation carefully with an attorney and an accountant.

Owners are called *members*, not partners, and those who manage the business are called managers. Almost all states allow an LLC to be formed with only one person as the owner. Some members can be investors with little or no management or actual work involvement in the firm. Like any business formation, the LLC can have employees who are not owner members.

Before forming an interior design business as a limited liability company, the entrepreneur should understand the laws that govern such a formation in his or her state. An LLC is organized under state law, and the requirements differ between states. It is very common that specific legal forms for organizing an LLC must be filed with a state agency such as the state's secretary of state office. Filing fees are also required. Table 9-4 mentions some additional points about the limited liability company.

The name of the company must contain the words "limited liability company," using the initials LLC or LC. For example, Robert is considering "IDS, LLC" rather than using his name. That name will have to be researched and approved by the state corporation commission or other appropriate agency before he can begin using the name.

TABLE 9-4.

Advantages and Disadvantages of an LLC

Advantages

- It is simpler to organize than a corporation. However, articles of organization and possibly an operating agreement will be required by the state.
- Special meetings such as corporate annual meetings of stockholders are not required. Records must be kept to document decisions.
- There is flexibility in how profits and losses are allocated among the members versus a partnership.
- It is managed similarly to a general partnership, assuming there is more than one member.
- There are few limitations on the number and nature of members.
- LLC members are not employees, so the business does not have to pay unemployment taxes on the members.

Disadvantages

- Licensed professionals such as lawyers and accountants are prohibited from registering the business as an LLC. This might affect interior designers who work in states that have licensing for interior design.
- Members who manage the firm must pay self-employment tax, since they are not employees. (Self-employment tax is discussed in Chapter 10.)
- The loss of a member might result in the dissolution of the LLC.
- If the company does business in other states, it may need to register with those other states. This depends on state law. If the LLC was formed with only one member, it may have limited ability to conduct business in other states.

One of the most attractive aspects of the limited liability company is that it is granted the limited liability protection of a corporation. The liability is limited to a member's investment, thus personal assets are protected. A member has no personal liability even if the company is sued or faces large debt. The business, of course, faces these liability issues, not the members personally.

It has certain tax advantages of a partnership or sole proprietorship in that the member can pass the tax responsibility in one of those two ways rather than a corporation. Thus, profits are taxed as either a partnership or sole proprietorship; the choice was made by the members. For this reason, the firm's accountant should be consulted before this formation is elected. It is possible for a design firm that has started out as a sole proprietorship or partnership to change its business formation to a limited liability company. Often a short form is required to be submitted to the state secretary of state office, or articles of organization need to be prepared and submitted to that same state agency for this change in formation. Changing from a partnership to an LLC may be more complicated, but not impossible. Item 9-2 on the CD is a worksheet to help develop the information most often required in applying to form a business as an LLC.

CORPORATIONS

Barbara and Jane have had a design business for five years in partnership called Excellence in Design. They have become specialized in an area of commercial interior design. It is important for both of them to protect the assets of the company and their personal assets. A recent problem with a client has had them wondering about changing their business formation. In addition, Jane knows that Barbara wants to retire or at least only work part-time in another two or three years. They have two full-time employees and one part-time employee.

Forming a business as a corporation is the most time-consuming and expensive method of legally forming a business. There are advantages as a firm grows and sees its existence living on beyond that of a sole proprietorship or partnership. A *corporation* (sometimes referred to as a C corporation) is an association of individuals created by statutory requirements and, as such, is a legal entity. As a legal entity in and of itself, a corporation exists independently of its originators or any other person connected directly with the firm. The originators may sell their interest in the corporation to other stockholders or to outside parties at any time, and the corporation goes on. If the principals or any of the stockholders die or otherwise withdraw from the operation of the business, the corporation still remains legally intact. Table 9-5 defines important terms concerning the corporation form of business.

The states establish regulations concerning chartering a corporation and its general organizational and operational limitations. If a firm engages in interstate commerce, it also will be regulated by the federal government. Although some states allow businesses to incorporate without hiring an attorney, it is a good idea to seek an attorney's advice for this legal formation. Firms generally incorporate in the state in which they do business. Firms doing business in other states may be required by those other states to be incorporated in those other states.

A corporation may be formed by one or more persons, depending on the state of origination. The organizers of the corporation must prepare a document called the *articles of incorporation*. Table 9-6 shows the general outline of articles of incorporation. This information is also included on the CD as Item 9-3.

TABLE 9-5.

Terms Related to Corporations

Corporation. An association of individuals created by statutory requirements and, as such, is a legal entity; sometimes referred to as a C corporation..

Incorporate. To create a corporation.

Incorporation. The act or process of forming a corporation.

Private, or general, corporation. Formed for private, profit-making interests. It is the most common type of corporate structure.

Public corporations. Formed by some government agency for the benefit of the public, such as the U.S. Postal Service. A public corporation can also refer to companies that sell stock on one of the formal stock exchanges, such as the New York Stock Exchange, the American Stock Exchange, or NASDAQ.

Close corporation. All the shares of stock are owned by a few individuals and is not traded on any of the public markets; also called family corporation or closely held corporation.

Domestic corporation. A corporation formed in one state and doing business only in that state.

Foreign corporation. A corporation formed in one state but doing business in another state is referred to as a foreign corporation by the other state. A foreign corporation does not have an automatic right to operate in the second state.

This document is most often prepared by an attorney and is submitted to the proper authority in the state. The name of the corporation must be approved by the state's secretary of state office or other appropriate state agency. When the articles of incorporation are completed, they are usually sent to the appropriate authority in the state, along with a filing fee. After approval, a certificate of incorporation is returned, along with the articles, by the state's secretary of state.

The first organizational meeting, the date of which is stated in the articles of incorporation, is then held. During this meeting, the board of directors is elected, the bylaws are prepared, discussions or actions concerning the sale of stock take place, and so on. When this agenda has been completed, the corporation may formally begin operation.

Corporate officers are required to inform the stockholders of the financial condition of the corporation and to conduct other such business as might be dictated by the board of directors or stockholders. An annual financial report must be prepared by an accounting firm and must be provided to the stockholders. Numerous reports must be filed on a monthly or quarterly basis with appropriate jurisdictions, making the corporation form of business a more intensive management challenge, especially if the corporation has employees.

TABLE 9-6.

A Basic Outline of Items in the Articles of Incorporation

An articles of incorporation document is required for a new corporation. Note that specific details will vary from state to state.

1. The name of the corporation
2. The purpose and nature of the business in which the corporation will engage
3. The initial capital structure
4. The number and classes of shares of stock
5. Shareholders' rights
6. The place where the corporation will do business
7. The names of the initial board of directors
8. The names of the original incorporators and statutory agents
9. Other information as might be required by the state for that type of business

A corporation is legally and financially separate and distinct from any of its originating or ownership members (called stockholders or shareholders). Because it is a legal entity, the corporation can sue and be sued by others, it can enter into contracts, and it can commit crimes and be punished. If a suit occurs and the court finds against the design firm, only the corporate assets can be used to pay the business's debts. The corporation is legally and financially responsible, like any individual person. A stockholder's liability extends to the value of his or her stock. Individual stockholders of a corporation cannot be sued, cannot enter into contracts, and so on.

Capital to start a corporation is generally obtained from selling stock. People who wish to invest in the company will buy shares of stock. When the corporation is formed, the initial board of directors determines how many shares of stock will be issued and how much of this first issue will be sold. Later, the corporation may sell additional stock to raise more capital. Unlike limited partnerships, however, stock ownership does not automatically mean they share in profits. Stock of a corporation that is some type of interior design firm is not openly traded on the stock market, so a large infusion of funds through the sale of stock is not easy.

It also can raise capital by going to lending institutions and pledging future assets as collateral in order to secure loans. Although this method is open to partnerships and sole proprietorships as well, it is much easier for a corporation to obtain loans than it is for these other forms of business. However, a purely service-oriented design firm that carries no inventory and has little other collateral will still have difficulty obtaining a loan from a bank.

Corporation tax issues are complex. The corporation must pay income tax on its profits. In addition, stockholders pay taxes on dividend income. Corporation officers also pay employment taxes, Social Security and Medicare contributions, and unemployment taxes. The corporation must pay these same taxes for all employees of the corporation. If a designer forms an interior design business as a corporation, that designer/owner becomes an employee of the corporation. Technically, clients hire the corporation for design work, not the individual owner. The owner must sign contracts in the name of the corporation, not in his or her own name. As an employee, you are paid a salary—assuming you wish to be paid. Payments for withholding and Social Security must be paid to the federal government for salary paid to the owners just like any other employee. And, of course, income tax will be paid on that salary.

Table 9-7 offers a summary of advantages and disadvantages of the corporation formation.

S Corporation

The *S corporation* is a special form of corporation that utilizes many of the benefits of a corporation but does not pay taxes as a corporation. If a designer chooses to utilize the S corporation, he or she is as much choosing a formation as electing a manner to which he or she will be taxed. At one time, this form was formally called a subchapter S corporation. Because of the popularity of the LLC, the S corporation is not used as frequently today.

The S corporation is formed in a very similar manner to a corporation and is expected to meet all the same requirements for articles of incorporation, stockholders' meetings, election of a board of directors, and so on as the corporation. Businesses are formed as an S corporation because the formation provides liability protection and has a different tax responsibility that is often more favorable to owners. To understand the liability benefits, please review the corporation form of business in the previous section.

TABLE 9-7.

Advantages and Disadvantages of a Corporation

Advantages

- The corporation is a legal entity separate from owners. No other business formation has this status.
- Financial liability of the originators (or principals) and stockholders is limited to the amount of money each invests in the corporation.
- The personal assets of the principals and stockholders cannot be used to satisfy legal judgments.
- Corporations have continuity, even if the originators cease to be involved.
- Capital for the business can be raised by selling stock.
- A corporation can obtain debt financing (loans) more readily than other forms of business.
- Shareholders elect the board of directors. This gives shareholders a say in the management of the corporation.
- The nature of the corporation, even if it is only by legal appearance, may make it easier to attract employees.

Disadvantages

- A corporation is the most complicated and expensive of the business formations.
- Business continuity as a corporation requires a great deal of paperwork.
- Annual stockholders' meetings must be held.
- The officers and directors of the corporation are liable for any criminal actions that they or their representatives perpetrate in the name of the corporation.
- Stockholders can only influence management by participating in the stockholders' meeting and election of the board of directors and officers.
- Business activities are limited to those described in the articles of incorporation.
- Corporations are more heavily regulated by state and federal agencies than the other business formations.
- A corporation must qualify and register to do business in other states.

If a business elects to be an S corporation for tax status from the Internal Revenue Service, it then pays taxes as a partnership or sole proprietorship.[1] Most states follow the federal government's requirement on taxation. However, a few states tax the S corporation as a regular corporation. Check with your state treasury department or secretary of state office to be sure what is in effect in your state. The corporation must file special tax reports with the government.

Designers also may wish to elect S corporation status in the early years of the business, when it is most likely to experience business losses. These losses are absorbed by the owner's personal income taxes and shareholders personal taxes rather than by the business, since the business itself does not pay income taxes. Owners and shareholders pay income tax on the profits of an S corporation in proportion to the share of stock they hold in the corporation. These payments are called distributions.

The owner of a design business who chooses to qualify it as an S corporation must apply to the Internal Revenue Service. The eligibility requirements include the following: (1) the firm must be a domestic corporation (incorporated within the United States); (2) the shareholders can only be individuals, not other corporations; (3) there cannot be more than 75 shareholders; (4) all shareholders must be American citizens; (5) the corporation has only one class of stock; and (6) the S corporation obtains no more than 25 percent of its revenues from investments. Any changes in these will result in the termination of S status for the corporation. Because of these requirements, it is common for smaller, family, or closely held corporations to elect to be treated as S corporations. It is necessary to change to the corporate form when the firm no longer meets the eligibility requirements of an S corporation.

Since the advantages and disadvantages are very similar to those of a corporation, they will not be repeated here. Business owners who are considering the S corporation election should carefully discuss this issue with their accountant.

Professional Corporation

If your state has interior design licensing, you may be able to use the professional corporation as a legal formation. A *professional corporation* (referred to as a professional association or professional service corporation in some states) is a corporation formed by persons in professions such as law, medicine, dentistry, accounting, engineering, or architecture. In many states, only professional services that are licensed or have other legal authorization by the state may register as professional corporations. The letters PC (professional corporation), PA (professional association), or PSC (professional service corporation) follow the name of the firm, identifying it as a professional corporation. All shareholders must be licensed to practice the service being provided, and the business is limited to a single profession.

Merely because your state has licensing for interior design practice does not mean you may use the professional corporation for your legal business structure. Each state has guidelines governing which professions may use this business formation. Some have very limiting restrictions related to the professional corporation. Restrictive laws concerning professional corporations were passed in the latter part of the twentieth century because many felt that professional service businesses were taking too many tax advantages with this business formation.

The professional corporation is formed similarly to an ordinary corporation. Registration is done through filing documents with a state secretary of state or corporation commission office. Many professional corporations are considered professional service corporations, meaning they provide services but sell no products. When this is the case, the tax burden is higher than the regular corporation and is in fact a flat 35 percent in 2006.[2]

All shareholders are liable to clients, even if only one member is negligent. Personal assets of shareholders are protected from business debts. Any shareholder of a professional corporation who is guilty of a negligent act is personally liable for the injury and damages.

JOINT VENTURE

Let us say that the design firm you work for has been approached by another design firm to respond to a request for proposal (RFP) for a boutique resort. (See a further discussion on RFPs in Chapter 20.) The resort will be located near your firm rather than the firm that approached you, which is located at a distance from the resort site in the state. The other firm is owned by a designer you met through your professional association activities. They want your firm to join them in responding to the RFP and doing the project together. They have proposed the two firms create a joint venture for this project.

When two or more persons or firms agree on a temporary basis to share in the responsibilities, losses, and profits of a particular project or business venture, they have elected to create a *joint venture*. The key to the joint venture is its temporary status. Neither firm loses its original identity, since the joint venture is almost always formed with a new name for the temporary partnership for the duration of the project. Both generally go on with other projects that are separate from the joint venture project. When the project has been completed, the temporary partnership ends, and each firm goes back to working on a completely individual basis.

The joint venture is treated much like a partnership business formation, but it is for a limited time period or for a certain activity. Since two (or more) firms are creating a new firm—even for a temporary time frame—a formal agreement should be prepared. This agreement needs to explain the responsibilities of each party, the conditions of the arrangement, the manner in which the profits and losses will be divided, the method for paying employees, and so on. Following the outline of items in a general partnership agreement is common.

Not being a legal entity, it cannot be sued, but the individual members of the joint venture can be sued. Each firm independently and the joint venture as a whole is liable to the client. Depending on the state in which the joint venture is formed, the profits and losses of the venture are usually taxed as they would be for a partnership or are passed along to the participating members of the joint venture.

This kind of business relationship most often is entered into for one of these reasons:

- A project is so large that no single firm—large or small—would have the time and support team within the existing firm to do it alone.
- Obtaining design projects in other states. An out-of-state firm could benefit from the reputation and licensing of a local firm, should the interior designer come from a state, for example, that does not license interior designers.
- Gain experience in the kind of project for which it has little or no experience. Perhaps one firm has experience in lighting and kitchen design for restaurants but needs additional staff for aesthetic design solutions. The joint venture creates a full-service design package for the project.
- The combined firm creates a large staff to complete the work even though each firm continues to do independent work. If one firm were to obtain the contract, it might be necessary to hire additional designers. It takes time to train new employees, and this can be quite costly. The temporary partnership would bring the staffs of both firms together and might negate any need to hire additional employees on a short-term basis.
- A joint venture gives the two firms an opportunity to learn from each other in areas other than design. Although competing firms do not willingly give away their design and business secrets, some ideas and concepts can be shared while respecting the integrity of both firms.
- The joint venture also provides a very strong design team. For the client, using the expertise of two firms can mean better design and follow-through. One firm may not have the support staff or expertise to complete the project in a timely fashion.

A joint venture is not the same as "partnering" with the various parties involved in a project in order to manage a project. Partnering is not a business formation. It is a way of managing a project. A joint venture *is* a type of business formation. Through the joint venture, both firms continue under their own individual identities and with projects other than the joint venture project. If the firms did not create a joint venture but wished to join together, one firm would have to merge with the other. This, of course, would mean that one firm would no longer exist.

SUMMARY

Anyone wishing to work on his or her own must make many important decisions when developing the business idea before the work of the design firm begins. Chief among those decisions is determining which business formation to use. The decision impacts the amount of funds required to initiate the business, legal liability, and personal responsibility should legal actions be brought against the company, to name just a few considerations. Understanding the many differences in the formations helps all practitioners appreciate the obligations of owner(s).

As the business changes and grows, the owner of the design firm also may wish to consider changing the business formation. For example, the sole proprietorship that seemed very appropriate for the practitioner working on her own often finds it more professionally practical to change to a different type of legal formation as the firm grows. In addition, business owners change legal formation for financial or tax reasons, as well as for liability protection.

This chapter has briefly outlined key points about the different legal forms of business that can be used by the interior designer for a new interior design practice. These same points may help the existing business owner determine if a different legal formation would be more appropriate as the interior design firm grows. The next chapter will discuss the legal filings that are necessary for the major business formations.

REFERENCES

1. Nolo, "S corporation Facts," 2005, www.nolo.com.
2. Nolo, "Professional Corporations," 2006, www.nolo.com.

CHAPTER 10

Business Legal Filings and Licenses

Key Terms and Concepts

These key terms and concepts are important to material in this chapter. Many of these terms will be utilized in other chapters as well. Be sure you understand these items as you read this chapter.

Terms and Concepts

Doing business as (DBA)

Legal name

Trade name

Unemployment taxes

Workers' compensation insurance

Resale license

Seller's permit

Estimated taxes

Self-employment tax

Personal property tax

Intellectual property law

Copyright

Patent

Trademark

Copyright notice

Publication

Shop right

Work product

Infringement

Filings

Employer identification number (EIN)

Fictitious business name statement

Work authorization verification—Form I-9

Employee's withholding allowance certificate—Form W-4

Employer's wage and tax statement—form W-2

Form 1099 Information Forms

Transaction privilege (sales) tax license

Use tax certificate

Contractor's license

Organization

Foundation for Design Integrity (FDI)

Critical Issues

After completing this chapter you should be able to:

▨ Explain the importance and necessity of the employer's identification number.

▨ Define when a fictitious business name statement is required.

▨ Explain what types of interior design business is required to obtain a transaction privilege tax license.

▨ Explain who must file self-employment tax and why.

▨ Compare the sales tax license to the use tax license.

▨ Discuss the basic process of protecting copyright protection for design drawings and documents.

▨ Compare copyright protection for a sole practitioner versus an employee of a design firm.

One of the challenges of owning a design practice is the regular completion and filing of various forms required by federal, state, and local jurisdictional laws. Serious consequences can impact the business if the owner neglects to prepare and file required documents with the jurisdiction. For example, failure to collect and pay sales taxes as required in a jurisdiction can lead to fines and even forfeiture of the business.

Some states may not require all those listed, and other filings may be required by a specific state. Advice as to proper filings can be obtained from the firm's accountant and attorney. Each city and county may also have particular licenses, property taxes, or tax requirements that the business must obtain and file. The interior design business owner should check with local city and county authorities to be sure that these requirements are satisfied.

Some of the forms discussed in this chapter are needed to originate the business. Recall that some forms needed to originate a business were discussed in Chapter 9 concerning business formations. Other filings are needed on an ongoing basis through the life of the practice. A few specialized filings that do not necessarily relate to starting a practice but that may be required or needed are also covered in this chapter. Such filings as interior design licensing and copyright protection are important topics in this chapter.

A caution needs to be expressed about legal filings. Changes are made annually to many of the requirements for business filings, especially those applied to tax laws. The business owner or prospective business owner must consult with his or her accountant and attorney to be sure the correct forms are filed each year. The documents discussed in this chapter are broad guidelines of what is required.

BUSINESS LEGAL FILINGS

Legal filings for a new business will vary based on the business formation. As you will recall from Chapter 9, a sole proprietorship has very few forms that must be filed to start the business, while a corporation has several. This section discusses the most common forms required to start a business beyond those required for the legal formation. The forms and filings discussed concerning employees are not a one-time filing and are needed throughout the life of the business. Additional forms may be required in your jurisdiction.

Form SS-4: Application for Employer Identification Number

The most common form required of a business is *Form SS-4 Application for Employer Identification Number* (EIN), issued by the federal Internal Revenue Service. This *employer identification number* identifies the business to the federal and state government. It will be used on income tax forms that must be submitted to the federal and state revenue services. Many states also require that the business obtain a *state employer identification number* using a different form. A copy of this form is included on the CD as Item 10-1.

All forms of business must obtain an EIN with the possible exception of the sole proprietor. The owner of a sole proprietorship can use his or her Social Security number in place of an EIN. Most accountants recommend that the sole proprietor/sole practitioner obtain an EIN, since it will be required when the business hires employees. In addition, banks also require an EIN to open a commercial account. States where a state employer identification number is required usually require an EIN whether or not the business has employees.

When the interior design practice has been formed as a corporation, anyone working for the corporation is an employee. This means that even if only one individual actually generated income for the corporation and was a member of the board of directors/stockholders of the corporation, that individual would be considered an employee.

Sometimes a business must get a new EIN. If the business formation changes to a different type of formation, a new EIN will be needed for the new business—even if the name has not changed. For example, Mary Anne, the owner of Overview Interiors (a sole proprietorship), has taken on a partner, James. Since the business has changed from a sole proprietorship to a partnership, a new EIN must be obtained. The firm's accountant or attorney can provide guidance on specific issues.

Since the privilege of operating a corporation rests with the states, the states require that all businesses formed as corporations be registered with the state before operations begin. In most cases, corporation identification numbers are obtained from the state department of revenue. This number may be different from a state employee identification number.

Fictitious Business Name Statement

Selecting a name for the new business is a very important task. Many sole practitioners use their legal name as their business name. Others choose a fictitious name. If the business is operating under a name other than that of the owner(s), the state requires that the business file a *fictitious business name statement*. Many businesspeople refer to this as a *doing business as* (DBA) statement. This filing is required of all sole proprietorships and partnerships and is usually filed with the county clerk or the state secretary of state.

Instead of a fictitious business name statement, corporations and LLCs must register the business name with the corporation commission and/or the state secretary of state (depending on the laws in the jurisdiction). Generally, a corporation or LLC would not need to also file a fictitious business name statement. The reader should check with the jurisdiction in which the business will be located to know how to correctly and legally file the business name.

When the business uses a fictitious name for its business, the owner must be sure that no other business in the state is already using that name. Research must be done to be sure that a fictitious business name is available. If the name is already being used, the state or county clerk will not allow another company to use the name.

What's in a Name?

The choice of the business name is very important. A business name is needed to open bank accounts for the business and to use on stationery and other marketing materials. In reality, a business can have two names: the legal name and a trade name. A *legal name* is the business's official name, which must always be used on legal documents such as contracts and tax returns. The *trade name* is the one used in public, such as on stationery, on business cards, and a Web site. The choice of a trade name can be dependent on the type of legal business formation used.

Many sole proprietors use their name as their business name. "Mary Smith" is the legal name for the interior design practice started by Mary Smith. If she adds terms like "interiors," "consulting," "design group," or "interior designer" to her name, it has become a trade name—"Mary Smith Interior Design." Adding terms like "interior design" to a person's name helps in marketing by clarifying the business. But there is no legal requirement to do so.

The legal names desired for limited liability companies and corporations require research and permission from a state agency. The state agency—often the office of the state secretary of state or corporation commission—will have the register of company names that are already in use. An LLC must register the name even if its business name is "Mary Smith, LLC." Partners that use their own name as the name are handled similarly to a sole proprietorship. However, partnership names should also be checked, since a partnership such as "Smith and Randolph Partnership" might already be taken by another company.

A trade name can be any name not used by some other company. It can contain the name of the owner of the company, such as "Thomas Campbell Interior Consultant," or it can be a name that is made up. A made-up name is also referred to as a fictitious name. Even a sole practitioner can use a fictitious trade name such as "New Visions." When a sole practitioner wants to use a fictitious trade name for the company name, it must be registered with the county clerk or state secretary of state, similarly to what must be done for trade names for all other types of business formations.

Using a fictitious name gives the small-sized firm a marketing opportunity. "New Visions" sounds like a larger-size company than "Thomas Campbell Interior Consultant." Even adding terms like "interior designer," "consultant," "design studio," or "design" provide some clarity to the name, indicating the type of business. The experts say that the more your company name communicates to potential customers, the greater the chance they will consider your firm. Also remember to keep the name short. A long name can be confusing. If you plan a fictitious name, test it with friends and relatives to be sure it conveys the meaning you want. And then perform a name search to be sure it can even be used by your company.

Name searches can be done by using an Internet search engine such as Google (www.google.com), by checking local phone books in your area, and by reviewing trade name lists with the U.S. Patent and Trademark Office. You might also want to check Internet domain names if you feel that one day your company will want to have a Web site. www.register.com or www.networksolutions.com are two large registration Web sites.

When you use a fictitious name, you may wish to also register the name as a trade name or a trademark. This is done through the U.S. federal government U.S. Patent and Trademark Office (www.uspto.gov). You can also go to a private Web site (www.uspto.com) to search trade names. Registering the trade name or trademark gives you exclusive use of the item. This might be particularly important for a firm that plans to have offices in other jurisdictions than its home location. As long as your jurisdiction says that the name is usable, you do not have to register the name with the federal government.

The main purpose in registering a fictitious business name is to identify to the state and to the general public the owner(s) responsible for any business formed within the state. In some states, it may also be necessary for the new business to publish a statement of ownership. This is required dependent upon the legal form of the business. It is relatively common for corporations to print a copy of the corporation papers in the business section of the local newspaper. The federal government does not involve itself in business names other than through trademark registration. Trademarks are discussed later in this chapter.

For Firms with Employees

There are several documents besides the EIN that must be filed when a firm has employees. The first is the *Form I-9 Work Authorization Verification*. As of the time of this revision, this form was also called the Form I-9 Employment Eligibility Verification. In 1986 the Immigration Reform and Control Act was passed by the U.S. Congress. This act makes it unlawful for individuals and businesses to hire aliens who do not have proper authorization to work. Since it is also unlawful for the company to discriminate in its hiring practices, companies are required to have all applicants hired after November 6, 1986, submit acceptable identification and work authorization information, primarily by using the Form I-9. A copy of the latest form available as of January 2007 is included on the CD as Item 10-2.

The business owner can obtain Form I-9 from the Bureau of U.S. Citizenship and Immigration Services, which is now part of the Department of Homeland Security, to ensure compliance with the law. Not only must the applicant be asked to provide acceptable documents, but also the individual or business that is doing the hiring must keep a record of the request and verification on file. Several different kinds of documents can be used to verify identity and employment eligibility.

Two additional federal forms the reader is probably familiar with are Forms W-4 and W-2. Federal *Form W-4, the Employee's Withholding Allowance Certificate*, is filled out by an employee upon being hired. The employer is required to keep this form on file and must send a copy of the W-4 to the IRS if the employee claims ten or more exemptions or claims an exemption from withholding. This form indicates the number of deductions to which the employee is entitled, which determines how much income tax is withheld from wages.

Federal *Form W-2, the Employer's Wage and Tax Statement*, is prepared by the employer and is sent to the employee no later than January 31 of the calendar year. Form W-2 shows all wages paid; federal, state, and city taxes withheld; and Social Security taxes shown as FICA withheld for the employee. By the way, FICA stands for Federal Insurance Contribution Act. Social Security is the more common name for FICA. Other information also may be reported on this form, depending on the firm's structure of benefits and wages.

Similar forms must be filed with the state. In most states, this will require obtaining a withholding number and an unemployment number from the state. The manner in which these are collected, their amounts, and the reporting methods vary from state to state.

Businesses with employees must pay contributions to the Social Security and Medicare tax responsibilities for their employees. The employee also will have a portion of wages withheld (and paid to the federal government by the employer) for the employee's share of the taxes that appear as "FICA" on the employee's wage receipt.

Design businesses with employees must budget and pay funds for unemployment taxes to the state. *Unemployment taxes* provide funds to eligible employees in the event that they are laid off from their job. Federal financial requirements for unemployment tax responsibility are set at a low threshold, and almost all businesses with employees, even if there is only one employee, pay unemployment tax. The exceptions are sole proprietorships and partnerships that do not have to pay unemployment taxes on the compensation to the owners.

Another cost to the business with employees is workers' compensation insurance. A state mandated program, *workers' compensation insurance* is an insurance program that provides funds to the employee to cover the expenses of work-related injuries. State laws generally require that most businesses, regardless of their size, provide workers' compensation insurance. Some states require that sole proprietors and partners also be covered by workers' compensation insurance.

It is very important that businesses owners with employees check with appropriate state agencies concerning their obligations regarding unemployment tax contributions and workers' compensation insurance obligations. Failing to pay these funds to the state can have serious consequences for the business. Likewise, other filings may be required in the jurisdiction of the business location. The interior design practice owner is advised to check with the firm's accountant to clarify which forms must be filed and when for individual needs.

Federal *Form 1099* is called an informational form, and it is used to report taxable income for individuals who are not employees of the firm. At times a practitioner may need special assistance for many kinds of tasks related to the business but not need a regular full-time or even part-time employee. Individuals working for the design firm who are not true employees are considered independent contractors. An example is an outsource CAD technician who produces drawings from time to time for the firm. Discussed in depth in Chapter 15, independent contractors are not employees and are not supervised by the hiring firm. The only filing that is done related to the work of the independent contract is the reporting at the end of the tax year of income paid to the individual. At the present time, only amounts to independent contractors that total over $600 must be reported on 1099s.

There are many different types of 1099 that are used to report other kinds of income or other types of specific information. In certain circumstances, the employer will have to file one or more copies of Form 1099. Some special types of income include dividends on stock and nonemployee compensation, such as compensation paid to contract labor. Other 1099s may have to be filed depending on the exact nature of the business and the benefits program offered by the firm.

What Would You Do?

Eric has owned a small design studio in a market area that has few competitors. His company has enough business that he has two student interns from a local design program, along with a full-time designer and an office manager. The full-time designer has moved here from another state and is a professional-level member of one of the associations. She was also registered in that state.

Eric's advertising in the local paper has recently included the association logo. One of the interns has talked to a professor, saying that she is pretty sure that Eric is not a member of any association, since she has never seen any evidence to support that achievement. The student doesn't want to say anything to Eric and doesn't know what to do.

LICENSES

The licenses that an interior design practitioner may need to obtain for a new business will vary based on local, state, and/or provincial laws. It is not possible to discuss fully all the specific licenses that might be required by the various jurisdictions. The owner of an interior design practice must check with the proper counsel to be sure he or she is fulfilling the requirements of each state in which the firm will be doing business. An important point is to also understand that a firm that is located in one state and that is doing business in another state may need to file specific forms or obtain licenses to operate in that other state. Note that "operating" can mean simply doing a project in that other jurisdiction. It does not mean that a branch of the business is in the state/jurisdiction.

The following is a brief discussion of the most common state licenses that are required of interior design practices. Note that there are no federal licenses required related to the interior design services or businesses. An exception to this statement might be an industry-related business involved in the manufacturing of certain goods used in interiors.

Interior Design Licensure or Title Registration

The exact nature of the laws in the jurisdictions in the United States and Canada that have laws related to the practice or work of interior designers varies, since these laws are enacted by the state or provincial government (see Chapter 2). Students and professionals must keep abreast of any new laws being formulated in their jurisdiction and must be prepared to meet the specific requirements of the statutes. In general, the state board of technical registration (or other like agencies) set the standards for licensing and title registration in conjunction with approval by state legislatures. The state boards are also responsible for enforcement and termination of license privilege.

Interior designers who are working in states where title registration or licensing requirements have been passed must meet those regulations when they open a business, even if it is a sole proprietorship. If the designer was not previously licensed in a regulated state because he or she worked for someone who was licensed, the designer might not have to be individually licensed as an employee. Depending on state laws, a designer working in a nonregulated state might be prohibited from doing projects in regulated states. Regulated states generally allow a registered designer in another state to work in his or her state. This is referred to as *reciprocity*. Of course, if the designer changes jobs or starts a business, the designer would need to obtain this important license or certification. Interior designers working in nonregulated states should consider meeting standards that they see being adopted in neighboring states so that they will meet requirements when their state enacts any type of regulation.

State and City Transaction Privilege (Sales) Tax License

It is imperative for businesses that intend to resell goods to the end user to obtain a state and city (if city sales tax is collected) *Transaction Privilege (Sales) Tax License*. This license is commonly referred to as a *resale license* or *seller's permit*. Many states require and accountants suggest that a business obtain this license whether or not the business will be selling goods.

In some states, the owner can obtain a city tax license form at the same time that he or she applies for the state license; the taxes are then collected by the state and are forwarded to the appropriate cities. If this joint license is not available from the state, the city license can be obtained from the offices of the city in which the business is located. The city license serves the same function as the state license.

Sales tax is required on almost all goods (food being a notable exception) that is purchased by the end user/consumer in almost all states. The exceptions, as of this writing, are Alaska, Delaware, Montana, New Hampshire, and Oregon.[1] Some jurisdictions require that sales tax be collected on design services as well. This is less common, but legislators have increasingly started to require sales tax on some services as a means to gain extra state income. The designer needs to carefully check to be sure whether or not sales tax must be charged for services.

When interior designers sell merchandise to clients, they must charge the client the sales tax. However, the seller (interior designer) does not pay sales tax on goods that he or she buys and resells to a client. The sales tax license allows the interior designer to pass on the state sales tax to the client. If the design firm has offices/stores in more than one city or state, separate sales tax licenses will likely be required for each jurisdiction.

The business must collect required sales tax from clients and pay this tax money to the state and/or the city department of revenue. If a designer does not charge the client the sales tax, the firm will have the obligation of paying that tax. If the business fails to do so, the taxing authority will hold the business responsible for the tax monies. The amount collected must be reported and paid on a monthly basis, whether or not sales for the period have occurred. These monthly reports must be filed as long as the business remains in existence. Additional information about sales taxes are discussed in Chapter 25.

Use Tax Registration Certificate

Use tax is a companion to the sales tax. If the business will be purchasing goods from out of state for use or sale and these goods are taxable in the state in which the interior design firm is doing business, the business is required to obtain a *use tax certificate* and to pay sales tax on those items. This ensures that sales taxes or use taxes are collected either by the state that is selling the goods to the interior design firm or by the firm to the state if the goods are sold to end users.

Contractor's Licenses

The hiring of trades to do construction work and the supervision of that work and/or the supervision of the installation of architectural finishes that an interior designer might specify for a client need to be done by a licensed contractor. This generally applies to residential and commercial interior projects. Of course, the requirements related to the use of licensed contractors vary from state to state.

There are few states with exceptions to this requirement unless the work is considered to be casual work for a small sum of money (specifics of this varies with the jurisdiction). Projects that would be designed by a professional interior designer rarely fall under "casual work." Thus, such items as structural work, carpet laying, wall-covering installation, plumbing, and other items that are attachments to the building must be done only by a licensed contractor.

This is not to say that an interior designer must also be a contractor or have a general contractor's license. In fact, it is rare for interior designers to be required to obtain a general contractor's license or one of the several specialized contractor's licenses for supervision of this work. However, some states require these licenses or a specialty contractor's license to sell, contract for, or supervise the installation or construction of these types of products. For example, if the design firm purchases and contracts an installer to install wall covering and if payment for both is made by the interior design firm, then the designer must have the appropriate specialty license or contractor's license.

If the interior designer does not have the contractor's license, he or she should instruct the client to hire contractors who hold these licenses to do the work. Other designers focus on design rather than construction and installation, and provide consultation regarding these activities to the client. In this situation, the client, or a third-party contractor hired by the client, reports back to the tradesperson, construction project manager, or general contractor and asks that person to take care of the problems.

Most states require that work done for private residences and commercial facilities be performed only by licensed contractors. If the designer hires unlicensed contractors to perform work that a licensed contractor must perform, the client may not have any legal obligation to pay the designer. It may also be a criminal offense for the interior designer to use the unlicensed contractor. The owner of the interior design firm should be familiar with the statutes of the state in which the firm is located, and of any state in which it may be doing business. Questions should be directed to the state registrar of contractors or other appropriate authority.

INCOME TAX BASICS

All businesses must pay federal income tax on business profits. The amount of tax that a business must pay on its income is based on many factors. The employer identification number discussed earlier is needed to file tax reports. The exact taxable amount is affected by legal business deductions. These deductions generally relate to costs of operating and maintaining the business. Items such as marketing efforts, office supplies, and rent are just a few of the kinds of expenses that are deductible. It is beyond the scope of this book to discuss tax deductions. This issue should be covered in detail with the practitioner's accountant so that proper record keeping can be instituted at the very onset of the business. A brief discussion on income tax related to the different formations of businesses is presented in the preceding chapter. Table 10-1 lists the type of federal tax forms that must be filed for each type of business formation discussed in Chapter 9.

States also require that businesses pay state income tax on business profits. Since most states model their income tax reporting on the federal laws, the reporting methods are similar. Forms and actual reporting methods are, of course, different for each state.

All forms of business have to pay *estimated taxes* because federal and state income tax is a "pay-as-you-go" tax. That means that the company must pay taxes quarterly on the amount of taxable income it expects to get. In a way this is similar to the portion of an employee's wages that is withheld from each paycheck to help offset the eventual total amounts of income tax due to the IRS or to his or her state's revenue department.

TABLE 10-1.

Income Tax Forms

Type of Legal Entity	Form
Sole Proprietorship	Schedule C (Form 1040)
	Form SE Self-employment
Partnership	Form 1065
	Form K-1 Partner's profit or loss statement
Regular corporation	Form 1120 or 1120-A (short form)
Single-member LLC	Schedule C (Form 1040)
S Corporation	Form 1120-S
Multimember LLC	Form 1065, 1120, or 1120-A

Note that other filings for income taxes for owners and investors will be required depending on the form of business.

Although estimated taxes are important for any size business to calculate and pay as required, it can be particularly important to the self-employed. With a self-employed individual, there is no employer to withhold a portion of wages with each paycheck. In fact, many self-employed people pay themselves on a very irregular basis. Thus, they will be required to pay estimated taxes based on the previous year's taxable amount.

Self-employed individuals pay quarterly estimated taxes in lieu of withholding taxes. The amount due each quarter is based on the level of taxes that were paid the previous year. Penalties are imposed for underpayment of estimated taxes. Sole proprietors and other business owners should discuss the method of calculating and payment of estimated taxes with the firm's accountant.

A portion of the amount that is paid in the estimated tax for the self-employed who own a sole proprietorship or partnership is a self-employment tax. The *self-employment tax* is paid on the income that a sole proprietor and any partners receive on their share of the owner's income of the business. It is the equivalent of the Social Security and Medicare tax paid by employees and employers on an employee's income. The form that is used in this case is Schedule SE (Form 1040), as shown in Figure 10-1. A copy of this form is also included on the CD as Item 10-3. A copy of another form important for the self-employed is Form 1040-Schedule C. A copy of this form is also included on the CD as Item 10-4.

Since the income for those who have ownership in certain business formations is considered self-employment income and is not subject to normal withholding taxes, the self-employed individual must report and pay this tax at the time at which normal income taxes are due. The government acts as an agent to collect this tax for the Social Security Administration.

In addition to income tax, many states tax the personal property of the business. In most cases, the personal property taxes cover furniture and equipment that are used in the business. Sellable inventory is not taxed. If a business owns any real estate, the business will also pay property tax. In most cases, these filings are sent to the county attorney or county assessor of the county in which the business is located rather than to the state revenue department. The county tax assessor automatically bills the owner of record annually for personal property taxes that are due.

Note that many tax guides are available from the IRS, some of which can be downloaded from www.irs.gov. Local and state agencies have numerous publications available that can help the new business owner clarify requirements within each jurisdiction.

COPYRIGHTS, TRADEMARKS, AND PATENTS

Barbara produced a set of working drawings showing the demolition and new layout and equipment specification on a remodeling of a kitchen and family room for her client. The fees for these drawings were included in the contract for the design services. When Barbara showed the client the drawings, the client suddenly said that he did not want to continue with the project with Barbara. The client gave no reason for terminating the project contract. The client wanted the drawings but Barbara refused without a payment of $1500 for the development of the drawings.

The creation and development of floor plans (and other types of construction/equipment drawings), sketches, and sample boards are frequent and common in the practice of interior design. Naturally, it is hoped that these intangible items will result in a completed interior or, possibly, a custom-designed product.

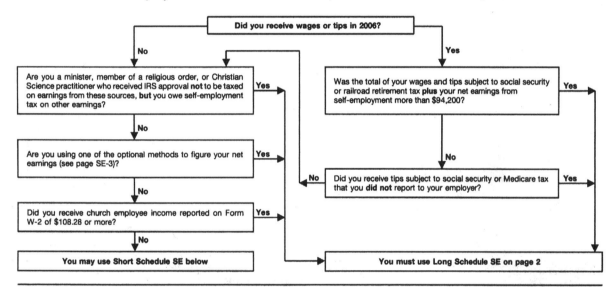

SCHEDULE SE
(Form 1040)

Department of the Treasury
Internal Revenue Service (99)

Self-Employment Tax

▶ Attach to Form 1040. ▶ See Instructions for Schedule SE (Form 1040).

OMB No. 1545-0074

2006

Attachment
Sequence No. **17**

Name of person with **self-employment** income (as shown on Form 1040)

Social security number of person
with **self-employment** income ▶

Who Must File Schedule SE

You must file Schedule SE if:

- You had net earnings from self-employment from **other than** church employee income (line 4 of Short Schedule SE or line 4c of Long Schedule SE) of $400 or more, **or**
- You had church employee income of $108.28 or more. Income from services you performed as a minister or a member of a religious order **is not** church employee income (see page SE-1).

Note. Even if you had a loss or a small amount of income from self-employment, it may be to your benefit to file Schedule SE and use either "optional method" in Part II of Long Schedule SE (see page SE-3).

Exception. If your only self-employment income was from earnings as a minister, member of a religious order, or Christian Science practitioner **and** you filed Form 4361 and received IRS approval not to be taxed on those earnings, **do not** file Schedule SE. Instead, write "Exempt–Form 4361" on Form 1040, line 58.

May I Use Short Schedule SE or Must I Use Long Schedule SE?

Note. Use this flowchart **only if** you must file Schedule SE. If unsure, see Who Must File Schedule SE, above.

Section A—Short Schedule SE. Caution. Read above to see if you can use Short Schedule SE.

1	Net farm profit or (loss) from Schedule F, line 36, and farm partnerships, Schedule K-1 (Form 1065), box 14, code A	**1**
2	Net profit or (loss) from Schedule C, line 31; Schedule C-EZ, line 3; Schedule K-1 (Form 1065), box 14, code A (other than farming); and Schedule K-1 (Form 1065-B), box 9, code J1. Ministers and members of religious orders, see page SE-1 for amounts to report on this line. See page SE-3 for other income to report	**2**
3	Combine lines 1 and 2	**3**
4	**Net earnings from self-employment.** Multiply line 3 by 92.35% (.9235). If less than $400, **do not** file this schedule; you do not owe self-employment tax . . . . ▶	**4**
5	**Self-employment tax.** If the amount on line 4 is: • $94,200 or less, multiply line 4 by 15.3% (.153). Enter the result here and on **Form 1040, line 58.** • More than $94,200, multiply line 4 by 2.9% (.029). Then, add $11,680.80 to the result. Enter the total here and on **Form 1040, line 58.**	**5**
6	**Deduction for one-half of self-employment tax.** Multiply line 5 by 50% (.5). Enter the result here and on **Form 1040, line 27** . . .	**6**	

For Paperwork Reduction Act Notice, see Form 1040 instructions.   Cat. No. 11358Z   **Schedule SE (Form 1040) 2006**

FIGURE 10-1.

IRS Form Schedule SE (Form 1040), used to calculate the self-employment tax.

Schedule SE (Form 1040) 2006   Attachment Sequence No. **17**   Page **2**

Name of person with **self-employment** income (as shown on Form 1040)	Social security number of person with **self-employment** income ?	: :

Section B—Long Schedule SE

Part I   Self-Employment Tax

Note. If your only income subject to self-employment tax is **church employee income,** skip lines 1 through 4b. Enter -0- on line 4c and go to line 5a. Income from services you performed as a minister or a member of a religious order **is not** church employee income. See page SE-1.

A   If you are a minister, member of a religious order, or Christian Science practitioner **and** you filed Form 4361, but you had $400 or more of **other** net earnings from self-employment, check here and continue with Part I . . . . . ? ☐

1	Net farm profit or (loss) from Schedule F, line 36, and farm partnerships, Schedule K-1 (Form 1065), box 14, code A. **Note.** Skip this line if you use the farm optional method (see page SE-4)	**1**	
2	Net profit or (loss) from Schedule C, line 31; Schedule C-EZ, line 3; Schedule K-1 (Form 1065), box 14, code A (other than farming); and Schedule K-1 (Form 1065-B), box 9, code J1. Ministers and members of religious orders, see page SE-1 for amounts to report on this line. See page SE-3 for other income to report. **Note.** Skip this line if you use the nonfarm optional method (see page SE-4)	**2**	
3	Combine lines 1 and 2	**3**	
4a	If line 3 is more than zero, multiply line 3 by 92.35% (.9235). Otherwise, enter amount from line 3	**4a**	
b	If you elect one or both of the optional methods, enter the total of lines 15 and 17 here . .	**4b**	
c	Combine lines 4a and 4b. If less than $400, **stop;** you do not owe self-employment tax. **Exception.** If less than $400 and you had **church employee income,** enter -0- and continue . . . . . ?	**4c**	
5a	Enter your **church employee income** from Form W-2. See page SE-1 for definition of church employee income **5a**		
b	Multiply line 5a by 92.35% (.9235). If less than $100, enter -0-	**5b**	
6	**Net earnings from self-employment.** Add lines 4c and 5b	**6**	
7	Maximum amount of combined wages and self-employment earnings subject to social security tax or the 6.2% portion of the 7.65% railroad retirement (tier 1) tax for 2006	**7**	94,200 | 00
8a	Total social security wages and tips (total of boxes 3 and 7 on Form(s) W-2) and railroad retirement (tier 1) compensation. If $94,200 or more, skip lines 8b through 10, and go to line 11 . . . . **8a**		
b	Unreported tips subject to social security tax (from Form 4137, line 9) **8b**		
c	Add lines 8a and 8b	**8c**	
9	Subtract line 8c from line 7. If zero or less, enter -0- here and on line 10 and go to line 11 . ?	**9**	
10	Multiply the **smaller** of line 6 or line 9 by 12.4% (.124)	**10**	
11	Multiply line 6 by 2.9% (.029)	**11**	
12	**Self-employment tax.** Add lines 10 and 11. Enter here and on **Form 1040, line 58** . . .	**12**	
13	**Deduction for one-half of self-employment tax.** Multiply line 12 by 50% (.5). Enter the result here and on **Form 1040, line 27** . . . **13**		

Part II   Optional Methods To Figure Net Earnings (see page SE-3)

Farm Optional Method. You may use this method **only** if **(a)** your gross farm income[1] was not more than $2,400, **or (b)** your net farm profits[2] were less than $1,733.

14	Maximum income for optional methods	**14**	1,600 | 00
15	Enter the **smaller** of: two-thirds (⅔) of gross farm income[1] (not less than zero) **or** $1,600. Also include this amount on line 4b above	**15**	

Nonfarm Optional Method. You may use this method **only** if **(a)** your net nonfarm profits[3] were less than $1,733 and also less than 72.189% of your gross nonfarm income,[4] **and (b)** you had net earnings from self-employment of at least $400 in 2 of the prior 3 years.

Caution. You may use this method no more than five times.

16	Subtract line 15 from line 14	**16**	
17	Enter the **smaller** of: two-thirds (⅔) of gross nonfarm income[4] (not less than zero) **or** the amount on line 16. Also include this amount on line 4b above	**17**	

[1] From Sch. F, line 11, and Sch. K-1 (Form 1065), box 14, code B.

[2] From Sch. F, line 36, and Sch. K-1 (Form 1065), box 14, code A.

[3] From Sch. C, line 31; Sch. C-EZ, line 3; Sch. K-1 (Form 1065), box 14, code A; and Sch. K-1 (Form 1065-B), box 9, code J1.

[4] From Sch. C, line 7; Sch. C-EZ, line 1; Sch. K-1 (Form 1065), box 14, code C; and Sch. K-1 (Form 1065-B), box 9, code J2.

Schedule SE (Form 1040) 2006

FIGURE 10-1.

(Continued)

There will be instances in which the designer will wish to legally protect these design ideas so that they cannot be duplicated or copied without permission and fair compensation. In some cases, the client may also wish that these designs not be duplicated.

The section of law that deals with the protection of these creative achievements that are protected by copyright, trademark, or patent is called *intellectual property law* and is governed primarily by federal statutes. Creative work such as design drawings, fine art, CD-ROMs and DVDs, photography, furniture designs, and writings such as this textbook are examples of items that are considered intellectual property because they are essentially intangible.

Copyright is the method by which written, artistic, and graphic forms of intellectual property are legally protected. A *trademark* protects words and/or symbols specific to a person or a business that are very creative and out of the ordinary. Distinctive names, logos, packaging, and the like are commonly registered as trademarks. A design firm's logo could be considered a trademark if it were distinctive and not used by any other business. If a designer wishes to protect the original design of a piece of furniture, he or she would seek protection under *patent* law. The process of obtaining a patent is quite complex. Readers who may want information on this process are urged to contact the U.S. Patent Office or to discuss the process with an intellectual property attorney. This section focuses on copyright protection, since most of what an interior designer creates can be copyrighted.

The actual law that protects copyright at this time is the Federal Copyright Act of 1976. The rights to a copyright last for a substantial period of time. Any written or graphic work that was created on or after January 1, 1978, is protected by copyright for the life of the author or designer, plus 70 years for an individual. If the work was created by an employee, the copyright, which belongs to the employer, lasts for 95 years from the date of publication or 120 years from the date of creation, whichever comes first. The difference between works created as an individual and as an employee is discussed later in this section.

The design idea itself is not what can be copyrighted. It is the expression of the idea as a written, graphic, or artistic work that is protected. In other words, the idea must become a physical, tangible form such as a floor plan, a sketch, or the written word before it is something that can be copyrighted. That expression must be in some way original as well, but it does not have to be unique. The tangible medium does not have to be in final form for copyright protection to exist. It would include a designer's scribbled floor plan on a napkin when the designer and client met about the project. Thus, floor plans for a prototype fast-food restaurant would be copyrightable, but the idea for that restaurant would not be. The idea for a custom-made dining room table is not eligible for a patent or copyright protection until the design of that table has been put down on paper.

The copyright begins at the moment at which the interior designer begins the act of completing the work. This means that the moment the interior designer begins drafting the working drawings, sketches, or specifications, the right to legally protect the work begins. Thus, common law provides the creator of an artistic work automatic protection—to a limited degree.

If the work is distributed—let us say that you provided a drawing or sketch to your client—without any copyright notice protection, then the work is considered to be in the public domain and can be used by anyone in any way without compensation to the creator. The work must bear a copyright notification prior to its being "published" (distributed) and must be registered with the copyright office in order to receive full, legal statutory protection.

So what exactly is a copyright "notice" and "publication"?

Copyright notification must contain the following elements:

1. The word *copyright*, or the abbreviation *copr*, and the copyright symbol (©)
2. The year of publication
3. The name of the copyright claimant for the copyright

For example, on a set of drawings, the notice should look like this: "Copyright © by Tracy & Jones Interiors, 2006." Or for a sole practitioner it might read: "Copyright © by Fraser McKain, 2007."

Placing these three elements on a drawing, sample board, or specification sheet does not fully protect and begin copyright. Notice serves to protect what the claimant publishes. Remember that copyright begins at the moment of creation. For full protection under the law, the creator must also register the copyright with the United States Copyright Office. A form can be obtained online at www.copyright.gov. There is a fee for registration. Please see the insert that provides additional information on registering a copyright.

Copyright Registration

The material within the chapter discusses the importance of including a copyright notification on drawings and written material the designer or firm wishes to protect. The copyright notification itself, however, does not provide complete legal protection. The proposed copyrighted materials must be registered with the federal government in order for the interior designer to be able to file suit in a federal district court for copyright infringement. To register a copyrightable item, the creator must obtain the proper forms from the copyright office. The "VA" form is used for graphic works, and the "TX" form is used for books, articles, and other general written works. The best way to obtain information and forms is to contact the copyright office at www.loc.gov/copyright. Note that this office is within the Library of Congress. Forms can be downloaded from the Internet. For your information, a copy of the TX and VA registration forms are included on the CD as items 10-5 and 10-6.

An original form, not a photocopy of the form, must be accompanied by one copy of the work if the work is unpublished and by two copies of the work if it has already been published. Instructions on the Web site inform you how to do this. The copy of the work must be a "best-edition" copy. Since originals cannot be readily submitted, properly prepared photocopies, photographs of the work, or plots of floor plans may suffice. What constitutes a best-edition copy, however, is up to the copyright office. A fee to process the copyright is also required.

It is not necessary to send each project under a separate copyright form. A bulk of work, called a collection, may be submitted at one time. A collection can constitute any work that has been created within the same year, as long as all the work is of the same basic type and falls under the same form.

For full statutory and actual damages to be awarded, registration must exist either prior to the work's being published or under specific circumstances. If the work is registered within three months of first publication, the copyright holder is still able to claim statutory and actual damages. If the work is registered up to five years of first publication, there is a presumption of a valid copyright. After five years, the claimant has to prove that he or she is the original author. In these example cases, the copyright claimant may receive actual damages but not statutory damages or attorney's fees and costs.

Statutory damages refer to amounts determined by the court for each infringement. Actual damages relate to damages that the copyright holder suffers as a result of the infringement. Actual damages may mean payment of design fees, profits the designer may have lost, and profits the infringer may have made by the infringement.

Publication occurs when the creator has somehow distributed the work to others for review without restriction of use by the creator. It does not mean that the work has been published by a publishing house. For example, if an interior designer gives a floor plan to a client for his or her review, the floor plan has been published. Providing to the client or to others copies of the work for the purpose of display constitutes publication. To protect the designer's ideas, those plans and copies should include a copyright notice.

Copyright ownership is different for individuals who are employees. When the design work is created by an employee of a design firm, the copyright belongs to the employer, not the employee under the concept of "work for hire" and shop right. *Shop right* is a concept that means that the employer holds the exclusive rights to anything that the employee produces as part of his or her normal work expectations. Any design that has been created by an employee as part of the normal responsibilities of the employee and for clients of the employer belongs to the employer, not the employee. Those drawings are also sometimes called *work product*, since the work is a product of the employer even though they are actually produced by an employee. Legally and ethically, the employee cannot take the project work he or she has done as an employee and show it as his or her own without also showing that the work was created as an employee. Taking work you have done as an employee and showing it as your own without permission of the employer is a legal and ethical matter.

As was mentioned earlier in the chapter, sometimes a firm will hire an independent contractor to produce certain work for the design firm. For example, Ann—an independent contractor, not an employee—was hired by Jones Interiors to prepare computer drawings for a project. The hiring firm would own the work only if the independent contractor—Ann—signed an agreement that the drawings are "works for hire." Otherwise, the independent contract—the creator of the finished floor plan—retains ownership. The definition of an independent contractor is a very important issue, and the distinctions between an individual defined as an employee and an independent contractor are discussed in Chapter 15.

Interior designers frequently hire photographers to shoot photos of completed projects. The interior designer wishes to use those photos in some sort of marketing effort. Of course, the interior designer has paid the photographer for taking the pictures, but who owns the rights to using the photos? The answer to this question depends on the contract between the designer and the photographer. The photographer is an independent contractor and as such owns the images taken for the designer unless the photographer's contract has specifically stated that he or she has given up his or her rights. If the photographer has not given up rights in whole or part, the interior designer must obtain permission (and may have to pay a fee) for each use of any of those photos. The photographer's contract can assign certain rights of use to the interior designer as part of the fee, but this generally does not include ownership. Interior designers need to negotiate the use and rights to photos taken of their projects so that they are legally using images taken by someone else.

What if the employee creates an item that can be patented? The shop right doctrine applied to patents says that employers hold a nonexclusive free license to any creation or invention of tangible products an employee designs that result as a part of employment.[2] "The theory is that because such inventions are developed with the employer's funds or property, the employer should at least be able to use them."[3] The employee is still the patent holder, however. An example might be a situation in which an interior designer creates a software program that provides a new way to handle the firm's data processing, and the program is, for some reason, sold to a local software company. If the program is created on company time, the employer has an interest in using the program without paying royalties to the employee.

This distinction is important because designers, being creative and thoughtful people, often dabble in works that stretch their job responsibilities in different ways. Generally, designs created on the employee's own time, using his or her own materials and facilities, belong to the employee, unless there is a statement to the contrary in an employment agreement.

Another important component of copyright is unauthorized use of materials that have a copyright attached. This unauthorized use of copyrighted materials is called *infringement*. This can best be explained with a few examples. Michael Smith Interiors has prepared a set of working drawings for the interior of a prototype fast-food restaurant in a specific location. The drawings contain a copyright notice. If the owner of the fast-food restaurant later duplicates the restaurant using those plans in another location without consent and compensation to the design firm, the restaurant owner has infringed on the copyright. In another example, George prepares drawings for a custom table and hires a cabinetmaker to build one table. The drawings provided to the cabinetmaker had the proper notices concerning copyright, but the designer has not patented the table drawings. The cabinetmaker not only produces the table for the interior designer but also begins to produce the design for his or her own clients. Since the plans were provided to the cabinetmaker for the exclusive use of producing one table, the cabinetmaker has infringed on the designer's ownership of the design by producing additional copies of the table without the designer's permission.

On the other side of this issue, infringement also occurs if a designer uses the design created by someone else to create a "custom-made" piece of furniture. Even making very small changes, such as using a different finish, can be construed as infringement. Assuming the original designer copyrighted or even obtained a patent on the design, then the second interior designer has infringed on the original designer's copyright when he or she "knocks off" or imitates the original design. Of course, this is not legal and is not ethical. Numerous court cases have been heard over the last several years about just such an issue. The Foundation for Design Integrity (FDI) represents numerous manufacturers and designers and aids them in the protection of their product designs and litigation for design infringement by other designers. The mission for the FDI is as follows:

> The Foundation for Design Integrity honors those who conceive, design, engineer and develop innovative new products for the Interior and Architectural Design Community and their clients. By educating and informing the industry, and the public, about the importance of original design, FDI fosters integrity in the specification and procurement of interior and architectural products. FDI helps set standards, protects original design and serves as the voice of the industry.[4]

The address for this organization can be found in the Internet Resources.

Placing a copyright notice on design documents is needed for legal protection. In addition, interior designers should include a clause in their design contract concerning copyright and ownership of documents. It has been upheld in court that work commissioned by a client from a designer belongs to the designer or company, even if there are no clauses in the design contract that gives ownership to the designer or company. Full statutory protection, however, is afforded only when the work contains the proper notification and meets registration and publication requirements.

An interior designer or firm may not always be concerned about copyrighting all the design documents that leave the office. Depending on the practice and projects, there may be instances in which certain projects or parts of projects would require this protection. Knowing how to prepare the documents for legal protection is very important. Including a clause in the design contract related to "design ownership" or "copyright permission" would also aid in legally protecting the designer.

SUMMARY

Starting an interior design business of any kind is an exciting and challenging endeavor. Many decisions have to be made, and many different kinds of documents or forms must be filed with appropriate jurisdictions. Some filings like income tax and reporting of sales taxes collected are ongoing filings that the firm must prepare quarterly. The business owner must be willing to complete this paper work in order to not run afoul of jurisdictional authorities.

There are also specialized filings or documents necessary in the practice of interior design. Those discussed were interior design title registration or licensure, contractor's licenses, and copyright registration of design ideas. One or more of these specialized filings affect almost all interior design practices in some way.

Whether you are a professional who is considering opening your own practice or a student, you should now be able to see that there is much work involved beyond design skill and ability in establishing a practice. The next chapter brings all of this research and decision making to a conclusion with the development of a business plan.

REFERENCES

1. Nolo, January 2006, www.nolo.com/article.cfm.

2. Garner, 1999, p. 1384.

3. Elias, 1999, p. 288.

4. Web site for Foundation of Design Integrity, www.ffdi.org as of January, 2006.

Preparing the Business Plan

Key Terms and Concepts

These key terms and concepts are important to material in this chapter. Many of these terms will be utilized in other chapters as well. Be sure you understand these items as you read this chapter.

Terms and Concepts

Mission statement	Building standards
Business plan	Build-out allowance
Pro forma	Demising wall
Zoning restrictions	Rentable area
Zoning variance	Trade fixtures
Conditions, covenants, and restrictions (CCRs)	Tenant improvements
	Tenant work letter
"As is"	Inventory

Critical Issues

After completing this chapter you should be able to:

▓ Explain the importance of a mission statement.

▓ Discuss the purpose and use of a business plan for a new practice.

▓ Discuss the common parts of a business plan and their purpose.

▓ Define a fictitious interior design business using the section "Define Your Business" in Table 11-1.

▓ Compare the advantages and disadvantages of operating a practice from a home office to one located in a commercial site.

▓ Discuss the advantages and disadvantages of being a sole practitioner.

Whether the business is entered into alone or with several partners or co-owners, many critical decisions must be made. A key aid in making those decisions is by creating a written business plan before the doors are opened. Evaluating the business idea through a business plan helps the entrepreneur determine how feasible the idea might be. Interior design practice is more

TABLE 11-1.

A Questionnaire to Help the Potential Business Owner Define the Business Idea

Carefully answer these questions in order to help you define your overall business idea. Remember to be as specific as possible in your responses. The information from this questionnaire can be used to develop your business plan.

Have you clarified your design and business skills? (If you will have partners, answer these questions for them as well.)

What experience do you have in interior design, architecture, and/or construction?

What experience do you have in sales and marketing?

What experience do you have in managing other individuals?

What business experience or knowledge do you have?

Define your business.

What services (exactly) will you offer initially?

Will you sell products?

Do you plan to have inventory?

How will you price your services (fee methods)?

How will you price the products you sell?

How will you receive and deliver goods to clients?

Have you considered what language will go into design contracts?

Do you know who your customers will be?

How many potential customers are in your business area?

How many of these customers do you think you can attract?

Will your customers perceive your prices as competitive?

Will your customers see a difference in your services from your competition?

What income group will your business appeal to?

What kind of finances will be required to start your business?

What business licenses will be required? Cost?

Are you going to start your business at home? Is this legally possible in your community?

If you are going to have your business in a commercial space, have you investigated rental costs?

What kind of equipment and furniture will be necessary to start your business? What is the estimated cost of purchase?

What are the possibilities to lease these items?

What kind of income are you seeking for yourself for the first year? Use this (along with estimated expenses) to determine how much revenue you will need to generate monthly. Is this possible, considering your business idea, number of potential customers, and competition?

Have you researched the competition?

Who are your main competitors?

How many other firms like yours exist within two miles?

How many other firms like yours exist within your business area?

What can you do that your competition is not already doing?

Do you know how much your competition charges for its services/products?

Why would your customers buy from you rather than an existing competitor?

How will clients find out about your business?

Will you do mass mailings?

Will you use advertising? What kind and in what media?

Are you going to develop marketing tools, such as a brochure?

Have you considered the design of your letterhead and other business stationery?

than creating a library, finding sources, and obtaining a few initial clients. As the previous chapters have indicated, there is much that should be thought out in starting any type of business, regardless of the specialty or size of the practice.

Merely obtaining a degree of any kind in interior design and having some funds to start the practice does not automatically mean success. According to the U.S. Small Business Administration, the lack of experience and insufficient capital are two of the biggest reasons that new small businesses fail.[1] Another reason that businesses fail is the lack of a plan that will help the owner through those early months and years of trying to find clients, and funds to keep the business in operation. Businesses also fail because the services the owner wishes to provide are unwanted or there are too few potential customers in the area.

Is it possible to start a design practice without a thorough business plan? Of course it is. However, a plan helps the budding business owner to clearly consider the business idea. A plan helps the entrepreneur establish such things as which design services will be offered, how many customers might potentially be interested in those services, and the amount of financial resources that will be necessary until revenue starts coming in.

Anyone who might consider starting a design practice needs to do serious research, thinking, and planning. Business skills and experience must be matched to the type of clients one chooses to pursue. In addition, the potential business owner must also evaluate his or her motivation for starting a design practice. Planning helps the potential business owner see if the idea is feasible and what will be required to make it work. It provides an operational tool for the owner to handle potential problems with thought rather than by pure gut reaction. A business plan does not guarantee success. A business succeeds through an enormous amount of hard work and dedication by the owner to make the practice viable.

The chapters in Part III have provided information to help the prospective entrepreneur and student understand what types of information should be researched in order to plan a new interior design practice. Other chapters in this text will provide information on specific operational activities and issues regarding the professional practice of interior design.

This chapter looks in detail at the steps that need to be taken in developing the research material required to prepare a business plan and provides a general outline for the business plan. It also includes information on operational topics in starting up a practice, including location, the design library, and inventory issues.

WHAT'S YOUR MISSION?

In business parlance, a business's mission is its purpose and direction. It is the reason for its existence. "That's easy," one might say. "To provide interior design services to residential clients." Yes, that can be and is the mission of thousands of businesses although most business consultants would say that is hardly a sufficient mission statement. Clarifying a mission helps the business determine how it is different from the dozens, maybe even hundreds, of other businesses that provide interior design services to residential clients in the same area.

Any size and type of interior design practice can benefit from defining its mission. It does not matter that the firm is a sole practitioner working with clients out of a home office or a large multifaceted design firm. In order to survive for many years, the new firm must know what makes it different from all the others.

Thus, a mission helps the owner define the purpose of the business and the services that will be offered in order to help create a positive start-up.

Taking the time to define a design firm's purpose and direction is a positive practice strategy. Careful consideration of a mission helps a firm know where it is trying to go in the long run. It will also help the owner with many decisions as the business is organized. A good starting point is to answer the questions in Table 11-1 to help the interior designer appraise the fundamental business idea. When this has been completed, it will be easier to create a draft of the business's mission statement. A worksheet of Table 11-1 is included on the CD as Item 11-1.

The *mission statement* is a philosophical statement that provides a concise explanation of a firm's direction and purposes and why it exists. The mission statement is a clear definition of the business and helps owners and employees realize what unique qualities the business brings to prospective clients. Defining the business with a mission statement helps the prospective owner with marketing decisions, operational choices, hiring employees, financing, and many other management issues along the way. For example, financing choices becomes easier when a clear picture of the purpose and direction of the firm has been established.

A mission statement generally contains information such as a description of the business, a description of its customers, the services and products offered, and the geographic area served; however, it does not always contain all these items. It does not have to be long, and it commonly consists of only a few sentences. Figure 11-1 is an example that is very simple and straightforward.

A mission statement obviously might change through the life of the company. Examining and redefining the company mission statement is part of the ongoing strategic planning process for the future of the interior design firm presented in Chapter 13.

THE BUSINESS PLAN

What is a business plan? A *business plan* is a detailed definition of a business idea and explains how the business of this potential company will be executed. The business plan is prepared to provide substantive thought as to what the business

---

Mission Statement

We create architecture
sensitive to people and place.

Vision Statement

We are a team of professionals with
unique talents, enriched through rewarding
architecture, recognized for
excellence and innovation.

Knoell & Quidort Architects, Phoenix, Arizona

FIGURE 11-1.

A sample mission statement. (Reproduced with permission, Knoell & Quidort Architects, Phoenix, AZ.)

is all about and how it is going to operate. Some new businesses will need financing beyond what the potential owner can obtain from savings. The business plan may well be the key to obtaining necessary funding from banks or other investors.

A business plan provides the owner a far greater chance of success in the immediate future and for the long duration. Time and time again, it has been shown that a business that starts with a detailed plan has a greater chance of succeeding than one without a plan. Although preparing a business plan will not guarantee success, the process of thinking the business through will help the prospective owner face the realities of starting a business. A plan, if it is thoroughly done, also provides an opportunity to anticipate problems and to avoid them, if possible—or at least to know how to cope with them as they arise. Evaluating and planning the services to be offered, researching the customer base, determining operational procedures, and clarifying financing help the prospective business owner map a strategy for the business's start-up.

Business owners who neglect to create a plan before the doors open often find themselves immersed in the challenges of running the business. They never seem to get around to planning how to effectively manage business operations. For many, handling the operations becomes a burden, requiring more and more time away from the reason they started the business in the first place—getting to do interior design. Avoiding taking care of one or the other of these facets always impacts the other. Although a plan will not eliminate problems, it helps the business owner understand what kind of assistance might be needed and how to better manage the whole of the business venture.

Preparing a business plan takes time. A prospective business owner should realize that it may take weeks or even months to prepare it, depending on how much time can be devoted to research and writing it. If it is necessary to obtain outside financing from a bank or investors, more information will be needed, perhaps requiring additional time for the research and writing of a plan. Advice from an attorney, accountant, banker, or consultant could be needed as well. Some of the decisions about how to structure the business can be made easier with advice from these types of professionals.

Understand that the business plan is a personal expression of what the owner feels the firm is all about and how he or she hopes it will grow. Once completed, the business plan helps the prospective owner determine if the idea is realistic and feasible in order to reach the goal of having his or her own practice. In developing a business plan, the owner should be setting goals and objectives of the firm for the immediate future. Having goals, which can be measured by the firm's performance, can help the owner determine what is going well and what needs to be looked at to get back on track.

One more important point is that a business plan should not be considered a static, carved-in-concrete business tool. Once the plan is completed and the doors open, new opportunities might occur that are outside the original plan. The business owner certainly needs to look at opportunities. The business plan helps him or her determine if the opportunity is truly an opportunity for the good of the design practice. This aspect is why a design practice owner should never assume once the plan is finished, that's it. Ongoing planning called strategic planning—discussed in Chapter 13—is important to grow a business.

An important ingredient of all business plans is research. The items in Table 11-2 provide a suggested sequence in which the research should be conducted to help prepare the sections shown in the outline. A typical outline is shown in Table 11-3, and it details the subject content of a well-thought-out business plan. As the reader can see from Table 11-2, research in areas of skills and abilities, the marketplace, and operational considerations, such as pricing,

TABLE 11-2.

Information to Research for Preparing a Business Plan

1. Analyze personal abilities and interests related to owning an interior design business.
2. Carefully consider the purpose and mission of the business, who prospective customers might be, and why the business is being started.
3. Develop a personal income plan that ensures payment of all personal expenses during the first year of the life of the business.
4. If you have hired employees or anticipate hiring additional employees, analyze operational needs and their required skills.
5. Analyze the potential market for the firm's services. Do not forget to research existing competition.
6. Draft a marketing plan that includes the aspect of the market that the firm will address. Determine what services the firm will offer, target market, pricing policies, and considerations for advertising and/or promotional activities.
7. Determine which type of business formation will be used: a sole proprietorship, a partnership, a form of corporation, or possibly some other legal form.
8. Determine legal responsibilities and tax obligations. Consult with an attorney concerning contracts and liabilities, an accountant concerning record keeping, and an insurance representative regarding insurance obligations.
9. Estimate how much capital will be required to "open the doors." Estimate the first year's expenses. Determine sources of initial capital.
10. Develop a financial plan and income projections. Include projected balance sheets, income statements, and cash flow forecasts.
11. Develop a concept of the firm's image: appearance of letterhead, business cards, exteriors of delivery trucks, title blocks for drawing paper, and so on.
12. Prepare an organizational plan that includes projected personnel needs, job descriptions, employee benefits, and purchasing procedures.
13. If the firm will engage in retail selling of inventoried goods, develop an inventory plan of what will be purchased, when it will be purchased, and where it will be stored.
14. Produce the business plan.

expected capital required, and projected financial planning, must be thoroughly investigated and considered.

We discussed in the previous chapter how important it is to understand personal motivations when contemplating starting a design practice. Naturally, skills and abilities are critical to the practitioner who desires a practice. Yet as we have already pointed out, there are many other issues that the prospective business owner must consider and plan. Table 11-4 provides a list of questions that the prospective owner must answer about the proposed organizational structure of the new business, which will help in the research for the business plan. Providing answers to these questions before the doors are opened will go a long way to allowing those figurative or literal doors to remain open for years to come. The items in Table 11-4 will be of valuable help the prospective business owner research other important information needed to complete a business plan.

START-UP COSTS

Analyzing the financial needs and revenue expectations of the business is an important consideration for the prospective business owner when developing a business plan. In Chapter 7, we addressed the evaluation of personal financial risk. Knowing the amount of financial resources needed to pay for personal living expenses during a business start-up is only one critical consideration in planning

TABLE 11-3.

Business Plan Outline

I. Business summary
   A. Provide name of owner or board of directors.
   B. Give location of business.
   C. Identify type of business formation (legal structure).
   D. Describe business, including types of services to be performed.
   E. Provide a summary of the owner's and/or manager's expertise in running the business.

II. Market research
   A. Describe how the information concerning the business was obtained.
   B. Describe the need for the firm's services in the community; include the number of potential clients.
   C. Describe as much as possible the known competition.
   D. Detail existing sales for this kind of firm in the community; might be available from the local chamber of commerce.
   E. Describe any industry or local trends that might affect the success of the projected business.

III. Marketing plan
   A. Detail what portions of the market the business will address.
   B. Describe what services the business will offer; may be detailed enough to explain how sample boards will be done.
   C. Determine how services and/or products will be priced.
   D. If a warehouse/delivery service is used, determine how these charges will be passed on to clients.
   E. Outline what kinds of advertising and promotional activities will support the business.
   F. Describe any problems concerning expected seasonal business, if applicable.

IV. Operational plan
   A. Provide the organizational structure of the business.
   B. Analyze hiring of personnel and job descriptions.
   C. Describe how records will be kept and controlled.
   D. Analyze employee benefits.
   E. Project dealings with suppliers, delivery people, and subcontractors.
   F. Frame customer relations.
   G. Project personnel needs.

V. Financial information
   A. Project initial capital and first-year estimates for keeping the business operating; detail how the money will be spent.
   B. Estimate additional revenue (monthly) beyond break-even points.
   C. Provide month-by-month, projected profit-and-loss statements.
   D. Decide on accounting practices that will be used, especially those related to depreciation, leasing, and inventories.
   E. Provide a beginning balance sheet.
   F. Explain how projections were made.
   G. Provide any additional information required of a corporation.

a new business. In this part of the chapter, we will look at the issue of start-up expenses.

The kinds of financial needs of a design practice will be similar regardless of the location of the business or type of practice. Table 11-5 is a list of start-up expenses composed of items that are one-time and ongoing expenses. The

TABLE 11-4.

Key Questions to Ask about the Organizational Structure of a Business Start-up.

Select a legal structure (see Chapter 9).

Sole proprietorship?
Partnership?
Corporation?
Limited liability company?

What licenses are required (see Chapter 10)?

Interior design registration?
Contractor's license?
Business licenses?
Transaction privilege tax license?

Select the name of the business (see Chapter 10).

Use your own name?
Use a fictitious name?

How will the business be financed for the first year (see Chapters 5 and 8)?

Personal investment by owner(s)?
Investments by friends or relatives?
Will loans be required?
Have an estimated cash flow and pro forma income statement been prepared for the first year?
Have personal living expenses for the first year been estimated?
Have start-up costs and expenses for the first year been estimated?

Where will the business be located (see Chapters 10 and 11)?

In a residence (will this violate zoning laws)?
In a commercial site?
Will customers easily be able to find the business location?
Can the business location (home or commercial site) easily be modified to meet your needs?
Will you rent or lease space?

Will the business have employees other than the owner(s) (see Chapters 10, 14, and 15)?

Are any federal or state filings required?
What type of benefits will be provided to employees?
What kind of equipment will be provided for employees to do their jobs?
How will employees be recruited?

How will business financial records be maintained (see Chapters 16 and 17)?

What accounting bases will be used?
Who will do the daily bookkeeping?
Who will keep payroll and tax records?
Who will prepare any formal accounting records that are required?

Insurance requirements (see Chapter 8)

What kinds of insurance are needed initially?

How will the business be promoted and clients obtained (see Chapters 18, 19, and 20)?

Do you have a marketing plan?
Do you know who your target clients are?
What marketing tools (such as a brochure or Web site) will be needed?
Will you market to clients only close to your business location?

Have you thought about how fees will be set (see Chapter 23 and 25)?

Will services only be provided, or will merchandise also be sold?
On what basis will fees be set?
How will fees be set?
Will compensation requirements be considered using more than one method?
Are you comfortable in quoting more than one fee method?
Do you know how to price any merchandise you purchase for clients?

Will design contracts or letters of agreement be used (see Chapter 24)?

What needs to be in a contract for it to be legally binding?
Have possible clauses been discussed with an attorney?
Will clients be billed for services covered in a design contract?
Will reimbursable expenses be billed?

Will the business require inventory (see Chapter 11)?

What will the initial inventory consist of and where will it be displayed and/or stored?
How will the purchase of initial inventory be financed?

one-time expenses essentially required at start-up include such things as legal fees and other business filing fees; start-up promotional items like advertising or mailings; sellable inventory, if any; utility deposits; and purchase of equipment and furniture for the office. Certain start-up expenses become ongoing overhead expenses. Items such as stationery, office supplies, telephone and fax charges, insurance, and promotional activities will be part of the overhead of the company. A third group of expenses that need to be considered are those that are ongoing yet are not necessarily needed at the initial start-up of the business. Items such as owner's salary or draw, inventory (unless you open with inventory), payroll for assistants, and interest on loans and credit cards are examples. Worksheets have been included to help create an estimate of start-up and on-going business expenses that should be budgeted for a potential new practice. They are shown as Items 11-2 and 11-3 on the CD.

Developing an outline of business expenses as discussed in this section can be sufficient for a sole proprietorship that will not need any outside financing for the first year. However, a firm that will require outside financing will have to pay more detailed attention to the part of the business plan concerning finances. Of course, anyone planning a new business would benefit from preparing detailed financial projections. Documents that are useful in this case are the pro forma income statement and other accounting reports. The business owner's accountant might help prepare any of these documents. In business terms, *pro forma* means a projection. It can also mean in advance. So, a pro forma income statement is one that has been created with projected numbers instead of actual numbers or in advance of actual numbers.

The basis of a pro forma income statement (also called a profit and loss statement, or P&L) is any known numbers, such as expected overhead expenses

TABLE 11-5.

Common Start-up Expenses for a Typical Interior Design Firm.

Initial, essential one-time expenses:

Office furniture (desks, files, shelves, etc.)

Office equipment (computer, printer, copy machine, and other electronic equipment)

Remodeling of office/studio space

Initial inventory (if any)

Utility and lease deposits (for commercial location)

Licenses and permits

Catalogs, samples, and so forth

Miscellaneous office equipment (coffee maker, radio, small refrigerator, etc.)

Ongoing expenses needed at start-up:

Stationery

Utilities

Phone and fax

Internet provider

Drawing supplies

General office supplies

Insurance premiums—related to the practice of interior design

Marketing materials, such as brochures, direct-mail items, and so forth

Possible consultant fees, such as accountant, attorney, insurance agent

Cleaning and janitorial fees

Transportation

Additional items or expenses that may be needed to initiate a design practice, as required.

---

like rent and utilities. If you are unfamiliar with overhead expenses, it would be helpful for you to read that section of Chapter 16 before working on this section of the business plan. Assumptions and "best guesses" as to what might happen in the future are factored in to produce the numbers on the pro forma income statement. People more often overestimate than underestimate the projected revenue for a business. The designer utilizing a pro forma statement must do some real homework on such things as the current and potential future economic situation, inflation, and changes in expenses.

By estimating the total amount of start-up and ongoing business expenses for one year, the prospective business owner will have an estimate of the minimum amount of revenue needed for the year. When the amount of revenue collected in a year just matches the amount of expenses estimated for the year, the firm has only reached a break-even point. At this point, the firm is neither making nor losing money and thus has experienced no profits.

The actual writing of the business plan can begin after the research has been done or while this process is ongoing. There is no surefire way to prepare a business plan, as the numerous books on the topic testify. A lender will be looking for certain kinds of information that you might not need if you are not seeking a loan. Software programs exist to also take the prospective owner through the business plan process. Many of the books listed in the References at the end of the book provide several outlines of business plans. Table 11-3 shows a common suggested outline. A sample business plan has been included on the CD as Item 11-4. This sample will help you understand a more complete version of a business plan.

BUSINESS LOCATION

Where the interior design practice is located is another of the many decisions included in business planning. Even though operating a business from a home office location continues to be an option by many designers, clients want to know they are dealing with a business professional. The location of the business can definitely have an impact on potential clients' opinion of the design professional. "It is often hard to be taken seriously when your office is at home, because clients think it's just a hobby rather than a business," says one Arizona sole practitioner. Determining which location is the best—at home, in a commercial office building, or in a retail center of some sort—depends on many factors, including the type of services that will be offered, the firm's expected client base, and available funds for start-up expenses.

Let's start by first looking at issues concerning a home office. It is economical, since no additional rent is required. With the many electronic resources available, having a home office is also desirable for many business owners. For example, floor plans can be transmitted via the Internet, product searches can be done using Web sites, and even teleconferencing can take place from a home office. In addition, the federal government has been more lenient in allowing tax deductions for a home office. However, extra record keeping is needed on certain expenses related to the home office and the residence in general. The home office worker's accountant should be consulted about using the tax deduction for home office space.

Another important consideration is that most home owner's insurance will not cover any furniture and equipment used in the home for business purposes without the addition of a special insurance rider. The designer needs to confirm what will happen to office equipment that will be used in the home in the case of theft or fire, in order to ensure that the business will not suffer irreparable harm should something like this happen.

There are two considerations that might make a home office location impossible. Cities have certain *zoning restrictions* as to where businesses may operate. This is done to keep residential neighborhoods quiet and safe for families and to keep commercial and industrial facilities in restricted areas. Single-family dwellings are zoned R-1 in most communities, and it is expected that the primary use of the land will be for homes. Any business may be restricted as to what it can do in an area that has been zoned R-1. Regardless of the huge increase in the number of home-based businesses and those who are working at least part-time from home, cities remain earnest in their enforcement of zoning restrictions.

Residential areas zoned R-1, which permit home-based businesses, generally do not permit employees to work at the home office location. Delivery trucks arriving at the residence and visits of clients to the home generally result in neighbors complaining to the city that the designer is operating a business in a residentially zoned area. The designer may be liable to pay a fine and relocate the business. In some cases, it may be possible to apply for a zoning variance. The *zoning variance* allows the business to operate legally in the residentially zoned area. A request for a zoning variance usually requires notification of neighbors and a hearing before the zoning commission. It is best that the owner check with the local zoning office before applying for a city business license.

Home-based businesses are also affected by home owner's associations' restrictions and covenants. *Conditions, covenants, and restrictions* (CCRs) are specific regulations for condominiums, townhouses, and even single-family dwellings in planned communities. Even if the city allows a home-based

TABLE 11-6.

Home Office Location

Locating the design practice at a home office has many economic advantages. It also has challenges in terms of operating the business in a professional manner.

Location of home office:

- A studio with its own private entrance
- Build an addition to the house—perhaps enclose the garage
- Dedicated room within the house

Operational issues:

- Privacy for telephone calls and faxes
- Separate business telephone line
- Minimal family background noise
- Privacy for concentrated work
- Where will meetings with clients take place?

Other considerations:

- Storage space for sample books and binders
- Will CCRs prohibit small deliveries for items such as fabric?
- Insurance for business activities conducted from home
- What will happen when an assistant is needed?
- Will you be able to create the appropriate business image from a home office?

Note: that this is not an all-inclusive list. Other issues not discussed in the chapter or on this list may impact the practice.

business, CCRs may prohibit even a quiet business, such as an interior design practice, from working out of a home. Other issues concerning a home office are listed in Table 11-6.

A business office that is located in a commercially zoned part of town gives an impression of professionalism required by many clients. The location might be influenced by the target client market. For example, a design firm that seeks primarily the office corporate client often locates in the downtown business district. Residential design studios are often located near retail stores for furniture, carpet, lighting, and the like. This relationship could bring a client to the designer when he or she visits these other establishments. A residential practice that has a small showroom for retail sales may want to locate in a shopping area where the design firm's potential customers shop.

Interior designers locate in low-rise office complexes, where street entry and visibility are available. Some locate in mixed-use centers with other professionals, like accountants and operators of small retail stores of various kinds. Locating near peer groups and related professionals should be a primary consideration when the designer is selecting a commercial location. Some interior designers find this conducive to business, while others feel it is not a good idea to be located near potential competitors.

Naturally, an office in a commercial location has added expenses. The amount of the rent, the terms of the lease, and how much of the utilities, insurance, and maintenance costs will be covered by the landlord are important factors to consider. The amount of rent is directly related to the square-foot amount of space taken by the business; thus, careful planning of that space

TABLE 11-7.

Selected Leasing Terminology

As is. Space is rented without any changes to the interior.

Building standards. Interior finishes provided by the landlord without charge to the tenant.

Build-out allowance. Landlord provides a dollar amount per square foot to build partitions and to install basic mechanical systems such as lighting fixtures and provide basic architectural finishes.

Demising wall. A partition that divides one tenant space from another. Each tenant pays for one-half the thickness of the wall.

Rentable area. The total amount of space required by the tenant on which the rent dollar amount (usually by the square foot) will be calculated.

Tenant improvements. Upgrades to a leased space paid for by the tenant.

Tenant work letter. A supplemental contract that details how the space will be finished by the landlord and what will be provided by the tenant.

Trade fixtures. Items attached to the rented space by the tenant. Depending on the lease, they can be removed if no damage is done to the structure.

is needed before looking for rental space. If there is too little space, the office/ studio will become quickly cluttered and will look unprofessional. Too big a space requires greater overhead expenses, possibly draining away revenues from other needs.

In a commercial space, the interior design practice owner will negotiate with the landlord concerning improvements to the space to suit the firm's needs. The amount of allowance for interior partitions and improvements that will be covered by the landlord is important. Some locations do not provide for much more than very basic painting, floor covering, and drop-in ceiling fixtures. If the allowances are minimal, the interior designer must decide to pay for *tenant improvements* (also called leasehold improvements) out of his or her own pocket. Everything that is done to the space by the landlord and tenant should be spelled out in the *tenant work letter* (also referred to as a building standard work letter). Tenant improvements are expenses that can be deducted in all likelihood, but they are not recovered upon vacating. A few additional terms related to renting commercial space are provided in Table 11-7.

What Would You Do?

Julie had been working as a designer at a residential furniture store for seven years. She had many satisfied clients and had also won a design award recently. Julie decided to start her own studio and spent a few months writing a business plan and budget before finally giving notice to her employer.

She has been open for business, located in a small executive office suite location. Julie was fortunate in that a few of her previous clients have come over to her business because they liked Julie's work very much. One of those clients had signed an agreement for the redesign of the client's living room two months after she left the employer.

The client, Mr. Griffin, has become irritated with Julie because of the high prices for some of the items specified by Julie and signed for by Mrs. Griffin. The plans for the living room were reviewed by Mr. and Mrs. Griffin but none of the sales agreements were signed until a few weeks later. Mrs. Griffin signed the sales agreements while Mr. Griffin was out of the country on business.

He e-mailed Julie to tell her he would not pay the invoice of $12,540 for an area rug and $23,978 for a sofa and two wing chairs, since he did not sign the sales proposal for these items.

Another option for office space is to rent space in an executive office complex. In this case, the suites are already planned to meet specific size requirements. The tenants utilize a common conference room, group kitchen, and copy and mail room, and pay for a receptionist that answers the phone and greets customers. This option provides a commercial solution to a sole practitioner who does not want to work out of a home office or get involved in a long lease at another type of office location. However, it is more expensive and space is limited. As the design firm grows to add an employee, the executive office rarely provides that "growth" space. As many a designer in an executive office location has said, it is also very expensive to pay for an extra office space to house the catalogs and samples of the business.

EQUIPPING THE OFFICE/STUDIO

The equipment needed for an interior design office varies based on the focus of the business and the types of services to be performed. Readers who have worked in the interior design profession for several years will have some idea as to what kind of equipment will be needed for their studio or office. Equipment needs, however, should be based on an evaluation of specific needs. It is always important to consider future needs and the ability to upgrade equipment or software for computers before purchase.

Table 11-8 provides a list of equipment items that are common and might be needed for a new office. Naturally, this list is not all-inclusive. Some items in the list might not be needed at start-up, and other items not on the list might come to mind. It provides the potential practitioner who is considering starting his or her own design practice with an idea of what needs to be planned for and budgeted.

There are several kinds of basic computer software applications that can help in the design office. A new business is tempted to save money by buying inexpensive software. However, using software programs with proven track records helps prevent errors in the data management. Software should also be chosen that is compatible with what is used in the industry. Being able to transmit any kind of document via e-mail or on a computer disc is important for both residential and commercial interior designers.

Combination packages that provide word processing, data management, contact management, and presentation graphics capabilities are common in many offices. There are also a few specialized programs related to interior design and architecture practice that some designers find useful. Although I do not recommend specific software companies, I suggest that you use software that is standardized across industries so that work can be easily transferred to clients and industry consultants.

DESIGN LIBRARY

The Internet has given many designers the opportunity to reduce the size of their library. However, maintaining actual samples of certain products and materials as well as catalogs of information and photographs of furniture and equipment are mandatory for all interior design studios and offices. Design firms located away from trade showrooms generally have larger libraries, since they cannot easily go to a mart or showroom for samples.

It is easy for large numbers of catalogs, tear sheets, and sample books to accumulate. Samples and catalogs in the firm's library should be maintained only because the items are expected to be needed at some point in the near future. Just

TABLE 11-8.

Typical Office Equipment for an Interior Design Practice

Office furniture

Desk, credenza, computer table

Desk chair

Guest chairs

Conference room table and chairs

Display cabinets or shelves

Display accessories or other items

Drafting equipment

Drafting table for manual drafting

Diazo machine for prints

Plotter for computer printing (also see "Electronic equipment")

Storage units

File cabinets for office documents and records

File cabinets for client project files

Shelves for office supplies

Shelves to hold storage tubs; might be used to store client samples

Shelves for binders; might be used to store client job books

Electronic equipment

Telephones, one or more lines

Voice mail for messages if office has no receptionist

Mobil/cell phone

Internet connection; high speed preferable

Fax machine; plain paper is best bet

Copy machine; size based on company needs

Computer; one or more for office work and CAD work

Printer; one for letter-size work

Printer or plotter; for oversized sheets for drawings

Scanner to scan photos/drawings into computer

All-in-one printer; combines fax, copy, printer, and scanner

Software

Word processing for business communications of all kinds

Accounting; daily financial and reportable record keeping

Data management/contact and client list information

Project management, including scheduling

CAD drafting, production of plans

Specialized software available for the design industry

Library

File cabinets for price lists, cut pages, small catalogs

Shelves for sample books, material samples

Shelves for catalog binders

Peg board and hooks for fabric sample books

Work table

like clothing that has been hanging in the closet for years but has not been worn, catalogs and samples that have been in the library for several years but have not been used should be reevaluated and discarded.

Samples and catalogs are not always free. The design firm must carefully evaluate the importance of taking or keeping a set of samples or catalogs with the likelihood that the products will be specified and perhaps sold to clients. Large fabric memo samples and cuttings often must be paid for if they are not returned.

Some manufacturer and vendor representatives will visit the small studio to update catalogs and price lists; however, this vendor service is more common for the larger office/studio. The business owner must take care of this chore on a regular basis so that it is less likely for the designer to inadvertently price goods at prices that are out-of-date or specify discontinued goods.

As indicated in Table 11-8, storage shelves, cabinets, file cabinets, and work tables are common equipment items in the library. Some firms also place a small table and a few chairs in the library so that items can be arranged to see how the color scheme will work out. Stand-up-height work tables are useful for creating sample boards. Many designers display fabric books on peg board, creating a backdrop that can be attractive if kept neat. Of course, a key to an organized library is to locate like items together. Catalogs in one area and samples in another are very logical even in the one-person office. The easier it is to find a catalog or sample, the quicker the project can be completed.

It is easy to find all kinds of residential and commercial products on the Internet today. Manufacturer's Web sites are inviting and easy to navigate. Many have photos that can be downloaded, as well as detailed information on the products. In some cases, pricing is also available online. Practitioners need only locate the Web address of vendors and suppliers—numerous ones are available in trade magazines—to obtain detailed product information. In some situations, direct orders also can be placed with the supplier over the Internet.

It is also possible to utilize reference libraries where product catalogs and samples are maintained by an independent business serving interior designers, architects, and contractors. A membership fee is often required in order to have access to the materials. Samples and catalogs are checked out and must be returned or an invoice for the items will be sent to the designer. These reference libraries may also offer lunch seminars presented by vendors. The seminars, open to all in the industry, may require a small fee for the seminar if the designer is not a member of the reference library.

INVENTORY ISSUES

Every design firm accumulates some inventory. Any type of goods purchased and held by the business for potential resale to clients are considered *inventory*. For accounting purposes, any goods being held at the design studio or a warehouse awaiting delivery to clients is technically also called inventory. For many small interior design firms that do not have a showroom, inventory can be items that have been rejected by clients that cannot be returned to the vendor. Some inventory can also be accumulated as a designer finds items for one client and locates some unique item that might be used for some future client. These last two examples one might define as unplanned inventory items.

Regardless of how that inventory is obtained, the owner must be clear as to the purpose of accumulating inventory items. Rejections are going to happen, no matter how careful the design firm is in specification of products, approval by the client, and delivery methods. And this is an important point. Good procedures and policies in place to prevent as many returns and rejections by clients as possible are especially important for the small firm. Purchasing extra items for some future client might seem like a good idea if the item gets sold in a reasonable length of time. These inventory items represent dollars that cannot be used by the firm for anything else until the items are sold. Inventory held for possible sales also create storage costs and insurance liability, which result in additional drains on financial resources.

Ideally, inventory items should be purchased based on an idea that an item can be sold in a reasonable length of time—perhaps within a few months or weeks, certainly within the year. The designer should make sure that these items are not so special that none of the firm's other clients might be interested in buying them. For example, the designer should not stock up on Oriental-style vases if most of the firm's work is in eighteenth-century Georgian historical restoration.

Of course, maintaining some items in inventory that turn over quickly and are common needs for your specific target client can be very good for business. Having immediate access to some items represents an additional revenue source. Higher income margins might also be possible for some of these items.

For the small firm, inventory can be expensive. Many more manufacturers now have quick-ship programs where a wide variety of goods can be obtained within a short period of time—often as quickly as two to five days—versus their regular shipping time of several weeks, even months. There are fewer options with quick-ship items, but when speed is the issue, it is an excellent alternative in many cases.

The design firm should keep good records on these items as to how long they have been in inventory and even where they are located. The records will be needed for tax purposes. I have heard many designers comment on the fact that they had lost track of some items because they had been in storage so long. If inventoried items become damaged or stolen, the records will help the firm recover insurance claims. Good records also help the design firm's owner know how to get rid of items—possibly at a designer's "ding-and-dent" sale through an association or even by making a donation to a charitable organization.

SUMMARY

Through research and analysis, the best possible decisions about the organization and future of the practice can be made with a well-thought-out business plan. The business plan could very well be the most important piece of "design" work that the owner/manager does in his or her career. Poor planning is a frequent reason for business failures, according to the SBA. A carefully considered business plan gets the new business off on the right foot.

Regardless of the type of practice, sound financial planning is also critical. There are many unexpected expenses in starting a business, from the fees needed to register the name and filing of origination documents to the equipment and supplies needed to begin functioning. Stationery is not the only expense, as many catalogs and samples are not complimentary for a fledging design firm.

This chapter includes brief discussions on business location, equipment procurement, and inventory. These topics are relevant considerations for any size interior design business. They certainly impact the initial operations, marketing, and impressions of the business as it starts its existence and can have a long-term impact as well. There are many references for preparing a business plan, some included in the general references. Other sources may be found at the public library, bookstores, or from the SBA.

Chapter 11 concludes the chapters providing the overview for planning a new practice. The next part of the text focuses attention on the management of the business both as it starts its life and into its continued future.

REFERENCE

1. U.S. SBA Web site, www.sba.gov/starting_business.

*T*he future of interior design in the twenty-first century is dependent upon two major factors: 1) the recognition of the true value of ideas-ideas that are valuable solutions to problems, and 2) the efficient and effective use of technology to maximize time efficiency.

Interior design professionals must fully realize the value of design solutions, and the overall impact these solutions have on the quality of life within the built environment. They must realize the true value of their creative abilities. The focus must be on ideas, not products.

Linda Elliott Smith, FASID is President of education-works, inc., a professional development seminar group in Dallas, TX. She is a Past National President of ASID and served three years as President of the National Council for Interior Design Qualification and has held numerous positions within the ASID and NCIDQ organizations. In addition to her seminar development group, Smith is President of Smith and Associates, Inc., an award-winning interior design firm specializing in contract, hospitality, and residential interior design in Nashville, TN.

Growing the Practice

CHAPTER 12

Practice Organization and Management

Key Terms and Concepts

These key terms and concepts are important to material in this chapter. Many of these terms will be utilized in other chapters as well. Be sure you understand these items as you read this chapter.

Terms and Concepts

Management	Decision making
Functions of management	Business or product life cycle
Autocratic management style	Stages of a business
Planning function	Market introduction
Organizing function	Market growth
Leadership function	Market maturity
Empowerment	Market decline
Control function	Chain of command

Critical Issues

After completing this chapter you should be able to:

- Describe the functions of management, giving examples of how they correlate to an interior design firm.
- Explain the stages of a business as can be related to interior design.
- Explain how planning decisions can affect the growth of a company.
- Describe how empowerment can benefit a firm during the design development and contract administration phases of a project.

With the large number of interior design businesses started as sole proprietorships by a single practitioner, it is not difficult to understand that the business organization of a small interior design practice is often not very complicated. Once the practice begins to grow, structure becomes increasingly necessary. The purpose of this organizational structure is to aid employees in understanding the various activities of the firm and to show who is responsible for those activities. The larger the firm is, the more complex the organizational structure will become. Very large multidisciplinary firms even have departments to structure the work and personnel.

Three years ago, Nancy started her design business, Nancy Smyth Interiors. She operated by herself for the first year and a half and then added a part-time assistant, Sue, who was a nearly graduating intern from the local college. Six months later, Nancy hired Sue full-time. A few months later, Angie joined Nancy's company. Angie is an experienced designer with five years of practice. Angie and, to some degree, Sue have been able to bring in some additional projects so that now Nancy is considering hiring an office manager. Nancy is concerned about Angie and the direction of the company, since Angie has increasingly designed projects in "Angie's style" rather than Nancy's. Nancy is unsure of how to handle the situation that Nancy believes is occurring. Another complication is that Sue now feels she can ignore Nancy's directives just as Angie does.

The organizational structure of an interior design firm should emerge through thoughtful consideration and decision making by the owners and managers. These activities of planning and decision making are two of the important functions or responsibilities of managers and management. The more the firm grows, the more important these responsibilities become. For, as the firm grows, the "pact" between owner and employees grows. This pact is that the owner and/or managers vow to keep the interior design firm viable and income-producing so as to meet all of its financial and legal obligations. Design talent and creative problem solving are naturally important to the continued life and growth of an interior design practice. Effective organization and management skills are also necessary to keep the business growing. Thus, management responsibility grows and becomes more time-consuming as the firm grows.

This chapter provides a brief section about the functions of a manager. These roles apply regardless of whether the firm consists of a sole practitioner or a design director with several interior designers on staff. The chapter also explains the most typical ways a design firm grows from a very small firm to something larger. It concludes this organizational discussion with an explanation of typical stages of the growth of a business based on the model of the product life cycle.

FUNCTIONS OF MANAGEMENT

Interior designers often start their own business in order to "do it their way." The lure of having the freedom to operate a design practice the way they would like and work with the clients they most want to attract are big reasons for venturing on one's own or in conjunction with others. Ownership of an interior design practice comes with responsibilities that many have not faced before. Most interior designers do not receive much formal management training. Few schools require that interior design majors take a basic management course. The lack of understanding of the functions of management is unfortunate, since even if the designer has no desire to own a practice, understanding the manager's job will help him or her be a better employee.

Management involves the effective direction of staff members and financial resources under a manager's control toward the goals and objectives that the owners of the firm have established. It does not really matter if the operation is a small firm with a sole practitioner or a large multidiscipline design firm with layers of employees.

Management involves a multitude of tasks and responsibilities. In a small practice, the owner wears many hats, marketing for new clients, producing design project work, drafting contracts for new projects, billing and ordering goods, perhaps hiring and supervising an employee or two. And these examples are but a very few of the tasks involved in managing a practice. In a large firm, tasks may be delegated to different responsibility areas, each with a separate manager. For example, it is unlikely in a large firm that the manager supervising design employees is also directly responsible for typing up invoices to clients.

Regardless of the size of the interior design practice, a manager performs four broad, generally accepted functions: planning, organizing, leading, and controlling. An important overall task related to these functions is decision making. Within these four broad functions are the important tasks that all successful managers undertake. Although the term "manager" is used extensively in this section, this discussion applies to the owner of the small business or those working in a large design firm.

The first very important function of management is the *planning function*. By engaging in business planning, managers help chart the future direction of the firm. Planning also gives the owner or manager ammunition to anticipate problems and act proactively. By consistently using the planning function, managers are better able to see the big picture as well as be concerned about the day-to-day details. What is meant by seeing the big picture? The manager must understand the workings of the entire company—all of its parts and responsibility centers. The big picture involves future plans for the company as well as its day-to-day operational issues.

Fully understanding the components of the company is used to formulate the firm's strategic plan. The strategic plan (discussed in detail in the next chapter) will outline the direction of the company for the future. Managers also prepare goals, objectives, and strategies for the coming year and as part of the strategic plan. These goals, objectives, and strategies involve every aspect of the firm: its operations, including personnel and production; marketing; and financial planning. Whether the owner of the firm wishes to remain small or grow with added employees, the planning function is a business tool that helps make that happen. Successful businesses plan for their future. Businesses that fail are often those who have ignored the planning function.

The *organizing function* occurs as the manager determines how best to use the resources at his or her disposal in order to carry out the plans and perform the work activities of the firm. Determining roles for the different employees is part of the organizing function. For example, if the firm is large enough so that a division of labor for completing projects is desired, the manager determines who will perform which tasks and how these tasks will interrelate. Establishing how projects will be done is another aspect of the organizing function.

Leading employees is a very important function. Everyone works a little differently. The manager or owner must marshal the individual talents and skills of the group into a cohesive whole. That, simply, is leadership. Of course, leadership involves inspiring others, delegating responsibility and authority, and guiding others to meet the goals of the design firm. Additional information on leadership is presented on the CD. It is labeled Item 12-1.

In interior design practices a big part of the leadership function involves empowerment. *Empowerment* can be defined as "giving employees [who are] responsible for hands-on production or service activities the authority to make decisions or take action without prior approval."[1] When employees are empowered, they make things happen themselves, without having to check with the boss. This responsibility is very satisfying for most interior designers, who want to "do it right" for the client and the job.

Management Styles

Owners and managers of design firms must effectively communicate, lead, and motivate their employees in order for work to be done productively. Although there are many people and each will bring his or her own personality to management, authorities in business management feel that there are two extremes of management style: autocratic (or authoritative) and democratic (or facilitative).

If a manager uses an *autocratic style*, planning and decision making comes down from the manager to the staff. Very little staff input is requested or even tolerated. This autocratic style of management is often apparent in small firms, where the owner performs all the management functions. A sole proprietor is naturally very connected to making decisions as to how things will be done. After all, it is his or her business. However, it can also exist in larger firms that often require more structure and organization. Accepting a position with a company that has an autocratic manager does not mean that the manager is going to be a difficult person to work for. It will mean that the employees are expected to do the design work and project management the way in which the owner/manager dictates it, with little room for individual decision making and initiative.

In a company that is managed in a *democratic* or facilitative style, staff input is desired and responsibility is often given to staff members to accomplish certain managerial tasks. Sometimes a democratic style of management can be a problem for the design firm. If employees start making promises, for example, that cannot be kept by the firm, the reputation of the design firm diminishes. Or maybe the promises can be kept but only through the extraordinary efforts of some or all of the staff. It can be argued that extraordinary efforts can sometimes be justified for the goodwill that it can create with the client. However, if a firm begins to make extraordinary efforts frequently, then clients may begin to expect them. Now the extraordinary becomes practically impossible without adding employees or stretching workloads into overtime. This also adds to the overhead costs of the firm, which might be more than the revenues obtained from the added projects.

A democratic type of manager can exist in any size firm, just as the autocratic type of manager can show up in any size firm. There is no way to predict which management style will exist in a particular interior design firm. Design employees prefer the democratic style of management, since most creative people like the freedom that this style of management provides. Knowing which style of management under which you work best can help you make a decision as to the firm from whom you will accept an offer of employment. Knowing one's own style of management will also help when you are hiring employees.

In the *control function*, the manager monitors the activities of the interior design department and takes any necessary steps to ensure that the plans, policies, and decisions of the manager and the firm are being carried out. This is done, in part, when a manager reviews the kinds of reports that will be discussed in Chapter 17. It also occurs when the manager makes adjustments or develops new evaluative mechanisms to help the firm achieve its goals and objectives.

Overlying all of the management functions is the owner or manager's decision-making ability. *Decision making* is the act of making reasonable choices between the alternatives available. It is a part of all the other management functions and seems to occur almost all the time in the manager's day. For example, in firms where new projects are generated through a manager, salesperson, or marketing individual, the manager must decide which designer will be responsible for completing which project. A scenario and exercise concerning decision making is included on the CD as Item 12-2.

Although each of these functions is discussed separately, they are continually intermixed. Managers find themselves engaged in all these functions every day. This reality is part of the stress and excitement of the management role. There are many fine books on management in libraries and bookstores. The reader may wish to review one or more of these books or even take a course in management to gain a more complete understanding of the management function.

ORGANIZATIONAL STRUCTURE OF AN INTERIOR DESIGN PRACTICE

The two most common organizational structures for a new practice are as a sole owner/practitioner and a partnership. The organizational structure of a sole proprietorship is quite simple, as the owner carries out all the work of the firm. In this smallest of interior design practices, the owner is the president, business manager, marketing director, designer, salesperson, draftsperson, order entry clerk, expediter, complaint department, bookkeeper, secretary, librarian, installer, and any other person required to get the job done. In a partnership, the partnership agreement spells out the responsibilities of the different partners, with these same tasks divided between the partners or employees. A new design practice also might start out as a small retail studio/store, offering design services to supplement sales of merchandise. Maybe the new design practice is a joint venture that later merges to form a new, large design firm.

A very large number of design practices began as one-person practice. The first employee added to the sole practitioner's interior design practice is often a full- or part-time design assistant or a part-time bookkeeper. A design assistant in the smallest of firms is commonly a recent graduate from a nearby college or university's design program or perhaps an upper-level student fulfilling an internship. A part-time bookkeeper might be hired once the workload has increased to the point where the practitioner cannot keep up with the records him- or herself. Of course, the practitioner is still responsible for the accuracy of these financial records.

If the design firm starts as a partnership or any other form of business that involves additional owners or managers, decisions must be made as to which of the two partners (for simplicity) will be responsible for which business functions, as well as to who will be responsible for the creative design work of the company. The partners need to sit down and honestly evaluate their strengths and weaknesses in order to determine who will do what. Egos must be put aside to ensure that each owner brings appropriate skills and resources to the venture.

As the firm grows in size as well as revenues generated for the year, additional attention must be paid to organizational structure. Depending on the size of the design firm and the focus of the business, there are likely to be at least three or more divisions of work responsibility within an interior design practice. Ownership and administration is one group, with the design staff making up the second primary group. A design firm will likely have someone to handle the bookkeeping and order-processing functions, creating the third group. In very large firms, a separate marketing staff is possible, as well as company-owned warehouse and delivery service employees.

Authority must be delegated within these work groups in order that each group is managed properly. When the group is large enough, the staff will require titles that differentiate seniority and responsibility. Decisions as to who will manage each work group need to be established as the number of employees increase. The owners will need to evaluate each of the existing employees to see if any of them can take on the management responsibility. If the owners do not find any employees who can take on management responsibility, then they will need to determine what to do until individuals can be interviewed and hired.

Job descriptions are helpful for any size interior design firm, but they are especially necessary when multiple employees are hired with different levels of experience and responsibility. An employee handbook describing specific personnel policies also needs to be prepared. In addition, policies regarding work activities for each group needs to be established. And, assuming that this was not done in the past, a procedure for developing yearly marketing plans, financial plans, budgets, and strategic planning for future growth has to be established—overwhelming tasks for many business owners. Yet these are things that must be done to assist the practice in continuing to achieve healthy, profitable growth.

Organizational structure goes beyond clearly defining personnel responsibilities as the firm adds employees. When the sole practitioner obtained a client, it was very obvious who was responsible for all the design activities. When a partner joined the firm, each partner most likely was responsible for his or her own design project work. Then, as design employees are added, project responsibilities are delegated among employees. However, few designers work exactly alike when given the freedom to do so. In a design firm with a number of interior designers, the owner will likely establish standards on how work is to be completed. This might include how the drawings are to be prepared, the style of sample boards, and many other project-related tasks. This standardization is necessary to be sure tasks are completed professionally, preventing errors or omissions that could create liability problems for the firm.

The structure of the operations and procedures of the growing design firm need to be addressed. Like it or not, the bigger the design firm, the more structure will be required to keep the CAD plotters humming and design revenues coming in the door. There is nothing wrong with staying small, and many practitioners are content working on their own in their own way. Growing the practice from its inception to whatever the owners would like it to be takes planning, organization, and structure.

What Would You Do?

Joy Anderson specified window treatments, flooring, and furniture for two different clients living in two different high-rise condominiums located in the same city in the Southwest. The unit for the Joneses was on the twentieth floor of a building in the central city. The living room is positioned in a corner and has windows on the south and west. The Brown's unit—located in a building eight miles away, is on the ninth floor of her building. Mrs. Brown's bedroom space has windows on the west, but the living room has windows facing north.

Joy completed the design of the unit for Mrs. Brown last year. She had permission from Mrs. Brown to show photos of the residence in her portfolio but could not indicate the location other than it was in a high-rise building.

Mrs. Jones wanted the drapery treatment that she saw in the portfolio, which happens to be in the Brown residence, for her living room. Mrs. Jones insisted on the drapery fabric shown in the photo of the Brown residence and a dark color carpet. Joy ordered the merchandise. Both products are now ready for installation. In the meantime, Mrs. Brown and Mrs. Jones met at an art guild association's meeting a week ago. Mrs. Brown was lamenting about the sun fading of her drapery to Mrs. Jones. Mrs. Brown also told Mrs. Jones that she was having a hard time getting the interior designer (whom she did not name) to do anything about the fading. Now Mrs. Jones wants to cancel the order because she is afraid of sun fading as well.

THE STAGES OF A BUSINESS

One could suppose that a business exists on a continuum from start-up to its closing (for whatever reason). However, that is not really what happens. A business goes through several different stages as it grows and survives in the highly competitive interior design market. These stages reflect the energy put into the business by the owner and employees, as well as the general viability of the business. To understand these stages for an interior design business, we need to look at the life cycles of products.

Marketing textbooks describe product life cycles. When a new product hits the market, sales are low, as consumers have not really seen the need for the new product. Consider cell phones, when only certain businesses incorporated car phones for their employees but few individuals had a cell phone or car phone. This first stage is called *market introduction*. The next phase, called *market growth*, happens when sales of the product increase substantially, providing increased profits to the company. Depending on the product, this increase in sales and resulting profit can last a long time—as is the case with cell phones—or can be shorter-lived until competitors start to sell a similar product.

When a product becomes successful, competitors come into the market and sales of the original product decrease or the profit margin decreases. In the third phase, called *market maturity*, sales for the originating company fall off as competitors enter the market and siphon off sales. Unless something dramatic is done, the product enters the fourth and final phase—*market decline*—as sales of the product diminish for the original company as well as for most of the competition (see Figure 12-1). Obviously, in our example of cell phones, the market has not declined or even matured yet. It is still in a growth stage for all producers of this product. It continues to grow as the product goes through design and feature changes, creating a market for new sales.

The premise here is that similar stages exist for interior design businesses (Figure 12-2). In the earliest stage of any new practice, the emphasis is on introducing the company to the marketplace, obtaining clients, and earning sustainable revenues. A client base must be established, and a good design reputation and excellent customer service must be developed. The main concern is survival, and the focus is on producing the work that will result in revenue. This is comparable to the market introduction stage of a product's life cycle.

When employees are added as the firm grows, the focus changes. This stage is akin to the market growth stage in a product's life cycle. New organizational structure is needed to handle the added employees and many challenges of increased business. The owner must consider whether he or she will spend time on design projects, marketing, or managing the firm. Owners quickly find that management and organizational issues become very important as the business

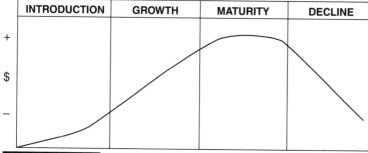

FIGURE 12-1.

The standard product life cycle.

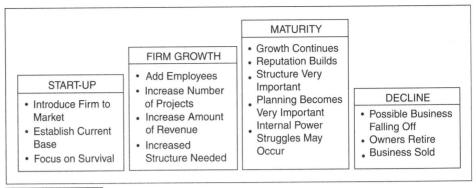

FIGURE 12-2.

The growth cycle of a typical interior design firm.

grows, perhaps overwhelming any opportunity to do creative project work. The small, personal, "family" business of the early days begins to disappear, because the owner has to be in too many places at the same time. Chaos can soon occur if the owner is uncomfortable with the added management responsibilities. This is often the time when the owner seeks out individuals with specialized management or other business skills so that the owner can continue to generate designs.

Let us assume that the interior design firm continually expands services and adds employees. When this happens, additional pressure exists to increase revenues in order to pay for the added overhead. Most likely the firm also finds itself competing with many other interior design firms and architectural offices, which are providing services to similar clients. In a sense, this situation can be compared to the market maturity stage of a product's life cycle. Organizational structure is very important at this stage. It is necessary to define how things are done with so many projects and employees. In addition, planning for the future becomes even more important.

Continued growth and expansion finds the firm in a mature stage that, hopefully, will never duplicate the last stage of a product's life cycle, market decline. The design firm now has a confirmed reputation, perhaps even an award-winning staff. It probably also has become more specialized and can to some degree be choosy about clients and projects. It may have grown to the point that strong departmentalized units have been formed around specialties or services. Department heads have been given the responsibility to organize and manage their departments in such a way that the overall goals of the company have been met. A more formalized reporting structure referred to as a *chain of command* between one level of employee and another could be necessary in the larger firms. Good yearly planning to retain the freshness and drive that will keep the design firm from losing customers and seeing revenues decline is now necessary to guarantee the future of the design firm.

Of course, any interior design firm can enter the decline phase of the life cycle. A major contributing member of the firm might move on to start his or her own practice. Maybe the owner reaches a point at which doing design and managing the office are no longer of interest. Some owners reach retirement age and desire to retire. And, of course, some firms simply decline due to poor management, poor marketing, and mediocre financial management.

Regardless of the size of the firm these stages or cycles are going to occur. Naturally, the larger the firm grows, the increasingly critical and complex these issues become. Planning for growth, regardless of what form that growth takes, is important to the success of the company. A discussion of how to plan for continued growth occurs in Chapter 13 with the discussion of strategic planning.

SUMMARY

Taking an interior design practice to another "next level" is a decision that affects all business owners. Growth puts different pressures on the owner and employees at each stage of the firm's development and as it moves from one stage to another. Growing a firm often means that procedures need to become more formalized. Job responsibilities become more specialized, and roles must be defined. Free-wheeling procedures of the early years do not provide an adequate framework for controlling project management and internal operations. One of the biggest changes for owners is that they find it necessary to spend more time in managing the firm and its employees rather than in primarily creating design work for clients. It is safe to say that some owners relish this challenge, while others long for simpler days.

With growth comes the need for management activities and skills, whether they are provided by the owner or employees. This chapter briefly described management responsibilities and functions as they relate to an interior design practice. Developing the design practice takes the business beyond the entrepreneurial beginnings discussed in Chapter 7. In some way, the interior design practice must be organized and managed as it moves into its next and subsequent stages. The chapters in this revised Part III have brought together topics critical to the development of a new practice and continued growth of an interior design firm.

REFERENCE

1. Ivancevich, Lorenzi, and Skinner, 1994, p. 261

CHAPTER 13

Strategic Planning

Key Terms and Concepts

These key terms and concepts are important to material in this chapter. Many of these terms will be utilized in other chapters as well. Be sure you understand these items as you read this chapter.

Terms and Concepts

Strategic planning

Mission statement

SWOT analysis

External factors

Secondary sources

Primary sources

Goals

Strategies

Tactics

Budgeting

Zero-based budgeting

Critical Issues

After completing this chapter you should be able to:

- Explain the purpose of strategic planning and its benefits for a sole practitioner.
- Explain how and why planning is important for any interior design practice.
- Identify through SWOT analysis at least three external factors that can have a positive impact on a firm.
- Discuss potential external threats that can impact a design firm.
- Discuss why budgeting is such an important part of any planning process.
- Establish a business goal, along with strategies and tactics to make the goal achievable.
- Search out and investigate secondary sources of information to establish better planning information for an interior design firm.

In Part III we discussed the many issues and decision points necessary in the planning of a new interior design practice. A successful interior design practice that grows and matures does not stop planning once it opens its doors. Planning for the future of the company is critically important to its ongoing success and growth. By the way, growth does not have to mean in size or numbers of employees. Growth can also mean the amount of revenue produced in a year.

Planning the business is an ongoing task for any owner who wants the company to grow. In fact, planning is necessary even for the owner who wants the firm to stay small and not become a huge management headache. Strategic planning is a specific process of planning that helps the business owner and employees determine where it wants to go in the future. This important planning process is a benefit to any size firm. The design firm does not have to be large to need to think about its future. The sole practitioner should be looking to its future goals as well.

There are many kinds of plans that can be developed to manage and grow a practice. Plans can specifically be developed for marketing efforts, financial needs, and any other part of the business operations such as human resources needs. However, the type of planning that develops a future-oriented viewpoint and direction for a business is strategic planning. This chapter focuses on the strategic plan as a management tool for any size interior design practice to develop a positive future direction. It will also discuss budgeting as part of the planning process and concludes with information about the importance of measuring performance of the planning process.

OVERVIEW

Many forces continually affect a business, especially the small business, and planning is an important way for the owner to keep control and be responsive and competitive in the marketplace. According to Ivancevich, Lorenzi, and Skinner, "Planning enables a firm to respond quickly to changing business demands, market conditions, and customer expectations."[1] Understanding the importance of planning is essential whether the reader is a business owner, employee, or student. Important points concerning the necessity of ongoing planning are presented in the following box.

The Importance of Planning

Planning is second nature to an interior designer when it applies to projects for clients. Many owners, but especially those with small practices, never seem to find time to use strategic planning for their business. This is very unfortunate, as planning helps them find a clear direction and define a purpose. Please remember that a strategic plan is a road map that is on paper, not in stone. When an interesting opportunity comes along, that opportunity needs to be evaluated and explored. It is perfectly okay to modify the plan when opportunities occur, just as the plan may need to be changed to handle unexpected challenges. Let's look at a few important reasons why planning is important.

First, planning helps the owner define and update his or her mission or vision of the firm by use of a mission statement. The mission statement, remember, is a philosophical statement that explains the direction and purpose of the design practice, its values, why it exists, and who it serves. Each year the owner and employees of a firm must revisit the mission statement to see if it is still valid and remains in touch with the desired future of the firm.

Planning helps a firm set priorities. Planning will help a firm determine how to use its human and financial resources to the best advantage. Maybe the firm needs a brochure to assist with marketing, while it also needs to update computers and software. Through the use of planning, the owner and staff determine which wants and needs are most important, setting the priorities to determine the items of greatest need. Planning provides a formalized mechanism for the owner to determine what is needed and when so that resources can be budgeted to obtain or achieve desired results.

Planning provides a yardstick to measure and evaluate success. A written plan makes it much easier to evaluate what was planned versus what actually happened. Reviewing progress is an important part of planning. Six months or a year later, the owner and employees can then carefully look at what was done and what was not accomplished as they prepare to plan for the next year. These variations or variances in planned versus actual can help the owner evaluate what happened so that negatives can be dealt with quickly before they become financial problems.

Planning helps to integrate management and employee thinking so that they both have a common purpose. It has been proven time and time again that small businesses are more likely to be successful when the employees really feel that they are a part of the business. This means that they are taken seriously by the owner, their input is respected, and they are made to feel that they have a stake in the firm beyond their expected work responsibilities. Involving employees in the planning process helps create this common purpose and feeling that they are important to the overall success of the design firm. When the employees are involved in planning, it is also much more likely that they will work to achieve the goals of the company. If the owner hands down the goals without having requested any employee input, employees may be resentful and may assume that their ideas are not wanted, with the probable result that the plans will not be achieved or the employees will leave the company.

The primary reason it is important for any size business to use planning on a periodic basis is that businesses that fail to plan are more likely to fail. Managing by the "seat of the pants" often leads to difficulty in handling problems that occur. Not knowing where the company is headed can lead to disjointed efforts, with confused priorities. Planning helps the design firm determine a destination and forces the owner and staff to create a road map of how to get to that destination in a logical manner.

Strategic planning is a process for creating a specific written vision for the design firm and its future. It is comprehensive and future oriented, requiring the business owner and employees to predict what they would like to see for the business concerning the many operational and organizational areas of the design firm in the future. Goals and objectives are set for a minimum of one full year into the future, with an emphasis on two to three years ahead. Table 13-1 represents a partial strategic plan. Strategic planning helps a business to act in a positive way to the inevitable forces that will affect it rather than constantly reacting and being in a crisis mode.

As one might assume from the name, strategic planning comes from military planning. In the mid-twentieth century, big business looked for a way to better plan and become proactive in their markets. They turned to the concept of strategies as part of a detailed plan used by the military. Over time in the twentieth century, the concept merged into a process of looking carefully at the internal resources a company had and the external forces that impact a business and utilizing this information to create a plan for the future of the company.

A strategic plan primarily focuses on the long term—three to five years into the future. However, many businesses create a "rolling strategic plan" that takes into consideration the current (or short-term) as well as the long-term goals of the company, making a separate annual plan unnecessary. A small firm might even use strategic planning to plan for only one year, although ideally the plan looks further into the future than the coming year.

Strategic planning is not just a plan. It is a process that in a sense forces the owners and employees to look internally and externally in order to analyze where

TABLE 13-1.

A Portion of a Strategic Plan for a Small Interior Design Practice.

Goal 2: Increase marketing and promotional efforts in order to create potential client awareness of Johnson/Clark Designs.

– **Strategy 1:** Review existing promotional materials.

   Tactic 1: Collect copies of promotional materials used in the last three years.
   Tactic 2: Categorize materials into types of promotional tools.

– **Strategy 2:** Identify potential venues for speaking programs.

   Tactic 1: Develop database of local target client professional associations.
   Tactic 2: Develop database of target client professional associations in the three adjoining states.
   Tactic 3: Develop database of any other possible clubs or groups that might host a program.

– **Strategy 3:** Brainstorm with staff for at least six possible topics for programs.
– **Strategy 4:** Identify potential venues for informational and educational articles to show our company's expertise.

   Tactic 1: Obtain copies of all local magazines and other print media in our local market.
   Tactic 2: Obtain copies of local magazines in major cities of the three adjoining states.

---

the firm is and where it wants to go. Many have said that the analysis process can be more valuable than the plan that results. However, it should be obvious that a plan is also very valuable, since a plan creates a road map for the owners and employees.

Businesses that do not plan often end up reacting instead of acting. What this means is that forces outside the business have more effect on the future—and even present circumstances—than what the owners would like to see happen. With strategic planning, owners can act in the best interests of the company in line with the strategic plan.

It is important to realize that there are other types of plans sometimes used by businesses. The business plan discussed in Chapter 11 is the blueprint for thinking through a new business. Once the business is rolling along, other plans are of value to the business owner and others who have a stake in the business. A common supplemental plan is the marketing plan. Whether the firm is large or small, having a detailed and specific marketing plan helps that firm understand what it perceives to be its place in its market. A firm's market is the overall range of potential customers that might be attracted to the business. A marketing plan helps the business think through the marketing efforts the firm will use to attract clients to the firm. Marketing plans are discussed in detail in Chapter 18. Large design firms might use other specific plans to map out how to resolve critical components of the organization. One example is a human resources or personnel plan to help determine hiring and training needs. Another is a capital spending plan, which will help the firm budget funds to purchase equipment or even own an office building rather than leasing space.

Of course, it takes time to develop any of these plans. Many owners of small firms give this as the primary reason for neglecting this important management task. A compelling reason to plan is that, according to the Small Business Administration, failing to plan is one of the biggest reasons that small businesses fail. Even a sole practitioner can gain from strategic planning and the development of other plans when called for. The remainder of this chapter focuses on the strategic planning process most facilitators and users of strategic planning employ.

MISSION STATEMENTS

A common component of the strategic plan is the mission statement. As discussed in Chapter 11, a mission statement is a concise philosophical statement that explains a firm's direction and purpose. It generally has an external focus, telling clients and other outsiders what the purpose of the firm is. A mission statement is a crucial part of strategic planning, since it is assumed that a firm's mission *might* change over time. Reviewing the existing mission statement at the early planning stages helps a prospective business owner think about the overall purpose of the business and determine if it needs to be modified.

For reference, you may wish to review the section on mission statements in Chapter 11. The CD contains additional sample mission statements and an opportunity to develop a company statement. See Item 13-1 on the CD.

Another example of a simple mission statement is this: "Defining Interiors, LLC is a full-service interior design firm providing the highest level of professional skills and creative solutions for the corporate client." Another example is, "AB & C Interiors is a client-oriented residential interior design firm dedicated to providing creative design solutions that meet the client's needs first."

A mission statement starts with the concept of where does the firm want to go. It is important that it be focused, not vague, though it is still a philosophical statement. Some confuse a mission statement with a vision statement. A vision statement comes from the values and convictions of the owner of the firm and expresses what the firm hopes to become: the best, most creative hospitality design firm in the country. Vision statements are more internal and used to focus and direct the staff and are less often communicated to clients and outsiders. Some of the references on strategic planning use "vision" instead of "mission" and vice versa. The point is to develop a simple expression of what the firm is trying to do so as to clarify its direction in the goals and other activities and tasks of the company.

Many texts on how to go about making a strategic plan suggest writing or revising the mission statement before completing the rest of the work of the plan. Others put it off until the end. The in-depth analysis that a firm should do as part of the strategic planning process often leads design firms in slightly different directions than might even be expected. If it is reworked at the beginning of the process, it is recommended that it be revisited one more time after the rest of the strategic planning process is completed to be sure it does not need any slight changes.

BUSINESS ANALYSIS

It would be unwise for an interior designer to start working on a project for a client without knowing the current situation of the space and requirements of the client for the new plan and specifications. Likewise, it is unwise to create a plan for the future of the business without first analyzing the firm's current condition. It is very difficult to determine what the possibilities for the firm are until the owner and employees know what they can do right now. By carefully looking at the forces that affect the design firm, the planning team can make better judgments for the future.

A very important part of the strategic planning process is called *SWOT analysis*. SWOT stands for strengths, weaknesses, opportunities, and threats. Much useful planning information is obtained through SWOT analysis as a firm investigates what it does well. Equally important to a business (or individual) is investigating what can't be done or what is being done in an inferior manner. As Peter Drucker points out, strength analysis "shows where there is need to improve or upgrade existing strengths and where new strengths have to be acquired."[2] Looking at a firm's weaknesses is also important so that actions can be taken to overcome and improve these areas.

SWOT analysis also means the firm should be looking at external opportunities and threats. These external forces can impact the firm in different ways. A developer announcing potential construction of hundreds of new high-end residential homes in the area can be a tremendous opportunity for new business. Of course, that same opportunity can bring added competition from designers outside the area. Opportunities need to be analyzed to clarify the positives. Depending on the actions of the firm, a threat could be a problem or it could lead to other opportunities. Analyzing strengths and weaknesses requires investigating the internal resources and activities that the design firm can control. They would include such things as the services the firm offers, financial resources, project management, and the way in which the firm is marketed. Understanding what the firm does very well is one consideration. Reviewing customer complaints is an example of a weakness that needs to be addressed. Another type of weakness is related to the type of work the design firm may wish to obtain. Perhaps an essentially residential firm wishes to enter the hospitality market. Having no experience in that specialty would obviously be a weakness.

External factors are the opportunities for, and threats to, the firm. Firms that are busy keeping up with its current day-to-day practice often miss seeing potential opportunities. Not reading the newspaper makes it nearly impossible to know if a new corporate headquarters is moving into the area. A contact with the real estate brokerage company that is helping a corporation locate housing for its headquarter's personnel's move into the design firm's city is a way to exploit an opportunity. Other external forces such as government regulations, competition, technology, economic forecasts, and the firm's customers can be opportunities or threats depending on exactly what is going on. New legislation limiting aspects of traditional interior design practice, such as requiring contractors' licenses for supervision of materials installation, is a potential threat.

Examples of SWOT items are shown in Table 13-2. Additional examples are included on the CD as Item 13-2. These examples should help you write your own SWOT analysis.

This kind of formal analysis helps the design firm to understand what it can do, what it wants to do, and what it must work on to improve present services so that the firm will be in a position to offer additional services. It also helps define outside influences on the firm that can affect its mix of services and its ability to offer services to specific groups of clients.

The easiest way to begin SWOT analysis for the strategic plan is by reviewing the skills and interests of the owner and all the staff. Once the firm knows what skills and knowledge exist within the staff, analysis of how the firm operates and processes of the company are important—especially when a desire to enter a new market is considered. If customer service has been notoriously bad, this factor will not help the company when it seeks to obtain a new market. Competition and existing or expected customer base is also important. Interior designers do not feel they have competition, but they do. Every residential

TABLE 13-2.

Examples of Items That Might Be Included in a SWOT Analysis.

Strengths

Our firm is well known.
Our firm has a strong financial position.
Our firm has a focused client target market.

Weaknesses

Our firm receives too many customer service complaints.
Some support staff members have a bad attitude.
None of our designers are NCIDQ qualified.

Opportunities

Angel Carpeting is offering co-op advertising.
Our studio will be relocating to an uptown location in order to increase our potential for high-end clients.
A major competitor has overextended itself financially.

Threats

Three strong competitors have moved into our market area.
A former employee has taken away two former repeat clients in the last six months.
State licensing will be required for supervision of installations.

interior designer in a given city is in some way a competitor to every other residential designer. Knowing what they do and how they do it can be an important part of a firm's strategic plan. These are important issues that can only be resolved through external analysis and research.

When the analysis shifts to external factors, it is often necessary to use primary and secondary sources of information. The easiest sources of information to obtain are from secondary sources. *Secondary sources* are generally those sources of information that are already in existence or are produced by others. These include such things as government, trade association, and general business publications such as the *Wall Street Journal*. Local business reports in newspapers, chamber of commerce publications, and reporting services such as the McGraw-Hill Construction Services (formerly referred to as the McGraw-Hill Dodge Reports) are other secondary sources of information. Any information that the firm gets from some source other than its own work is considered a secondary source. Such information as general economic trends, new firms opening in the local area, economic outlooks and forecasts, and census bureau reports all provide valuable hints as to potential clients for the residential and commercial interior designer.

Primary sources are sources of information that provide specifics from people who may have direct knowledge about the information being sought. Surveys, questionnaires, observation, and interviews are considered methods of primary research. The most common method of gathering primary data used by design firms is a casual interview, or, more precisely, casual conversation. It is expensive for a design firm to formally collect primary information using a method such as a formal questionnaire. Although primary sources of information can be the most helpful to the design firm, the cost and time involved usually limit its use to large practices.

Successful firms know that much can be learned from networking and casual conversations with past clients talking to design professionals at conferences and seminars, and talking with professionals such as architects, contractors, and developers. Good networking and developing a strong group of contacts with government agency employees, manufacturers' representatives, vendors and subcontractors, and even employees of the firm will provide information that can be used in developing a strategic plan.

Another relatively easy form of primary research—observation—can be done whenever anyone who is working for the firm is driving around town. Everyone should keep his or her eyes open for new construction, remodeling, or work in progress related to the interior design firm's practice. This kind of observation might not bring an immediate lead but could result in a contract at a later time.

GOALS, OBJECTIVES, STRATEGIES AND TACTICS

In the strategic planning process, the first part of the process is to focus efforts on the analysis of the internal and external environment and development of or revision of a mission statement. When all the analysis and research have been completed, it is time for the design firm to begin developing the actual plan— often thought of as the action plan. Goals and objectives are developed for as many operational areas of the company as are practical. In the best case, considerations are made for such areas as marketing, project management, operational management, finances, and personnel.

Establishing goals and objectives is an important aspect of financial and overall management control. An organization's *goals* are broad statements of what the firm wishes to achieve, without regard to any time limit—although in strategic planning, it is often recommended that a goal be something to achieve in three to five years. One of the goals for an interior design firm might be "to become an award-winning residential design firm within three years." Some goals do not have to have a time limit, such as "become the most respected medical office design firm in the state." *Strategies* are specific statements that describe how the firm plans to achieve a goal. They are almost always combined with time limits. An example strategy might be, "During the next year, we will refine our resource library to obtain materials on the highest quality merchandise." Also, "The owner will begin submitting articles on interior design to a local shelter magazine to gain publicity." By the way, shelter magazines are generally considered to be those sold to the general public on newsstands or by subscription such as *Architectural Digest*. Magazines such as *Contract* are considered trade magazines and are rarely available to the general public on the newsstands.

To further ensure successful accomplishment of these goals and objectives, more specific tactics must be established. These *tactics* are highly specific actions that are needed to accomplish the strategies. A tactic for the goal concerning medical office design might be, "the owner and senior project manager will attend the Health Care Symposium scheduled in October." All the goals, strategies, and tactics of the strategic plan must relate back to the firm's mission statement.

After the goals, strategies, and tactics have been defined and prioritized, the next step is to implement a review of the budget. Having a goal to become the premier in any kind of firm, with well-thought-out strategies and tactics, is certainly a positive step. However, not having the funds to achieve even the simplest of the tactics will discourage even the most enthusiastic owner and employee.

What Would You Do?

Sandy works in a state with interior design licensing legislation. She meets the requirements for registration, and has submitted her application to the board of technical registration. She is an employee of a design firm with six other designers, including the owners, who are registered. Two other designers are registered. When meeting with clients, the owners indicate that the company is registered and that their designers are also registered.

After a particularly problematic project, a client has reported Sandy to her professional association claiming she was working without a license and breached the contract. In addition, the client claimed the faux finishing was not done properly and has "ruined" the appearance of the house. The faux finisher has been to the house three times to try to solve the concerns of the client. In the meantime, the client has refused to pay the invoice for the faux finishing (billed by Sandy's company) and also refuses to pay the outstanding design fee. Those amounts total $23,000.

BUDGETING

Budgeting, which is a part of the management planning function, involves creating annual managerial goals that can be expressed in specific, quantitative monetary terms. We all work with a budget—a limited amount of money for a specific period of time to take care of bills and miscellaneous expenses. Businesses must budget as well. The difference between personal budgeting and business budgeting is that as an individual, you will know what your funds will be every two weeks represented by your expected salary. A business's funds fluctuate from month to month, since revenues fluctuate while expenses stay reasonably the same. This makes budgeting very important. Strategic planning requires budgeting because many of the goals and tasks outlined in the plan necessitate funds that the company might not have yet but must plan to obtain.

Budgeting encourages the owner and manager to plan for the financial needs of the company in a thoughtful and organized way. It helps them control the budget in a proactive rather than reactive manner. When there is no plan or budget, owners must "react" to what happens to them. This is thought of as "stamping-out-the-fires" management. Using a budget provides just one more opportunity for success. Budgeting also permits the discovery of potential problem areas and provides the opportunity to determine a course of action prior to their occurrence. Wanting or even needing new computer equipment, for example, can be planned, but it also must be budgeted. That may mean that the owner might not take a draw of salary for a few months in order to retain funds for that new computer. Finally, budgeting focuses the efforts of the whole organization toward the firm's annual goals by coordinating all the various individuals' and groups' efforts.

As part of strategic planning, budgets can be done as plans are developed. However, it is more common for budgeting to be done when all the goals, strategies, and tactics are determined and prioritized. This timing makes it easier for the owner and manager to estimate the financial and even human resources necessary to accomplish important, agreed-upon goals and, if necessary, make adjustments to them. It is the prioritizing that most affects the budget part of the process. Something that at first seemed to be of highest priority might have to slip when the cost of that goal or task is budgeted.

Strategies and tactics are the items that receive budget consideration, whereas goals are budgeted based on the total cost of the strategies and tactics that are needed to achieve the goals. Each strategy and tactic should be reviewed, and preliminary cost estimates for each item should be established. Revenue production strategies and tactics also should be budgeted. It is just as important for the firm to create revenue budgets as it is for the firm to determine what level of revenue is needed and is possible to accomplish for all the items that require "costs."

Forecasts of revenues and basic expenses for the coming year or future years begin by reviewing figures of prior years (see Figure 13-1). With further analysis, budgeting for what the company will actually attempt to accomplish becomes more realistic. However, budgeting should not be done by merely adding a modest percentage of increase for the coming year. This might work for expenses that do not fluctuate from month to month and year to year. It does not provide an accurate budget for activities like marketing in a new geographic market, or the designer to host an educational seminar for potential clients. It is better to develop more accurate cost estimates when the firm creates the budget.

The simplest and most common method of budgeting in many firms is to look at figures of the prior year and then, by applying various percentages of increase or decrease, come up with a new budget. This can work fairly well in normal circumstances but could be disastrous in a slow economy or during a

Design Department Proposed Budget 200x		
Revenue		
From Fees	420,000	500,000
Cost of Sales		
Direct Labor	271,875	290,000
Supplies	8,500	7,000
Reproduction Expense	9,350	7,500
Telephone (long distance)	3,700	4,800
Total Cost of Sales	293,425	309,300
Gross Margin	126,575	190,700
Total Cost of Sales	293,425	309,300
Gross Margin	126,575	190,700
Operating Expenses For Design Dept.		
Salaries	61,990	84,000
Payroll Taxes	16,000	24,000
Group Insurance	1,750	1,700
Promotion	2,750	2,000
Travel Reimbursements	6,800	7,000
Supplies and Postage	6,300	6,000
Professional Dues	3,000	2,500
Printing and Reproduction	8,400	10,000
Technical Consultants	12,900	5,000
Total Operating Expenses	119,890	142,200
Net Income	6,685	48,500
Profit to Sales	2%	10%

FIGURE 13-1.

A simple budget report helpful to owners in planning the upcoming business year.

period in which the economy goes down or becomes volatile for some reason. The past is always a good starting point, but it should be used in conjunction with good research and planning.

When totally new tactics are called for as part of the plan, the firm, naturally, will have to do some research through appropriate consultants to determine budget figures. For example, if the plan includes developing a Web site, it will be necessary to check with Web site designers to establish a budget for the design of the site as well as the ongoing costs of a Web master and provider fees.

Some firms use the zero-based budgeting method as their starting point. This budgeting method received a lot of attention during the presidential administration of Jimmy Carter. Zero-based budgeting assumes that each year the managers of the firm start with a zero budget level and must justify all costs, as if the department or activity were starting new. This means that no costs are considered as ongoing from year to year. It also means that the firm must accurately forecast revenues to cover and, of course, to exceed the amount of the expenses.

MEASURING PERFORMANCE

Inherent in all types of business plans are the means of measuring performance. Utilization of strategic planning as part of the overall planning process is no different. Establishing goals and objectives with no way of determining success results in a meaningless expenditure of energy in the planning and writing process. Establishing some of the control mechanisms that can be used to evaluate financial and organizational success is also very important.

Performance evaluation not only is part of the individual employees' productivity results but also relates to all other planning. It is useful to see accomplishment whether it is personal accomplishment or business accomplishment. As with crossing off items on a personal to-do list helps the designer feel that he or she has actually completed required tasks, sometimes simply crossing off the accomplishment of preparing job descriptions—and using them during hiring—provides a very simple measure of performance for the strategic plan and the business.

A more formal measure of performance is variance analysis. Briefly, an example of variance analysis would involve comparing financial projections that have been prepared for the business plan to actual performance. Another measure of performance can be accomplished by doing post-project reviews at the conclusion of all significant projects. This can be very formalized, and a standard report form can be created by the design owner in order to obtain such information as revenue dollars and reports on expenses, or it can be informal. In fact, a sample is included on the companion CD for Chapter 32. The numerical/financial data can also be supplemented with a short narrative review of the project. This post-project review is discussed further in Chapter 32. Additional control reports might well be suggested by the firm's accountant, attorney, or the experience of the owner/manager. Many of these control and evaluation reports are discussed in Chapter 17 on financial management control.

It does not matter if one is monitoring a strategic plan, a marketing plan, a personnel plan, or any other type of plan. Stopping to review progress is essential to good business practice. A large firm might only have time for a formal annual review. A small design firm needs to look at the big picture painted by the plan a little more often—at least twice a year. Scheduling a half-day to review progress or the lack thereof is just as important as developing the plan in the first place.

SUMMARY

Planning in general and strategic planning in particular are necessary functions of management regardless of the size and specialty of the design firm. A strategic plan helps chart the future and helps an interior design firm owner achieve success. Owners generally know where they want to go with their business—though, of course, some do not! But far fewer think about how they are going to achieve their business goals.

The strategic planning process has become an increasingly important part of the business practice of interior design, since it helps create a road map to help the firm achieve its goals, whether those goals are lofty or not. Commitment to a planning process for the future is especially useful to the small-practice owner and sole proprietor. These owners rarely take the time to consider where they are, let alone where they are going with their practice. Yet planning helps a small practitioner remain in business rather than becoming part of the large number of small businesses that fail each year.

This chapter has provided a brief but detailed introduction to the process of strategic planning. Information has also been provided on the overall importance of planning, regardless of the use of the plan. It also discussed the importance of putting budget figures to the plans and monitoring the progress of the plan. A plan will not guarantee overwhelming success for the firm, but it will provide an important basis for proper decision making in the present and the future.

REFERENCES

1. Ivancevich, Lorenzi, and Skinner, 1994, p. 166.
2. Drucker, 1995, p. 43.

CHAPTER 14

Human Resource Management

Key Terms and Concepts

These key terms and concepts are important to material in this chapter. Many of these terms will be utilized in other chapters as well. Be sure you understand these items as you read this chapter.

Terms and Concepts

Job classifications	Gross margin
Organizational chart	Hourly wage
Chain of command	Gross salary
Job description	Incentive compensation
Compensation	Merit pay
Fringe benefits	Bonus plan
Straight salary	FICA
Compensatory time	Cost-of-living adjustments (COLA)
Commission	Performance evaluation
Gross sale	Employee handbook
Net sale	Implied contract
Gross margin method	Mentoring

Critical Issues

After completing this chapter you should be able to:

- Discuss the responsibilities of the job classifications of a design staff.
- Discuss how an entry-level designer would likely interact with the other office job classifications.
- Discuss the importance of job descriptions in general and how each section helps employers and employees.
- Identify the different compensation methods found in interior design.
- Explain the importance to employees for performance evaluations, and outline the process.
- Discuss the pros and cons of an employee handbook for a small design firm.

- Explain why mentoring is important to entry-level designers, and outline how you might approach securing a mentor after graduation.
- Describe the different incentive compensation methods.

Managing employees is almost always a difficult and certainly challenging task for many owners and design department managers. Interior designers in general are self-motivated and do not need or like someone to stand over their shoulders to be sure they are working. Owners often find it difficult to delegate tasks to other designers assuming—generally incorrectly—that only the owner can do the work "correctly." The creative process is personal and individual, yet the interior designer must often work as part of a team. Job satisfaction comes from making a client happy with the design created by the designer.

Personnel issues are important to any business organization. Individuals enter the interior design profession for many reasons. As with any professional, interior designers expect to be treated fairly, receive adequate compensation, and be given greater responsibility as their worth to a company and the industry grow. When the industry or a market area is highly competitive, employers must be more than normally concerned with employer/employee relationships and personnel policies. There is no documentation concerning the number of lawsuits filed that involve personnel issues within the interior design industry. It is easy to assume that the number of suits concerning employee/employer practices has increased in this industry as with all others. It is certainly time for employers to be more formalized and careful in their dealings with employees.

Processes that formalize personnel management can assist in the hiring, development, and retention of effective employees. Formalized processes also protect the employer should employees feel they have been treated unfairly. At the same time, formal personnel processes help employees understand what is expected of them and that the design firm intends to treat its employees fairly.

The areas of personnel management discussed in this chapter are job classifications, job descriptions, compensation and fringe benefits, the performance evaluation, and the employee handbook. A new section discussing mentoring has been added to help both the employee and employer build better staff members. Legal considerations of personnel management, including the concepts of employment at will and employment contracts, will be discussed in the next chapter.

JOB CLASSIFICATIONS

The decision to hire an employee comes from a realization that the owner or current staff cannot accomplish certain tasks with the existing staff and skill levels. Adding design staff, or any staff for that matter, should not be taken lightly. It takes the owner a lot of time just to progress through the hiring process. Regardless of a new employee's skills, a certain amount of time is needed to train that new employee. It also costs the firm a considerable amount of money to train even an experienced designer to be part of his or her new design "family."

Searching for and then hiring a new staff member should only be done after careful analysis of what that new hire should be doing is accomplished. Looking at office procedures and defining project responsibility is an important part of that analysis. When the design department has several interior designers who have varying amounts of experience and expertise, job structuring can make the hiring effort less difficult and continuation of effective work among the existing staff less traumatic. Structuring of job responsibilities leads to defining job classifications or job titles within the various responsibility centers of the firm.

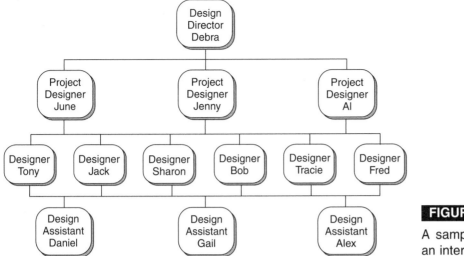

A sample organizational chart for an interior design firm.

As a firm grows, an organizational structure or chain of command emerges. This structure helps everyone in the organization understand the formal communication patterns. In a very large firm, this structure is often graphically represented by an organizational chart. The *organizational chart* is a graphic representation of the chain of command (see Figure 14-1). Interior designers who work with corporate and many other commercial clients are very familiar with the idea of an organizational chart that shows the layers of responsibility. Although the issues of chain of command are more critical in larger firms, they actually do impact a small interior design firm with a few employees. A formalized chain of command with an organizational chart rarely exists in smaller design firms. An informal structure representing the same concepts, however, does.

The job classifications discussed in this section also provide the titles that define responsibility level. Furthermore, a job title provides a sense of value to the firm for some individuals. Even the entry-level, recently graduated intern appreciates a job title when working full-time. In a large firm, job titles help show employees a way up the ladder of responsibility. Job titles also relate to the job descriptions that more specifically define responsibilities and required experience within a design firm. Job descriptions are discussed in detail after this section.

In many companies—even large corporations—the "real chain of command" does not always reflect the organizational chart. It is a useful tool to show the formal flows of official communication. Figure 14-1 shows an organizational chart that includes the various job classifications common in an interior design office. The descending order of responsibility reflects no specific organization.

Principal

The job title "principal" or "president" is often used by the owner of the interior design firm. If there is more than one owner, the title principal is often used by the different owners. In some firms, the principal can be joined in upper-level management by a partner. A partner can be an owner or an upper-level employee who may or may not have some financial vested interest in the company. In large, multidisciplinary firms, the top officer of the design firm is often called chief executive officer (CEO) rather than principal or president.

The principal (for simplicity) provides the vision and direction of the company. He or she is the most direct link to clients and is responsible for the majority of initial client contacts and presentations to obtain new design work. A principal often finds the time to spend on designing a project is reduced because of the greater administrative and marketing responsibility. Many find it important to remain involved in projects and hire others to take on many day-to-day management or administrative responsibilities.

Should a principal or partner be involved in a design project, his or her time would be billed at the highest rate quoted by the firm. The principal as a designer would be supervising project managers and other design staff in the execution of the needed design work.

Design Director

In some design firms, the individual responsible for managing the interior design professional staff has the title "design director." Firms might also use the title vice president of design, design manager, or perhaps some other title indicating this person's leadership role. Responsibilities for this individual vary with the size of the firm. However, it is common that they include administration, marketing, and design. Understand that any of these responsibilities can be assumed by the principal rather than a design director.

Administrative duties include all the management functions not reserved by the principal or CEO. Such tasks as planning, hiring and firing, assigning work, and preparing contracts are often the design director's responsibility. In addition, the design director is responsible for preparing various management control reports, establishing policies, and attending management meetings. The training and development of the design staff is an important part of the design director's responsibilities.

The design director often works with the principal or on his or her own to make client contacts and subsequent presentations to prospective clients. The design director is often involved in the development of marketing tools, such as brochures. In many firms, the design director is also the company's liaison with the public. And, of course, he or she is involved in planning and participating in the development of marketing plans.

The design responsibility of the design director may be minimal in large, very active design firms, or it may be an important part of the manager's responsibility—especially in a small firm. By design responsibility, I mean that the design director is in charge of design projects when he or she plays the role of the project designer. In this situation, the design director makes client contacts, prepares design documents (or supervises others in their preparation), prepares and reviews purchase orders, and makes him- or herself available for supervision during the installation phase of a project.

In addition, the design director, with guidance from the principal, sets the minimum standards for all design work that leaves the office. This means that the design director (and possibly the principal) reviews projects during their progress and before they are presented to clients. In this situation, the design director remains involved with project activities without actually doing them.

In very large design firms, the leadership role concerning managing the design professional staff might be broken down into two or more areas. The design administration and marketing group might be responsible for all administrative functions, such as hiring, and all marketing activities of the interior design department. The design production group might be responsible for ensuring the quality of project execution. It would be common for these two groups to be headed by different individuals, who would report to a design department head, such as a vice president.

Senior Designer

In previous editions of this text, the discussion of senior designers was included as part of the discussion of a project manager. Due to the increasing specialization within growing firms, the two job classifications have been separated.

Senior designer or senior associate is the title that is often given to the most experienced interior design professional. Senior designers generally have five or more years of experience in interior design—similar to what would be expected of a project manager. A senior designer has extensive project responsibilities, is the lead designer, and may supervise other designers. Good communication skills are a must in order to manage a design team for a large project and to effectively work with clients. He or she has critical client contact via assigned projects and perhaps during marketing presentations. As the lead designer, he or she meets with clients to determine their needs, prepares or directs others in the completion of design documents, and is responsible for order entry supervision and installation supervision. It is not unusual for the senior designer to also have specific administrative responsibilities assigned by the design director, or principal.

Project Manager

The project manager often has different responsibilities than a senior designer and can be on a different "level" on the chain of command. Depending on the size of the firm, the project manager may have limited involvement in developing design concepts. Rather, many project managers find themselves primarily involved in administrative management of the project. Their job requires good communication and organizational skills. In some firms, the project manager may be required to market the firm's design services and may even be required to negotiate the design contract. Specific tasks of a project manager are discussed in Chapter 28.

Designer

At the next level of the organizational chart, professional employees are given such titles as designer or staff designer. Designers commonly are required to have two or more years of professional experience and well-developed technical design skills. On large projects, these individuals work under the supervision of a senior designer or project manager.

A designer-level employee may be involved in client interviewing and any information gathering research needed for the project. They may be asked to prepare preliminary drafting and other documentation, preliminary product specification, or other tasks assigned by the senior designer or project manager. On smaller projects, they may be responsible for all phases of the project. Administrative responsibility is limited.

Design Assistant

The entry-level position for most firms is commonly called design assistant or junior designer. Entry level means that these individuals have little professional experience other than as interns. They work under the direction of a more experienced designer for one or more years. The kinds of work performed most commonly are drafting, preparation of sample boards, preparation of specifications lists for furniture and furnishings, perhaps some installation supervision, maintenance of the library, and other tasks assigned by the design director. After working for several months in a smaller firm, the design assistant usually is given full responsibility for small-sized projects. As in the case of the designer, administrative responsibilities include only time and record keeping for his or her efforts.

Depending on the actual interior design practice and size of the firm, there may be some additional, specialized job classifications. Many firms have support personnel that provide administrative assistance. Larger design firms may have additional professional staff providing specialized assistance to the design staff. These other job classifications are noted in Table 14-1.

The incredibly active market has led to a fast growth for Paul's commercial design firm. In the last year, he and his business partners, Ron and Judy, have had to add an office manager and four designers. One is a senior-level designer, one a project designer, one an entry-level designer hired after an internship, and one a technician to exclusively do CAD work. Paul is the managing partner and has been completely stressed by the overwhelming personnel management issues that keep occurring. Judy thinks they need to add two more employees, but Paul feels the office is in a certain amount of chaos as it is. Adding people might not be the right choice even though everyone is working 10- to 12-hour days six days a week to keep up. Sometimes hiring additional people without careful consideration of personnel needs solves one problem but will also cause additional management headaches. Careful analysis of what skills are needed in each job along with preparation of job classifications help to alleviate the kind of problem that Paul now faces.

TABLE 14-1.

Other Interior Design Job Classifications.

Space planner: Work responsibilities focus on space planning and use of space, not the specification of furniture and fixtures. Also called TI (tenant improvement) specialist.

CAD operator: Experienced in the use of computer-aided design equipment and software. Might be an interior designer or a computer operator.

Specification writer or estimator: Responsible for the preparation of finished specification documents and project budget estimates. May be interior design trained.

Librarian: Responsible for maintaining resource materials. In some firms will also be involved in writing purchase orders and the expediting functions. Might be an intern or entry-level designer or non-design-trained individual.

Renderer: Major responsibilities include production of perspectives and colored renderings. Might also be responsible for building models.

Graphics designer: Responsible for the design of graphics for such things as business cards and brochures, presentations, and presentation graphics for clients, as well as for similar graphics for the interior design firm.

Business development specialist: Exclusively works to identify and qualify potential clients, assists in developing presentations to obtain contracts, and is the liaison between the design firm and public relations and/or advertising specialists. Also called marketing director.

Administrative staff: Non-design staff providing secretarial, bookkeeping, and order-entry assistance to management and design staff. Also includes receptionist.

Human resource manager: A position in larger firms, professionaly trained in dealing with hiring personnel and almost all other personnel issues not the responsibility of department heads.

JOB DESCRIPTIONS

Once job classifications and essential responsibilities of each are developed, the next step is to prepare job descriptions for each classification. The *job description* communicates the qualifications, skills, and responsibilities of each job classification within the firm. As was discussed earlier in the chapter, the title assigned to the job description helps create a feeling of identity and value within the firm. In a small firm with five or fewer employees, a job description or even a differentiated title is almost an anomaly. The reader will find that even in many large design firms, job descriptions are rare even though the firm has job titles to differentiate rank and responsibility.

Job descriptions do have a place in interior design firms. Job descriptions help growing firms organize and control the employee search task. They also help to organize the work in the office and keep work on track. Job descriptions should be provided to individuals when they are seriously being considered for a position or upon being hired. Job descriptions also should be available to existing employees so that they can see what qualifications and skills are required of higher-level positions. Formalized job descriptions also are often necessary to help satisfy equal-opportunity complaints that might be raised by employees. Of course, this is more a consideration in a large firm than a firm with only a few employees. However, if a complaint is filed, job descriptions help explain why one individual is paid less than another.

Job descriptions do not need to be elaborate. The small firm may find a simple structure, such as the one shown in Figure 14-2, satisfactory. Larger firms may find that detailed job descriptions are of greater value (see Figure 14-3). Prepared in outline form, they should contain statements that are specific enough to differentiate among individuals, yet broad enough to allow the manager some flexibility in hiring. The content of the job descriptions must be kept current and complete. They also must accurately reflect the desired skills required to perform the responsibilities of the positions. As much as possible, the descriptions should be stated in measurable terms to aid in performance evaluation. Included on the CD is a worksheet to help organize a job description. It is labeled Item 14-1.

As can be seen from the samples, job descriptions should contain statements related to responsibilities, qualifications, and skills required. The Responsibilities section must be detailed enough so that the individual in the position knows what is expected of him or her. Large corporations, which have a great deal of experience in the preparation of job descriptions, often have very detailed outlines of responsibilities. Interior design firms have limited experience in this area. However, the owner and senior designers will be able to outline responsibilities and define the required tasks as they are needed for the particular firm at each job classification. Remember that the job classification helps define the responsibilities that will be outlined in the job description.

The Qualifications section outlines the minimal educational requirements. This section also specifies the minimum amount of work experience in years that is required. Statements such as "graduation from at least a four-year college or university, with a major in interior design" sets one of the minimum criteria for an interior design position. Statements concerning specific technical abilities, along with any skills or abilities of a general nature, are outlined in the Skills Required section. Although this section often comes second in a job description, it is often easier to finish writing this section after the Responsibilities section has been completed. It is important for the skills required to correlate with the responsibilities expected and the qualifications demanded. It is important that these skills and general abilities be listed in the order of their significance. For a firm that is involved in commercial interior design, CAD skill may be of primary

---

Interior Design Consultant
Creative Design Consultants, Inc.

This job classification requires that the employee assist the owner with projects. The employee is also expected to bring his or her own clients to the company.

Responsibilities:
Assist clients.
Evaluate and specify products to meet client needs.
Prepare layouts, plans, and other documents as required.
Prepare color boards.
Obtain signed sales orders.
Prepare cost estimates for all work required on a project.
Complete all required purchase orders.
Coordinate installation and delivery.
Share in housekeeping chores in the office/studio/warehouse.

Qualifications:
Bachelor's degree in interior design. Associate's degree in interior design with work experience in interior design would substitute for a college degree.

Work Experience:
Minimum of two years' actual sales and interior design experience required.

Skills:
Portfolio should show training in color and product coordination, and the ability to space plan.
Excellent manual drafting required; CAD knowledge preferable—AutoCAD.
Knowledge of Microsoft Word, Project, and Excel.
Knowledge of residential products and how to specify those products.
Proven sales record.

FIGURE 14-2.

A basic job description that can be used to define a design staff position in a small interior design firm.

importance for an entry-level design assistant, and therefore it should be listed first. For a firm that is involved in residential interior design, color coordination may be of primary importance for an entry-level design assistant.

A reference as to whom the person reports, either in a separate section or within the responsibilities section, should be provided. This helps clarify the chain of command and also aids new employees in learning who will be their supervisor. Since people do leave positions, reference is best made to job title rather than to an individual's name.

COMPENSATION AND FRINGE BENEFITS

Personnel expenses for a design firm are one of the largest if not the largest expense item for a firm. Employees expect fair compensation for the skills and experiences they bring to a firm and for the contribution they make to the design firm. Exactly how an employee is paid can be as important to the employee as the amount. Because of the high expense, some employers try to hire staff at the least

Job Description

Job Title: Senior Designer

Reports To: Design Director

Pay Rate: Salary

Responsibilities:
The following describes the essential responsibilities of this job classification. Other duties may be assigned from time to time by the Design Director or Owner.

☐ Determine scope of services required for projects.

☐ Assist Design Director with development of design contracts and project scheduling.

☐ Responsible for all phases and activities of design projects assigned, including but not limited to programming and data gathering, space planning, furniture layouts, development of contract drawings, product specification, budgeting, presentations to the client, and job site supervision.

☐ Maintain client confidence and good client relations.

☐ Supervise design team members to complete projects. Team members will be assigned by Design Director.

☐ Maintain client files for projects assigned, including all correspondence, drawings, and other materials, as described in our standard client file processes booklet.

☐ Keep Design Director informed of project status on all projects and other duties assigned.

☐ Attend all in-house meetings and programs.

☐ Be available to meet with manufacturer's representatives as assigned by the Design Director. Maintain design proficiency by attending seminars and workshops.

☐ Provide accurate time records to the Design Director each week.

☐ Provide marketing assistance by participating in marketing presentations as requested and by informing Design Director of possible projects that might become known to the designer.

Supervisory Responsibilities:
This job has no direct supervisory responsibilities; however, some direction of team members will be expected from time to time. This position does not participate in performance evaluations of team members.

Qualifications:
☐ Education: Bachelor's degree from a four-year college or university with a major in interior design; or an associate's degree and a minimum of four years of experience in lieu of a four-year degree.

☐ Previous work experience: A minimum of four year's full-time work experience.

FIGURE 14-3.

A job description for a senior designer in a firm with numerous employees.

☐ Portfolio and resumé should show ability and competence to perform the required tasks of a senior designer with full competence and skill.

☐ NCIDQ qualification required

☐ Qualified to be licensed in this jurisdiction

☐ Competence with AutoCAD minimum. Competence with other computer applications is expected, or training will be required.

FIGURE 14-3.

(*Continued*)

amount possible. Naturally, the concept of "you get what you pay for" does impact this kind of thinking, as low pay may bring in an employee, but that individual may not have the experience to make a very positive contribution to the firm's revenue. Consequently, determining fair and reasonable compensation is an important consideration for a design firm owner.

Although most readers think of their "pay for work" as salary, in reality there is more than one way for employees to be paid. Being paid a salary is only one of those ways. The method of paying someone to work as an employee is better thought of as compensation. The term *compensation* is any kind of payment made to an employee for work performed. In addition to compensation, employees may receive other payments or other considerations. *Fringe benefits* are other kinds of payments that are optional or that may not even be provided by an employer. Fringe benefits, such as paid vacations and health insurance, also make a significant contribution to the total compensation package. We will first consider typical methods of compensation and then discuss some common fringe benefits. You may also want to read a brief article located on the CD concerning compensation in interior design. The article is Item 14-2.

Compensation

Harry works for a design firm that expects him to be in the office and prepare design documents, as well as perform other tasks common to either a residential or commercial designer. He is not expected to sell any merchandise, although he specifies FF&E (furniture, furnishings, and equipment). Harry is paid a salary. Joanne is an interior designer working for a furniture store, where her responsibilities include the sale of merchandise that the company stocks on its showroom floor or orders for clients. Joanne is paid a commission on the amount of goods she sells each month. Rob is a part-time employee who does CAD work for a design firm. He works anywhere from 15 to 20 hours a week while he attends classes. Rob is paid by the hour. Harry and Joanne have received a bonus at the end of the calendar year during some of the years they worked.

These examples are the most common methods of compensating employees—straight salary, commission, and hourly wage. Bonus plans, technically called incentive compensation, are sometimes tied to any of these. The compensation program used by a particular firm is up to the owners and managers based on factors such as competition, company mission, type of practice, target client market, and, of course, that it meet state and federal laws. Please note that the examples above provide some work situation specificity. However, this is not meant to convey that any one compensation method is only used by the work situation described.

Let's look more closely at how Harry is compensated. The *straight salary* (or salary) method of compensation provides a fixed amount of salary to the employee no matter how many hours in the week Harry works. Of course, the firm still requires that Harry and other employees paid the salary method work a normal workweek of 35 to 40 hours. The actual number of hours varies, since the workweek in offices varies from 35 to 40 hours per week. By the way, that 40-hour workweek is merely a standard. Interior designers often find it necessary to work longer than a 40-hour week. Harry's weekly salary is determined by dividing the yearly salary by 52 weeks. This is often paid every other week rather than once a week. This is the most common method of compensating interior design and other design professional staff, especially when product sales are not part of the compensation arrangement.

Some weeks it is necessary for Harry to work more than 40 hours in a week because of project schedules. Straight-salary employees are not eligible for any overtime pay when they work more than 40 hours in one week. They are also not expected to work "extra" for free, as that would not be fair compensation practice. In this case, the employee is usually expected to, at some convenient time, utilize compensatory time. *Compensatory time* is time off during the normal workweek that makes up for the overtime hours that an employee has worked. In all cases, the utilization of compensatory time must be approved by the manager so that the absence of the employee will not be detrimental to the regular office work. In other words, when Harry has worked extra hours, he will ask permission of his boss to miss work on an agreed-upon day. Firms generally have an additional policy that compensatory time cannot be "saved up" for an extended period nor added at the beginning or end of a vacation period.

Joanne's work responsibilities are more involved with the selling of products or services, even though she also prepares floor plans for her client's projects. Joanne is paid a commission on the amount of merchandise or services she sells to clients. *Commission* refers to some percentage of the gross sale, net sale, or gross margin of the merchandise sold, or the amount of the contract. Being paid a commission is riskier for the employee because the amount paid is never guaranteed. The employee's compensation is solely based on what is sold. Consequent with that risk is that employees paid a commission might earn more over the course of the year than an employee paid a salary. Of course, they might also earn less if they have a bad year!

There are a few common methods of calculating commission; thus, some explanations are appropriate. Let's say that Joanne is paid some percentage of the *gross sale*. This means that the commission percentage is paid on the amount for which the client has actually been billed. For example, if the designer is paid 10 percent of the gross sale and the client has been billed $50,000, the commission owed to the employee is $5000.

Another way to compensate an employee by using commission is basing the commission on the net sale. When commission is based on the *net sale*, the percentage is calculated after certain items have been deducted. Deductions could include discounts, freight charges, delivery charges, returns—even interior design services of in-house designers. For example, assume that same gross sale of $50,000 with a 10 percent commission on the net sale. From the $50,000, a $1000 deduction for delivery and freight charges is made by the company. The commission that should be paid to the designer would be $4900.

Many companies that sell commercial furniture items pay commission on the goods and other products sold based on the gross margin of the sale. In the *gross margin method* of paying a commission, the commission percentage is not based on the selling price to the client. *Gross margin* (also called gross profit) is the difference between the selling price and the cost price of the goods or services being sold. In the preceding example of a $50,000 gross sale, with a 10 percent commission, assume that the cost price of the sale is $25,000. The amount of commission that should be paid in this case would be $2500.

The preceding example makes it seem like someone who is paid based on the gross margin is not making much for his efforts compared to the other commission methods. In some respects, this is correct. To provide greater incentive, some firms utilizing the gross margin commission method might incorporate a sliding scale of commission. In this situation, different percentages are paid depending on the amount of the gross margin percentage. For instance, if the gross margin is 90 percent (nearly retail price), the commission percentage might be 45 percent. If the gross margin is only 5 percent (nearly cost price), the commission percentage might only be 2 percent. Designers are motivated to sell merchandise and services for the highest gross margin possible in order to receive the most commission possible. It should be noted, however, that depending on the type of work (residential or commercial) and competition, it might not be possible to sell merchandise at a very high gross margin.

Another common compensation method is the hourly wage. When an employee is paid an *hourly wage*, he or she is paid some rate for every hour that he or she works. Although most firms talk about how they pay employees based on an hourly wage, interior design professional staff are rarely actually paid by the hour. Because of the nature of interior design work, the hourly wage is used less often as a method of compensation, except when the monitoring of the employee's productivity and work responsibilities is relatively easy. More common is to compensate entry-level employees and "production" employees, such as secretaries, bookkeepers, tech employees such as CAD specialists, and delivery people.

At the beginning of this section, it was pointed out that Rob was paid an hourly wage. Rob only works part-time, so this compensation method is very appropriate. William is another employee whose job responsibility it is to prepare CAD drawings and other production documents for other designers. William is a full-time employee, and he is also paid an hourly wage. The weekly salary of William is computed by figuring the average workday (e.g., 8 hours) and the average workweek (e.g., 40 hours). If an employee is paid $20.00 an hour, his or her weekly gross salary would be $800 per week for a 40-hour workweek. (This same concept holds true, of course, for Rob or any other part-time employee.) Some firms, however, have slightly shorter workweeks. It is possible for a company's workweek to be 35 or 37 hours rather than 40. It is up to the individual company to determine the length of its normal workweek. Since the federal wage and hour laws apply to design firms and employees who are not considered professional staff, the firm has to pay hourly wage employees overtime for any hours worked beyond the normal workweek when they are a full-time employee. This amounts to time-and-a-half for weekday overtime work and double time for work done on Sundays and holidays.

Another issue to discuss is the concept of an employee's gross salary, not what the employee "takes home" and is free to spend. *Gross salary*, as anyone who has held some kind of a job realizes, is the amount of employee compensation before any deductions. The employer must withhold (deduct) amounts for federal income tax, Social Security[*] and Medicare contributions, possibly state income taxes, and possibly voluntary contributions for such things as health insurance. The amount of compensation left after these

---

[*]Social Security contributions show up on the paycheck stub as FICA. FICA stands for Federal Insurance Contributions Act. Social Security is the common for FICA.

deductions is called net pay, or take-home pay. It is common for the basic withholding deductions for taxes and Social Security to amount to 20 to 35 percent of gross pay.

Often, larger design firms provide methods for employees to earn or achieve supplementary income in addition to their regular compensation. *Incentive compensation* is the term for any payment over and above regular compensation. Incentive compensation is primarily awarded to hourly and salaried employees. Two common types of incentive compensation are merit pay and bonus plans. *Merit pay* is an amount added to an individual's basic annual compensation amount, often as a reward for quality work done in the past. It is commonly referred to as a raise or salary increase. For example, Gail is a senior designer at a firm specializing in hospitality projects. During the last year as the senior designer on a major project, her work was recognized with a competition award for outstanding design using sustainable design concepts. Due to the extra publicity this award gave the design firm, the owner gave Gail a merit pay increase in her salary. This increase in her salary remains in effect into future years with the company. Merit pay is an increase that can go to all employees but usually is given to those individuals whose high level of performance during the past year warrants it. Merit increases are rarely paid to employees on commission.

A *bonus plan* is a method of paying extra compensation to employees based on their producing more than a specific personal quota. Bonuses most commonly are paid to design employees who sell merchandise. If they meet or exceed their sales quotas, the employees are paid some kind of bonus. Since designers who are responsible for creative design work cannot easily establish a quota of design work, bonuses are less often paid to these individuals. However, some interior design firms do have a bonus plan that rewards creative staff. Bonuses are usually based on the employee meeting or exceeding the amount of contracts budgeted or on exceeding a budgeted amount of specifications on a certain kind of furniture or furnishings. A bonus is not an ongoing compensation increase, but only for the year it was awarded. Of course, individuals can achieve bonuses every year. The bonus is the type of incentive compensation that is most commonly paid to those on commission and not eligible for a merit increase.

Another kind of compensation that is added to the basic annual compensation is a cost-of-living adjustment. *A cost-of-living adjustment* (also referred to as COLA) is generally given across the board, meaning that all employees may receive a cost-of-living adjustment to help offset increases in inflation.

Fringe Benefits

Individuals working for a design firm carefully consider the compensation amounts offered when interviewing for a job. They also consider additional payments or benefits that the company has to offer employees. Depending on the size of the firm and allowances for a potential wide variety of fringe benefits, these items can represent from 25 to 40 percent of the overall payroll, with approximately 30 percent of hourly compensation being the most common amount.[1]

There are many kinds of fringe benefits offered by interior design firms. In a very small firm, the fringe benefits will be quite minimal—paid vacation for full-time employees might be the only fringe benefit. The larger the firm is, the more benefits will be provided. Federal and even state labor laws are an important factor in the benefits packages offered. Only the largest of the multidisciplinary design firms will have enough employees to be required to offer or have a wide

TABLE 14-2.

The Most Common Employee Benefits Provided by Businesses.

Actual required benefits will be different based on the size of the firm.

Voluntary benefits

Health insurance

Life insurance

Supplemental insurance such as dental, disability, and vision care

Retirement plan, such as profit sharing

Paid holidays, vacations, and sick leave

Employee purchase discounts

Payments for employee professional association dues

Payments for NCIDQ or other testing and licensing fees

Reimbursements for employee use of personal automobile

Payments for employee educational enhancements

Required "benefits"

Unemployment taxes

Social Security insurance

Workers' compensation insurance

range of benefits. Most firms are too small under federal rules to have more than a few employee fringe benefits. Of course, competition during a tight labor market also can have an impact on benefits paid to employees.

The kind of fringe benefits and the amounts that can be paid to an employee and consequently deducted by the owner of the company vary based on the type of legal business formation. This is an important consideration for companies that begin as partnerships and corporations or experience rapid ongoing growth, as offering fringe benefits can entice highly qualified individuals to work for a particular firm.

The most common fringe benefits given or paid directly to employees are paid vacations, paid holidays, group health insurance, and employee discounts on purchases (see Table 14-2). Other benefits offered to employees might include supplemental health insurance such as dental programs, paid sick leave, and professional-growth benefits. Professional-growth benefits include such things as paid educational benefits for continuing education classes, partial or full payment of professional association dues, and partial or full payment of NCIDQ exam fees.

Other benefits that would not be paid directly to the employee but must be paid by the employer include Social Security tax contributions, workers' compensation taxes, and unemployment insurance taxes. These are benefits that the employee may or may not draw from for some time. Social Security is not payable until the employee retires (or is physically disabled and can no longer work). Workers' compensation covers on-the-job injuries, and unemployment insurance is only paid, under certain circumstances, if the employee has been laid off from the design firm.

When an individual is applying for a job, is considering a promotion, or is weighing the merits of staying with the present employer, he or she must look carefully at the complete benefits package. A position with one firm with a slightly lower salary but a good employer-paid health insurance program may be better than another position where the salary is a bit higher but there is no health insurance program available to employees.

What Would You Do?

Monica has had an unfortunate bout of illness recently. In addition, her young son has also been sick with colds. This has meant she has missed several days, even a few weeks of work, each month for the last six months. Although she is entitled to some sick leave each month, the amount of time she has missed exceeds that amount. Her work as a project designer at the firm has had to be repeatedly done by others. However, the work she has accomplished herself has been at a high level and complimented by clients.

Her boss called her in to his office the other day and informed her that if she misses any more work, he will have to let her go. "All this personal time off is interfering with your ability to get projects completed on time. Other designers have to pick up your slack," her boss told her at that meeting.

THE PERFORMANCE EVALUATION

Management decisions concerning who gets a raise, a promotion, or extra training should someone be laid off or replaced are decisions that owners and managers must deal with throughout the year. The management tool that can be used for these types of decisions is the performance evaluation.

A *performance evaluation* is a systematic evaluation of the positive and negative work efforts of an employee. It is an evaluation based on objective criteria that helps make the process of determining raises, promotions, and the like as fair as possible. The performance evaluation is a positive management activity that always gets a bad rap as an unpleasant task for both the employee and the owner/manager. Part of the reason this is so difficult for design managers is that few have any training in, or experience with, the performance evaluation process.

In many design practices, the performance evaluation consists of an informal mental review of each employee's work contribution. This informal review is almost always based on the manager's subjective opinions rather than on any objective evaluation of the employee's performance of job responsibilities. Considering the increase in employee lawsuits with regard to discrimination, harassment, and unfair termination, it is important for owners and managers to apply performance evaluations.

Conducting performance evaluations as a positive process does take time. It is not easy for owners or managers in busy smaller-sized design offices to consider each employee's past performance and discuss these impressions with the employee. Too often it is anxiety producing for employees as well, since many employers use performance evaluations as a time for negative criticism rather than as an opportunity to help direct an employee's progress and development.

Performance evaluations should be for the development of the employee, not the punishment of the employee for past performance. Maintaining a philosophy that evaluations must be based on the responsibilities that the employee understands to be within his or her control during the period of the evaluation is critical to making the process a positive one. Objective evaluations can help employees be more effective, productive, and loyal to employers. Table 14-3 provides some guidelines for the use of the performance evaluation.

From a legal standpoint, written evaluations also help protect the employer if an employee files a formal grievance. Written notes and evaluations placed in each employee's personnel file provide the owner of the design firm with a credible document that can be used if any employee claims that some type of discriminatory practice exists or unfair termination has occurred.

TABLE 14-3.

Guidelines for Performance Evaluations.

A performance evaluation should be designed to do the following:

- Encourage employee development.
- Aid the employer–employee relationship.
- Provide for supervision and training of design staff as needed by staff member.
- Provide an objective aid in determining compensation increases and promotions.
- Define guidelines for how a performance evaluation impacts dismissals.
- Help motivate employees to achieve agreed-upon goals related to responsibilities and job performance.
- Provide aid in determining needs of new hires.
- Protect the employer from false claims by employees.
- Make available written records of performance and reprimands if a former employee claims wrongful discharge.

A well-conceived and administered performance evaluation should tell each employee how he or she is doing and where he or she can likely progress in the future. Clearly defined job responsibilities in a job description and performance levels for each position level or employee helps this happen. Performance levels also need to be discussed and agreed upon. They can be negotiated each time a formal evaluation occurs. Interim evaluations—especially useful for new employees—should focus on the achievement of goals, and where satisfactory progress does not exist, constructive criticism should be given to help the employee succeed. A discussion regarding new goals and how current and future responsibilities and performance levels fit into these goals becomes the performance criteria for the next evaluation. Two sample performance evaluation forms are included on the CD. They are Items 14-3 and 14-4.

The Performance Evaluation Process

Performance evaluations can be a very valuable task for both the person being evaluated as well as that person's supervisor. It is most valuable, of course, when done to provide constructive criticism to help the employee improve his or her contributions to the company and improve personal skills. In this section, we will discuss the performance evaluation process.

Although informal performance evaluations may occur at any time for any level of employee, most companies find that a formal evaluation should take place on a yearly basis. It is a very good idea, however, for new employees to be evaluated more frequently during the first year. The first evaluation generally takes place at the end of the probationary period, which is usually 90 days. Many firms find it advantageous to have reviews at 30-, 60-, and possibly 75-day intervals for new employees during the 90-day probationary period. Subsequent evaluations occur after the first six months and then after one year. The one-year date can be either on the anniversary date of hiring or on a day set for all evaluations.

The performance evaluation should be performed by the employee's immediate supervisor. In design firms, where people often work in teams to complete projects, individuals who are not truly an employee's supervisor may be asked to evaluate an employee's performance. If this occurs, the employee should be made aware of who is making the evaluations and why he or she is involved, if that person is not, in fact, the employee's supervisor.

Often individual evaluations are supplemented by self- or peer evaluations. Self-evaluations can be helpful, but it is not uncommon for employees to be either harder or easier on themselves than their superior. Peer evaluations, in which employees rate their coworkers, only seem to work when employees trust each other, when they are truly in a position to be very familiar with each other's work, and when they are not competing with each other for raises or promotions. Experience has shown that peers will be either too easy on each other (so as not to get their coworker angry) or too hard on those individuals whom they do not like.

It is best to use a formalized performance evaluation form. The criteria on this form should deal only with those factors that are relevant to an individual's performance. For example, a design assistant may be told that drafting is a primary responsibility of the position. If the quantity of work produced is not relevant but the quality of work (i.e., no mistakes) is, then only the quality of work should be evaluated.

The evaluation form and its application to personnel matters must be written as objectively as possible. Dealing with specific skills and skill levels as they relate to job responsibilities is one way to maintain objectivity. Being sure the evaluation form does not contain a lot of questions that focus on either the personality, attitude, or appearance of the employee also helps to maintain objectivity. The evaluation form also should not evaluate the employee based solely on the employer's personal opinion, especially if that personal opinion has not been satisfactorily communicated to the employees. The correct kind of evaluation form will help maintain objectivity in the evaluation, which is necessary to make it fair for all employees.

A performance evaluation interview should be scheduled so that both the manager and the employee can adequately prepare themselves to discuss the employee's past performance with respect to previously agreed-upon goals. The evaluation interview—generally one hour in length—should be private and held without interruptions. Only the employee and the manager should be present.

The manager should start the performance evaluation interview by making a positive statement. This helps put the employee at ease and avoids putting him or her immediately on the defensive. The employer should seek to be as descriptive as possible in positive and negative comments, and these comments should be based on performance criteria, not on personal feelings. This attitude will help the employee understand more precisely what he or she is doing right or wrong. During the performance evaluation interview, the employee should be asked to evaluate his or her own progress. It is necessary for the employee to comment about his or her own performance so that the employer can understand how the employee views his or her own role.

The last portion of the evaluation interview should focus on the future, with discussions concerning what the employee can do to resolve any performance deficiencies. Discussion and negotiation must occur so that the course of action becomes an agreed-upon plan, not one dictated by the employer. Success comes from focusing on two or three of the more important negative areas. This is a more satisfactory approach, since it is difficult for people to try to improve on many things in which they have been deficient and, at the same time, maintain a positive attitude. A realistic timetable for improvement should also be agreed upon as an aid in future evaluations.

The evaluation interview should be concluded with a summary of the satisfactory and unsatisfactory areas of the employee's performance, as well as an action plan for the resolution of agreed-upon unsatisfactory areas. The evaluation interview should end on a positive note, with the employee understanding clearly how his or her performance is viewed by the employer and what the future will bring for that employee.

After the evaluation, the employer should prepare some notes related to what occurred during the evaluation interview and place the performance evaluation form and notes in the employee's personnel file. It is a good idea for the employee to keep notes as well. The goals and timetable should be prepared as soon as possible. It should then be reviewed individually, and any discrepancies should be discussed and agreed upon immediately.

The employer should follow up the performance evaluation with monitoring of the employee's progress. Some areas may need special monitoring, and the manager must be ready to spend the time either training or working with the employee. Remember that performance evaluations fail when the employer thinks only evaluation and development are the important issues in a formal performance evaluation process.

THE EMPLOYEE HANDBOOK

Adding one or two employees does not generally cause confusion in terms of everyone adhering to the rules and policies of the company. However, when multiple employees exist, it is important for an employee handbook to be developed. The purpose of an *employee handbook* is to provide owners, managers, and employees with a concise reference regarding the company's policies. It can include general operating policies, such as those related to special-ordering merchandise for clients, as well as personnel policies. Some design firms decide to have one handbook that describes personnel issues and one or more additional handbooks that explain operational policies.

Personnel policies are the primary reason that employee handbooks are developed. Having written policy statements helps ensure that policies are applied fairly and consistently. To be sure all policies are current, the owner should review the handbook once a year. The state Department of Labor can advise the owner on current labor policies. Of course, the firm's attorney can also advise on specific legal issues that might arise regarding the contents of the handbook. It is also advisable that all employees sign a form acknowledging that they have received, reviewed, and understand the contents of the handbook.

Employers must recognize that employee handbooks can create legal issues if the handbook is written carelessly. Language in an employee handbook can create employment obligations that the employer did not intend. Many courts have determined that promises or statements that indicate continuing employment in a handbook create an implied contract. An *implied contract* is one in which "a contract [is] implied by the direct or indirect acts of the parties."[2] Implied contracts are also discussed in Chapter 15. Interpretations of the law may make the small-business owner shy away from preparing an employee handbook. On the contrary, it is a useful management tool for any size interior design business.

The handbook is most often prepared by the owner of the company with the assistance of staff. Many policies may already exist in writing, or employees may already know what they are, even if they are not written down. Some information, such as paid holidays and vacation or sick time allowances, may have to be obtained from company records. An employee handbook should be reviewed by the firm's attorney before being issued to the employees.

The organization and contents of the handbook should be logical and concise. For example, the firm may wish to use a format that mirrors the logical sequence of events of an organization. In this case, issues related to hiring would be placed first, hours of work, absenteeism, and employee benefits would be placed in the middle, and the policy when an employee leaves the company, including termination, would be placed at the end.

As much as possible, clear and concise wording is important. Terminology that everyone understands or is in common usage should be adopted. Policy statements are meant to inform employees, not impress them with flowery prose. Also remember that some employees are not interior designers and may not be familiar with some of the jargon of the interior design profession.

TABLE 14-4.

Common Parts of an Employee Handbook.

A. **Overview**
B. **Introduction.** Provides an overview of the company.
C. **Organization.** Provides a description of the responsibility areas and organizational structure.
D. **Employment and hiring policies.** Details hiring procedures, if performance evaluations are performed, and promotion policies.
E. **Compensation.** Details compensation policies for all levels of employees. This section commonly defines pay periods, bonuses, and fringe benefits (if any).
F. **Time off.** Details company paid holidays (if any), vacation policies, sick leave, and other paid or nonpaid days off.
G. **Training.** Provides information about any company training or reimbursement for training for educational purposes.
H. **General rules and policies.** Details workweek, overtime, tardiness, and such things as use of company phone and mail for personal business, dress code, and other general work conditions.
I. **Leaving the company.** Includes information on termination policies, expected notice, severance pay (if any), and policies on references.

It is important for the owner and/or managers to meet with employees to explain why the handbook was prepared, to define the purpose of the handbook, and to go over its contents with employees. Even if employees have not been a part of the process of creating the handbook, at least they will feel less threatened by a new set of rules if the rules are explained to them before the rules are put into effect. Revisions also need to be reviewed with employees before they take effect.

Precisely how much information should go into an employee handbook will vary with the size and complexity of the design firm. It should provide the policies needed to aid managers in control and decision making. However, the business owner must always remember that strictly enforced rules may lead to a disgruntled group of self-motivated, self-directed individuals—the type of person that often seeks a career in interior design. Table 14-4 summarizes the common parts of employee handbooks.

Written policies related to operational and personnel issues aid the owners and managers of the firm in running the practice in a professional manner. Written policies also help clarify how things are done and where employees stand in their relationship to the firm. Policies that are clear and can be easily followed will be adhered to by all employees. Employers need to keep in mind that an employee handbook is never really finished. It needs to be reviewed periodically and modified if necessary to meet the changes in company policies. Items 14-5 and 14-6 provide sample sections of an employee handbook.

MENTORING

It costs a firm a considerable amount of money to train a new employee. Some feel that it can cost up to one year's salary to train someone to really be a benefit to the firm. Those funds are in addition to the actual salary, by the way, and represent time that the owner or others in the firm must spend in training a new employee, along with the normal slowness of someone unfamiliar with procedures in a company.

Mentoring is training or advising someone to help that individual attain a higher level of success. Although mentoring can be a kind of training, it is also more than training an employee in how to do the operational procedures of a firm. Someone that can be a mentor to another designer can provide career advice that goes beyond what might be appropriate to the immediate situation.

Large design firms often have a formal mentoring program where a senior designer works with entry-level and junior designers to help them learn the ropes and improve skills. In a small firm, it is hoped that the owner will mentor new employees and, of course, he or she does so at first. Small firm owners rarely have sufficient time to mentor employees after the first few weeks or months.

Mentors come from many different places. A mentor can be someone in the firm; others find mentors outside the design firm in which they work. Perhaps it is someone that the designer meets at an association meeting or an alum from the designer's college. A mentor within the firm helps the individual increase worth and understanding within that company. Having a mentor from some other firm or part of the industry gives the individual someone to talk to about issues that he or she might not want to discuss with a colleague.

When someone comes to you seeking a mentor—whether or not you own the company—remember to:

Keep the discussions confidential.

Only accept a mentorship relationship if you can be sincerely helpful to the other person.

When the person asks you to critic his or her work, give constructive criticism.

Don't talk too much! Ask them questions and let the person think out loud.

SUMMARY

Does it seem strange to consider that even a one- or two-person design firm should have a defined structure as to how to go about doing the tasks needed in the firm? It should not, since having a defined operational structure ensures that even the sole practitioner has a checklist of what must be done for each project, thus ensuring quality control in project execution and management.

As an interior design firm grows, it becomes increasingly important for the owners and managers to review and define the organizational structure. Job responsibilities become more specialized, and roles must be defined. The development and utilization of job classifications and job descriptions assist owners of growing design firms in managing employees.

Fair compensation and fringe benefits vary widely in the interior design industry. Employers do not want to pay more than they have to, and at the same time, employees want to feel they are being treated fairly. Compensation and fringe benefits are particularly important issues during a tight job market when a few extra benefits can make the difference between an employee accepting a position or not. Of course, these issues are also important in a good job market, when design firms, frankly, become less concerned about keeping employees. Fair methods are needed to attract and retain qualified and appropriate employees.

To keep good employees, research has shown that more must be done for employees than give them occasional raises. Performance evaluations that are keyed to job descriptions help employees understand how they are doing. They also show employees how they can advance in the firm. In addition, performance evaluations help protect employers when disputes concerning termination occur. Employee handbooks clarify work rules and operational procedures. Mentoring employees (or an employee finding his or her own mentor) is another important part of ownership. Employees are expensive to train and retain, and mentoring does not automatically mean a well-trained designer will go some-where else. A well-trained and fairly compensated designer will frequently be willing to stay with a company than try to make it somewhere else all over again.

All these issues are of critical importance to the owner and managers of an interior design practice. A firm is really made up of individuals who must be managed and motivated to achieve the business goals of the firm. Without effective office organization and employee management, the smooth operation of the firm becomes difficult, if not impossible. In the next chapter, we will cover legal issues of employment, such as the employer–employee relationship and employment contracts.

REFERENCES

1. U.S. Small Business Administration, 2005, p. 1.
2. Brown and Sukys, 1997, p. 98.

CHAPTER 15

Legal Issues of Employment

Key Terms and Concepts

These key terms and concepts are important to material in this chapter. Many of these terms will be utilized in other chapters as well. Be sure you understand these items as you read this chapter.

Terms and Concepts

Agency relationship

Agent

Principal

Employer–employee relationship

Employment at will

Wrongful discharge

Implied contract

Employment contract

Noncompete agreement

Restrictive covenant

Work product

Independent contractor

Sexual harassment

Quid pro quo

Workers' compensation

Equal Employment Opportunity Commission (EEOC)

Federal Employment Laws

Title VII of the Civil Rights Act of 1964

Equal Employment Opportunity Act of 1972

Civil Rights Act of 1991

Age Discrimination in Employment Act of 1967/1990

Americans with Disabilities Act Title I

Executive Order 11246

Rehabilitation Act of 1973/1974

Equal Pay Act of 1963

Occupational Safety and Health Act (OSHA) of 1970

National Labor Relations Act (Wagner Act)

Family and Medical Leave Act of 1993

Pregnancy Discrimination Act (amendment to Title VII)

Consolidated Omnibus Budget Reconciliation Act (COBRA) of 1986

Critical Issues

After completing this chapter you should be able to:

- Discuss the agency relationship and how it impacts the employee–employer relationship in an interior design office.
- Explain why (or why not) a design staff member is an agent for an interior design office.
- Outline the legal duties the employer has to an employee, as well as the legal duties an employee has to an employer.
- Discuss employment at will from the employer's point of view.
- Compare employment at will with a situation where a designer has an employment contract with his or her employer.
- Explain how a noncompete clause in an employment contract might affect a designer (currently an employee) starting his or her own business; going to work for another firm in the same geographic area.
- Outline the differences between an independent contractor who does interior design work for the company and an employee.
- Explain why it is important for an employer to have a written contract with an independent contractor providing CAD services.
- Discuss an example of wrongful discharge and how this situation could have been avoided.
- Understand how to protect yourself from situations that might be considered sexual harassment.
- Briefly explain why the federal government has instituted employment laws.

Mary worked for a large commercial interior design firm where the number of men employees outnumbered the women. For the most part this was not a problem, as several of the men were willing to provide guidance and help and good camaraderie to Mary. But two of the men constantly told off-color jokes and, at lunch meetings at some restaurants, not only ignored Mary in the discussions but also made comments about waitstaff that seemed out of line. After one exceptionally difficult in-house meeting of the staff, Mary complained to her boss about their rude behavior. He said he would look into it, but after a few weeks, nothing had changed.

More and more employees are utilizing the courts to satisfy their grievances. In the interior design profession, lawsuits occur as a result of misunderstandings about work requirements, company policies, or layoffs, for which there is seemingly little reason. As women claim their right to be treated fairly and equally in the workplace, sexual harassment and discrimination complaints are increasing. Far too many interior design employees find out about their legal rights and obligations only after some unpleasant experience.

Employers are responsible for abiding by many federal and state laws regarding the hiring and firing of employees and meeting regulations about keeping a harassing environment out of the office. Although some statutes have an impact only on large design firms, many affect the small interior design firm as well. Meeting the spirit of employment laws is, at the very least, the ethical thing to do in any size or type of interior design firm. Added to this ethical consideration is the fact that the number of employees suing employers over some issue or another has increased. Although there are no actual figures for the interior design industry, it is likely that interior design firms are being affected by employee lawsuits.

Interpretations of older laws and the enactment of new laws to protect employees have made it difficult for employers to hire or fire individuals when they do not perform as expected. Firms that never before found it necessary to have job descriptions and performance evaluations are busy developing them in order to clarify the responsibilities of their employees. Strategies that were seldom used by design firms in the past are now being used to protect the employer. Employment contracts and more formalized record keeping of disciplinary actions and performance evaluations have become necessary in the interior design industry. Since the number of designers who have left companies to start their own small firms has grown over the last few years, the misuse of independent contractors has unfortunately grown in this industry. Even small design studios are looking to develop formalized personnel management systems in order to protect themselves from the possibility of employee complaints and lawsuits and to meet government regulations.

In this chapter, we will look at many issues related to legal regulation of employment. We will briefly discuss federal laws regulating employment, the agency relationship, the concept of employment at will, implied contracts, and employment contracts. This chapter will define the difference between employees and independent contractors and will discuss sexual harassment. Legal issues concerning interviewing for a position are detailed in Chapter 34.

Please note that the information on legal issues of employment are provided as a brief overview and do not constitute a complete legal discussion of these topics nor considered legal advice. Employers and employees who have questions concerning potentially unfair treatment should discuss this matter with an attorney familiar with human resources law.

THE AGENCY RELATIONSHIP

Individuals who are employees of a company are naturally expected to follow the rules and policies of the company. They perform duties required by the company and are expected to act in the best interests of the company. The employer–employee relationship is important to understand, since actions by either party can occasionally lead to civil lawsuits between the parties as well as between one of the parties and an outsider such as a client. Of course, misunderstandings about the responsibilities and expectations can also lead to a lot of bad feelings without resort to lawsuits.

Many readers are familiar with the fact that agents represent professional athletes during negotiations for contracts with sports teams. Agents also frequently represent a home buyer or seller. In common law, an *agency relationship* occurs when one person or entity agrees to represent or do business for another person or entity. In the agency relationship, an *agent* is empowered to represent another party, called the *principal*. The agency relationship gives the principal the right to control the conduct of the agent in the matters entrusted to the agent. The agent for a sports figure cannot make a deal with a sports team if it is not agreed to by the principal—the sports figure. The individual working for the interest of the sports figure or a home buyer is an agent, not an employee.

The employer–employee relationship is a type of agency relationship. An employee is defined as "a person who works in the service of another person (the employer) under an express or implied contract of hire, under which the employer has the right to control the details of work performance."[1] The principal of the interior design firm is the owner (or controlling board member), whereas the agents are all the employees, whether they are in management positions or staff positions.

In a pure agency relationship, the agent can negotiate and make contracts for the principal. In most cases, this aspect of the agency relationship does not exist in an interior design firm. In general, only certain individuals in the design firm other than the owner should be able to sign the actual contract for services. An employee is a legal agent of the firm only if he or she has the authority to act in place of the owner, although in many other ways, employees are also agents, since they also represent the owner. For example, Roger, Phyllis, and Kelley work for Marjorie. All four designers are expected to call on clients, obtain the information to prepare a design contract, and prepare the required design activities to complete the project. Only Marjorie, who is the owner, is allowed to sign the design contracts. If Roger, Phyllis, or Kelley signed a design contract, the contract would not be binding on the firm.

Agreeing to go to work for an employer means that the employee understands that there are certain expectations and duties concerning the work relationship. Agency relationship is the legal concept that specifically spells out the extent of the relationship between the employer and the employee. Unlike most contractual relationships, the conditions of the agency relationship do not have to be in writing. There does have to be an agreement to the effect that the employee is willing to be an employee or agent for the employer. It is, of course, highly recommended that any employee who is an actual agent and who can sign contracts of any kind should also sign an employment contract upon hiring. Accepting a position and knowing what the responsibilities of the position cover imply agreement. Since all positions in the firm have different responsibilities and different levels of trust within the employer–employee relationship, it is important for employees to fully understand their responsibilities. Carefully prepared job descriptions, as discussed in Chapter 14, explain most of these responsibilities.

Employees and legal agents of the design firm understand they are being hired to perform certain responsibilities and the performance of these responsibilities involves certain duties to the employer. The employer also has responsibilities to the employee and agent. Each party has a primary duty to the other to act in good faith toward the other party. There are specific legal duties of each party in an agency relationship. Let us look first at the duties that the employer has to the employee.

Employer to Employee

When Michael agreed to work for Paul as design director, they had negotiated Michael's salary and benefits. Providing the employee with a reasonable amount or kind of compensation for the completion of the services that Michael would be expected to perform is one of the duties that the employer has to an employee or agent. What this reasonable amount of compensation entails is not defined by law for most types of employees, except that the law states that it must conform to what would be customary compensation for the services performed. Of course, there are federal laws that outline minimum wages for certain types of employees depending on the size of the company. The employer is also required to provide reimbursement to an employee for reasonable expenses while the employee is working for and under the direction of the employer. For example, since Michael will be using his car to travel from the office to many job sites, Paul will reimburse Michael (as well as other employees) when he uses his own automobile when traveling on company business. The amount of that reimbursement is negotiable, but it is commonly set to the amount per mile allowed as a deduction on federal income taxes.

Another important duty of the employer is to assist and/or cooperate with the employee so that he or she is able to perform the agreed-upon services. For example, Paul will provide computer equipment and office furniture in the office for Michael to do his job. If he expects Michael to provide his own computer, it can be interpreted that the employer, Paul, is inhibiting Michael from performing his duties. It could be construed by a judge as a violation of the employer–employee agreement if the employer prevents or inhibits the employee from performing his or her duties.

Federal and state regulations as well as basic common law requires that the employer provide safe working conditions for employees. Should an employee feel that his or her working environment is unsafe, the employer cannot dismiss the employee for reporting unsafe conditions.

The preceding examples relate to general duties of the employer to the employee. Other duties may also be required of the employer, depending on the exact nature of the agreement between the employer and employee and changes in prevailing federal or state laws.

Employee to Employer

Accepting compensation from an employer automatically means that the employee has a duty to do the work assigned and follow the policies of the company. Whereas Paul has certain duties to Michael, Michael also has several basic duties to Paul and the design firm, and may have additional ones, as outlined by any formal agreement or written contract.

Michael, and all other employees, have an obligation to perform duties with reasonable diligence and skill. What distinguishes that level of diligence and skill is related to what would be considered common for the services required and experience level expected. For example, if Erica is hired on the basis of her skill in, and knowledge of, architectural CAD software—purported by her to be at a high level after working with CAD for eight years—her employer has a right to expect that the work performed be representative of someone who fully understands the software. Rick, an entry-level designer, would not be expected to produce CAD drawings at the same level as Erica.

Many say that loyalty to employers (and vice versa) has diminished over the years. However, a second duty of the employee is to be loyal to the employer. An employee is expected to act in the interests of the employer, not for the benefit of any outside party or even of the employee. This means, for example, that a designer such as Michael who prepares the design work for a major company cannot be hired by that client company to design an additional area in the company "on the side." If the designer engaged in moonlighting—which is when an individual holds or engages in work outside his or her main job—the employer would have the right to terminate the employee for breach of the agency relationship because of this conflict of interest.

Another important duty of the employee or agent is to keep the employer informed of anything related to the relationship or work undertaken for the employer. "What the agent actually tells the principal is not relevant; what the agent *should have told* the principal is crucial."[2] The following provides an example. Sara, working at an office furnishings dealer as a designer, mentions to her boss that a client appears to be ready to order 50 traditional desks and credenzas from a certain manufacturer. The boss, thinking that this would be a good opportunity to order some of this popular desk for their inventory, orders another ten units. After the order has been placed, Sara learns, but neglects to tell her boss, that the client has changed his mind and will not order the desks for at least six months. The boss, who now is responsible for paying for all the desks and credenzas because it is too late to cancel the order with the manufacturer, could consider Sara in breach of the agency relationship.

Employees not only must be loyal to their employers, but they also owe a duty to be obedient to the employer's rules concerning business activities. In other words, the employee is required to follow all legal and clearly stated instructions or policies of the employer. Creative individuals have a tendency to dislike rules and want to work in a manner that suits them. Unfortunately, this does not always work out, as working for someone else does mean that the individual must follow company policies and processes. For example, if the company has a policy that the sample boards and drawings are to be completed in a certain way and use specific conventions, all the designers will be expected to complete their work according to those policies. Deviations of policies without permission from the right supervisor technically violate this duty to the employer. In another example, if policies state that warehouse workers may not use the company vehicle for personal business, it would be a violation of this duty if one of the drivers used a company truck on the weekend without getting permission from the proper supervisor. Only certain emergency situations would allow the employee to deviate from these obligations.

Employees are hired because of the skills they possess, which match the tasks and responsibilities required by the employer. The employer expects that those tasks and responsibilities will be performed by the employee, not a third party. It is unlikely that an employee will hire someone else to perform the work required by that employee without telling the employer; however, this duty is part of the relationship and personal service that are required by the agency relationship.

Finally, some employees, Michael for example as design director, may have access to company funds (petty cash to purchase supplies) or property (perhaps the opportunity to take home a company-owned laptop computer). The employee has a duty to keep a proper accounting of the inflows and outflows of funds or use of property. A designer who has authorization to sign purchase orders for supplies would be breaching this duty if he or she used one of the purchase orders to obtain supplies for his or her own needs. In this case, the breach is also a criminal act, and the employer could press charges.

There are other kinds of issues that can be involved in the duties and responsibilities of both the employer to an employee and an agent to the principal. The issues discussed here are the key issues especially in the employer–employee relationship. It is also important to note that when an interior designer is hired by a client, a form of agency exists. It is not quite the same, however, as the employer-employee agency. Interior designers are not employees of the client in the same sense as has been described in this section. Comments about this form of agency relationship are included in Chapter 24 on design contracts. Employers are advised to discuss other specific issues with their attorney. Employees may also wish to consult with an attorney or read more about agency relationship in a business law book, several of which are mentioned in the references.

EMPLOYMENT AT WILL

Sandra was hired by Hayden, Mill & Williams Designs three years ago. She has been working in the interior design department as a designer/project manager. A month ago, Ms. Mill discussed some problems that clients had been expressing about Sandra's performance over the last several months with Sandra. She was told at that time that she needed to correct the attitude and lack of communications issues that the clients had become upset about and reported. Another client called the primary owner, Jim Hayden, and was very angry about some things said by Sandra at a meeting. Can the design firm fire Sandra?

In the vast majority of cases, an interior designer joins a firm after one or more interviews and without signing an employment agreement and begins work after a brief introduction to the other employees and a complete explanation of job responsibilities. In other words, the firm has done what it wishes to do in terms of investigating the qualifications and personal attributes of the employee and sets him or her to work with the conditions of employment as stated in those interviews. This situation describes the common concept of employment at will.

Employment at will relates to the doctrine that an employee, who is not bound by a written contract and who has no written terms of his or her employment spelled out, can be fired by the employer at any time without any explanation. Traditionally, the courts have ruled that, since the employee may quit at any time without giving a reason, the employer has the right to fire the employee at any time without giving a reason, as long as the firing does not violate any federal or state employment laws. Although the basic concept of employment at will includes the right of the employer to fire someone with very little reason, the employer must be careful when terminating any employee. The courts have also ruled that if promises were made during the interview, the employer might have implied an agreement, which then makes it harder to fire an employee.

Interior design has grown to be a very competitive business. Many design firms who never before thought of needing employment agreements with the professional staff have begun to do so. Designers who work for a firm for a few years later decide to start their own firm and often take some clients with them. If there is an employment-at-will situation with no contract, the designer perhaps has a legal right to do this, but no doubt does not have an ethical right to take clients.

There are some restrictions on the employer's right to terminate an employee under the employment-at-will doctrine. An employee cannot be fired merely because of his or her sex, race, religion, age, or physical condition. An employer cannot fire an employee out of malice, in retaliation, or because of bad faith. Unless there is a contract between the employer and the employee, the employer can fire the employee without giving any reason. Of course, an employer can have many reasons to terminate an employee that are perfectly legal. A few examples of these include insubordination, violating company rules, excessive absence or lateness, low productivity, misappropriating company property, or a downturn in business.

With the increased number of lawsuits and challenges over firings, the employer must be more careful in terminating an employee even when an at-will state exists. Employers are being more thorough when investigating a potential employee. Employers should also document problematic activity of employees as an important employer safeguard. In the same sense, the employee should have documentation or copies of materials concerning any employment discussions concerning poor work performance.

Unfortunately, some employers take advantage of the employment-at-will doctrine and terminate employees unfairly. If an employee believes that he or she has been fired unfairly or not in accordance with his or her written or implied contract, the employee may have grounds for a wrongful discharge suit.

Ralph has worked for the design firm for a little more than a year. Clients from three projects of the eight he has been responsible for have complained to the owner about his sometimes poor attitude, as well as a consistently poor record of responding to client communications about projects. Even so, three of the projects he worked on during the year have won industry awards, including one in which the client complained to the owner. The owner decided to fire Ralph after a client called and threatened to file a suit against the firm and an ethics complaint against Ralph. After talking to some colleagues at another firm, Ralph decided to look into suing the firm because of the termination.

Wrongful discharge basically means that the employee has been fired without good cause. Was Ralph wrongfully discharged? Wrongful discharge litigation, also called unjust dismissal, stems from rulings by judges who feel that the employment legislation passed by federal and state governments have not always gone far enough to protect employees. Common-law wrongful discharge is based on legal precedent rather than on statutes. Under the concept of wrongful discharge, workers cannot be fired for performing "public obligations," such as jury duty or voting. Employees also cannot be fired for reporting company violations of health or safety laws (called whistle-blowing). These are examples of a public policy tort and are grounds for an employee lawsuit.

Yet employers must have reasons for terminating an employee—what attorneys often call "just cause." A few examples that show cause are excessive absences or tardiness, violating company policies, being dishonest and stealing from the company, and poor job performance. The last is often the most difficult for the employer to justify unless a pattern of performance that has been documented can be shown.

Another aspect of wrongful discharge involves implied contracts. Many courts have ruled that verbal agreements about working conditions constitute an implied contract between employer and employee. An *implied contract* is a contract formed by the actions of the parties rather than by an expressed written agreement. A written or oral assurance made to an employee by the employer can restrict the employer's right to fire the employee for anything other than cause. It is thus very important for employers to not make any long-term promises or statements about employment during interviews. In handbooks, during interviews, and when an offer of employment is actually made, the employer should be clear that the hiring is at will and no contract exists between the parties—unless, of course, a contract is desired.

According to Lewin G. Joel, to see if an implied contract exists, the courts will look at such things as how long the employee has worked for the firm, if records show a lack of criticism of the employee, whether promises or assurances have been given to the employee, and the firm's overall employment practices.[3]

Although it is a good idea for a firm with several employees to have an employee handbook, the owner of the firm must be careful about what is included. Judgments in some states have found that statements in an employee handbook can constitute an implied contract related to the firing and possibly other conditions of employment. In the case of terminations without reason, if the handbook describes the procedure for dismissal, an employee cannot be terminated unless the firm has followed that procedure. For example, if a company named Business Office Furniture has the statement "No employee will be dismissed without good cause" in its handbook, an employee cannot be fired unless the employee has been told what that "good cause" reason is. To avoid this problem, it is necessary to add a statement in an employee handbook such as "the employee has no contract for employment unless the contract is in writing and has been signed by the employer" and/or that "the company reserves the right to fire the employee for reasons that may have been stated in the handbook (such as insubordination) or for no reason at all." These kinds of statements help protect the employer.

Employees like Ralph may feel they have been fired wrongfully or illegally. The burden to prove that will be on the employee. The employee must be able to prove in court that the firing was due to discrimination or wrongful discharge or that for some other reason he or she was fired illegally. This can be very difficult for the employee to prove. The employee can protect him- or herself by requesting written information regarding expectations and performance evaluations on a regular basis. It is also important for the employee to document any events that might relate to the firing. The employee should also maintain copies of performance evaluations that have been signed by the supervisor, as well as notes about any meetings concerning job performance.

Small and large firms should protect themselves from potential charges by changing management practices as employees are hired. Regular performance evaluations of all employees hired "at will" is one way to prove that a terminated employee has been fired because of inadequate job performance. Documented meetings, during which the manager talks to and warns an employee that he or she is not meeting expectations, is another method the employer can use to protect his or her right to fire noncontract employees. Adding disclaimer statements to employee handbooks also affords the employer protection against lawsuits.

Although it is harder for an employer to fire an employee for little or no reason, the courts still support the idea that the employer must retain the right to fire employees who are incompetent, unqualified, unwilling to work, and so on. As more and more court cases related to improper termination occur, it is important that both employers and employees take the hiring, evaluation, and termination process more seriously. Consider this example. Alice has worked for a 25-person commercial design firm for only about three months. She was hired right out of school, and her hiring was based in part on a terrific portfolio. Her portfolio and her comments at the interview indicated she had very good drafting skills. By the time of her 90-day performance evaluation, it had become obvious that Alice was struggling with the drafting assignments given to her by the design director. During her 90-day performance review, she was asked about problems and then was asked to bring in her portfolio for a second meeting. At that second meeting, Alice admitted that some of her portfolio work was done by a friend. Alice was subsequently fired.

Both employers and employees should be aware of each other's rights with regard to employment and termination. Employers no longer can terminate an employee capriciously if the employee is fulfilling his or her duties in accordance with satisfactory levels of performance. And employees have the right to retain employment without fear of retaliation, sexual harassment, and discrimination.

What Would You Do?

A good friend of yours who works at another design firm in town told you about a situation that happened to her two weeks ago. She went on a trip with her boss to an out-of-town job site. The meetings lasted two days. Your friend told you that her boss made a pass at her. "It wasn't the first time," she said. "He has made comments at work that I just don't think are appropriate," she continued.

She said that she doesn't know what to do because she likes working there and in every other respect the firm is a great place to work. "I don't know what to do. I already told this jerk designer that I am not interested." she said.

EMPLOYMENT CONTRACTS

Interior design firms all have a valuable intangible asset that they work hard to obtain and to maintain. That asset is their client list. There have been many instances when an interior designer works for a firm for a few years and then leaves, taking clients of the firm with that designer. This is a primary reason why many interior design firms have resorted to the use of employment contracts when hiring staff in today's competitive market. Losing clients in this way can be financially damaging to the employer. However, it is important to note that preventing employees from taking clients to another job is not the only reason that a formal employment contract is used.

An *employment contract* or agreement is used to spell out conditions of employment or special perks and benefits. Employment contracts have always been more prevalent for management and sales positions. Professional staff positions in interior design are more often considered to be employment at will. Tighter job markets and increased competition have resulted in an increased use of employment contracts for the design staff as well. Of course, disagreements also occur when an employee was not asked to sign a written contract but the employment situation has been considered "at will." Figure 15-1 shows a sample employment contract.

An employment contract does not have to be in writing. An oral employment contract would be formed technically when the employer and employee have agreed about things with respect to responsibilities, compensation, and terms of employment. As previously discussed, these discussions and/or clauses in an employee handbook create restrictions that lead to implied contracts. For the most part, written contracts are prepared to clarify more complex issues that may be of interest to the employer or the employee. An interior designer who is responsible for sale of goods or is otherwise eligible for a commission or a bonus may want a written contract to spell out what will be paid and how the commission or bonus will be paid. Some firms that sell substantial amounts of goods seek contracts to protect company policies such as discount structures that competitors would like to have if an employee goes to a competitor. And many employers seek written contracts to limit the employee from taking clients to competing firms if the employee quits.

In general, the written employment contract covers the following:

1. *Compensation.* This section explains whether the employee will be paid hourly, on a salary, or by commission. If by commission, the method of payment should be spelled out.

2. *Employee benefits.* The firm may wish to explain specific employee benefits that have been negotiated. It is likely that they are the same as all other employees, but it might be feasible for some employees to have a different benefit package than other individuals. This is especially true for management and senior designer staff.

3. *Employment responsibilities.* The employee's responsibilities will be explained in sufficient detail so each party knows what the employee will be expected to do for the firm. Many companies refer to and attach a copy of the appropriate job description.

4. *Grounds for termination.* It is critical for both the employer and employee that statements about procedures and policies concerning termination notice and the manner in which either party must give notice are included in the contract. For the protection of the employee, statements should also outline how any outstanding commission (if commission is part of the compensation method) is to be paid.

5. *Termination for cause.* This clause protects the employee from being terminated for some capricious reason. Reasons for termination for cause include negligence, incompetence, dishonesty, disloyalty, and nonadherence to company policies.

Corporate Interiors Group, Inc.
7000 N. Lincoln Avenue
Anywhere, Pennsylvania

August 200x

Mr. Tony Smith
8142 E. Dempster St.
Anywhere, Pennsylvania

Dear Tony:

Let me welcome you to the Corporate Interiors Group, Inc. family! We are very pleased you have decided to join our company.

The following constitutes the employment contract between Corporate Interiors Group, Inc. employer, and Tony Smith, employee.

Employment

You shall devote your full time and best efforts to interior design activities and perform these activities to the best of your ability. You are not allowed to work for clients or other design firms outside the employ of Corporate Interiors Group, Inc.

The starting job classification for your employment is **Project Manager.** The duties and responsibilities of a Project Manager include: marketing presentations, project design and specification, production of contract documents, working with designers and design assistants, job site supervision or coordination, and other duties and responsibilities as called out on the attached job description.

Compensation

Project Managers are compensated on a salary basis. Your starting salary will be _____ annually. This salary will be paid on the basis of 26 equal pay periods.

You are eligible for the bonus program after you have worked full-time for a period of three (3) consecutive months. Bonuses are determined based on a percentage of income. The details of the bonus calculations are outlined in the attachment, "Corporate Interiors Group, Inc. Bonus Policies." This attachment is considered part of this employment contract.

Project Managers are entitled to a _____ percent commission on all accessory specifications. Payment is made only after receipt of payment from the client.

Merit and cost-of-living increases are only awarded at the beginning of the calendar year. Merit raises are determined on the basis of performance reviews. Any salary increase thus earned will begin at the next regular pay period after the completion of performance reviews. Performance reviews are conducted for all employees during November and December. Cost-of-living increases are at the discretion of the owners, not the design department manager.

Benefits

All benefits are described in detail in the company handbook. There is a company retirement plan. Eligibility and details are available from the Personnel Manager.

Termination

Your employment may be terminated by either party upon written notice. This notice must specify the date of termination and be hand-delivered or delivered by certified mail.

FIGURE 15-1.

An example of an employment contract for an interior design position.

A. Within thirty (30) days of termination, you will be paid outstanding commission on sales of accessories made prior to your termination where all the merchandise has been delivered and accepted to the customer.

B. Commissions due on sales begun prior to your termination but not delivered prior to your termination will be paid within 30 days of receipt of payment by the customer.

C. Bonus payments will be prorated on the number of calendar days you worked between the last date of the previous bonus payment and the date of termination notice.

Noncompetition Provision

The employee may not go to work for a competitor of Corporate Interiors Group, Inc. for a period of 15 days from the date of termination of employment with Corporate Interiors Group, Inc.

The employee will not make available to a subsequent employer any confidential information concerning the operations and clients of Corporate Interiors Group.

Return of Company Property

Upon termination of employment, the employee will surrender all handbooks, files, equipment, price lists, catalogs, customer information, and other company records or property. The use of photographs for a personal portfolio of projects which the employee was primarily responsible when an employee of Corporate Interiors Group can be used only if Corporate Interiors Group is cited as the employer.

Modifications to the Contract

No changes, modifications, additions, or deletions shall be made to this contract unless those changes, modifications, additions, or deletions are in writing, and are signed by both parties.

The above constitutes the total legal agreement between the parties named. Signatures below signify agreement to the terms of the employment contract. One copy shall be placed in your employment file. The second copy should be retained by the employee.

_____   _____

Tony Smith, Employee   **Date**

_____   _____

Jordan Jones, President   **Date**
Corporate Interiors Group, Inc.

Attachments:
 Job description, Project Manager
 Corporate Interiors Group, Inc. Bonus Policies

FIGURE 15-1.

(*Continued*)

6. *Territory rights*. Sales personnel especially are limited to working with clients only in certain territories. This territory might be certain cities or states, or even certain clients. If the employee is limited to a territory, this fact should be stated in the contract.

7. A *noncompete agreement*. The noncompete clause is also often called a *restrictive covenant*. This type of clause affects the employee after leaving the company and places some limits on where and/or how the employee may work after leaving regardless of the reason. A non-compete clause is used by interior design firms most frequently to prevent an interior designer from taking clients from the employer with the employee. It may also be written to prevent employees from taking other company privileged information such as discount structures to another job situation.

    The length of time of the restriction is the most contentious part of this employment contract clause. The noncompete/restrictive covenant can effectively prevent the employee from working for a competitor of the employer or from starting his or her own business, and can limit the territory in which the employee seeks new employment. A restrictive covenant is enforceable by the court as long as it does not last for an unreasonable length of time or unfairly restrict the individual from making a living in the same location as the former employer. What the length of time is and what the area is that are considered reasonable is up to the court in the area.

8. *Ownership of work*. Another clause that has become more prevalent in contracts for interior designers is a clause dealing with ownership of what is called *work product*. Recall from Chapter 10 that the design work undertaken as an employee belongs to the employer. Even without a clause of this type in an employment contract, the interior designer must have permission of the employer to use any drawings or documents created for the employer's clients in the designer's portfolio. The use of work product in a portfolio when one is looking for another job or starting one's own firm without permission can also be an ethics violation.

There may be other clauses in the contract to protect either party. A clause regarding return of company property may be in the contract. Although most employment contracts in the interior design profession would not have an ending date, the employer or the employee might wish to have a duration clause that specifies a fixed date when the contract would expire. It is understood that the contract remains in force as long both parties agree to the employee's continuing employment.

Employment contracts can protect both the employee and the employer. If the employer requests that a written contract be signed, the prospective employee should be certain that he or she understands all the terms of the contract. If an oral agreement is made, the same advice is suggested. In fact, many authors on employee rights suggest that the employee prepare a letter that summarizes the oral agreements discussed during the job interview and then send this letter to the employer. It is far more pleasant for both the employer and the employee to be in agreement concerning the terms of employment, compensation, and other conditions of the employment relationship rather than at odds about those conditions later on in court.

INDEPENDENT CONTRACTORS

Fred recently obtained a contract to remodel the kitchen and family room of a large house. He generally does his drawings using manual drafting; however, the contractor retained by the home owner only works with CAD drawings. Fred did not feel he had time to learn CAD for the project, so he contacted Emily, an architect he met a few months ago at a professional association event. Fred and Emily discussed whether she could do the drawings for Fred from his sketches.

There are many occasions that interior designers utilize the services of individuals who are not employees of the firm. A very common example is all the tradespeople who install goods purchased for clients in residential and commercial projects. For example, a designer who hires a wallpaper hanger is hiring an independent contractor, since the wallpaper hanger has his own business. The delivery crew that has been hired by the design firm on an as-needed basis to deliver furniture for a design firm is considered an independent contractor, as that crew works for a company providing warehouse and delivery services to many designers.

Individuals who work on the design portion of a project can also be considered independent contractors. A design firm can intermittently supplement its staff with design personnel when necessary to handle a work overload or to complete work that in-house staff does not have the expertise to handle. These individuals might be designers who had been laid off by an employer but are asked back on an as-needed basis. Some designers started their own businesses and freelance their design services to design firms. In some cases, it might be a designer working for another firm that has been given permission to work with another firm on a small part of a project.

These temporary workers are often thought of as independent contractors. According to the IRS, the general rule is that an individual is an *independent contractor* if the employing company has the right to control or direct only the result of the work and not the means and methods of accomplishing the result.[4] The independent contractor usually has a specific, short-term working relationship with the firm, and the work often is defined by a written contract. The hiring firm is not required to pay benefits to an independent contractor, since that individual is not an employee.

Designers and others who work freelance are generally independent contractors. *Freelance* is generally accepted as meaning a self-employed worker. Wallpaper hangers, floor covering, installers, contractors, and subcontractors are all examples of independent contractors, as long as the work that they do and the equipment that they use to do the work are *not* controlled and provided by the designer who has hired them. Obviously, the materials or goods that they are installing have likely been provided by a designer, but the tools to install the goods are not. Designers who hire architects to review drawings that have been produced by the designer are hiring an independent contractor. Design firms that hire consultants are hiring independent contractors.

Some design firms have taken advantage of the independent contractor designation when they hire individuals to prepare many kinds of design work. Whether this occurs by mistake or is intentional, this practice can have serious consequences for both the employer and the workers.

Matthew has his own interior design firm specializing in office and hospitality projects. He was hired by George to help George complete the space planning and tenant improvement drawings needed for a large corporate project contracted to George's design firm. Matthew worked at George's office on the project and then became involved in other projects George had obtained.

TABLE 15-1.

Guidelines for Defining an Independent Contractor.

> According to the IRS, the following factors will be considered when determining whether an individual is to be considered an independent contractor or an employee. Individual state departments of revenue and workers' compensation insurance providers also may be called to audit whether an individual is an employee or an independent contractor.
>
> - The person hiring the independent contractor has no control over how, when, or where the contractor does the work for which he or she has been hired. This is a very key issue in determining the status of an independent contractor.
> - An independent contractor uses his or her own methods and receives no training from the person who buys the services.
> - An independent contractor hires his or her own assistants when necessary to complete the assignment.
> - An independent contractor works when and for whom he or she chooses. He or she also sets the hours of work, though this may be negotiated by the requirements of the assignment.
> - The independent contractor provides his or her own equipment and supplies to perform the job duties required.
> - The independent contractor is usually hired for a short time, with no expectation of permanent employment. Often the independent contractor is hired "for the job," which means only for a specifically defined task.
> - Payment for services is commonly at the end of the job or by means of one or more partial payments (depending on the length of the job).
> - The expenses of working are borne by the independent contractor, though some expenses may be billed to the buyer, based on the assignment.
> - An independent contractor can work for more than one company or individual at a time.
> - The independent contractor must engage in professional work that is distinctly different from that of the person hiring the contractor. Interior designers hired by interior design firms to do interior design work might not be considered independent contractors, especially if the other conditions mentioned in the preceding are not met.
> - An employee can be fired or quit at any time. An independent contractor agrees to work until the assignment has been completed and cannot be fired as long as he or she produces a result that meets the specifications of the assignment.
> - If the employer withholds federal income taxes, Social Security taxes, and pays unemployment taxes on the individual, the individual is likely to be considered an employee.

Source: From IRS Publication No. 15-A. (U.S. Department of the Treasury, Internal Revenue Service)

Matthew has spent so much time at George's office that the time Matthew spent obtaining and completing work for his own firm has vanished.

The primary issues that define a worker as an independent contractor or employee focus on the degree of control that the employer has over the worker. The greater the control, the more likely it is that the worker is an employee. Along with this is the degree to which the worker controls his or her own work schedule, whether the worker is working solely for one employer or is working for more than one at a time, and where the contracted work is being performed. Again, all these issues relate back to control held by the employer. There are strict guidelines for defining independent contractors. Table 15-1 summarizes these guidelines. If you are considering hiring someone as an independent contractor or are working as an independent contractor, you are urged to obtain IRS Publication 15-A for clarification of this type of employment status.

There are several advantages for employers to consider the use of independent contractors when staff needs become evident. Independent contractors are not employees of the design firm and have no rights to the benefits that employees have. Employers save money by hiring an independent contractor even though they may need to pay them more per hour. Employers are not required to withhold deductions for income tax withholding. They are generally not required to pay or withhold Social Security, Medicare contributions, or workers' compensation insurance for an independent contractor. Also, employers are not liable for the negligent acts of independent contractors while they are performing their contractual work responsibilities.

As far as the independent contractor is concerned, he or she cannot file for unemployment insurance when the work has been completed. He or she also is most likely not entitled to workers' compensation insurance if he or she is injured while working for the contracting business. The independent contractor must pay self-employment tax on this supplemental income. If the worker does not report the supplemental income and pay self-employment taxes in accordance to IRS regulations, the worker can be subject to penalties by the IRS.

An advantage to the independent contractor that is a disadvantage to the employer is that the copyright to that design might belong to the independent contractor rather than to the employer. The contract between the two must clarify that ownership of the drawings and other documents prepared by the independent contractor belong to the employer.

Part-time workers are not considered independent contractors by the IRS. It may be that the part-time employee receives little, if any, company benefits, such as health insurance; nevertheless, the employer is required to withhold Social Security, workers' compensation, and other mandated contributions for all part-time workers.

A lot of problems that can arise concerning independent contractors can be reduced if not eliminated if a written contract is developed between the parties before the work begins. Issues such as a specific description of services to be provided, duration of the agreement, how the contractor will be paid, and other issues that relate to the work required and working arrangement should be spelled out. Figure 15-2 is a sample of a contract with an independent contractor.

 There are two items on the CD that impact this section. The first is a scenario focusing on whether or not an individual should be treated as an independent contractor. It is Item 15-1. Item 15-2 discusses outsourcing as it applies to interior design practice.

January 30, 200x

TO: Evanston Smith Jones, Interior Design

This agreement is made between Evanston Smith Jones, Interior Design (Client) and Caroline Miller (Contractor).

Services to be performed by Contractor:

The Contractor agrees to perform the following services concerning the Client's _____

_____ project:

  A. Prepare accurate and complete design development floor plans for non-load-bearing walls using sketches and other drawings provided by the Client.
  B. Prepare accurate and complete elevations and other needed drawings for custom cabinets using sketches and drawings provided by the Client.
  C. Revise the above into finalized plans and elevations using information provided by the Client.
  D. Contractor will provide the Client with deliverables consisting of:
    Two printed sets of each sheet of drawings as are needed.
    Computer disc containing the final drawings at the completion of the project.

FIGURE 15-2.

An example of an agreement for contract work between an independent contractor to be hired to do specific interior design tasks and an interior design firm.

It is agreed between the parties that the drawings will be completed using CAD software available to the Contractor. The Contractor will provide all materials otherwise needed to provide the services described.

Payment Terms

The Client will pay the Contractor a fee of_____ per hour for preparing all drawings described above.

A retainer of _____ is due upon signing this agreement. Hourly charges will be billed monthly thereafter. All invoiced payments are due within 30 days of invoice.

The Client will also reimburse the Contractor for reasonable expenses for travel to the Client's place of business from the Contractor's place of business. All other expenses related to this project are the responsibility of the Contractor. The Contractor will submit an itemized statement of Contractor's expenses along with invoices for drafting services. Payment for expenses is due within 30 days of invoice.

Understandings

- It is understood that the Contractor is an independent contractor, not an employee of the Client.
- The Contractor has the right to perform work for others during the term of the Agreement.
- The work under this agreement will be performed at the Contractor's place of business.
- The Contractor has the right to control and direct the manner of providing the services described.
- The Contractor has the right to hire assistants or subcontractors if necessary to provide the services required.
- Contractor is responsible for all income taxes and FICA incurred while performing services under this agreement.
- This agreement does not create a partnership or joint venture with the Client.
- With reasonable cause, this agreement can be terminated by either party by giving written notice of termination. Contractor shall be entitled to full payment for services performed prior to termination of the agreement.

This Agreement will be governed by the laws of the state of_____.
No changes, modifications, additions, or deletions shall be made to this Agreement unless those changes, modifications, additions, or deletions are in writing and are signed by both parties. Any additional work requested by the Client on this project or a different project requires a separate agreement.
The above constitutes the total agreement between the parties named. Signatures below signify agreement to the terms of this independent contractor agreement for this project only. The retainer is due upon signing the agreement.

Client:

_____   _____

Brad Evanston, Principal   Date
Evanston Smith Jones, Interior Design

Contractor:

_____   _____

Caroline Miller, Owner   Date
Miller Design Services, LLC

_____
Contractor Taxpayer ID Number

FIGURE 15-2.

(*Continued*)

SEXUAL HARASSMENT

Arthur took Jane to lunch to discuss a design project they were both working on at the time. During the lunch meeting, Arthur, who was the senior project designer on this project, repeatedly touched Jane's hand and shoulder as they talked about the project. He also suggested that it would be necessary for them to travel to the job site to meet with the client's construction project manager. Arthur made some veiled suggestions to Jane that if she was "nice" to him, he would get her a raise after the project was completed. What should Jane do?

Sexual harassment is a type of discrimination, covered under federal statute Title VII of the Civil Rights Act of 1964, and is governed by the U. S. Equal Employment Opportunity Commission (EEOC). "Sexual harassment is generally defined as sexual advances, requests for sexual favors, and other verbal or physical conduct of a sexual nature when submission to such conduct is made either explicitly or implicitly a term or condition of employment or some related activity."[5] Sexual harassment can affect women or men, gay or straight. It can happen in the interior design office, whether large or small, and in other firms involved in the built-environment industry. Unfortunately, many in the industry have been exposed to, or have been recipients of, sexual harassment at one time or another. Obviously, this issue is very important, since many cases have come before the EEOC and the courts in recent years.

We most often think of sexual harassment occurring when a business owner or supervisor of an employee makes unwelcome sexual advances toward an employee or subordinate. For example, Rachel is told she will receive a promotion if she gives sexual favors to a superior. Remember that harassment can occur to men and women. This example is an illustration of the type of sexual harassment called *quid pro quo*, which is Latin for "something for something." It is associated with the most commonly understood type of sexual harassment.

Another common type of sexual harassment is the situation when actions by others create what is called a hostile work environment. This second type is more subjective, since it is harder to prove and it is generally not tied to a promotion, raise, or the like. Examples are the posting of explicit cartoons in the work environment; the telling of offensive jokes or the use of offensive gestures or language can also create a hostile work environment.

Most cases of sexual harassment occur between employers and employees, but some peer harassment is also considered illegal sexual harassment. However, peer harassment is not illegal under EEOC laws. For example, Bonnie is a relatively new interior design employee at a design firm with several men and one other woman designer. The group goes out frequently on Friday late afternoons for drinks at a restaurant after work. The owner rarely joins the group, with the exception of special occasions. Bonnie, trying to fit in and get to know everyone, felt it was necessary for her to attend these Friday afternoon socials even though it seemed that two of the men in particular seemed to enjoy telling off-color jokes. Bonnie did not appreciate and was even offended by some of these jokes but wasn't sure what to do.

In some cases, the employer might be liable for sexual harassment of an employee by a customer, especially if the employer has been informed of the situation and does nothing about it. Of course, the customer might also be liable. There are interior designers who can tell stories about a client making sexually suggestive comments to a designer. Perhaps that client has been an especially good client of the firm or represents a firm that could bring a large contract to the design firm. Of course, this kind of behavior by a client should be reported to the firm owner.

Sexual harassment is not easy to prove. In many cases, it is one person's word against the other's. The first thing that should be done is to tell the person exhibiting the unwanted behavior to stop. This can be very difficult for the person being harassed, but experts say that it is actually very effective. Telling the offending person to stop lets the person know that the words or behavior are unwelcome and offensive to the individual. Experts suggest that a brief letter demanding a stop to the behavior can be effective if a face-to-face discussion is uncomfortable. Of course, keeping a copy of the letter is *always* imperative.

Documentation of any situation is also imperative. When harassment occurs, the employee should check with other employees to determine if the harassment is widespread. Documentation of harassment by supervisors is very important because employees are often fired when these situations occur and the employer often cites work deficiencies as the reason for termination. The documentation will help show that it was the discrimination, not work deficiency.

The individual should file a written complaint with the proper supervisor or person in authority if the behavior is coming from a coworker, client, or others outside the firm. If a designer feels that he or she is being harassed by a supervisor, he or she should, as soon as possible, document for his or her files any details about the episode. If the individual is working in a small firm and the harassment is coming from the owner, the designer should still submit the letter to the owner. In larger firms, the individual might need to file the complaint with the human resources manager—who might be different than the interior design supervisor.

If nothing positive results from the written complaint, the designer should speak to someone at the U.S. EEOC or state fair-employment office before going to an attorney and filing a lawsuit. In fact, it is necessary for an individual to have filed a complaint with the EEOC before filing a federal lawsuit. If they feel your complaint has merit, the EEOC will issue a letter that allows you to take the case to court. Delays in contacting the proper authority might be interpreted as acceptance of the behavior and could result in jeopardizing a claim, if one is filed later.

Sexual harassment is unwanted sexual advances or sexual connotations. If the individual accepts the behavior, he or she cannot later claim that the actions constitute harassment. Do not tolerate this kind of behavior from coworkers, bosses—even clients. Learn more about sexual harassment by reading one of the books in the references or any of the other numerous books and articles that have appeared recently.

FEDERAL LAWS REGULATING EMPLOYMENT

An employer must use diligent care in hiring, working with, and terminating employees. Because of a lack of training in employment issues, the owners of interior design practices—especially the small firm—can easily fall victim to inappropriate behavior in the supervisory relationship with employees. Numerous laws at the federal and state levels were written during the twentieth century to protect employees. Many of the laws written to protect employees have more of an impact on firms that are unionized. Since it is almost unheard of for an interior design firm to be unionized, there will be no attempt in this text to discuss those laws. However, several federal laws do affect employment in the nonunion professional interior design office.

Workers' Compensation

Kimberly is an interior designer working for a firm with a contract to do the interior design of a small resort. She went to the job site prior to the installation of the furniture to check that the interior finish work was completed and the site was ready for the delivery of the merchandise. She was coming down a short flight of stairs in a two-story cabin when she tripped and fell down the last three steps. Kimberly tried to break her fall, but instead she broke her wrist and sustain a bad bruise on her left knee. She will have to miss about one week of work. Who is responsible to pay for Kimberly's medical care and loss of work: Kimberly, her boss, or the client?

There are actually many ways that an interior designer can be injured on the job. This profession is no different from any other in that things happen and people get hurt. *Workers' compensation* is actually state law mandating that the employer pay for medical treatment of employees should the employee be injured on the job—regardless of who was at fault. In essence, the employee gives up the right to sue the employer related to the injury by accepting workers' compensation coverage. The employer must have insurance, pay into a state fund, or be in essence self-insured to cover the medical expenses if an employee is injured or dies on the job.

The compensation limits are defined by state statute, and the level of responsibilities will thus vary. The key is that regardless of what state the design firm is located, if the firm has employees, it will have to have workers' compensation insurance. It is thus a very good idea to always check with the state where you are working or where you own your company to know what is expected in that state. The department names are different from state to state, but information can be obtained by going to the phone book or the State Workers' Compensation Officials page of the U.S. Department of Labor's Web site.

Employment Discrimination

Alan has worked in the interior design profession for 33 years. He worked in a residential design firm for 12 years and commercial design firm for 14 years. He has been a sales representative for a vendor for the last seven years. Because of his experience and conversations with his boss, he thought he was in line for a promotion as the sales manager of one of the district offices of the vendor. His boss informed him a week ago that Alan was going to be laid off in 30 days when the vendor was merged with another vendor. Alan just heard that his boss had hired a woman with only five years' experience for essentially the job that Alan has had.

Congress and state legislatures want to be sure that individuals are able to fairly obtain and hold jobs. Although these laws generally apply to firms with 15 or more employees—either full-time or part-time—all interior design firms should abide by their intent. Even a small design firm with only one or two employees must avoid discriminatory hiring and working relationships with employees.

One type of discrimination has already been discussed—sexual harassment. Other forms exist in the workplace. There are several federal laws to protect employees from job discrimination. Title VII of the Civil Rights Act of 1964, along with the Equal Employment Opportunity Act of 1972 and the Civil Rights Act of 1991, prohibit an employer from discriminating against an employee in terms of hiring, on the basis of sex, race, color, religion, or national origin. These laws prohibit an employer from discriminating against an employee related to hiring, promotions, pay raises, benefits, firing, or many other work-related issues. For example, Jane has repeatedly asked for flexibility in her work hours to take a class at the community college. Without being given a reason, her requests are refused each time. Harvey has been granted the same request the first time that he has asked. On the face of it, it appears that Jane has grounds for filing a discrimination complaint.

Civil rights and equal opportunity employment laws also make it illegal for employers to ask verbally or on a job application for such things as the employee's (1) age, (2) date of birth, (3) maiden name, (4) marital status, or (5) gender, or for any other information related to age, gender, religion, national origin, race, or marital status. It is possible for the employer to obtain information in less direct ways, if the information has significance as to whether the interviewee is capable of performing the job responsibilities. For example, it is legal for an employer to ask something like, "Are you between the ages of 23 and 50?" or "Are you a citizen of this country?" The key, of course, is whether the questions and the way in which they are asked are being used to discriminate against potential employees. Additional sample questions that are illegal in the hiring situation are given in Chapter 34.

The Age Discrimination in Employment Act of 1967, which was amended in 1990, prohibits employer discrimination based on the age of the employee. It specifically prohibits discrimination concerning employees 40 years old or older. This is another federal law that impacts larger-sized businesses—those with more than 20 employees; however, state laws may impact smaller firms.

A most familiar law to the reader is the American Disabilities Act. This act concerns accommodation in public buildings, yet it also affects the workplace. Title I of the Americans with Disabilities Act affects the hiring and promoting of employees. This portion of the ADA restrains employers from discriminating against any handicapped person who is otherwise qualified for a job. Employers with 15 or more employees are required to comply with the law.

Furthermore, the employer is required to make "reasonable accommodation" in the structuring of the job and/or modification of the work as necessary for the employee to do the job. For example, a paraplegic designer who has the qualifications and skills required for a design position must be given equal consideration as a nondisabled person. If the disabled person is hired, the employer must attempt to make reasonable changes in the work areas. The drafting station, for instance, could be reconfigured using modular furniture that is more flexible and accommodating to a person's specific needs.

Commercial interior design firms often seek to obtain projects with the federal government. When they do so, the firm would need to comply with some additional federal laws. Executive Order 11246 requires that firms that do more than $10,000 of business with the federal government have non-discrimination clauses in their contracts. If an interior design firm does more than $2500 of work for the federal government, the Rehabilitation Act of 1973 and 1974 requires that the design firm accommodate disabled employees. Other requirements may be enforceable, depending on the exact nature of the design firm's work with the federal government.

The first line of defense for an employee in any kind of discrimination matter is discussed in the section on sexual harassment. Documentation by the employee of what transpired in a conversation or other actions will be necessary. Complaints are most commonly reviewed by the EEOC and/or state labor relations departments. This should be done before any lawsuits are filed. Should the EEOC determine there is sufficient cause, it will file a civil lawsuit against the employer in the name of the employee. If the employee wishes to talk to an attorney, it is important that the discussion occur with an attorney who has specialized in labor law. Not all attorneys will understand the intricacies of discrimination in the workplace to be able to best advise a client.

Other Employment Issues

Mike and Jennifer started working for a design firm as junior designers at the same time right after graduation. Jennifer had just completed an internship with the hiring firm, while Mike had done an internship in another state. They both graduated from accredited design programs and had essentially the same grades and showed similar skills in their portfolios. At the time of the 60-day review, Jennifer was told that she would receive a pay raise that she knew was equivalent to what Mike was given when he started.

An important federal law dealing with pay and wages is the Fair Labor Standards Act, commonly called the wage-hour law. First passed in 1938, it primarily governs wages for employees who are working in companies that are involved in interstate commerce and hourly wage employees. For the most part, interior designers are exempt from the minimum wage and overtime pay requirements of this act, since they are most often considered "professional employees."

The Equal Pay Act of 1963—an amendment to the Fair Labor Standards Act—requires that employers pay all employees who have the same basic work responsibilities and work experience the same amount of salary or wages. In this case, if two employees with the same job title and job responsibilities are hired at the same time and start with approximately the same work experience, each must be paid the same starting wage. If future proven performance or responsibility issues become different for the two individuals, then each can be paid a different amount.

Employees are all expected to be given a safe place to work. The Occupational Safety and Health Act (OSHA) of 1970 regulates workplace safety. OSHA inspectors, although primarily found in production facilities, do make inspections in the office environment. In the interior design studio, an OSHA inspector may look for properly located and functioning fire extinguishers, first-aid kits, and a proper reporting procedure for employee injuries. In 1999, OSHA proposed dramatic requirements related to ergonomic workstations for office workers. Additional proposals by OSHA would also affect home office workers. At the time of the writing of this fourth edition, these changes have not become law.

The National Labor Relations Act, also called the Wagner Act, protects employees from many kinds of tactics by employers that could cause unfair labor practices. Most of these laws protect union employees and will not be discussed here. One issue that might affect an interior design practice is this example: Suppose an employee was fired or otherwise discriminated against as a result of the employee's filing any kind of charges or giving testimony against the employer. An example might be that an employee is fired after he or she files a complaint related to wage discrimination with the Federal Wage and Hour Board. Depending, of course, on the exact nature of the complaint and the manner in which the firing took place, the employer would be liable for illegally firing the employee.

Additional laws affecting the employer–employee relationship for some companies include the Family and Medical Leave Act of 1993. In companies with 50 employees or more, the Family and Medical Leave requires that an employer give employees up to 12 weeks of leave for child, spousal, or parental care without jeopardizing the employee's job. This leave is not automatic and does not accrue until the employee has worked at the company for at least one year on a full-time basis. The Pregnancy Discrimination Act (1978), which is an amendment to Title VII, prohibits employers from discriminating against an employee due to her pregnancy. They cannot force a pregnant woman to take a leave of absence or fire her once her pregnancy is announced.

When an employer provides some sort of health insurance as a benefit, the employee is entitled to continue that health benefit even after he or she has been fired or quits. An exception is if the employee is fired for gross misconduct. Employees of companies with 20 or more employees are covered under the federal law called the Consolidated Omnibus Budget Reconciliation Act of 1986 (COBRA). This law requires that the employer continue health benefits for the employee and the employee's spouse and dependents. The time period of the benefits is generally 18 months. Of course, the employee must pay the insurance premiums. Note that states have variations on the law and requirements regarding the length of time that the insurance must be made available.

State legislatures have also passed many laws that affect legal issues related to employment. Employers are urged to speak to an attorney to be sure that their business is in compliance with employment laws. Prevention is cheaper than having to deal with employees through the court system. Employees should speak to an attorney or contact the EEOC if the employee feels that he or she may have experienced any kind of employment discrimination.

Of course, this section does not discuss all the federal statutes that in one way or another affect employment. There are also many state statutes that affect employment. The reader may wish to review one or more of the books listed in the references or check online for additional information on employee rights and/or employer responsibilities.

SUMMARY

Employers have many obligations to employees that go beyond providing them a reasonable and appropriate salary for the work they are expected to perform. Laws regulate the hiring, retaining, and firing of employees that apply to the interior design firms, especially those with more than 15 employees (depending on the law and the jurisdiction). Employers and employees should be familiar with these laws to avoid government intervention or lawsuits. The employer–employee relationship itself also involves specific legal obligations on the part of both parties. Increasingly, employers are using employment contracts with their staff to protect the company from losing confidential company information to a competitor or the designer leaving to start his or her own business using documents from the former employer.

On the other hand, employees have rights in the design office, and they should become informed about those rights. Discrimination in all phases of the work situation and sexual harassment are among the most widely occurring problems in employee–employer relationships. Employees—even those who work part-time—are entitled to certain benefits that are paid in part or entirely by the employer. It is important for the employer and the worker to understand when the worker is classified as an employee and is entitled to certain benefits and when a worker is truly an independent contractor.

The legal issues discussed in this chapter are not meant to handcuff the employer or employee. Rather, both sides must realize that hiring employees or accepting a position with a company must be done in good faith and within legal restraints. It is too expensive for companies to hire, train, and fire, or watch employees leave design firms. It is too emotionally draining for the employee to have to sue or even threaten to sue over employment misunderstandings or mistreatment. As the profession continues to grow and change, employers must accept the responsibilities related to employees just as it accepts responsibilities related to the client.

REFERENCES

1. Reprinted from p. 543 in *Black's Law Dictionary*, 7th ed., by
   Bryan A. Garner, ed., 1999, with permission of the West Group.

2. Jentz et al., 1987, p. 479.

3. Joel, 1996, p. 55.

4. IRS, 2006. Publication 15-A.

5. Jones and Philcox, 2000, p. 92.

CHAPTER 16

Basic Financial Accounting

Key Terms and Concepts

These key terms and concepts are important to material in this chapter. Many of these terms will be utilized in other chapters as well. Be sure you understand these items as you read this chapter.

Terms and Concepts

Financial accounting

Accounting methods

Accrual accounting method

Cash accounting method

Revenue

Expense

Income statement

Profit and loss statement (P&L)

"Pass through"

Net income or profit

Gross revenue

Cost of sales

Gross margin

Direct labor

Direct expenses

Overhead expenses

Balance sheet

Assets

Current assets

Fixed assets

Cash

Petty cash

Accounts receivable

Prepaid expense

Depreciation

Amortized

Liabilities

Current liabilities

Accounts payable

Accrued expenses

Deferred revenues

Owner's equity

Drawings

Retained earnings

Statement of cash flows

Transactions

Single-entry system

Double-entry system

Chart of accounts

Accounts

T-account

Debit

Credit

Journal

Posting

Ledger

Trial balance

Cash management

Work in process

Critical Issues

After completing this chapter you should be able to:

- Compare the differences between the cash accounting method and accrual accounting method.
- Explain the purpose of the income statement, balance sheet, and statement of cash flows.
- Understand and discuss the terminology of the income statement and balance sheet and relate the terminology to business examples.
- Explain the basic formula or financial outcome of a balance sheet.
- Correctly place dollar amounts into an income statement and balance sheet to show understanding of what the basic documents report.
- Discuss the difference between assets and liabilities.
- Identify items that are direct and overhead expenses.
- Discuss the basic concept of the chart of accounts, debits, and credits.
- Analyze a cash management forecast.
- Discuss some techniques that would be useful in ensuring good cash flow.

Ralph has been considering moving to a new, larger office to better accommodate his growing design firm. After considerable research, he has decided to purchase an office condominium rather than rent space. He will need to bring several types of documentation to the bank with him in order to expedite his loan. Why is it important for him to bring a copy of a current income statement and balance sheet as part of that documentation?

It is critical for any size interior design firm's owners to have a firm handle on the finances of the company. Financial recording and the reports that can be generated from the data are tools that the owners need to have to make decisions about many operational issues. Accurate financial recording is also critical for income tax purposes. It is especially important for a firm's owners and management to be able to read, interpret, and analyze the primary accounting reports. Regardless of whom the firm may hire to take care of the daily bookkeeping described in Chapter 8 or prepare the formal reports discussed in this chapter, the owner has the ultimate legal responsibility for those record keeping and reporting.

This record keeping is referred to as *financial accounting*, which is the day-to-day and periodic measurement and reporting of a firm's monetary resources. The owner and managers of a design practice use financial record keeping and reports to analyze and understand the financial position of the design firm. This measurement and reporting is also of interest to individuals outside the firm, such as bankers, government agencies, stockholders, and auditors.

The basic financial recording of business financial transactions begins with the various accounts, journals, and ledgers set up to record the daily transactions of the design firm. These records are then used by the firm to prepare reports to help the owners maintain a firm hand on the finances. Income statements, balance sheets, and statements of cash flow are the most common reports that are part of financial accounting.

Financial accounting reports can be prepared by the firm's accredited business accountant, a public accountant, or a certified public accountant. It is important to hire an accounting consultant who is familiar with the interior design business. Many general accountants, who are unfamiliar with the seeming peculiarities of this industry, have problems in properly advising interior designers.

Reliable and inexpensive accounting software programs make the preparation of reports easy for even the sole practitioner. Of course, formal audits and reports for tax purposes generally are still prepared by trained accounting personnel. Software programs, however, give the sole practitioner and the owner of any interior design firm many useful reports in order to keep up with the financial position of the firm at any given moment.

This chapter introduces the reader to several essential components of financial accounting and financial management. The chapter begins with a discussion of the different accounting methods used to record information. A review of the elements of the income statement, balance sheet, and the statement of cash flow (formally, the funds flow statement) follows. These reports are critical management tools for any size firm and owner. The chapter also discusses other accounting documents, such as the journal and ledgers, that will introduce the reader to basic concepts of the daily bookkeeping records. This chapter will not cover how to actually do daily bookkeeping. Finally, the last sections of the chapter explains cash management, a very important factor in the financial health of a business, and the use of the computerized accounting systems for financial record keeping.

ACCOUNTING METHODS: ACCRUAL VERSUS CASH ACCOUNTING

It makes little difference to the IRS or state revenue departments whether an interior design firm utilizes a manual or computer system for financial record keeping. A sole practitioner or very small business might feel more comfortable with a manual system even though there are relatively simple software programs available. The system should be appropriate to the needs and skills of the owner and chosen and refined with the advice of the firm's accountant.

However, aside from the manual-versus-computer issue, the firm must decide which accounting method to use. The two most common accounting methods (or bases) are the accrual method and the cash accounting method. Central to the difference between the two methods is the time when revenue and expenses are recognized (recorded). *Revenue* is the amount of inflows from the sale of goods or the rendering of services during an accounting period. An *expense* is the amount of outflows of resources as a consequence of the efforts made by the firm to earn revenues. Rent, monthly utility bills, salaries, and advertising costs are examples of expenses.

With the *accrual accounting method*, revenue and expenses are recognized at the time they are earned (in the case of revenue) or incurred (in the case of expenses), whether the revenue has actually been collected or the expenses have actually been paid in the time frame (month and/or year) in which they have been incurred. For example, during May, Maximum Interiors received a total of $11,400 in revenues. Of that, $5600 is from cash sales and $5800 is from invoices to clients that have not yet been received. In the same month, expenses of $6500 have been incurred for the period—$4500 has already been paid and $2000 is still due. Using the accrual method, there is a $4900 gross profit for the month. In this case, the profit is a "paper profit," since $5800 has not been collected yet (see Table 16-1). The accrual accounting method requires the use of double-entry accounting, making it somewhat more difficult to master. Double-entry accounting is discussed a little later in the chapter.

A design firm that has an inventory of goods or otherwise sells products will have to use the accrual method to determine its income tax responsibilities. It is also required for businesses with over $5 million in annual sales or a firm whose

TABLE 16-1.

Comparison of Accrual and Cash Accounting Methods.

	Accrual Method	Cash Method
Revenue	$ 11,400	$ 5,600
Expenses	−6,500	−4,500
Gross income	$ 4,900	$ 1,100

business structure is a regular corporation (not an LLC). Understand that furniture ordered for a client is technically inventory in accounting. The accrual method is also recommended for any business that sells on credit, as the accrual method is a more accurate picture of revenue and expenses.

In the *cash accounting method*, revenue and expenses are recognized in the period in which the firm actually receives the cash or actually pays the bills. In the preceding example, only $5600 of revenue and $4500 of expenses are recognized for the month, since this is what actually has been received or paid out. Using the cash accounting method, Jane Doe Interiors shows a $1100 profit for the month. Cash accounting is commonly used by small design practices for daily book-keeping purposes. It is simpler to use than the accrual accounting method and allows for use of single-entry accounting.

A firm generally can use whichever accounting method it chooses, although many accountants recommend the accrual method for firms that sell goods and maintain some inventory. It is also possible to use a hybrid of the two methods. Cash accounting could be used for service fees but accrual for the sales of goods and inventory. However, if the firm is a regular corporation form of business, it cannot use the cash method. The cash method can be used for daily or nontax accounting needs. Since tax laws change annually and accounting standards also change on a regular basis, it is important for the business owner to discuss appropriate accounting methods with the company's accountant.

It is commonly recommended that all firms use the accrual method for an additional reason. Even though the accrual method may require extra account-ing time, it provides a more comprehensive picture of profit and loss for the firm at any given period. Having a more accurate financial picture of the firm at all times helps the owner/manager make more intelligent management decisions. Moreover, with cash accounting, it is too easy for unpaid invoices to accumulate, thus allowing debt not to be obvious, which would put the firm in a serious situation.

This chapter discusses accounting principles based on the accrual method.

THE INCOME STATEMENT

The financial report that provides the clearest indication of whether the firm has made a profit is the income statement. The *income statement*, commonly called a *profit and loss*, or *P&L*, formally reports all the revenues and expenses of the firm for a stated period of time. The period of time may be a month, a quarter, or a year. The result shows the net income (or loss) for the firm during the period. This example shows the essential format used for an income statement, showing the main items reported to determine profit or loss.

Net revenue – Cost of sales

Gross margin (or gross profit) – Operating expenses

Profit (loss) before taxes

It is important to point out that just because a particular income statement shows a profit or loss does not mean that the company is operating at a profit or loss for the year—unless, of course, the income statement is for the whole year. Rather, it indicates that for a particular time the design firm was operating at a profit or loss. Understanding the items are included in the income statement and why they are there helps the owner make decisions that can positively or even negatively affect the overall profit and continued financial health of the firm.

As mentioned, revenues are the inflows of moneys to a company from the sale of goods and services. For an interior design firm, revenues may result from the fees it charges clients or from the amounts received from the sale of goods. For the sale of goods to yield revenue for the firm, the goods must be goods that *pass through* the design firm. What does "pass through" mean? To define the term, let us look at an example. James Smith specified furniture items for a several areas of a doctor's office. James ordered those items from the vendors and supervised the installation of those goods. The client paid James for the goods. In this case, the order for the goods passed through the design firm and would represent revenue. If the doctor had purchased those goods from someone other than James, then the goods—although specified by James—would not be considered revenue. The design fee to specify those goods, however, would be revenue for James, since those funds were billed through James's office. Goods that are specified by the designer but are sold to an end user by someone else are not revenue producing for the design firm. This distinction is very important with regard to sales tax funds and income taxes for the firm.

Also as mentioned, expenses are the outflows of assets used to generate revenue and operate the business. There are many kinds of expenses. Some expenses are directly related to generating any kind of revenue for the firm. An example is the time the interior designer works on the drawings for the project. Another example is the cost of the goods that the designer must pay a vendor when ordering goods for a client. Many other expenses are not related to generating income per se but are necessary to operate the design firm. Rent and utilities are common operational expenses as are any monies spent on marketing.

Net income (or *profit*) is the eventual difference between revenues and expenses. A loss occurs when expenses are greater than revenues.

A more complete example giving details to the primary sections of an income statement is shown in Figure 16-1. Note that this figure should be referenced for the discussion of the income statement. This example is formatted with the consideration that the firm uses the accrual basis for its accounting method. Figure 16-1 also has been prepared to show more detail concerning the utilization of cost accounting to measure and evaluate costs of doing business against the revenues that the firm has generated. In a cost accounting system, certain, if not all, costs directly related to the generation of revenue are "costed" or charged to the particular revenue-producing activity. For a design firm, this means that all costs related to a particular job are recorded for that job. These costs show up on the income statement under the category of cost of sales as either direct labor or direct expenses. In my opinion, it is important for a design firm to use this method in order to have an accurate view of the activities of the firm. This point will be discussed further. Another sample income statement is included on the CD as Item 16–1. That example shows income and expenses for a smaller design company.

The easiest way to understand the parts of an income statement is to start at the top entry and work down to the various parts. The income statement in Figure 16-1 shows income generated from fees and goods sold. First note the heading. The date indicates the status of the firm prior to the date shown in the

Income Statement
Grand Designs
For Year Ending December 31, 200X

Income

Gross Revenue

From Fees	185,350	
From Reimbursable Expenses	11,540	
From Sale of Goods		
Product	227,820	
Freight-in	24,680	
Delivery	14,100	
Installation	8,610	
Total Gross Revenue		$ 472,100

Other Revenue

Interest	3,575	
Net Revenue		$ 475,675

Cost of Sales

From Fees:		
Direct labor	35,800	
Supplies	2,350	
Reproduction expense	3,760	
Telephone / Fax (long distance)	1,290	
CAD—contract labor	6,750	
Reimbursable expenses	9,540	
From Products:		
Cost of Goods	177,699	
Freight-in	19,750	
Delivery	10,200	
Installation	7,650	
Total Cost of Sales		$ 274,789
Gross Margin		$ 200,886

Expense

Operating Expenses

Salaries	30,940	
Payroll taxes	15,200	
Group insurance	6,000	
Rent	28,800	
Heat, power, and light	9,800	
Telephone	7,500	
Advertising and promotion	10,000	
Travel reimbursements	12,600	
Supplies	4,800	
Postage and express	1,300	
Depreciation expense (furniture and equip.)	5,600	
Depreciation expense (auto)	2,500	
Insurance	5,700	
Dues and subscriptions	2,750	
Professional development	1,800	
Professional consultants	3,000	
Printing and reproduction	2,200	
Interest expense	4,800	
Bank charges	1,750	
Web/Internet provider and serv.	2,400	
Misc. expenses	2,575	
Total Operating Expenses		$ 162,015
Net Income Before Taxes		$ 38,871

FIGURE 16-1.

An income statement showing the separation of direct expenses from overhead expenses.

heading. In our example, the heading indicates that the time period for this income statement is for the whole year.

It is not uncommon for a firm to look at additional time frames. A quarterly report produced every three months provides an extra management tool for the owner to recognize financial performance. With accounting software, it is possible to have monthly reports as well. Annual reports are necessary to expedite income tax preparation. Quarterly reports are useful, since businesses—even sole proprietorships—must pay estimated taxes on a quarterly basis. How often income statements are produced is a decision the owner should make with the firm's accountant. Note that a blank income statement worksheet for a three-month period has been included on the CD. It is labeled Item 16-2.

Gross Revenue to Net Revenue

For our purposes, we will break gross revenue down into revenue from fees, which are the design fees for interior design services, and revenue from sale of goods, which are revenues related to the sale of products to clients. *Gross revenue* consists of all the revenue generated by the firm for the period of time noted. The term "gross" in accounting indicates that the figure represents funds prior to any deductions. We further break down the revenue from sale of goods to show (1) product, or the amount the client paid the design firm for the goods; (2) freight-in, the freight charges the client paid for goods; and (3) delivery, the delivery and/or installation charges that the design firm has billed to the client.

Total gross revenue is the total amount of revenue generated from all means by the firm for the period of time noted. Adjustments are made for deductions to gross revenue for such things as returns and allowances, damages, or any extra discounts that the designer has offered to clients for prompt payment. For example, perhaps the designer agreed to take back some small accessories the client originally agreed to purchase. The original revenue from these accessories is deducted from gross revenue when the funds are returned to the client. These types of adjustments are subtracted from the total gross revenue to obtain net revenue.

Cost of Sales to Gross Margin

Selling merchandise and design services results in expenses that are directly related to the generation of revenue. *Cost of sales* refers to those costs paid in the direct generation of revenues. In retail sales businesses, such as a clothing store, this is called cost of goods sold and relates to changes in inventory. In an interior design firm there are generally two parts of these expenses: from fees and from products. These expenses relate to the revenue categories from fees and sales of goods.

Under Cost of Sales from Fees, there are four items. The first, direct labor, should be the easiest to determine. *Direct labor* is the time the designers spent directly involved in the generation of the designs under contract for which fees for services are charged. The amount of direct labor can easily be determined from the time sheets kept by the design staff. This would include such activities as time meeting with clients, drafting plans, developing product specifications, and even traveling to the job site. This amount can be calculated against the salary paid to the various designers. Direct labor also can include the time that secretarial and management staff are involved on the projects under contract. Since this is often harder to keep an accurate account of, the time spent on projects by management and support staff is more commonly figured as overhead.

In Figure 16-1, other line items under cost of sales from fees are amounts shown for supplies, reproduction, and long-distance telephone charges. These are legitimate costs against projects done under contract. They are presented to give a more accurate view of the profitability of the firm's activities. In accounting they are called *direct expenses*. Many firms do not show these charges at all, putting them into appropriate categories of overhead expenses.

Under the section Cost of Sales from Products in Figure 16-1, there are three lines corresponding to those in revenues. The first is cost of goods, which shows the change in inventory and any special orders delivered during the period. The second, freight-in, shows the actual charges the firm has been billed for goods that have been delivered to the firm. The third is delivery and installation, which shows the cost of delivery and/or installation of products to the company (this includes salaries paid and cost of trucks, equipment, and so on that are needed to deliver products to the customer).

All these adjustments (costs) are totaled and subtracted from net revenue. The result is gross margin, which is sometimes called gross profit but which does not represent profit. Thus, gross margin (or gross profit) is the amount left after expenses have been subtracted from revenues. "Gross margin is the difference between the revenues generated from selling products (goods or services) and the related product costs."[1] Gross margin shows the amount of revenue that is available to cover overhead expenses in order to keep the firm in business. Gross margin can also be expressed as a ratio and is discussed in the next chapter.

Overhead Expenses

Margery is planning to redesign all of her firm's stationery, including the business cards, letterhead, and title block. These overhead expenses as well as a new computer have been carefully planned by this sole proprietor, since adding to her overhead expenses reduces her profits. *Overhead expenses*, also called selling and administrative expenses, are those expenses that are incurred whether the firm produces any revenues or not. They are often thought of as those expenses needed to keep the doors open. They are reported in as much detail as is needed by the firm for anyone who would be looking at the income statement. Expenses listed in Figure 16-1 represent the many expense items that are common to an interior design firm.

Some of these items need explanation for readers who have not taken an accounting class. "Salaries" represents the amount of expense paid out for non-revenue-generating labor activities (or activities that cannot be easily costed to projects). This usually includes salaries for secretaries, accounting personnel, and management personnel. If the firm is using a true cost-accounting methodology, it also would include that portion of the design staff's salaries that cannot be considered direct labor. To be clear, a design employee some days will not be 100 percent involved in billable design work. That portion of the designer's salary not billable is an overhead expense. Assuming accurate cost accounting, then the nonbillable time would be included in the "salaries" category in the overhead expenses.

"Telephone" represents those normal telephone charges and other telephone charges that the firm cannot or chooses not to cost back to specific revenue-generating activities. "Advertising and promotion" can be actual promotional expenses such as magazine advertising or the cost of placing the firm's ad in the yellow pages, but it can also represent the expense of a business lunch.

As can be seen from Figure 16-1, a firm can go into quite a bit of detail in order to have an accurate picture of its financial standing. The detail also helps the interior design firm and especially the small firm deduct legitimate business expenses to reduce income tax payments. If an interior design firm has invested in a good computer system, the detailed record keeping and data entry that are required is made easier. Many management reports that would be helpful in the control of the design firm can then be generated. More detail on this topic will be covered in Chapter 17.

All these expenses are totaled and subtracted from gross margin to obtain net income. *Net income* (or loss) represents the amount of income (or loss) that results when all remaining expenses (deductions) are subtracted from gross revenues. If the result is positive, net income represents the dollar amount of profit that the firm has made for the period reported. If expenses are greater than revenues, then a negative result or loss is reported for the period. If the design firm is a corporation, this result would be called net income before taxes, since it is necessary for a corporation to show its estimated income taxes on the income statement. Unless the firm has some extraordinary expenses, such as a loss from fire, the next line should show a "provision for income tax," which is the estimated tax for the period. This amount is subtracted to determine Net Income. If the firm receives income from sources other than from those brought in as a result of the normal operation of the firm, such as interest earned on checking or savings accounts, it is added before the net income before taxes result is determined.

This is not true for sole proprietorships or partnerships, since the income of these types of businesses is personal income and is reported along with any other income made on individual or family tax statements. These forms would not necessarily show a provision for income tax. The next line, in these cases, would be net income.

THE BALANCE SHEET

Financial statements are essential documents to help the owner of the design firm evaluate the financial performance of the activities of his or her business. Regular review of a business's financial statements is a critical part of business ownership. They are also documents that are needed to prepare income tax forms, are often required to obtain loans or other financing, and help identify the financial strengths or weaknesses of the design firm.

The financial statement that shows the financial position of a firm at a particular moment in time and provides a statement of its assets (resources) and liabilities (claims against total resources) at that moment is called the *balance sheet*. The balance sheet is still sometimes called a statement of financial position. This form is composed of two parts that must equal each other—thus the term balance sheet. These two parts are called assets and liabilities. *Assets* are any kind of resource—tangible or intangible—that the firm owns or controls and that can be measured in monetary terms. *Liabilities* are claims by outsiders and/or owners against the total assets of the firm as a result of past transactions or events. A design firm's assets are typically shown on the left side or top of the page, and the liabilities are shown on the right side or bottom of the page. Figure 16-2 is a sample balance sheet for a small interior design practice that will be referred to in conjunction with this discussion.

There are two important formulas you should keep in mind when reviewing a balance sheet:

Total assets = Liabilities + Owner's equity

Total assets − Liabilities = Owner's equity

Balance Sheet
Bently and Jordan Interior Designs
As of January 31, 200x

Assets

Current Assets:

Cash	$ 8,625	
Accounts Receivable	31,750	
Inventory	11,900	
Supplies	1,250	
Prepaid Expenses	2,250	
Total Current Assets		$ 55,775

Fixed Assets:

Plant and Equipment:

Office Furniture at Cost	$ 25,500	
Less: Accumulated depreciation	−2,400	
Office Equipment at Cost	11,500	
Less: Accumulated depreciation	−1,800	
Automobile at Cost	19,500	
Less: Accumulated depreciation	−5,600	
Net Plant and Equipment		46,700
Total Assets		$ 102,475

Liabilities

Current Liabilities:

Accounts Payable	$ 8,725	
Notes Payable	4,000	
Accrued Expenses	7,000	
Deferred Revenues	6,750	
Total Current Liabilities		$ 26,475

Other Liabilities:

Long-Term Debt		29,500
Total Liabilities		$ 55,975

Owner's Equity

Common Stock	$ 35,000	
Retained Earnings	11,500	
Total Owner's Equities		46,500
Total Equities		$102,475

FIGURE 16-2.

A typical balance sheet for the corporation form of a interior design firm.

The first reflects the final outcome of all balance sheets. The total amount of asset accounts must always equal the total amount of liability accounts. The second formula shows the breakdown of the two sections that make up the liabilities side of the balance sheet. Liabilities are moneys that the firm owes to creditors. *Owner's equity* represents moneys invested in the firm by the owners or stockholders. It is important for you to understand that liabilities accounts always have first claim on the assets of a firm. Further, it is critical for you to understand that those liability accounts such as bank loans and the utilities companies—in other words, anyone other than owners or investors in the design firm—have first claim on the assets over the owners/investors.

Assets

As mentioned previously, assets are resources owned or controlled by the design firm. In accounting there are three kinds of assets based on how quickly the asset can be converted to cash. *Current assets* are resources that the firm would normally convert to cash in less than one year. The second type of asset are *fixed assets*, also called property, plant, and equipment, which are the long-lived items used by the firm. The third category of assets is called *other assets,* which are such assets as patents, copyrights, and investment securities of another firm. These "other assets" are often considered as intangible assets.

Current assets typically include the following accounts: cash, accounts receivable, inventory, prepaid expenses, supplies, and marketable securities. *Cash* is the cash on hand in the firm's bank account, checking account, cash register, or petty cash box. *Petty cash* is currency used to purchase small or minor items, such as office supplies, with cash on hand. *Accounts receivable* is the account that shows what others owe to the firm as a result of sales or billings for services. Funds owed to the design firm from clients are the primary source of accounts receivable amounts. *Inventory* shows those items purchased by the firm for resale to the firm's customers. For an interior designer, a chair that the designer has purchased for sale to a client is inventory; a chair that the designer has purchased that is used by the bookkeeper in the office is equipment, the value of which is recorded in the fixed assets account. A *prepaid expense* is early payment of expenses, such as insurance policies paid on the equipment that the firm owns or rent that may have to be paid in advance. The term "supplies" on the balance sheet represents the value of normal office supplies. If a firm has purchased stock in other companies and the owners expect to sell that investment within the year, then a line for "marketable securities" will appear on the balance sheet.

Items that have long-term value to the design firm are considered to be fixed assets. One category of fixed assets is called building and equipment. If the design firm owns the building they use for their business location or any other building the firm owns—perhaps a small warehouse—these buildings are a fixed asset. Equipment owned by the firm such as the furniture used by the office staff, computers, plotters, copying machines, delivery trucks, and so on are considered in accounting to be capital equipment—another category of fixed assets. The accumulated depreciation on these items is also shown on the balance sheet. Property or land is shown as a separate entry, since it is not depreciated—land does not "wear out." Note that in Figure 16-2, the company does not own its building, so it is not listed as an asset.

Depreciation results from the concept that capital equipment has a limited useful life. It is intended to express the usage of a fixed asset in the firm's pursuit of revenue. Although many think of depreciation as a way to express the wearing out of an object, it more accurately relates to the usage of the object, not its wear and tear. Accountants predict what will be the useful life of the equipment and determine the depreciated value of the equipment for each year the firm owns the item. Depreciation is set for a fixed period of time and varies based on current tax laws.

The category for "other assets" includes investments that the firm has made in other firms. If the investments are to be held for more than one year, they are listed here. If they are expected to be sold within a year, they are listed under current assets. As mentioned, other types of items that are considered "other assets" are the value of copyrights, trademarks, patents, licenses, and similar intangible assets that the firm might own. Of special interest to the design firm is the value placed on copyrighted designs or patents on any furnishings the firm may have obtained. Recall that copyrighted designs or patents solely belong to the design firm and cannot be used by others without the permission of the firm. Patents and copyrights are *amortized*, which is the practice by which the value of the patent or copyright is reduced over time to record its usage in the firm's earning activities. Amortization is essentially the same as depreciation, except that it applies to intangible assets.

Liabilities

At any given time, a design firm will owe funds to others for some reason or another. It might be to the electric company, a custom cabinetmaker, or an employee—or many others. The firm also has an obligation to those who have invested in the firm either as owners or purely for investment purposes. These examples—and they are only a small fraction of the types of entities that the firm may owe money to—are considered liabilities.

The liabilities side of the balance sheet is made up of two sections: liabilities, which can be current and noncurrent (or long term) liabilities and owner's equities. Liabilities always have first claim on the firm's assets. Should a business cease operation for any reason, all outstanding liabilities must be paid before owners or stockholders receive any funds.

Current liabilities are obligations that are due within one year or less. Probably the most typical current liability account is the accounts payable account. Claims from suppliers for goods or services ordered (and possibly delivered) but not yet paid are examples of items in *accounts payable*. Short-term loans such as lines of credit often obtained by design firms to pay for special orders for clients are called *notes payable*. *Accrued expenses* are those expenses owed for the period but not yet paid. Examples of accrued expenses are salaries due, rent, utility bills not yet paid, and so on. *Deferred revenues* are revenues received for services or the future sale of goods, but the services or goods have not been delivered yet. The most common source of deferred revenues for a design firm is retainers or deposits that the client has paid to the designer.

Depending on the type of business formation (sole proprietorship, etc.) and how the firm's accountant sets up the balance sheet report, there might be two other current liabilities accounts on the balance sheet. One is most commonly referred to as *taxes payable* (sometimes called estimated taxes). This line represents the amount of income tax or other taxes owed to government agencies but not yet paid. The second is a line for the *current portion of long-term debt*, which shows how much of the long-term debt, perhaps resulting from the purchase of a delivery truck by the firm, is to be paid during the next one-year period.

Another item that might appear on a balance sheet regardless of business formation is for liabilities that will not be paid within the coming year. As shown on the example in Figure 16-2, this situation is noted under "Other Liabilities." It is also referred to as noncurrent liabilities, since these amounts owed will not be paid during the coming one-year period. The main item listed would be most often for an interior design firm the balance of principal owed on a long-term loan. That long-term loan might be for the purchase of a vehicle or the outstanding principal on the mortgage if the firm owns its office/studio building or space.

Owner's Equity

Owner's equity represents the amount of funds the owners have invested in the interior design firm. The Owner's Equity section on the balance sheet is actually part of the Liabilities, but it is common to report it as a separate section, as shown in Figure 16-2. It is a liability account, since the owners have claims to the assets

TABLE 16-2.

Reporting Format of Owner's Equity for a Sole Proprietorship on a Balance Sheet.

Owner's Equity	
Michael Smith, capital as of January 1, 200x	$25,000
Deduct: 1999 drawings	−5,000
Michael Smith, capital as of December 31, 200x	$20,000

of the business. However, it bears repeating that in the case of a business's failure, the owners are not provided any assets related to their owner's equity until after all other liabilities are paid.

You might see the term "net worth" in other references on basic accounting and the balance sheet. This is a term that some accountants use in place of owner's equity. If it is used, it most often applies to the small business. The majority of accountants do not like to use this term on the balance sheet because it gives a false idea that the amount represented as net worth actually represents the value of the company. This is not true, as this net worth/owner's equity amount is only "worth" actual assets after all liabilities are paid. In principle it represents that the company has a worth on its own, but that is only the case if the total assets of the company actually exceed the total liabilities.

How this section is shown on a balance sheet will vary, based on the legal business formation. For example, if the firm is a sole proprietorship, owner's equity would be shown as "Michael Smith, Capital" and the amount Michael Smith invested to start the firm. If Smith invested additional funds at a later time, those additions would also be listed. For a partnership, it is customary to indicate the amount invested by each partner as a separate line, in much the same way as for a sole proprietorship. Tables 16-2 and 16-3 show the Owner's Equity section in these business formations. A partnership and a sole proprietorship also show a beginning and ending balance to show any withdrawals (or drawings) made by the owners against the assets as shown in Table 16-2. *Drawings* are amounts withdrawn by proprietors or partners as salaries. Drawings are not truly salaries, however, and are not treated as salaries in the bookkeeping process. A separate drawing account is set up for each partner. It is not uncommon for the balance sheet for a sole proprietorship not to show an owner's equity section. However, it is also not uncommon for these types of businesses to retain earnings by maintaining all or most profits within the company assets rather than taken out as drawings by the owners. In this way, a sole proprietorship, for example, has additional funds for future purchases of equipment needed as the firm grows.

A design firm that is a corporation would use the term "stockholders' equity," since the corporation is owned by stockholders. The amount of money obtained to run the corporation is listed as capital stock and paid-in capital stock. Par value of issued and outstanding stock is reported to represent the legal

TABLE 16-3.

Reporting Format of Owner's Equity for a Partnership on a Balance Sheet.

Owner's Equity	
Helen Sampson, capital	$15,000
Margaret Wallace, capital	10,000
Burt Anderson, capital	10,000
Total Partnership Equity	$35,000

minimum claim on assets associated with the stock itself. Paid-in capital stock is the excess of par value representing the claims on assets arising purely from the value of stock at the time of its issuance.

Recall that an interior design firm that is formed as a corporation issues or sells stock as one means of obtaining capital. When this is the case, the corporation may at the end of its year determine to set aside an amount of profits for some future use by the corporation. These funds are called *retained earnings* and represent the claim on assets arising from the cumulative undistributed earnings of the corporation after dividends are paid to stockholders for use in the business. Retained earnings do not refer to cash in and of itself. It may be in some other form, such as a vehicle, equipment, or marketable securities. There is no retained earnings section on the balance sheet of a sole proprietorship or a partnership. Earnings are treated as noted above for these forms of business.

Each general category is added to obtain total assets and total equities. Total assets must always equal total equities.

What Would You Do?

The sales agreement for Turbo Designs clearly states that once the agreement is signed by the client, orders cannot be canceled after seven business days and that the cancellation request must be in writing, but not via e-mail. A few weeks after the agreements were signed, the client contacts the designer and tells her that the custom rug that was ordered must be canceled, as the husband feels it is too expensive. The designer reminds the client that the sales order has a no cancellation policy. The client's husband e-mails the designer and says unless the rug is canceled, he will cancel everything and, if necessary, sue the designer.

THE STATEMENT OF CASH FLOW

Design firm owners often need to project the flow of cash into and out of the company in order to ensure that bills are paid and possibly to purchase equipment or other assets. The statement of cash flow reports all the inflows and outflows of cash due to the various activities of the company. A formal statement of cash flow will detail the changes in cash from operations, any investing, and other financial activities over a given period of time.

Cash, for accounting purposes, is money, checks, or items such as money orders that are accepted by banks. The statement of cash flow also reports the inflows and outflows of cash equivalents. Cash equivalents are very liquid, short-term investments, such as money market funds, that can be converted to cash quickly. However, if these kinds of investments are made only for the temporary investment of excess cash, they are not to be considered a part of the data that make up the statement.

The inflows and outflows come from three areas: operations, investments, and financing. Operations activities are those that are involved in the normal revenue-generating activities of the firm. Operations flows come primarily from the payments and receivables from clients, and the payments that the firm makes to others in the generation of revenues. Depending on the nature of the firm, operations flows also can come from interest earned, if the firm has loaned money to someone, or from dividends from certain kinds of investments. Investments inflows and outflows result from lending money and receiving payments on those loans; purchasing or selling certain kinds of securities; and purchasing or selling assets such as property, buildings, or equipment that the firm owns. Financing inflows and outflows comes from the finances that the owners have invested in the company and subsequent payments to those owners for the investment, as well as payments received and returned to creditors, such as banks, for mortgages.

The information in a statement of cash flows is used by owners to make decisions concerning the firm. For example, perhaps the company is considering moving to a new office location. This report will help the owner understand if sufficient cash is regularly going to be available to pay higher rent. In case the owner is considering the purchase of an office space, creditors will want to review this report before a decision to offer a loan is made.

The information used to prepare the statement of cash flow comes from the balance sheet, from the income statement, and, for corporations, from the retained earnings portion of the income statement. Although the report can be useful for those who need to review the financial condition of any business formation, it is primarily prepared for the corporation form of business ownership. Many lending institutions require a cash flow statement when a business seeks loans.

Prior to 1987, this type of financial information was reported as part of the statement of changes in financial position (sometimes called the funds flow statement). This statement reported the sources and uses of funds during a given period. Because of an increased emphasis on reporting this information on a cash basis format, the Financial Accounting Standards Board recommended that cash flow information be recorded in the statement of cash flows format. The most widely used format for this information is the indirect method, shown in Figure 16-3.

Tanner Interior Design, LLC
Statement of Cash Flows
For the Year Ended December 31, 200x

Net Cash Flow from Operating Activities:	
Net Income	$ 120,400
Adjustments to Convert Net Income to Net Cash Flow from Operating Expenses:	
Depreciation Expense	10,600
Increase in Accounts Receivable	−25,650
Decrease in Inventory	22,300
Increase in Prepaid Expenses	−12,300
Decrease in Accounts Payable	−22,360
Increase in Accrued Expenses	−8,700
Net Cash flow from Operating Activities	101,690
Cash Flows from Investing Activities:	
Purchasing of Equipment	−$ 22,500
Net Cash Used by Investing Activities	−22,500
Cash Flows from Financing Activities:	
Proceeds from Customer Retainers	18,900
Proceeds from Customer Deposits	33,000
Proceeds of Long-term Debt	27,000
Payments on Long-term Debt	−7,750
Cash Dividends Paid	−1,250
Net Cash Provided by Financing Activities	69,900
Net Increase in Cash	$ 149,090

FIGURE 16-3.

An example of a statement of cash flows using the direct method.

The methods for actually constructing these forms are quite complicated and are generally done by the firm's accountant. They will not be discussed here. Interested readers may want to review appropriate material that can be found in one of the references or, as a necessary part of business management, may want to discuss the statement of cash flow with the firm's accountant.

ACCOUNTING RECORDS AND SYSTEMS

The daily financial activities of the design firm must be diligently recorded. Each purchase or payment from clients must be documented as a record of the revenue generated by the firm. In the same sense, each payment the design firm makes to a vendor or pays bills to others must also be documented. These accounting records are commonly referred to as the daily bookkeeping records. The income statement, balance sheet, and statement of cash flow are summary reports generated from the information that the firm has maintained in its accounting records.

In accounting terminology, events that affect the financial activities of a firm, either as revenue generating or expense generating, are called *transactions*. It is critical that all these transactions be recorded accurately to meet legal and ethical standards of practice. Revenue and expense transactions must be recorded in an organized manner so that reports can be generated as needed to review the firm's financial condition and meet obligations concerning the reporting of profits or loss at tax time.

Many interior design businesses utilize some sort of computer software to aid in the recording of financial transactions. A small firm such as a sole proprietor may choose to use a manual method of bookkeeping. In making that determination, the firm is also determining what bookkeeping system it will be using. Bookkeeping systems are either single-entry or double-entry systems. The firm's accountant should advise the owner about what system is appropriate.

A *single-entry system* is very simple. It is set up based on the income statement and includes business income and expense accounts. Because of its simplicity, it is used by many small businesses. Many accountants feel that it is not an adequate way of properly accounting for transactions.

Most accountants recommend using the *double-entry system* because of its built-in checks and balances. The double-entry bookkeeping system uses journals and ledgers (discussed below), and the accounts are based on the entries found in both the income statement and the balance sheet. In the double-entry system, transactions are first entered in the journal and then summary information is transferred to the appropriate ledger. The next section provides additional information about the double-entry system.

Chart of Accounts

Financial organization is established in accounts. *Accounts* show additions (increases) to the account and subtractions (decreases) to the accounts that are represented in the income statement and balance sheet. Look again at the terms, noting the parts of the income statement in Table 16-1 and the balance sheet in Table 16-2. Each of these terms is, in a sense, a summary term that is generated from dozens of separate subaccounts.

Because the amount of assets of a firm must always balance with the liabilities of the firm, the account record looks like the letter "T" in its simplest form. Accountants refer to these as T-accounts (see Figure 16-4). The left-hand side of the T-account is called the *debit* side, whereas the right-hand side is called

T-Accounts

Assets		Equities	
(Increases on left, decreases on right)		(Decreases on left, increases on right)	
Cash		**Accounts Payable**	
DEBIT	CREDIT	DEBIT	CREDIT
300	900	900	
1,700	450	450	
1,000			

Accounts Receivable		Fees Revenue	
DEBIT	CREDIT	DEBIT	CREDIT
8,700	9,100		8,700
7,500			7,500
1,700			12,000

Note: These Accounts are not represented to balance.

FIGURE 16-4.

A sample format of typical T-accounts.

the *credit* side. In these accounts, debit and credit have no meaning in accounting other than "left" and "right," respectively. They are not substitutes for the words "increase" or "decrease," since, for some accounts, the increase side of the T-account will be on the right and the decrease on the left. Figure 16-5 shows this accounting situation.

Even a small interior design business will have numerous accounts. A logical format must be created to manage all those accounts. This logic is managed by the chart of accounts. A *chart of accounts* is a list of all the accounts that a firm is using. Typically, the major headings of the chart of accounts are set up to have account names that mirror the items shown on the balance sheet and income statement. Figure 16-6 is a portion of a chart of accounts indicating many of the major accounts typical of an interior design practice. Accounts are set up for cash, accounts receivable, fixed assets, accounts payable, payroll, telephone, rent, sales revenue from fees, and so on. The chart of accounts is a statement about how the firm categorizes the events that it seeks to control. These accounts can be further detailed to indicate such things as each customer's account or each vendor's account, to cite a few examples.

The chart of accounts is numbered in a logical order, and the example in Figure 16-6 is typical of the order. These code numbers are the ones used to cross-reference journal entries to posting entries. The chart of accounts should be set

Assets		=	Liabilities		+	Owner's Equity	
increase	decrease	=	increase	decrease	+	increase	decrease
(+) debit	(-) credit	=	(-) debit	(+) credit	+	(-) debit	(+) credit

FIGURE 16-5.

This example shows how some accounts show *increases* as a debit, while other accounts show *decreases* as a debit.

Sample Chart of Accounts

Account #	Description	Account #	Description
Assets		**Revenue**	
1000	Cash	6000	Sales of goods/products
1010	Cash: checking	6100	Freight in
1020	Cash: savings	6110	Delivery fees
1030	Petty cash	6200	Professional fees
1099	Total cash	6300	Reimbursable expenses
1100	Accounts receivable	6400	Cash discounts
1190	Allowance for bad debts		
1199	Total accounts receivable	**Expenses**	
1200	Inventory	7000	Cost of sales
1299	Total inventory	7100	Cost of goods sold
1300	Fixed assets	7125	Freight in
1310	Office furniture & fixtures	7200	Direct labor
1320	Office equipment	7300	Telephone
		7325	Supplies
Liabilities		8150	Payroll tax
2000	Accounts payable: cost of sales	8200	Rent
2050	Accounts payable: general	8300	Telephone
2100	Accrued payroll	8320	Utilities
2110	Federal withholding	8400	Group insurance
2120	Unemployment compensation	8450	Insurance
2125	Social security	8500	Professional consultants: attorney
2200	Note payable	8550	Professional consultants: accountant
2300	Interest payable	8600	Supplies
2400	Sales tax payable	8625	Catalogs/samples
3000	Long-term liabilities	8650	Postage
3010	Note payable long term	8675	Promotion
4000	Capital	8900	Depreciation expense
4100	Owner's capital	8925	Bank charges
4300	Owner's drawings	9000	Federal income tax
		9999	Net Income

FIGURE 16-6.

A partial chart of accounts for an interior design practice. (Excerpt from Christine M. Piotrowski, *Interior Design Management*, 1992, John Wiley & Sons.)

up so that it can increase in complexity as the firm grows, with appropriate accounts added as needed.

The Journal and Ledger

Following a business transaction, entries are made in a journal. A *journal* is a chronological record of all accounting transactions for the firm (see Figure 16-7). Journal entries show the date of occurrence, the name of the account to be debited or credited, the amount of the debit or credit, and a reference to the ledger account to which the entry has been posted. Entries are posted to different ledger accounts from the journal. *Posting*, therefore, is the transferring of a journal entry to the correct ledger account.

The *ledger*, often called a general ledger, is a group of accounts. If the bookkeeping is done manually, then an actual general ledger book will be used to record all the entries. When computer software is utilized, the ledger will likely be the first place the data is entered and the software would then update accounts as appropriate. The general ledger is often supplemented by various subsidiary

200X		Accounts	Ledger	Debit	Credit
Oct	6	Cash	1	1,250	
		Sales	26		1,250
	6	Accounts Receivable	2	3,400	
		Design Fees	3		3,400
	6	Inventory	5	17,700	
		Cash	1		7,000
		Accounts Payable	21		10,700

FIGURE 16-7.

An example of journal entries.

ledgers. These provide detailed information to support the general ledger. For an interior design firm, an important subsidiary ledger is the accounts receivable ledger (see Figure 16-8). This ledger has separate accounts for each client who purchases on credit from the designer. A few other ledgers are as follows:

Cash receipts ledger: Shows all the moneys received by the firm

Cash disbursements ledger: Records moneys paid out to cover expenses

Accounts payable ledger: Records amounts that the design firm owes to others

Purchase order ledger: Shows outstanding orders for goods and/or services for clients or the firm

Payroll ledger: Records payments to employees

Sydney Orlando								Client #: R842	
1526 E. Seaport Drive									
Date		Explanation	Debit		Credits		Balance		
May		Balance					150	00	
	9	Sales Check # 6801	325	00			775	00	
	14	Received on Account			500	00	225	00	
	29	Sales Check # 7002	120	00			345	00	
June	8	Received on Account			300	00	45	00	

FIGURE 16-8.

A sample page for an accounts receivable ledger.

Trial Balance

Remember that assets must equal liabilities and debits must equal credits. This does not mean that debits and credits will be equal within each account but that when all accounts are considered, they will be equal. A test to see if accounts are balanced and if all the account balances with the debit and credit side are totaled separately is called a *trial balance*.

There are two purposes of a trial balance. One is to check the accuracy of the posted entries to see if total debits equal total credits. The other is to establish summary balances in all accounts in order to prepare the balance sheet, income statement, and changes in financial condition. A trial balance can be done whenever the accounts are up-to-date.

CASH MANAGEMENT

Lillian and Robert's residential interior design firm (they are partners) has experienced a flurry of very recent project work. Due to the inflow of expected revenue, Robert ordered several thousands of dollars of accessories to have on hand in their small studio/showroom for future customers. The day before those accessory items were due to arrive, one of the customers canceled a contract for design services and an expected $100,000 of furnishings.

The example situation described above is exactly why it is important for the design firm to have a firm grasp on cash management. The statement of cash flow, discussed earlier, reports to those outside the firm the sources and uses of funds for a given period. Although this report provides valuable information for the owner for long-range planning, the constant inflow of cash that is needed to meet the cash demands of a firm in order to pay bills is not as easily seen by this report. A more simplified cash flow statement that helps the owner with cash management is a critical tool for more frequent review. In this section, we will briefly discuss a simple cash flow statement that can easily be prepared by a manager and can be used in cash management.

Cash management is really cash forecasting. The firm estimates how much revenue will be realized each month (or quarter) and how much expenses will be for that same time period. Because it is a forecast, the estimate for cash receipts (revenue) can never be 100 percent accurate. All kinds of things may happen to upset forecasts for obtaining revenues. As we see in the example, a project can fall through or clients might not pay on time. These are just a few common potential problems that make cash management challenging.

For this reason, it is also a good idea to project a small, though realistic, percentage above expected and needed cash receipts for the period. If this is done, then it is easier to meet actual needs if (and when) forecasts are lower than actual receipts. Of course, it is also important to meet that cash inflow forecast if at all possible. It should also be remembered that not all income turns into cash immediately. Accounts receivables may take 30, 60, even 90 or more days to be received. So although the cash could be recorded for several months, it should not be forecasted as in hand until the income has been actually received.

Cash forecasting for expenses is much easier. These outflows are usually known for any given period and are more easily controlled. Although the firm might forecast the purchase of a computer or inventory, these items can often be put off when cash receipts do not materialize as forecasted.

The important thing is to keep reviewing cash flow. An existing business would probably want to do a cash flow report monthly. Computer programs allow this to be done fairly easily.

Cash Flow Statement: December to March 200x				
Description	Actual December	Projected January	Projected February	Projected March
Beginning Cash Balance	$ 8,000	$ 6,500	$ 19,100	$ 21,200
Projected Revenue	95,000	92,000	100,000	105,000
Other income		1,100	1,100	1,100
Projected Gross Revenue	103,000	99,600	120,200	127,300
Operating Expenses	77,000	78,000	79,000	81,000
Purchase computer	17,000			3,400
Purchase office furniture			17,500	
Line-of-credit debt	2,500	2,500	2,500	2,500
Ending Cash Balance	6,500	19,100	21,200	40,400

FIGURE 16-9.

A simple cash flow statement. Notice how it repeats the format of an income statement.

A simple cash flow statement for the purposes of cash management begins with the current, known cash balance (see Figure 16-9). Notice how this report mimics the appearance of the income statement. If the cash flow statement is for projected cash flow, then the beginning cash balance for each month can be estimated. In order to show how the cash flow statement works, however, the beginning cash balance is the actual balance (as determined by revenue minus expenses). The next line shows the known and projected revenues for the months being projected. The projected revenues combine the known work-in-process amounts for each period with forecasts of additional work in each month. *Work in process* means work under way for any clients that have not yet been billed. Adding the beginning cash balance to the projected revenue provides the projected gross revenue.

Under the expenses, operating expenses are the projected combined expenses for each month. These include salaries, fringe benefits, rent, utilities, and other costs of doing business as well as direct expenses. On another line is shown each month's responsibility for a bank line of credit that has been obtained in a previous month. This amount is the amount of principal and interest due each month. Note that in March, the firm expects a one-time expense of $3400 for a computer. The last line shows the ending cash balance for each month. This balance is carried up to the beginning cash balance line in the forecast months. The reader may wish to fill in April's figures to obtain the ending balance for the month (and to see how well the firm is doing). An additional sample cash flow statement sample and worksheet is provided on the CD as Item 16-3.

A positive ending cash flow does not necessarily mean the firm is a profitable firm. Even a company with good cash flow can be losing money. Sometimes the assets of a firm can be tied up in receivables or fixed assets. These assets help make a "profit" at the end of the income statement, but do not represent cash that is available to pay bills. Bills to vendors or others that are not paid or are deferred will have to be paid one day. And Murphy's Law says that those will always be due when the cash reserves are low. Design firm owners and managers must not let this happen but should constantly review the cash flow statements against the P&L to help them make management decisions that will keep them out of financial trouble with creditors.

A cash flow budget allows the owner to compare actual results of the business against forecasted goals. When the revenues are lower than forecasted, the owner will want to renew marketing efforts or possibly find new revenue sources. The owner can also look at how he or she has been extending credit to customers or may want to change payment requirements. If expenses exceed forecasts, the owner can look quickly at what has happened and determine ways in which he or she can hold down expenses.

Many small design firms operate in markets in which they must survive on seasonal design business such as the design of second homes in resort areas. Understanding on paper what the cash flow situation will be in the slow months when these example second home owners are not procuring interior design work can help the owner determine how to generate alternative revenue sources for those slow months. For example, perhaps the owner can work with real estate agents, providing brief consultations for sellers. Alternately, the owner may need to generate larger pools of revenue or hold down costs during busy periods.

New firms and those in the first year also have a built-in cash flow problem. A new firm has many first-time expenses such as stationery, office equipment, and marketing activities. If the firm also sells merchandise, it may be extending credit to clients several months into the future. Revenue is often delayed as the firm waits for full payment on delivery. On top of this problem is the requirement for many new businesses to pay up front for merchandise that they have purchased for clients. Recall from Chapter 8 that this is often referred to as pro forma credit. Obviously, the cash could easily be going out faster than it is coming in, unless the firm has a well-thought-out retainer and deposit policy. Even if the firm has no debt expense for a line of credit from a bank (operating on an all-cash basis), the design firm can quickly get into financial problems.

For design firms that do not sell merchandise, the cash flow cycle is relatively short. Firms that sell merchandise often have a constant cash flow problem because they have not received enough cash from some source to pay for the merchandise that is on order. Whatever the case, there must always be enough cash available to pay current bills. Employees expect to be paid within 7 to 14 days of completing their work. Suppliers generally have a 30-day grace period before they start charging penalties. The faster the firm can collect on its receivables, the more efficient its cash flow cycle will be. However, it is not uncommon for a firm to have a significant percentage of its receivables over 120 days outstanding.

It is important for you to realize that cash management and cash flow falls back on the cash accounting method rather than on the accrual accounting method. Good cash flow records of cash receipts (deposits of cash) and outflows (when a check to a supplier or other liability account clears the bank) are necessary. To accurately record cash receipts, the owner must keep track of new orders or contracts for services, when deposits or retainers are to be received, when partial payments are expected, when delivery of goods are expected, and so on.

Tips to Help Monitor Cash Flow

When the owner sees cash needs months in advance, that information encourages the owner to market beyond what is needed to pay today's bills. Small firms frequently have an uncanny habit of looking at the work that they are doing right now, neglecting marketing until the current project is done. When this happens, a business may be without any revenue for weeks or even months as the owner finally gets around to seeking new business. Cash management actually forces the owner to recognize marketing efforts as an ongoing part of his or her ownership responsibilities.

Cash management has a relationship to other business operations. Good, basic business practices aid in keeping cash flow operating efficiently. Here are a few examples:

- Constant monitoring of outstanding orders and receivables aids the firm in protecting narrow margins of profit.
- The firm must have good pricing policies for both fees and products.
- Credit reports on clients with whom the firm is unfamiliar should be obtained before the firm orders merchandise.
- Inventory, returns, and exchanges must be carefully monitored so that cash is not tied up in inventory. This cash cannot be used to pay other expenses.
- The firm must prepare design contracts to help protect from possible stoppages or losses of revenue.
- The firm should require substantial retainers and deposits before work is begun or products are ordered.
- Careful time keeping, scheduling, and project management are also helpful in cash flow forecasting.
- A thorough monitoring of budgeted versus actual time estimates and fee estimates can eliminate project shortfalls.
- Monitoring of outstanding product orders and receivables aids the firm in protecting narrow profit margins on the sale of goods.
- Constant monitoring of outstanding orders and receivables aids the firm in protecting narrow margins of profit.

Positive cash management can be helped by establishing policies that require substantial retainers and deposits as well as tracking and collecting receivables. When the firm needs cash, the owners may be able to obtain short-term loans from the firm's banker. Keeping the banker informed of the financial situation of the design firm helps the firm in the loan approval process, as does a good history of prompt repayment of those loans. Going to the bank every time the firm needs cash to pay bills is not the best solution. Good management of the firm and the firm's cash flow is the answer.

COMPUTER APPLICATIONS FOR ACCOUNTING

With the many computer accounting software systems becoming easier to use, interior design businesses increasingly utilize the computer to maintain financial records regardless of the size of the design firm. A manual system may be preferable to some sole practitioners; however, utilizing one of the simplified, computerized accounting software programs to assist in this important management activity provides many advantages.

Accounting software accommodates check writing to pay bills, preparation of payroll and payroll tax reports, and preparation of sales tax reports. Software programs help the owner create managerial reports of many kinds that can be useful to the owner as well. The documentation created with the software will be utilized by the firm's accountant to prepare income tax statements as well as many other kinds of financial record-keeping documents.

Software programs exist for both Windows® and Macintosh® computer systems that can be adopted by interior designers. I do not recommend any one particular accounting software program, but three common ones used by interior design firms are QuickBooks Pro®, Peachtree Accounting®, and

MYOB®. There are other specialized programs available that have been created specifically for interior designers that combine accounting functions with other functions such as purchasing, project management, and order tracking. Computer programs should not be used with the idea of eliminating any involvement of a qualified accountant. Selection of appropriate software should be made after the owner discusses all pertinent issues with the firm's accountant. The firm's accountant generally is familiar with different software programs for accounting needs and can help the design firm owner with this decision.

SUMMARY

A basic understanding of accounting is important to the student and all interior designers whether or not they intend to own their own business. Knowledge of the concepts of revenue and expense as they relate to eventual profit impacts every interior design employee. If a firm is not profitable, there are no funds for the owner to offer bonuses or raises or even perhaps simple discounts to employees for the purchase of personal goods.

It is important to understand the financial aspects of the interior design business and to be conversant with the terminology and concepts of financial accounting. No matter who does the daily bookkeeping in the long run, the owner of a design firm is responsible for accurate recording of financial transactions.

Countless owners of small firms likely take care of the daily bookkeeping chores. Many leave the day-to-day bookkeeping chores to bookkeepers, accountants, or others who better understand these financial matters. Accountants are engaged by design firms to prepare the formal accounting statements that are needed periodically, to check accuracy of accounting records and prepare income tax statements. Regardless of the involvement of others in the financial record keeping, the owner should still have knowledge of the firm's financial condition, since he or she is ultimately responsible for the company's finances.

This chapter has introduced the reader to the basic concepts, definitions, and parts of the income statement, balance sheet, and statement of changes in financial condition. We also have looked briefly at the concepts related to accounting records and systems, and cash management.

In the next chapter, we will discuss managerial accounting and some brief concepts concerning management control systems. These concepts relate to reporting methods generated from the financial statements, which have been created to help owners and/or managers plan, organize, and control the finances of the design firm.

REFERENCE

1. Anthony, Robert N., and James S. Reece, 1983, p. 908.

CHAPTER 17

Financial Management

Key Terms and Concepts

These key terms and concepts are important to material in this chapter. Many of these terms will be utilized in other chapters as well. Be sure you understand these items as you read this chapter.

Terms and Concepts

Financial management	Favorable variance
Ratios	Break-even analysis
Information reports	Break-even point
Performance reports	Variable costs
Variance analysis	Fixed costs
Unfavorable variance	

Critical Issues

After completing this chapter you should be able to:

- Explain the importance of understanding financial management concepts for any interior design practice owner.
- Calculate the ratios shown in this chapter.
- Discuss the implications of the ratios and percentages in the chapter.
- Discuss how financial management reports can be useful to the owner of an interior design practice.
- Explain "favorable" and "unfavorable" in variance analysis.
- Discuss ways to control overhead.

Wallace Design Group experienced a 35 percent increase in net income during 2006. During that year, the owner added one interior designer and hired a full-time office assistant. The owner has been aggressively marketing for additional office projects, along with the high-end residential work they have already been obtaining. In their prime market area, new housing starts for homes over 3000 square feet have decreased by 20 percent over the last three months. What kind of analysis should the owner do to ensure a continued high level of net income?

Financial resources for all interior design businesses are limited. Expenses must be met, salaries have to be paid, loan interest is due monthly, and vendors expect prompt payment. The smaller the design practice is, the greater this pressure on financial resources can become. Some firms need to pay out dividends to stockholders or at least some sort of return on financial investment. At the very least, the sole proprietor wants to be paid a salary or possibly to draw against the profits. Regardless of their size control and management of financial resources is a critical management function.

The development of the income statement, balance sheet and cash flows statement discussed in the previous chapter is the primary type of information that an owner uses to manage the financial resources of the firm. For many firms, these reports do not provide enough information to assist the owner in making important financial decisions. Owners and their accountants turn to other financial management techniques for assistance.

Financial managerial reports as well as other types of reports can be developed from data available to the firm from internal data resources or outside sources of information. These reports provide additional information that the owner or manager can use to assist them in decision making. As the interior design firm grows, this function becomes more important. This chapter reviews several useful financial ratios and percentages, as well as a variety of reports that the owner can use to make financial decisions.

One way to improve the financial status of a firm is by controlling overhead expenses. Although reporting overhead expenses is part of basic financial accounting, controlling those expenses is a function of managerial control. A brief discussion concerning controlling overhead has been included in this chapter to assist the reader in understanding the importance of this important management responsibility.

WHAT IS FINANCIAL MANAGEMENT?

Each month, Sally was responsible for developing two key reports on the activities of the interior design department. One of those reports showed the status of work in progress for the previous month and estimated work for the next month. A second report detailed design fees that were booked via new contracts, billings for the previous month, and expected billings for the next month. This report also compared this year's billings to last year for the same months. Sally also generated a report on the direct expenses for last month and the expected direct expenses for the next month. Even without having a sample of each of these reports before you, how would these reports help Sally manage workload and operational decisions for the design department?

The reports mentioned in the above scenario reflect some of the reports that managers and owners develop and analyze as part of their management functions. They represent some of the common reports developed as part of the financial management responsibility and activities of a business. *Financial management*, or managerial accounting, is concerned with the analysis and reporting of all the financial aspects of the firm. The reports that are prepared are used to help individuals within the firm to manage and control the performance of the firm.

As the example above shows, financial management goes beyond financial accounting. By means of financial management, owners and managers generate reports that will help them analyze any kind of financial or numerical information that is of interest to them. These accounting reports can show many things. One simple example is a report that summarizes how much of all possible work time for each designer is billable to clients as opposed to house or nonbillable time. This is commonly called a utilization report. That is one of the kinds of reports mentioned at the beginning of this section. A second type of important report is called an aged receivables report. It provides information about how many dollars are owed to the firm by clients and for what period of time that money is owed.

Financial management is the responsibility of the owners and possibly the business manager and design director—those in the firm who are entrusted with the responsibility of planning, organizing, and controlling the organization. In small firms, financial management is always the responsibility of the owner, who receives assistance from the firm's accountant in developing reports. In medium- and large-sized firms, the reports are usually generated and analyzed by the managers.

In addition to reports that look at larger amounts of financial and other data, financial management also involves the review of ratios. These ratios can be applied to the data that can be obtained from the balance sheet and income statement. Financial ratios help the owner by giving him or her evidence of performance (or the lack of performance) of such things as the amount of profit actually realized from the revenues generated, the amount of working capital that actually results from comparing current assets to current liabilities, and even the relationship of direct labor to nonbillable labor.

Perhaps a design firm is considering locating a branch office in another state. The owner might hire one or more consultants to analyze the business potential of this new location. The consultant would likely prepare a narrative report—another type of managerial report—that can combine numerical data and narration describing parameters that are important to help the owner make a decision about the potential viability of the branch office.

There are many kinds of computer software to help generate many of these reports. Accounting, project scheduling, database, and many other kinds of software can be used by owners and design directors to help them make decisions on day-to-day and long-term financial limits or opportunities that can benefit the firm. Analyzing appropriate data helps the owner make sense of the efforts of staff and the business as a whole. Financial management reporting assists the owner in determining ways in which he or she can keep the firm viable. It is not necessary for the small-business owner to become an accountant in order to do this. It is incumbent upon the owner to seek appropriate help from accredited public accountants and certified public accountants or other business consultants until he or she becomes familiar with reading and interpreting results.

FINANCIAL RATIOS AND PERCENTAGES

Understanding the data and implications of the financial reports detailed in the previous chapter is only part of really understanding whether a business is financially successful. Looking at ratios and percentages provides many important clues to the success of, or possible problems in, the financial performance of an interior design firm. These ratios and percentages give an even clearer message as to the overall financial success (or lack of it) of a business.

By using ratios and percentages, a designer can evaluate almost anything that can be measured in numerical terms. Ratios are quite common and are used every day by almost everyone in one way or another. In our everyday experiences, we might use ratios to determine the miles per gallon our car gets or to simply calculate a tip at a restaurant. A ratio, you will recall, is one number over

TABLE 17-1.

Financial Ratios to Determine the Financial Performance of the Business.

1. Profit margin on sales = Net income / Total sales
2. Return on total assets (ROA) = Net income / Total assets
3. Return on equity (ROE) = Net income / Owner's equity
4. Return on investment (ROI) = Net profits / Total assets
5. Current ratio = Current assets / Current liabilities
6. Quick ratio (or acid test) = Current assets - Inventory / Current liabilities
7. Debt ratio = Total debt / Total assets
8. Working capital = Current assets–Current liabilities
9. Net profit = Earnings before interest and taxes (EBIT)/Net sales
10. Return on investment = EBIT / Total assets–Total liabilities
11. Average collection period = Accounts receivables × 360 / Total sales
12. Inventory turnover ratio = Cost of goods sold / Average inventory
13. Gross margin percentage = Gross margin dollars / Net revenue
14. Receivable turnover ratio = Annual sales / Total outstanding receivables

another—the relationship between two or more things. With ratios, we are comparing two numbers. A ratio can become a percentage when we divide one number into another. Of course, for a ratio to become a percentage, the large number (the denominator, in this case) must be divided into the small number (the numerator). For example, if we divide 75 by 100 (75/100), we will get a percentage of 75. When using ratios, remember that when comparing a part to the whole, the whole is always the denominator.

There are many ratios that accountants and financial analysts use to evaluate a business. In this brief discussion, we will discuss only a few of the key ratios. Table 17-1 shows several financial ratios. Realize that analyzing financial ratios is not difficult to grasp. The information that they provide can be critical to an owner's decisions about the current state and future of the firm.

Profit ratios help a design firm owner analyze how effectively the company is earning more income than spending in expenses. Obviously, a business can only remain viable if it sustains a profit. As a rule, profitability (or income) is affected by increases in volume and changes in price, or both. There are three primary ways a design firm can increase its profitability. The first is to increase its fee base. For example, charging $100 per hour rather than $90 per hour or $3.25 a square foot rather than $2.75 per square foot. Another is to bill more hours at its design fee. This might simply involve being more productive and more accurate in billing time to a project. And a third can be to find ways to reduce expenses.

The profit margin on sales ratio tells the business how much profit has been obtained from every dollar of sales. Using the information in Figure 17-1, you can see that the firm's profit margin on sales (fees only) is 17 percent. Find the data in the income statement that you can use in the formula in Figure 17-1 to calculate this percentage. How can the firm increase this ratio? What might some consequences be if the ratio was decreased?

A second important profitability ratio is the ratio that tells the return on (total) assets, often expressed as ROA. This ratio measures the amount of profit generated by the use of the assets of the company. The ROA for Wallis Design Group is 5 percent. Is this firm using its assets effectively to achieve a reasonable profit?

Income Statement
Wallis Design Group
Period Ending December 31, 200X

Gross Revenue	
From fees	$18,400
From sale of goods	
Product	$37,500
Freight-in	2,625
Delivery	3,250
	43,375
Total Gross Revenue	$61,775
Net Revenue	$61,775
Cost of Sales	
From products:	
Cost of goods	$25,000
Freight-in	2,500
Delivery	3,000
From fees:	
Direct labor	12,750
Materials supplies	185
Reproduction expense	95
Telephone (long-distance)	105
Total Cost of Sales	43,635
Gross Margin	$18,140
Operating Expenses	
Salaries	10,500
Payroll taxes	1,900
Rent	850
Heat, power, & light	250
Telephone	265
Promotion	225
Supplies & postage	225
Insurance	200
Dues & subscriptions	57
Printing & reproduction	50
Interest expense	200
Total Operating Expenses	$14,722
Other Revenue	
Interest	350
Net Income Before Taxes	$3,418
Less: Provision for income taxes	−627
Net Income	$3,141

FIGURE 17-1.

A sample income statement for an interior design firm.

Numerous efficiency ratios can be developed to review how well the business is operating. One very important efficiency ratio is the average collection period ratio. This ratio tells the business how many days, on average, it takes to collect accounts receivable. The faster clients pay their bills, the sooner the firm can pay its bills—a very positive situation for any size interior design firm. If this ratio is low, it means that the business is receiving payments from clients quickly. If it is high, it means that clients are taking a long time to pay, and this can seriously affect cash flow for the business. The data for the average collection period ratio comes from the balance sheet and income statement. Note that the 360 in the denominator of the formula represents the number of days in the year. When calculating ratios, accountants generally use 360 rather than 365 days to determine the number of days in a year. Should this firm try to improve its collection policies? Can you think of some strategies that the firm can use to improve its collection policies?

Another ratio that reports a reference concerning cash flow is the receivable turnover ratio. This is determined by dividing annual sales by the total amount of outstanding receivables. Let us say that a design firm has $500,000 in annual sales and currently has $75,000 in receivables. Doing the math, the ratio in this case is 7, meaning the receivables turn over 7 times per year. But this is not enough information to be fully useful. To find out how many days on average it takes for an invoice to be paid, 360 days needs to be divided by the ratio of 7. In this example, that would be 52 days. This information helps the owner know that cash flow is a little slow. Instituting procedures and collections so that this average is lowered even more would be a very positive strategy.

Interior design firms often have some inventory of goods. In some companies, this is a purposeful display of merchandise in a showroom space open to the public. For many others, it is an assortment of goods that the design firm has accumulated because of returns from the client that could not be sent back or simply purchased by the design firm to have on hand. It is important for the owner and manager to know how long the merchandise in inventory has been in stock. The longer the inventory is held in the office or warehouse, the longer dollars are tied up that can be better used in some other way. Design firms, like any business that sells from its inventory, needs to turn over that merchandise and keep what it sells fresh. The information for this ratio comes from the balance sheet and the income statement. It appears that the firm is turning over its inventory quite quickly. Is it possible that this might not actually be true?

Larger design firms that have obtained investors to help capitalize the company are going to be interested in two other groups of ratios called the liquidity ratios and debt ratios. Liquidity ratios show the design firm's ability to pay its debts. Of particular importance is the firm's ability to pay its current liabilities with available current assets. A second liquidity ratio is the working capital ratio. It measures the amount of cash that is available to operate the business on a daily basis. If a firm's working capital is less than its operating expenses, it may not be able to pay all of its current bills. Debt ratios indicate how much of the firm's financing has come from debts—loans and lines of credit—rather than direct investment by the owners and/or stockholders. Potential new investors will be concerned about high debt ratios, since they mean that the loans must be paid off before any return is made on investments in the firm.

Ratios help determine the financial health of the firm and locate some of the potential financial or operational problems. Ratios are more important to the owner or manager than to employees. However, employees should understand that there is a lot of number crunching that goes on behind the scenes in the operations of a design practice. Awareness brings about concern, and concern brings about the realization that every employee in the design firm affects the financial health of the company.

An additional income statement that can be further used for discussion of concepts in this section and others in the chapter is provided on the CD as Item 17–1.

What Would You Do?

George's firm has been working on the design and specification of a very large public utility office building in another state. The design contract calls for space plan coordination with the architect, specification of all the furniture, and coordination with the architect on architectural finish specification. The project will be going out to bid for the purchase of the furniture.

The person from the utility that George has been working with has asked him to specify ergonomic desk seating for the offices. That amounts to 195 small executive chairs and another 57 large executive chairs. George wants the client to purchase a specific manufacturer's chairs, as they have the right design look that George and the rest of the design team want for the project. The client likes the chair but is concerned about the price.

George talked to a sales rep from another chair manufacturer who wants to bid on the project, and the rep said, "A good price can be obtained if you can convince the client to let me make a presentation so that the utility negotiates a contract directly with the factory. I know I can get a deal from headquarters, especially if the company will also negotiate the desks."

REPORTING PERFORMANCE

The larger the firm, the greater the likelihood that management or owners will ask for written reports from staff or consultants that provide information valuable to management and other employees. Two important types of reports that are used by management to determine if the firm's plans are being accomplished are information reports and performance reports. *Information reports* are generally reports of financial or other numerical data. They are prepared in a narrative form and are used to provide information that is needed in the operation of the organization. A report prepared by a consultant offering commentary and/or suggestions on changes in operations to improve work flow is an example. A summary of an article related to general economic forecasts for the geographic area of the design firm, which also discusses how these forecasts may affect the design firm, is another example of an informational report.

The second type of report, which is more important to our discussion here, is the performance report. The *performance report* consists primarily of financial or other numerical information. The data to develop many performance reports can be found in the financial reports discussed in the previous chapter or from other data collected by the firm. Detailed performance reports can be generated from information such as time records, accounts receivable records on design fees, and reimbursable expense records, to name a few.

Computer software programs create many kinds of reports with relative ease. However, not all reports that can be created are necessary. In fact, too many reports can confuse rather than help the owner. It is therefore necessary for the owner and the firm's accountant to determine which reports will be reliable and timely. What this means is that any report must be based on accurate data or information.

A report is only useful if it is accurate. If the information inserted into a reporting format is inaccurate or in any way comes from improper data, then the usefulness of the report will be questionable. Let us look at a simple example. If an owner is concerned about the revenue productivity of the firm's senior designers, he or she will want to analyze accurate time records for those individuals. If the designers have not kept accurate time records, the resulting analysis will be of little use to the owner. Of course, providing inaccurate time records is very serious, if the design firm is billing the client for that design time.

Reports must also be timely. Knowing where the firm stands with aged receivables—that is, monies owed to the firm but not yet paid—on a monthly basis is timely. Only seeing that report when the firm is strapped for funds to pay bills is not as useful. An aged receivables report is needed monthly at the very least, but it might be needed on a weekly basis if a firm has a serious cash flow problem. Those responsible for marketing and obtaining new work need to know the current status of all projects on at least a weekly basis. Accepting new design projects when the staff is completely booked and overworked might look like a good idea, but when the work cannot be accomplished, the staff's enthusiasm will backfire. Some firms may want daily time sheets; others can live with weekly or even monthly reports.

The business management methodology of variance analysis is a helpful management tool for owners and department managers when reviewing many performance reports. Basically, what happens in variance analysis is that data can be reviewed to see differences in planned performance versus actual performance. To be more technical, in *variance analysis*, the owner or manager looks at financial and numerical data in relation to the differences between planned (or budgeted amounts) and actual amounts. In variance analysis, accountants use the terms favorable and unfavorable. An *unfavorable variance* generally means that the actual amount is more than the budgeted amount. A *favorable variance* generally means that the actual amount is less than the budgeted amount. For example, if the budgeted amount of direct labor for a project is 300 hours and the actual amount of hours worked is 365 hours, there is an unfavorable variance. Assuming there is the same number of budget hours, if the actual hours were 280, there would be a favorable variance. In Figure 17-2, you can see that there were unfavorable variances for several of the overhead expense items. If this trend continued, including the overall total expense variance, what affect would that have on the potential profitability of this particular firm? Item 17-2 on the CD provides another more detailed variance report.

A manager must not only look at the quantitative differences. For the data to be truly meaningful, he or she must also ask questions as to why the variances occur. There are always reasons for a variance that can be logical. For example, in Figure 17-2 the expense for heat, power, and light may have exceeded the budget because of a large amount of overtime required to complete a project. Can you think of some reasons why the salary expense was less than budgeted? The manager uses his or her judgment after meetings with the individuals involved or further review of billings before decisions are made concerning what to do about the variances.

These types of reports help the owner clarify if the firm is on track to accomplish strategies and tactics spelled out for the goals in the company's strategic plan. Certain reports are especially important, such as reports related to

Expense Report($)
April 200X

Expense	Actual	Budget	Variance over Budget
Salaries	$75,000	$78,500	$-3,500
Payroll taxes	4,575	5,000	-425
Group insurance	750	750	0
Rent	1,500	1,500	0
Heat, power, & light	650	500	150
Telephone	375	300	75
Promotion	450	525	-75
Travel reimbursements	790	600	190
Supplies and postage	450	500	-50
Depreciation expense	900	900	0
Insurance	750	750	0
Dues & subscriptions	250	150	100
Professional consultants	2,300	1,000	1,300
Printing and reproduction	570	450	120
Interest expense	875	875	0
Total Expenses	90,185	92,300	-2,115

FIGURE 17-2.

A sample performance report showing various analysis for the overall expense report.

revenue generation (see Figure 17-3), expenses, and profits. To have the most use, performance reports should be prepared on a monthly basis.

Some examples of specific reports that can be useful, depending on the size and complexity of the interior design firm, are as follows:

1. Revenues from sources—fees and sales of goods
2. Work in process and aged receivables
3. Aged accounts payables
4. Deferred income
5. Employee utilization and productivity
6. Comparisons of fees earned with budgeted estimates
7. Revenues by client type (or size of project)
8. Month-by-month profit and loss statements (with variances)
9. Budgets for capital equipment purchases
10. All overhead expenses or specific overhead expenses month to month

Figures 17-4 and 17-5 are examples of some of these reports.

These example reports are optional accounting and managerial information. Essentially, they should be prepared depending largely by the firm's ability to produce the required reports and on the owner's need to have the information. As mentioned, computer applications allow for fast turnaround of many reports. In some cases, assuming data are available, a report can be generated on the computer by the end of a business day. If the report is done

Creative Interior Design Projected Revenue by Client Type 200X, 200X (Est.), 200X (Est.)			
	200X	**200X**	**200X**
Open Office Planning:			
Under 15,000 sq. ft.	$23,500	$65,000	$75,000
15,000–30,000 sq. ft.	12,000	36,000	40,000
Over 30,000 sq. ft.	20,800	27,000	35,000
Subtotal	$56,300	$128,000	$150,000
Medical Facilities:			
Physician's suites	32,500	48,000	55,000
Hospitals	35,000	40,000	25,000
Subtotal	$67,500	$88,000	$80,000
Banking Facilities:			
Branch offices	10,000	20,500	28,000
Corporate offices	15,500	20,000	30,000
Subtotal	$25,500	$40,500	$58,000
Professional Offices:			
Attorneys	28,700	42,000	55,000
Accountants	13,600	25,000	30,000
Corporate	45,900	55,000	60,000
Real estate	5,000	7,500	10,000
Others	10,000	20,000	25,000
Subtotal	$103,200	$149,500	$180,000
Hospitality:			
Restaurant	65,500	80,500	90,000
Lodging	38,500	49,000	72,000
Subtotal	$104,000	$129,500	$162,000
Grand Total	$356,500	$535,500	$630,000

FIGURE 17-3.

Performance report showing projected revenue by client type.

manually, as is the case for many small design firms, getting it done on a monthly basis can be considered fast, since some reports are prepared only every three to six months—if at all. Ideally, most reports should be prepared on a monthly basis when the previous month's data is available within the first ten days of the month.

Even small design firms or sole proprietors can take advantage of performance reporting by using accounting and database management. Computer systems can link accounting and other numerical data to generate tabled reports relatively easily. Software that also can automatically prepare charts and graphs from the numerical data provides additional aid for the manager.

CONTROLLING OVERHEAD

When an interior design firm spends too much on overhead expenses, the profits of the company are diminished. Losing control of overhead expenses not only means diminished profits, but it can result in a critical financial situation

Excellent Interiors, Inc.
Work in Process/Age Analysis
As of July 200X

Client	Total	Work in Process	Current	30 Days	60 Days	90 Days	120 days and Over
				Accounts Receivables			
Nelson's Real Estate	$8,900	$2,250		$900			
Smith, Jones Corp.	15,000	5,000	$5,000				
Astro Business Park	12,500	3,000	2,500	1,000	$2,000*		
University Computing Center	29,500	9,750	7,750				
Phoenix Corporation	25,500			5,500	2,000*		
Financial Trust Bank	8,500	5,000	3,000	500			
Oceanview Development Co.	70,500					$21,000*	
Carter Residence	5,000	1,500					1,550*
Robbins Residence	6,500	2,000	1,500	1,500			
Totals	$181,900	$28,500	$19,750	$9,400	$4,000	$21,000	$1,550

*Sent letter: work stopped until account is current.

FIGURE 17-4.

Another performance report that shows the work-in-process/age analysis.

leading—in the worst-case scenario—to the closing of the company. Keeping overhead expenses under control is an important task in producing a profit for any size design business. Obviously, the larger the design firm, the more important controlling costs becomes. Yet even the sole practitioner who works out of a home office needs to control overhead, or profit margins will be nonexistent. Although this section is directed to the interior design firm with employees, the sole practitioner will find key concepts to assist in cost control.

Manpower Utilization Report
Excellent Interior Design, LLC
Week Ending April 1, 200X

Week ending	No. of employees	Total hours	Billable	% Billed	House	Meetings Admin.	Misc.
3/3	8	335	280	84%	55	42	13
3/11	8	365	274	75%	91	73	18
3/18	8	385	375	97%	28	13	15
3/24	8	330	300	91%	30	21	9
3/31	8	342	320	94%	22	15	7
4/01	9	355	337	95%	18	12	6

FIGURE 17-5.

This performance report shows employee productivity based on billable and nonbillable time.

Break-Even Analysis

Few interior designers consider their businesses to be a "nonprofit." Yet many find themselves barely making a profit at the end of each tax year. This happens despite their best efforts at creating excellent interiors and being wonderful problem solvers for their clients.

Low profitability often occurs because many designers do not carefully control the operating expenses. These expenses must, at minimum, be in balance with the revenues that are generated. When this doesn't happen, a low profit or loss occurs.

One management tactic that can help with this situation is to plan for profit by establishing the firm's break-even point. The *break-even point* is when the dollars to operate the business are exactly equal to the dollars generated from revenues from all sales activity. Since too many designers forget to consider all the costs of operating the business as well as the costs of doing projects, estimates for fees (and other sources of revenue) can easily fall short of revenue needs. When that happens, the firm is operating below the break-even point. When revenues exceed costs, then the firm is operating above the break-even point and making a profit.

Accountants look at the costs of operating and generating revenue in terms of variable and fixed costs. *Variable costs* are those costs (or expenses) that vary with the volume of revenue generated. In other words, a variable cost such as CAD expenses goes up when the volume of design work goes up and goes down when business is slow. The biggest variable cost in an interior design firm is the direct labor—or time actually spent on projects that create revenue—since it varies with the amount of projects that are done. Labor costs are also the highest expense of any firm.

Fixed costs are those that are commonly thought of as overhead items and stay essentially the same or nearly so every month. Generally these do not vary with the volume of work being done by a firm. Fixed costs increase somewhat as an expense such as rent or heat/power/light increase but do not vary as much as the variable cost items. The reader may want to go back to Chapter 16 and read the sections on revenue and expenses discussed as part of developing the income statement.

Calculating a break-even point involves carefully determining the fixed costs on a monthly or quarterly time period. Another monetary factor that is needed is the salary cost of all employees. If the firm is a sole practitioner without employees, this amount is represented by the draws that the practitioner takes from the company's funds. Remember to include all salary and employee benefit costs such as payment for NCIDQ dues and Social Security contributions paid for by the employer as part of the fixed and salary costs.

Another factor that comes into play in calculating break-even is the billing rate of all employees. If the firm only charges design fees and makes no revenue from the sale of goods, the dollars of billings must equal the fixed costs to break even. Should the firm also sell goods—quite a variable item—that impacts the break even point, which means less time is required to be billable in order to break even.

By example, let's say that the total fixed costs (including salary expenses) for one month is $10,000. If we only consider funds from fees as the source of revenue, and the billing rate is $125 per hour for the owner, he or she must bill 80 hours in the month (assuming a 40-hour workweek or 160 hours per week) to break even. That might not seem like a lot of hours, but if the designer is a sole practitioner who also must take care of all the other tasks involved in the operation of a business, it means that the designer is only billing approximately 50 percent of his or her time per month. That really isn't a lot of productive use of the workweek!

Information about break-even analysis can also be found in many of the books listed in the references, including *Interior Design Management*, by this author.

As you will recall from the previous chapter, overhead consists of those expenses that are necessary to keep the doors of the design firm open. For almost all businesses, overhead expenses exist even if no revenue is produced during a business day. Common overhead expenses were highlighted in Chapter 16.

Ideally, monthly reviews of overhead expenses are the starting point for controlling overhead. Reviews need to be made so that the owners can see if any areas of the business have increasing overhead costs. For example, the owner may see that the utility bills have risen and stayed high for a series of months. Cost control should result in a review to determine if this increase is solely due to an increase in utility rates by the supplier or if a sudden amount of overtime is the culprit. Working longer hours means an increase in the use of utilities. Although it might not be possible to eliminate this increase—the workload is the workload—it can be taken into consideration when the owner is determining billing rates and fee methods for future projects.

Indirect labor is an important factor in the overhead expense totals for a firm. You will recall that indirect labor is any work performed that cannot be directly charged to a particular revenue-producing account or project. When the design staff meets with manufacturers' representatives and vendors who drop by the office for a general visit unrelated to a particular project, this time is an example of indirect labor. Many firms limit when vendors can meet with design staff for such general sales calls to keep this to a minimum. Deciding not to have the secretary keep track of time spent typing and preparing specifications for projects is another example of indirect labor that can create big overhead expense problems. The drop-in visit by a vendor cannot be billed to a client. The secretary's time for typing can be billed or at least costed to the project only if the secretary keeps a time record of his or her work.

Here are several other ways in which overhead expenses can sometimes be reduced to help improve profit margins:

- Purchase equipment rather than renting or leasing.

- Negotiate for the best cell phone contracts as possible—perhaps using multitasking services to include the office landlines and Internet. Cell phone charges can be a huge expense and are difficult to track to individual clients. This is a major expense for firms with multiple designers who must be in contact with clients and others involved in the project.

- Make sure staff members are aware that business cell phones are not to be used for personal use. Although personal cell phone use by employees is difficult to monitor, cell phones provided by the company are an expense item.

- Sublet office or studio space from another design firm (for the sole practitioner).

- Rotate designers who are sent to major market shows.

- Contract for a payroll service to administer the payroll.

- Depending on the size of the firm, schedule quarterly meetings with the accountant or other business professional advisors rather than monthly.

- When working with business professional advisors such as an attorney, have your questions prepared ahead of time so that the time with the professional is efficient.

- Arrange for in-house training seminars rather than sending designers out of state. A firm could sponsor a CEU and invite non-firm designers to participate.

The most important way to control costs is to know what the costs are. Many smaller interior design practices keep minimal records on direct or indirect expenses of operating the practice. "It takes too much time to record all my time" and "It's too much trouble to keep track of how many copies I make for a client" are common excuses for minimal expense recording. Yet anytime the firm charges the client by the hour, accurate time records are mandatory. Carefully recording time and other expenses should not be considered an intrusion. This type of record keeping is good business practice. Working from knowledge allows the owner to make better estimates of fees and to come closer to meeting expected profit forecasts, both of which make it easier to expand the business and obtain needed equipment or hire experienced personnel.

It is also easy for the detail-oriented interior designer to create methods and procedures to control overhead that can be obsessive. Controlling overhead should not be an intrusion into the orderly completion of work in the firm. Determining which overhead activities will be controlled and studied should be carefully limited to ensure positive assistance to the owner while not creating extra work for the staff. For example, I remember hearing about a firm that expected designers to keep track of the number sheets of plot paper used in the development of a project. This type of micromanaging is generally a waste of time and rarely helpful in lowering expenses. Discussions with the firm's accountant to determine which areas of overhead need to be controlled, along with meetings to carefully explain to the staff the importance of these procedures, are vital when the owner is instituting methods to control overhead.

A last thought for sole practitioners and any size design firm: It is absolutely necessary to have accurate records and receipts for overhead expenses in order to list these expenses as business deductions. Expenses for entertainment, travel, and meal expenses are looked at very carefully by the IRS. Good record keeping for those receipts from employees should be mandatory, along with records for major purchases made for operational equipment and use by the firm. Records and receipts are critical in case of an audit.

SUMMARY

As an interior design firm grows, the importance of understanding reports and processes to better manage the company increases. Far too often, an interior design firm has had to close and lay off employees because of poor financial management. Managerial financial reports provide important information to the owner to help him or her make decisions related to many financial, personnel, and operational issues of the interior design practice.

Many of these reports can be quickly created from existing data entered into computer-based accounting software packages that most firms use today. The variety and complexity of these reports must aid the managerial function, not burden it with the preparation and analysis of useless documents. Discussions with an accountant will help the owner know which reports to prepare and guide the owner until full understanding is achieved. Companies or managers who become slaves to the numbers may miss other opportunities for exciting projects or to explore other issues associated with the overall mission and goals of the design firm. Finding a balance is critical to providing needed information for effective decision making.

*I*n a time when more evidence is needed to substantiate value, there is a transformation from the perception of interior design as a luxury to interior design as a necessity to improve behavior in the built environment. What this means is that as interior designers, we can no longer be complacent to just know design trends. We must be well versed in all aspects of our future, i.e., political, economic, environmental, sociological, and technological trends. With a more evidence-based approach to our problem solving, our clients will begin to value us as an important ally in the achievement of their strategic plans.

Rosalyn Cama, FASID, is the President and Principal Interior Designer of a healthcare evidence-based interior planning and design firm CAMA, Inc., in New Haven, Connecticut. Founded in 1983, CAMA, Inc. is noted nationally for the work it has done in the Acute Care health setting. A frequent lecturer and author of many articles on the topic of evidence-based design, Ms. Cama has served as National President of The American Society of Interior Designers and is currently Chair of the Board of The Center for Health Design.

Marketing and Business Development

CHAPTER 18

Marketing Interior Design Services

Key Terms and Concepts

These key terms and concepts are important to material in this chapter. Many of these terms will be utilized in other chapters as well. Be sure you understand these items as you read this chapter.

Terms and Concepts

Marketing	Target marketing
Personal selling	Market segment
Marketing mix	Demographics
Four "Ps" of marketing	Psychographics
Product	Niche
Price	Market analysis
Promotion	SWOT analysis
Place	Marketing plan
Branding	

Critical Issues

After completing this chapter you should be able to:

▦ Explain how selling is different from marketing.

▦ List and name the four Ps of marketing.

▦ Explain what the product is in an interior design firm.

▦ Discuss how a client's perception of a design firm impacts its ability to attract clients.

▦ Evaluate a design firm's brand based on its Web site.

▦ Discuss why some firms' established brand helps them attract business without needing to do any marketing.

▦ Describe target marketing and the factors that are analyzed to determine a firm's target market.

■ Explain how a market analysis is important before developing a marketing plan.

■ List the topics that need to be explained in a firm's marketing plan.

■ Discuss how a marketing plan can be useful to a small practice.

Many interior designers do not think about marketing because they are too busy with projects—fortunately for them! Others think that marketing is selling and refuse to consider themselves salespeople. Most, however, do not have sufficient knowledge about marketing to feel they can be effective at the task. Referrals are certainly an effective way to obtain prospects or commissions. However, it is also important for design firms to actively market their design services through other means.

Design professionals who are committed to the expansion of their business must always be thinking past the current project and look for ways to attract a constant flow of new projects. This is especially the case in commercial design, since contacts may be promoted, change companies, transfer to other cities, retire, or lose responsibility related to the interior designer's interests. Residential designers must also look beyond today's client in order to keep their firms active, growing, and profitable. Waiting until today's project is completed to market for the next client can mean that the designer suddenly has plenty of time to do many other kinds of things—often not the choice desired when owning a business.

Expanding competition is another reason that designers should actively market their firms. Many manufacturers open their catalogs to the end user. Architectural offices and residential developers continue to offer design services to clients. And the Internet allows firms in one part of the country—or world—to make contact with potential clients anywhere. It is easy for an interior design firm to get lost in the crowd of new design firms. Many interior designers were "forced" to go out on their own in the 1990s because of the poor condition of the economy at that time. The economy has been very active since the last edition of this book was published. However, it has slowed in some markets with the housing boom peaking. Various components of the commercial market have also been affected. This means that interior design firms must always be vigilant to what the economy is doing, as it will impact the interior design industry.

This chapter introduces the reader to some of the basic underlying concepts of marketing. These concepts serve as the basis for the use of specific marketing techniques to execute a design firm's marketing plan. We will begin with some definitions of marketing and will follow with brief discussions of other marketing strategies, specifically branding and target marketing. The chapter continues with a discussion of marketing analysis and the development of the marketing plan. Chapters 19 and 20 explore many of the promotional activities and tools used by interior designers. Personal selling techniques are reviewed in Chapter 21, and Chapter 22 concludes the part of the book devoted to marketing, with a discussion of some techniques used to make presentations.

DEFINITIONS

Do you know what marketing means? If a survey would be taken, it would not be surprising to find out that most interior designers would define marketing as something rather simple such as using different ways to obtain more clients. Marketing is actually quite a bit more than that. There are many actual definitions of marketing. Most include the concept of moving goods and services from

TABLE 18-1.

Marketing Dynamics.

- Identify customer needs and wants.
- Develop new products or services.
- Manufacture or offer the new products or services.
- Understand buyer behavior.
- Understand cost to offer the service or products.
- Analyze customer interest and demand.
- Develop awareness of competitive pricing.
- Determine feasible selling price.
- Price to ensure sales and reasonable profit margin.
- Determine which marketing tools to use.
- Develop a brand.
- Advertise to create awareness.
- Use personal selling techniques.
- Utilize publicity and public relations.
- Establish how the services and products will be made available to clients.
- Determine where the services will be offered or products sold.
- Locate best place for business location.
- Investigate possibilities of offering services at multiple locations.
- Evaluate customer satisfaction.

producers to consumers. One definition says "marketing is a societal process by which individuals and groups obtain what they need and want through creating, offering, and freely exchanging products and services of value with others".[1] For comparison, the American Marketing Association defines marketing as "the process of planning and executing the conception, pricing, promotion, and distribution of ideas, goods, and services to create exchanges that satisfy individual and organizational goals."[2] The well-known management consultant Peter Drucker has written, "The aim of marketing is to know and understand the customer so well that the product or service sells itself."[3] Obviously, there can be many definitions of marketing. There are also many factors that impact marketing definitions and activities. These are shown in Table 18-1.

An important part of the marketing process for interior designers is selling. As a service business, interior designers must be able to sell themselves to obtain a meeting with a client to have an opportunity to convince the client that he or she is the right person for the job. Then, the designer must continually sell concepts to the client as the design process goes through its different steps. At some point the designer must also sell the client on the final plans and solutions.

But what is selling? According to one source, personal selling is "a two-way flow of communication between a potential buyer and a salesperson that is designed to identify the customer's needs, match those needs to one of the firm's products, and convince the customer to buy the product."[4] Of course, this definition, though not specifically mentioning services, applies to the personal selling of services as well. In selling, the designer must explain his or her services or perhaps his or her solution to the design project in a personal way in order to instruct and bring the client to accept the company or design idea.

Many marketing texts insist that selling involves "an inward-looking function in which you persuade the customer to take what you have.... Marketing, on the other hand, is an outward-looking function in which you try to match the real requirement of the customer."[5] Interior designers, it can be argued, must do both. It takes personal selling to explain design concepts to clients, yet it also takes marketing to find out what the client really needs from the designer in order for the interior designer to secure new clients. Chapter 21 discusses personal selling techniques used by the designer to obtain a commission or to finalize a project presentation as part of the marketing process.

THE FOUR Ps OF MARKETING

The marketing mix is another factor in how the firm will market and the development of a marketing plan. The *marketing mix* consists of operational elements that the design firm can control in the process of marketing and selling goods and services. Traditionally, the marketing mix consists of what are called the four Ps of marketing.

The *four Ps of marketing* are four basic variables—product, place, promotion, and price—that create a firm's marketing mix. An interior designer's product is generally considered to be professional design services. For simplification, I will only use the term "product" in this discussion. The types, styles, and quality of goods that some interior designers choose to sell is another part of the product variable. The style of design—contemporary versus some version of traditional, for example—must also be something that satisfies potential customers' needs. Designing in a contemporary style in a very traditional market like Boston is likely to be a somewhat futile venture. A designer's wish to do contract labor CAD work in a small town could also be futile if there are few users of such a service in the area. The firm must utilize its internal analysis and its preferred market area to determine which products are needed by potential clients.

The second variable is place. The reader has no doubt heard the comment "location, location, location" associated with businesses. The place variable deals primarily with location. This means that the firm must find ways of getting its product to the places where potential customers exist. Business owners must recognize that the client drives the need for products and that the products must be offered or made available where potential clients exist. The need is not based on the designer's desire to offer products that only the designer perceives as necessary or that exist only in a location where the designer wishes to reside. Someone offering contract CAD work is likely to need to market the services to larger cities rather than depend on the local market.

The potential client finds out about the availability of a product through the third variable, promotion. Promotional activities inform potential clients of the existence of the design firm and the services that the firm offers, whether or not the designer is located in the same geographic area as the client. Promotional activities include public relations, the use of brochures, referrals, advertising, Web sites, and many other promotional techniques. These are discussed in detail in Chapters 19 and 20.

The last of the four variables of marketing is price. Establishing the right price for the interior design firm's "product" is a difficult management activity. If the firm sets a price for services that is too high in relation to competition, the firm will not secure work with many clients. If the price for fees is set too low, clients will suspect the firm's ability to do the work and may not seriously consider using the design firm. To some clients, a price that is too low in comparison to others might also mean to the client that the designer isn't very good or experienced. Pricing is a very delicate decision. Compensation pricing for services is discussed in Chapter 23 and pricing for products is discussed in Chapter 25.

There is one other variable to be factored into the determination of a marketing mix: perception. Although perception is not in the accepted list of variables of the marketing mix, it is an important factor in marketing. Perception is an intuitive process of gathering information about people, places, events, and so forth, with which we come into contact. Clients perceive the designer in terms of such things as image, business professionalism, and, of course, design ability. If a designer's image does not meet the client's perception of the image of a designer, the client is less likely to hire the designer. Clients develop a negative opinion of interior designers who are not business professionals. Being consistently late for meetings, neglecting to return phone calls, making mistakes in estimates, and not following through on promises are all factors that sour the perceptions of clients. Perception also impacts on the client's willingness to pay the price the designer is asking. If the designer's creative reputation, quality of service, and methods of doing business have a high value to the client, the client is more willing to hire that designer and even conceivably to pay a higher price for the design services. If the client does not perceive the high value of a designer's services, the client will not be willing to pay the price, even if the designer is a truly creative professional.

All these variables are important and must be investigated by the firm at its inception and throughout its existence. They all have an impact on the design firm's marketing plan; one is not really more important than another. Each is important by itself as well as in relation to the others. Ignoring one variable could upset the marketing mix and make it difficult, if not impossible, for the design firm to successfully market its services.

BRANDING

Regardless of the size of the interior design firm, gaining a competitive advantage can only help a firm obtain a steady stream of new clients. One method that has received a lot of attention in recent years is the concept of branding. A brand is "a type of product manufactured by a particular company under a particular name. Branding is the promotion of a particular product or company by means of advertising and distinctive design."[6] In other words, *branding* is the combination of images and encounters that the customer perceives, accepts, and experiences with a product. It is not just a logo on a business card.

As you can see by the definitions, branding is most commonly associated with a product, but services can also be branded in a positive fashion. Think of FedEx, which provides shipping services, and Southwest Airlines, which provides low-cost travel. The American Society of Interior Designers recently had the society's logo and color scheme redesigned to enhance its brand. Even a person him- or herself can become a brand in consumer's minds. Consider Oprah Winfrey or Donald Trump. Certainly, an interior design firm can work at developing a positive and lasting brand.

A brand becomes a valuable commodity for a firm when it automatically conjures up positive thoughts by clients and potential clients. Consumers and businesses are bombarded with products and service solicitations. There are simply too many choices sometimes, and often a client cannot see the difference between one design firm and another. Brand identification helps at least to focus attention on a particular firm.

Many design firms develop and market an image—after all, image is part of the profession. That image can and should go beyond the style of interior design the firm performs, if it indeed has a specific style. The image can be translated into its logo, design of stationery, manner in which documents are completed, its marketing materials—even the way business is conducted. Branding activity and a brand are not just what the firm tries to create. It is heavily dependent upon how the client perceives the firm and accepts the brand.

To create a brand, a firm needs to carefully consider and develop these elements:

Company name. A strong name helps develop the brand. Chapter 10 discussed some of the issues surrounding the selection and registering of a company name. Many designers use their own name, since many clients associate the work of an interior designer with the person. It is harder for a name such as ABC Designs or IntDeCon to become a brand, since it is harder for a client to relate the name to an individual or group of individuals for some time.

Logos. Discussed in the next chapter, logos are usually a graphic that helps identify a business. A logo can bring instant recognition without even including the company name. Consider the apple logo for Apple computers.

Tag line or slogan. This is a few words that provide a strong concept of what the company does. Not very many interior design companies try to use a tag line or slogan, since so many include the terms "interior design" or the title "interior designer" on their business cards and stationery. An example, however, is "Designing productive work spaces," which might work for a commercial firm specializing in corporate offices as well as other types of commercial facilities.

Business color scheme. Choosing a color scheme that is carried out on all stationery and marketing materials add to brand identification. Consider IBM blue as an example of how color helps identify a brand.

A brand can also be established by providing exceptional customer service and customer responsiveness. When was the last time you were in a store and the sales clerks ignored you as they talked amongst themselves? Probably today, right? In interior design exceptional customer service can be done by returning phone calls and e-mails promptly or at least when you say you will. It also can be provided by making the process for the client as easy for him or her to understand as possible. They should not have to ask the designer three times for the answer to a question.

For a service business such as interior design, it is critical for the firm to emphasize its value to the client. Many clients will hire an interior designer who can show the client how they can provide value to the client. Materials suggestions and detailing in a residence add to the resale value of the house. The specifications also create status and even perhaps a unique look that no one else in the circle of friends of the home owners have. An office is designed to improve employee productivity, while the restaurant interior is so exciting that guests line up to get in to see the interior. An assisted-living facility is designed to help patients be very comfortable in the environment, or a school is sensitively designed and specified to ease maintenance and security. Design solutions such as these are valuable to the client, and the reputation of a designer for providing these types of services makes the designer valuable to the client.

In this book, it is not possible to discuss branding in detail but only to provide an overview. Two additional important points about establishing a brand are in order, however. If the design firm or designer has been practicing for a few years or more, a brand of sorts has already been started. The firm or individual's brand begins with the reputation that the designer has in the industry and market already. Continually working to maintain an excellent reputation in the field is critical in this highly competitive business. Establishing a stronger brand identity builds on this reputation.

The second point is that everything that the firm does somehow relates to the brand. Names, reputation, logos, corporate colors—all these are certainly important parts of the brand. But so are things such as how the phone is answered, the way employees or others working in the name of the design firm interact with clients, how easy it is to read the fine print on sales proposals and contracts, professional business attitudes with clients, and even, to some, how the designer dresses.

A successful brand starts with knowing what the firm is all about—its purpose and its values. The purpose and values of the firm is the framework enhanced by excellent service, which results in client loyalty and trust. Loyalty and trust brings back clients when they need design services again or creates willingness to refer their friends to the design firm.

What Would You Do?

In the last three months David's design firm has been experiencing some financial problems. He has not paid his installers on two jobs and is 45 days behind in those payments. He also owes a cabinetmaker $5000 for a custom cabinet. The installers are refusing to do any more work for David's company until they are paid in full for outstanding work. The cabinetmaker is angry because this has happened before, and he is threatening to put a lien on David's company if they are not paid in the next ten days. All of David's current clients are up-to-date with their payments for any work or products needed for their projects. In other words, he has no outstanding receivables.

TARGET MARKETING

Margaret was finally in a financial position to venture out on her own and open a small studio. She told herself that she would wait until she had funds to have a studio in a commercial location rather than work from home to better attract the clients she wanted. After a great deal of thinking and research, Margaret located in a low-rise office building near a new residential development that was soon to also be the general location of a new sports stadium and a lot of retail space. She wanted to focus on residential clients in the new development as well as on small professional offices, since she had experience in both areas of design.

A very important decision for a new interior design practice—and existing practices as well, for that matter—is to determine the type of clients they seek to attract to the business. In the most rudimentary sense, this decision is whether to seek clients who wish residential or commercial interior design services. This decision can be considered the beginning of a business strategy, called target marketing.

More precisely, *target marketing* is a marketing method that helps a firm identify one or more groups of potential customers who are most likely to utilize the services of the firm. When a firm uses target marketing, it develops identifiable groups within the firm's total market, called market segments. A *market segment* is a group of customers that has some common characteristic. For example, everyone living within the city of Beverly Hills can be a market segment for a residential designer located in Beverly Hills, California. All doctors practicing in Boise, Idaho, can be a market segment for a commercial designer in Idaho.

However, those examples are rather broad. Firms have greater success in target marketing when they are as specific as possible, because they cannot get every customer who may want some type of design services in these broad segments. By specifically defining segments within a broad segment, firms will have greater success in attracting clients and thus will utilize marketing resources to the best advantage. Of course, a firm can make a mistake and create too narrow a focus or target, thus limiting the number of potential clients. An example of this would be a firm that is located in a medium-sized city but has targeted a very specific type of commercial work, such as spas. Unless the designer is willing to travel for business, that narrow of a target might "run out" within the local area.

Knowing what the design firm can do and wants to provide is only part of the challenge in reaching the right clients. The interior designer who is intent on expanding his or her market to high-quality clients must also find out what the client wants from an interior designer. As with any business, an interior designer cannot survive on providing what he or she thinks is needed, rather than what clients actually need. That is like the traditional marketing example of the companies who continued to make buggy whips when automobiles became popular. Target marketing provides a way to help designers solve both these problems.

Target marketing begins with an understanding of what services the firm can offer. A thorough analysis of what each employee can do and the kind of projects the firm has done in the past helps the firm determine what it can do in the future. This analysis also may help a firm determine if it can offer new services. Any new services may open up a new market segment and produce additional revenue for the firm.

Internal analysis of strengths, weaknesses, and previous general market interest should be followed by in-depth research in order for the design firm to more clearly identify the market segments that most likely want and need the firm's services. Table 18-2 provides the characteristics that are most frequently used to differentiate market segments.

Information to develop target market segments comes from many sources. A firm's historic data on completed projects is where many firms start their target

---

TABLE 18-2.

Target Characteristics Used to Help Define a Target Segment and Market.

1. *Demographics.* These encompass characteristics such as age, gender, occupation, level of income, stage in family life cycle, religion, and race.
2. *Psychographics.* These concepts define a person's lifestyle interests and attitudes, such as hobbies, sports interests, personality traits, and abilities (or lack of abilities).
3. *Geographic.* These define a location of the targeted clients. For example, is the design firm willing to work only within the confines of the city in which the business is located, or is the firm willing to go out of state for work?
4. *Industry type.* This can be explained by differentiating the exact type of specialty within interior design. A commercial designer has many areas in which he or she can specialize, such as health care, retail, lodging, and so on. Residential designers can specialize as well; for instance, they wish to limit their practice to designing apartments and condominiums rather than single-family dwellings.
5. *Benefits.* What is the client looking for? Benefits are related to why the customer buys. For example, the client may be looking for a more productive office staff and therefore may be seeking a design solution that will help accommodate that need.
6. *Product usage.* This defines how often the product or service is purchased or used. Although this factor relates more to product sales marketing than to design services marketing, it can be used to target services. Knowing how often a certain type of client will use design services will help the firm understand the type of marketing methods that it must use to attract repeat and new business.

market research. Additional data can be obtained from reports and publications at the library, the local chamber of commerce, city building departments, and small-business development centers located at many community colleges, to name just a few other sources. In our example, Margaret likely looked not only at her previous clients at the firm she was working for but also researched demographics of the type of customer for the housing development and what kinds of retail stores were planned near the new stadium. Occasionally, large firms may fund a questionnaire or interviews. This is done to obtain very specific information that the design firm needs. Information gathered from the library or other sources by someone other than the design firm is called *secondary research*. When research such as a questionnaire is undertaken to answer specific questions, it is called *primary research*. Primary research, obviously, is more expensive than secondary research.

Creating a clear focus of the firm's target market is very important in the firm's overall marketing efforts. All firms have a limited amount of resources to put into marketing. Through target marketing, a firm can expand its limited marketing resources, trying to locate potential clients who are most likely to be interested in the firm's services. It is one way of using scarce marketing dollars and time to fullest advantage. In addition, when a firm determines its target market, it is then easier to establish what marketing methods will work most effectively to attract target clients.

ESTABLISHING A NICHE

Some design firms have found that it is advantageous to establish a particular specialty in interior design. A few examples include HOK Sport + Venue + Event, a division of HOK that many consider the premier sports stadium design firm; Gensler in corporate design; and Wilson & Associates in hospitality. Specializing creates a targeted focus of the firm on some area of the industry that the owner finds particularly interesting and rewarding. It is easy to see how this would help a commercial designer. Residential designers can also specialize. Consider a residential designer who only does condominiums in high-rise buildings or someone who will only do contemporary-styled interiors of contemporary homes. When the specialty has some very refined focus or is somehow unique, the firm has targeted a *niche*. According to Martin and Knoohuizen, a niche is "a design specialty that focuses its services to meet the needs of a specific group—or segment—of the total market."[7]

Some marketing books do not even mention the term niche; they simply refer to this concept as *market segmentation*. The idea is to choose a specific segment or part of the total market in which the designer has an interest or expertise and to work only with clients in that segment. Of course, some designers choose to specialize in two closely related segments. By becoming an expert in one or two segments, the designer can provide specialized services and a focused use of the firm's resources. Rather than market to all residential clients, consider the niche of condominiums in high-rise buildings. In a community of empty nester baby boomers, perhaps the niche helps clients downsize their homes by providing evaluation, restoration, and even disposal through resale of furnishings. A commercial designer with experience in the design of medical offices might further specialize by determining a niche of dermatologists' offices.

When a designer has a niche area of design rather than trying to be all things to all people, the designer has the opportunity to become very experienced in the niche area. More time can also be spent productively researching and learning the peculiar functional problems of that niche. This allows him or her to be of special value to potential clients. When a designer is very knowledgeable about a particular niche, the client will not feel like the designer is learning on the job about the client's particular needs. In addition, the designer is also able to find unique specialty products and materials appropriate to that niche. Designers who do not specialize do not always know about specialty products for the distinctive needs of the niche.

If a designer decides to specialize in a particular niche, he or she must be sure that sufficient work exists to support the goals of the design firm in terms of meeting business expenses and generating a profit. Targeting a specialized segment can mean that the designer does not have enough clients to keep working if the number of clients are too small due to an extremely small focus. Any size firm may find that not enough work exists in the area to support its business if the niche is too unique. This is why most niche designers market outside their immediate geographic area into different cities, states, and even outside the country.

The niche should be something that the designer also has a passion for. If the designer does not like doing residential design very much, taking up a niche in assisted-living facilities is not a good idea. Success is more likely to result for the interior designer when the niche is related to a special interest or passion. If a designer has gained some expertise in a particular area of interior design, then the designer may be on the way to establishing a niche. The specialty options listed in Tables 6-2 and 6-3 represent numerous potential niches; however, the possibilities are almost endless if one wishes to be very narrowly focused.

Good market research is needed to establish a business niche. Everything discussed in this chapter becomes vital. Coming up with an idea for a niche that has few potential clients or is past its prime is a disaster waiting to happen. The numbers of clients, the competition, and potential growth of the specialized area of design are all important factors. The experience level of the designer and the ease in which the designer can enter the niche also play a part in the designer's determining whether a niche is a possibility and which niche might be right for the firm.

MARKETING ANALYSIS

Marketing analysis involves similar research to what is done for target marketing and information gathered for the strategic plan discussed in Chapter 13, with the focus on gathering marketing data. *Marketing analysis* involves gathering and analyzing data about such things as the abilities and interests of the staff, potential clients, the economy, and the competition. This research and analysis allows the firm to make better plans and decisions about the direction of the firm's business efforts. The goal of marketing analysis is to find out what the client wants and then to determine if and how the firm can provide it.

Marketing research and analysis is done by consulting firms that specialize in this kind of work. Sometimes advertising agencies do marketing analysis. Small firms and designers who are just beginning their practices often try to do their own marketing analysis. Although they can meet with success, it is a time-consuming and detailed process. Firms that are determined to do this work internally must be prepared for the fact that the designer who is responsible for the marketing analysis will generate less revenue for the firm.

An important first step in market analysis is answering the question, "What business are we in?" If a strategic plan has been done, then this question has already been answered. If the firm believes that it is in the business of providing interior design services, it has done little to really answer the question in a way

TABLE 18-3.

Questions to Determine "What Business Are We In?"

These questions will be helpful in developing a marketing plan, a mission statement, and a strategic plan.

1. What design services do we offer?
2. What design services could we offer that are needed in the marketplace?
3. What products do we intend to specify and sell?
4. Are there sufficient potential clients for the firm's services within a reasonable distance?
5. Who do we see as our primary and secondary customers?
6. How do we do what we do?
7. What quality of service do we endeavor to supply?
8. Is anyone else offering the services in the way our firm does?
9. Why should/would customers buy from our firm rather than from one of our competitors?
10. What are the trends in the profession, and how will these trends affect the firm's potential business?

that will help the firm market itself to new clients. In many ways, almost every interior design firm and others in the built-environment industry could say the same thing, thus not differentiating the firm at all from its competition. In order for the design firm to answer the question about what business the firm is in, it must answer other questions. The key questions in Table 18-3 help the firm understand what business it is in (or wants to be in) and help the firm realize the direction it wishes to take.

These questions relate to significant issues, especially for new or relatively new firms, or firms that are seeking to move into some sort of new market. In a large city, there may be thousands of companies that can provide similar services. However, if a firm is really interested in attracting new clients, it needs to understand what business it is in so that it discovers ways in which it can make itself appear different, even unique, from its competition.

A second step in marketing analysis is to conduct an in-depth review of the internal and external forces that can and do affect the firm. SWOT analysis, described in Chapter 13, is a common method that can be used to accomplish this. If you have not reviewed that chapter, please do so now. The focus of conducting a SWOT analysis to develop a marketing plan is to look at internal and external factors that can affect the firm's marketing goals.

Competition analysis is a critical part of conducting a marketing analysis once the issue of understanding what clients want has been resolved. Many small firms do not even recognize other designers within their local association chapter as potential competitors. Yet they may well be. Understanding a competitor's design style and method of business, regardless of the size of the firm, will be an asset to a design firm that is interested in expanding its own market.

Marketing analysis should assist the design firm in determining marketing goals and budgets. It provides a body of knowledge about the firm's practice and staff, the kind and amount of clients available, general economic and legal trends or restrictions prevalent in the area, and the competition. The design firm can then use this knowledge to prepare a definite plan in order to achieve results that are specifically related to the firm's overall marketing or strategic plan.

Marketing analysis must not be a one-time endeavor. It should be considered a critical part of strategic planning and of the annual business plan.

THE MARKETING PLAN

A marketing plan should be developed in connection with a strategic or annual plan. It can be very formal, discussing the items listed in this section of the chapter, or it can be a less formal action plan that addresses similar topics in a less formal manner. Regardless, the development of a plan will be a benefit to any size interior design practice, as it will help the firm determine what it intends to do to meet its marketing goals.

Marketing plans help create goals that set down what the firm wishes to accomplish. The plan also helps establish how the firm intends to accomplish the goals through various strategies and tactics. For the most part, a marketing plan looks at the future year's activity, while the strategic plan, you will recall, is long-term. Goals, strategies, and tactics should also be developed for the long term—those that are expected to take from three to five years or more to accomplish. The establishment of long-term goals is important so that the design firm can keep thinking ahead and anticipating the changing needs of its basic or desired market.

Marketing goals can take many forms. One might be to increase awareness of the firm in its present market. Perhaps it is to target a specific group of new clients. Conceivably the goal is to introduce the design firm to a totally new market location. Maybe the goal is to gain greater recognition as an expert in a certain area of design.

Whatever the goals might become, the process of creating a marketing plan and actually writing it down helps the owner and employees see the goals before them and create the means to best accomplish those goals. By developing a plan, the design firm considers which promotional tools (discussed in the next chapters) are most appropriate to help achieve its goals. This decision then help's the firm, in turn, produce budgets that will ensure that the resources are available or need to be obtained to develop the appropriate tools and strategies.

Just as there is no perfect business plan, there is no one outline for a marketing plan for all interior design firms. Some firms will want to have a very formal plan with a table of contents, references, and budgeting information. If the plan is to be used internally so that the owners, managers, and staff know what is going on, a more informal format can be used. An informal action plan focused on marketing can outline goals with appropriate strategies and tactics for each goal in a logical sequence.

Many design firms find that hiring a marketing professional to consult with them for the preparation of a marketing plan can save time. Other firms decide to venture into this area on their own. If you are considering a professional marketing consultant to help with your marketing plan or any other aspect of your marketing needs, the information in CD Item 18–1 will be of help.

A portion of a formal marketing plan is shown in Table 18-4. A sample informal action plan is shown in Table 18-5. The informal action plan is more common in the small firm, while the formal plan is predominantly used by larger interior design firms. Some of the items that the formal plan should cover include the following:

1. *An introduction*. Statements based on the information that was used to prepare the plan and statements about the use and purpose of the plan.

2. *Goals statement(s)*. A revised statement of general business goals based on the information gathered in the analysis.

TABLE 18-4.

A Page from a Sample Marketing Plan.

II. Client Base

A. Current Year

1. Our current client base is primarily from the Midland area. Current clients within the city limits represent 80 percent of total sales. The remaining 20 percent is made up of clients outside the city limits but within a 30-mile radius.

2. The majority of current work is residential. Eighty-five percent of clients purchase merchandise and services for homes. Fifteen percent of clients purchase merchandise and services for offices or other commercial facilities.

3. Services versus Merchandise

   Of residential sales, 70 percent of all revenues are merchandise sales.

   Twenty percent are from design fees, and 10 percent represent other services, such as repairs, which do not require the purchasing of additional merchandise.

   Of commercial sales, 90 percent of all revenues are merchandise sales.

   Design fees only represent 10 percent of revenues from commercial projects.

4. Type of Purchaser

   Sixty-five percent of residential customers purchase goods or services for their existing home.

1. Sixty percent of purchases are for only a few replacement items in one or two rooms.
2. Thirty percent of purchases are for new floor coverings, window coverings, and/or wall coverings.
3. Ten percent of purchases are for many items in two or more rooms.

   Twenty percent of residential customers purchase goods or services for a new house.

1. Forty-five percent of purchases are for new floor coverings, window coverings, and/or wall coverings.
2. Thirty-five percent of purchases are for only a few replacement items in one or two rooms.
3. Twenty percent of purchases are for many items in two or more rooms.

   Fifteen percent of residential customers purchase goods or services for a second (vacation or rental) house.

1. Fifty-five percent of purchases are for only a few replacement items in one or two rooms.

---

3. *Capabilities.* A discussion of the firm's abilities, related to the kinds of clients who previously hired the firm.

4. *Services.* A listing of the services the firm can and is going to offer. Subsequent sections should discuss who will be responsible for these services and how they will be done.

5. *Clientele.* Quantitative information as to potential numbers, market share, and possible growth in each client category. Both existing and new client objectives should be stated.

6. *Policy decisions.* A discussion of such things as how the firm will charge services to clients, how the firm will charge for consultants, whether or not the firm will bill reimbursable expenses, whether or not the firm will sell merchandise, and what policies there will be related to purchasing of products for resale.

7. *Marketing organization.* A statement of who will be responsible for ongoing marketing analysis.

8. *Marketing effort.* Answers to such questions as, "In what ways will the firm accomplish its goals?" "How will it use advertising and public relations?" "How will results be monitored to see whether or not they are successful?" "How much financially will be committed to marketing?"

TABLE 18-5.

Sample Action Plan for a Small Design Firm.

Goal: To increase client awareness of this design firm

Increase networking activities.

  Become a member of a good networking group.
  Take two realtors to lunch each week.
  Discuss interrelationship with builders.

Advertise in low-cost magazine.

  Determine which local magazines are available in this market.
  Obtain their advertising rates.
  Work with a graphic designer to create a one-quarter page ad.

Enter association awards competition.

  Make arrangements to photograph Jones residence.
  Obtain competition entry and follow through.
  Consider entering a national competition with Jones residence.

Goal: To change image/brand of this firm

Attend a seminar on branding.
  Read a book on branding.
  Contact three graphic design firms to discuss costs on redesign of logo, stationery, etc.
  Discuss image and "brand" with at least six past clients.

9. *Evaluation*. A discussion of how the goals will be measured so as to indicate the success of the marketing plan.
10. *Forecasts*. Amount of sales, profit, number of new clients, and additions to personnel. These should be stated as both quantitative and qualitative measures.

It is wise to involve the entire staff in the analysis and the planning for the yearly marketing plan. Final decisions, of course, should be made by management. It is almost always true that when plans are passed down by management without staff input, the staff feel resentful. If the staff do not believe in the plan, it will not be very successful.

As with any plan, it is important for a process of monitoring the progress and success of the plan to be instituted. It does no good and is, frankly, a waste of time and resources for the firm to go through the process of developing and writing a marketing plan if it is not committed to its execution. Monitoring the plan's progress helps, though it cannot guarantee the success of the plan.

SUMMARY

Competition, whether from other design firms and others in the built-environment industry, and the economic ups and downs of a local market make it imperative for all interior design firms to look carefully at marketing activities. Responding to, or depending upon, referrals is a common marketing technique that is used by interior design firms of any size. Referrals, however, are oftentimes not a sufficient method to provide a steady number of clients.

Thinking through the entire marketing process is a valuable endeavor for the owner of the interior design practice. Finding more and better clients is a continual problem for most firms. Good, professional business practice requires the analysis of possibilities and a focus on those aspects of the market that are reasonable for the firm to undertake, considering the resources that are available.

This chapter has explained the four common factors of product, place, promotion, and price that are considered in the developing of marketing strategies, and it provided a brief overview on the concept of branding. The chapter also discussed target marketing and establishing a niche in the profession. It also discussed the analysis process that is necessary for developing a formal marketing plan. Other chapters in this part of the book will explain numerous promotional tools that can be used in the marketing effort and in the personal selling of design services. Various presentation methods are also detailed.

REFERENCES

1. Kotler, 2000, p. 8.
2. Bennett, 1995, p. 166.
3. Drucker, 1973, p. 64.
4. Keegan et. al.,1995. p. 654.
5. Czinkota et al., 1997, p. 19.
6. *Oxford American College Dictionary*, 2002, p. 167.
7. Martin and Knoohuizen, 1995, p. 6.

CHAPTER 19

Promoting the Interior Design Practice

Key Terms and Concepts

These key terms and concepts are important to material in this chapter. Many of these terms will be utilized in other chapters as well. Be sure you understand these items as you read this chapter.

Terms and Concepts

Promotion	Press release
Public relations (PR)	Brochure
Publicity	Collateral materials
Promotional tools	Referral
Graphic image	Testimonial
Logo (or mark)	Networking
Photo portfolio	Internet marketing
JPEG format	Advertising
TIFF format	

Critical Issues

After completing this chapter you should be able to:

- Discuss the differences between promotion, public relations, and publicity activities.
- Explain promotional benefits of well-designed logo and business stationery.
- List several ways the press release and company brochure can be used to promote a design firm.
- Discuss several ways that referrals can be used to improve the chances of promotional success for a design firm.
- Prepare a simple press release.
- Describe the way networking works to help uncover new clients.
- Analyze the Web sites of interior designers, and discuss how effective they are in attracting a client to the designer.

■ Evaluate the Web sites of interior designers, and discuss the ease that a site visitor has in obtaining needed information about the firm.

■ Describe the good and bad points of magazine advertising by interior designers.

You are invited to try to compare the number of listings for interior designers in the yellow pages of your local phone directory against an old one (you might still find an old one in the library) to see how many new firms have opened in your community. You will probably be surprised that it is possible that dozens of new firms with numerous new designers were started in the reader's hometown over the last decade. Many new practices have opened because of the generally robust economy and huge home buying and selling market of a few years ago. Existing firms have merged with other existing firms or designers have broken away to start their own practice in a good economy.

Existing firms, as well as new businesses, must cultivate new clients and new projects to keep employees actively involved in generating revenue. No firm, regardless of its size, specialty, or reputation, can afford to let its message be lost among the competition. How is this done? Through various promotional strategies and tools that are deemed appropriate to the design firm's mission, goals, and budget.

Promotion is the method used to get the designer's message—even existence—before the client. In practical sense, promotion "includes all the activities the company undertakes to communicate and promote its products [and services] to the target market."[1] Many people use the term promotion to mean public relations, but promotion is much more than public relations. Promotion also includes publicity, publishing, advertising, personal selling, and all the other strategies or techniques that help get a business's message to potential clients and its market in general. Promotional activities help a company grow regardless of its size and focus.

Competition plays an important part in what promotional activities a firm may decide to utilize to increase public awareness and attract new clients. Many firms have added Web sites to their arsenal of promotional activities, since so many clients are now very comfortable in surfing the Web to find new service providers. Newer firms might also want to publish a brochure that gives them a defined "leave-behind"—something that reminds clients about the firm that the designer can give away. Perhaps a firm is considering how beneficial would it be to enter a project in a competition in order to gain publicity? Is it proper for the firm to advertise in local magazines? Should the firm attempt to get a project published in one of the trade magazines? Can a new graphic image or logo help to change the client's perception of the design firm? These questions and many more are being asked in design firms every day as a part of the continual search for new clients, new markets, and greater recognition. In this chapter, we explore many of the ways in which the interior designer can get his or her message across to prospective clients.

The chapter begins by clarifying the strategy of public relations and publicity activities. It continues with a brief discussion of essential promotional tools—the company's graphic image and photo portfolio. Other promotional tools discussed in this chapter include how to use and prepare press releases, brochures, use referrals and networking, and Web sites. These are important promotional tools, since they are the kinds of activities or tools that all design firms can use effectively to promote the design practice. Additional promotional tools and strategies are discussed in the next chapter.

PUBLIC RELATIONS

In a profession where creativity and image are very important, how an interior design firm goes about expressing its public image is very important. *Public relations* (or PR) is a term that refers to all the efforts of the firm to create an image in order to affect the public's opinion of the firm. In a sense, it is an umbrella for all the activities, tools, and efforts used to communicate information about an interior design firm to the public and especially to potential clients.

The public image often starts with the design of the company logo and stationery and the design of the studio. Public relations and creating a public image is about communicating information concerning the design firm through a Web page, producing a brochure or newsletter, and placing news releases in local newspapers or national trade publications. Public relations can consist of educating potential clients by writing and submitting articles on design-related topics to local publications or trade magazines; conducting an in-office product seminar for the public or other professionals; or even writing a book on a design topic. It can also consist of making contributions to professional organization fund-raisers, becoming involved in legislative efforts, and participating in special events in the community. Public relations refers to all of these and much more.

A firm should never take developing the public image lightly. Small or large, crafting a positive image of the interior design firm can and does make a difference in the ability of the firm to attract new business. This kind of work can be done internally and is often the responsibility of the owner or a few key senior staff members. Many firms hire a public relations or marketing professional to help them decide what activities and tools will best serve their marketing goals and resources. The public relations professional can then produce the tools him- or herself, or hire subconsultants to produce the desired materials or activities.

Through the firm's research about itself and the public, and the marketing plan that was discussed in the previous chapter, a picture of the activities needed within public relations, publicity, and general promotional activities will emerge. The public relations professional makes suggestions as to which activities are going to lead to success—that is, more client contacts and potential sales. For a firm that has been in existence for several years, one suggestion might be to redesign the company logo and graphics. Although we saw how developing a brand is important to any firm—and the logo is definitely part of that brand identification—even major firms reevaluate and redesign their graphics from time to time. A firm without a Web site might want to begin the research and development of a site or redesign an existing brochure. Whatever the strategy is, the result is to gain positive recognition for the design firm in the public's mind. And this recognition will eventually lead to future business and greater revenues.

PUBLICITY

Several interior designers participated in their local chapter's show-house fundraiser. Their projects were published in the local home-design magazine, and each firm was able to purchase reprints of that section of the issue.

A direct form of promotion is publicity. "Publicity is what you use to get attention without paying for it. Publicity is the key to letting people know what you do."[2] The aim of *publicity* is to attract attention or awareness without having to pay any media charges. Designers who participate in events like a show-house, home tour, or design competitions benefit from the publicity those types of events are able to provide. This is the kind of promotional communication that design firms strive to achieve as much as possible. Traditionally, this has been the accepted form of promoting professional services. When the firm has to pay for media attention, that promotional activity is called advertising. This form of promotion is discussed later in this chapter.

Publicity takes many forms. It can be planned (good publicity) or accidental. Unfortunately, most accidental publicity is bad publicity. Bad publicity, such as being named in the papers following a personal injury suit, is not something that a design firm desires. Design firms seek to create planned publicity that will help potential clients view the firm in a good light and seek them out for design contracts.

Good publicity could be the publication of a press release sent out by the firm about its winning a design award. Good publicity can be obtained by providing a free lecture about accessibility guidelines to a professional business group, such as accountants. Home sections of newspapers often run articles on very special home designs. Sometimes they will include the name of the interior designer in the article. These examples are activities that the design firm may pay to develop, but the firm does not pay to place promotional information in some type of media.

Other examples of activities resulting in good publicity are charitable and community service work related to interior design, for example, helping the community theater with props and set designs; volunteering services on restoration projects; and getting members of professional organizations involved in designing rooms in model houses or a display house for the benefit of a charitable group.

ESSENTIAL PROMOTIONAL TOOLS

There are few interior design firms that are lucky enough to never need to engage in some kind of promotional activities or need promotional tools to get the word out on the firm. Marketing and promotion of the design firm is a critical activity for all interior design firms. Certain promotional tools are essential to any practice. Others are utilized as the firm grows and/or changes directions in its mission.

Promotional tools are the mechanisms and devices that are used by the interior design firm to create awareness and are created for relatively nonspecific general audiences. The firm's graphic image, stationery, and a photo portfolio are examples of essential tools. The simplest essential tool is the designer's business cards and other stationery. Others might come into play when a firm is more experienced or is trying to enter new markets. Press releases can also be thought of as an essential tool, since they can be used by any firm at any stage in its life to get information about the firm out to a wide audience. A Web sites an all too necessary way for interior designers to make themselves known to clients who enjoy surfing the Web for service providers. Designers can also cast a wider net by publication of their work in magazines and books, and even with speaking engagements.

Promotional tools need to be selected that will be most useful for the design firm and are naturally cost-effective. One advertisement placed in a magazine or newspaper can cost thousands of dollars. The return on that one ad often, however, is negligible. Those same funds spent on quality photography or graphic design work for a brochure or Web site can bring numerous returns. Which promotional tools to use, when to use them, what goes into them, and how they are delivered to prospective clients all play a role in furthering the image desired by the firm.

The Graphic Image and Basic Stationery

By *graphic image*, I am referring to the package of materials that the interior design firm uses to identify itself. This includes the company logo, business cards, letterhead and other stationery, business forms, and drawing paper identification. The firm's graphic image is usually incorporated into many of the tools that are discussed in this chapter and the next.

There are many design options for stationery. This graphic image is the first impression potential clients have, which is so important for establishing a relationship with clients (see Figure 19-1). The color used for paper stock and ink, the type size, the typeface, and the size of the finished format are just some of

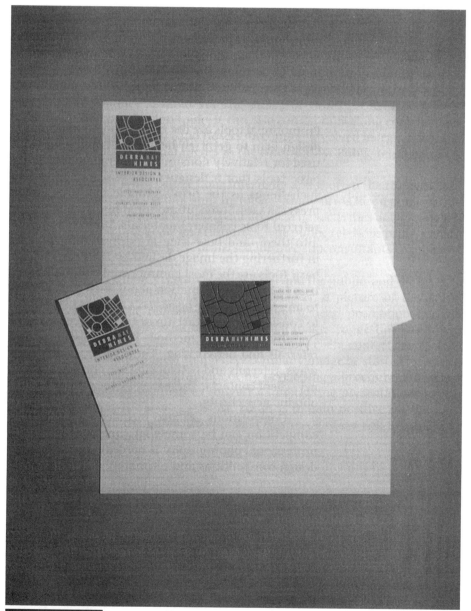

FIGURE 19-1.

Sample of a design firm's stationery and logo. (Reproduced with permission, Debra May Himes Interior Design & Associates. Mesa, AZ; photo, Dawson Henderson)

FIGURE 19-2.

A sample design firm's logo, used on the firm's stationery and related materials. (Reproduced with permission, James Tigges, Pinnacle Design, Inc. Phoenix, AZ)

the factors that the design firm must consider when it is developing the firm's graphic image and stationery. Some typefaces are overly decorative and may look great on some items but may be difficult to read on others. It is a good idea to consider hiring a graphic designer to create any logo and stationery designs. Even though the interior designer may feel that he or she is capable of doing so, a graphic designer is more familiar with products and processes that can be used to create the graphic image.

 A *logo*, or mark, is a symbolic image of the company (see Figure 19-2). It can be a strong identification symbol for the firm, which will eventually help make the firm easily identifiable. It can be used for all of the firm's written communication, as well as on many other items that are related to the firm's business. The business card is a key tool incorporating the logo. Additional tips on developing a logo are presented in CD Item 19-1.

Business Cards

Business cards remain an important component of the array of promotional tools used by a design firm. This small piece of stiffened paper, generally 3.5 inches by 2 inches, serves many purposes and can be designed in many ways. They are sometimes thought of as tiny billboards by which a company can leave an impression of sophistication, whimsy, or seriousness. Its simplest form is black type on white card stock or many other more sophisticated designs with color on one or both sides, foil, metallic inks, or whatever the interior designer, graphic designer, and printer can put together to create the image desired by the designer. A business card can be single-faced, double-sided, folded, square, embossed, or it can have cutouts.

The purpose of the business card is to help people remember the designer—especially potential clients or others who can help the designer in some way. We also obtain business cards from those who can help us with specifications, might lead us to other clients, or provide other opportunities. An interior designer looking for new business should never be without a few business cards. That is not to say that one tries to give out these cards indiscriminately. There actually is a bit of etiquette concerned with handing out business cards. Here are some tips:

■ Do not offer your card as a way of starting a conversation.

▥ Offer a business card after the conversation is drawing to a close.

▥ If someone offers you his or her card, you generally provide him or her with yours as well, but it is okay not to exchange as well.

▥ Always hand out clean, unbent cards. Carry them in a card holder.

▥ It is okay to write on the back of the card info about the person. Depending on what you write, you might want to do this out of sight of the person.

▥ If the other person says they are "out of cards," you could offer one of yours for them to write information. Be aware that some people don't carry cards just to play a power game of collecting them from others.

It is becoming increasingly difficult to include all the information that a design firm may want on its business card by using only one side. Positioning the firm's logo, name, address, phone number, fax number, e-mail and Web addresses, cell or pager number, and, finally, the person's name, affiliation, and license number makes for really tiny print! When the design includes a logo or the company name is done in a large-sized and elaborate font, it also makes it difficult to include contact information. Many design firms have started using both sides of the card or a folded card. Other design firms are deleting some of these items and choosing to include only key contact points, such as the phone and fax numbers and e-mail addresses.

In the late 1990s, some companies chose to use small CD-ROMs as business cards, sometimes incorporating multimedia. These high-tech cards can store video, text, graphics, audio, and even links to Web pages. They are expensive, and while still used by some companies, they have not gained broad use.

The design and color of the logo should be the same on all materials related to the firm. This will help clients identify the logo with the firm and help bring about client awareness and identification. Logos are displayed in many of the figures found throughout this chapter. The rest of the design of the business card, stationery, and so forth must be compatible with the logo (see Figure 19-3).

Interior designers like to design their own logos, graphic image, and basic stationery. It is always a good idea to talk to a graphic designer about the graphic image in order to ensure that the design is going to "work"—that is, that it can be reproduced effectively and project the image desired by the designer. There are many subtleties to the designing of graphic image and stationery, which are too numerous to discuss here. A graphic designer as well as a high-quality, professional printer can provide advice about paper color, weight of the paper stock, typefaces, color on the stationery, and many other things.

Photo Portfolio

Clients are most concerned about how you can help them and if you can do the kind of design that they envision for their home or commercial space. What the designer needs to assist in convincing the client that their firm is the firm to do the project is a portfolio of project photos. The *photo portfolio* is a selection of project photos preferably taken by a professional architectural photographer. It is a very important tool to help any interior design firm and especially the newer firm show what it can do in meetings with prospective clients. A photo portfolio in today's design world is really a generic term for the establishing of a library of project photos that can be used as part of many kinds of promotional tools.

Many designers use digital cameras to take their own photographs. An advantage to a digital photograph is that the image can be checked immediately, and if there is something wrong, such as underlighting or overlighting, adjustments can be made and a new image can be taken. Digital photographs also can

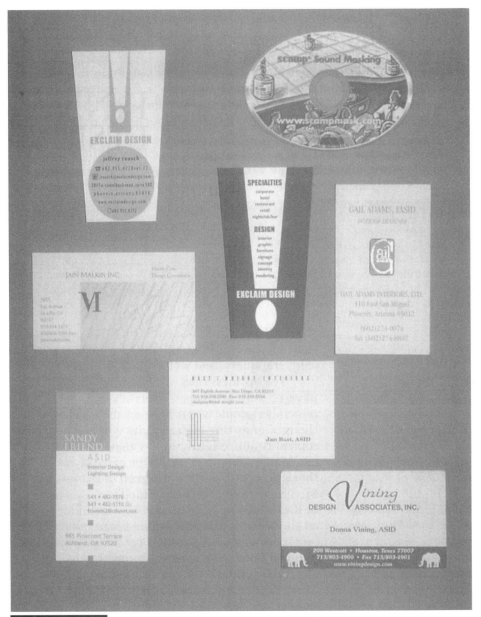

FIGURE 19-3.

Examples of logos used on business cards. Clockwise from top right: Scamp Sound Masking Systems by K. R. Moeller Associates, Ltd., Ontario, Canada; Gail Adams Interiors, Phoenix, AZ; Bast/Wright Interiors, San Diego, CA; Vining Design Associates, Inc., Houston, TX; Sandy Friend, Ashland, OR; Jain Malkin, Inc., La Jolla, CA; Exclaim Design, Scottsdale, AZ. (Photo: Dawson Henderson)

be manipulated on the computer with software like Photoshop®. Subtle changes—even dramatic ones—can be made on the computer in order to improve the photo or to incorporate other elements.

Higher-quality reproductions of digital photos can be achieved when the image is available as a TIFF format image. It is a style of storing images so that it retains a color and depth to a greater degree than other digital formats—the most common being JPEG. In storing the images, a JPEG version is more compressed, while a TIFF is less compressed, retaining a better-quality image when printed.

Many magazines and other publishers will only want digital photos that are TIFF format images.

Although digital photography with high-quality cameras and formatting is satisfactory for many interior designers, numerous professional photographers retain the use of film for their work. Photographs that are shot in a transparency or negative format generally produce sharp, high-quality photographs required of many magazines and book publishers. Enlargements made from negatives or transparencies are generally sharper than from most digital photos unless the camera is capable of taking photos with high pixel counts (resolution). A book filled with photographs of installations can be shown to the client during the marketing stage of a design project. They will also translate a bit better when they are used to create color copies on copying machines for proposals.

It is important to get the permission of the client and to have anyone appearing in the photo sign a release, especially if the photo will be published. This protects the designer from being sued for invasion of privacy. There should always be a clause in the design contract that gives the design firm permission to photograph and submit for publication all work, whether the firm expects to do this or not. The photographer generally has the release forms in case there are people in any of the photos.

It is important to know that when the designer hires a photographer to shoot an installation, the rights to that photo are retained by the photographer. Recall the discussion on copyright in Chapter 10 where the creator owns the rights to the creation. Thus, a photographer—the creator of the photo—owns the rights. Designers pay for use of that photo and must be clear with the photographer what uses are included in the fees. Merely because a designer has a photo of a project does not mean the designer has the right to have that photograph published.

PRESS RELEASES

Alex was excited to receive word that a project his firm had completed in another state was to be awarded a special commendation by that state's environmental office for its excellence in sustainable design. Alex has been working for several years to make a major impact in sustainable design, and this award, she thought, would help bring her firm to a primary position in her state as well as for future promotion in other states. She has decided that a press release to the local media in her state would be the first step in promoting this prestigious accomplishment.

When the design firm has some important news such as Alex's award, the primary way to get that news out to the public is through a press release. A *press release* is a method of providing information about the design firm that might be of interest to the news media. It is an effective, inexpensive way for any size design firm to achieve increased public awareness.

Almost any kind of news or announcement can be prepared as a press release. Newspapers and magazines, however, only have a limited amount of space and usually only use those items that they feel are about significant, newsworthy events. If the firm has recently been named the primary design firm for a large or unusual project, a press release is in order. Perhaps the firm is sponsoring a seminar or a workshop of interest to a wide variety of businesses or consumers. A press release is also in order if the interior design firm has won a design award—especially a prestigious national award. Even the opening of a new interior design firm or the relocation of an existing interior design firm can be announced with a press release. Due to space constraints, in most cities, announcements about promotions and new hires are relegated to a minimal statement in a business briefs column of the newspaper.

PR professionals have experience in preparing press releases; they also have many contacts with local and national print, radio, and television media. These contacts can be utilized to obtain the best coverage for press releases. If an in-house individual uses good journalistic techniques, however, then he or she can prepare a press release. Since preparing a press release is a relatively easy assignment and is an inexpensive way to obtain some publicity for any size firm, it will be covered in some depth.

PR professionals know that editors do not have a lot of time to read unsolicited materials. Thus, it is critical to give them only information that is really considered newsworthy. It should also be submitted in a form that the publication essentially uses. Interior designers preparing their own press releases should make a habit of learning what type of news is used by the local media. They must also realize it must be timely and newsworthy—not just promotional information.

Promotional information in press releases that is often used by the media is prepared in a standard, concise journalistic style, using the classic five "Ws" and "H": who, what, when, where, why, and how. The most significant information should be presented in the first paragraph, and additional details can be presented in subsequent paragraphs. Text should be typed double-spaced, with wide side margins for editorial comments. A one-page release has the best chance of reaching the media. When the editor or news director reads a press release, he or she may have additional questions. The contact information—name, address, telephone number, fax, and even the e-mail address of the contact person—should be placed at the top of the first page (see Figure 19-4).

Often press releases are prepared for immediate release. The words *Immediate Release* indicate that all the information in the text is timely and ready for publication. If this is the case, it should be indicated at the top of the press release, as shown in Figure 19-4. Otherwise, the date of preferred release should be clearly indicated. A preferred release date might be used when the news relates to something that will happen in a week or more in the future such as announcing a nationally recognized speaker at a design firm sponsored event.

Supplementary materials, such as line drawings or photographs, provide information that the text cannot easily explain. They also may make an otherwise routine story more interesting. Magazines prefer color transparencies or TIFF format digital photos rather than color photographic prints. If a black-and-white photograph is sent, it should be a glossy print. Newspapers readily use black-and-white glossy prints but are less likely to use color photographic prints. When line drawings, such as floor plans, are submitted, be prepared to send PMTs or high-quality mylar reductions. PMT (for photomechanical transfer) is a diffusion transfer process that results in a positive reproduction of line copy or artwork (sometimes called a "photostat" or "stat"). A TIFF version of a CAD drawing is also usable to the media. Not all the media has the capability of opening a CAD drawing.

If people are in the photographs, their names and titles, along with signed model releases, should be provided. Not providing a model release with the photograph could prevent the photograph from being published. Be sure that the client or organization has been informed about your press release and model releases, and has provided written clearance for the information to be released. If a project photo taken by a professional photographer is included, be sure that you have the rights from the photographer included as well as the appropriate credit line for that photographer.

Interior Associates, LLC
Contract Interior Designers
1776 E. Commerce Street
Atlanta, Georgia

For Immediate Release

For further information,
Contact: John Adams
404–555–3506

Interior Associates, LLC Awarded 200x Golden Achievement Award

Atlanta, January 10, 200x—Interior Associates, LLC is the recipient of the twenty-sixth annual 200x Golden Achievement Award presented at the_____Community Service awards banquet on February 20, Patrick Smith, President, announced.

The award is granted to an interior design firm within the metropolitan Atlanta area that has achieved an outstanding record of community service during the year.

_____ notes the achievements of Interior Associates with the Northside Hospice, MacAlister Center for Battered Women, and the Home Start Youth Center as representative of the outstanding interior design work contributed by the firm. Jillian Connell, administrator for the MacAlister Center for Battered Women, said, "The sensitive design of our resident areas by Interior Associates has provided an atmosphere desperately needed in this facility."

Interior Associates, LLC has been specializing in health-care facilities as well as facilities for the aged for 25 years. The firm has completed projects throughout Georgia, as well as Florida, North Carolina, Tennessee, and Alabama.

FIGURE 19-4.

A sample press release. Please note that this is a fictitious release.

Being selective, especially at a local level, about who receives the press release may help get it noticed and published or even broadcasted. All areas of the media like to "scoop" their colleagues. Knowing that the design firm has attempted to provide that scoop just may help to get the press release noticed—especially for very special news.

Review the policy of the publication before you send an e-mail. Many editors do not like to receive press releases from unknown sources via e-mail. Like everyone else, editors receive lots of e-mail every day, and some find it annoying to get a press release in this way. It is also a good idea to save and send your e-mail messages in plain ASCII text so that they can be read by any word-processing software that the publication uses. Do not e-mail graphics or other attachments with an unsolicited press release. Attachments such as graphics are a big reason that e-mails are classified as spam by many computer systems today. Mention that graphics are available and briefly describe them. The editor will let you know if you should send the graphics by a messenger or mail.

Remember to follow up with a phone call to the editor when you send a press release. Public relations professionals do this to ensure that your message has been received, and you should do it as well. Even if the editor is not going to use your press release, it gives you the chance to talk to him or her briefly in order to better understand what they look for, so that you will be prepared when future newsworthy items occur at your firm.

BROCHURES

A *brochure* can provide information to interest clients, grab their attention, and allow the design firm to showcase its design style and expertise. A brochure is sometimes referred to as a *collateral material*, along with other kinds of marketing publications such as flyers, calendars, and inserts that can be sales materials (see Figure 19-5). A brochure is most useful to a design firm when clients do not know about the design firm and it still needs to build credibility in the marketplace. Brochures are least useful to interior design firms that have frequent repeat customers or that rely on referrals to generate new business.

The brochure gives the interior design firm the opportunity to show selections of its best work and to tell clients something about itself in a relatively easy to produce leave-behind. Although a four-color brochure on standard letter-sized paper can be expensive, small brochures can be produced at a reasonable cost by using computer software available to any design professional. An example of a small size "brochure" or leave-behind is the postcard. Figure 19-6 is an example of how a postcard format can be successfully used for promotional purposes.

The images on the brochure should mirror the firm's image. If a folded brochure is used, the cover should be attention-getting and interesting. It should have the highest-quality photography that the design firm can afford. A few excellent photographs of very good installations are far superior to many inferior shots and wordy copy. The graphic identification should relate to the other graphics. If the brochure is done in-house using some type of publication software, the brochure should still be prepared using high-quality images.

Copy must be well written and brief, written with the client's point of view in mind. Too many designers include a lengthy history or design philosophy that clients often do not have time to read. The copy and photos of a brochure are meant to provide just a taste of what the design firm is about and to invite the potential client to call the designer so that a face-to-face presentation can be scheduled. The copy should tell potential clients about the firm and the services it offers, and perhaps should list former clients. Graphic designers and PR professionals recommend that the copy be written using the second person (you/your) rather than the first person (we/us). It needs to be attractive and written in a language that the potential client can understand and set the stage for further discussions. Item 19-2 on the CD is a worksheet that can help you focus on identifying your capabilities in interior design. This information can be utilized in the copy of a brochure or other types of promotional materials.

Care must be taken that the photographs chosen do not date the brochure. Featuring photos of the design staff is a compliment to each designer, but when one of them leaves the design firm, his or her photograph in the brochure can date or even negate the brochure. Always remember that a brochure is not, by itself, going to win new clients. It is a promotional and sales tool to help in the long-term process of attracting new clients to the interior design firm.

Creating a high-quality brochure takes expertise in graphics, composition, photography, and copywriting. Although the firm may wish to prepare the conceptual content of the brochure, it is recommended that the actual production be left to public relations professionals or professional graphic designers.

REFERRALS

Relationship building in interior design is critical, since so much of this profession is very personal and successful client relationships are based on personal interaction. These good relationships are particularly important to residential interior designers, since clients might tell their friends about who designed their

PHOENIX CITY HALL

Size: 550,000 s.f.
Estimated Cost: $55.3 M
Construction Cost: $53.8 M
Completion Date: 1993
Location: Phoenix, Arizona
Client/Contact: City of Phoenix
Sheryl Sculley
Assistant City Manager
602.262.7915

Project Features

• Careful programming consolidated 20 city departments into a centralized, citizen-friendly facility which has become an icon in the downtown Phoenix landscape. The project has received numerous awards including AIA Award of Merit, APS Energy Award and Valley Forward Crescordia Award.

• City staff were relocated to a highly flexible and efficient 80% open office and 20% closed in the new building from approximately 80% closed offices and 20% open. New workstation standards were developed, enabling the City to more efficiently utilize space.

• Security is accomplished inconspicuously with carefully planned access to sensitive areas, and bullet-resistant panels in millwork, providing protection for staff and officials, and a level of comfort for visitors.

LANGDON WILSON ARCHITECTURE PLANNING INTERIORS

FIGURE 19-5.

One-page inserts used by many firms in place of formal brochures. (Reproduced with permission, Langdon Wilson Architecture Planning Interiors, Phoenix, AZ)

FIGURE 19-6.

A postcard mailer used as a "pass along" when a firm has an extensive Web site for promotion. (Reproduced with permission, Suzan Globus, FASID, Globus Design Associates, Red Bank, NJ.)

home. For some interior designers, referrals may be the primary way in which a sole practitioner obtains new clients. Word-of-mouth or referral marketing is an effective way to market interior design. A *referral* occurs when one client tells another person who may be looking for interior design services about a particular design firm—hopefully your firm. For years, many design firms have depended on this method of promotion for finding new clients. It costs nothing, since no promotional materials are needed for a client to recommend the design firm to someone.

Referrals do not just happen, however. Satisfied clients may not think about mentioning your firm to a friend or a business associate without prompting from the designer. On the other hand, they will tell everyone they know if the work was done incorrectly or poorly. It is human nature for clients to complain to even total strangers about poor service rather than mention positive service. What this means is that the designer must "manage" referral marketing.

One way to do this is to develop strategies that will encourage the client to refer the design firm to potential clients. This starts with doing everything for each existing customer as perfectly and as positively as possible and not allowing errors or problems to occur. If a problem does occur, it should be taken care of with a smile and as quickly as possible. "Studies have shown that each time customers had a positive experience with you or your place of business, they will tell 4 other people. On the other hand, any time they have a negative experience, they'll tell 11 people."[3]

Most clients will not give referrals unless the designer encourages them to do so. This is done by many designers by using strategies to help the client help the designer. One way is simply to include a sentence in a follow-up letter or thank-you card at the end of the project—perhaps with a sentence that says something like, "My business depends on referrals. Please consider mentioning my company to people whom you feel may benefit from my services." Another strategy is to not only thank the client for a referral but also to give the client a thank-you gift, such as a gift certificate to a restaurant. In fact, some firms make it a practice to offer incentives to obtain referrals. Perhaps the incentive is a gift certificate, a special discount, or something else that might have value or meaning to a former satisfied client.

Related to referrals are client testimonials. *Testimonials* are statements that the client has made in a letter that he or she sends or gives verbally to the designer concerning their satisfaction with the design firm's work. "Eric Smith provided our family with an outstanding solution to our needs to add a small living space for my mother. His design solutions were supportive of our needs and managed the project with great concern for detail" is an example of a testimonial.

Another type of related referral is a letter of reference that states positive attributes about the design firm to either a specific client or in general. When design firms respond to requests for proposals from clients, letters of reference are often required or submitted along with the other documents. Letters of reference are often longer than a testimonial and often provide greater detail about the designer or the designer's work. It is also possible that an interior designer will ask the person writing a letter of reference if a sentence or two can be used as a testimonial.

Testimonials and letters of reference lend credibility, because someone else is making the positive comments or lending evidence to claims made by the design firm. These testimonials and letters can also be used on Web sites, brochures, and other collateral marketing materials.

A word of caution about referral marketing and asking clients for referrals is in order. Never make it look like the firm is begging for work. The firm must focus on satisfaction and how it can help acquaintances of the client rather than on the design firm's need for business. If the designer somehow makes it sound like the firm is desperate or in real need of business, the client will wonder if something is suddenly wrong with the firm.

Here are some tips to improve success with referrals:

- Always provide a positive experience with existing clients. Do not let problems sour a relationship. Make sure that your reputation keeps improving.

- Make it a policy to always deliver more than you promise and never promise what you cannot deliver. When a client gets something positive that he or she did not expect, the client will generally be more interested in referring your company to others.

- Join association referral programs. These programs might exist on the local chapter level or come from a national database of designers who sign up for the program. The organization usually gives a client at least three names of designers in the area.

- Develop an in-depth mailing list of existing and past clients. Send them something each month, such as article reprints, newsletters, or announcements about seminars that you may be giving. This will keep your firm in their minds.

- Identify the clients who are most likely to provide referrals, and focus your efforts on them. Do not be a pest, but sending them article reprints about your firm or a brochure with a well-written letter explaining how referrals are important to your business can help them help you.

- If the firm has employees, do not forget to instruct them in appropriate ways of obtaining referrals from people with whom they come in contact.

- Consider joining a referral group. There are groups of professionals in many major cities that get together to discuss general business topics. These referral groups then try to help each other with referrals.

- Position yourself as an expert. Being very good at your niche in interior design means you will be thought of first when a client hears of someone who needs your expertise. If your firm provides excellent service and is an expert in an area, clients will feel very comfortable recommending your firm to others.

NETWORKING

Robin and James joined a professional group consisting primarily of contractors. They joined the group in order to meet with individuals working for or owning companies that might create referrals and collaborative work in commercial design. Robin and James had a plan that each meeting they would both try to get to know at least three new people at the meetings. Their only marketing tool along for the visits was a good supply of business cards. The next day they met to discuss who they met and how to take the next step in developing the relationship.

Networking is another word-of-mouth marketing technique. In this case, the designer is the one who is doing the talking, not the client. According to the *American Heritage Dictionary of the English Language*, a network is "an extended group of people with similar interests or concerns who interact and remain in informal contact for mutual assistance or support."[4] *Networking* is the cultivating of mutually beneficial relationships; it is getting to know people you can help and who can help you. *Mutually beneficial relationships* are the key words here.

Many interior designers think about networking as an opportunity to get together with colleagues at professional association meetings. Certainly, this is true, and it is always enjoyable to meet and mingle with designer friends whom you have not seen for weeks, months, or even years. However, the purpose of networking is to use it to meet people outside the design industry who might help in other ways. This kind of networking goes on at social and community clubs, seminars, church groups, schools, and the like. Because many of the reasons that a client will work with an interior designer are based on relationships, it is important to build contacts at organization meetings and groups with which potential clients may affiliate.

Of course, many designers have had positive work-related networking experiences from professional association meetings. Yet attending events where one can meet potential new clients or others that can help provide referrals or tips on potential business needs to go beyond the interior design chapter meeting.

Whether your purpose in including networking as a marketing tool is to meet colleagues in your area or to uncover possible clients, remember that networking is a two-way street. Do not expect the other person to help you more than once if you are unwilling to help them. Becoming involved with your church's building committee just to meet clients and not really contributing to the committee will leave a very sour taste in the mouths of the rest of the group. Asking colleagues at an association chapter meeting about suggestions for vendors without at some time giving them similar or other information will turn your colleagues away from you.

Determine what your purposes are for networking and who you want in your network. Will they be strictly designers and maybe vendors who can help you with sources? Are you looking for new clients? What other sources of help are you looking for? Go through your computer contact files or list the names of people whom you think can help. Be sure to ask yourself, "Why these people?" and "What kind of help am I hoping they can give me?" Invite them to coffee or lunch to talk about mutually beneficial topics. If the purpose of your networking is to obtain a reference or a recommendation, you are, in effect, saying to them that you respect their opinions. And when you are asked, it means that other people respect yours. It is extremely flattering to be asked your opinion. Be willing to share information, and others will think of you as well.

Networking, like any other kind of marketing, works better if you have a plan. If you are looking to meet people at various kinds of meetings or groups, you need to learn to "work the room." Ask the greeters if the people whom you are hoping to meet are expected. Perhaps they can even introduce you. When you attend a seminar or workshop, get to the class early so that you can introduce yourself to other participants and the speaker. In fact, keeping abreast of seminars offered by various associations and groups can lead you to very good networking opportunities to clients you otherwise might never be able to meet. Look for these announcements in the business section of the newspaper.

Always have some small talk or conversation openers prepared: "Do you come to the meetings every month?" "This is a beautiful facility. Have you been here before?" It is never wrong to consistently know what the local sport teams are doing. "How about those (insert your local team) Saturday!" is always a great opening. Open-ended questions like these can get the other person to start talking, and before you know it, you will find yourself in a conversation. If your purpose in attending the event or meeting is to meet potential clients or others who can help you generate business, do not simply find people you know and stay with them all through the event. You already know them. Say hello, be friendly, and move on to meet others. Make sure that you have enough business cards, and ask for cards from people who really interest you. Get back to those individuals whose cards you have obtained. If you want something from them, do not wait for them to get in touch with you.

Another important and successful networking tactic is to get to the meeting early and plan to stay as late as you can. Getting there early allows you to scope out the meeting place and participate in the social part of the business or organization meeting. Staying to the end—even helping with the cleanup— can get you noticed. Some of the best contacts can be made at the end of the

TABLE 19-1.

Tips on How to Work a Room for Networking Effectiveness.

- ☐ Place your name tag on your right side. As you shake hands, the other person's eye will be directed to your name tag. Of course, some people believe that putting the name tag on their lower jacket pocket or belt is more interesting. If it suits your personality and the occasion, go for it!
- ☐ Have a ten-second introduction prepared. When asked the common question, "What do you do?" have something to say besides, "Oh, I'm an interior designer." Perhaps you might say, "I help create unique home interiors" or "I assist companies improve their bottom line."
- ☐ If you want to give your business card to someone, ask the person for his or hers first. If the person does not offer you a card, then it is okay to ask for one.
- ☐ Arrive early and stay until almost the end. It is the best time to meet the decision makers or VIPs.
- ☐ Take care of eating at a meeting first, if possible, since it is difficult to balance a drink and a plate of food, and get at your business cards. Freshen up and then progress to meeting people and exchanging cards.
- ☐ Know why you are attending the meeting. If you want to meet people, plan to introduce yourself. Do not complain later that the meeting was a waste of time if you end up spending the evening with an old friend or sitting like a wallflower.
- ☐ Do not drink too much alcohol. Sometimes it is a good idea not to drink at all during a meeting if you are trying to meet business contacts. At the very least, know your limit. Getting even a little tipsy is not a way to make a good impression.
- ☐ Always have a sufficient number of business cards for the occasion. Nobody is impressed when you say, "I just gave out my last one." Use a card holder or put a few in your jacket pocket.
- ☐ Make others feel comfortable at meetings. If you have been to the meeting before and you see someone new, go up and talk to the person. Introduce the person to others. In a way, appoint yourself a hostess. At the very least, you will get to meet one or two new people and will gain experience at extending yourself.
- ☐ Be sure and follow up in an appropriate manner. If you have promised to call or to send something to someone whom you have met, do so promptly. Be sure to get in touch with the chair, if you volunteered to help out at the next meeting. And do not forget a thank-you card, if one is needed.

evening or meeting. The leaders of the organization almost always are among the last to leave a meeting or event.

Using networking to expand your group of acquaintances and to meet potential clients is a very effective and inexpensive marketing technique. Realize that gaining a positive relationship with someone—even a business colleague—does not happen overnight. Take the time to build your network with positive sharing, and before you know it, you will be called upon to share your knowledge in ways that you never expected. Pushing yourself on someone whom you have not met before can backfire, because they may find you aggressive or manipulative. Wanting to tell your story or ask your questions without giving something back is also impolite. Table 19-1 provides some additional tips on how to work a room in order to meet new people and expand your network.

INTERNET MARKETING

Interior design professionals have certainly embraced Internet marketing and the importance of having a company Web site. All types of consumers are turning to the World Wide Web to find interior design service providers and to even pre-shop for products. Surfing the Web is not only an activity for the young, as older consumers of every age group have become computer savvy.

The meaning of the two concepts—the Internet and World Wide Web—still sometimes causes confusion. The Internet is a large, worldwide network by which all computers around the world can be connected to one another. The World Wide Web (also called the Web) and even is a subset of the Internet, made up of servers—large computers—that store the information that Internet users

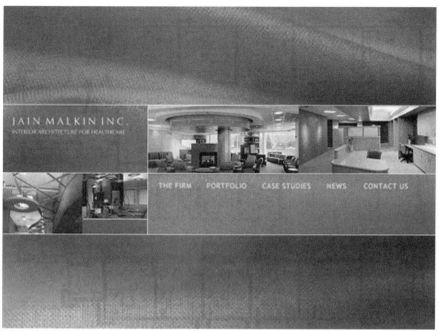

FIGURE 19-7.

The home page from the Web site of Jain Malkin Inc. (Reproduced courtesy of Jain Malkin Inc., San Diego, CA.)

can access. The visual that most readers are familiar with is the Web page (see Figure 19-7). The Web page is a document that is written using a special programming language, referred to as HTML (Hypertext Markup Language). With the use of secondary software, commonly called plug-ins, the HTML basic document can use text, graphics, animation, audio, and video to create a finished Web page.

At first, the Internet and the World Wide Web was just a great place for people to find information. It opened up libraries around the world to researchers, educators, and students. In addition, it provided a place for writers to submit material on an almost limitless assortment of topics. The Internet quickly grew from being a vehicle for government agencies and the military to exchange information to being a wide-open highway of information, commerce, and marketing venues for anyone with access to the Internet.

The Internet has become a tremendous tool for all types of interior design firms and others in the business world to market their services and products. Interior designers had a Web presence fairly early. Large firms, in particular, were the first to embrace Web marketing, since they were already very familiar with the use of CAD in the 1980s. The opportunity to have a worldwide marketing presence was understood immediately by these firms. Smaller firms have found the possibilities of the Web more slowly, but their use of the Web has increased significantly.

As with any type of promotional tool under consideration for development, a firm should first decide why it might be necessary to have a Web site. Does the firm seek a Web site because it seeks clients in its immediate area or around the world? Is it prepared to work with clients on the other side of the globe, or is it content to stay in its area? If the design firm thinks having a Web site will immediately bring dozens of new clients, it is wrong. A Web site does provide exposure—no question—but, like advertising, it rarely provides clients instantly.

FIGURE 19-8.

The home page from the Web site of Brannon Design Associates, Inc. (Reproduced with permission, Brannon Design Associates, Del Mar, CA.)

What should be on the Web page is another decision that the firm needs to make. The firm can display photos of recent jobs, award-winning projects, text that can describe the firm's design philosophy, and service offerings and client list (see Figure 19-8). The firm can integrate graphics, animation, and video to make the pages different from others. Since there is so much that can be put into a Web page, the firm must decide what information about the company will intrigue someone who finds its Web site.

Thought must also be taken in what to leave off the Web site. Including pricing for services or quoting discounts might seem like a way to attract a client; however, it can also frighten them away, as the dollars or percentages quoted may be high in comparison to other competitors. Exaggerated promises should also be avoided, as these exaggerations become expectations, and the lack of performance could lead to legal and ethical problems. The owner of the design firm must be absolutely certain that everything on the Web site and linked pages is truthful about the company.

What does the firm want the viewer to do after he or she surfs through the Web site? Certainly, the firm wants the viewer to communicate with the firm, so contact information is necessary. The simplest way to do this is by e-mail. Thus, the Web site should include a link to the e-mail address of the owner or other staff. It is also possible to have a space where the viewer can leave contact information. Perhaps the firm wants the viewer to request information, make a personal phone call for an interview, or purchase something offered for sale on the Web site. Many Web sites have a link to a frequently asked question (FAQ) page, where the viewer will find a list of things that are often asked by other clients. To save both the viewer and the firm time, the viewer can go to this page for many inquiries. However, a danger is that, if the firm provides too much information in this way, the prospective client may not bother to contact the firm for an interview.

When the design firm chooses to market itself on the Internet, the relationship between client and design firm is harder to achieve. Because of the lack of a physical connection, the relationship starts with the image projected on the Web site. Image definitely comes across on a Web site. The quality of the photos, the style of language in the text, and the colors used for backgrounds all play a part, similar to a printed brochure or hard-media promotional pieces. Small firms often cannot afford a site designed by a specialist in Web site design nor use the tools of Web design to create a stunning site. A site that is as well designed as the firm can afford, especially with quality photos and informative text, will stand up against fancy sites, however.

Finding ways to get the viewer to stay at the Web site is very important. If the design firm has a lot of graphics and/or animation on the Web site or has a very large site, it may take some time for the site to load on the viewer's computer, and not every business and household has a high-speed connection. In addition, some people have a short attention span and may not wait for the page to load or be willing to wade through a site if the information or the site is very complex. There are little things that can be done to get the viewer to come back. The first is to have a clean, easy-to-navigate, and interesting home page that will direct the viewer to the links that are important to that viewer. Another is a changing page of tips—perhaps a "hint of the week"—where the designer can provide design ideas or information to target consumers. A commercial designer could include code information, while the residential designer might supply hints on color trends or holiday decorating—with the seasons correct. This should be something that the design firm can commit to upgrading, or the viewers will not come back.

Investigate several Web sites of other interior designers. Maybe there are colleagues in your area who have Web sites. You can probably get their addresses from association directories or just type "interior design company" into a search engine and start looking. Watch your spelling and try more than one search engine. Make notes on what you like and bookmark sites that you like. You also may want to read books or attend seminars on Internet marketing.

Now reexamine why you want to be on the Internet and start creating specific notes for your Web site designer. If you don't have a mission statement, write one. You might not include your mission statement, but the philosophy of why you are in the business of interior design will be important in the creation of your Web site. Then gather your information and get the Web site designed!

This discussion is necessarily brief as the total discussion on how to design a Web site is beyond the space available in this book. There are many different opinions about how and what information should be placed on a Web site. In addition, so much is changing relative to hardware, delivery, and software that it would be impossible to speak with sufficient depth in this text. After reviewing Web sites of other interior designers, you may wish to refer to the many references available at bookstores and those included in this book. One very interesting and complete book on this topic is *Communication and Design with the Internet* by Jonathan Cohen. It focuses on the architectural profession, but the concepts Cohen presents are applicable to all design areas. Table 19-2 provides some additional tips and considerations on the use of Web sites for marketing.

There are, of course, all kinds of uses for an Internet connection. Besides using the Web as a marketing tool, the Web can be searched for product information. There are several design library sites that provide information, graphics, and even purchasing capabilities for the products that the interior designer specifies and sells to clients. This resource makes many products that were not available before to the designer very accessible. Some designers prefer these sites, since they free up office space by reducing the amount of space for keeping a library of catalogs. In addition to design libraries are the Web sites of manufacturers. Designers can get information on a wide variety of products directly from manufacturers by going to their Web sites. Depending on many

TABLE 19-2.

Tips for using a Web site for marketing an interior design business.

Why do you want a Web site?

- Increase awareness
- Sell products
- Develop leads for design consulting
- Provide information about the firm
- Market worldwide
- Develop a mailing list through the "hits"

What information will you include?

- Job photos
- Owner and staff photos
- Owner and staff resumés
- Client list
- Design philosophy
- Services list
- Photos and descriptions of products to sell
- Online place information distribution

Tips for creating a successful site

- Make sure you know why you want a site
- Keep it simple
- Provide a reason for the viewer to come back to the Web site
- Target the audience through design techniques
- Respond quickly to inquiries
- Keep it updated on a regular basis
- Promote your Web site
- Provide an easy way for potential clients to contact you
- Keep your links to other sites at a minimum so that you don't lose the reader

---

factors, it also may be possible for the designer to order directly from the manufacturer. This use of the Web is discussed in Chapter 29.

By now all readers are familiar with the use of the Internet for e-mail. Electronic mail is fast, reliable (for the most part), and certainly cheap. Business communications of every kind can be sent by e-mail as attachments. Many design firms use e-mail to communicate with clients around the country and the world. Some were beginning to use e-mail in the early years of the Web to transmit orders for goods from suppliers. Others find the speed of transmitting drawings electronically an amazing advantage. Care must be used when including attachments, since different computer operating systems might not translate these attachments in the receiver's system. Graphics and photographs are particular problems when sent as attachments. The two parties need to communicate ahead of time on the best way to send graphic attachments so that the receiver actually receives what is sent.

E-commerce and e-tailing (electronic retailing) are quite common. A great deal of thought must go into this issue should a firm that handles inventory on a regular basis decide to sell via the Internet. It involves deciding what will be sold, pricing, purchasing arrangements, security for purchasing, display of product photos, and much more. Ordering via the Internet using e-mail or direct placement systems is commonplace for businesses, with consumers also accepting this method of purchase if they trust the privacy and security of the site.

What Would You Do?

"It takes days for Roger to return my phone messages. I even try to leave messages on his e-mail, and more times than not, he doesn't respond. Yesterday, the three e-mails I sent to him bounced back undeliverable like he is blocking my e-mails!"

These statements came from a disgruntled client who was complaining to Roger's boss at a large, multidiscipline design firm. The boss did what he could to calm down the client, but it didn't work very well. "I'll talk to Roger and make sure he returns your calls right away. I will also remind him that company policy forbids anyone from blocking e-mails," said the boss.

When Roger came to work the next day, the boss called him into his office and told him about the complaining client. "Oh, for goodness sakes! He's calling me all the time, asking stupid questions and wanting me on the job site every day. I'm working on five other projects and can't give him all my attention," claimed Roger.

ADVERTISING

Gail and Martin have decided to include a quarter-page advertisement in their local business "List of Best Businesses" publication. They feel the ad will be a good supplement to the fact that they are included in the list of Best Commercial Interior Design firms for this year.

Advertising is defined as any kind of paid communication in media, such as newspapers, magazines, television, or radio. If a design firm pays the newspaper to run an announcement of some kind about the firm, it is considered advertising. If the newspaper runs an announcement or article about the firm and the firm does not pay for it, it is considered publicity.

Advertising as a means for professionals to promote their services has been controversial until about the 1980s. Professional associations at that time loosened up their stand against members' advertising. For example, in 1981, the Institute of Business Designers (now IIDA) stated in its code of ethics that "members may purchase dignified advertisements and listings in newspapers, periodicals, directories, or other publications."[5] Today, even professional associations themselves regularly use advertising in print and television media. Perhaps you have seen ASID's and IIDA's advertisements in major business magazines.

Although there has always been reluctance on the part of the professions to engage in advertising of services, many interior design firms have embraced print advertising. There is no standard as to the use of paid advertising by interior design firms. For some firms, advertising plays an important part in the firm's overall promotional plan. Others never even consider using a paid advertisement for any reason. Most firms fall somewhere in between these two extremes, as competition in many markets has grown quite strong.

Firms that are designer/specifiers and who do not sell much if any merchandise may occasionally advertise in special editions of trade magazines in their local market. This type of ad normally is a general awareness advertisement in which a photograph of a client installation is featured. Designers who produce revenue from selling products advertise more often. It may be an advertisement

FIGURE 19-9.

Magazine advertisement for an interior design firm. (Reproduced courtesy of Wagner Somerset, Clifton, VA.)

announcing a sale on inventory or special purchases. Of course, retail stores in this industry regularly advertise in local magazines and newspapers. In general, the more the firm depends on product sales and showcases products in a retail store or a studio, the more the firm will use advertising (see Figure 19-9).

Part of the decision to advertise or not is also affected by the firm's clients. If the design firm's clients are exclusively or primary commercial, the advertising used consists of print ads placed in trade magazines or newsletters targeted to commercial specialties. In business-to-business (B2B) advertising, the design firm needs to target where the business's clients are, and the local newspaper may or may not be a satisfactory location for a B2B ad. Residential designers locate print advertising in local home magazines, a regional publication such as *Western Interiors*, or national home magazines like *House Beautiful*. Today there is a wide assortment of business, trade, and residential consumer-oriented publications in which a design firm may choose to advertise.

Service-oriented interior design firms generally limit advertising and usually have limited success in using advertising to obtain new clients. Advertising for service businesses rarely brings an immediate response. Instead, it is a way for the interior design firm to create awareness when it places an advertisement in publications that reach its target audience. A viable client might not contact the design firm until months after the advertisement has been published. As some designers have reported, other times clients call asking about specific product items in a project photo rather than expressing interest in design services.

A common form of direct advertising that all designers use is a yellow-page advertisement in the phone book. Many rely on ads in which the firm's name, address, and telephone number are printed in very small type. These ads are placed to announce the firm's presence in the local area. Firms that sell furniture out of retail showrooms or small studios often take out larger-size yellow-page ads, calling more attention to their company. Those who have an open retail studio—regardless of the size—might decide to place phone book ads in both the interior designer section and the appropriate furniture section.

Manufacturers of many kinds of products use photographs of their products in installations in paid advertising. Designers should seek to negotiate for the project designer's and the firm's name to be incorporated into the ad. These manufacturers' ads can go into trade or shelter magazines, in the company's brochures and catalogs, on their Web page—almost anywhere that the manufacturer chooses to advertise. This type of advertising is commonly called *co-op advertising*. This means that the manufacturer and designer generally share in the cost of the advertising, or the manufacturer provides an incentive to the designer to sell a particular product. While this type of promotion is not truly public relations, it does serve to market the firm to new clients.

Advertising is expensive. One ad can use a small design firm's total marketing budget for the year. For example, a quarter-page black-and-white advertisement in many local magazines starts at $1500 for a one-time use. Color ads can run over $3000 for a quarter-page insert. National magazines will charge far more. Of course, ads in the newspaper announcing a sale on a particular product can bring in results quickly but can also cost easily over $500 for a small ad. It is important for the design firm to understand what the goals are for placing and paying for an ad.

Newspaper advertisements are cheaper than those placed in magazines. They can reach a broader audience, but they also reach a generally untargeted audience. An ad in the newspaper may get response from callers who really are not prepared to work with the interior designer or to pay the designer's fees. Yet the designer will have taken the time to talk to the prospective client on the phone or during an interview. As with any other promotional tool or strategy, care must be taken in considering the why, when, how, and where of advertising. These are the kinds of issues discussed in Chapter 3 that are related to target marketing and marketing plans.

SUMMARY

When a design firm neglects to do any marketing or promoting of the business, it is likely that business will eventually dry up. That is especially true of any interior design firm that has not developed a substantial following of former clients who will be happy to provide referrals to their friends. Should the design firm be new or be trying to enter a new market, it will likely need a variety of promotional strategies to make itself known to potential clients. However, no firm can succeed without using some of the marketing tools discussed in this and the next chapter. Potential clients will want to know something about the firm, so having a brochure or marketing letter available to give them, or even prepared resumés of staff for inclusion in a proposal are needed.

The promotional concepts discussed in this chapter suggest that there are many tools that the firm can utilize to promote itself to potential clients. Used independently or in combination, all sizes of design firms must promote themselves to a target market. Whether this is accomplished by using a well-designed Web site, press releases, a brochure, or any of the other tools discussed in this chapter and the next, keeping the design firm's name in the client's mind is very important.

REFERENCES

1. Kotler, 2000, p. 87.
2. Fletcher and Rockler, 2000, p. 1.
3. Burg, 1999, p. 114.
4. *American Heritage Dictionary of the English Language*, 2000, p. 1181.
5. Institute of Business Designers, 1981, p. 3.

CHAPTER 20

Additional Promotional Methods

Key Terms and Concepts

These key terms and concepts are important to material in this chapter. Many of these terms will be utilized in other chapters as well. Be sure you understand these items as you read this chapter.

Terms and Concepts

Project submissions

Newsletter

Case study

Direct mail

Premium

Proposal

Request for qualifications (RFQ)

Request for proposal (RFP)

Letter of interest (LOI)

Short list

Hot-button issue

Critical Issues

After completing this chapter you should be able to:

- Discuss the pros and cons of submitting projects to magazines as a promotional method.
- Explain the benefits of writing articles as a way of exposing the design firm/designer to potential clients.
- Compare the purpose and content of a newsletter to a case study.
- Provide insights into the benefits of entering design competitions.
- Compare the promotional benefits of speaking at an interior design professional meeting to speaking at a meeting of potential clients.
- Discuss how the RFP and RFQ system aids clients and interior designers.
- List the items that are traditionally needed in an RFP.
- Discuss the pros and cons of effective ways for the sole practitioner to promote him- or herself.

▓ Discuss the pros and cons of effective ways for the design firm with a small design staff to promote the firm.

▓ Explain how a hot-button issue can be the focus of promotional methods other than RFPs.

The previous chapter discussed several methods or tools for promoting an interior design practice that have become essential and commonplace for any design firm. The methods discussed in this chapter can be used by any size or kind of interior design firm. Many are more commonly used by the larger firm, because a larger firm has greater financial resources. Exactly which marketing and promotional methods are used by a firm should be carefully considered in light of a strategic plan and budget constraints. A design firm does not need to nor is it likely to afford all the promotional methods discussed in this chapter.

A tool or method that most interior designers look forward to utilizing includes one or more types of publication opportunities. Some of these publications are available to the sole proprietor with a limited amount of experience, while others will require experience before they can be utilized. Competitions are a very good way to obtain publicity for any size firm. Reprints of the award announcements in magazines can be used as a supplemental item when a client is looking for general information about the designer. Other promotional tools such as direct marketing mailings, seminars, and premiums are provided to give the practitioner some additional ideas on how to promote the practice. The chapter concludes with a discussion of the preparation of a proposal in response to a request for proposal (RFP) from a commercial client. The RFP is a very important marketing tool for many firms.

PUBLICATION

Evelyn was very proud to see that the article she wrote for a local residential magazine was finally published. It took her many hours to create and write and then revise, but the result was already garnering comments from friends who saw the piece. She was able to include a photograph of a project related to the topic that she hoped would get her some additional notice from potential clients. The magazine was gracious to include her contact information at the end of the article.

There are many possible ways for the interior designer to utilize print media to gain publicity for the firm beyond the press release. Excellent-quality photographs are very important for many of these publication methods. In some cases, the publication will pay for the photography and even prepare the editorial material (the text), though this is not common. For the most part, the publication of photographs and text (or editorial copy) is a relatively inexpensive way for the design firm or designer to obtain publicity, since the interior designer does not pay for it. However, preparing materials to submit for publication takes time and not every submission will result in publication. This section will discuss four ways of using publication as a promotional tool: (1) project submissions, (2) general design articles, (3) newsletters and case studies, and (4) books.

Project Submissions

A most sought after kind of publicity and promotion is publication of projects in trade and shelter magazines. Trade magazines or journals often focus on a particular profession, business, or industry. These publications are sold by subscription primarily to those within the publication's target market. Shelter or consumer magazines are sold by subscription or on newsstands for the general public. A few trade magazines cross over to the consumer market.

A firm must carefully consider to which magazine or other print publication it submits materials. Each publication has a slightly different target market and audience. This needs to be part of the consideration by the design firm, since some magazines will simply not publish even great material if it does not fit its focus. ASID has prepared a pamphlet called *How to Get Your Work Published*. This informative pamphlet is available to members. The pamphlet lists general guidelines for preparing publication material for many of the trade and shelter magazines. The pamphlet also provides information concerning the type of projects and kinds of materials each of the magazines might be interested in publishing. Designers can also contact a magazine's editorial offices to receive information about submission requirements. This type of research is commonly part of a public relations professional's responsibilities.

There is a more limited audience for work published in an interior design or built environment trade publication. Most readers of interior design trade magazines are other professional peers. The opportunity to have a project published in these magazines is an impressive accomplishment, although it might not reach new clients. Residential designers may want to have projects published in local or national shelter magazines or possibly the home section of the local newspaper. Many cities have local magazines that are used for promoting the good qualities of the city or state. These magazines often include articles on residences or commercial properties, giving designers an outlet to consumers. Some of these magazines even have special issues that focus on the local design community. In addition, many of these publications welcome articles or even have ongoing columns written by local designers. These articles help educate the reader on various topics in the interior design field.

Commercial designers may seek to publish their projects in the trade magazines that are read by the target clients. For example, if the purpose of the publication of a project is to have clients gain more awareness of the interior design firm, the firm can obtain reprints and mail or give them to prospective and former clients. Such magazines as *Hospitality Design*, *Law Practice Management*, *Modern Physician*, and *Corporate Design* run articles on outstanding interior design projects. To locate a publication that focuses on a particular design specialty, refer to *Ayer's Directory of Publications*, published by Ayer's Press and available in most public libraries. Information on magazines can also be obtained on the Web at www.gale.com, the current resource for Ayer's.

General Design Articles

"Publications provide one proof of who is real and who isn't ... Published work tells [a potential client] that the author must have substantial experience, and that she has reflected more deeply on her businesses than some."[1] Everyone wants to learn more about a wide variety of topics in this information age. And there are certainly a wide variety of topics covering the interior design and built environment industry. Designers who are comfortable with gathering information and writing find that proposing general design articles is an effective way of marketing themselves and their businesses.

Clients many times view designers who have articles published in print media as experts or at least as having more expertise than others. And clients like to hire experts. When a potential client sees an article by a designer in a magazine or a newspaper, this indicates to the client that the designer must have some expertise that his or her peers do not. Article publication also gives the designer exposure to potentially a very wide audience that the designer might not be able to reach in other ways. The fact that a magazine has printed an article by a designer might also inspire a trade association to ask the designer to speak at a meeting.

Material submitted to a magazine is reviewed and considered by an editor who is looking for good information that will be appropriate for the publication. The writer must have some credentials, along with an ability to write, in order to be considered a columnist or even a contributing writer to a publication. The editor also is looking for good writing and a sense that the person who is writing the article knows what he or she is talking about.

What is another benefit of writing an article? Once an article has been published, the author can request reprints. These reprints can then be used as part of the design firm's total marketing plan and strategies. Reprints can be included in packets that are given to clients during marketing presentations or in packets that are mailed to prospective clients. Designers can also send along a reprint when they are writing to a former client.

In order to achieve publication, the designer must do some homework. First of all, the designer should investigate the publications in the firm's geographic area. Determine what kinds of articles are commonly found in those publications. Major cities have local resident and tourism magazines that cover issues of interest to local residents but also are used to attract out-of-town tourists. This type of magazine occasionally has a few issues that contain articles on interesting interior design and architecture. Magazines such as *Phoenix Magazine*, *Los Angeles*, and *Chicago* are of this type. There are other local magazines that focus on residential topics, including interiors or business topics. You are encouraged to investigate the variety of magazines that might be available in your area, since it is not possible to list all of them in this book.

It is essential to research some back copies of magazines you think target your potential clients to see what style of writing and types of editorial material the magazine publishes. If what you want to submit does not fit the editorial content of the magazine, you will be wasting your time and that of the publication's editorial staff. Most magazines review unsolicited manuscripts, but usually they do not return them if they are not used. Query letters should be sent to the magazine editor before time is spent developing an article. A query letter explains the concept of the article and even gives a little taste of it by including the first paragraph. If the editor is interested, he or she will send you information about the magazine's style guidelines, which include information about margins, word count, requirements for camera-ready photographs or drawings, and basic grammatical style that is appropriate for the publication.

Come up with an idea that is interesting to the magazine's readers. Make sure it is something you know something about and can easily research for additional background, if necessary. Provide a good focus to the article—most magazines limit the length of articles submitted from nonstaff writers to 500 to 1500 words.

Although an article will not result in the phone ringing off the hook from new clients' inquiries, it does provide one more promotional tool that the interior design firm can use. Articles provide awareness; they get the design firm's name or designer's name in front of more clients than can be reached by the efforts of the designer alone. And writing can be fun!

Newsletters and Case Studies

With today's desktop publishing software, design firms of all sizes are using newsletters and e-letters to help get information about the firm out to clients and to pose information that might be useful to potential clients. Newsletters have long been popular with architects and larger interior design firms, but small firms sometimes find the time to produce them as well. There are two basic kinds of *newsletters*. One is the simple in-house newsletter that tells everyone whose birthday it is and other tidbits of interest to employees. The other is the promotional newsletter that is used to inform clients about projects or otherwise provide information that clients might find valuable (see Figure 20-1). This discussion focuses solely on the marketing newsletter.

It takes commitment to begin publishing a newsletter, regardless of whether it is a printed collateral item or published on the Internet. Once the firm begins to publish a newsletter, it must follow through and be ready to produce this marketing piece on a consistent basis. One of the first decisions that the firm will need to make is to determine what will be the purpose of the item, determining the basic content, how often it will be published, and the budget for producing it. With a large in-house staff, a design firm might be able to produce enough project announcements or other information to issue a newsletter on a quarterly basis. A small firm might plan on publishing a semiannual newsletter. Of course, a monthly newsletter is best, but any regular publication is better than none. Other considerations include the number of pages and what type (if any) graphics will be included. Of course, the basics, like type style, format (two or three columns?), and use of color also must be determined.

Then the firm will need to decide on the overall content of the newsletter. Perhaps it will be primarily announcements about project contracts and completed projects. Maybe the firm intends to provide useful information, such as changes in code requirements, that clients should know about. Finally, a determination must be made as to who will have the responsibility of producing the newsletter. Someone in-house may be able to take on the responsibility, but this means that the hours spent on this task are not billable. A freelance writer or consultant can be hired, which saves time for the staff but will raise the expense of producing the newsletter. None of these decisions can be taken lightly.

Of course, a newsletter can also be integrated into the design firm's Web page or be an e-mailed newsletter or e-letter. Numerous types of businesses are creating e-letters for clients, potential clients, users of product, and even members of the general public who subscribe. In fact, many firms have given up producing a printed promotional newsletter and have put all this information on their Website or e-letter. The Web will be discussed further later in this chapter.

A promotional tool used by larger firms, especially in collaboration with manufacturers, is the case study. A case study of a particularly interesting or challenging project can be produced as a separate publication. A *case study* tells what the design program was and some unique features of the project, and may include before and after photographs. A case study can also discuss the solution and ideally contains some quotes from the client regarding the quality of the project.

Many commercial design firms develop a variety of simple case studies to include in materials needed for proposal submissions. A case study can be short enough to fit on one page, with space for a photograph. Complex projects, obviously, will require a longer case study in order to include several photographs. They also can be inserted into a brochure to show the firm's special expertise. Some firms also include case studies as part of their Web page. The same kinds of considerations mentioned for a newsletter need to be taken into account when the firm is determining whether or not to utilize case studies as a promotional tool. A sample case study is now included on the CD. It is Item 20-1.

Perkins&Will

Chicago. New York. Washington
Architects. Engineers. Planners. Interior & Graphic Designers

PROGRESS

Facilities Management: Controlling Physical Assets

Reduction in demand for basic and consumer goods and services, slow receivables, lay-offs, and changing capital markets are phenomena almost all sectors of the economy have faced to some degree during the early 80's. The result has been commitment to tighter management of an organization's assets. Asset management includes people, equipment, and facilities. It is no surprise, then, that a full service architecture, engineering and interior design firm like Perkins & Will has experienced increased interest from its clientele in a specialized section of this process—Facilities Management.

In its most comprehensive sense, facilities management is the process of inventorying and evaluating the location, condition, function, and economic value of an organiza-

tion's physical assets. In other times we called this systematic effort Master Planning. While the terminology has changed, the intent has not. Whatever it is called, the objective is to make the best economic use of the real estate owned and/or occupied by an institution. The required activities fall into two categories.

- Identification in an organized and retrievable manner of all pertinent data related to real estate and property assets.

- Analysis of this data to determine the most appropriate means of using and managing the asset.

These analyses take on many different forms depending on an organization's specific objectives. They can deal with land, build-

ings, improvements, interior space, or furnishings. They can address immediate needs for space or cash, or they can position the company to respond intelligently to future conditions.

Furnishings

Beginning with the most tangible facilities, companies are looking at their furnishings, carpeting and other moveable equipment to determine whether they are functional, for how long, and what they are worth. When one real estate investment trust recently acquired two neighboring, but dissimilar office buildings, it decided to market the buildings as one unit. To achieve this, the public had to view the two buildings as related even though the architecture, bay

continued on page 2

HARTFORD PLAZA
Chicago, Illinois

Two downtown Chicago high-rises were the focus of efforts to unify the buildings visually through new signage programs and renovation of main floors and public areas. Tenant standards were developed

for various interior design elements; the overall conceptual scheme was designed to allow for phased implementation so the buildings could remain open while renovation proceeded

April 1983 1

FIGURE 20-1.

A sample of a newsletter that provides information about projects with which this design firm recently has been involved. (Reprinted with permission, Perkins & Will, Chicago, IL; Photo: Eugene Balzer)

Neither the newsletter nor the case study needs to be printed in color but should be well done. Today, high-quality color laser printers and color photocopiers make it much easier for smaller design firms to incorporate color into their newsletters and case studies.

Books

Writing a book is another way of demonstrating expertise and authority and can be a very effective promotional tool for the interior designer. Books take a substantial amount of time to write and require greater commitment than writing an article. However, it is a way of showing more expertise and credibility, especially if the topic is related to the designer's specialty.

Perhaps a designer's expertise is in retail store design and he or she writes a book on that topic. A book about the many considerations that go into designing an effective sales background for a retail store can be a very useful contribution to the design industry body of knowledge, as well as a promotional tool for that designer. The book will give prestige to the interior designer, and the designer can add this to his or her resumé.

Books take time, a great deal of time to research, write, rewrite, obtain photographs or other graphics for, and go through the editing process. Practicing interior designers who decide it might be nice to write a book as a way to contribute to the profession should have discussions with publishers or someone that has written a book before they begin the process of starting a manuscript proposal. Do not contemplate writing a book as a promotional tool if you are disorganized and your business does not allow your being away while you write the book. Publishers only give the writer a certain length of time to complete the manuscript. They expect to receive it on time—or nearly so.

You can find complete instructions on how to submit a manuscript proposal from many book publishers. In fact, you can go to the Web site for John Wiley & Sons and obtain information concerning submitting proposals to this publisher. There are also numerous reference books at bookstores on this topic.

COMPETITIONS

Even though entering a competition can be somewhat time-consuming and even expensive (because professional photography is needed), any size or type of design firm can enter design competitions and potentially gain publicity from the entry. It is also a promotional activity that can bring a designer or a design firm a great deal of publicity. Interior designers may produce incredible design work, but sometimes only a few people get to see how creative this work is. Competitions provide a great deal of publicity. Since the competitions are judged by design peers, peer recognition for outstanding work is recognized.

Many organizations and venues sponsor design competitions. The first place to look for competitions is on the local level. Most professional association chapters sponsor annual competitions. With the client's permission, the designer can enter recent work. These competitions are juried by other interior designers or those in the interior design industry. The award itself is always something that can be displayed in the office and serves to announce to potential clients that the designer has a reputation for doing exceptional work. In addition, the competition organization generally submits information about the award winners to the local media. When the awards are announced in a local magazine, the designer can obtain reprints to give out to potential clients. Local awards are sometimes announced in national trade publications. Some chapters also have student design competitions that are juried by members of the local chapter.

Competitions occur on the national level, sponsored by professional associations or manufacturers. Awards are announced at national conferences, and information about the awards is often published in trade magazines. The information is commonly submitted to the local media in the award winners' hometowns. Many competitions have categories for student entries. The Fuessler Group publishes the *Publicity Directory of the Design, Engineering and Building Industries* on their Internet site listed in the Internet References. It is also a catalog of award programs. It can generally be found in most large libraries. You can find out about competitions through associations' announcements on their Web site and announcements in trade magazines, and direct mailings to interior designers from various sources.

Design firms must target which competitions to enter, since there are numerous opportunities for entering competitions throughout the year. Entering a project in a competition is not without expense. A fee is almost always required and can range from $50 for a local competition to over $300 for some national ones. Of course, time is needed to prepare the materials in the required format.

Professional photographs of the project are needed as well. A particular competition may not require that photographs be taken by a professional, but few interior designers win competitions, especially at the national level, with nonprofessional photographs. Photographing a project can cost several thousands of dollars. Like any other promotional tool, however, the cost of photos must be weighed against the possible benefits. The designer needs to be sure that the contract with the photographer grants the designer rights to use the photos in other marketing tools. The photographs taken for a competition can be used in many ways—for the firm's photo portfolio, as well as in brochures, newsletters, case studies, and direct-mail programs. They might be needed for proposal pamphlets, and they also can be integrated into the firm's Web site.

The professional recognition that comes with winning or placing in a competition is very worthwhile. Recognition from peers is especially nice to receive, and recognition from peers in one's professional association is even sweeter to some designers. Entering and winning or placing in national competitions gains publicity for the designer beyond its local market. The fact that the designer has won an award often plays an important part in a client's decision to hire a designer, as it is another evidence item of the designer's expertise.

It is advisable to prepare entry materials very carefully and professionally. Jurors are likely to respond to a dramatic presentation as much as to the creativity shown in the project; however, the design firm must prepare its entry to meet the requirements of the competition. Deviating in any way can eliminate an otherwise excellent project from consideration. Do not forget to get the client's approval before submitting drawings and photographs. In fact, many competitions include a required release form as part of the competition package. If your firm is new to the awards competition scenario, start on the local level or with smaller competitions. Get your feet wet and then move up to the more prestigious ones. Remember, the larger the pool of competitors is, as in a large, national, or international competition, the more difficult it will be for you to win. Good luck!

What Would You Do?

The design process for a large second home progressed very satisfactorily with client approvals at each stage of the process. Client approvals were obtained before any product was ordered, as was stipulated in the design contract. The interior designer specified and provided all the movable furniture and custom cabinets except the cabinets in the kitchen and bathrooms.

The interior designer had convinced the client to purchase a custom entertainment center for the master suite and a custom entertainment center for the family room. The clients were excited about the design of both cabinets, especially when the designer explained the fine finish of both units and all the features that could be built into the cabinets.

As the cabinetmaker was installing the custom unit in the family room, he realized it didn't fit right into the alcove. He told the interior designer and client—who happened to be there at the time—that the cabinet had to go back to the shop for some adjustments for it to fit. The client asked the cabinetmaker who made the mistake, and the cabinetmaker said he made the two pieces according to the drawings sent by the interior designer. "Didn't you check with the builder on the size of the alcove and verify that dimension before constructing the cabinet?" asked the interior designer. "I did check with him and nothing had changed from the drawings," retorted the cabinetmaker.

Two weeks later when the designer faxed a revised drawing and cost estimate for the family room cabinet, the client e-mailed back and said he would not pay for something that the designer did not do correctly. He also canceled the entertainment center for the master suite, saying that he could no longer trust the designer.

DIRECT MAIL

Shelia and Tom decided to send a letter to former clients—those that they had done work for over the past three years—inquiring about a "tune-up" and special price for that tune-up of their projects. They did a mix of commercial and residential design work, so the letters went to both of these types of clients. Five clients contacted them and set up appointments.

Direct mail can mean just about anything—from mailing letters to sending out brochures or newsletters. Since printing and postage are ongoing expenses, the key is to get the mailed items to the right people. To do this, the firm must have a good mailing list. For many firms—like Shelia and Tom—the mailing list for direct-mail promotion starts with former clients. Additions to the list might come from researching chamber of commerce membership lists, appropriate professional association membership lists, or buying a mailing list from a service.

We all receive a huge amount of unsolicited junk mail. A promotional mailing from a design firm will be considered junk mail by many receivers. Most junk mail ends up in the wastebasket. Often, junk mail that is sent to businesses ends up the same way. Even the best-prepared mailings from business to business receive a small return rate when they are mailed to unknown people.[2] Therefore, it is important to consider carefully what is being mailed, why it is being sent, and to whom it is being sent.

If a letter is being sent to former clients, it should be a document that the designer has taken time to prepare. It should be flawlessly written with no grammatical errors and certainly no typos. If the designer is not a good written communicator, have the letter checked by a trusted mentor or consultant. When a more generalized mailing is considered—meaning it is not necessarily going only to former clients—it must have impact and should be designed to catch the eye of the receiver. Direct-mail items need to be well designed and creatively thought out. A good graphics designer or marketing specialist might be the answer for designing the mailing. Direct mailings to generate business from totally new clients might be announcements of sales, holiday promotions, and seminars. They give the firm a chance to see how the receiver reacts to the mailing and to make an appointment to further discuss its contents or answer any questions that the receiver may have.

Direct mail can be sent to residential clients as well as to businesses. The items sent should be prepared for, and focused on, that particular audience—a letter or brochure for a commercial client, obviously, will not be received well at a residence, and vice versa. The items sent should provide information and should be sufficiently interesting to entice the receiver to call or write for more information. But nothing will happen automatically. For the greatest-possible number of leads from direct mailings, the designer should follow up with a personal call.

Now it is becoming increasingly common for direct-mail items to arrive via e-mail. Of course, e-mail spam is a problem, and these direct mailings should only go to people that the designer knows, such as former clients, who will be less likely to object—and reject—the e-mailed letter. Unsolicited faxes are not permitted by law, and the designer should not use facsimile broadcasts to a potential client that is unknown to the designer. It is important to check with your attorney to find out if unsolicited e-mailings and faxes are permitted in your jurisdiction.

There are a great number of techniques and strategies in direct mail that the designer can use as a promotional tool to develop client leads. The professional who wants to consider using direct mail is urged to check the references. For direct-mail programs to businesses, the best book that I have found remains Robert W. Bly's *Business to Business Direct Marketing*. A simple worksheet has been included on the CD to help you develop an idea for the contents of a direct mail item. The designation for this Item is 20-2.

SPEAKING AT SEMINARS AND MEETINGS

Melissa, who teaches a building codes class at the interior design program at a local community college, has developed a 60-minute overview that is suitable for developers and business owners who are not interior designers. She markets the program within the state to various trade groups.

Whether the designer is in residential or some area of commercial interior design, speaking at seminars can be a very rewarding process and effective promotional tool. Residential clients are interested in all kinds of topics related to the design of homes, and interior designers who make themselves available to speak to civic and club groups may find a ready group of listeners, as well as potential customers. Local business trade associations look for experts who can provide them with information at their monthly meetings. The designer may even be asked to speak at regional or national conventions of professional groups of potential clients. Many interior designers have found this to be a successful way to market themselves or their design firm while giving something back to the profession through the seminar information they disseminate.

As with articles and books, the designer should choose a topic of interest to the potential audience and something that can help project expertise. For example, an interior designer was asked to speak to a local accounting group shortly after the Americans with Disabilities Act went into effect in the 1990s. This professional group was concerned about how the law would impact their offices. A presentation was made on the law, in general, and how design issues could resolve the impact of this law on their offices.

Speaking at a national conference involves research and preparation before asking to be involved in a conference. The first step is to obtain conference proceedings or convention brochures from last year's convention to help determine what an appropriate topic might be for the next convention. After determining a topic or two, the next step is requesting information about how to go about sending in a proposal. National meetings receive numerous proposals for seminars, and many now have advisory groups to help determine the speakers. Send your proposal in early. The next year's convention is planned shortly after this year's convention ends. If you want to start speaking at the local level, contact association or club program chairs. They often set schedules a year in advance as well.

At the presentation, bring along plenty of business cards, your brochure, or other handouts that the audience can take with them to keep your name in front of them. This is completely proper, unless the organization has a policy against it.

If you are afraid of making a presentation—and this is feared by a great number of people—work up to giving a presentation by speaking to smaller groups. Volunteer to give a presentation or critique at interior design program classes. Chair an association committee so that you have to speak before groups. Take a public-speaking class—a good idea for students and also for professionals. The class can help you polish your presentation techniques and build confidence. Joining a group such as Toastmasters® is another way to learn to speak before a group. This type of group is a mixed group of professionals who use the meetings to learn how to speak to groups.

If you do not want to actually give the seminar, host one. Playing the host will force you to speak before a group. This will, again, help you gain confidence so that someday you will be ready to take the podium yourself! There are many books on how to prepare presentations. Check the references for suggestions.

PREMIUMS

Have you been to a trade show or conference and received something like a ballpoint pen with a company name on it? Or perhaps you received a bag with a company logo when you registered for the trade show. Maybe it was a stack of memo pads with a company name. Interior designers are used to receiving these types of premiums from vendors and suppliers. A *premium* is a product that has a logo, slogan, or other words or graphics printed on an object. Other examples are coffee mugs, letter openers, architectural scales, small calculators, and numerous other items with the firm's name and logo. A premium can also be something that the company sells, such as the classic logo T-shirt. Giving a premium is an easy way for the firm to get its name recognized by a reasonably wide audience. Just think of how much recognition Mouseketeer ears have brought Walt Disney Corporation!

Premiums can be reasonably priced or quite costly. They come in all types, colors, and price ranges. Even the small firm can offer a premium by having its logo and name printed on something small and useful, such as memo pads or pencils. Remember that the premium itself says a lot about the firm, just as the message you have printed does. If you want your firm to be known for quality, do not send out cheap pens that break after a few uses or a scale that is not in scale!

PROPOSALS

It is not unusual for a residential client to interview at least three interior designers before deciding on a firm for a project. In fact, three seems to be the minimum number of designers that associations provide to clients through association referral programs. In commercial interior design, a client might want to research and interview many more interior design firms than three before making a decision on hiring a firm. As competition has increased, clients have had their pick of design firms.

The proposal process has been around for many years. The term "proposal" has been used to mean a contract proposal or an overview of how the designer intends to proceed with a project. In this context, however, the *proposal* is a response to a request for a proposal---often abbreviated into the acronym RFP— issued by a client. It is not a contract in this context.

When a client decides to use the proposal process to obtain an interior design firm, the process might start with a *request for qualifications* (RFQ). The request for qualifications—sometimes called a *letter of interest* (LOI)—is a way that clients can prescreen a number of firms, focusing on the experience and qualifications of firms. Generally, the RFQ asks for staff resumés, brochures, references, and other experience documentations. After a client reviews these RFQs, he or she will use this prequalified group as the primary group to receive RFP responses. It is most commonly used on very large projects and might be something that only the largest interior design firms ever encounter. A sample RFP letter that a client would send to numerous design firms has been included on the CD. Look for Item 20-3.

The RFP, on the other hand, is something that many interior designers are very familiar with for a variety of projects, especially in commercial interior specialties. It is an efficient way for clients to obtain information and, to some extent, ideas on how to solve their project issues. A client issues an RFP to design firms whom it might like to consider to have execute a project. An RFP can also be issued to search the design market for a design firm that has the qualifications the client feels are important for the project. Proposals have thus become an important, even critical, marketing tool for many interior design firms (see Figure 20-2).

From the client's point of view, the RFP involves gathering a lot of information on perhaps dozens of design firms. The proposal prequalifies the firms, because the information required is very specific, and if a firm cannot meet the requirements and supply the information requested, it generally will not even bother to reply. Since developing a proposal takes so much time, it also results in proposals being returned only by firms that are seriously interested in the project. The proposals are reviewed by the client, and he or she can eliminate any other firms that do not meet the qualifications spelled out in the RFP. This actually saves the client time and money, since the client (1) gets responses from firms that he or she might never have thought of for the project; (2) reviews proposals at his or her convenience; (3) does not invest a large amount of time interviewing a large number of design firms, some of which may be unqualified; and (4) may find a group of highly qualified firms (theoretically).

From the interior designer's point of view, an RFP gives firms sufficient information about the project so that they can decide if they wish to take on the project. Since the client prepares the RFP, the design firm may have the opportunity to be considered for some projects the firm might never have known about. In carefully reviewing the RFP, the design firm also can forecast the possibility of obtaining an interview with the client—that is to say, if the design firm has an insufficient amount of experience in executing certain sizes of retail spaces, it is unlikely that it will be granted an interview. In such cases, it would not be reasonable for the design firm to spend the time putting the proposal materials together. Table 20-1 is a standard outline for a proposal.

The decision as to which firms the client will interview rests on the material provided in the proposal. This makes the proposal a very important document. Clients do not make a decision about a design firm purely on the basis of the proposal. After the proposals are reviewed, a list of design firms that the client most wants to interview emerges. This list is usually called a *short list*, because the number of firms is commonly limited to three to six (depending on the size and complexity of the project). Interviews are then set up with each firm on the short list.

It is very important to realize that the client controls the content and format of the proposal. The design firm must respond with the required information in the proposal. Exactly what is required is spelled out in the RFP. This control is

FIGURE 20-2.

Proposal materials in response to an RFP. (Reproduced with permission, Fred Messner, Phoenix Design One, Tempe, AZ; photo by Dawson Henderson.)

used by the client so that all proposals will be treated equally. The design firm has an obligation to provide all the information requested and to present it in the order required. Leaving out sections or making the proposal presentation different from what was requested can lead to disqualification.

A typical proposal contains the information outlined in Table 20-1. If a design firm decides to respond to an RFP, it will have to include information pertinent to each of these issues and perhaps others. The instructions in the RFP will inform the design firms as to how much latitude they have in what is to be stated and what additional information can be included. Each part is critical and

TABLE 20-1.

A Typical Outline of a Proposal in Response to an RFP.

Note that the actual content of the proposal is governed by the information requested by the client.

- Cover letter
- Title page
- Table of contents
- Executive summary: Overview of contents
- Problem analysis: Design firm's opportunity to explain its understanding of the client's needs
- Scope of services: What will be done in response to what was required
- Project experience: Information about projects similar in nature to the proposed project
- Project approach: Information about how the firm will provide services and will manage the project
- Staffing: Who will be responsible for the project

    Staff resumés

- Schedule
- List of deliverables: Documents the firm expects to prepare for the project
- Budget and fees
- Financial information on the design firm
- References
- Miscellaneous optional information:
  Additional project case studies
  Article reprints
  Other information the firm wishes to provide

must be written in response to the specific project, client, and instructions. Although many proposals allow room for what amounts to "boilerplate information," that is, standardized sections that can apply to more than one project, the proposal must still read as if it were written only for the client. Other parts are written specifically for the project. For example, information on past similar projects may very well be reusable boilerplate information, while comments about a firm's experience with sustainable design may be very specific to the project's needs. Proposals for commercial projects can easily run about 25 pages for a small project and more than 50 pages for complex projects. So this activity should not be taken lightly.

Table 20-2 provides several tips on preparing a RFP proposal. Many of the references can provide additional help and ideas on preparing a proposal. Chapter 1 provides information concerning the presentation phase of the proposal process.

Design firms that have been successful with the proposal process are exceptionally good at identifying hot-button issues within the RFP. A *hot-button issue* is one of critical concern to the client. For a school district, the hot-button issue might be quality design at an economical price. Other frequent hot-button issues include a concern for sustainable design, a very tight schedule, a concern for value engineering, a desire for innovative design ideas, and a concern for cultural design influences. Clients do not always describe needs succinctly or as obviously. The design firm would then have to attempt to identify the issues. This, obviously, is more difficult and challenging for the design firm.

TABLE 20-2.

Tips in Preparing an RFP.

- Good writing is a must.
- Always be clear and factual, using language that will be easily understood by the client.
- Ensure perfect spelling and grammar.
- Make sure it completely speaks to the issues the client has stated.
- Follow the outline the client has used rather than your own outline.
- Be sure that content has addressed client hot-button issues.
- Ensure that scope of services is not vague and that it contains sufficient descriptions to clarify what you will be doing.
- Create an interesting-looking proposal with the use of photography and color photocopying.
- Present material in two or three columns rather than one column.
- Include testimonials from references using excerpts in quotes followed by the source name.
- Integrate color in bullets or headlines.
- Use loose-leaf pages rather permanent binding to make it easier to insert additional items and move things around.

In this context, proposals are not design contracts. A proposal is a marketing tool by which a design firm gets to tell its story as to why it is best qualified to do a project. Generally, the proposal does not include the same information that a contract must have. However, RFPs from clients may ask design firms for their desired fee for the project. This is usually provided under a separate cover letter in a sealed envelope.

SUMMARY

As the reader can see from this chapter and Chapter 19, there are numerous ways that the interior design firm can use promotion to make its existence known to potential customers. Deciding how to go about promoting the interior design practice is never an easy one. The small firm has a limited amount of resources in both dollars and time to devote to finding new clients. Yet, in some ways, it has the greatest need to market itself. Larger firms can often depend upon its reputation and referrals. Nevertheless, it must budget for many kinds of promotional tools when collateral items are needed for presentations, proposals, and prospective client requests.

Chapters 19 and 20 have presented a great deal of information and ideas on the kinds of promotional tools that are available to interior design firms. Which items are right for any one firm can best be determined by a review of Chapter 18 and the marketing plan. The next two chapters essentially discuss what a design firm should do once a prospective client shows interests in the firm. Chapters 21 and 22 focus on the selling and presentation processes.

REFERENCES

1. Harding, 1994, p. 24.
2. Bly, 1994, p. 42.

CHAPTER 21

Selling Strategies

Key Terms and Concepts

These key terms and concepts are important to material in this chapter. Many of these terms will be utilized in other chapters as well. Be sure you understand these items as you read this chapter.

Terms and Concepts

Selling	Lead
Intangibles	Qualifying
Services are perishable	Probing
Services are actions yet to be performed	Open probe
	Closed probe
Prospecting	Features
Prospects	Benefits
Cold calling	Etiquette
Warm calling	

Critical Issues

After completing this chapter you should be able to:

- Explain how selling is only one part of promotion and marketing.
- Discuss how the information on why it is harder to sell services than products can be used to improve the marketing of services.
- Explain what it means for services to be "perishable."
- Explain the importance of building a professional relationship with clients.
- List the steps in the selling process, and describe activities in each step.
- Discuss several ideas on where to develop leads of potential customers.
- Explain the selling technique of probing, and offer a suggested sequence of questions to help uncover a client's specific needs for interior design services.
- Compare the use of features versus benefits in the offering of interior design services and a typical type of interior design product.
- Summarize why it is important for a design professional to be aware of and use good business etiquette at all times.

As you will recall, personal selling is one of the many ways that a design firm markets its services to potential clients. Personal selling is also important in selling the design contract (or any other method by which they wish to be compensated) in order to begin the project. Designers must also sell their design concepts as the project progresses. Designers also sell products—literally and figuratively.

Only very rarely does an interior designer have the opportunity to become involved in a project without using some selling strategies. The best design idea will become a reality only if the designer and design firm can convince the client to buy it. Most of the time, a relationship between the client and the designer must be built, and the designer must work very hard to finally obtain agreement from the client. Most of the time, the designer needs a lot of skill in selling to achieve an agreement.

Some designers find it extremely easy to sell concepts or products. Others feel frustrated by a lack of success in this area. We hear about the proverbial "born salesperson." But designers who can successfully sell ideas and products are not just "born." It is a skill that becomes easier with practice and experience. Learning techniques about how to sell more effectively also helps make the selling situation more successful.

This chapter discusses several selling techniques that are used by designers. The focus of this chapter is on selling interior design services; however, much of what is discussed applies also to the selling of products. We begin by discussing the differences in selling services versus products. This section is followed by comments on relationship building. The chapter continues with an overview of the selling process and includes a few techniques that can help bring the sales encounter to a successful conclusion. Working with clients includes understanding a certain amount of business etiquette, and this topic has been added to this chapter. Chapter 22 will focus on design presentations and discuss the parts of the selling process that relate to making a successful presentation.

WHAT IS SELLING?

Amanda and Tom were just finishing up their presentation to the building selection committee for a project at the university that would involve the redesign of the interior of the student union. They had made the short list and were very happy that they had an opportunity to explain how their firm would approach the project should they be awarded the contract. Amanda has great one-on-one presence with clients, and so she really worked hard relating to the five committee members. Tom focused on discussing the technical methodologies they would use.

Selling, like marketing, involves finding out what the client wants and providing it. But unlike marketing, *selling* consists of personal, often one-on-one, communication. According to the *World Book Encyclopedia*, selling "involves two-way communication between a salesperson and a customer. It enables the buyer to ask questions about a product [or service] and receive additional information about it immediately."[1] Some people do not like selling or salespeople, because they believe that selling involves manipulating people to get them to buy what they do not want. Unfortunately, this kind of selling is practiced by many so-called salespeople, but this is not the kind of selling we wish to talk about.

In their interaction with clients, interior designers do their utmost to find out what their clients really want in the way of design services and products, and then try to provide those services and products. Satisfying clients and making a sale makes both parties winners. It is not necessary for the designer to try to sell clients what they do not want. In fact, it is bad for business.

The activities of this profession find interior designers involved in many selling situations. Interactions with clients create a constant stream of one-on-one and small-group communications exchanges that are, in essence, sales encounters. The most successful interior designers learn techniques that help them navigate through these encounters as effortlessly and productively as possible. They use sales techniques to obtain initial interviews and to make marketing presentations. Sales techniques are then utilized during that type of meeting to convince the client to hire the designer. All the mini-presentations and meetings held during the course of the project are other sales types of opportunities. Many times clients pose objections to concepts, floor plans, colors, and products that the designer has worked so hard to research and prepare. The designer must find ways to handle these objections, explain why certain things have been specified, and bring the presentation to a successful conclusion. These back and forth communications form the heart of the sales association with the client. And, as many interior designers will tell the uninitiated, none of this is easy to do.

SELLING SERVICES VERSUS PRODUCTS

Interior design, above all else, is providing a service to the client. That service is to gain an understanding of what the client needs and then providing ideas, applying knowledge, preparing documents, and in many ways taking care of bringing the project from concept to completion. A more detailed definition of what an interior designer does has been presented in Chapter 1 and the appendix.

What makes selling interior design services so difficult is that the service and the proposal are intangible; it is, after all, a concept that the designer is selling the client. At first, it exists only in the mind of the designer. The designer must translate that concept into words and graphics so that the client understands it and "sees" it as the designer sees it. It only becomes real when the project has been completed. However, the designer must convince the client to trust him or her in order for it to be completed.

It is very important for professionals and students to understand that what they are selling to clients is not the chair, sofa, desk, or other products. Certainly, many interior designers wish to sell those tangible items. Interior designers are first selling trust that they can do what is required in a professional manner, concepts and ideas on how to meet the client's needs, knowledge to know which products are most appropriate, knowledge to meet codes and good planning precepts, and the ability to execute any other tasks needed to complete the project requirements. Most of these concepts involve intangibles.

Selling a service is selling an action that is yet to be performed. For the client, it is difficult to know what he or she is going to get until it is done. In addition, the client does not keep the service; the client keeps the result of the service—in this case, a beautiful interior. Perhaps this is why so many people have difficulty understanding what goes into doing an interiors project. The client often does not "see" all the work that is done to complete the concept of a project before he or she is presented with floor plans, boards, and specifications.

A lot of what constitutes interior design service is the creation of a concept and getting the client to buy that concept. How the living room will look or how the restaurant will look is difficult for many clients to understand. Most have a difficult time visualizing the colors and fabrics on the pieces being recommended. Many clients also are not used to reading floor plans, which makes it difficult for them to visualize the interior space plans. The designer must use all of his or her technical training and verbal selling skills to explain how the space will look—before it has been completed.

It is generally a lot easier to sell a product, because it is tangible. Clients can see it, feel it, and use it. They like it or they don't like it. They either agree with the designer that the piece would be perfect in the living room or office or they don't agree.

"Whereas most goods are produced first, then sold and consumed, most services are sold first and then produced and consumed simultaneously."[2] The designer must sell the client on his or her ability to solve the client's problem, execute the requirements of the project within a budget, and actually make it all happen. The client has to have a great deal of trust in the designer's ability to follow through with the plans. This is why experience in a design niche, reputation, knowledge of the design process, and knowledge about products are so important for the interior designer to develop and for the client to accept.

Finally, a service is said to be "perishable." What this means is that, since a service only takes place *as* it is taking place, it cannot be inventoried or resold. Goods, of course, can be inventoried and sold or subsequently returned, and the product can then be resold to someone else. Once a designer has committed to work for a client, he or she cannot spend that *same* time working for another client. Of course, designers may work on more than one project at a time, but not literally. He or she cannot draft a floor plan for one client and literally draft a different floor plan for another client at the same time anymore than a student can be studying for an exam and having fun at a party at the same time. If something happens that causes the client to not be satisfied with the results, the designer might not get the compensation that he or she was expecting. In addition, if the designer is committed to one project, he or she probably cannot take on another project that perhaps might be more interesting.

Successfully selling the design concept is the culmination of the design-selling responsibilities of the interior design professional. Understanding the differences between selling services and selling products points out how important it is for the interior designer to understand the selling process and learn how to be successful in navigating that process. Neglecting to learn these differences will impact the designer's ability to sell services and produce sufficient revenue to maintain the business.

The Buyer Decision-Making Process

Buyers consciously or unconsciously go through a process when they desire to purchase something. It doesn't matter if the purchase is a product or service. It does matter, however, if the good or service has special value—such as the selection of a doctor or interior designer—or the cost of the good or service is rather high as defined by the buyer. The process is very similar for a residential and commercial client. It is often suggested that the commercial client may take longer to make a decision, as many decision maker levels might be involved in the decision. Residential designers also say that many of their clients seemingly take forever to make a decision!

The recognized buyer decision-making process involves five steps.

Step 1 is the recognition of a need for something. The stronger the need, the more quickly the buyer moves through this step and into the rest of the process.

Step 2 is where the buyer seeks information about the purchase need. The buyer might seek general information directly from providers, or from friends and relatives, and advertising. Today buyers often research products and service providers via the Internet. Some buyers want a lot of information before they purchase. They will research more deeply on the Internet or, in the case of goods, spend time at stores asking questions of salespeople. For services, the client might want to interview three or more interior designers before making a decision to hire.

Step 3 can be thought of as an extension of Step 2. As they gather information, the buyer evaluates alternatives. A buyer obtains some information about the different possibilities and begins to narrow choices. Exactly what is important is very personal to the buyer. What may be of importance to one client is likely to be of less importance to another. For example, one client may feel that the interior designer's project management responsibility is a key importance. Another client may be more interested in the designer's creative skills.

Step 4 brings the purchase decision. We have all purchased things impulsively—that's why all that candy and gum are positioned at the cash register in grocery stores and accessories are placed near the cash wrap in a clothing store. Interior design services are rarely purchased impulsively. The purchase decision on interior design services and many types of goods for interior spaces are deliberate decisions, often taking a lot of time.

When a purchase decision is made or nearly so, then the price becomes a more important factor. Of course, the price of the goods or services was probably a factor in the evaluation of alternatives step as well; however, now is the time that price negotiation really takes place. In general, a reasonable price is relative based on how the client perceives price. Naturally, the more money the client has, the more reasonable a high price will seem to them—within reason. Everyone has his or her ceiling on how much they are willing to pay for services or goods. A reasonable price is also tied to the concept of value in the buyer's mind. The more the buyer values something, the greater price they are willing to pay.

Step 5 is the inevitable post-purchase evaluation. Depending on the buyer and what transpired during his or her evaluation of alternatives, the price, and numerous other issues, the buyer may have "buyer's remorse," a feeling that he or she may have made a bad choice. On the other end of the spectrum is the buyer who is elated with the choice made and can't wait to proceed. Most are somewhat in the middle, happy to have made the decision or purchase and pleased to get the goods to the home or office or begin the actual design process.

There is much in the general business literature on this topic, as in general the buyer has more disposable income right now than ever before. Several books are listed in the references that might be of interest to the reader.

BUILDING CLIENT RELATIONSHIPS

If you go to a particular restaurant on a regular basis, do you ask for the same waitress? Do you have a favorite sales clerk at your preferred clothing store? Marketing and sales experts continually discuss the importance of building client relationships in this highly competitive world. In building client relationships, the focus is on helping the design firm and the client become partners—ideally working toward long-term commitments. It pays for the designer to build an ongoing relationship with the client, since the cost of prospecting for new clients is greater than that of maintaining existing client relationships. Designers and clients may become friends, not only working with each other but also socializing, although this is not always the case. Clients prefer to work with someone whom they already know rather than to find a new interior designer. Relationships should be built so that clients think of the same designer and firm whenever they need interior design services.

Certainly, it is not easy for designers to develop this type of partnership with many clients. For some clients, interior design services are something that they purchase once, maybe twice in a lifetime. These encounters may happen many years apart. Because these encounters happen with many intervening years, a relationship with an interior designer is not easy to sustain. Furthermore, for some clients, the relationship does not last, because they had a bad experience. On the other hand, sometimes the designer does not want to continue the relationship because there are many very difficult clients.

The interior design of a residence is an intensely personal experience for clients. It is their home. It is where they will raise the children, share family accomplishments and perhaps tragedies, and entertain friends and business associates. Bringing a stranger into the home can be difficult for the family. The designer must show concern, thoughtfulness, and empathy for the clients' interiors problems. Being totally businesslike certainly has its place, but so does having a sense of humor and knowing when it is all right to relax and be casual.

The interior design of a commercial space is less personal, but the relationship that must be built between the parties is no less important. The client may trust the designer to specify hundreds of thousands of dollars worth of construction and products, using the client's financial resources. The client certainly must trust the designer to create an interior that solves whatever the goals and needs of the client may be. This trust is a very important part of the relationship. Since many commercial projects take several months or even years to complete, a personal relationship may also develop between the client and interior designer.

Developing a sustainable relationship with clients is not an easy task. Despite the difficulties that may be encountered, doing so will very likely result in repeat business, referrals, and success for the design firm. The trust that must be built between the designer and the client takes time; it is easy to lose and difficult to gain but worth every effort to achieve.

What Would You Do?

Rose Marie has started her own design practice after having been fired from Miller/Jones Interior Architecture. Rose Marie was a competent designer, but about three months before her boss decided to fire her, she started making mistakes that cost the design firm in extra services. One example of her recent problems is that when she had to leave town on family business, she did not leave any instructions for anyone else in the firm about her pending jobs. Rose Marie also failed to leave a forwarding phone number and didn't get in touch with the office for ten days.

During a presentation that Rose Marie was making to a new client, the client commented that he is also talking to the Miller/Jones firm Rose Marie used to work for. Rose Marie makes very disparaging comments about Miller/Jones, which seem to dissuade the client from considering that firm.

THE SELLING PROCESS

In all selling, a flow of activities and communications takes place in order for the selling process to be successful. The reader already understands the design process; now we will discuss the selling process. It is generally accepted that there are seven steps in the selling process (see Table 21-1). The first three—prospecting, qualifying, and preparation—are covered in this chapter, whereas the last four are discussed in the next chapter.

Prospecting

It would be nice if clients purchased services from interior designers on a regular basis—once a happy customer, always a happy customer! Unfortunately, interior design services are not a commodity such as apparel items that can be repeatedly

TABLE 21-1.

The Steps in the Selling Process.

1. *Prospecting.* Locate viable prospective clients.
2. *Qualifying.* Clarify if these prospects can work with you.
3. *Preparation.* Do homework and prepare everything needed for the presentation.
4. *Presentation.* Make appropriate presentation to the client.
5. *Overcome objections.* Resolve client questions or concerns.
6. *Close.* Ask for the sale or job.
7. *Follow up.* Provide documentation or actions promised during the presentation.

obtained by the client in a sustained manner. Some types of service firms have a continuation of service—attorneys and accountants, for example. Of course, clients do sometimes come back to the same designer. That is a big reason why developing a good business and professional relationship with clients is so important. However, finding new clients is really an important activity for all types and sizes of interior design practices.

Finding new clients does, to some extent, include "digging around" for them. That is probably why the term "prospecting" has been associated with the sales process. *Prospecting* is the process of locating new clients and obtaining appointments with them in order to discuss how the design firm may assist the client. *Prospects* are potential clients in the firm's business area or target market who may require design services. They include clients who have worked with competitors, though not clients who already are under contract with competitors.

Target market research and the marketing plan are used to identify potential clients in the firm's business area (see Chapter 18). Potential clients or prospects can also be found in other places. They may be members of social or civic groups to which the designer belongs. They can result from any one of the promotional activities discussed in Chapters 19 and 20.

Another method of finding prospects that designers sometimes use is cold calling. The technique of *cold calling* means that the designer is contacting potential clients whom the designer has not met before. Telephone solicitations and unannounced visits are forms of cold calling. Drop-in visits like door-to-door salespersons or telemarketers are not an effective way for interior designers to find clients. However, some individuals who work in commercial design make drop-in visits to potential clients. Designers do not particularly enjoy cold calling; many feel that it is unprofessional. However, competition sometimes forces designers to make use of cold-calling techniques in order to obtain an initial in-depth meeting with potential clients. Still, cold-calling techniques such as telephone solicitations and drop-in visits are not the most effective means of marketing one's services.

A variation on cold calling is referred to as *warm calling*. In this case, the designer has received some sort of entrée to the client through a referral or mutual acquaintance. A warm call is still a sales call on someone that the designer does not personally know, but it is more inviting because of the referral or introduction by another party.

When a prospect begins to show interest in a firm, he or she might be referred to as a *lead*. Clients who call after seeing an article about the design firm in the newspaper or a trade magazine can be considered leads. Those who respond positively to the idea of a face-to-face meeting to discuss possible design services are leads. By generating leads, the design firm identifies the best prospects for selling the interior design firm's services. When leads are identified, the designer begins the crossover into the next phase of selling—qualifying prospects.

It is not uncommon for the designer to make a brief prospecting presentation before the client allows the designer to make a full presentation. Some designers might refer to this encounter as the initial meeting. Initial meetings are discussed in the next chapter, since they are more a type of presentation than a true prospecting activity. It is difficult to know exactly where this falls in the selling process. Is it part of prospecting or qualifying? Or is it really a type of presentation? Most designers would agree that it doesn't matter; it just needs to occur!

A prospecting presentation requires that the designer gather enough information to explain to the client who the designer is and why the designer is contacting him or her. Since such contacts are usually quite brief—perhaps occurring over the telephone—the designer must get to the point quickly. For example, the following might be the kind of opening a designer could use to make a cold call on a potential client: "Hello, Mr. Stevens. My name is Rhonda Tower, and I am the design director at Robbins and Porter Commercial Interiors. I saw in the Dodge Reports that your firm is planning to add office space at your Dallas facility. It would be our pleasure to make a presentation to you on how Robbins and Porter Commercial Interiors might be of service to your company." Depending on the client's response, Rhonda either has a solid lead or should go on to the next lead on her list.

The goal of prospecting presentations is to obtain an appointment with the client so that the designer may then make a marketing presentation. In order to make a prospecting presentation, the designer must prepare carefully, just as he or she would for any kind of presentation. The designer should script what it is he or she wants to say beforehand. This allows the designer to anticipate questions and objections. It is important for the designer to emphasize the benefits for the client of the potential meeting, not simply how great the designer or firm is. The details of the firm's services can be given at the marketing presentation. Through the script, the designer must tell the client that he or she is interested in being of service to the client.

It is important for the designer to take notes as he or she talks to the potential client. The script may have room for notes below each question. Some designers develop contact sheets or cards to record calls. It is also important for the designer to keep track of names, titles, and key words that might give the designer a hint about the potential of the contact. The call should not be tape-recorded. Recording a telephone conversation or a face-to-face meeting without the other person's permission is unethical and may be illegal.

Qualifying

Identifying potential prospects is only the first step in the process. The designer must also qualify prospects. *Qualifying* means that the designer determines whether or not there is sufficient reason to pursue a prospect. A qualified prospect is one who has been determined to be reasonably likely to contract with the interior designer. Not all prospects will meet this criterion.

A key point about qualifying clients is to devote time to those potential clients who have the greatest likelihood of retaining the designer. Clients who have the greatest likelihood of retaining the designer are those target clients identified in the marketing plan. Qualified prospects must have a need for interior design services, and not all potential clients in the firm's business area are really viable prospects. For the design firm that specializes in restaurant design, for example, facilities that have been open for only a year or so will not need design services for some time. Restaurants that have been open for several years, however, may be looking for some kind of assistance.

Qualified prospects must also be able to pay the fees expected by the interior designer. Can the potential client afford the level of fees the designer requires? There are certainly many potential clients that can utilize the services of an interior design professional, but not all will have the means to afford the fees nor might they be a good credit risk. Credit ratings of commercial clients can be checked, and diplomatic discussions and questioning can be used to check whether the residential client has the income level to afford hiring the designer. Of course, credit checks can also be conducted on residential clients.

Another qualifying criterion most associated with commercial design is whether the prospect has the authority to make a purchasing decision. The designer must get to the person who is in charge, or he or she could be wasting time. Sometimes it is not easy to get to a decision maker. Assistants to upper-level management personnel are very good at keeping unsolicited callers from getting to the executives.

A fully qualified lead usually results in an appointment for a face-to-face meeting. Now the designer is ready for the next step—the preparation of a marketing presentation.

Preparation

You have no doubt heard of or seen presentations made by a colleague where it is obvious that very little if any preparation was made for the presentation. Students frequently make the mistake of presenting their projects without thinking through what they want to say. Designers run to their next meeting with only a vague concept of how they plan to present their company and ideas to a potential client. Whatever the purpose of the presentation, a certain amount of preparation is wise. The more important the presentation is, the more preparation should be undertaken.

I have heard of many designers who like to "wing" a presentation—they simply go to the meeting and discuss things as they come up. This technique might work for a project presentation to clients with whom the designer has a good relationship. It is very unwise for the designer to use when he or she is trying to win a contract with a new client or make the final presentation. And we are talking about marketing presentations where we are trying to impress a potential client so that he or she will hire the designer for that great new project.

Marketing presentations require a great deal of preparation. Whoever has made the initial contact with the client already has obtained some valuable information about the direction and content of the presentation. The following are just a few of the questions that the designer must answer in order to prepare the best possible marketing presentation.

1. What are the prospective project requirements?
2. To whom will the presentation be made?
3. How many people will attend the presentation?
4. Where will the presentation take place?
5. Who from the design firm should be involved in the presentation?
6. What is it about the design firm that the client will want to know?
7. What kind of graphics will be used to evidence the design firm's design expertise?
8. What materials and documents will be given to the client to keep?

The answers to all of these questions and perhaps others will have an influence on the content and format of the presentation itself.

The designer must set the objectives of the presentation yet must keep in mind the concerns of the client. In fact, it is critical in today's highly competitive market that the designer needs to ensure that the presentation addresses the prospective client's questions and concerns or, frankly, the designer will be wasting his or her time. Obviously, the design firm's objective is to obtain the go-ahead to prepare a design contract. But there can be other goals as well. Clarifying the client's needs and showing how the firm can address those needs is at the top of the list. Making sure the prospective client learns about the design firm's design philosophy, methodology in project management, and expertise is very important. With these goals in mind, the designer needs to make decisions about the questions posed above.

An important step is to clarify the identity of the *decision makers*—the person or persons who have the authority to hire the designer. This seems obvious (whoever the designer has contacted to arrange for the presentation); however, this is not always the case. In commercial design, for example, it is not uncommon for the design firm to make the initial contact with a purchasing agent, not the owner or the principal of the company. In such cases, the designer may make an initial presentation to the purchasing agent and a more formal presentation to the owner at a later time. Presentations for many commercial projects often are made to a group of clients. For example, a medical office building may be owned by a group of doctors. In residential design, the designer rarely consults in this early stage with anyone but the owner of the home and the family, but who is the decision maker in the family—the husband or wife?

Who from the design firm will be involved during the project impacts the presentation preparation. This is obvious in a small firm; however, in large firms, the owner or design director must establish who will be expected to execute the project at about the same time that the firm is still trying to secure the project. Some designers may need to be involved in the presentation, since the client likes to know who he or she will be working with during the project. Be careful not to have so many representatives from the firm at the meeting that the client is overwhelmed. Commercial design firms commonly intimidate clients by bringing great numbers of people to the presentation, thinking that the client wants to see the entire team. That is most often only true of presentations after an RFP selection has been made by the client. A good rule of thumb in general is that anyone from the design firm who attends the presentation must participate in the presentation, or he or she should not be there.

Deciding and preparing what to show the client are also very important. For example, clients do not really care to see slides showing how many doctors' offices a design firm has designed if the project involves a retail store. A variety of materials and strategies can be used for the content of a marketing presentation. For a few people, a photo portfolio of previous projects would work quite well, but for a larger group, it would be more effective to use slides, a video presentation, or a computer-based presentation. Whatever type of media is used, it is critical to customize it to the specific client project. Equipment should be checked to make sure that everything works as it is supposed to. Backup equipment, such as a projector bulb or an extension cord, might be necessary if the presentation is at the client's home or facility.

Preparation includes determining where the presentation will take place. Designers generally like to make presentations in the firm's office or studio, if at all practicable. This allows the designer to control the environment, keeping distractions to a minimum while the designer is putting his or her best foot forward. More will be said about the presentation environment later in the next chapter.

The designer will probably have about one hour, maybe two, to make the presentation. It is very important to stick to the time limit, unless the client allows the presentation to continue. An outline is always a good idea to best plan the time. Notes, key words in slides, or a computer-based presentation help the designer cover all the important topics and help ensure that nothing is forgotten. Memorizing the presentation is generally not a good idea, no matter how critical the presentation is. A memorized presentation usually sounds just like that— canned and not personalized for the client.

In organizing the outline of the presentation, the designer should follow the basic form for outlining and organizing material for any report or presentation:

1. Tell them what you are going to tell them.
2. Tell them.
3. Tell them what you have just told them.
4. Ask for the sale.

The first step, "Tell them what you are going to tell them," is quite simply to prepare the information that will create an overview of what will be discussed at the meeting. Key items include reviewing the agenda, introducing other members of the design firm, and briefly describing what each person will discuss. The purpose of the first step is to stimulate the potential client's attention and interest. Even though the client has agreed to meet with the designer (which automatically suggests interest), the client still needs to be given a reason to listen to the presentation. The designer must provide that reason during this step.

The second step, "Tell them," consists of giving the body or the presentation itself. All of this section on preparation indicates the kinds of information that the design firm likely needs to tell the client. What is important as to the "telling" is for all the presenters to be enthusiastic, alert to the client's body language, and responsive to the client's questions. Questions, by the way, are not bad. Questions mean the client is listening. In fact, the designer should involve the client by asking questions of him or her. If the discussion digresses from the outline, the designer should go back to any item that he or she feels still needs to be covered.

Step 3, "Tell them what you have just told them," consists of giving a summary of the points that you have made during the presentation. Do not forget to remind the client of the important points that he or she has heard. Remember to highlight the features and benefits of your services as they relate to the needs that the client has expressed. We will discuss features and benefits in this chapter.

The last step, "Ask for the sale," amounts to requesting that the client give the go-ahead for the firm to prepare a design contract, sign the already prepared contract, or in some other way provide a positive conclusion to the presentation. In other words, this is the "close" of the marketing presentation. More about closing will be discussed in the next chapter.

The last part of the preparation involves making an impression. There is an old saying that you only have one chance to make a first impression. Even though the designer may already have met the prospective client, he or she should not let this mean that appearances can be taken lightly. Everyone should dress professionally and appropriately to meet the client's expectations. Refer to the discussion on business dress for more information on this topic.

The biggest mistake that the designer can make during the marketing presentation is to ignore the client's goals and questions during this very early phase of a potential project. Too many designers get carried away with telling their story and forget to tell the client what he or she wants to know. The designer who has been careful to cover what the design firm wishes to tell about itself as well as to answer the client's questions will conclude the presentation on a positive note.

The remaining parts of the selling process are discussed in the next chapter. We continue with a brief discussion of some verbal techniques that can be used throughout the presentation, regardless of the type of presentation undertaken.

Dress for Business

What we wear makes a difference in how people perceive us. Put on any well-tailored garment and you will probably find yourself standing up a little taller. In business, clothing does speak volumes to those with whom you interact. Whether you are designing a home or an office for the chief executive officer of Sony or the managing partner of a local law firm (or whoever the client may be), what you wear to the interview and subsequent meetings will influence whether or not you get the project.

We all play roles in our interactions with clients, vendors, peers, coworkers, friends, and associates. What is appropriate dress for one role is not necessarily appropriate for another. You may hear people talk about dressing for a particular situation. When you meet clients for the first time, your appearance should impress on them that you are a serious businessperson. Your portfolio and what you say should convince them of your talent. For subsequent meetings, you can dress more on the "business casual" side leaving the navy blue suit at home and wearing something less traditional. Of course, this still depends on who the client is and the design firm for which you work.

A creative career such as interior design allows—even encourages in some firms—the wearing of outfits other than a conservative-colored suit. In fact, some clients probably expect an interior designer to wear trendy attire. Others are looking for that conservative suit. Nonetheless, there are some conventions or standards that apply to appropriate business attire in the interior design profession. The business's owner sets the tone for what is appropriate at a particular time.

Designers who work in commercial design firms tend to wear more traditional, conservative apparel. The well-tailored suit is always appropriate for meetings and giving presentations to clients. Pantsuits in the office may be permissible for women depending on the firm and the designer's position in the firm.

In residential design, women have more flexibility than men in terms of what they can wear. Women residential designers often wear dresses with more flair and color. Others like to wear lighter-colored business suits, especially during the summer. Pantsuits or pants outfits in the office and perhaps to see a client are also appropriate. Men generally still need to wear a suit for most business situations.

It is important for you to dress for the situation. Take into consideration the type of design firm you are working for and the type of clients (traditional, conservative, professional, trendy, or budget conscious) with whom you will interact. However, remember that casual Friday never means shorts and sweatshirts or revealing sundresses.

SELLING TECHNIQUES

It is hoped that the reader has not gotten the impression that this chapter focuses on selling products. On the contrary, as the chapter title indicates, it is important for the professional and student to understand that design services do not sell themselves. The interior designer must use many kinds of communication techniques to arrive at the point that the client is comfortable in making a decision to hire a designer to provide services that will create that outstanding residential or commercial interior. Using selling techniques described throughout this chapter help that outcome to occur.

It is not possible to turn the reader into an expert salesperson in these few brief pages. The topics of probing, features, and benefits as techniques that help a designer sell have been used by successful designers and salespeople for many years. Perhaps these, as well as those discussed on giving presentations and the ones that will be discussed later, will assist you in taking steps to improve your selling and presentation skills.

Which techniques will help the designer sell his or her services and products is a very personal business. What works for one designer can lead to frustration and failure for another. Although interior designers use many techniques to help them sell, two important characteristics have always been present in the presentation methods used by successful designers: *enthusiasm* for what they are doing and *interest* in the needs of the client. Successful professionals must have a genuine interest in their clients and the needs of their clients. When the designer realizes this, it is a lot easier to bring the encounter with the client to a successful conclusion.

Clients come to interior designers for help in solving their problems in making their home or business attractive and functional. Clients also come to designers to help them make decisions, because many have a difficult time making decisions or are reluctant to do so. Showing a sincere interest in trying to help the client will achieve positive results for the designer. However, because clients are afraid that they will be blamed by a boss, coworker, or spouse if the decisions they make are wrong, interior designers must help them make that decision without coercion but with concern for the client. Sometimes certain techniques can be used to help that decision become reality. These techniques come from tried-and-true methods of selling products, but the reader will see how they can be applied to the discussion of and selling of interior design services.

Probing

"Mr. Jones, I understand that you need to remodel your office spaces due to the increases in the number of employees. I believe you said earlier that you are interested in using open office systems as a possibility to increasing the number of employees you have in your existing space," said Arthur Thompson, an interior designer.

The brief comments above provide an example of the concept of probing for information. *Probing* is a technique for asking different kinds of questions in order to uncover the needs of the client. Some questions that the designer may ask will elicit what is referred to as a *closedprobe*, which generally results in a closed response—"yes" or "no." Other questions that the designer may ask will hopefully force the client to provide a response so that the client is encouraged to talk. This second kind of probing question is called an *open probe*. Which type of probe has Arthur used with Mr. Jones?

Closed-probe questions are geared toward eliciting specific information. They are also used when the client is not particularly responsive to other kinds of questions. For example, a designer might ask this short series of questions:

Designer: Do you have a preferred color scheme?

Client: Not really.

Designer: Do you prefer warmer colors, like oranges, rusts, and yellows?

Client: No.

Designer: Do you prefer cool colors, like blue and green?

Client: Yes.

Designer: Would a color scheme combining blues and greens together be satisfactory to you?

Client: I think I would like that.

Open-probe questions, on the other hand, attempt to get the client talking freely about some topic. They are also used to try to get the client to expand on previously mentioned information or to talk about broader concepts. For example, an interior designer is interviewing a doctor who plans to open a new family practice medical suite with other doctors. The designer might say, "Tell me about any ideas you have on how to accommodate small children and their parents in the waiting room." Hopefully, such a question will get the doctors to provide ideas on this important topic.

What types of questions could Arthur ask in order to clarify the information he needs to expand what was said in the opening example? What questions might Arthur ask to move on to other important programming information related to the opening example?

By means of a careful combination of open and closed probes, the designer can obtain the information required to discover the actual needs of the client. Discovering the needs of the client allows the designer to find out what the client's goals and needs are for the project and help the designer determine what should go into the design contract. These kinds of questions also can be used successfully when the designer is handling objections that the client has raised during the actual progress of the design project.

Features and Benefits

Another important selling technique that is useful in any kind of selling situation is one of describing features and benefits. *Features* are specific aspects or characteristics of a product or service; for example, a plastic laminate top on a desk is a feature of many desks. *Benefits* are features of a product or service that directly relate to a client's need for that product or service; for example, a benefit of the plastic laminate desktop might relate to the ease of maintenance (it will not mar as easily as a wooden desktop).

When the designer is discussing services, it is far more important to discuss the benefits of the service than any features, because it is more difficult to explain and understand features of services. A feature of the design firm's services could be error-free working drawings. However, the client expects this to happen. What, then, might be a benefit of the firm's service of preparing working drawings? One benefit is that the designer provides a one-stop, single-source for documents needed for the client's project. When the designer is trying to think of benefits of services, he or she should think of outcomes that provide value to the client. What are some benefits of interior design services for a couple who is planning to build a custom home or for an organization that is planning to build a convention center?

Once the designer knows the needs of the client, it is relatively easy for him or her to point out the various features and benefits of the services or products as they relate to those needs. If the services and products meet the needs of the client, obtaining confirmation and closing the sale is much easier and quicker.

Using probing, features, and benefits can assist the designer in the selling situation. Other techniques related to the selling process are learning how to overcome objections, to negotiate, and to close. These are discussed in the next

TABLE 21-2.

Tips on How to Have a Successful Selling Outcome.

- Listen carefully to the client.
- Ask questions that are thoughtful and that show you are listening.
- Be sure to let the client talk; don't monopolize the conversation.
- Have a positive attitude and be enthusiastic.
- Never interrupt.
- Never, ever argue!
- Be polite and respectful toward the client.
- Do not sound like you are begging for work.
- Do not sound insincere.
- Always work toward a win-win outcome.
- Dress and sound like a professional.
- Use third-party testimonials as evidence of the firm's expertise.
- Remember that it takes time to build a relationship. Do not feel bad if you have to come back three or four times to close the sale.
- Always say thank you and follow up promptly on any promises.

chapter. A few other ideas on how to have a successful selling outcome are offered in Table 21-2.

BUSINESS ETIQUETTE

Interior designers are hired by executives, professionals, and those at the upper end of the residential market who are in positions of power and influence. Individuals who have power and influence expect those that provide services to them understand their world—even if in reality it is unfamiliar territory for the designer. Appropriate business etiquette, or manners, is part of being the consummate professional, whether one's client is Bill Gates of Microsoft, a senator, the owner of a mansion in a city, the homeowners of a medium-priced home in Anywhere, USA, or the owner of a small family business. According to Letitia Baldrige, former chief of staff for Jacqueline Kennedy, "An atmosphere in which people treat each other with consideration is obviously one in which a customer enjoys doing business.... A company with a well-mannered, high-class reputation attracts—and keeps—good people."[3]

This section has been moved to this chapter in order to provide an interior designer at any level of experience some tips on common courtesy, business travel, and entertaining. These topics are provided because all designers find themselves affected by situations that demand appropriate business etiquette.

Common Business Courtesies and Etiquette

There are common courtesies in the business world that everyone should follow. When dealing with clients who are used to receiving preferential treatment, such as older clients, executives, and the affluent, you will be expected to show certain courtesies to them as well.

- Always use the client's surname when you address him or her until the client gives you permission to use his or her first name.

- If you are seated and someone approaches to shake your hand, always stand up, whether the person is a man or woman.
- Never stay seated behind the desk in your office when a client or other person who is introduced to you arrives.
- Always introduce the person with the highest "status" to the people with lower status; that is, introduce the client to your boss, your boss to a coworker or a friend.
- If you are a smoker, do not smoke if you are speaking to a group and there are nonsmokers in the group, even if you are the host.
- If you are sharing a cab, the person of junior rank should be prepared to take care of the fare if the boss does not.
- The designer should always take care of the fare when in a cab with a client.
- If you have traveled to visit a client, your time is really the client's time.
- On any kind of business trip, your boss, accountant, or the client will want receipts for tax or billing purposes.
- When you fly during the workweek, it is best to wear business clothing, even if you are traveling alone.
- Be sure you have any documents, computer discs, or other items that you will need to conduct business in your attaché case or carry-on bag.
- If you are eating with a group of colleagues and you all need receipts, ask about requesting separate checks.
- If you invite someone to lunch, the guest will assume that you will be paying for it.
- Never order the most expensive item on the menu, even if you are the host.
- Do not pull out business papers during the meal. Discuss business, if you must, after you have finished eating.
- Be aware of time restraints. Check with the client regarding the amount of time he or she has and stick to that time limit. If necessary, instruct your waiter and tip extra for faster service in a slow restaurant.
- Do no personal grooming at the table. This includes applying fresh lipstick. Excuse yourself and go to the restroom.

Business Travel

Interior designers in all specialties travel on business. Sometimes you will travel with a client, colleague, or your boss. It might be to make a presentation to a client, revisit the job site during construction/installation, or attend a professional meeting or seminar. Having the opportunity to travel on business does not mean that you should leave good manners at home. In fact, they may be even more important when you are traveling. You never know if the person sitting next to you on the airplane might turn out to be a potential client. If you are traveling with a client or your boss, then good manners are particularly important.

Business travel does not mean it is appropriate to dress in casual clothes—even when traveling alone to the meeting or job site location. Luggage can always be lost, and making a presentation in jeans does not offer proof of professional awareness. It is also critical to carry any essential documents within a briefcase as carry-on luggage, rather than checking CDs, contracts, handouts, and so on in luggage. Just because you are out of town does not mean that your manners and good sense should be forgotten. There is nothing funny about seeing a colleague get drunk at a conference and embarrass the design firm. Use the same business etiquette that you would use at home. The companion CD contains a brief article highlighting a discussion on international business etiquette. Please see Item 21-1 for this article.

Business Entertaining

A significant amount of business is conducted across a table in a restaurant. Interior designers often meet with clients at a restaurant after a presentation or to discuss a topic that does not require reviewing of plans and samples. Manufacturers' representatives often invite designers to lunch. An employee may go to lunch with a supervisor or the owner of the firm. The designer meets colleagues at professional associations, and they often meet to chat and network.

Table manners can play a part in a job interview as well. Some companies have daylong interview sessions. It is quite possible that the interviewer is carefully evaluating the job seeker's etiquette during the lunch or, for that matter, all day. The firm does not want to hire someone who does not know basic etiquette. It is quite obvious that there are all sorts of situations in which an interior designer will need to use appropriate table etiquette.

The main purpose for a business meal is to continue to develop rapport between the designer and the client, colleagues, or the boss. Business *is* discussed, but it is usually done after some small talk has occurred. Naturally, a business meal between colleagues may well be a purely social event. As for meetings with clients, it is not only acceptable to ask the client about his or her hobbies and interests, but also helpful in developing a business relationship with the client.

You can find several specific tips on business etiquette while dining on the companion CD. Look for Item 21-2.

Telephones, Cell Phones, and E-Mail

Interior designers spend quite a bit of time on the phone and using e-mail to communicate with clients, coworkers, vendors, and others. There are common courtesies regarding telephone communication that have been used for many years. Cell phone courtesy is a hot topic, since it seems almost everyone, from children to the highest-level executive, has a cell phone. E-mail courtesy is also becoming a concern. The amount of e-mail many receive, including spam, creates a time-consuming task for reviewing and writing e-mail.

A business telephone is for that purpose—business. Not calling family and friends or, for some, using it to find another job. A telephone greeting says a lot about the design firm, including the staff that answers after the initial pickup by a receptionist. An overly casual manner can affect a potential client's impression of the firm. A sole proprietor working from home should have two lines: a personal phone line and a business line. When the person the designer needs to contact is not available, ask when the person might be available. The usual rule is that the one who has something to gain from the conversation should call back.

Return messages from others promptly—no later than the next day, if this is at all possible. Clients especially expect responses right away even when that is not practical for the designer. Letting them know that it might take 24 hours to return a message at least establishes a ground rule of expectation.

Courtesy and cell phones sometimes do not seem to go together. The ubiquitous ringing phone and people who seem to be talking to themselves can be annoying. The best practice is to believe that the person you are with is the most important person—not the cell phone. If you must use your cell phone around others, be conscious of how loud you are talking. Not everyone is interested in hearing your conversation. Since most cell phone plans allow for voice messaging, turn your phone off while you are dining in a restaurant or are in another quiet place. Only you are impressed by your own self-importance when you feel you must respond to a call on your cell phone in such environments.

It seems that everyone is comfortable with e-mail communications, disregarding the large amount of spam that arrives every day. One very important tip about e-mail is to take care in what is sent via this electronic mail system. Be assured that clients and others are maintaining a copy of the e-mail they receive. Likewise, the designer should maintain copies of e-mails received from clients and others involved in projects. In-box files are a good idea until a hard copy can be produced. Because they are saved, be careful about what is said. A promise in an e-mail is expected to be fulfilled by the client. In fact, Chapter 26 comments on the fact that a person's name at the end of an e-mail can be interpreted as creating a contractual agreement. Here are a few courtesies concerning the use of e-mail:

- DO NOT USE ALL CAPITAL LETTERS. It is considered shouting.
- Once you click the Send button, there is no way to take back what you have sent.
- Take care that the e-mail is going to the right address and person.
- Always check your spelling.
- Large attachments or e-mails with graphics take a long time to load.
- When sending attachments to people who do not know you, it is likely to be considered spam and disregarded.
- Be careful when you "Reply to All" or "Forward" an e-mail. The original document goes with these, and something may have been said that someone else should not read.

SUMMARY

"Selling" should not be a dirty word in this profession. Selling is personal communication with potential and actual clients to reach a point where the client agrees to hire the designer and approve the plans and specifications created. Throughout this book, we have seen that there is more to interior design than being able to put colors, fabrics, and furniture together into a workable floor plan. One of the most important nondesign activities of the interior designer is selling.

In this chapter, we have reviewed concepts that explain why selling design services can be difficult and introduced the buyer decision-making process. We have discussed the first three phases in the selling process, which help the designer do a better job of making a sale or a presentation end more satisfactorily for the designer. Some of the many techniques that are used by designers to sell their services and products also have been briefly explained. All these processes and techniques, and those that will be covered in the next chapter, will help the designer conclude the sales presentation for services or products.

REFERENCES

1. *World Book Encyclopedia*, 2000, p. 62.
2. Zeithaml and Bitner, 1996, p. 20.
3. Baldridge, 1985, p. 3.

CHAPTER 22

Design Presentations

Key Terms and Concepts

These key terms and concepts are important to material in this chapter. Many of these terms will be utilized in other chapters as well. Be sure you understand these items as you read this chapter.

Terms and Concepts

Marketing presentation	Selection committee
Initial interview	Objections
Relationship building	Closing
Feasibility studies	Trial close
RFP proposals	Third-party testimonials
Short list	Negotiating

Critical Issues

After completing this chapter you should be able to:

■ Compare any differences in an initial presentation to a marketing presentation.

■ Compare a marketing presentation in general to one given related to an RFP.

■ Discuss why it is important to know something about the people on a selection committee.

■ Discuss why it is important to prepare for any type of presentation.

■ Compare the focus of presentation points in a preliminary project presentation versus a final project presentation.

■ Discuss strategies to overcome objections.

■ Discuss why it is important for a designer to ask for the sale rather than waiting for the client to say something like, "Okay, where do I sign?"

■ Discuss what kinds of things should be noted when following up on a marketing or initial meeting and the final presentation beyond notes on the project scope itself.

■ Explain what is meant by creating a win-win situation in a negotiation.

■ Describe why the environment where a negotiation takes place can have an impact on the negotiation outcome.

Sara received a good lead on a project for an advertising agency. She is the owner of a commercial interior design firm that has been in business for eight years specializing in corporate and small-business office facilities and some small hospitality projects. She called the agency and was able to obtain an appointment to make a presentation of her firm for the project. Sara's firm has a staff of four interior designers and holds a contractor's license, and all the designers are NCIDQ certificate holders and are licensed in the state. This would be an important project for Sara and the firm, since the agency represented many important clients of the type that Sara would like to have for clients. She is working carefully with her senior designer to determine what should be said and brought to the presentation.

The selling of interior design services is not a cut-and-dried matter. High levels of competition in many markets require that the professional practitioner consider all presentations to prospective clients very carefully. In the previous chapter, we reviewed the first three stages of the selling process: prospecting, qualifying, and preparation. The focus of this chapter is on design presentations.

This emphasis is given to professional design presentations because it is so very important to the overall activities of the designer. The presentation made after the potential client has shown an initial interest in the design firm is arguably the most important of these activities. If the encounter does not go well and the relationship between the designer and the potential client is not built, there will be no project to execute.

The initial marketing presentation is only one of the many meetings that occurs during a project. After a marketing presentation or initial meeting, it is normal for the interior designer to meet once again with the client to go over a design contract. Designers make mini-presentations each time they meet with the client during the course of the project. And, of course, designers often make a final presentation at what they hope concludes the design development stage of the project. Other meetings with the client are in a sense also marketing presentations even if the meeting is to discuss the ongoing schedule of the project, since all encounters with the client should be considered a part of marketing.

Making any kind of presentation can be very stressful for many professionals and students. Public speaking is one of the most feared activities. Although giving a design presentation is not the same as public speaking, it still requires the designers to stand up (figuratively or literally) in front of one or more people and be in the spotlight. Selling design involves listening as well as talking. If you do all the talking, this does not give the client a chance to tell you anything useful.

This chapter provides some basic guidelines for making three common types of design presentations used in professional practice: (1) the marketing presentation to obtain consent to begin a project; (2) the proposal presentation, whose end result is the same; and (3) the project progress presentation. It also discusses the other stages of the sales process that bring the process to a conclusion: overcoming objections, closing, and follow-up. This chapter includes negotiation strategies and concludes with numerous general guidelines for making any kind of design presentation. Although the focus of this information is on the presentations made by practitioners, students can learn important tips about how to present their class projects.

MARKETING PRESENTATIONS

One of the most important types of presentations made by a member of a design firm is the presentation to obtain a new client. It doesn't matter if the client came to the firm because of a referral, the company Web site, or any other promotional method, the job is not confirmed until the presentation is successfully concluded. For our purposes, a *marketing presentation* occurs when the designer finds him- or herself discussing why a prospective client should hire the interior designer for a project. Many interior designers—especially those in residential interior design—refer to this presentation as the *initial interview.*

Conducting an Initial Client Interview

It would be nice if there was one surefire way to conduct the initial meeting with the client. Unfortunately, this important contact has as many ways to approach and conduct the meeting as there are designers and clients. There are several points that should be kept in mind regardless of the type of client or specialty.

Many designers strongly suggest having a plan for the meeting. "Winging it" is not a very professional way to walk into any type of client meeting. Some outline each meeting after the initial contact call. Others use forms such as the one shown in Figure 28-1 to help gather needed information. The most important information that the designer must obtain during this initial meeting is an understanding of the scope of the project and the client's ideas on what needs to be done. Not getting the scope right easily dooms a promising project to failure. Another key piece of information is the budget. Clients are very likely to say that they don't know what the budget will be yet. You must do the best you can at determining budget constraints by your careful and diplomatic questioning. That will save you time and possible grief in the future. Naturally there are many other key points that need to be determined, and they will be listed on your outline or form.

Where is the best place to hold the presentation meeting? That will depend upon personal preference of the interior designer and the type of project. Many interior designers like to visit the project site for the initial presentation in order to help them get a feel for the project. Sometimes this is impractical if the project is under construction and a good space for the meeting is not available. Residential interior designers tend to like to have an initial presentation at the client's home or site. Commercial interior designers prefer to control the presentation environment and conduct the meeting at their office. Commercial designers often use PowerPoint presentations as part of that initial meeting and prefer to do that program at their office.

"Take notes, take a lot of notes, always take notes" was advice given to me when I was just starting out in the profession. It is easy to forget small details as you run from one meeting to another appointment. You shouldn't tape the meeting unless the potential client gives you permission to do so. Don't forget to bring a tape measure in case you need to measure the space right away—although this is really a service you should do after the contract is signed.

Avoid the temptation to give away design ideas at the first meeting. Clients of all types are often anxious to pick your brain for ideas and then possibly hire someone else. Make it clear that the initial meeting is to obtain a clear picture of what is needed and not to make design suggestions.

Of course, you must also be prepared to talk about you or your firm and how you proceed through the stages of a project. Bring along the brochures or other leave-behinds that you want to give clients to help them decide about you. They will also want to know how you charge. You certainly can discuss this issue in a broad sense by saying something like "I charge an hourly fee." Refrain from getting too specific. You can do that after you prepare a contract proposal.

Whether or not you should charge for the initial meeting is another question that often comes up. Many residential interior designers charge for that initial meeting. Some of them credit that charge to the project once a contract is signed. Those designers who do charge do so because they know the client intends to interview three or more designers and the designers just don't have time or honestly doesn't want to waste their time on calls like that. Others feel that initial meeting is a marketing expense and do not charge. Commercial designers—except those at the very highest echelons of the industry—do not charge for an initial meeting. If you do charge for the initial meeting, it is very important that you make that clear to the client when you set up the meeting, not at the meeting itself.

The initial meeting is very important, of course. It should be planned and prepared for as with any meeting. The information in the other sections on this chapter and the next will also be applicable to the initial meeting. Oh, yes—don't ever be late, don't ever be rude, and don't forget to be enthusiastic—even when you realize that this client is not a right fit for you. One never knows how this client might be able to influence others!

The marketing presentation can take many forms. It can be a formal or informal, one-on-one meeting between the interior designer and the client held at the designer's studio, the client location, or even at a restaurant. It also can be a very structured and formal meeting with numerous clients and designers participating—as is often the case for presentations for a commercial project. The purpose of a marketing presentation is to determine enough information for the designer to understand what the project is about and then for the designer to explain how he or she plans to do a project. Of course, the interior designer will also explain to the client why the client should select the designer to do the project. Only the larger design firms really think of this first in-depth meeting with the client as a marketing presentation. Many designers simply think of this presentation as the initial interview and do not even think of it as a presentation. Whatever it is called, it is important because it introduces the designer to the potential client, and so it should always be handled thoughtfully and professionally.

Relationship building is a primary goal of the marketing presentation. Although this is true for any kind of project, the residential client often puts the relationship and how well he or she feels he or she will get along with the designer as a key element to the decision to hire an interior designer. This relationship, as we saw in the previous chapter, is necessary so that the client will have confidence in the designer's ability to handle the project.

Another goal of the interior designer during this presentation is to clarify the extent of the firm's experiences, ability, and interest in undertaking the potential project. To varying degrees, clients will want detailed information about the designer's experience in general but specifically with similar projects. A qualifications sheet clarifying the designer's education, experiences, awards, and other pertinent information on experience can be prepared so the details do not have to be explained. A folder with this qualifications sheet along with brochures, article reprints, and other collateral materials can be presented to the client as a leave-behind. Interest in the project can be projected with enthusiasm, regardless of how small the project might be.

It is very important for the designer to establish how he or she can and will solve the client's concerns and meet the client's goals. For as much as the client wants to know that the designer has the experience and skills to do the project, he or she is most concerned that the designer is interested in helping this client and has some ideas on the approach. Avoid the temptation and requests from clients to give free ideas during marketing presentations. Providing concepts, ideas, even any sketches at an initial meeting that might be done at no charge to the client might seem harmless, but it is generally not advisable, regardless of the size of project.

Building rapport, explaining the design firm's abilities and interests concerning the project, and clarifying client needs are key issues that generally make up the bulk of the marketing presentation. So the goal is to finish the presentation with a request by the client for the designer to prepare a design contract or otherwise go forward with the project. It does not matter if a firm making this initial marketing presentation is a sole proprietor or someone working for a larger firm; preparing and making the presentation—along with developing any information that is provided to the client in a marketing packet—take time and money that need to be carefully budgeted.

The client will have concerns that he or she wishes the designer to address. Project management is a key consideration of both residential and commercial clients, since so many clients are too busy to worry about the project themselves. They expect the professional to take care of the details and keep the client informed of its progress, problems, and solutions if problems do arise. Interior design projects have become more complex, and the designer's ability to manage the myriad details is very important to clients. Then again, some clients will not care for a discussion of process and management ability, as they assume the designer has the experience to do this task. Potential clients also want assurance that the designer has the experience and ability to handle the creative and technical tasks of the project. They do not want to find out sometime during the project that the designer does not have the expertise to satisfactorily complete the project. Clients are very concerned about the project costs and how long the project will take. As mentioned, it is generally better to not be specific about design fees at such an early juncture. It is best to speak in generalities and return with a contract for design services a few days later. Except for small projects, designers should also refrain from specifically quoting project costs for products and/or construction at this time. If the client requires estimates for products and construction, *feasibility studies*, which are in-depth estimates of the cost of planning and providing specifications, can be accomplished within a few days or weeks. Some designers provide ranges of costs when pressed for this information. However, providing ranges might lock the client into the lower end of the range rather than the actual costs that will be arrived at later. The remainder of this section provides many tips on conducting a marketing presentation.

Preparation

The kind of preparation that we discussed in the previous chapter is generally required of a marketing presentation. The information will not be repeated here. Refer to Chapter 21 for ideas on how to go about preparing a marketing presentation.

The Presentation

A presentation to be made to a group of clients and/or requiring participation from two or more people from the design firm requires careful preparation and coordination of the meeting. An agenda or outline for the presentation should be prepared, and the role of each participating member of the firm should be determined. The outline helps make sure that everything that needs to be said will be said. This agenda can be distributed to the client for the most formal of presentations. It can be done verbally for other situations.

A conference room at the design studio or office is preferable as the location for the presentation. Holding the meeting at the designer's office allows the designer to control the meeting and control potential interruptions. This allows the designer to show the client a professional "face" through the design of that space. Should the interior designer work from a home office or have a small office without a conference room, an arrangement might be made to use an executive office suite conference room for a fee.

If the presentation must be held at the client's office or facility, ask for the use of a conference room. It is impossible to show slides or computer-based presentations in an office. Besides, a conference room—even though it is at the client's place of business—is somewhat neutral territory. A presentation held in the client's office is not only awkward but also allows the client to be distracted by phones, people dropping in, and other interruptions.

Residential designers, when presenting at the client's home, should request the use of the dining room or the kitchen rather than the living room. For most families, the living room is the formal room, where they can easily say "no." The dining room allows the designer to sit directly across or at a right angle to the client, which is considered a more satisfactory informal situation.

Seating or positioning has been shown to make a difference. Ideally, the client should be positioned directly across from the designer or at a right angle to the designer. This allows the designer to easily see and evaluate the client's body language. Observing the client's body language can help the designer evaluate whether the presentation is going well or whether the client has lost interest. If the presentation is to a group, the designer might want to be at the head of the table if visuals are presented or at the center position, which allows the designer to see all of the clients. Being near the decision maker is an ideal position as well. If at all possible, try not to be in a situation so that the design firm team is on one side of the table while the client group is on the other. This seating arrangement seems confrontational.

During the presentation, the designer should be aware of his or her own body language and that of the client. Body language is a very powerful communication device. Nonverbal communication is said to be 75 to 90 percent of effective communication.[1] Experts such as Julius Fast believe that body language is a more accurate indication of a person's true feelings than the words that are said.

Body Language

A very powerful nonverbal communication tool is body language. The study of body language comes from the scientific study of the meaning of body positions and gestures, called *kinesics*.* The clues we give through body positions and gestures often more accurately reflect what we are thinking than the words we use. Knowing how to read these signals helps designers to interpret whether a client is really interested in what you are saying or even upset at what is being discussed— even though he or she hasn't said anything. We also are giving clues to what we are thinking through our body language.

One of the most important elements of body language is eye contact. Not making eye contact can be interpreted as meaning that you do not really think the other person is important. When you fail to use eye contact, you are also sending a message that can be interpreted as arrogance: "I'm better than you." Both of these messages are bad to send to your client or to anyone else, for that matter.

Another body language signal involves what we do with our hands. We shake hands; we put our hands in our pants pockets, behind the back, or sometimes over our mouth slightly while talking, or we put our fingertips together to make a triangle. What do these gestures mean? We shake hands, of course, as a way to say "hello." Putting your hands in your pockets, however, can be interpreted as meaning that you are secretive or unsure of yourself. Placing your hands behind your back can be a power stance. Many police officers do this when they walk a beat. Someone who puts his or her fingers over his or her mouth while talking is commonly interpreted as not very confident about what he or she is saying. It can also mean that the person is not being completely truthful. Let your hands fall naturally to your side or perhaps fold them softly (so it does not look like you are madly gripping your hands) at your waist. If you are seated, fold them softly in your lap or rest them comfortably on the arm of the chair.

Placing your fingertips together to create a triangle with the hands is referred to as steepling, since the shape resembles a church steeple. People who use this gesture usually feel they are in a powerful position. They may be considered smug or egotistical.

Work at being relaxed, maintaining good posture when you stand to give a presentation. Face the client or group as much as you can rather than place your back to them. Keep your hand movements slow and small; don't flail around with your hands or arms. Stand with an easy stance, without slouching. Walk with your head up but not with your nose in the air!

When you are sitting, you can lean forward to show interest in what you are saying and what the client says in response to your statements. If the client leans or pushes away from the table, then possibly he or she is losing interest in what is being said. If you are standing and lean over the conference table or desk toward the other party (or this is done to you), it is generally considered to be an aggressive posture. Most people will then lean away from the person who is leaning toward them.

There are many other gestures and body positions that can help you better understand what your client, boss, coworkers, or others are actually saying when speaking. Here are a few more quick body language tips you might find useful:

A person shows impatience by

    Pushing away from table or desk

    Taps fingers or a pen or pencil on the table

    Shifts from one foot to another while standing

Boredom is indicated when a person

    Turns body toward exit

    Rests head in the hand

    Doodles

Possible secretiveness and suspicion is indicated when a person

    Looks everywhere but at you

    Smiles superficially or glances sideways

*Fast, 1980, p. 1.
Other sources: Nierenberg and Calero, 1993; Delmar, 1984.

Many perceive eye contact as an indication of honesty and trustworthiness and the lack of eye contact as either a lack of confidence or disinterest. Good eye contact does not mean staring down the client to make him or her uncomfortable; it does mean looking the client in the eye from time to time. Maintaining eye contact with an individual for about five seconds, looking away for awhile, and then returning to eye contact so that eye contact is maintained about 50 percent of the time is a beneficial technique.

How you say what you say is also important when you are communicating a favorable message. Beware of using fillers like *er, well, okay, you see,* and *umm.* These words are indicators of powerless language and nervousness. To the astute client, these fillers also show lack of preparation and lack of confidence in what the presenter is trying to say and sell. Do not say things that will dilute the feeling of confidence in you that the client needs to have. Hedges, fillers, and other meaningless words that are combined with slumped posture will make a client think twice about your ability to execute the project.

Handouts, including the contract (unless the review of the contract is the actual purpose of the meeting), should not be distributed until the verbal portion of the presentation is nearly completed. When handouts are given to the client while the presentation is being made, it is almost a certainty that he or she will look through the handouts rather than listen to the presentation. If the client is looking through handouts while the designer is continuing with the verbal presentation, the client will miss important points and ask questions about what was said. This can result in the designer's not being able to present everything that he or she wants to present because information must be repeated. Enough time should be allowed at the end of the presentation for distributing and going over any handouts that have been prepared for the client.

Interest in any visuals such as slides, PowerPoint programs, charts, or other graphics should be built upon some portion of the verbal presentation. It is better to first get the client excited and interested in what he or she will be seeing in the visuals. When the visuals are presented, be careful not to show so many that the client falls asleep. Present a sufficient number of visuals to make a strong impression without boring the client.

Multimedia Presentations

Gone are the days in which a designer was confined to using glossy photographic prints in a portfolio or a slide presentation. That is not to say these items are unimportant today. For the small firm, they are the primary way of telling part of the presentation story to the client.

Interior designers today have many forms of media to choose from for possible promotional assistance. Photographs and slides are scanned onto compact discs and integrated with animation on film or as part of a PowerPoint presentation. Digital photographs can be incorporated into multimedia presentations in many different variations. Live interviews or other action clips are also integrated into PowerPoint or other forms of multimedia presentation. The opportunities are now limited only by the budget of the design firm.

A multimedia presentation takes some thought and time to produce. Someone needs to be in charge of the production. It can be an in-house project, but this takes time away from billable hours. A consultant might be necessary to help with development and production, especially if the presentation will take the place of a printed brochure. It is necessary to determine what should be included and to prepare an outline so that a script or a story board (sketches of each frame or page) can be created. Then the actual integration and production will take place. A narrator may be needed as well.

Obviously, a multimedia presentation is not an inexpensive promotional tool, unless the firm is using a tailored slide presentation or prepares a PowerPoint presentation that can easily be done in-house. As with any other promotional tool, the firm must consider it in light of the budget and the goals of the firm before it commits to anything.

After the summary and the "ask for the sale" portion of the presentation are concluded, thank the client for your taking up his or her time. Do not forget to shake hands, and use the last few minutes for small talk about continued interest in the project. Be friendly and continue to show confidence in obtaining and completing the project.

PROPOSAL PRESENTATIONS

Commercial interior design firms know very well that the commitment to developing a response to an RFP is only the first step in obtaining projects that start with this document. When a design firm sends a proposal in response to an RFP, the hope is that it will be received in a more than satisfactory manner so as to make the *short list* and be allowed to make a presentation. The proposal is the key to having the opportunity to make the presentation, whereas the marketing presentation is requested after the designer has made a few prospecting and qualifying phone calls.

Unlike the basic marketing presentation, the presentation made after a proposal submission may be the first time the designer has actually met and talked with the client, other than brief conversations on the phone or possibly during a tour of the facility for firms interested in responding. A key issue, therefore, besides being able to tell the firm's story, is to develop rapport with the client. This is difficult for many designers, since the presentation is likely to be given to a group. Many find it more difficult to speak before a group than to one or two people. These client groups, referred to as the *selection committee*, however, want the designers to succeed in the presentation. Having to make a presentation to a group should guide the designer in preparing the materials and selecting the type of materials that will be used.

Remember from our discussion in Chapter 20 that the RFP is often used by larger client organizations that want to investigate a number of design firms for a project without having to talk to each and every one of the firms. A firm that makes the short list is therefore already considered capable of doing the project. The presentation must help the designer establish the relationship that is so important when executing an interior design project.

It is essential that the presentation address the goals and needs of the client, as stated in the RFP, and address the key issues that are on the client's mind. It is critical for the designer who takes the lead role in the presentation to convince the client that his or her design firm is the only one who truly understands the issues the client has and that they are there to meet those challenges. It is not the time to brag about how great the firm is. This was done in the proposal.

These presentations are commonly given at the client's place of business. It is necessary to find out about the room, what audiovisual equipment can be supplied, what the presenter must bring, and the seating configuration of the space. Some designers prefer to use a conference table; others like a U-shaped table for a group. Since the designer is using the client's facility, he or she will need to ask what is available and whether arrangements can be made to accommodate the presentation style. It is likely that more than one firm is presenting in a day, and changes in the arrangement of the conference room might not be possible.

All the strategies and techniques discussed in the "Marketing Presentations" section apply to this presentation as well. The decision as to who will participate in the presentation is very important. Most of the time, a principal of the firm will lead the presentation, with the project manager or lead designer making a significant contribution to the proceedings. If the project is large enough for partnering with another firm, then a representative from that firm must be included. Each person plays a part, explaining some important points about the project concepts and/or methods that will be employed to execute the project. Which presentation tools to use is also important and can be keyed to the expected group.

Knowing who is to be on the selection committee is not unethical. Asking about the committee members and then finding out something about each one is a good presentation strategy. This is not always easy to do, but phone calls to colleagues who have dealt with the client before can be helpful. Some members might be especially budget conscious, while others prefer highly creative solutions to the project. Certainly it would be helpful to know their concerns about the project. This not only clues the firm into what to say but also how to strategize the presentation. For example, a budget-conscious group may not appreciate a computer-based presentation (too slick) but may think the use of flip-charts is just great.

It is very important for the firm to stick to the time limit established by the client. Most likely, all the other firms will be waiting to make their presentations that same day (if a small number of firms constitutes the short list). Stealing time from someone else is very unprofessional. Practicing the presentation ensures that it will stay within the designated limits. Leaving something out because of poor time management or forgetting to bring along a particularly important graphic can infer that the firm is not up to the challenge of the project.

Appearances are important. Appropriate business apparel, clean and neat presentation materials and handouts, and working audiovisual equipment are a must. The designer may be asking the client to trust him or her with millions of the client's dollars. The interior design team must look like it can meet that challenge in a businesslike manner.

It is important to involve the client in the presentation. Encourage questions and rehearse questions to ask members of the committee. Listening is an especially important skill and component of what the lead presenter and everyone else on the design team must master and then do. Listening to the comments and questions that the client makes as well as watching body language are critical to developing rapport and showing the client that the design firm will listen to the client's concerns and needs. Involving the client helps gauge client interest and confirmation of the ideas the firm is offering.

Find out when you are going to present. If it is late in the day, bring along some refreshments to wake up the selection committee. Even if you are first, it is a good idea to bring the refreshments. Do not count on the client to supply you with coffee or soda! Some firms like to go first; they feel they can make a good impression that way. Many other firms like to be last—giving the last ideas and concepts that the client hears for the day. Presenting last also means that the client has been "educated" a little about the process and pros and cons of other firms. Questioning might be more intense because of what other firms have said. On the other hand, if minds have begun to be made up, the client might not be as interested in your story when you are last. Naturally, these are gambles every firm faces. Some firms bring along a small, fun "gift," like the small toy construction vehicles a firm brought to a presentation. However, some clients are not allowed to take even this small gratuity.

Now it is actually time to make the presentation. Everything has been rehearsed, checked, and rechecked. Everyone knows his or her part and what to wear. Plan to arrive a little early so that you can set up your materials while the committee members are breaking between presentations. Arrange the space (if that was cleared ahead of time), and then take a deep breath and relax!

Even if this is a project that your firm really wants to get, it should not feel like the end of the world if your firm does not win. So relax, be at ease with the committee members, and exhibit warmth, enthusiasm, and interest. Do not try to show off or hard-sell. Most clients do not care for overly aggressive presentation styles any more than they care for the prima donna designer. Only a few designers can get away with this kind of behavior and still get plenty of work. Make sure that your presentation has focused on what the client needs to know about your firm and how you are going to solve their challenges. Do not bore them with too many slides, charts, graphs, slick multiple presentations, or anything that seems to get away from their primary concerns.

When it is over, say thank you, gather your materials, and leave without trying to hang around. It will probably take the committee a few days or weeks (depending on how many design firms are making presentations) to get back to you with the results. If you have had a lot of questions or the group is particularly lively when you have finished, you can assume that the presentation is successful. If they are subdued, well, you tried!

Always go back to the office and critique the presentation: What seemed to go well? What went wrong? Learning from mistakes makes the firm better at making a presentation the next time. It is also appropriate to send the selection committee chair a thank-you letter within a few days. This is not only a polite bit of business etiquette, but also it gives the firm one more chance to say a few words about how interested it is in executing the project.

What Would You Do?

The sales agreement for Turbo Designs clearly state that once the agreement is signed by the client, orders cannot be canceled after seven business days and that the cancellation request must be in writing. A few weeks after the agreements were signed, the client contacts the designer and tells her that the office furniture for the conference room that was ordered must be canceled, as one of the partners feels this particular product is too expensive. The designer reminds the client that the sales order has a no-cancellation policy. The partner e-mails the designer and says unless the order for the conference room furniture is canceled, he will cancel everything and, if necessary, sue the designer.

PROJECT PRESENTATIONS

Interior design professionals must make numerous presentations during the course of any type of project. Each one is important in itself, even if it is a brief encounter or a lengthy meeting. Project presentations should also be considered important marketing encounters, since any encounter with a client or potential clients is an opportunity to enhance or diminish the reputation of the designer with the client. The preliminary presentations conducted periodically to ensure that the designer is on track with his or her design decisions are the most frequent project presentations. The other project presentation is the final presentation conducted when the designer has completed all of the planning, design, and specifications for the project that are required in the contract, usually at the end of the design development stage, preceding the technical move into the contract documents phase of the project.

Preliminary Project Presentations

The goal of the designer during preliminary presentations is to obtain client approvals of whatever is being discussed. Obviously, approvals will not be obtained for everything at each presentation. Designers, especially entry-level designers, should not be discouraged when clients object to plans or specifications at this stage. Some objections are very common. It is necessary for the designer to learn that not all suggestions made by the designer at this stage will be automatically approved by the client. Some designers even make certain types of suggestions so as to guarantee that one of them will be vetoed in order to direct the client toward the solutions that the designer wishes to pursue. In many cases, educating the client is a big part of the preliminary presentations. Clients sometimes want the darnedest things in an interior, and part of the designer's responsibility is to explain why they might not be appropriate for the client's situation and needs.

Plans and other graphics discussed during preliminary presentations are often rough sketches and preliminary CAD drawings. In this way, the client or designer can sketch on the rough floor plans or make notes on the sketches. Although CAD drawings at this stage look "final," the designer should be clear to the client that changes are still possible at this stage. Product selections can be informal as well; the designer can use the pages from catalogs and loose fabric and finish samples. Psychologically, it also makes the client feel like the designer is not forcing decisions on him or her, since the plans and selections are still in the preliminary stage.

It is important for clients to sign off on approved products and floor plan proposals. A form such as the one in Figure 22-1 can be used to detail preliminary and final product specifications. A worksheet is also included on the CD. Look for Item 22-1.

Note that the form provides a place for the client to initial or sign it. Signed approvals allow the designer to move on through the project with confidence. A client signature or even initials on the marked-up copy of the floor plan or specification, which signifies agreement to what has been shown, also provides a mechanism for the designer to charge clients for work that has to be redone if the client changes his or her mind *after* the initial approval.

Whether the preliminary and final presentations are held at the client's location or at the designer's office is really dependent on the designer's style, the size of the project, and the demands of the client. The client wants to feel in control of the project, so when the designer comes to the client, the client feels in control. "We have found that going to the job site or office is good psychologically for clients. They are paying us to develop design ideas, but they want to be serviced. Going to them in the early stages is one of the ways we service the client," related one design director. Residential designers often find that it is helpful to make the preliminary presentation at the client's home. Oftentimes this is not practical for a commercial project, since the space may be under construction or could interfere with business. Making the preliminary presentations at the designer's office provides access to additional resources, such as product materials and print machines, if it should be necessary to make copies or additional prints. Table 22-1 provides several characteristics of a preliminary presentation.

Final Project Presentations

It is customary to have a final presentation of the project documents at the end of the design development stage of the project. This final presentation is done to review the design decisions one last time. The goal of the final project presentation is to obtain the go-ahead to begin the preparation of contract documents, including any formal specifications needed for bidding, to proceed with the ordering products if bids are not necessary, and to prepare construction drawings and construction specifications. Ideally, the designer is hoping for approval of all the design concepts and product selections. It is common that a few changes will still be necessary, however.

For very large projects, a substantial amount of time may have elapsed since the last preliminary presentation. Final presentations pull all the earlier decisions together into one package. They also are used to show the client specialized graphics, such as detailed, rendered floor plans; perspectives; sample boards; models; and computer simulations. All the last-minute hesitations by the client must be resolved at this time so that the project can move forward.

Presenting the final cost estimates (for bid situations) or actual final cost of the project is also done at this time. The designer must be ready not only to defend design decisions but also to answer any questions about costs of the project. It is advised that the designer once again obtain signed approvals on product

Product Control Sheet

Job Name: _____ Job #: _____

Room/Area: _____ Control Number: _____

Item Specification

Manufacturer:	
Catalog Number:	
Case/Frame Finish:	
Hardware Finish:	

Size   W: D: Ht: Sh:

Other:

Special Installation Instructions:

Fabric:

    Grade: _____ Yards Required/Unit: _____

    Repeat: _____ Stain Repellent: _____ Fire Retardent: _____

    COM Supplier:

Sketch/Photograph   **Fabric**

Delivery Time: _____ Shipping Location: _____
_____
_____

Unit Price (net): _____   Quantity: _____

Upholstery: _____

Special Handling: _____   Freight: _____

Total Item Net _____   Delivery: _____

Client Signature: _____

© 1993, Christine Piotrowski

FIGURE 22-1.

A typical control sheet that can be used for client sign-off on each item on which agreement has been reached.

TABLE 22-1.

Characteristics of a Preliminary Presentation.

- They are usually less formal than marketing and proposal presentations. Informality allows for the necessary give-and-take that must occur in the early stages of the project.
- Presentation style should create a comfortable atmosphere to involve the client.
- Always give the client some choices during the presentation.
- Changes in the plans can be sketched on the CAD sheets or on tracing paper.
- Take plenty of notes to be sure all changes are incorporated into revised documents.
- Obtain client sign-offs on all drawings and changes, as well as all product specifications.
- Involve the client in the presentation by asking the client questions.
- Questions that bring acceptance of the concepts under discussion usually lead to agreement for the whole concept.

selections and plans. The signed documents become part of the project files, just like those obtained during the preliminary presentation.

Most designers prefer that the final project presentation be made at the designer's office. Presenting a relatively simple project to one or two clients can be done successfully over a conference table, the client's desk, or even a dining room table. When the project is complex and several representatives of the client need to be present, a different set of presentation graphics may need to be prepared, just as with the marketing presentation. Controlling the environment of the presentation is very useful in bringing this phase to a satisfactory conclusion.

Reviewing project materials with the client is an important professional activity. Designers need to have thought as much about how to show the drawings and other documents as what is to be said. Involving the client in the presentation, using professional language without getting hung up on jargon or highly technical descriptions, exuding confidence, and creating excitement and enthusiasm in the design solutions are all important parts of conducting successful preliminary and final presentations.

As with the other types of presentations, it is a good idea for the designer to spend time after the presentation has been made to review what went right and wrong during the presentation. Obviously, this is more important if the client had lots of questions and problems with the final presentation documents. Generally, however, this presentation requires only that minor changes to the plans, specifications, and other documents be made so that the project bid documents or purchase orders can be prepared. Item 22-2 on the CD is a post presentation review form that can help formalize the notes on what happened during the presentation.

OVERCOMING OBJECTIONS

Frequently, interior designers hear something like, "I don't think I like that color (style, arrangement, etc.) Can't you come up with something else?" from a client. In any selling or presentation situation, the client will have some objections to what is being discussed or proposed. To become successful at presenting concepts and selling services or products, one must understand how to

TABLE 22-2.

Common Objections Raised by Clients during Presentations and Selling Encounters.

- Your price is too high.
- Your service was not very good the last time the client worked with your firm.
- There is a question about the designer's experience for this type of project.
- The client does not like what has been proposed.
- The competition is cheaper.
- The client cannot afford the service or product after all.
- The client does not believe your firm is big enough to handle the project.
- A competitor is willing to do the design work on spec (for free).
- The designer has not met the needs of the client.
- The client must get approval from someone else.
- The client likes the ideas but will purchase from a friend or relative in the business out of state.
- Your low price as compared to the competition makes the client suspicious.
- The client is not convinced that you can meet the client's schedule.
- The client's priorities have changed, and the client needs to spend the funds on something else.

overcome these objections. Many of the top salespeople feel that unless the client makes some kind of objection, it is quite possible that the designer is not even making any headway. Others feel that an objection means the opposite—they are giving you a signal that they want to buy but you have not convinced them as of yet.

Objections can occur because the client does not understand what the designer is talking about but is embarrassed to say so. Sometimes objections are raised because the client really cannot afford what is being discussed but will not admit it. And other objections are raised because the client is afraid of making a mistake and would rather not buy than make a mistake. Some of the most common types of objections are listed in Table 22-2.

One of the most common objections has to do with price. It is rare for price not to be an issue. "Your competition charges less per hour," "I can get free design services from another studio," or "The sofa is too expensive" are typical comments heard by interior designers. The literature on selling services and products strongly suggests that price is rarely the only factor in a price objection. For the high-end residential client, price is generally not an actual concern, while quality certainly is. Perhaps the designer can overcome such objections by restating quality characteristics of the product or by discussing how his or her services are different from the competition. A commercial client might be objecting to price because the concepts presented do not represent the needs of the client or because something has gone wrong in the relationship and the value of the services or experience of the designer has now become a question that translates into "the price is too high."

A second common objection is, "I need to talk this over with my spouse" (e.g., partner, boss, etc.). This objection often comes up for two reasons: First, the client is afraid of making a mistake and will not make a decision unless someone else agrees; second, the designer has not been careful in setting up an appointment with the decision makers in the first place. In the first situation, there is not much the designer can do, unless he or she can review information about the service or product to help alleviate the client's concerns. This may lead to the client making the decision without consulting with the other party. Be careful about becoming a pushy salesperson, which could result in losing the sale altogether. In the second situation, the designer must be sure that he or she understands who is making the decision as the designer gathers information during the initial presentation. The presentation should be arranged so that all the decision makers are at the meeting. In this way, the designer only makes one presentation.

Another common objection develops over a question of the designer's experience or credentials. The interior designer may feel he or she is perfectly qualified to design the project, let us say a restaurant. However, the client does not see the experience of the individual in the qualifications and experiences list, nor does the designer convey knowledge of what is necessary in the design of restaurants. This might have occurred because the designer did not take the time to customize the leave-behinds nor update a brochure with recent restaurant photos. A situation could also have occurred where the client heard some unflattering information about your firm. Don't ask who told them something unflattering, but ask them what they heard so that you can explain how things are not that way. By the way, never argue with the client. That attitude will never work.

An obvious part of overcoming objections is actually listening to the objection. This sounds simplistic, but it is brought up because too many designers do not listen to the client and miss the cues or even the words of the objections. It is imperative that the designer listen carefully to everything that the client is saying so that the designer will not be in the following sample situation. Sally Jones, a designer, was on a call with Bill Preoccupied, one of the project's designers. They both were at the office of Anthony Smith. Smith was responding to a question by Jones concerning color and style preferences for the remodeling of the office, and in the middle of that discourse, Smith said that he really did not like a lot of browns and tans. Bill Preoccupied looked up from his notebook and said, "I really think that browns would be great in your new office." Both Jones and Smith looked at Preoccupied and then looked at each other. Although the names have been changed to protect the guilty, it is a true story and shows that even the most experienced designers may not pay attention and potentially can lose a client. "Listening is a selfless act. You must suspend your own ego and interests and focus on the other person."[2] Listening also involves focusing your mind on what the person is saying rather than on what you are trying to say. Most people can tell when someone is truly listening or pretending. Do not pretend. Listen, learn, succeed.

When objections occur, keep your sense of humor and perspective. The client is not going to like everything. Repeat the objection back and then ask questions to clarify what the problem might be. Then review the information you have already gathered about the needs of the client and summarize your point of view in terms of the client's needs and objection. It is not necessary to assume that the client is right concerning the objection. However, be respectful, since the client may not be familiar with industry concepts and terms. Never tell the client that he or she is wrong—this will only put the client on the defensive.

Whatever the objection is, the designer must listen to the objection and be ready to deal with it in a professional manner. Successful designers do not become successful by giving in to these objections without trying to understand the nature of the objection and to sway the client. However, never argue with the client. Getting him or her angry not only means that the problem will remain unresolved but also that the designer may lose the client.

CLOSING TECHNIQUES

If one of the hardest things for interior designers to do is speak before a group and another is to talk about his or her value without sounding egotistical, the next hard thing in selling is asking—that is, asking the client for the go-ahead to create a contract, asking the client to sign the contract, asking the client if the plans and products specified are approved. *Closing* is the art of knowing when to ask for the sale. If you are lucky and the client says, "I'll hire you," or "I'll take it," without your having to ask first, you probably do not even need to read this chapter at all. If you have developed a positive relationship with the client, most likely you will not have to utilize any of the techniques discussed in this section. When a good relationship exists, the designer has a better feeling about how to answer the questions the client asks or doesn't ask, for example, what the client's face and body language may be saying to the designer about agreement or disagreement. Getting a signature or approval in order to move on with the project will then be easy.

Not asking for the sale is among the most common reasons that the client does not buy the designer's services and/or products. Why? Because some clients just want you to ask. Interior designers are very comfortable in designing elaborate, complex residences or commercial spaces. Some of these same designers, however, become very uncomfortable when the time comes to present and sell those concepts. Why are designers afraid to ask for the sale? Fear, plain and simple—fear of the rejection that comes when the client says "no." A fact of life is that sometimes the client is going to say no or "I'm not sure."

Some object to the idea of discussing techniques to sell and get a client to buy. We are not talking about hard-core, aggressive techniques to force someone to buy something or sign a contract. There are closing techniques that are very acceptable in this profession, as well as other service professions, where words and actions can be used by the designer to ask for the sale. The sooner the designer asks, the sooner the client may sign the agreement, and the sooner the designer can move on to another project. In a very real sense, asking for the sale assumes that agreement has been reached on the issues being discussed. However, many people neglect to ask the questions that slowly confirm agreement. When this happens, when the designer then tries to close before the client is close to saying yes, the designer is often met by one more objection. Remember that objections do not necessarily stop the presentation in its tracks; they are just obstacles to be overcome through additional questions and answers.

There are many techniques that are recommended by numerous how-to-sell books. Some of those books are listed in the reference section. The following will recount some of the techniques that other professionals use with great success. They are easily applied to selling services and products in the interior design industry.

In the previous chapter, we discussed using features and benefits to help sell services and products. Try this closing method in combination with features and benefits. When you can meet at least two needs of the client based on your features or benefits (or those of a product), use a trial close. A *trial close* is simply asking for the sale; that is, you are trying to close. Supporting the client's needs with features and benefits shows the client that you are really trying to solve the client's needs and provide him or her with only what is needed, not what you want to sell the client. Remember, trying to close the sale means that you have reached an agreement on needs. Consider the following situation:

Designer: You said that you are looking for a comfortable sofa bed for the guest room, which will have a fabric that will be easy to maintain. Is that correct, Ms. Smith?

Smith: Yes, it is.

Designer: I have already shown you that this sofa bed, made by company X, has been rated by an independent testing company as having the most comfortable mattress on the market. This nylon basket weave fabric, which you liked, will be easy to maintain. Why don't I work up the final price with this fabric and see when we can deliver it to your home?

Assuming that the price is not an issue, if the client says this will be fine, you can finish with the sale and only need to write up the paperwork. However, if the client says no, you must assume that something needs still to be resolved. You must ask more questions and discuss other features and benefits, and then try again to close.

Another frequently used closing technique is to close when the client agrees to a secondary issue concerning the sale. In the preceding example, when the designer obtained agreement about the fabric choice, he or she would then follow with questions related to the color of the fabric. When these two issues were resolved, then the designer would be ready to close.

Many designers use *third-party testimonials* (or references), which are statements or stories to help with the close. "A testimonial is a statement from a satisfied client praising you and your services."[3] Recalling how a previous client was satisfied by the firm's service or products often helps to alleviate fears of the decision-making process. "Grey Fox Restaurant felt our project management techniques were outstanding and was a major reason why their fast-track restaurant project opened on time" is an example.

Third-party testimonials or stories are very powerful. They do not represent the designer's opinions but a neutral third party. It is reasonable to ask clients who were particularly satisfied with your work for a testimonial. Do this by asking for comments and criticisms to improve your service in the future. You will likely gain a sentence that can then be used as part of your closing techniques or in other promotional situations. Always ask for permission to quote the client.

A closing technique that many designers use, though perhaps reluctantly, relates to a forthcoming event. For example, a client who might be hesitant to close the sale today might be encouraged if he or she knew that the price on the goods were going up in a few weeks. "I can only guarantee this price for the next ten days, since we have already been informed of a price increase on January 1," the designer would say. This technique is perfectly legitimate *if it is true*. It should, however, only be used in complete honesty. Telling a client that the price of the goods is going to go up when, in fact, it will not or telling the client that the plant will close for two weeks when it will not is not ethical.

These closing techniques and others are discussed in many sales books as methods that can help the designer obtain the client's signature on a design contract, perhaps achieve agreement to design concepts when reviewing plans, and sell products. Whether you use them or not is up to you. They are provided as a conclusion to the discussion on the overall sales process.

FOLLOW-UP

A designer related a story that he had been contacted by a client who, as he later found out, interviewed five designers for the remodeling of her kitchen. He said that about ten days after the interview, he received a call back saying that the client wanted to hire him. One of the reasons for this positive development is that he sent her a brief note thanking her for her time. He was the only one who did so, and the client liked this very special courtesy.

Many times we are too busy to follow up promptly with thank-you notes after the project is completed. Think how much of an impression it might make on clients to be thanked with a quick note after a marketing presentation! The designer should follow up on the marketing or proposal presentation with a letter and/or a phone call. The follow-up should cover such things as thanking the client for his or her time, restating important points of the presentation, and emphasizing continued interest in working with the client. Any information or document that might have been promised during the presentation must be taken care of at this point as well. Delays in sending these additional documents could hurt the designer's chances of closing the sale.

Losing a sale can be a great lesson—that is, if the designer takes the time to evaluate why he or she did not get the job. Whether the designer is experienced or new to the professional presentation process, his or her understanding of why he or she lost the job may be more important to future success than closing one sale. It is not pleasant to lose a sale, but it is important for the designer to try to find out why he or she did.

Records should also be kept on the results of marketing presentations and at the completion of a project. This activity was discussed in part in this chapter, at the end of the discussion on proposal presentations. A post-project presentation evaluation form has been added to the CD as Item 22-2. A post-project review discussion is in Chapter 32.

NEGOTIATING

Martha had presented her design contract to Dr. Jones and Dr. Smith. All through her presentation and discussion of how she worked and how she saw this project progressing, she felt that obtaining the doctors' signatures on the contract would be easy. Questions arose concerning the scope outlined and a few clauses in the contract, as well as the overall fee. Martha wanted this project, as it would get her foot in the door of a large medical office building that was only partially leased to tenants. The developer of this building had also started another next door. She began by asking the doctors about their questions concerning the scope of services.

You undoubtedly have already been involved in many negotiation situations, even if you have not yet worked in the interior design field. Perhaps it was to get a few extra days from a professor to complete a project or a paper. Or it could have been to obtain a raise at a part-time job. Of course, the professional designer is negotiating all the time—for better pricing from a vendor or a more favorable installation date from the wallpaper hanger, or even the hourly fee charged by the designer's accountant. In many respects, a negotiation is another form of a presentation. When you (or your client) want something that perhaps the other person does not want you to have, you are probably getting into a negotiating situation.

Negotiating is an activity wherein two parties are trying to reach agreement about some point of discussion. In the ideal situation, the negotiation proceeds so that the two parties who start out on opposite sides of an issue come to a mutually agreeable conclusion. In other words, negotiating should create a "win-win" situation so that both parties are satisfied. If a negotiation reaches a "I win, you lose" situation, then it is not a successful negotiation, since only one party is happy. The "I win, you lose" situation is not a negotiation but, rather, manipulation. And manipulation has no place in the bag of skills of a successful interior designer.

Successful negotiation requires the use of strategies that are similar to those used in any other type of presentation. To be successful, you have to know what it is you want in order to understand your goals and objectives for entering into the negotiation. You also have to think like the client and try to determine what the client might be looking for or object to. Preparing to negotiate includes having your facts straight concerning your position and knowing what the "bottom line" is as well. What is the less satisfactory solution that is considered acceptable? Perhaps you are requesting $10,000 in fees to execute a design project. That is your position. Are you really willing to go below that, and if so, how far below? And why are you willing to lower your fee?

As it might seem to suggest, negotiation involves discussion. Both you and the client (or whomever you are negotiating with) will state a position and wisely explain how you feel about the other person's position, not being negative, but to show the positive side of your position. The other party will counter with their position and their reasons that their position is best. Negotiations that are win-win will always have some give-and-take, as hopefully each side sees some value to what the other person is saying.

For example, a client has told you that a $10,000 design fee is too high. She says someone else quoted only $7000. You might counter by explaining the steps that will be needed to accomplish the scope of services, how you go through the design process, and the value that your services will provide. You could decide that deleting a few of the steps in the scope are feasible though the end result you understand the client wants may not be the same. Of course, many other approaches can be taken in this type of a negotiation.

Eventually, after discussion and counterproposals, an agreement is reached. Or not. One or the other party to the negotiation can sooner or later hit their bottom line, where they are no longer willing to budge. Someone gives in or they both agree to disagree and walk away.

Knowing when and where to negotiate is also important. Control of the environment is why designers prefer to make marketing presentations in their office or studio rather than at the client's location. If the client greets you at the entry with a scowl and tells you about the terrible time she just had with the maid, it is no time to negotiate or make a presentation with the expectation of obtaining a positive outcome. Reschedule if possible when the client is no longer frantic and perhaps angry. This type of thinking of when and where applies to other kinds of negotiations as well. If it is possible, carry on the negotiation for a raise somewhere other than your boss's office. Take your boss to lunch and discuss this topic in a neutral place.

Understand that conflict is inevitable in many business situations. Not every client the designer calls on can actually afford the services of a particular designer. The designer might not really be interested in every project that he or she obtains a lead on. It is very easy for the designer's philosophy or style to be in conflict with what the client was looking for. A client might not understand what the "design process" is all about and why it should take so long to determine what the interior should look like and what they should buy. It happens so fast on television, after all! Always giving in may obtain work for the designer, but eventually it will make themselves feel less valuable, making harder each time to negotiate for what is really fair. On the other hand, being hardheaded and demanding his or her own way creates an impression of the dilettante designer. Not very many clients in today's competitive market will stand for that anymore.

Success in negotiation is not a gift that comes naturally to most professional designers, but it can be learned. Each successful negotiation affects how you conduct future negotiations. And how you go about a negotiation session will also affect the future relationship between the individuals involved. Table 22-3 lists some tips that might help in negotiations.

TABLE 22-3.

Ideas for Negotiation.

- Start with a plan. When you are about to negotiate an important design contract or a salary increase, do not fool yourself into thinking that you can pull it off without planning what you are going to say.
- Only negotiate for what you are prepared to do or are able to do. Do not put anything on the table that you have no intention of doing or cannot accomplish.
- Always be truthful. A successful negotiation depends on trust between the two parties. If the parties to a negotiation do not trust each other, they will never be able to successfully negotiate anything.
- Have patience. The best negotiators know that it takes patience to work toward a win-win conclusion. Nobody likes being browbeaten or intimidated into making a decision. You gain an advantage when you take your time rather than rush.
- Use your "power." Power is based on perception. If you think you have it, you do. Using your power means having confidence in yourself and your point of view.

ADDITIONAL GUIDELINES FOR MAKING PRESENTATIONS

In this chapter, we have discussed many tips for making specific types of design presentations. Frequently, these tips overlap and are a useful part of any kind of presentation. In fact, many of the items discussed can be applied to job interviews, asking for a raise or promotion, and even dealing with personal relationships out of the office. Following are several additional presentation guidelines that students and designers alike might find useful in their professional practice.

- You only have one chance to make a first impression. Remember that the first 30 to 60 seconds create the strongest impression. Do your best to make this initial contact as professional and confidence-building as possible.
- Dress appropriately. Business clients expect designers to look as though they understand business. Residential clients generally are more comfortable with trendy attire than with conservative business clothing.
- Use professional language. Part of being a professional is sounding like a professional. Use proper language and speak distinctly. It is okay to use technical words, but be prepared to explain any technical language that you incorporate into your presentation.
- Tailor your presentation to the client, and be sure you are focusing on determining and understanding their needs.
- Use good posture. Stand and sit straight, shoulders back—just like Mother always said!
- Anticipate the other person's responses and questions. Trying to determine the other person's concerns will make you more thorough and professional.
- Be enthusiastic. Clients cannot get excited about a project if you are not enthusiastic.
- Stick to your time limit. Never exceed the time limit, unless the client gives you permission.

- If you make a mistake, do not make a big deal out of it. Calling attention to the problem only will make you feel worse and may totally throw you off balance. Say something like, "Let me clarify that last point," and move on.

- Never be late for the presentation or begin the presentation late. In fact, plan on arriving a little early. In that way, you will always have time to repair a board that has been damaged in transit, freshen up, and relax before you must begin.

- Be respectful of the client's time by not spending a lot of time making small talk, then having to rush through the presentation or taking up too much of the client's time.

- For especially long presentations like a proposal presentation, plan a break. Use the time to set up additional visuals and arrange for providing refreshments.

- Prior to a presentation, do not consume milk products, salty foods, or alcohol. These items dehydrate most people. Be sure you have a glass of water handy in case your mouth is dry.

- Use gestures carefully. Gestures are helpful to emphasize important points. Hands that are constantly in motion are distracting.

- Talk to the client, not to the board or the screen. Too many presenters direct what they are saying to the board or screen rather than to the audience. The client does not want to admire your back. He or she wants to see your face as you are talking.

- Do not criticize your competition. If the client asks you what you think of a competitor, say something simple like, "I understand that he is a competent designer." Bad-mouthing the competition is unprofessional and will only come back to haunt you later.

- Relax! Don't scowl so that you appear as if you are about to have a root canal. If you know what you are going to say and have confidence in your ability to pull off the presentation, it will be easy to look as though you are having a good time.

- Define your goals for the presentation. If you do not know what you want to say or accomplish in your meeting, you will almost always be dissatisfied at the end.

- If the potential project is out of the country or with a foreign company, bone up on body language and customs of the other country. This kind of homework is absolutely necessary if your firm seeks to work with international clients.

- Make sure your projector works and sample boards hold together for the presentation. If a problem occurs, have one of the other members from the design firm fix the item while you continue presenting other information. If this is not possible, suggest taking a short break so that you can fix the item without the client watching.

- It is okay to use an outline or script—just don't read it back to the client. Designers who lack in presentation experience or are uncomfortable with making presentations need to write out what they want to say.

- Practice, practice, practice! The more often you run through a presentation, especially with a colleague who can critique it and the more often you make presentations, the easier and more effective they will become.

SUMMARY

Interior designers make all types of presentations in the course of their professional practice. It makes little difference if the presentation is to gather additional information after an initial meeting, actually make a marketing presentation of some kind, or defend design plans and specifications during the course of a project. Designers are constantly making presentations. Marketing presentations are among the most important, as without successful marketing presentations, not much interior design work will be required of even the most creative practitioner. Successfully navigating through each succeeding presentation will help the designer build confidence and increase his or her professional competence.

Educational programs strongly emphasize giving critiques of design work. Although this is a great way to understand the good and bad points of a project, it does not focus attention on the type of presentations that designers have to make in the professional world. Students should consider taking a speech or acting class in order to gain confidence in speaking in front of a group. Professional designers often join networking clubs, where they must make a brief presentation from time to time. Of course, a professional who is uncomfortable in front of a group can also gain from taking a speech or acting class.

In this chapter many techniques have been discussed and numerous guidelines on structuring and performing design presentations have been provided. Utilizing these concepts when faced with making a presentation should help students and professionals become more effective.

REFERENCES

1. Twitty-Villani, 1992, p. 2.

2. Excerpted with permission of Chandler House Press, from *Knockout Presentations* by Diane DiResta. Copyright 1998 by Diane DiResta www.chandlerhousepress.com. p. 516.

3. Bly, 1991, p. 30

C lients demand high-performance buildings that are beautiful, functional, agile, and address the demands of their customers, employees, and stockholders. Many methodologies have changed from the days of the master builder working with craftsmen. However, the underlying processes remain highly collaborative, requiring the expertise of many disciplines working together to develop creative, new solutions.

Highly performing and successful collaborative teams operate on trust and respect, with members being skilled listeners and critical thinkers. Effective team collaborations share the characteristics of clear direction provided by the team leaders; essential in creating the environment for collaboration and a commitment to continued learning from shared experiences.

Beth Harmon-Vaughan, FIIDA, is an award-winning commercial interior designer who has been an officer in several internationally known design firms. She is currently Managing Director for Gensler, in Phoenix, Arizona. This distinguished designer has chaired panels and presented professional papers at conferences around the world.

Harmon-Vaughan is a Fellow and a past international president of International Interior Design Association (IIDA) and has recently served on the Boards of the Council for Interior Design Accreditation as chair. Currently she serves on the Dean's Council for Design Excellence at the College of Design at Arizona State University, the AIA national Interiors Committee, and chairs the Missouri Licensing Board for Interior Design.

Louise Bourgeois

Art is a Guaranty of Sanity, 2005–2006

Aluminum, stainless steel, steel, glass, and diodes

H 94'5" × W 32'3" × D 20'

Commissioned by the City of Phoenix, through the Phoenix Office of Arts and Culture's Public Art Program

Photo: Bill Timmerman

Project Compensation and Agreements

Statute of Frauds
The Sales Contract
Electronic Agreements and Signatures
Title
Risk
Sales on Approval
Seller's Rights and Obligations
Buyer's Rights and Obligations

27. Warranties and Product Liability

Warranties
Products Liability

CHAPTER 23

Project Compensation and Fees

Key Terms and Concepts

These key terms and concepts are important to material in this chapter. Many of these terms will be utilized in other chapters as well. Be sure you understand these items as you read this chapter.

Billing rate

Multiple

Multiplier

Direct personnel expense (DPE)

Hourly fee

Not to exceed limit

Daily rate

Fixed fee

Flat fee

Lump sum

Square foot method

Value-oriented

Percentage of merchandise and product services

Double dipping

Cost plus percentage markup

Retail method

Percentage off retail

Consultation fee

Combination

Indirect job costs

Critical Issues

After completing this chapter you should be able to:

- Calculate a billing rate based on the DPE.
- Discuss several factors that impact which fee method is used for a particular project.
- Compare the pros and cons of the hourly fee method to the cost plus percentage markup method.
- List and compare other fee methods discussed in the chapter.
- Determine which fee method to utilize based on a specific project description.
- Discuss how to use the value-oriented fee method.
- Explain how to control indirect job costs from negatively impacting overall fee profitability.

Marsha charges a consultation fee that she feels covers the majority of her time working on a project. Occasionally the consultation fee is based on an hourly fee, and sometimes it is a fixed fee. Marsha added the consultation fee when she realized that clients were not recognizing the value she provided through her design solutions when she only charged a cost plus markup on the goods she sold. She also added a consultation fee when it became clear that the markup percentage alone—which was very competitive in her market—was not providing a sufficient profit margin to cover expenses.

For many interior design firms, the only source of income for the firm is from fees charged to the client for services. These fees must cover the cost of the designer's time or salary expense and overhead expenses, such as electricity, cost of drafting paper, and telephone calls, and must provide a margin of profit as well. Other interior design firms generate revenues from the sale of merchandise. Still others generate the revenues from both merchandise fees and service fees.

It can be argued that charging a professional fee versus selling merchandise is one additional factor in "professionalizing" the profession. Some might argue that it does not take an educated, certified, licensed individual to sell desks or sofas. It might further be argued that most clients do not come to interior designers solely because of the good deals they can get on furniture anyway. There are many interior designers who argue that a professional interior designer should be seeking compensation based on the same things any other professional is compensated for—training, knowledge, their ability to solve the client's problems, and capacity to produce the work product of the profession. Selling product should not, it is argued, be the purpose of the work of an interior designer but a consequence of that work. Of course, selling goods produces revenue, and so it is likely to continue until clients accept and understand the value of the interior design professional's skills, and fewer and fewer designers sell merchandise directly.

Be that as it may, there is no one way to satisfy all situations and all types of interior design practice. Each firm must decide which fee method and revenue method is appropriate for its purposes. Many factors will impact this decision. The methods used by local competition may force the design firm into using certain fee methods, since clients may be used to specific practices. The type of design in which the designer chooses to specialize may mean that the firm must use one fee method over others. The designer's own experience and knowledge may direct the designer to use a particular fee method.

The variety of fee methods allows the design professional to choose a method with which he or she is comfortable in order to "sell" it to the client more easily. Various fee methods allow the professional to customize how he or she charges clients to suit the client's needs and the specific project. However, the different fee methods can create confusion. Inconsistency can be a problem if the designer is working with clients who talk to each other a lot, such is often the case in residential interior design practice.

This chapter emphasizes fee methods related to compensation for interior design service as might be used by a designer or a firm. However, fee methods used alone or in combination with service fees are also discussed. Pricing methods for the sale of goods is discussed in Chapter 25.

CALCULATING THE BILLING RATE

John charges $125 per hour regardless of who in his firm works on the project. At her firm, Susan determines a fixed fee that she relates to the salary of each employee team member on the project. At his company, Otto insists on a flat consultation fee of $750 for a two-hour meeting. Each of these examples—which are all fictitious—show that designers charge many different ways. And each in some way is determined by the billing rate of each design staff member.

The *billing rate* is a dollar amount charged for each design professional, staff member, or, in some cases, the type of service provided. Most typically, the billing rate is expressed as an hourly rate. Some situations might call for a day rate, in which case the billing rate is for a full day's work rather than determined on an hourly basis. A billing rate is used to calculate fixed fees and most other types of fee methods as well, once a determination is made as to how long the project is expected to take to complete.

The billing rate is based on the salary rate of the employee. Since the salary rate alone does not cover expenses for the employee as well as overhead expenses and provide a profit, the rate is actually calculated based on the firm's *multiple* (also called a multiplier). A multiple is calculated to include these other factors. For some fee methods, especially the fixed-fee and square-footage method, the billing rate is primary to the determination of the total fee. In other methods, such as cost plus or percentage off retail, it has an indirect bearing on the fee itself. The multiple is multiplied by the salary rate, and the individual's billing rate is then established.

Traditionally, the most commonly used multiple is 3.0. No one seems to know where this factor came from. It might be interpreted as meaning that one part is equal to the salary rate, one part covers overhead burden, and one part allows for profit. However, this is not necessarily accurate, since some firms have a carefully calculated multiple that is below 3.0 and some firms have one that is slightly above 3.0. The size of the firm has a major affect upon overhead and, of course, salary expenses. A method commonly used in interior design and architectural offices is to determine the multiple of direct personnel expense. The *direct personnel expense* (DPE) is a number that includes the salary of the employee and costs of employee benefits such as unemployment taxes, medical insurance, and paid holidays. The calculation of the DPE is the most accurate way to determine a firm's multiple.

It is not simply a combination of the salary and benefits. The DPE, to be accurate, must include direct and overhead expenses, as well as profit; otherwise, the fee multiple will not provide adequately for these critical parts of the profitability of projects. For example, on average, the cost of employee fringe benefits can add up to 30 to 60 percent to the cost of the employee. Sixty percent is quite high and probably only impacts the largest multidisciplinary firms. Even a 30 percent factor for a small firm can make a serious dent in profitability of the firm if not factored into the fee. Too often a sole practitioner and other owners of new design firms forget that paid vacations and health insurance for an individual or small group can be a very expensive, though important, benefit. Many new owners of an interior design firm are very surprised to find a net profit of only 2 to 4 percent—if they find any net profit at all—because they have not carefully considered their expenses in operating the firm when determining their compensation. Net profit rates of around 10 to 15 percent are more common, especially in firms that carefully control costs and accurately estimate profit plans into billing rates.

A multiplier based on the DPE is a factor that is based on the direct labor expense plus the cost of employee benefits. You will recall from the discussion in Chapter 16 that direct labor and expenses are those that are incurred when employees are actually working on revenue-producing work. This discussion follows the numbers shown in Table 23-1. This table has also been included on the CD as Item 23-1.

TABLE 23-1.

Direct Personal Expense and Fee Multiple	
Total annual salaries	$100,000
Total fringe benefits	20,000
Total overhead expenses	32,000
Total Expenses	$152,000
Total profit goal (20% of revenue)	38,000
Total Net Revenue (income goal for year)	$190,000
Direct labor $100,000 × 0.70	$70,000
Indirect Expenses:	
Indirect labor $100,00 × 0.30	30,000
Payroll taxes and benefits	20,000
Overhead expenses	32,000
Total of indirect salary and expenses	82,000
Total of Direct Salaries and Indirect Expenses	$152,000
The DPE multiplier would be:	
Direct salary divided by direct salary: $70,000 divided by $70,000	1.00
Total indirect expenses divided by direct salary: $82,000 divided by $70,000	1.17
Adding profit: $38,000 divided by $70,000	0.54
Total DPE multiplier	2.71

All of this information could be obtained easily from the financial records of the design firm. First, the total annual salary of all employees is determined. Then the total of employee fringe benefits expenses are found, such as unemployment taxes, workers' compensation, medical and/or life insurance, FICA, sick leave, pension plans, and paid holidays. Table 14-2 in Chapter 14 provides examples of common employee benefits. Next, the owner needs to determine the total of overhead expenses for the year. Adding these three items together gives the total annual expenses for the firm. At this point, the owner should add on a factor for a profit goal. In Table 23-1, we have added a percentage that would give a reasonable profit goal of 20 percent.

The total net revenue shown in the example is revenue that does not include any sale of furniture. It is purely related to the offering of design services. In this situation, the revenues are realized when designers work on design projects; thus, it is necessary to determine a factor for direct labor. Since it is very difficult for all professional staff to work at 100 percent billable time and little of the support staff's time is billable, it is necessary to create a multiplier based on direct personnel expense (DPE to be accurate).

This is done by the calculations shown in the remainder of Table 23-1. Assuming that only 70 percent of possible work time is billable (referred to as a utilization rate), then $70,000 would be direct labor. A 70 percent utilization rate is reasonable if the designer also has nonbillable responsibilities such as marketing, administration, and employee supervision. Designers whose primary responsibility is to be fully engaged in designing projects are expected to have a utilization rate closer to 100 percent. The remaining salary expense is indirect labor—that salary expense that cannot be billed to clients. The amount of payroll taxes, fringe benefits, and overhead expenses is restated in the lower portion of the table for clarification. Employees whose time is billable are the professional design staff. Secretaries, office assistants, and bookkeepers generally are not employees whose time can be billed. The time that a secretary spends preparing specifications and certain other written documentation specifically needed as part of a project *can* be billed, as it directly relates to the completion of a project. However, it is not very common for design firms to charge for this time.

The net multiplier is then calculated against the salary rates to get the billing rates. For example, if the senior designer is paid $42.50 per hour, his billing rate would be $113.82, or probably rounded to $114.00 per hour. An entry-level design assistant who is paid $20.00 per hour could be billed at $54.20, or $55.00 per hour. Note that actual billing rates at the time of this writing vary widely from those noted. These numbers are provided merely for you to see how the calculation is accomplished.

When the owner is determining the expense portion of the billing rate multiple, there is another concept that he or she should consider. As the business expands, the cost of direct expenses will expand as more revenue is generated. What is sometimes forgotten is that as business expands so might overhead expenses. It may be necessary for the owner, manager, and employees to stay after normal business hours in order to complete projects, adding to overall utility bills. This extra work could also mean additional work for support personnel. As business expands, simple overhead expenses, like supplies, telephone services, and many other costs of doing business and those related to generating income, also increase. Calculating these extra overhead expenses into the multiplier may not be an easy thing to do, but recognition of their impact should be taken into consideration. Failing to consider the effect that overtime work will have on the costs and fee estimates of projects will, at the very least, lead to a reduction in planned profit margins.

Billing rates also can be used to determine if the fixed fee and the percentage rate methods are sufficient. The fee divided by the billing rate multiple will give the amount of salary dollars that the owner can use for that project at the profit margin that is normally maintained. This method helps the owner determine if the amount of salary dollars available is sufficient to cover the expenses and desired profit for the project. If it is determined that the project cannot be done for that amount, then the owner can either reject the project or try a different fee method or a combination of methods in order to ensure that there will be proper compensation.

WHICH COMPENSATION METHOD?

Professionals have many choices as to how exactly they are going to determine which fee method is appropriate for their business. Fee methods may also vary because of the nature of the project, the client, shifts in competition, and other personal and business reasons. No one method is better than any other all the time. Interior designers tend toward one or two methods most of the time. This may be because it is one they are used to or has worked before or better fits the way in which they do business with a majority of clients. There are several factors that must be considered when determining which compensation method to use and estimating the amount to charge. Following are a few that are discussed in detail. A discussion of estimating considerations is provided in the next section of this chapter.

- *Scope of services.* It can be argued that all projects involve some measure of the complete design process. Yet some projects do not require many drawings or contract documents. What has to be done impacts the amount of time and work required—naturally. And thus the scope of services has probably the major impact on what method to use and the amount of fee that will be negotiated. Interior designers who tend more toward the decorative side of design and who work little in the overall planning and limited architectural services often charge no fee for their services and earn revenue from the markup of furniture that they sell to their clients. Of course, more can go wrong with a complex project that requires a large number of services. Contingency planning in the selection of fee methods and amounts is necessary in a large, complex project. Thus, detailed discussions with the client concerning what needs to be done are critical in determining which fee method to use as well as what that amount will be.

- *The designer's experience.* The less experienced the interior designer is with a particular type of project, the longer (logically) it will take him or her to execute the project. There is a learning curve with every project because the designer does not know a particular client or a project in depth. Perhaps new programming methods and tools must be found and used to elicit the needed information. In a commercial project, the designer may lack background information about the client's business and may find that research is in order. Maybe the client and project call for product specifications that are unfamiliar to the designer or are so unique that extra time is required to find the products. All of these examples and many others affect the amount of time that the designer needs to complete the project, thus requiring that he or she be compensated for that time without making the client pay for all the "learning" that the designer needs in order to complete the project.

- *The client's experience with an interior designer.* Clients—residential or commercial—who have had no previous experience working with an interior designer require more of the designer's time and patience, and more educating. These clients ask more questions, want more choices, and deliberate more before they make decisions. They also change their mind more often and generally challenge the interior designer more frequently. The client who has worked with a designer before, for the most part, will be just the opposite—though no cinch to work with either! And if the designer has never worked with the client before, the client will also require more of the designer's patience and time, even if the client has worked previously with other interior designers. Projects generally will take longer to complete for the client who has not previously worked with a designer.

- *Size and complexity of the project.* The larger and more complex the project is, the more time the designer will have to spend on the project. There is no argument that the designer must make carefully considered decisions when designing and specifying a custom window treatment for a residence or creating a new look and furniture specification for the patient waiting area for a doctor's office. Much more, however, must be determined and prepared in the design of a 10,000-square-foot high-end residence, a multilevel condominium in a high-rise, a hospital, or other commercial interiors. On the other hand, there are some large projects that are large in terms of square footage but that do not require a lot of unique designs. For example, hotels may have hundreds of rooms, but most of the rooms have the same floor plan and use perhaps a few different color schemes in the same pattern. Creating the prototype guest room is where the intense design effort occurs; less time is spent on the "copies."

- *Residential versus commercial.* Residential interior designers tend to charge fees or earn revenue based on the sale of goods. Sometimes, charges for their design services are commonly "buried" in the price of the goods and are not charged directly. These designers frequently charge retail, a discount from retail, or at cost plus a markup percentage for the goods. Other residential interior designers charge a small fee for their services and then sell merchandise at some sort of markup from cost or discount from retail in order to cover the remainder of the revenue that is required to cover the expenses of performing design services, paying overhead, and earning a profit. Naturally, some residential designers do not sell furniture and other furnishings at all and charge clients based on fees for services.

  Commercial designers, on the other hand, predominately charge for the services they perform and less frequently sell merchandise. Commercial interior designers use a variety of fee methods but commonly use the hourly fee, fixed-fee methods, the square-footage method, or perhaps some other method. The hourly fee is the most remunerative way of charging for design services, because the client pays for every hour (or potentially every minute) of design work. Clients, however, may be concerned that the designer may take too long to finish the project if the work is based on an hourly rate. This is why many commercial designers use other methods.

Which method to use depends on all the factors just discussed, as well as many others that are particular to the design firm. Competition, the desire to do a particular project, the cash flow situation of the design firm, and many other factors are considered by the owner every time the client wants to know "How much will this cost?" Now let us look specifically at the typical fee methods that are used in the professional practice of interior design.

ESTIMATING DESIGN FEES

Design projects are often complex endeavors and can involve several people to design and many months to execute the plans and other documents. A design project can also involve one designer for only a few days. Regardless of which fee method the designer uses, the key to profitability in providing design services is properly estimating the design fees. Several issues to consider that effect the design fee are shown in Table 23-2. Two key issues are (1) understanding the scope of services to be provided and (2) carefully calculating costs to ensure that the fee method satisfactorily covers the costs of executing the project and provides a profit margin. These both have a significant impact on the fee estimate and potential profitability of the project.

The first step must be a detailed analysis of what must be done—that is, determining the scope of services required—how much time each design activity will take, and how much time the project will take. Firms use estimating sheets, such as the one in Figure 23.1, to assist them in calculating what has to be done and how long it will take. The experience of the designer in doing similar projects helps the designer create an estimate of how much time the project will take once the designer determines what has to be done. Another example of a form that can be used for project fee estimating is provided on the CD as Item 23-2.

TABLE 23-2.

Factors That Impact Fee Estimates.

Scope of services
Estimates of direct expense items
Overhead expenses
Experience of design staff
Existing office schedule
Project location versus design firm location
Client familiarity with design process
Client expectations
Client budget expectations
Need for meetings with consultants such as architects, contractors, and lighting designers
Jurisdictional limitations—codes, licenses requirements
Competition—are other designers being interviewed?
Research time for codes or other special issues
Research for product specification
Custom design of products and millwork
Preparation of formal bid specifications versus equipment lists
Extent of design drawings/construction drawings required

Note that this list is not all-inclusive but represents major impacts on fee estimate.

Interior design projects include costs beyond the time involved. Supplies of various kinds are needed, from stationery to plotter paper and CDs to files for storing information. A telephone, cell phone, and fax machine are necessary for researching information for the project and coordinating the execution of the work. Each of these communication tools have costs associated with their use. Support personnel are needed to assist the interior designer with many phases of the project. And utility bills must be paid to keep the lights on and the heat or air conditioner working as the studio remains open to work on the project. Naturally, these are just a few expenses associated with completion of an interior design project. Of course, some of these expenses are straight overhead expenses, such as utilities. Others can be considered direct expenses, such as telephone calls. Regardless of how the owner determines to categorize expenses, they all play a part in the cost of operating the business and generating revenue. Somehow they must be included in the estimate for design work.

The other items in Table 23.2 must also be factored into the fee estimate. A client who has never worked with an interior designer before is likely to take longer to make decisions. If consultations with a consultant such as a lighting designer are required, these meetings must be factored into the design fee. A client budget that is too low paralleled by high expectations likely will require extra resource research time and meetings with clients. In estimating a fee, knowing that the client is interviewing two, three, or even several other firms will definitely influence the final fee estimate.

Determining Billing Rate Based on Salary

Many interior designers determine their billing rate based on a relatively simple manner. First an individual's annual salary is determined. Then a factor for fringe benefits is determined. A fairly common noncalculated factor, according to the U.S. Small Business Administration, is 30 percent of salary.* However, that varies greatly based on the actual array of fringe benefits and their cost. Next, the designer must determine how many weeks per year he or she is expecting to work and divides this into the salary expense. Not every sole practitioner, for example, chooses to work 50 weeks out of the year. A further calculation of the number of expected billable hours is needed in this method. That factor varies widely based on the individual and how carefully the designer or firm keeps track of billable time. A positive standard is to assume that on average a design staff member should be billing a minimum of 75 percent of his or her time per week. A multiplier is determined and an hourly billing rate results from the calculations as follows:

Annual salary	$50,000
Fringe benefits (30% of salary)	15,000
	$65,000/50 weeks = $1300 per week
Average of 40-hour week with	
75% billable on average	$1300/30 hrs = $43.34

A 3 times multiplier would result in a $130.00 per hour billing rate

(rounded for simplicity)

However, what this method fails to accurately include is how much overhead expenses impact the multiplier. A sole practitioner working out of a home office will have far fewer overhead expenses to impact the multiplier than a firm with commercial office space and support staff members. Office space rent, utilities, and extras can create a substantial overhead expense. Another factor involves the number of billable hours. Many designers do not charge for all their time, since they also earn revenue from the sale of goods. Even more important is that many small business practitioners fail to accurately keep track of their time working on projects versus taking care of administrative responsibilities.

Although it might seem that this method of determining an hourly fee is simpler than using the DPE calculations shown in Table 23-1, the DPE method is recommended because it is more accurate.

*Source: U.S. Small Business Administration, August 2005, Executive Summary. Available at www.sba.gov/advo.

With this information in hand, the designer or manager can apply one or more fee methods to the project to determine which method provides the greatest profit for the particular project. As previously discussed, projects requiring a lot of meetings, drafting, and specification writing are best charged at an hourly fee. Projects that have a lot of similar design decisions (multiple spaces like hotels and hospitals) might work out better if the designer uses a fixed fee or a percentage of cost. Computer simulations can be set up that will compare costs and revenue generation based on the fee method that a firm generally uses. These simulations help the designer determine which fee method will generate the greatest profit for a particular job.

The owner of each design firm must make his or her own decision as to what method will be used to charge for design services and produce an appropriate level of revenue. Planning for a profitable business begins with understanding the financial side of the business. If a designer is clear about his or her expenses in operating the particular practice, then the designer has taken the first step toward maintaining a profitable and successful design practice. Understanding the scope of services required is a very important factor that will impact the profitability of a project. The designer must consider the kinds of clients with whom he or she will be working, the types of design spaces, and the local competition. The firm must be ready to modify its fee methods when necessary to remain competitive.

PROJECT SCOPE OF SERVICES

Project:

Address:

Size:

Budget:

Scope:

Project Goal:

Items Specifically Excluded:

Proposed Project Team:

Schedule:

PROJECT DELIVERABLES

Included	Not Included	Quantity	Project Deliverables
			DESIGN PHASE
			Interior Design
			Field Verification/CAD Setup
			Space Plan
			Design Details
			Furniture Selection
			Finish Selection
			Presentation Boards
			Illustration/Computer Rendering
			Programming
			Schedule
			Tenant Leasebook
			Furniture/Equipment Inventory
			Construction Budget Estimate
			Graphic Design
			Identity Development (logo, stationary, menus)
			Signage Development
			Design Sketches and Concepts
			City Code /ADA Research
			DESIGN PHASE MEETINGS
			Client
			Subconsultant
			Contractor
			Site Visit
			City Code Review

FIGURE 23-1.

A sample form that can be used to estimate design fees (partial). (Reproduced with permission, Jeffrey Rausch, Exclaim Design, Scottsdale, AZ)

METHODS FOR SETTING DESIGN FEES

There are a great number of factors that the owner of a design firm must take into consideration when determining which fee method he or she will use for each design project. No one method works for all projects for any one design firm, and there is no one fee method that can be guaranteed to work best all the time for a particular type of project. This section discusses the typical methods of setting design fees. Table 23-3 discusses several differences between residential and

Included	Not Included	Quantity	Project Deliverables
			DOCUMENT PHASE
			Interior Design
			Construction Specifications
			Demolition Floor Plan
			Demolition Reflected Ceiling Plan
			Construction Floor Plan
			Reflected Ceiling Plan
			Millwork/Finish Plan
			Construction Elevations and Details
			Millwork Elevations and Details
			Floor and Wall Finishes Plan
			Phasing Plan
			Site Plan
			Furniture/Equipment Plan
			Furniture, Fixtures, Equipment Specifications
			Furniture, Fixture, Equipment Bid Documents
			Construction Bid Documents
			ADA Compliance Survey
			Graphic Design
			Camera-ready Artwork (digital documentation)
			Design Intent Drawings
			Final Design Drawing
			DOCUMENT PHASE MEETINGS
			Client
			Subconsultant
			Contractor
			Bidding
			Site Visit
			City Document Submittal
			City Code Variance
			City Design Review
			Health Department Review
			PROJECT ADMINISTRATION
			General Project Management/Administration
			Punchlist
			CONSULTANT SERVICES
			Mechanical Engineer
			Plumbing Engineer
			Electrical Engineer
			Structural Engineer
			Signage Consultant
			Civil Engineer
			Fire Protection Consultant
			Landscape Consultant
			Audio/Visual Consultant
			Telecommunications Consultant
			Security Consultant

FIGURE 23-1.
(*Continued*)

commercial projects that can affect the choice of fee method and the amount of the fee.

Hourly Fee Method

An interior design project is often very time-intensive. Regardless of a practitioner's experience, it does take time to progress through the stages of the design process as defined by the scope of services. Everyone is granted the same 24 hours in a day, and an individual can only do so much in any one hour of that day. It is a big reason why all compensation methods at least start with the determination of an hourly fee even when some other compensation method is used.

Included	Not Included	Quantity	Project Deliverables
			Food Service Consultant
			Lighting Consultant
			Artwork Consultant
			Asbestos/Toxic Substance Consultant
			REIMBURSABLE EXPENSES
		Actual Cost + 15%	Document Reproduction/Plotting and Blueprinting
		Actual Cost + 15%	Camera Ready Artwork/PMT's
		Actual Cost + 15%	Messenger/Delivery Service
		Actual Cost + 15%	Long Distance Telephone Charges
		Actual Cost + 15%	Travel and Expenditure
		Actual Cost + 15%	Presentation Materials
		Actual Cost + 15%	Film/Photography
		Actual Cost + 15%	Digital Services (diskettes, zips)
		Actual Cost + 15%	Color Prints (color printer-high end color outputs)
		Actual Cost + 15%	Additional Insurance required by Client's Insurance Coverage
		Actual Cost + 15%	Government Fees/Permits

PROJECT SCOPE

In describing these design services, reference is made to various people:

The Designer: the professional firm or individual that will provide the design services described here.

The Client: the user for whom the space is being designed, landlord of the premises or the tenant of the building.

The Contractor: The individual or firm providing the construction or fabrication of the project design of the Designer.

Note that only those items identified on the attached basic service list are included.

DESIGN PHASE

FIELD VERIFICATION/CAD SETUP
The Designer will verify the accuracy of documents provided by the landlord, confirm "as-built" conditions, measure existing suites in order to correct discrepancies and calculate square footage. Existing building conditions may create difficulties in obtaining complete as-built measurements. Some measurements may require verification after demolition and during construction. The Designer will prepare as-built drawings on AutoCad from field verification mark-ups showing the following: walls, doors, windows, cabinetry, electrical and voice/data outlets.

SPACE PLAN
The Designer will prepare, and present for approval, a preliminary space plan that illustrates a planning concept and design direction. Calculation of useable square footage is done using Building Owners and Managers Association (BOMA) area calculations methods. This floor plan will include:

Preliminary: Preliminary plan is schematic only and does not include notes and specifications for budgeting purposes
- Walls, doors, windows
- Furniture, for reference (reception, conference, open staff areas only. Private offices are excluded.)
- Room names, sizes
- Cabinet, sink, plumbing locations

Detailed: Detailed plan may be prepared for use in preliminary budgeting including:
- Walls, doors, windows
- Furniture, for reference
- Electrical and Telecommunication locations
- Room names, sizes
- Cabinet, sink, plumbing locations
- Specifications in CSI format

FIGURE 23-1.

(Continued)

The *hourly fee* is very common in business, with the service provider paid an amount for each hour or part of an hour that work is done on behalf of the client. Many clients are familiar with this method, as many other professionals such as accountants and attorneys and other service providers charge by the hour.

As was recommended earlier in the chapter, the hourly fee in interior design is commonly determined based on the firm's DPE. Hourly rates vary considerably around the country, even within the same city. It is a very satisfactory way of ensuring that the firm will be compensated for all the work it does for a client, and it is used by those in residential or commercial practice. Not all clients will quickly agree to be charged an hourly rate, however.

TABLE 23-3.

Factors That Impact Commercial versus Residential Fees Compensation.

Commercial projects:

Are often large, starting at about 3000 to 5000 square feet.

Are very complex because of their size.

Require a considerable amount of coordination between the designer and other project stakeholders—the architect, contractors, and engineers.

Often can take numerous months or even years to complete.

Can also go through many changes, even during the design stages. Clients may add employees or change functional requirements during the course of the project.

May experience code changes, resulting in needed design modifications.

Can have construction and product cost increases due to long completion time, which can affect the fee estimate.

Require an emphasis on time management, time keeping, scheduling, and project management.

Commercial clients:

Generally make decisions quickly—they do not like to waste time.

Often will agree to the products presented at the earliest schematic and design development meetings.

Select fewer items that are custom-made, instead approving products available in manufacturers' catalogs.

Agree to using products from a limited number of sources, since pricing advantages result from the economy of single-source purchasing.

Residential projects:

Are, by a vast majority, portions of a home, townhouse, or other private living space with various sizes of project space.

Can be a complete single-family residence, although that varies with experience level of the designer.

Are most often single-family residences (SFR) from 2000 to 5000 square feet, with some projects 10,000 to 15,000 square feet.

Are often very complicated due to multiple architectural finishes, custom cabinets, and numerous other details.

Can be built in about six to nine months (barring weather or construction delays), though it can take longer for larger, more complex residential construction projects.

Often require revision of plans and extra research or "shopping" for the products that will go into the project if client is indecisive.

Can exceed delivery and completion expectations due to custom-manufactured items.

Require coordination with architects, contractors, and subcontractors.

Can also be affected by cost overruns if client makes changes.

Residential clients:

Often take longer to make up their minds concerning the decisions that must be made. Need assurance and servicing, described by professionals as "hand-holding," that can take considerable extra time.

Often insist on many more moments and hours of communication with the designer on what sometimes seem minor issues.

Are often reluctant to pay a reasonable fee for services when the designer also sells merchandise to the client.

Many clients are reluctant to agree to an hourly fee, since the meter, metaphorically speaking, is always running. The longer the designer works on the project, the greater the charges will be. The client is often afraid to allow the designer this much freedom in setting the time schedule. Clients are often afraid that the designer will take extra time so that he or she can increase the fee. Many firms get around this objection by setting a *not to exceed limit* on the

TABLE 23-4.

When to Use the Hourly Fee Method.

1. For the initial consultation if the designer decides to charge for that initial meeting
2. Specific project consultations on small-scale projects
3. Whenever the scope of the project is unclear, making it difficult to use any other fee method
4. When the project involves a great deal of consultation time with architects, contractors, and subcontractors
5. When the designer perceives that the client will have difficulty in making up his or her mind
6. To cover travel time to the job site, to markets, or for other travel time
7. When it is necessary to prepare working drawings and specification documents
8. Whenever it is difficult to estimate the total amount of time needed to complete a job, for example, a law office in which each partner wishes to have his or her office designed in a very individual manner

contract. What this means is that the designer must estimate the actual amount of time that he or she will spend on the project and must quote a maximum fee that will cover all the expected work. The client cannot be charged more than this maximum. The designer must be careful in estimating the time it will take to complete a project in this case. He or she should also be sure that a clause is included in the contract to allow additional charges if the cause for delays or extra work is due to the client (see Table 23-4).

Hourly billing rates are commonly charged in three ways. The first is to charge based on the professional level of the employees. Thus, work performed by principals and senior designers is charged at a higher rate than less experienced design assistants. These differences will be naturally occurring, since the principal and senior designers will be paid a higher salary rate than lower-level designers in the firm. Of course, local competition impacts what that hourly rate based on professional level can be.

Another way to charge an hourly billing rate is to average all the rates of the various levels of design staff and charge one rate no matter who is doing the work. The danger here is that if the principal or senior designer is largely involved in the project, his or her time will not be generating adequate income. When entry-level designers are involved in the project, they often take longer than experienced designers. The averaging method can result in undercharging or overcharging the client.

The third way of charging the hourly fee is to charge by the kind of service rather than the personnel. In this case, the firm's owner determines that three or more levels of service are needed and sets a fee amount to charge for each level of service. Three levels might be design (or creative) service (the highest level of service), documentation and drafting (such as the preparation of final drafting of floor plans and other drawings, texture boards or documents, and bid documents), and, at the lowest level, supervision and/or miscellaneous time (such as travel time within the city, meetings with architects and contractors, meetings with the client, site visits, and so on). This method has the same problems as the averaging method.

An hourly rate can also be calculated to create a *daily rate*. A daily rate might be used for travel to market with the client, out-of-town meetings with the architect and/or client, or any other services that can be accomplished in only a day or a few days. The amount of hours that constitute a "day" does vary, with six to eight hours common calculators. The day rate often is larger than the six hours times the DPE multiplier, but that also varies with the designer.

Fixed-Fee Method

The *fixed-fee method*, also called the *flat-fee* or *lump-sum* (or stipulated sum) method, requires the interior designer to calculate a fee that will cover all the work and expenses required in the scope of services, knowing that the fee cannot be increased beyond the fixed amount. An additional amount is added to allow for contingencies. The estimated fee is usually charged to the client whether the amount of time estimated is correct or not. The terms lump sum and stipulated sum are commonly used by architectural firms or large interior design firms.

The fixed-fee (for simplicity) amount must be carefully considered. If the firm's owner has estimated badly and the time involved in completing a project exceeds the estimated fee, the firm cannot be compensated for the extra time. If the firm has estimated too high and the project does not require the full amount of estimated time, the firm is not obligated to refund any of the fee to the client. Of course, it is improper to overinflate the fixed fee as a way of seeking to obtain a huge profit at the client's expense. The fixed fee includes charges for all services and expenses other than those that the firm charges as reimbursable expenses. This fee method is not recommended for the inexperienced designer, since she or he will not have a good idea or history as to how long it will take to complete projects.

This fee method appeals to those clients who clearly are interested in the bottom line. Designers who wish to use this fee method should have a database of previous projects that will help them determine the approximate average times and expenses that are needed to execute various kinds of projects.

In order to use this method, it is important for the owner or project manager to consider the salary and overhead costs for the design firm and to have a thorough understanding of the services that must be performed. He or she must also have a feeling for the decision-making ability of the client so as to predict if the client will be difficult or easy to work with and if the client understands the time element so that all phases of the project can be satisfactorily accomplished. It is also important for the owner or manager to have a record of job histories for similar projects, which can aid in estimating and can be used as a guide in making decisions on new projects. And, of course, the owner or manager should have a very good idea of the client's budget.

The owner or manager must be very comfortable in his or her ability to estimate the time that will be necessary to complete various kinds of projects if the fixed-fee method is used. The firm that has built up a history of time records and expense records from various kinds of projects is in the best position to use the fixed-fee method. The fixed-fee method, which can be used for both residential and commercial projects, is a satisfactory method of charging fees when:

1. The scope of work for the project is easy to determine and not expected to change.

2. The amount of supervision on the job site is limited or can easily be controlled by the designer.

3. It is easy to determine the time and requirements of the project.

4. The designer has a significant amount of experience with the type of project and scope of services required so that an estimate is clear-cut.

5. The client is not purchasing goods from the designer. This allows the designer to utilize goods that he or she might not normally use, since the designer is not selling the goods. For the client, this may mean that the goods specified are at a lower cost than those the designer might be trying to sell.

6. Whenever a large amount of the same items are to be purchased. This is often the case for projects such as restaurants and office complexes, in which standardized products are specified; little additional time is required for such projects after the final product selections are made.

What Would You Do?

Super Interiors always included a photographic rights clause in their design contracts. The clause said "Super Interiors reserves the right to photograph all areas of the project throughout the phases of installation and upon final completion of the project. By signing this agreement, the client acknowledges this right and gives permission for Super Interiors to use the photographs in any and all promotional media without the name of the client appearing in the photographs."

Six months after the project was completed, a client of Super Interiors saw photographs of his reception room and employee lounge in a trade magazine related to the client's business. In the photograph, the client's business name was clearly in the photograph and was listed in the caption.

The client was both flattered and upset that photos of his office spaces were shown in the magazine. No one from the company had given permission for the photos to be published.

Square-Foot Method

Another method that requires a good history with projects of particular types is the *square-foot method*. The fee is determined by some rate per square foot times the amount of square footage of the project being designed. Commonly used in commercial design and by some designers in residential practice, the square-foot method can be a profitable way of determining the design fee. It is crucial for the designer to have sufficient experience such that they can be comfortable with determining the square-foot fee rate that the final fee is based upon.

With the square-foot method, the owner must determine what factor will be used for charging for the various phases of the project. As mentioned in the discussion of the hourly fee method, the project can be broken down into phases. If the firm normally charges a different rate for each of these phases, the firm must determine what fee rate correlates with a portion of the square-footage fee.

A beginning point in determining the square-footage rate again relates to the expenses of doing projects and reasonable profits expected by the owner of the firm. An owner who has never used the square-foot method for determining fees can gather data on several completed projects, for example, similar-size doctors' suites or real estate offices. The actual design fee charged for these projects is divided by the square footage of the project, which provides a historical view of the square foot cost of the design work.

Fee amounts will vary based on the type of project, since different types of design work require longer or shorter time periods to complete the scope of services. The fee also varies based on the scope of services, since it is obvious to the reader that a more complex project will take more time, thus likely to increase the square-foot rate. In addition, regional factors, the design firm's experience, and local competition may drive rates up or down.

Value-Oriented Method

It is very important, even critical, for a design firm to consider its expenses and reasonable profit in determining a fee amount. The experienced interior designer also brings value to the project in his or her experience. Too few interior designers consider the value they bring to the client when determining compensation and fees. A designer with several years' experience doing hospitality projects, for example, should be able to bring to the client greater value and be worth more to the client than a designer with very little experience wanting the same job.

The *value-oriented*, or value-based, method uses the concept that the design firm prices services based on the value or quality of the services rather than totally focusing on the cost of doing those services. This fee method or concept will only work for a design firm whose services have, for some reason, additional value in the marketplace. It is critical for the reader to understand that the value judgment is made by the client and is based on his or her perception of the value of the interior design firm.

As we have already seen, most fee methods are based on time or cost rather than on value. With the value-oriented fee method, the designer must show the client how his or her services are valuable to the client's bottom line (or other concerns) and superior to those of competing designers. The perception of most clients is that all designers do the same thing and provide the same services. The designer must show how he or she differs from the competition and is thus worth the fees requested. If the client perceives that what one design firm offers has greater value than what other design firms offer, the more valued firm will win the contract.

In many cases, this perceived value also means that the design firm can charge a premium for its services. Firms with a lot of experience are expected to do a better job than a new firm or than designers who are trying to get into a different segment of the market. For example, a design firm that has specialized in restaurants for ten years has a far greater expertise in that type of facility than a firm that has done primarily offices for the same ten years. The first firm will try to show the client that experience has value and that value should be compensated fairly.

Clients who are unfamiliar with or do not appreciate the time and subtleties involved in completing a project react favorably to the value-oriented method. The fee is based on the designer's ability to meet the expectation of the client and experience to do the work rather than on the time that it will take to complete the project. When the designer can clearly differentiate how he or she can be of value to the company and his or her experiences and ability warrant this consideration, this fee method should be considered.

Percentage of Merchandise and Product Services Method

Commercial interior designers sometimes determine their design fee based on a negotiated percentage of the cost of the goods and installation (and possibly some portion of the construction) that will be involved in the project. This is commonly referred to as the *percentage of merchandise and product services method*. This fee method is similar to the architect's percentage of construction cost method and is used by firms who do not intend to sell merchandise to the client. This fee method is not very common for residential designers, who more often also wish to sell merchandise to clients. The amount of fee becomes the percentage that was negotiated multiplied by the budgeted or final costs of the project. This might include the furniture, wall coverings, floor coverings, ceiling and window treatments, lighting fixtures, accessories, built-in cabinets, and even general construction costs.

It is very similar in concept to the cost plus percentage method. It is sometimes used when clients suspect the designer of *double-dipping*, that is, of earning revenue from the design and specification of the products and also from selling the merchandise. By not actually selling the merchandise to the client, the designer is then not double-dipping.

The percentage rate varies with the size or complexity of the project. The larger the project is, the smaller the fee will be. The more complex the project is, the greater the fee will be. For example, a large project like a hotel, with a large dollar volume but a potentially smaller number of design decisions, would require a smaller percentage fee than a group of individually designed executive offices requiring a great deal of time.

There are definite advantages and disadvantages to this method. Since the project fee is based on cost, the client may actually save money if any extra discounts are provided on merchandise that the client purchases. The client also saves when products of a cheaper cost are purchased. On the other hand, the client may feel the designer will specify expensive items so that the total costs for the project rise, thus increasing the fees.

The designer must carefully negotiate the percentage of that discount, because the firm could lose a considerable amount of money when cheaper products are used or if projects are bid and won by vendors and suppliers trying to "buy" a project at a very low price. Budgets must be carefully considered to ensure that the project is done as required and that the designer is compensated fairly. This method should be used cautiously and only in combination with another method that will ensure fair compensation for design time and services.

The remaining fee methods are those that are used most often by interior designers who depend upon the sale of merchandise as their primary source of revenue. Although these following methods are most commonly used by residential designers, commercial firms may also use one or more of these methods to generate revenue.

Cost Plus Percentage Markup Method

A compensation method that many interior designers utilize when they also sell merchandise to the client is the *cost plus percentage markup* method. The client agrees to pay a specific markup on the actual cost of the merchandise and other items that the designer specifies and sells to the client. In this situation, the client obtains a better price on merchandise when he or she buys from the designer, since the designer passes on all the discounts that suppliers provide, arriving at a competitively low cost. Then the designer adds the specified markup in order to realize revenue from the project.The percentage determined must be sufficient to cover the design firm's costs and allow for the desired profit margin, if it is the only compensation method used. The markup might include design services or be a smaller amount when a design fee is charged as a separate fee. Remember that this markup amount is not really "profit" in and of itself, since it also must cover the designer's costs of doing business and direct costs of doing the project.

Cost plus percentage markup is more commonly used in residential design but can be effective in commercial design as well. It can be the least remunerative method, if a very small markup is added to the net price. It is critical especially for those designers who do not charge a design fee for services that the percentage be carefully considered and be sufficient to create an appropriate amount of revenue and remain competitive. This method can be used as the exclusive fee method, if the amount of goods to be purchased from the firm is sufficient to compensate for the time the designer must put into the project.

The key in using this fee method is to charge an adequate percentage. Residential designers might charge from 10 percent to over 30 percent. There is no average markup, as each firm decides what percentage to use based on business needs, competition, and what the client is willing to pay. When commercial interior designers use this method, the percentage is generally quite low. That is primarily due to the competition for the sale of goods in the commercial area of interior design. It works well for firms as long as:

1. The budget is not cut at the last moment.
2. The client does not use a lot of existing furniture in the new project.
3. The client does not decide to hold off purchasing any of the merchandise at a later time, thereby reducing the amount of fees the firm may collect.
4. The client does not decide to purchase any items from someone other than the designer.

Another segment of the interior design industry that uses the cost plus percentage markup method consists of those design firms that are just getting started. Many new design firms offer this method of compensation as a way of competing with larger, more established firms that can operate at the retail method. If a firm decides to use this method of obtaining fees, it must be sure it is covering the costs of its design practice. Without a careful calculation of costs, the designer may not be fully compensated for his or her design talents. Any firm that is considering the use of this method should use it in conjunction with some other fee method to be sure the firm receives a reasonable gross margin to cover costs and obtain a profit.

Retail Method

William's interior design business is located in a small retail showroom that he and his business partners also operate. The showroom is stocked primarily with accessories and an assortment of case goods. They do not stock seating. The showroom is located in a retail center near a high-end residential development. The combination of stores in the center attracts potential clients who purchase the items in stock. Customers do not receive a discount on any items they purchase from those stocked in the showroom. The retail business also attracts a small percentage of the interior design services work performed by William and his staff. Because of the store, William does not charge a design fee unless the client does not purchase any merchandise from him. He chooses to charge a very small design fee as long as the client purchases the goods from him. He prices merchandise except architectural finishes at suggested retail or above. William does not discount the sale of items that are in stock but does provide a discount to clients who purchase special-order furniture only items. He does this because he limits the amount of sellable inventory of furniture in the showroom.

In the *retail method*, the design firm charges the client the retail price suggested by the manufacturer or supplier. If the manufacturer does not provide a suggested retail price, then the design firm marks up the merchandise from the net or cost price to achieve the retail price. The retail method has always been a very common method of obtaining fees if a design firm actually sells merchandise to the client. Since both the suggested retail price and the common markup percentage used is 100 percent, the retail method provides a high gross profit margin for the firm. In recent years the markup to "retail" has grown beyond 100 percent. Designers say it is not uncommon for there to be a "double markup" of 200 percent or even more to reach "retail".

The retail method is more commonly used by residential design firms than by firms that are primarily involved in commercial design. And it is frequently used by firms that perceive that the amount of time needed on any given project or client is small in relation to the budget for merchandise. If it is estimated that a great deal of planning, custom design, drafting, specification writing, or supervision work is required, the retail method is not a suitable fee method for the firm to use. Even though the markup provides a reasonable margin to cover the expense of these tasks, there is no guarantee that the client will purchase merchandise from the designer, which means that the designer will not be fully compensated for time spent working on the project. Should these kinds of activities be the major part of the project, then another fee method should be used, or the retail method in conjunction with another method might be used.

Because designers have become more willing to quote a design fee for services, the retail method is used less often today. Of course, it is still used in many stores or showrooms that sell products such as lighting fixtures and furniture and might not be focusing on design services. Clients are becoming accustomed to the concept of paying for the professional services that an interior designer can offer and thus are willing to pay the separate design fees. In addition, clients are far more willing to shop around for a good price today. This has led many designers to use a different method for generating revenue.

Discounting or Percentage off Retail Method

The *percentage off retail* method is another common fee method that is directly related to the purchase of goods. Stores and showrooms that have an inventory of some sort of merchandise offer merchandise at a percentage off retail in order to gain a competitive edge over stores that are strictly retail priced only. They might do this because the firm expects that the volume of merchandise purchased by the client will offset the design services costs. It is a method that office furnishings dealers frequently use. This method is also used by those residential designers who sell large quantities of merchandise whether or not they have a showroom.

In this method, the design firm reduces the selling price of the merchandise by some percentage off the suggested retail price. Care must be taken when the design firm determines what that discount will be, since the resulting difference between the selling price and the net price (the gross margin) is needed to allow for a profit and to cover overhead costs. As long as the discount allows for the needed gross margin and that the gross margin amount covers overhead expenses, and provides a profit margin, this fee method works. However, the larger the discount is, the smaller the gross profit margin will be and the less there exists the potential to pay off expenses and maintain profits.

Office furnishings dealers have found that this method does not always cover the cost of design services. This has become true because of the rash of deep discounting on systems projects and the highly competitive market in office furnishings. Because of these deep discounts (which will be discussed in Chapter 25), dealers have been forced to charge design fees, such as an hourly fee, to make sure the designer's time is covered.

Consultation Fee

Mr. Jackson knew he should have some help with his small office suite because it was important to him for the suite to have a very professional look. Through client contacts he was able to purchase furniture. He asked Dianne Dawson, an interior designer one of his clients knew, if she would provide ideas on what he could do himself. They negotiated and she agreed to provide four hours of consultation at a flat fee.

In some situations, a client may feel that he or she wants some ideas from a designer but does not need complete design services. The interior designer would then charge the client a fee for the consultation. The designer would provide ideas but generally would not execute plans or other documents. The consultation is generally limited to a maximum of a few hours, though any arrangement that the designer wishes to develop is possible.

Goods are generally not sold in this arrangement. Of course, the client may later decide that he or she does need the full services and/or purchasing ability of the interior designer. Generally, the interior designer applies this consultation fee later to the project, although this is not standard.

Combination Method

In many cases, using only one of the described fee methods will not provide sufficient compensation to cover all the expenses and desired profit margin for the firm. It is often necessary for almost all commercial firms and many residential firms that are not primarily retail showrooms to use more than one method for obtaining design fees.

Since projects involve a variety of activities, it is defensible for the firm to charge the client a variety of fees. For example, let us consider a project that involves a lot of the designer's time in meetings with the client, contractors, and the architect for specifying interior finish materials but not a large dollar amount for the actual materials to be purchased. The designer might find that an hourly charge for meetings, travel, and on-site supervision in combination with either a cost plus percentage or percentage discount from retail for the merchandise sold would adequately compensate the designer in this situation.

In another case, a project might require that the designer spend a large amount of time in the preparation of contract documents and specifications for rooms that are basically the same. In this situation, it is common that the goods would be purchased from a vendor, not the designer. This might occur for a hotel project or a major office complex. In this situation, the designer might charge an hourly fee for the drafting and a fixed fee or a percentage of the selling price for the design and preparation of specifications for the areas that are basically the same. If properly considered, a combination of design fee methods can provide excellent compensation to the designer at a fair price to the client.

The two most common combination methods are the cost plus percentage markup with a fixed fee and cost plus percentage markup with an hourly fee. Both residential and commercial interior designers might use either of these methods when they sell merchandise as well as provide design services. In these cases, the designer charges a fixed fee or hourly fee for services and then sells the merchandise on a cost-plus basis. The fixed fee can be sufficient to cover direct labor and overhead when carefully considered against costs and provide some profit for the project. Markup percentages vary with type of client, competition, and location.

Some clients object to these combination fees—especially when they combine a service fee with product markup. Many clients see the markup (or the consultation fee) as double-dipping. Double-dipping to them means that the designer is making a profit on both the service fees and the product sales. It behooves the designer to explain that the fixed fee (or hourly fee) is calculated to provide only a portion of the revenues needed to cover labor, expenses, and profit. The remaining revenue to make the project profitable for the designer is generated by merchandise sales and that the client is obtaining the goods at a substantial discount from retail.

An important issue when the fee is an hourly rate along with a markup is the determination of which services will be charged at the hourly rate and which will be considered included in the markup of the merchandise. Designers who use this combination feel that they are more likely to cover all or most of the time that they actually work on the project. This does not always happen with a combination of the fixed-fee and cost plus percentage markup methods.

The danger in using either of these combinations is that the designer may rely on the client's purchasing goods to generate some of the revenue. However, if the client purchases from some other source, delays purchasing, or buys goods at a lower price, the designer will receive less income than estimated. Depending on the size of the fixed fee and/or the services to be included in the hourly rate charges, these fees may not be sufficient to cover the time spent on the project. Safeguards can be incorporated in the event that some of these problems occur. They will be discussed in the next chapter.

Any of the fee methods described in this section can be used by the interior designer for a reasonable and fair fee. Considerations for each situation that is most appropriate for the designer, the client, and the project impact the selection of fee method. There comes a time when any interior designer feels that he or she might want to charge more, whether in consideration of the competition or for personal needs. Table 23-5 provides some points concerning obtaining higher design fees.

TABLE 23-5.

Strategies to Increase Your Design Fees.

Know what the market charges. You must know what the market charges for services similar to yours. If you are charging too little in comparison to others, a potential client may think you are not very good. If you are charging more than the market, the client will want to know why you feel you are worth more. Remember that those with little experience will never be considered of the same value as those with a great deal of experience.

Establish and maintain your reputation. Always work honestly and ethically. Your reputation often precedes you to new clients, and a good reputation can even have a status or prestige effect on a client, thus positioning you for higher fees. Don't do anything that harms your reputation.

Provide excellent customer service. Be sure you understand what level of service is expected by your clients, and provide an even greater level than their expectation.

Your value relates to what the client values. The client must feel that what you provide has value to them, regardless of your reputation, background, or experience. If they do not see the value, they will be reluctant to hire you.

Build a good relationship. Interior design—especially residential—is a highly relationship-affected profession. Many times designers get hired because of the impression that is projected at the initial meeting and the relationship that is built as the project progresses.

Offer services that few others propose. Find a niche that is needed and not being serviced in your market or some other market. Then become very good at it. The more expertise you have in a specialty or when you are the first to offer something new, the more you can charge.

Pinpoint your value-adds. Determine what you can do better than other designers. You have to have something of value to clients for them to be willing to pay you more.

Add to your personal value. Continually update your knowledge of topics and tasks needed within the profession through continuing education. Obtain state licenses and certificates such as the NCIDQ. Go back and get a degree if necessary to improve your standing in the industry.

Why are you worth more? Have good reasons for why you charge more than others. You can't charge more just because the competition does. You must be able to explain your value to the client. You also need to have good reasons to explain to existing clients why you are raising your rates.

Charge differently. Maybe you have experience or abilities that can allow you to charge in a way that is different from the competition. Instead of charging by the hour, perhaps you can charge for a "menu" of services. This one is tricky, so consider it carefully before plunging in.

INDIRECT JOB COSTS

Unexpected events, poor estimating, doing extra work—all of these actions can impact any project for any size interior design firm and are considered indirect job costs. No matter how carefully the designer considers which fee method to use and thereby estimate the fee amount, it is possible for the firm to lose a certain amount of profit because of indirect job costs. Although some of these indirect cost factors can be mitigated through the clauses in a contract and contingency allowances, they still occur.

One of the most common indirect costs for firms that are doing strict cost accounting is overtime. No matter how carefully a project has been estimated, if the design firm must pay overtime salary to any of its staff, the gross margin of the project and potential profitability will decrease. A career in interior design is rarely a 9-to-5 job. However, careful supervision of projects by the design director or project designers will help to hold down the amount of overtime needed for projects. Some firms control overtime costs by paying designers, not on an hourly basis, but rather on a salary basis, as discussed in Chapter 14. This does help with direct salary expense but not with overhead expenses, which are still incurred when the office is working past normal business hours. In addition, it is common practice (as pointed out in Chapter 14) for the firm to provide compensatory time for overtime worked by salaried employees. This time does not generate revenue.

A second indirect cost that impacts profitability is the indecisive client. This type of client just can't seem to make up his or her mind about any number of things—colors, furniture styles, patterns, the furniture or space arrangement, and so on. Experienced interior designers learn to recognize the indecisive client during the initial interviews. But often even the most experienced designer gets a client who just can't seem to make up his or her mind. If the fee method used is the hourly method, this would have little bearing on the final outcome of the potential profitability of the project, since the designer continues to charge for all the changes and extra meetings. When a fixed fee that limits the amount of fee that can be charged, the designer must diplomatically find ways to urge the client to make up his or her mind and move on with the project.

Many times, the profit on a project is affected by changes and/or additions to the project, caused by the client. This is often called scope creep. A few examples include the client that asks the designer to select a finish or "take care of a problem" that was not included in the scope of services. Or perhaps the client changes his or her mind about some portion of the project, which necessitates extra planning or drafting work or perhaps respecification of products. It might be that the client asks the designer questions and may request design work for other parts of the residence or commercial space that originally was not part of the project. If the designer continues to take care of issues like these or design extra spaces, planned profit for the job can disappear. Interior designers are, after all, in business to generate revenue and hopefully make a profit. The best way to avoid this problem is to have in the design contract a very clear description of the project area to be designed and a detailed scope of services to be provided, and to specify charges for changes and additions to the project. This will also be discussed in the next chapter.

An added cost that occurs whenever a designer has ventured into a project that he or she has never done before is for unexpected technical or professional consultation. Oftentimes designers are asked to do projects that require the preparation of construction documents. Most jurisdictions have strict regulations as to who may prepare construction documents. Designers may suddenly discover that they must have an architect or other consultant prepare those documents.. This unexpected fee reduces the expected profit margin. Of course, the better action is that interior designers not become involved in a project for which he or she has limited or no experience.

Designers who depend on the sale of merchandise face another indirect cost. For example, Margaret had an agreement with the client that stated all merchandise would be sold at cost plus 30 percent. She had charged only a small consultation charge rather than a design fee. The client kept delaying the ordering of area rugs and some accessories. Margaret finally found out that the client purchased these items on his own. Clients who go along with design concepts but then purchases merchandise through some source other than the designer or perhaps purchase nothing at all obviously impact the revenue expected from a job such as the one described. Interior designers in this situation must protect themselves from the client who uses them for ideas but buys from some other source. If no fee for service has been negotiated at the start of the project, the designer has worked essentially for free. This is no way to build a successful and profitable professional practice. Techniques that designers can use to help with the client who does this will be discussed in the next chapter.

Unusual job site and delivery costs can also add to the cost of a project. In projects related to open-office systems, for example, it is common for thermo-stats, light switches, air-conditioning vents, and the like to end up right where the interior designer has planned to hang a wall strip or to attach a divider panel. In residential design, it is common for a client to make some kind of change at the site without telling the interior designer. Sometimes a designer may specify a very large piece of furniture, which may be very difficult to deliver. For example, a designer specifies a very large conference table that cannot fit inside an elevator but must be placed on top of the elevator cab or must be hoisted up on cranes from the exterior of the building.

Unless there is careful project management, furniture may be ready for delivery to the job site, but the job site may not be ready to receive the merchandise. In situations where the design firm does not have a warehouse to hold merchandise until it is ready to be delivered, extra cost is involved in storing and later delivering it to the job site. In many cases, this extra cost is borne by the design firm, even though the design firm has not caused the delay, since management of the project is considered to be part of the normal and expected services of the firm.

All of these examples lead to extra design time or in some other respect impact the expected revenue. All too frequently these factors have not been calculated for or otherwise considered in the fee and contract. The extra costs of some of these examples may be passed on to the client, if the proper clauses are in the design contract, which we will discuss in the next chapter. Unfortunately, the extra costs discussed in this section are often the responsibility of the design firm.

SUMMARY

All interior design firms are in business to make a reasonable profit while providing quality services to clients. The goals and operations of the design firm, as well as the clients whom the firm wishes to attract, all play a part in how the owner determines which fee methods to use and which revenue-generating strategies to use so that the firm will stay in operation.

The income that the firm generates, whether from fees for services only, from the sale of goods, or from a combination of both, must be sufficient to cover costs and to provide a net profit in order to sustain the firm. In this chapter, we have looked at the different ways in which a design firm can generate this income by means of several fee methods. No fee method is perfect for all circumstances for all firms. Each firm must determine for its own type of business which situations warrant a particular fee method.

Once the fee method for a particular project has been determined, the next step for the owner to take is to prepare a design contract or proposal. In the next chapter, we will look at the preparation of such a contract.

CHAPTER 24

Preparing Design Contracts

Key Terms and Concepts

These key terms and concepts are important to material in this chapter. Many of these terms will be utilized in other chapters as well. Be sure you understand these items as you read this chapter.

Terms and Concepts

Contract

Offer

Acceptance

Contractual capacity

Consideration

Mutual assent

Legality

Offeror

Offeree

Counteroffer

Mirror image rule

Restraint of trade

Letter of agreement

Statute of Frauds

Writing

Scope creep

Reimbursable expenses

Disbursements

Per diem

Designer responsibility disclaimer

Third party

Assignment

Delegation

Arbitration

Retainer

Performance

Complete performance

Inferior performance

Breach of contract

Damages

Compensatory damages

Nominal damages

Incidental damages

Consequential damages

Punitive damages

Specific performance

Uniform Electronic Transaction Act (UETA)

Electronic Signatures in Global and National Commerce Act (ESGNCA)

Critical Issues

After completing this chapter you should be able to:

- List and explain the basic requirements (or elements) needed to create a contract for services.
- Describe a counteroffer and explain what happens when a counteroffer is given by a client.
- Explain the concept of contractual capacity.
- Compare and contrast a letter of agreement to a contract.
- Discuss the benefits of a written contract over oral agreements.
- List and explain the elements that are needed for a written contract to be enforceable.
- Describe how the Statute of Frauds impacts contracts for services.
- Explain why it is important for the contract to clearly state the client's name and address and include a description of the project at the beginning of a contract.
- Discuss strategies for being certain that the appropriate clauses have been included in a contract for interior design services.
- Explain why a detailed scope of services is so important in a contract.
- Analyze a contract for services and determine its flaws.
- Explain the following: Charges for third parties, publishing rights, ownership of documents, and arbitration.
- Discuss the concepts of assignment and delegation.
- List and explain the forms of performance that signify completion or breach of a contract.

A contractual agreement between the interior designer and the client should never be taken lightly. Serious consequences occur when promises made in the contract are not fulfilled. Michael found that out when the client refused to pay for extra services, since there was no clause in his contract concerning extra work beyond the scope of services descriptions. Since the contract for interior design services originates from the designer, he or she must carefully compose and organize the various clauses in order to protect him- or herself and ensure that the work outlined can be accomplished.

There are many kinds of contracts that occur between an interior designer and some other party. The type that is the focus of this chapter is when the interior designer offers to provide services to a client and the client agrees to hire the designer to perform those services. Another contract related to design services is for the selling of merchandise to the client. Still another is when the designer makes purchases for the client from vendors. In these contractual relationships, it is the interior designer's responsibility to fulfill the contract. In many cases, designers and clients enter into contracts, but they do not know that they have done so. Or they should have entered into a contract but did not.

Designers and clients also may breach or break those contracts. Sometimes this is done knowingly and willingly (while hoping the other party does not sue, though this hope is not ethical practice), sometimes this is done by accident, and sometimes this is done by mutual consent (which is not really a breach at all). Interior designers also are sometimes faced with such threats as "I'm going to sue for breach of contract" or "I'm going to sue because we had a contract." Naturally, this can occur when the designer has actually done something to create that breach, or sometimes it is a threat when the client is in some way dissatisfied with the designer's performance.

In this chapter, we review the basic ingredients of a contract and contract law as they relate to a contract for services or a combination of services and goods. In the next chapter, we will discuss the specific differences concerning contracts for the sale of goods. The counsel of an attorney is strongly recommended for obtaining a complete explanation of the legal considerations of contracts. The information in this chapter is general in nature and should not be construed as legal advice.

DEFINITION AND BASIC ELEMENTS OF A CONTRACT

William met with his client, Andy, at a coffee shop after they had toured a spec office space that Andy wanted to acquire for his accounting practice. During their discussions at the coffee shop, William made notes about the project scope and wrote down an estimate for design fees for services only. William always dates his notes so that the date of the meeting was already attached to the notes. After reading these notes, Andy signed and dated the paper and said, "You've got a deal! When can you start?" Is this paper a valid contract for design services?

Suzanne returned from an initial interview with a client and was directed to prepare a contract for the interior design of a large high-end residence. Part of the project responsibilities would involve working with the architect and general contractor. The home was for a sports figure who met briefly with Suzanne and said he was leaving the rest of the particulars to his agent and girlfriend. What kinds of issues should Suzanne cover in the contract, and what problems might occur in this situation? Would you even take this project under the stated conditions?

A contract to provide interior design services is like any other contract. Although no one enters into a contractual situation expecting problems, a contract helps the interior designer clarify what will be done and, of course, how much he or she will charge the client to do that work. But what is a contract in a legal sense?

Developing a design contract and offering services to a client is a serious matter. Anything included in the contract and discussions concerning terms is also very serious. What technically is a contract? A *contract* is a promise or agreement that is made between two or more parties to perform or not perform some act. The performance or lack of performance of this act can be enforced by the courts. In interior design, the designer offers to provide a certain group of design services he or she has determined are needed, and when the client agrees, a contract has been formed. This simple example gives two important keys to a legally enforceable contract, but other terms must be included so that the interior designer has the force of law on her side.

A legally enforceable contract must have these basic elements:

1. *Offer.* One party proposes to do something or not to do something for another party.
2. *Acceptance.* The party to whom the proposal has been made agrees to accept the offer and is bound exactly by the terms set up in the offer.
3. *Contractual capacity.* Each party to the contract must have the legal ability to enter into the contract.
4. *Consideration.* Something of value that is exchanged as it relates to the contract. It must be legally sufficient enough for a court to take it seriously.

5. *Mutual assent.* The giving of the offer and acceptance of the offer must be done willingly.

6. *Legality.* The contract must exist only to support the performance of some legal act.

Let us now look at each of these elements in detail.

Offer

An *offer* in a contract is made by the party who makes the offer—the *offeror* (for our purposes, the interior designer). In legal terminology, the client is referred to as the *offeree.* Julie has prepared a contract for the interior design of a retail store. Thus, Julie—the offeror—has made an offer to her client, Heavenly Jewels, owned by Rita Jones and Sara Barrow—the offeree.

An interior designer's offer to do some outline of design services must be done with serious consideration and intent. If a designer makes statements in a contract that promise to do certain things and the designer is unable to achieve them or neglects to have someone else achieve them, this is very serious and can have legal consequences. Forgetting to put something into a contract can also have serious consequences. For example, if Julie's contract with Heavenly Jewels required a fee of $25,000, but in the terms of the contract, Julie neglected to require a retainer, Julie cannot later ask the client to pay a retainer, since that was not part of the original offer.

For an offer to be legally binding, there must be a serious intention by the offeror (the party who makes the offer) to the other party (the offeree). Merely expressing an opinion is not a form of valid intention. For example, if Julie says to her client that "the project can probably be completed in five days," her client cannot sue if it actually takes ten days, since the "five days" is an opinion, not a promise. Even though it is not a legal opinion, ill will is likely to occur when the project is not completed as mentioned by this opinion.

Common problems occur with contracts when the offer is vague. The terms of the offer must be definite enough for a court to determine whether the contract has been fulfilled or not. A statement such as, "select all finishes" can leave the firm responsible for selecting interior and exterior finishes when the firm only considered selecting interior finishes. Designers often mistakenly include a vague description of the scope of the job such as "design your house" when the job really involves the furniture and finish selections for the family room and kitchen. This vagueness leaves the designer open to services related to other parts of the house, probably without additional compensation.

The third element of a legal offer is that the offer must be fully communicated to the offeree so that the offeree knows of the existence of the offer. For example, unless the client knows that out-of-town travel expenses are over and above the design fees, the client is not expected to pay these expenses. Another example would be if Julie failed to inform the client in the contract that any architectural services that might be required would be over and above the stated fee.

The last element in a legal offer concerns the ability of the offeror to terminate the offer or the acceptance of the offer. If the designer's proposal states that the price for the services is good for ten days but the client responds on the fifteenth day, the designer is not obligated to provide the services at the stated price. It should be noted that the time period of the offer begins when the offeree receives the offer, not when it is prepared or mailed by the offeror. If there is no time limit stated in the offer, the time limit terminates at the end of a reasonable period of time, based on consideration of the circumstances of the offer.

Here is an example of another issue concerning the offer. Peter discovered that he had miscalculated his design fee for the services needed for the addition that the Emersons wanted for their home. To complete the work for the stated fee of $21,000, he would actually lose $6000. Peter wants to rescind the offer, since he cannot afford to lose that much money.

An offer can be terminated if the offeror withdraws the offer before the offeree accepts it. It is, of course, important that the offer be withdrawn prior to its being accepted. For example, if an interior designer discovers that he or she has miscalculated his or her bid to the City of Chicago but has already turned in the bid, he or she must revoke the offer prior to the closing date and time of acceptance of all bids. If all bids are due by Friday at 5:00 P.M. and the designer discovers the error on Friday at 5:30 P.M., it is too late to revoke the bid.

An offer can be terminated if the offeree (the client) rejects the offer, effectively ending the negotiation for that project contract. Should this happen, there is no obligation on either side to fulfill the contract. Should the client later wish to accept the offer, the designer can refuse, accept, or modify the original offer. This is because the client's refusal of the offer has terminated the original offer. But if the client says something like, "Is this the best price you can give me on design fee?" this does not constitute rejection of the offer.

This last example brings up the last method of terminating an offer, which is for the client to make a counteroffer. A *counteroffer* is an agreement to the offer in which the terms of the offer have been changed. For example, if Heavenly Jewels tells Julie, "Your design fee is out of the question. I am prepared to pay only $5000 for these services," the offer of $5000 is now a counteroffer. The designer is now in a position to either accept or reject this counteroffer. This also means that Julie's negotiation skills are needed as she discusses the original fee and counteroffer.

There is another important point to discuss concerning contract offers. Interior designers are often invited to bid on design projects or sales of goods. An invitation to bid or to negotiate is not an offer but merely shows a willingness on the part of the client to enter into discussions with the designer about a potential contract. For example, Steve is asked to respond to a proposal by the City of Phoenix on the specification of new furnishings for the mayor's office. The RFP is not a contract offer, but an announcement that a project exists.

Acceptance

Rita Jones and Sara Barrow, owners of Heavenly Jewels, read the contract prepared by Julie and indicated everything was fine with them. Each of the owners signed the agreement and were happy to learn that Julie could begin the project in only a few days. Since the offeree (the client) agrees to the terms of the offer, acceptance has been given. "In order to exercise the power of acceptance effectively, the offeree must accept unequivocally. If the acceptance is subject to new conditions, or if the terms of the acceptance change the original offer, the acceptance may be considered a counteroffer that implicitly rejects the original offer."[1] Unequivocal acceptance is referred to as the *mirror image rule* of acceptance in law textbooks. When someone accepts a contract proposal and does not make changes, he or she has "mirrored" the offer. If Rita and Sara had asked for some changes in the agreement—a smaller deposit, for example—then the original offer had not been accepted and agreement had not been reached.

It is not uncommon for clients to take some time before they respond by calling or mailing back a design contract. Even though the interior designer may feel that the client is likely to go through with the project and decide to start working on the project, the interior designer should not begin work without the signed agreement. Just because the client seemed inclined to go ahead does not constitute agreement. This type of "silence" should not be construed as acceptance. However, if by silence the client has received a benefit from the services that the designer has provided, then the courts will rule that the client has accepted the contract. For example, if a designer decides to proceed with the space planning of an office for a client, even though the client has not yet accepted the terms of the contract, the client is not obligated to pay the design fee for the services provided, unless the client has taken ownership (a benefit) of the space somehow. Yet merely beginning work on the space planning does not generally translate into receiving a "benefit." Interior designers should be very careful about beginning any type of work on a project in which the signed design contract has not been returned by the client. Good intentions or enthusiasm by the interior designer are often not rewarded by the unscrupulous client.

Finally, acceptance must be made within the time limit set in the terms of the offer. If no definite terms are stated, acceptance must be made within a reasonable time frame, considering the conditions of the offer and the subject of the offer.

Contractual Capacity

Harold, the owner of HRH Interiors, obtained a signature on a contract from the office manager of a physician's office. The doctor refused to pay the first invoice of the design fee, since the office manager did not have the authority to sign the contract. *Contractual capacity* relates to the full legal competency of the parties. Both parties in a contract must have the legal capacity to enter into a contract. It is very important for the designer to be sure that the person agreeing to and signing a contract has the legal capacity to enter into the contract. In residential design, the interior designer normally deals with a legally competent adult who is head of a household or a spouse. As an added protection and in some states an absolute necessity, both the husband and wife or the other owners of the residence should sign the contract. It is not that uncommon for a divorce or breakup of the family to occur while the project is under way. Signatures of all the owners of the property obligate all the owners to the contract.

In commercial interior design, the designer often deals with people other than the actual owner of the business or the chairperson of the board of the corporation. Rarely does a minor (under the age of 18) have contractual capacity. Julie had both Rita and Sara sign the contract for the design work for Heavenly Jewels, since she knew that they were partners in the business. As our example at the beginning of this section showed, in a commercial project, the interior designer must be sure that the person who signs the contract has the authority to bind the corporation or business to that contract. Not all employees, even those with fancy job titles, have that authority.

Consideration

Requiring and obtaining fair compensation for the design services provided to clients is an understandably important issue. Chapter 23 discussed the ways that compensation is charged to clients. *Consideration* is the term for the "price" that the offeree "pays" to the offeror for the offeror's fulfilling the promise made in the contract. Generally, in an interior design contract, the consideration is the design fees that the client must pay to the designer for providing the services agreed to by the client. The consideration must be adequate enough to be fair. What was the consideration that Julie was negotiating with Rita and Sara for Heavenly Jewels?

Consideration can be money, property, services, or anything else that is legal. For example, a designer might barter or agree to provide interior design services to his or her accountant in exchange for accounting services. An interior designer might also accept a piece of property, such as a painting from a gallery, for interior design services provided to the gallery. Frank accepted a small lot from his client as the full consideration for the design of a cabin for the client. Of course, money is the primary type of consideration.

A promise to give consideration for something that has already occurred or that the designer is already obligated to do is not binding. If the client says, "Because you did such a great job on finishing the office installation on time, I will give you a $500 bonus," the client is not legally obligated to pay the bonus, since it is consideration for something that has happened in the past. Considerations are negotiated for actions that take place in the future or in the present, not in the past. If the design contract says, for example, that the designer will provide a watercolor rendering of the client's living room and later the designer tells the client that he or she must pay the designer an additional $500 for that rendering, the client is not obligated to pay, since the design firm is already legally obligated to supply that rendering for the consideration outlined in the contract.

Mutual Assent

Roger kept insisting that Mr. and Mrs. O'Neil sign the agreement to order the new appliances for the kitchen remodel. He repeatedly mentioned during the meeting last week that the prices were going up on the commercial grade stove/oven "very soon," and they needed to sign the agreement so that he could get the order in before the price went up. Mrs. O'Neil had her heart set on the stove/oven, and finally her husband signed the agreement. Not completely happy about the pressure that Roger had used, Mr. O'Neil called someone he knew who had access to the stove vendor and found out that there was no expected price increase for at least two months.

The legal concept of *mutual assent* means that the parties to a contract must be willing and free to enter into the contractual offer and acceptance. Sometimes a contract that is made by two parties who have the full legal competency to make a valid contract may not be able to be enforced because the reality of that mutual assent of one or another of the parties is being called into question.

In our example, Roger's insistence that the client sign the agreement while effectively threatening an impending price increase that was not actually going to occur is an example of the lack of mutual assent. Our example is a case in point for undue influence, where one party exerts so much influence on the other party that that other party virtually is unable to exercise his or her own free will. Other occurrences of what a judge may consider a lack of mutual assent happen because of (1) a mistake (this must relate to a mistake by one or another of the parties with regard to the facts of the terms of the contract, not an error of judgment or quality), (2) fraudulent misrepresentation (the terms of the agreement have been intentionally presented with information that is incorrect in an attempt to deceive the other party), and (3) duress (this negates a contract if the offeree is forced under certain kinds of threats to agree to the contract). If any one of these occurrences is proven to exist for either party, then the contract is not valid.

Legality

All interior designers are required by law to conduct their business operations and procedures following legal statutes in effect. Naturally, the issuing of a contract for interior design services or even the selling of merchandise to a client falls under this concept. In addition, designers who belong to a professional association or who are licensed or regulated by a state agency must also abide by these legal concepts or face ethics disciplinary hearings. Thus, a design contract must describe legal acts. An illegal contract is any contract that, if performed, would constitute an act against legal statute, would break tort law, or in any way would be opposed to the public good. It is highly unlikely that an interior designer would develop a design contract that might broach the concept of legality unless an interior designer entered into a contract related to restraint of trade.

Contracts in *restraint of trade* are made intentionally to be detrimental to the public good and generally have an effect on the potential for fair competition in a given market. For example, if two or more interior design firms in a market area in which they were the only source for furniture got together and agreed to sell merchandise at the same markup, they would be guilty of collusion, and their agreement would be in restraint of trade. If one subsequently lowered prices and the other sued, saying they had an agreement, the lawsuit would be thrown out, and both firms would likely be charged with a crime.

Some contracts in restraint of trade are actually legal, however. Certain clauses in employment contracts that restrain the activities of former employees can be legal, if the restrictions relating to noncompetition are reasonable. This was discussed in Chapter 14.

These elements are primary to the formation of a contract for such services as might be offered by an interior designer. The interpretation of these elements and the enforcement of these contracts is governed by common law. When a designer sells goods to a client, these sales contracts are governed by the Uniform Commercial Code. These contracts will be discussed in Chapter 26.

LETTER OF AGREEMENT OR CONTRACT?

A *letter of agreement* is a contract that is generally less formal in content and terminology and looks more like a letter. A letter of agreement is a contract and affords the designer the same legal consideration for enforcement as a contract, that is, if it meets the criteria discussed in this chapter, as for any other contract. It is really a semantic difference in what the agreement is called. Many interior designers prefer to use the terminology "letter of agreement" rather than "contract" when discussing a written agreement for services with clients, as they feel that the word contract scares some clients. It has been traditionally more common for the term letter of agreement, along with its less formal style of writing, to be used for residential projects. The term contract is more commonly used for commercial projects. However, this is not a universal situation. Unfortunately, with the increasing litigation in the industry, letters of agreement are not very simple anymore. It is advisable for disclaimers—discussed and shown later in this chapter–to be included in any letter of agreement. This is a necessary protection for the interior designer and the client.

Although a letter of agreement is thought to be less formal, it is often quite detailed and may contain many of the same types of clauses as a contract. It is up to the designer to decide whether the term contract or letter of agreement is more appropriate to his or her interior design practice. Format examples of both a letter of agreement and a contract are shown in this chapter. Note that this chapter will more frequently use the term contract than letter of agreement. Please note that the sample letter of agreement shown in Figure 24-1 and all other contracts shown in this chapter should not be used as is without review by the designer's attorney for appropriate applicability to the designer.

Dear Mr. and Mrs. Jones:

It was a pleasure meeting with you on Monday to discuss your design project. This letter of agreement outlines the services, fees, and other responsibilities of this firm.

My understanding is that the spaces to be included in this project are to remodel your kitchen and family room and the design of a custom entertainment center for the master bedroom. It is also my understanding that you will be purchasing all new kitchen appliances and furniture for the family room. It is not expected that the designer will be selling you the products as part of this agreement. If you choose to purchase products from this designer, a supplemental agreement will be prepared.

The approach to this project will be the following:

- Measure the spaces in order to prepare accurate floor plans.
- Prepare preliminary drawings and specifications required to draft finalized floor plans and specifications.
- Prepare elevations of the kitchen cabinets, any built-in cabinets for the family room, and the custom entertainment center for the master bedroom.
- Prepare finalized floor plans after your approval of the preliminary drawings and draft architectural plans for the remodeling work.
- Prepare finalized drawings needed for custom cabinets and entertainment center.
- Prepare specifications and budget estimates for the kitchen, family room, and entertainment center.
- Consult with architects, contractors, or other advisors that might be needed for the project.
- Review all drawings and specifications with you and not proceed to the next step in the process until approved by you.
- Assist you with selecting qualified contractors and suppliers needed to complete the remodeling and finishing work.
- Supervision of the work of contractors to the extent allowed by our license.

Compensation

The client agrees to pay an hourly fee of _____ an hour for all services described above. The client further agrees to pay expenses by the designer required of this project at the designer's cost. Expected expenses include travel time to meet with consultants, and custom cabinet constructors, reproduction costs of plans and other project documents, and express charges if necessary. Other expenses may be necessary and will be discussed with you before they are incurred by the designer.

Consulting charges by architects, contractors or other advisors that are required shall be billed directly to you by the consultant.

Payment

1. The client will pay a retainer of $1000 upon signing this agreement. Additional time will be billed for actual hours worked on the project as follows:
2. An invoice will be sent after preliminary plans and elevations are reviewed with you.
3. An invoice will be sent after approval by you of finalized drawings and specifications.
4. An invoice will be sent at the completion of the project.
5. All payments are due within 10 days of your receipt of invoice. Payments to third party consultants are due in accordance to their billing procedures and are paid directly to the third party provider.

Other terms applicable to this project

Drawings and documents prepared for this project remain the property of the interior designer and cannot be used without permission of the designer.

The designer provides good faith in assisting you in obtaining the services of qualified contractors but cannot be held responsible for the performance, quality, or timely completion of work by these third parties. The designer is also not responsible for changes made by your or consultants without notification to the designer.

The designer will provide on site supervision during the construction as the designer deems necessary. Primary construction supervision remains the responsibility of the contractors hired to do the work.

Any work that the client requests of the interior designer in addition to the work described will only be started after an amended agreement has been prepared and approved by both parties.

This agreement may be terminated by either party upon seven (7) days written notice. In the event of termination by the client, the client agrees to compensate the designer for all work completed up to the time of termination.

The client and designer agree that this letter constitutes the complete agreement between the designer and the client. Both parties also agree that disputes are to be handled by a third party arbitrator.

Your authorized signature on a copy of this agreement and a check for the retainer are necessary before we can begin the services described.

We thank you for the opportunity to submit this agreement.

_____   _____
Jane Doe, Designer   Date
XYZ Design, LLC

FIGURE 24-1.

Sample letter of agreement. The project involves a professional services assignment

FORM OF THE CONTRACT

John Smith, an interior designer who owns S.I.D. Interior Design Group, met with his client, Paul Drummond, and said to him, "My fee for the feasibility study of your restaurant will be $8000." Drummond asked him a few questions and then said, "That will be fine. When can you start?" Have Smith and Drummond entered into a contract for services? On the face of what we know, yes, because an oral agreement has been made by Smith and Drummond for services. It is not unusual for interior designers to begin projects for clients without a written contract or agreement. An oral understanding or agreement, however, is not good professional practice in this age of increased litigation and ethical disputes.

There remain many interior designers who believe an oral agreement is the best way to work with a client. Perhaps the designer feels the client will be threatened by the contract and doesn't want to lose the job. Or perhaps the designer knows the person or the person's reputation and figures it is not necessary to have a written agreement. Whatever the reason might be, it is simply not a good idea and is also not very good business practice in today's world. But is an oral contract a legal contract? Yes, it can be legal, except in some specific instances that require a written contract—these will be discussed later in this section. Professional interior designers in the twenty-first century should not start any design work for clients without obtaining some sort of written agreement, whether it is required by statute or not.

When an interior designer's major source of income comes from performing design services rather than selling goods, a written contract should always be executed and signed by the client before work begins. In fact, goods to be sold to a client should also never be ordered or delivered until the client has signed an agreement as well.

A written contract is the strongest evidence that a designer has to show that a contract for services exists between the client and the designer. Although an oral agreement might be considered legal by many judges, a written contract shows definite parameters that a judge can use to make a determination should a dispute occur. Designers should be concerned about conducting themselves in a professional and businesslike manner and should therefore insist on a written agreement prior to beginning design work and/or ordering merchandise. Although it is true that an occasional client's feelings may be bruised by the contractual situation, it is better to lose an occasional client than to experience costly and time-consuming contractual disputes.

As the old saying goes, "an oral contract is as good as the paper it is written on." Some designers have worked for many years "on a handshake" and never have had any problems. Others work with some clients without a contract and use a written agreement with other clients. Considering how litigious our society has become today, it is not particularly good professional practice to offer design services and/or to sell goods to clients without having a written agreement.

A written contract or agreement is actual evidence of what the circumstances to the agreement actually are. Written evidence is always preferred over someone's word by the courts when they are determining the facts. If a designer has a dispute with a client over whether certain work has been performed or not, the written agreement should provide the evidence to help clarify what is to be done. A written contract helps protect the designer. It also helps to protect the client if a designer fails to fulfill his or her obligations to the client.

Given that it is harder to determine performance or lack of performance when an oral agreement exists, there is more opportunity for fraud and perjury when disputes occur. Laws or statutes dealing with preventing fraud and perjury in relation to oral contracts exist to reduce the opportunity for fraud when two parties enter into some sort of agreement. These statutes prescribe when a contract must be in writing and the form of that contract.

Each state has its own Statute of Frauds, and a statement of Statute of Frauds is contained in the Uniform Commercial Code (UCC). Of the six types of contracts that must be in writing, three relate to the interior designer: (1) contracts that cannot be completed within one year of their origination, (2) contracts for the sale of goods, and (3) contracts for the sale of real estate. There are other situations in which the contract must be in writing, but these do not apply to the work of an interior designer. Additional information on the Statute of Frauds with reference to the sale of goods and agreements for the sale of goods is presented in Chapter 26.

Contracts Whose Performance Will Take More than One Year

Residential and commercial interior design projects often take longer than one year to complete. These large-scale and complex projects should never be undertaken without a written contract. The Statute of Frauds requires that the contract for a project or the services to complete the project that cannot be fulfilled in one year be in writing. If the terms of the contract indicate that the project will be completed within one year, it is not necessary for the contract for services to be in writing, although good business practices require that it should be in writing. The time limit begins one day after the contract is agreed to by both parties.

Contract for Sale of Goods

Susan has worked with her client, Alice Greatly, for many years, completing many small projects for the Greatly's residence. Mrs. Greatly asked Susan to order $20,000 of furniture for her daughter's home, and Susan, as usual, did not ask Mrs. Greatly to sign an agreement prior to ordering the furniture. "I wouldn't think of asking Mrs. Greatly for a contract to order anything for her." Interior designers often take orders for furniture and furnishings without obtaining any written agreement from the client. Yet many of these same designers sometimes find themselves owning furniture and furnishings that their clients have refused to accept.

The Statute of Frauds requires that a written contract be in existence for the sale of any goods of an amount over $500. Changes in the UCC have a $5000 minimum. However, since not all jurisdictions may have adopted this higher number, the designer should check with his or her accountant to be sure what the minimum is in that area. This contract need not be any kind of formal contract but merely a written sale agreement document that states quantity, description, and terms of the agreement; it must be signed by the party or parties involved. The agreement can be very informal or completed on an appropriately designed sales agreement form as illustrated in Chapter 31. The written contract or agreement provides more authority for the designer to obligate the client to pay for the goods. A complete discussion on the Statute of Frauds is presented in Chapter 26.

Contract for the Sale of Real Estate

It would seem that everyone at one time or another becomes involved in the sale of real estate. The interior designer might purchase an office or studio location rather than lease office space. Of course, he or she will also likely purchase a private residence. A contract for the sale of real estate, which is any land and buildings, plants, trees, or anything else affixed to the land, must always be in writing. Any oral contract for this kind of transaction is not binding on either party.

CONTENT FORMALITIES

An enforceable written contract or agreement does not have to read like something put together by an attorney—although having the firm's attorney look at your basic outline is a strong recommendation. So then when a contract must be in writing, what does *writing* mean? "The writing should be intelligible. It may be embodied in letters, memos, telegrams, invoices, and purchase orders sent between the parties."[2] As this definition indicates, there are other documents besides contracts that are also legally called "writings." A contract can be written on a napkin or an envelope, although this is not recommended. A key element is that it be readable. The contract or purchase orders, as well as other documents and agreements, should be prepared on the design firm's stationery and other business forms rather than on random slips of paper.

Contracts and agreements can be prepared on a computer and transmitted electronically. The Uniform Electronic Transaction Act of 1999 (UETA) and the Electronic Signatures in Global and National Commerce Act of 2000 (ESIGN) are model laws adopted by most of the states that help to enforce contracts transmitted electronically.[3] Interior designers often send purchase orders via fax or e-mail. Commercial clients might utilize an electronic signature feature on contracts and agreements if acceptable to the interior designer. These laws help clarify that a paper-and-pen record is not always required if a properly executed electronic record is produced. This convenience is something that the designer should discuss with his or her attorney to be sure that the electronic signature is actually an acceptable way of obtaining acceptance from a client.

A written agreement concerning interior design services—and indeed almost all forms of contracts—must provide enough information to signify that an agreement has been made between the parties. To be more specific, to be fully enforceable, the contract must include the following information:

- Date
- Parties involved
- What services are to be provided
- How fees are to be charged and the terms of payment
- Signatures of the parties, especially the party being charged—the client

Such items as time limit of the agreement and other terms that seem appropriate are left up to the discretion of the designer. Many of these other items will be discussed in the "Interior Design Contracts: Content and Form" section of this chapter. There are differences in what is needed for a contract for the sale of goods versus a contract for services. That type of contract will be covered in Chapter 26.

Just as there is no such thing as an ideal way to charge, there is no ideal way to write a design contract. To protect the design firm from the potential loss of income, a variety of contracts should be developed with the assistance of the firm's attorney. These different contracts should focus on the various kinds of business in which the design firm is engaged. ASID and the AIA have standardized contracts that have been carefully developed based on input from interior designers and attorneys who specialize in contract law. Members of the professional organizations can obtain copies of these standardized contracts from the national office.

DEVELOPING THE DESIGN CONTRACT

A written contract can alleviate many disputes between the interior designer and the client. Disputes related to contracts remain among the major source of ethics complaints filed by clients against interior designers, according to the ethics committee of the major professional associations. Numerous tasks must be done through the different design phases, and getting the scope and needs right at the beginning when the contract is formulated is critical to a smooth project process and reducing the chance of a dispute.

Gathering the information needed to prepare a design contract that will protect the interior designer from future disagreements is very important. Designers regularly use questionnaires or other forms to help them obtain the necessary information (see Figure 24-2). To a great extent, this information is obtained directly from the client during the initial meetings and consultations. Depending on the exact nature of the project, others such as an architect, engineer, and employees for commercial projects will provide additional information necessary for the interior designer to complete the contract and subsequent project requirements. Note that Figure 24-2 has been included on the CD as Item 24-1.

Interiors projects are complex whether it is the design of a high-end residential project, including the design of custom cabinets, furniture, and architectural treatments, or a commercial project regardless of the type of space. Therefore, this task should not be taken lightly and should not be trusted to one's memory. Eagerness to become involved in a particular project sometimes leads designers to neglect finding out anything about the potential client. This same eagerness has led many interior designers to move ahead with a project before fully understanding the scope of actual needs.

One important issue before the contract is developed is clarifying the client's familiarity with working with an interior design professional. It is, of course, not possible to know each client well before beginning a project, but some investigation is possible. As the interior designer talks to a prospective client, he or she will begin to understand if the client is knowledgeable about the design process. Clients who have never worked with an interior designer before will need to be informed in more detail of the process and will probably have more questions and pose more problems during the course of the project. Clients who have worked with designers before have preconceived ideas on what will happen based on their previous experiences. Thorough interviewing helps the interior designer understand if the client has unrealistic expectations concerning budgets, time lines, and overall responsibility of the interior designer. Budget expectations are particularly problematic, as clients who have not budgeted sufficiently for the project may be afraid to say that they do not have the funds to cover the design suggestions. Later, they may accuse the designer of not meeting the budget that they had in mind or might otherwise create problems related to their unrealistic budget.

An interior designer may want to consider checking on the client's financial situation before proceeding with a contract. Many have been left suffering a loss when the client that lives in an expensive house was on the verge of bankruptcy and cannot pay the designer for services and goods. The designer can check on clients before proceeding in several ways. One is by obtaining credit reports. This is a natural safeguard if the designer is intending to sell the client merchandise and to request design service fees. The firm's attorney might be able to do a check of court records in order to determine if the client has a propensity for suing. The Better Business Bureau can tell the designer if other businesses have had problems with a particular client. And, of course, there is always the gut feeling that some experienced designers have that warns them to stay away from a particular client.

One of the most critical parts of the design contract is the scope of services. The scope of services details what must be done from start to finish. Clarity aids in the prevention of misunderstandings on both parties to the contract. Each design activity takes time. Some require expense items (like the materials to build a

Project Information

Date of Contact: _____   Project # _____

Appointment Date: _____

☐ Existing Clients   ☐ New Client

Move-in Date: _____

Client	Project Location
Address	Address
Phone	Phone
Fax	Fax
E-mail	Contact E-mail

Project Areas Involved:

Budget

Site Conditions:
     ☐ New Construction   Architect _____
     ☐ Renovation–Some Demolition   _____
     ☐ Renovation–Finishes Only   _____
     ☐ Movable FF& E Only

Scope of Services: Additional Comments:
   (See Fee Estimate Form)

FIGURE 24-2.

A type of form that designers can use to obtain detailed information about the design project in order to prepare the design contract.

Expected Deliverables:

☐ Design Concept Statement
☐ Programming Report
☐ Presentation Documents
    Specify
☐ Purchase Proposals
☐ Others _____

☐ Full Construction Documents
☐ Partial Construction Documents
    Specify
☐ Bid Documents

Expected Staffing

☐ Principal
☐ Senior Designer
☐ Project Manager
☐ Design Assistant
☐ Consultant:
☐ Consultant:

☐ Clerical
☐ Warehouse Service
☐ Other

Reimbursables:

☐ Travel: Airfare, Hotel, Per Diem
☐ Ground Transport
☐ Misc. Travel
☐ Printing / Copying Documents
☐ Other

Notes

FIGURE 24-2.

(*Continued*)

model). The small-practice owner may need to outsource CAD drawings to complete working drawings. A project may require utilizing a lighting designer who is not on staff of the contracting firm. Missing out on understanding the full scope of the project could mean that the designer might provide some services at no charge. Not including a complete scope of services could mean that, if part of the project is done improperly, there would be legal liability. Understanding the full scope of the project cannot be taken lightly by the designer. Table 24-1 provides some of the questions that must be answered prior to the writing of a design contract. CD Item 24-2 is a worksheet that will help you develop a design contract.

    It is unfortunately true that interior designers are sometimes tempted to work with a client on a project when their capabilities to do the project are marginal. Taking on a design project is a serious responsibility. The designer should not enter into a design contract for a project if the designer is not competent and capable of performing the work required. The errors that can be made can be costly in terms of both finances and reputation. If the project is something the designer wants to do in order to gain experience, then the designer might consider setting up a joint venture

TABLE 24-1.

Typical questions used to prepare design contracts.

Who are the owners?
What is the exact location of project?
What spaces will be involved in the project?
Is the project new construction or a remodeling project?
What is the square footage of the project?
Does the owner occupy or lease the building?
Will designer/client CAD networking be required?
What is the budget?
What is the targeted completion date?
Are architectural floor plans available, or will the space need to be site-measured?
Have you worked with this client before?
Has the client worked with a designer before?
Will presentation graphics, such as perspectives, be required? What media is appropriate?
Does the current design staff have the time and experience to do this project?
Will consultants or additional staff be required in order to do this project?
If it is a remodeling project, what code requirements must be researched and met?
If it is new construction, who is the architect?
Who and how will the contractors be selected?
What kind of presentation will be required at preliminary and final meetings?
Will sample and image presentation boards be required?
If it is new construction, what code requirements must be researched and met?
Who will obtain permits?
How much demolition is expected?
How much supervision must be done on site?
Will the project go out to bid, or has a purchasing agreement already been established?
Will the project be completed all at once or be done in stages?
What portion of the construction or interiors project will be handled by the client?
Does the client require moving services, or will the client take care of this himself or herself?
How much existing furniture will be used?
Who is responsible for production of construction documents?
What styles of new furniture are preferred?
Are new architectural finishes to be selected?
Are custom cabinets, custom furniture items, or treatments expected?
Are office systems furniture (or other furniture) evaluations required prior to specifications?
Will art, graphics, accessories, interior plantscaping be required?

Note: This list, of course, is not all-inclusive.

with an experienced designer. Otherwise, the designer should steer clear of working on any project in which his or her skills are marginal.

INTERIOR DESIGN CONTRACTS: CONTENT AND FORM

It has always been the contention of this author that the best way for a student or designer to understand the types of items that should make up the content of a contract for services is by reading brief explanations of the common clauses. These explanations are supplemented by examples that help the reader see these clauses in the context of different types of projects. It is not possible to offer samples to satisfy every situation. And these sample contracts should not be used without the advice of the practitioner's attorney to be sure the language suits the needs of the particular firm.

As previously mentioned, some designers do not like to refer to agreements for design services as "contracts." What the designer chooses to call the written agreement—a contract or a letter of agreement outlining design services—does not matter. What does matter is that the writing spells out information concerning the offer in sufficient detail so that the courts (if necessary) can determine the nature and facts of the offer and agreement. The minimal requirements discussed earlier in the chapter help create that legally enforceable contract. Utilizing a written agreement does not guarantee future lack of legal problems. Disputes occur even with the most diligently prepared contract. However, care in the preparation of a design contract is definitely beneficial.

The format is determined from information obtained in meetings with the client, the designer's knowledge and experience with similar projects, and a thorough knowledge of the abilities of the design staff of the firm. All three play an important part in determining which clauses should go into the contract and whether or not a contract should be prepared for the client. Depending on the project, there are certain specific items that should be in the contract to protect both the designer and the client. The form or outline to use depends on the scope of the project, the experience of the designer, the experience of the client in working with interior designers, and the compensation method.

Residential interior designers tend to use a less formal-looking letter of agreement. The length and complexity of this agreement needs to be prepared in consideration for the complexity of the project. They must contain the parts discussed in the "Content Formalities" section, with emphasis on the scope of services and charges/payment sections. Interior designers like to use less formal language in a letter of agreement. In today's litigious climate, any designer needs to realize that a written agreement is the safest way to protect the design firm and avoid disputes.

Contracts for a large majority of commercial projects are almost always relatively long and detailed, running about four pages at least. Some sample formal contracts used in commercial projects and architecture can even be as long as 12 pages, because detailed clauses are needed to protect the interior designer by clearly spelling out all the services, duties, and responsibilities of the designer, the client, and any other parties to the contract. The length and detail is always adjusted for the complexity of the project and operational needs of the design firm.

A final comment involving an agency relationship is in order before the details on the common clauses in a contract are discussed. You will recall from Chapter 15 that agents are hired to work for the benefit of the principal such as a real estate agent working for the seller/buyer of a house (the principal). An agency relationship also exists between employees and employers. Agency relationships exist between an interior designer and the client when the designer provides design services to the client and when the interior designer places orders for merchandise for the client that are purchased directly through the interior designer's company.

It is important for the designer to be sure that the contract for services as well as for the sale of goods spells out the scope of the authority of the designer as an agent for the client. In many respects that is accomplished primarily through the scope of services clauses in the contract and appropriate clauses suggested by the designer's attorney in a sales agreement. Providing the drawings and specifications as spelled out in the contract is an example of the designer fulfilling his or her agency relationship. Ordering merchandise that has not been approved by the client is an example of the designer failing in his or her relationship as an agent for the client. Both residential and commercial contracts have the same basic parts. Table 24-2 shows a list of the common items found in a contract for interior design services. Some projects do not require the entire list of contract terms. A very complex project may actually include terms not shown in the figure or discussed in this chapter. We will discuss each item in the list as they relate to residential and commercial projects, noting any differences between the two.

TABLE 24-2.

A checklist of typical types of clauses found in design contracts.

1. Date
2. Client's name and address
3. Detailed description of project areas involved
4. Detailed scope of services to be provided
5. Detailed purchasing arrangements
6. Price guarantees
7. Method and payment of compensation
8. Reimbursements for out-of-pocket expenses
9. Charges for extra services
10. Designer responsibility disclaimer
11. Charges and responsibilities of third parties
12. Photographic and publishing rights
13. Termination of contract
14. Responsibilities of the client
15. Assignment and delegation
16. Ownership of documents
17. Time frame of the contract
18. Matters of arbitration
19. Mutual understanding and legality
20. Conditions and amount of retainer
21. Signatures

These items are discussed in the typical order in which they would appear in a contract. Refer to Figures 24-3 through 24-5 for sample contracts.

1. *Date.* Contracts must be dated with the day, month, and year.

2. *Client's name and address.* The name of the client obligated to the contract should be clearly identified at the beginning of the contract. In residential design, it is important for the husband's and wife's names to be on the contract and for both to sign the contract. This obligates each in the event of divorce, separation, or death of either of the spouses.

   In commercial design, the name of the person having the authority to contract for the business should be listed, and the contract should be signed by that person. The address of the home office is listed when the business has several locations unless someone at a branch location has the authority to sign the contract.

3. *Detailed description of project areas involved.* It is important for the project areas involved to be detailed at the beginning of the contract. This is like listing the product number and description of a piece of furniture on a sales agreement. Clarifying in detail the project areas involved helps to avoid confusion and arguments over extra charges or threats of breach. In a residential project, this may mean including a clause as broad as "your residence at 1234 Hummingbird Lane," which means the designer is responsible for the scope of services to be defined in the contract for the entire house. If the services relate only to the living room, the contract should say this. Should the client later want to include additional areas, the designer can then charge for these new, optional design spaces or services over and above the original fee.

(*text continues on page 457*)

August 31, 200X

Mr. and Mrs. Michael Hamilton
1479 E. Stanford Drive
Hazelton, Rhode Island

Dear Mr. and Mrs. Hamilton:

This letter will confirm our agreement concerning the professional services we will provide for your residence at 1479 E. Stanford Drive, Hazelton, Rhode Island. It is understood that the project specifically involves the living room, dining room, family room, and kitchen.

We will provide the following services:

A. Design Concept Services

 1. Measure the existing spaces and prepare sketches or take photos of the existing interior.
 2. Discuss your specific needs and preferences.
 3. Prepare conceptual furniture floor plans.
 4. Make preliminary selections and color schemes for new furniture items to be purchased, as well as selections for walls, floors, and window treatments.
 5. Prepare a preliminary budget for the project.
 6. Review all of the above with you.

B. Purchasing Services

 1. Upon approval of the preliminary selections mentioned above, we will prepare finalized specifications and pricing proposals.
 2. It is understood that all items specified by the interior designer will be purchased only through the interior designer, should you wish to purchase them.
 3. All items to be purchased will be detailed as a specification and will require your signed authorization, as well as 75% of the total price for each item prior to placing the order. The balance, including applicable taxes, shipping, and handling fees, are due upon delivery.
 4. The price for each item shall be the regular or normal wholesale or cost price to the interior designer plus_____% purchase fee plus shipping and handling fees at actual cost. The fee is in addition to Design Concept and supervision fees, to be described below.
 5. As might be necessary, the designer will provide counsel and guidance in the selection of necessary contractors to perform the required work. Client will enter into any contract for these services directly with the contractor.
 6. Periodic visits to the residence will be made to observe that the work is being done in accordance with standard acceptable practice. Constant on-site observations are not part of the designer's responsibilities.

C. Compensation
The fee for the concept and supervision services described will be_____. Additional services requested by you that are beyond the scope of services outlined in this agreement will be billed separately at_____ per hour.

Billing for services shall be in the following manner:

   20% upon signing the contract (retainer)
   40% at the end of the preliminary review meeting
   30% when construction and furniture orders are placed
   10% upon completion of the project

All payments are due ten days after receipt of invoice.

The above fee does not include client-approved expenses for long-distance telephone calls, out-of-town travel to shop for resources, and special renderings. These charges, if required, will be billed separately at our actual cost plus 10%.

D. Other Matters

 1. The drawings and specifications are intended for design concept only and cannot be used for construction or architectural purposes.

FIGURE 24-3.

A sample design contract for a residential project.

2. The designer does not include any responsibility for the design of structural, electrical, plumbing, heating, or other mechanical systems that exist or might be needed for the project.

3. The drawings and documents prepared by the interior designer remain the property of the design firm and cannot be used by you for any purpose other than the completion of the project by the interior designer.

4. We will perform the services described in good faith but cannot be responsible for the performance, quality, or timely completion of work by others. Further, we shall not be responsible for any changes to the project that the client or contractor(s) make without informing the designer.

5. You are expected to grant reasonable access to the premises for the designer and the designer's agents, as well as to contractors required to perform the agreed-upon work. By signing this proposal, you understand that the peace and privacy of your home may be disrupted for the time required to perform the work.

6. This proposal may be terminated for any reason by either the client or the designer, provided ten days' written notice has been given. In the event of termination by the client, the client will pay the designer for all work done and expenses due up to the date of termination.

7. Upon completion of the project, the designer may require permission to photograph the project for the firm's records. The interior designer shall not use the photographs for promotional purposes without the permission of the client.

8. This agreement is the complete statement of understanding between the interior designer and the client. No other agreements have been made other than those stated in this agreement. This agreement can only be modified in writing, signed by both parties.

It will be our pleasure to begin your project as soon as we have received a copy of this proposal signed by both of you and a check for the retainer. We appreciate your selection of our firm for your interiors project and look forward to working with you.

Sincerely yours,

EastCoast Interiors, Inc.

_____
(Owner)

_____
Mr. Michael Hamilton

_____
Mrs. Betty Hamilton

FIGURE 24-3.

(*Continued*)

January 30, 200x

John Smith, Chief Executive Officer
Smith Serve, Inc.
1776 N. Adams
Boston, MA

Dear Mr. Smith:

We are pleased to submit the following proposal of professional interior design services for the space planning and interior design of your new office in Amherst, Massachusetts, at _____.

SCOPE OF SERVICE

A. **Programming and Schematic Design**
   1. Meet with you and/or selected members of your staff to determine all requirements that will affect the space planning and interior design of your project.
   2. Obtain floor plans from the architect.
   3. Inventory existing equipment that might be used in the new space plan.
   4. Conduct interviews with staff to determine equipment needs and adjacent requirements.

FIGURE 24-4.

An example of a design contract for a commercial project withan extensive scope of services.

5. Determine project objectives as well as budget considerations.
6. Review all programming findings with your project committee.
7. Prepare preliminary schematic layouts.
8. Develop preliminary furniture, color, and materials selections.
9. Review schematic layouts, selections, and sketches with your project committee.

B. **Design Development**
1. Finalize space plans showing locations of walls, furniture, and built-in equipment.
2. Finalize selections of all materials, finishes, and treatment for furniture, walls, flooring, windows, and ceilings.
3. Provide three-dimensional drawings of typical workstations.
4. Provide three-dimensional sketches of lobby and employee "think tank" space.
5. Finalize lighting specifications with lighting consultant.
6. Prepare a budget of all interior furnishings.
7. Present plans and product specifications for your approval.

C. **Contract Documents Phase**
1. After final approval of all space plans, furniture layouts, and product selections, prepare appropriate working drawings and documents for the construction of the space and installation of the interiors. This will include dimensioned floor plans, furniture plans, electrical location plans, reflected ceiling plans, and cabinet shop drawings as needed.
2. Prepare bid specifications for furniture and other movable equipment.
3. Consult with you on developing the qualified bidder's list.
4. Provide information for the preparation of bid specifications for floors, walls, windows, ceilings, and lighting fixture materials or products (bid specification to be written by your facilities department).
5. Coordinate with your facilities department to develop complete set of bid documents.

D. **Contract Administration Phase**
1. Assist you in obtaining competitive bids for furnishings and equipment.
2. Assist you in coordinating the schedule for delivery and installation of the work.
3. Make periodic visits to the job site to ensure that the work is progressing according to the specifications in the bid documents.
4. Supervise installation of furniture and movable equipment covered in the bid documents.
5. Upon completion of the installation, the designer shall prepare a punch list of items needing attention by the designer or vendors. This will be reviewed with you prior to transmittal to appropriate parties.

TERMS OF COMPENSATION

For the interior design and consultation services outlined above, you will be billed a fee of $57,500 payable according to the following:

You will be invoiced monthly for actual hours worked. Payment is due within ten (10) days of receipt of invoice. A late payment charge of 1–½% per month (18% per annum) will be added to invoices thirty days past due. Note that a retainer is required to begin work. The amount is detailed later in this proposal.

The total fee is based on a maximum of two revisions after each client review. Work required or requested beyond the two revisions will be charged at the described hourly fees, but will be in addition to the maximum estimate.

Additional services not outlined in this proposal but requested by you or required after client approval results in changes in the project will be billed separately at an hourly rate of _____.

Fees include provision of six sets of contract documents for the client's use. It is understood that your company is responsible for reproduction of all sets of contract documents required for the bidding process.

REIMBURSABLE EXPENSES

Reimbursable expenses are in addition to the charges detailed above. Such expenses as out-of-town travel and living expenses, long-distance telephone charges, special renderings, mock-ups, and reproduction costs other than those detailed shall be billed at actual cost to the designer.

Out-of-town travel in the interest of the project shall only be made with proper notification and approval of the client. At this time, it is estimated that a minimum of four site visits will be necessary during the progress of the project.

FIGURE 24-4.

(*Continued*)

GENERAL CONDITIONS

1. The designer shall not be responsible for the quality, workmanship, or appearance of products should you purchase products other than those specified.
2. The designer is not responsible if you, architect, or contractor(s) make changes to the project without notification to the designer.
3. The designer or representatives of the designer reserves the right to photograph the project upon completion in order to provide a record of the project. The design firm shall have the right to use these photographs for business purposes.
4. This contract does not include provision for fees by third party consultants required to complete the project. Contracts for these services will be negotiated separately and their contract negotiations must be completed within 20 days of the execution of this contract.
5. You shall make provision for the design firm and/or its agents access to the project site as needed for the completion of the project in a timely fashion.
6. This proposal may be terminated by either party upon seven (7) days written notice. In the event of termination by you, you shall pay the designer for all services performed and reimbursable expenses due up to the date of termination.
7. Drawings, specifications, and sample boards, as instruments of service, are the property of the designer. The designer reserves the exclusive copyright to these items and provides them to you for your use on this project only. Any reproduction or reuse of the drawings, specifications, and sample boards without the prior written consent of the designer is not permitted.
8. The timely completion of this project and the fees quoted is based on this signed return of this proposal to the designer within ten (10) calendar days.
9. Any controversy or claims arising out of or relating to this project or breach thereof shall be subject to review and settled by arbitration in Massachusetts. Arbitration shall be in accordance with the rules of the American Arbitration Association. The decisions of the arbitrator shall be final and binding on both parties.
10. This contract represents the complete understanding between the designer and the client. Changes and modifications must be made in writing and signed by both parties.

Approval of this proposal is signified by your signature in the space below. Work will begin on your project when the designer receives a signed copy of this proposal along with a check for a retainer of _____.

We would like to thank you for the opportunity to submit this proposal for professional interior design services. We look forward to a set of challenges which we pledge to meet with our best professional efforts and attention.

Sincerely,

Authorized:

Columbia Interior Design, Inc.

_____
(Company)

_____
(Design Director)

_____
(By)

_____
(Date)

_____
(Title)

_____
(Date)

FIGURE 24-4.

(*Continued*)

ASID Document ID123

RESIDENTIAL INTERIOR DESIGN SERVICES AGREEMENT

This **AGREEMENT** is

made this _____ day of_____ in the year of Two Thousand and _____

BETWEEN the **CLIENT**:
(name and address)

and the **DESIGNER**:
(name and address)

The **CLIENT** and the **DESIGNER** agree as follows:

The Project pertains to the following areas within Client's residence located at

_____ :

(List areas below:)

ID123-1996   1

FIGURE 24-5.

ASID document ID 122: Residental Design Services Agreement (fixed fee). (Reprinted with permission ASID, Washington, DC)

INTERIOR DESIGN SERVICES

1. Design Concept Services

1.1 In this phase of the Project, Designer shall, as and where appropriate, perform the following:

A. Determine Client's design preferences and requirements.

B. Conduct an initial design study.

C. Prepare drawings and other materials to generally illustrate Designer's suggested interior design concepts, to include color schemes, interior finishes, wall coverings, floor coverings, ceiling treatments, lighting treatments and window treatments.

D. Prepare layout showing location of movable furniture and furnishings.

E. Prepare schematic plans for recommended cabinet work, interior built-ins and other interior decorative details ("Interior Installations").

1.2 Prior to commencing Design Concept Services, Designer shall receive an Initial Design Fee of _____ dollars ($_____). This non-refundable Design Fee is payable upon signing this Agreement and is in addition to all other compensation payable to Designer under this Agreement. Not more than_____ (____) revisions to the Design Concept will be prepared by Designer without additional charges. Additional revisions will be billed to Client as Additional Services.

2. Interior Specifications and Purchasing Services

2.1 Upon Client's approval of the Design Concepts, Designer will, as and where appropriate:

A. Select and/or specially design required Interior Installations and all required items of movable furniture, furnishings, light fixtures, hardware, fixtures, accessories and the like ("Merchandise").

B. Prepare and submit for Client's approval Proposals for completion of Interior Installations and purchase of Merchandise.

ID123-1996   **2**

FIGURE 24-5.

(Continued)

2.2 Merchandise and Interior Installations specified by Designer shall, if Client wishes to purchase them, be purchased solely through Designer. Designer may, at times, request Client to engage others to provide Interior Installations, pursuant to the arrangements set forth in the Project Review services described in paragraph 3 of this Agreement.

2.3 Merchandise and Interior Installations to be purchased through Designer will be specified in a written "Proposal" prepared by Designer and submitted in each instance for Client's written approval. Each Proposal will describe the item and its price to Client (F.O.B. point of origin). The price of each item to Client ("Client Price") shall be the amount charged to Designer by the supplier of such item ("Supplier Price"), plus Designer's fee equal to _____ percent (____%) of the Supplier Price (exclusive of any freight, delivery or like charges or applicable tax).

2.4 No item can be ordered by Designer until the Proposal has been approved by Client, in writing, and returned to Designer with Designer's required initial payment equal to _____ percent (____%) of the Client Price. The balance of the Client Price, together with delivery, shipping, handling charges and applicable taxes, is payable when the item is ready for delivery to and/or installation at Client's residence, or to a subsequent supplier for further work upon rendition of Designer's invoice. Proposals for fabrics, wall coverings, accessories, antiques, and items purchased at auction or at retail stores require full payment at time of signed Proposal.

3. Project Review

3.1 If the nature of the Project requires engagement by Client of any contractors to perform work based upon Designer's concepts, drawings or interior design specifications not otherwise provided for in the Interior Specifications and Purchasing Services, Client will enter into contracts directly with the concerned contractor. Client shall provide Designer with copies of all contracts and invoices submitted to Client by the contractors.

3.2 Designer will make periodic visits to the Project site as Designer may consider appropriate to observe the work of these contractors to determine whether the contractors' work is proceeding in general conformity with Designer's concepts. Constant observation of work at the Project site is not a part of Designer's duties. Designer is not responsible for the performance, quality, timely completion or delivery of any work, materials or equipment furnished by contractors pursuant to direct contracts with Client.

3.3 Designer shall be entitled to receive a fee equal to _____ percent (____%) of the amount to be paid by Client to each contractor performing any work based upon Designer's concepts, drawings, specifications ("Project Review Fees").

ID123-1996   3

FIGURE 24-5.

(Continued)

3.4 The Project Review Fees shall be payable by Client to Designer as follows:

4. MISCELLANEOUS

4.1 Should Designer agree to perform any design service not described above, such "Additional Service" will be invoiced to Client at the following hourly rates:

Design Principal	$_____
Project Designer	$_____
Staff Designer	$_____
Draftsman	$_____
Other employees	$_____

Hourly charges will be invoiced to Client _____ and are payable upon receipt of invoice.

4.2 Disbursements incurred by Designer in the interest of the Project shall be reimbursed by Client to Designer upon receipt of Designer's invoices, which are rendered _____. Reimbursements shall include, among other things, costs of local and long distance travel, long distance telephone calls, duplication of plans, drawings and specifications, messenger services and the like.

4.3 Designer's drawings and specifications are conceptual in nature and intended to set forth design intent only. They are not to be used for architectural or engineering purposes. Designer does not provide architectural or engineering services.

4.4 Designer's services shall not include undertaking any responsibility for the design or modification of the design of any structural, heating, air-conditioning, plumbing, electrical, ventilation or other mechanical systems installed or to be installed at the Project.

4.5 Should the nature of Designer's design concepts require the services of any other design professional, such professional shall be engaged directly by Client pursuant to separate agreement as may be mutually acceptable to Client and such other design professional.

4.6 As Designer requires a record of Designer's design projects, Client will permit Designer or Designer's representatives to photograph the Project upon completion of the Project. Designer will be entitled to use photographs for Designer's business purposes but shall not disclose Project location or Client's name without Client's prior written consent.

ID123-1996   4

FIGURE 24-5.

(Continued)

4.7 All concepts, drawings and specifications prepared by Designer's firm ("Project Documents") and all copyrights and other proprietary rights applicable thereto remain at all times Designer's property. Project Documents may not be used by Client for any purpose other than completion of Project by Designer.

4.8 Designer cannot guarantee that actual prices for Merchandise and/or Interior Installations or other costs or services as presented to Client will not vary either by item or in the aggregate from any Client proposed budget.

4.9 This Agreement may be terminated by either party upon the other party's default in performance, provided that termination may not be effected unless written notice specifying nature and extent of default is given to the concerned party and such party fails to cure such default in performance within _____ (____) days from date of receipt of such notice. Termination shall be without prejudice to any and all other rights and remedies of Designer, and Client shall remain liable for all outstanding obligations owed by Client to Designer and for all items of Merchandise, Interior Installations and other services on order as of the termination date.

4.10 In addition to all other legal rights, Designer shall be entitled to withhold delivery of any item of Merchandise or the further performance of Interior Installations or any other services, should Client fail to timely make any payments due Designer.

4.11 Any controversy or claim arising out of or relating to this Agreement, or the breach thereof, shall be decided by arbitration only in the _____ in accordance with the Commercial Arbitration Rules of the American Arbitration Association then in effect, and judgment upon the award rendered by the arbitrator(s) may be entered in any court having jurisdiction thereof.

4.12 Client will provide Designer with access to the Project and all information Designer may need to complete the Project. It is Client's responsibility to obtain all approvals required by any governmental agency or otherwise in connection with this Project.

4.13 Any sales tax applicable to Design Fees, and/or Merchandise purchased from Designer, and/or Interior Installations completed by Designer shall be the responsibility of Client.

4.14 Neither Client nor Designer may assign their respective interests in this Agreement without the written consent of the other.

4.15 The laws of the State of _____ shall govern this Agreement.

4.16 Any provision of this Agreement held to be void or unenforceable under any law shall be deemed stricken, and all remaining provisions shall continue to be valid and binding upon both Designer and Client.

4.17 This Agreement is a complete statement of Designer's and Client's understanding. No representations or agreements have been made other than those contained in this Agreement. This Agreement can be modified only by a writing signed by both Designer and Client.

ID123-1996   5

FIGURE 24-5.

(Continued)

5. ADDITIONAL TERMS

CLIENT:

_____

_____

DESIGNER:

_____

_____

ID123-1996   6

FIGURE 24-5.

(_Continued_)

A contract for a commercial project often needs to be even more specific. If the address of the project is different from the main office, it should be listed. It may be necessary to list the specific area by department or room and even the amount of square footage. "The main dining room, foyer, and meeting rooms, but excluding the kitchen of your restaurant at the Harbor Hotel, San Diego" is a clear definition of what rooms in what building will be involved in this contract. Saying "your restaurant at the Harbor Hotel" leaves the designer open to a lot of unplanned additional design. Should the client want additional areas to be included or added, a secondary contract or addendum to the contract might be prepared to cover these areas and the services they require.

4. *Detailed scope of services*. Services required for a project vary greatly from one to another. In many cases, as a project proceeds, the client may desire additional areas to be designed or services to be performed. Some designers use the term *scope creep* to signify project requirements that become larger than originally intended because of client requests. In some cases, the designer may suggest additional services that were not obvious at the beginning of the project. However, clients are reluctant to agree to additional fees for services that interior designers say are needed, believing they should have been included in the first place. A detailed description of the scope of services outlined in the general order in which they will take place leaves little room for disagreements about doing or not doing something. Following the outline of the generally accepted phases of a project helps to create a detailed outline that is easier for the client to understand. Refer to Chapter 28 and Table 24-3 for detailed samples of the

TABLE 24-3.

A detailed list of common services for a "Scope of Services."

Scope of Services

Programming Phase

Interview client to determine user needs and goals.
Evaluate existing job site or review any drawings for new construction.
Inventory existing furniture that might be used in the project.
Obtain scaled floor plans of the project space from the client (the architect or landlord).
Measure job site to obtain necessary dimensions of site.
Determine style, color, etc. preferences.
Meet with landlord concerning building standards and regulations.
Ascertain potential building code, life safety code, and barrier-free regulations as might affect the project.
Develop project schedule.
Develop project budget.
Coordinate (if needed) with appropriate consultants.
Determine feasibility of meeting the client's requirements; determine and inform the client of any restraints that will affect the feasibility of the project.
Prepare final design program.

Schematic Design

Develop spatial and communication adjacencies.
Develop preliminary space utilization plans.
Prepare preliminary furniture plans.
Preliminary selections of interior architectural finishes.
Preliminary furniture, furnishings, and equipment selections.

Review applicable building, life safety, and accessibility codes, and apply as required.
Make preliminary color selections.
Refine budgets.
Prepare design drawings, such as perspectives, elevations, etc., as needed.
Meet with consultants, such as architect, contractors, or others as required.

Design Development

Finalize relationship diagrams or charts.
Complete space plans and layouts.
Complete furniture, furnishings, and equipment plans.
Complete working drawings concerning custom furniture, cabinets, or architectural treatments.
Determine specifications of architectural finishes.
Prepare specifications of furniture, furnishings, and equipment.
Prepare other drawings, such as lighting plans, elevations, and sections, etc., as required.
Prepare presentation boards.
Prepare presentation graphics, such as renderings of perspectives, isometrics, or axonometric drawings.
Prepare a budget of expected costs for all construction and furnishings, as specified.

Contract Documents

Prepare working drawings and schedules for the construction and/or installation of the space.
Prepare written specifications to accompany working drawings, schedules, and furniture, furnishings,
   and equipment.
Prepare furniture and equipment installation drawings.
Obtain approvals and permits from jurisdictional agencies.
Provide or assist client with the preparation of bid documents.
Qualify vendors, suppliers, and subcontractors.
Assist client in obtaining competitive bids for all phases of the project.
Provide guidance in the selection of necessary contractors.
Assist client with owner-contractor contacts.

Contract Administration

Assist with securing of bids.
Provide project management supervision of the job site during construction/installation.
Procure furniture and furnishings by submitting purchase orders to suppliers and installers.
Assist in the procurement of furniture and furnishings through bid administration.
Make periodic visits to the job site to ensure the work is being done in accordance with the contract documents and
   specifications.
Supervise installation of furniture, furnishings, and equipment.
Maintain project management and schedule records.
Assist in determination of substantial completion, payments to vendors, and securing releases.
Prepare and administer postoccupancy evaluations.
This list suggests a wide range of services and is not meant to be all-inclusive.

TABLE 24-3.

(*Continued*)

range of services that might be required of either a residential or commercial project. Naturally, only those services that the designer understands are to be performed should be listed in the contract.

On-site supervision is a common service. This service causes considerable misunderstandings between designer and client. To avoid misunderstandings and undue expense to the client or time spent on the site by the designer, it is important for the designer to be very clear with the client as to the extent of on-site supervision and what the designer can and cannot do during this phase of the project. Designers must also be careful when using words such as *supervise* or *manage* in relation to the installation of interior finishing materials or any actual construction. All states require that construction supervision be performed by licensed contractors, and many states require that the supervision of installation of interior finishing materials also be done only by licensed contractors. Additional information on this topic is in Chapter 28 on project management.

5. *Detailed purchasing arrangements.* When the sale of goods as part of the project is anticipated, a clause should be included in the design services contract to inform the client of the conditions under which the design firm will be selling any products to the client. This information introduces the client to the policies the design firm has concerning the ordering of goods for clients. It is also common for all these considerations to be spelled out in the contract for the sale of goods and for only a reference to these conditions to be made in the contract for services.

   The minimal information that should be covered in this clause is how the client will be charged for furniture and furnishings; the terms of payment; penalties for cancellation of orders; the design firm's responsibilities toward warranties of goods sold; charges for installation, freight, sales tax, delivery costs; and whether or not there is a late payment penalty on the sale of goods. Detailed confirmation proposals signed by the client should be part of these policies. This paperwork item is discussed in Chapter 31.

   An additional clause or statement should have specific language regarding what would happen if the client purchased the goods specified from someone other than the designer. In some cases, the only way in which the designer is receiving compensation for services is through the sale of goods. If goods are purchased from someone else, the designer would not receive compensation, unless this was covered in the contract.

   As part of completing the installation of certain types of goods such as carpeting and wall treatments, it is necessary to procure outside sources or contractors for these services. In some cases, the interior designer will want the client to hire these outside contractors rather than have to contract him- or herself with subcontractors. This section of the contract should inform the client as to expectations and requirements in this case.

6. *Price guarantees.* An important clause that ASID recommends deals with price guarantees. Interior design projects often last many months, sometimes a year or more. It is quite possible for the prices for products and services to increase as the project moves from conceptualization through design development and final approvals by the client. Although the designer is responsible for maintaining a tight control on the budget and is responsible for keeping the client informed of any price increases, this clause helps to provide some protection for the designer if the actual bid prices of construction and goods increase over time.

7. *Method and payment of compensation.* This is one of the critical clauses, since it helps a judge determine valid consideration for services rendered. It should begin by describing how the design fees will be charged. The compensation section is the most common changeable part in standardized contracts that are available from the professional associations. Table 24-4 provides examples of wording for three common compensation methods. An interior design firm is likely to have two or more different standard methods of explaining compensation, since it is rare for a firm to charge the same way for all projects.

TABLE 24-4.

Sample compensation clauses for three different ways of charging design fees.

Hourly Fee

1. For the design services as described, you will be charged on an hourly fee basis of_____ per hour. You will be invoiced monthly for all hours actually worked.

2. Compensation for the design services described will be billed:

   _____ per hour for Principles

   _____ per hour for Senior Designers

   _____ per hour for Project Managers

   _____ per hour for Designers

   _____ per hour for Design Assistants

   _____ per hour for Draftspersons/CAD

Fixed Fee Method

1. The design fixed fee for this project will be_____. You will be billed as follows:

   20 percent upon signing of contract as a retainer

   20 percent at the end of the preliminary review meeting

   40 percent at the completion of the preparation of drawings and specifications

   10 percent when construction begins and purchase orders are placed

   10 percent upon completion of the project

2. The design fee for basic services will be_____. You will be billed as follows:

   _____ Percent upon signing of contract as a retainer

   _____ Percent upon completion of Programming

   _____ Percent upon completion of Schematic Design

   _____ Percent upon completion of Design Development

   _____ Percent upon completion of Construction Documents

   _____ Percent upon completion of the project

Cost Plus Percentage Mark-up

1. Design Consultation
   The designer will be compensated for consultation services as described under the scope of services on an hourly basis at the rate of_____ per hour. Client will be invoiced on a monthly basis. Upon signing this agreement, the client shall provide_____ as a nonrefundable retainer for design consultation services. (Note that a flat fee could be substituted for an hourly rate.)

2. Purchasing Services
   The designer will be compensated at a cost plus percentage of markup on a basis of a_____ mark-up percentage of cost of furniture, furnishings, and equipment specified. Cost will be defined as the Designer's cost as stated by the manufacturer or supplier's invoice. The client will be required to pay an initial payment of_____ of the expected invoice cost prior to orders actually being placed with the supplier. The balance will be due upon delivery.
   Products specified shall be purchased only through the interior designer.
   (There are many other ways of stating the purchasing services section of a contract.)

Note that these examples may not include all the phrases or clauses you may wish to include in your agreements/contracts. Actual wording should be reviewed with your attorney.

The other part of this section details how the client will be billed and whether or not there will be any penalties for late payment. Payment terms must be clearly stated within the contract so that the designer is assured of being paid. The designer cannot charge a late payment penalty if the client is late paying invoices if this clause is not included in the contract. Such clauses as "payments are due upon receipt," "payment is due upon receipt of invoice," or possibly "payments are due within ten days" are needed to clarify how quickly the designer expects the client to send payment. Interior designers need to include a statement about late penalties, since any type of client for any type of interior project could be slow in paying invoices for services. The amount of the late payment penalty is commonly 1 1/2 percent per month on the unpaid balance, which is charged for any invoices that are overdue. The monthly percentage varies and should be determined with the advice of the design firm's accountant and in accordance with prevailing state law.

What Would You Do?

Dr. Milton and Dr. Sawyer hired George, Miller & Ross Design Group to plan and specify their new medical suite. They got along very well with Benjamin George, and the design of the project was moving into the design development phase.

Benjamin brought Alice Miller with him to the final review of the schematic plans presentation. At the end of the presentation, Benjamin reintroduced Alice and told the doctors that she would be taking over the remaining design and other responsibilities of the project. "I'm taking a year leave of absence from the firm, leaving the firm next week. Alice will be taking over," said Benjamin.

The clients suddenly became noticeably reserved but said nothing other than asking about Benjamin's absence. "I'm going to work on a master's degree with an emphasis in geriatrics," said Benjamin. "We want to specialize more in assisted living and other senior facilities."

Alice tried to contact the doctors three times in the next two weeks but kept getting excuses as to their availability. Three weeks later, the design firm received a letter from the doctor's attorney filing notice of breach of contract. The doctors alleged that since Benjamin was not completing the project, the design firm was in breach.

---

8. *Reimbursements for out-of-pocket expenses.* Projects might require the interior designer to travel to a job site out of state. Almost all designers find themselves making long-distance telephone calls or sending information or orders via faxes. These are just a few examples of out-of-pocket expenses necessary to complete the project. Out-of-pocket expenses are more commonly referred to as *reimbursable expenses* and are those expenses that are not part of the design contract but that are made in the interest of completing the project. Some designers refer to these charges as *disbursements*.

Projects that require travel to meet with clients or others involved in the project, travel to the job site, or even take the client to showrooms at a distant location is the most expensive type of reimbursable. *Per diem* ("for each day") refers to a dollar amount that is allowed to cover hotel, meals, and transportation costs for client-approved travel. These expenses are something that the client should pay for, but they should not be part of the design fee. Other typical reimbursable expenses are long-distance telephone calls, postage, blueprinting, computer time, and overtime. Some firms include the cost of renderings, models, and mock-ups in reimbursable expenses. Expenses such as blue-printing, telephone calls, and data processing are often considered costs of doing business and are not charged to the client, although they could be charged to the client when they are directly related to the project.

Most firms charge reimbursable expenses at actual cost. Some, however, add a service charge to the expense. If a service charge is added, this should be clearly stated in the contract. Many firms only put a clause concerning reimbursable expenses in the contract if they anticipate out-of-town travel, the need for renderings or models, or an inordinate amount of other kinds of expenses.

9. *Charges for extra services*. There is always the chance that the client will ask for additional areas of the project space to be done "while you are working here." Interior designers should never work on additional spaces or provide additional services requested by the client in the course of the project until an addendum or memorandum to the original contract has been executed. A clause concerning charges for potential extra services is provided to deal with these situations. This clause protects the designer so that he or she will not be required to perform design services for free. It also informs the client as to how additional work can be added to the contract or done at the same time, and how the client will be charged. If the designer is using an hourly rate, many charge extra services at a higher rate than stated in the original contract.

An important part of this section of a contract spells out what happens if the client makes changes to the project after certain phases of work have been completed. For example, if the designer has already received approval for certain phases of the project—let us say that the overall space plan was approved—and changes are then made by the client, the designer should be compensated for the additional work. This is considered extra work required by the client, not due to a mistake or omission by the designer, and compensation for redoing the work is appropriate.

10. *Designer responsibility disclaimer*. The *responsibility disclaimer section* specifically describes any portions of the project for which the designer cannot claim responsibility nor be held liable. Perhaps the client wants some other company to plan the lighting for an interior. If so, the contract should state that the firm claims no responsibility for the lighting design.

Many times the interior designer notes that there are certain services or limitations on the work that the designer can do on a project. For example, interior designers cannot in most states legally prepare construction drawings for structural load-bearing walls. This type of drawing must be prepared by a licensed architect, and the interior designer should disclaim any responsibility for errors in the drawings prepared by the architect. A wide variety of consultants and subcontractors are possibly included in these basic types of situations.

Designers are often advised to include a clause in this section disclaiming responsibility if the client purchased products other than those specified. This would protect the designer from potential negligence or product liability suits, if the products the client purchased were not the same as those specified.

Interior designers also want to protect themselves from responsibility when changes are made to the project or site by the owner, architect, or contractor without the designer's consent. Should the client or the contractor change the length of an alcove that is to receive a custom-made piece of furniture, the designer would not be held responsible if the furniture did not fit in the alcove, if he or she had not been informed of the change. The architect and client changing the types or sizes of windows in the kitchen or bath during construction can have multiple impacts on designs and products ordered by the interior designer.

11. *Charges and responsibilities of third parties.* You might think of this clause as a companion to the clause on designer responsibility disclaimer. At the conclusion of the initial consultation or meeting, the interior designer should know whether the project will require the consultation of any third parties, such as architects, lighting designers and commercial kitchen designers, contractors, or commercial space landlords. When a *third-party* consultant is required for a project, the ideal situation is to separate these charges from the interior designers fee. Short meetings with consultants are ordinarily included as part of the project, but the work they may need to do for the project should be considered a separate service. For example, if a project requires extensive architectural services, the services of that architect may be better dealt with as a separate contract between the client and the third party. However, the designer should still charge for the time that he or she will have to spend with the third party.

12. *Photographic and publishing rights.* A portfolio of projects is an important marketing tool for all design firms. Although it is unlikely that every project will be photographed, it should be standard practice to include a clause in all contracts to allow the designer to obtain permission to photograph projects. Clients should know up front how the designer intends to use the photographs of the project for publication. Some clients may object to allowing this kind of intrusion. In some commercial installations, it may be against company policy because of security reasons. When clients object to photographing their living or working quarters, the designer may be able to get permission if he or she does not publish the name of the client. Remember that releases must also be obtained from any recognizable people in the photographs, even if the owner of the space has given permission to photograph the interior. Refer to the section on copyright in Chapter 10 for other information on the use of photographs.

13. *Termination of contract.* A termination clause is included to ensure compensation for services rendered in the event that the project ends for some reason *other than* by the designer's wishes. If the client runs out of money, cannot take the space, and must end the project, it is important for the designer to be paid for design work that has been prepared. Without this kind of clause, it is more difficult for the designer to collect any fees. One example of wording is, "In the event the project is terminated through no fault of the designer, the designer will be compensated for all work actually performed." Other wording may be recommended by the firm's attorney to meet specific needs of the firm.

14. *Responsibilities of the client.* Certain tasks in some projects might need to be the responsibility of the client. Depending on state laws, it might be necessary for the client to obtain needed permits and approvals. Interior designers should only do this if they have the proper professional license. Another common client responsibility is to provide reasonable access to the job site and to provide a place to receive, unpack, and store

products prior to installation on the job site. Providing approvals expeditiously is a client responsibility necessary for successfully completing the project on time. For a commercial project, it is also necessary for the owner of the building or site to designate an employee as a liaison between the designer and the owner.

15. *Assignment and delegation*. Sometimes an event may occur that is unforeseen that prevents the designer (or even the client) from fulfilling the contract. For example, the designer/owner of a sole proprietorship might become ill, or the lead designer in a larger firm might quit in the middle of a project to take a position with another firm, causing the design work to stop. It might happen that the real estate office with which the designer is contracted to design is sold to another owner in the middle of the project. When these kinds of unforeseen incidents happen, it might be necessary to turn over the work and/or responsibility for the project to someone else. If the rights in a contract are transferred to another party, it is called *assignment*; if they are given to someone else, it is called *delegation*.[4] The assignment and delegation clause requires that the assignment or delegation of responsibility of either party to another cannot be done without written notice to and consent by the other party is recommended.

16. *Ownership of documents*. As you will recall from the discussion of copyright in Chapter 10, design ideas executed as drawings and specifications belong to the interior designer and are provided for use to the client. Some projects are of a nature that they could be copied in a different location. An ownership of documents clause prevents the drawings from being copied or imitated without the designer receiving fair compensation. The designer must copyright his or her design documents as an added protection. A sample clause might be, "Documents and specifications are provided for the fair use by the client in completing the project as listed within this contract. Documents and specifications remain the property of the designer and cannot be used or reused without permission of the designer." This will clarify the issue. If the designer needs or wishes to use this clause, he or she should become familiar with copyright law so that he or she can answer the questions of the client. Many clients do not understand why they do not own the drawings, since they are paying for the production of the drawings. Copyright law is the reference the interior designer should understand when discussing document ownership.

17. *Time frame of the contract*. The time frame or time limit of a contract is an important part of the offer. Interior design projects, whether they are residential or commercial, must work around some date, such as the move-in date. A time limit on the offer is often necessary, since designers often need to schedule projects as they continue with other work. Time limits on acceptance of the contract is also important to be sure the project can be completed by a move-in date. A sample clause is, "In order to complete the project as specified in the scope of services, the signed contract must be received by the designer no later than June 20, 20xx." This should help the client in making up his or her mind quickly as to whether or not he or she will engage the designer.

A clause related to time frame involves projects that might last longer than one year. In this case, it might be necessary to renegotiate a portion of the fee for the long-term completion. Of course, this should be taken into consideration when the contract is drawn up. This type of clause or situation often exists between the designer and the client when the designer is on a retainer for an extended period of time. In this relationship, design work may be scattered over time, and it may be necessary for the design firm to renegotiate a fair increase in its fees every so often.

18. *Matters of arbitration.* Although no one wants to think that a disagreement will occur during the project, something might happen leading to a disgruntled relationship. Contracts should all include a clause concerning arbitration as a solution to resolving contractual conflicts and disputes that cannot be resolved between the designer and client. *Arbitration* means that rather than going to court, an arbitrator (a disinterested third party) would be called in to listen to the arguments of both sides and then render an opinion of what must be done. Both client and designer must agree beforehand to abide by the decision of the arbitrator.

19. *Mutual understanding and legality.* Designers sometimes add a clause that clarifies that the contract, as written, is the full and complete mutual understanding of the terms and conditions of the agreement. This is done in case there are claims by the client that some verbal comment has been made that creates an addition to the contract or supersedes the original intent of the contract. If this clause is included and a later claim is made, the later claim is unlikely to be upheld by a jury. This positive protection for the designer is only one reason why changes to the project that the client requests or that the designer finds are needed should be made in writing as an addendum to the original contract.

    Along with this clause, the contract should note that the laws of a specific state or province govern the agreement and interpretation. The specific state or province generally is the one in which the design firm is located, since that is the legal location of the business.

20. *Conditions and amount of retainer.* Interior design professional services should, as a rule, not begin until a retainer is received along with the signed contract. A *retainer* is an amount of money that is paid by the client to the designer for professional services that will be done in the future. The retainer is applied by the designer to the total fee of the project as work progresses. In some ways, the retainer acts as "earnest money" from the client, showing his or her good faith in proceeding with the project. The retainer provides operating funds to the designer to purchase the needed production materials and services for the particular project in order to begin the design services portion of the project. If a retainer is expected, the amount and when it is due must be spelled out in the contract. It is a good idea also for the designer to explain briefly how it will be applied to the total fee. Typically, the retainer clause appears at the end of the contract.

    A deposit (or down payment) is similar to a retainer, but it is usually applied toward the purchase of furniture and furnishings. Refer to Chapter 25 for additional information on down payments and deposits.

21. *Signatures.* Space should be provided in the contract for the client to sign along with the date. Should there be more than one responsible client—such as husband and wife—then both should sign the contract. To enforce the contract, the client only must sign. The client, on the other hand, will want the designer to sign as a token of the designer's good faith.

    The type of information and clauses discussed in this section are those that are typically included in contracts or agreements for interior design services. Each contract, whether it is for a residential or a commercial project, must be developed to suit the individual project. Design firms create standard contracts to cover almost all contingencies, and then parts can be "cut and pasted" to make the final contract. A word processor makes this task very easy. This works because certain clauses are considered "boilerplate," meaning that they are very standard and apply to any kind of project. Two examples are the clauses concerning ownership of documents and arbitration.

Standardized contracts can be obtained from ASID and the AIA. These organizations have a variety of contracts that meet the conditions of many normal projects. Space is provided to type in standard information, such as the designer's name and address, and some can be imprinted with the design firm's name. Whatever the final form of the contract is, it should be periodically reviewed by the firm's attorney to be sure that the contract meets the conditions of the firm's individual practice.

Now let us look at what constitutes legal performance and termination of a contract.

PERFORMANCE AND BREACH

Alice had the final walk-through with her client on Tuesday. Alice had her client sign off on the punch list document that indicated that everything was delivered as required and no further work was needed. This allowed Alice to bill the client for the final design fee dollars as well as the last of the charges for goods. Thus, the contracts with the client had been completed as far as the designer's responsibilities were concerned.

A contract terminates—or, using the legal term, "discharges"—when both parties perform the acts or activities promised in the terms of the contract. This completion of the acts called for in the contract is also called *performance*. Sometimes there is disagreement as to whether or not the terms have been fulfilled down to the last detail. This is especially true when the contract insufficiently specifies the required services. In contract law, there are three types of performance: (1) complete, (2) substantial, and (3) inferior, or performance far below what is considered reasonable.

The preceding example describes complete performance. For *complete performance* to occur, the terms expressed in the contract must be fully accomplished in the manner in which they are specified in the contract. Here is an example of incomplete performance. If Alice's design contract for the project has as one of its terms the provision that "the designer provide two computer-generated color renderings of the dining room," the contract is not complete if these renderings have not been provided to the client. This is true even if all other terms in the contract have been fulfilled. In this case, the client has grounds to sue for breach of contract, if he or she so chooses.

Since it is sometimes impossible to satisfy a party's idea of complete performance, the courts hold that performance is complete if it is done so as to be substantially complete. *Substantial completion* means that the performance cannot vary greatly from what has been spelled out in the contract. If, in the preceding example, the designer provides two black-and-white computer-generated renderings of the dining room, the court might rule that the terms have been performed substantially and that the client must pay the designer for the services performed. However, it is also likely that the judge would rule that the designer must reduce or refund a portion of the fee, since the designer did not provide what was called for in the contract. Note that a substitution of a different medium, such as markers, technically constitutes a breach of contract and could result in a refund to the client for the difference in what was promised versus what was delivered.

In our example, should the designer provide only pencil or ink sketches of the areas, rather than the computer-generated color renderings, it could be argued that what was provided was inferior. *Inferior performance* is work that varies quite considerably from what is required. Inferior performance causes a material (or major) breach of contract and excuses the nonbreaching party from fulfilling his or her obligations in relation to the contract. A material breach would have occurred. The nonbreaching party would not have to pay agreed-upon fees and would likely be entitled to damages.

A *breach of contract* occurs when one of the parties of the contract does not perform his or her duties as spelled out in the terms of the contract. For example, an interior designer included in the scope of services that he would select and specify all the architectural finishes for an advertising agency office complex. It turned out that the architect made these selections as part of his contract and the client did not tell the interior designer of this change. Was there a breach of the interior designer's contract?

Oftentimes the breach is minor, such as when the designer does a black-and-white rendering rather than a color one or neglects to provide copies of her invoices to the client as agreed in the contract. When a minor breach occurs, the client would not be excused from his or her obligation to the designer, but the client generally would not have to pay until the designer has provided the services as were required or until some other agreement has been worked out. When the breach is material, such as the designer failing to provide accurate drawings as called for in the contract, the client is excused from the contract and may also be entitled to damages. A decision of a material breach terminates the agreement when major or material ones occur.

A breach of contract could also occur if the designer was negligent or had performed tasks in what could be considered an unskillful manner. Interior design services must be performed to standards considered reasonable for a professional in this profession. If, for example, drawings are submitted that do not meet code or the furniture as drawn does not fit into the actual rooms, the client can claim that the designer has breached the contract and is likely also guilty of professional negligence. "Wrongful performance or nonperformance discharges the other party from further obligation and permits that party to bring suit to rescind the contract"[5] or recover monetary damages as compensation.

Performance is, of course, one type of remedy that is enforced against the breaching party. Another could be the award of damages. The term *damages* refers to money awarded to the party that has been harmed as a result of the breach. There are several types of damages that can be awarded. The first is actual or *compensatory* damages. This type of damages represent a sum of money that is equal to the financial loss that the harmed party has suffered. They are compensatory because they are meant to compensate for the loss. Another type of damages is *incidental*, which are meant to cover expenses that have been paid out by the harmed party. *Consequential* damages might be given in order to cover losses that could have been foreseen by the party who has breached the contract. *Nominal* damages may be awarded as a token to indicate that the breaching party has done something wrong but that the harm is not very great.

The most serious kind of damages are *punitive* damages. In this case, the damages are given in order to punish the guilty party, because the harm is grievous in his or her breach of the contract. It is more common for punitive damages to be awarded in tort cases than for breach of contract and are most likely to be awarded when physical injury or malicious or outrageous conduct has occurred to the harmed party. The reader should note that there are additional kinds of damage awards and may wish to review these in a business law textbook. While they may apply to an interior design breach-of-contract case, they are less of a factor in our discussion.

A type of remedy that is related to breach of contract is specific performance. *Specific performance* is an equitable remedy when the court requires that the breaching party perform what it is required to perform according to the contract. For example, Phillip was supposed to provide sample boards and renderings suitable for display in the leasing agent's office. As the project progressed, he provided some sample boards, but they would not display well in the office. In fact, materials kept falling off the boards. If this situation went to a judge, in a strict sense, he or she would have required Phillip to provide boards and renderings for display in order to specifically perform this clause in the design contract.

As it relates to breach of contract and our example, the party that has breached the contract—Phillip—is ordered to perform whatever is required in the contract that he so far has not done. The nonbreaching party generally is satisfied with specific performance, since it requires that what has been bargained for actually is done. It is usually applied only if the monetary damages are insufficient to satisfy the party who has been breached. However, courts are reluctant to apply specific performance to service contracts, since such application requires that the courts force someone to perform a specific service.[6]

A breach of a contract can occur easily, especially if the designer has not been careful in the preparation of the terms of the agreement. And, in fact, it is generally easier for the interior designer to breach the contract than it is for the client to do so. It is extremely important for the designer to understand the scope of the project and what the terms of the agreement are so that the designer does not leave him- or herself open to a breach.

Performing to completion all provisions of the design contract is the natural desire of the interior designer and the client. Doing so while avoiding disputes is always the goal. Interior design performance is not perfect, however, and disputes can occur. Item 24-3 on the CD provides several ideas on how to avoid contract disputes.

TERMINATION BY AGREEMENT

Adam had been working on the plans for a small doctor's office for six weeks. The drawings were ready to review with the client for final approval before the orders were prepared. However, Adam was called into service by the National Guard, and he would not be able to finish the project. He visited the client for the approvals with another designer in the office, who would take over for Adam. When the client heard that Adam could not finish the project, he was unwilling to have the other designer take over, as he had a good relationship with Adam. The client sent a letter terminating the contract with the design firm.

Contracts can be terminated by agreement. Adam's design firm wanted to continue, but the client was adamant about terminating the agreement. The client did pay the firm fees due up to the point of the last meeting with Adam. We saw in a preceding section, in which we discussed the termination of contract, how the designer seeks to protect him- or herself if something occurs that is not the designer's fault. It is not necessary for there to be such a clause in the contract for the contract to be terminated by agreement.

It is possible at any time for the contract to be terminated if both parties agree to the termination. If a clause does not exist in the original contract, it is necessary for a second contract dealing with the terms of the termination to be written as a protection for both parties. An oral agreement to terminate the contract is not advisable. All terminations by agreement, regardless of who initiates the termination, should be spelled out in writing.

SUMMARY

Interior designers provide services and order goods for clients without developing a contract for the services or a sales agreement for the goods all the time—unfortunately. Too often, when this happens, a dispute occurs between the parties, as each claims he or she did (or got) what was agreed to verbally. As we saw in Chapter 3, disagreements concerning the contract is a common issue that causes clients to file an ethics complaint against interior design members of associations.

The major portion of what the interior designer does for clients can be covered by contracts of one sort or another. Not having a clear contract often results in a loss of fees to the designer. It is no longer acceptable to fail to understand what constitutes a contract or how to prepare one properly. The professional designer must realize that in order to protect himself or herself, he or she must insist on the preparation of contracts. The designer must also get the contract signed by the client before beginning design work. Regardless of the designer's enthusiasm to do a project, today the professional designer should not undertake a design project or order goods for clients until the appropriately prepared contract has been signed by the client.

This chapter described in a general sense what legally constitutes a contract and a contractual relationship. It then covered the kinds of clauses that are commonly found in an interior design contract. The chapter may not answer all the questions or special needs; therefore, the designer should discuss the matter and form of contracts with an attorney. Although most attorneys understand contract law, few understand the interior design, architecture, and construction professions. Ideally, the designer should work with an attorney who is familiar with the design industry. More information on contracts and contract law can be found in the references. A course in business law that emphasizes contracts can provide additional material for study.

You are advised that the information in this chapter does not constitute legal advice and practice concerning contracts may vary between jurisdictions. You should consult with your attorney to be sure that the contracts proposed to clients meet the needs of the designer and the jurisdiction in which the firm is in business.

REFERENCES

1. Clarkson et al., 1983, p. 129
2. Brown and Sukys, 1997, p. 167.
3. Emerson, 2004, p. 126.
4. Conry et al., 1993, p. 227.
5. Brown and Sukys, 1997, p. 197.
6. Jentz et al., 1987, p. 227.

CHAPTER 25

Product Pricing

Key Terms and Concepts

These key terms and concepts are important to material in this chapter. Many of these terms will be utilized in other chapters as well. Be sure you understand these items as you read this chapter.

Terms and Concepts

Price

Suggested retail price

Manufacturer's suggested retail price (MSRP)

Wholesale price

List price

Net price

Cost price

Selling price

End user

Retailing

Discount

Stocking dealer

Keystone

5/10 discount

Quantity discount

Multiple discount

Trade discount

Cash discount

Seasonal discount

Advertising allowance

Deep discounts

Buying the job

Markup

Gross margin

Markdown

Prestige pricing

Deposit

Down payment

Retainer

Pro forma credit

Freight

Piggyback

Free on board (FOB)

FOB, Factory

FOB, Destination

FOB, factory—freight prepaid

Zone pricing

Actual freight

Freight factor

Delivery

Installation

Door-to-door

Use tax

Tangible personal property

Fixtures

Designer/specifier

Competitive bidding

Price fixing

Restraint of trade

Price Discrimination

Critical Issues

After completing this chapter you should be able to:

- Discuss the meanings of the different price terms.
- Calculate a discount from retail, a quantity discount, and a multiple discount.
- Explain the purpose of price codes.
- Explain a cash discount and how it benefits the interior designer.
- Calculate a markup from cost and the markup percentage.
- Calculate a gross margin in dollars and the gross margin percentage.
- Describe prestige pricing and how it might impact the services of an interior designer.
- Explain the differences between a deposit and down payment.
- Discuss the retainer and how it is different from a deposit.
- Explain the differences in the freight terms presented in the text.
- Discuss why it is important to include charges for delivery and installation.
- Explain how sales taxes are to be collected and who has the responsibility for paying those amounts.
- Discuss the impact of the Sherman Antitrust Act on the interior design profession.
- Explain how the Robinson-Patman Act impacts interior design product pricing.

Specifying merchandise is one of the many key tasks of an interior designer. Selling merchandise to clients remains an important source of revenue for many interior designers even though an increasing number of design firms charge fees for services. It is critical for interior designers to understand how to price products whether or not the firm sells merchandise. Designers must know how products are priced by the manufacturers and suppliers to help clarify and, if necessary, establish a budget. In addition, many interior designers are hired to design and specify the furniture, furnishings, and equipment (FF&E), create specifications for competitive bidding, and they are not involved in the actual sale of the goods. In this case, product pricing knowledge helps the designer create an estimate of potential vendor bids to compare to the budget.

Designers who specify and sell merchandise to clients must be very aware of the prices they quote to clients. When the designer is depending upon FF&E sales for revenue for the firm, care in pricing is acutely important. Making a mistake in calculating and quoting products' selling prices is always costly to the design firm. Depending on how the designer is compensated, pricing errors can also come out of the designer's commission. For projects that are specified for bids, mistakes in pricing and budgeting can create projects that the client cannot afford to purchase from any supplier. Mistakes in budgeting for any reason can also leave the designer accused of professional negligence and ethics complainants.

The *price* is, of course, what something sells for. There are many factors involved in determining the price of a product or a service. And, unfortunately for the individual who is new to the interior design profession, there are many different prices with which the interior designer has to deal. A foundation for product pricing starts with an explanation of pricing terminology. The ways in which a "price" is determined will be explained and includes examples of how these various prices are calculated. There are other topics that impact product pricing that must be understood by the student and practitioner. Those covered in this chapter are deposits and down payments, shipping charges, and sales and use taxes.

Many designers do not sell merchandise but do have the responsibility of pricing and budgeting the goods specified in the project. This chapter briefly discusses the role of the designer/specifier in the pricing of merchandise.

Understanding product pricing terminology and the pricing practices used in interior design are critical for anyone involved in the profession. Clients are rarely nice enough to pay additional sums to the designer because he or she has made a mistake. Care in pricing and in budgeting merchandise is as important as determining how much to charge for a design fee.

PRICING TERMS

Marjorie told her client that the price of the products for the real estate office would be $36,140 plus tax and delivery. Marjorie determined this after she was quoted a total cost to her of $27,800 from the two key vendors. The vendor for the desks had quoted a net price of $21,000 for the desks, while another vendor quoted a 20 percent discount from suggested retail (SR) for a cost of $6800 to Marjorie for the chairs. (SR was $8500 for chairs.) SR for desks would be $42,000 at a 100 percent markup (MU). Her MU on the sale was 30 percent, or $8340.

As this example shows, there are many terms related to pricing in the interior design industry. Prices are quoted by the designer to the client, and prices are quoted by a supplier to the designer. To add to the possible confusion, some of these pricing terms often mean the same thing. Other terms can also be interpreted as a "price"; for example, "fee" is the term commonly used to represent the price of services; "rent" is the price for an office space. Students are familiar with the term "tuition," which is the price for classes; and "interest" is the price one pays for a loan.

Calculating and quoting the price accurately is obviously important. Quoting the wrong price means losing money rather than making it. Accurate pricing for design firms that count on product sales for revenues can mean a difference between making payroll and paying bills or losing credit worthiness with suppliers.

Knowing what price has been quoted by a vendor or in a catalog is also very important. Product pricing in catalogs varies by the manufacturer, and not knowing the prices quoted in a catalog or carelessness in determining pricing can easily mean that prices quoted to clients are below the designer's price from the vendor. This is no way to make a profit! It is important, therefore, to clarify the different terms that are related to buying and selling merchandise as they apply to the interior design industry.

Pricing from the Supplier to the Interior Designer

A price term that needs to be defined at the beginning of these discussions is suggested retail price. The term *suggested retail price* is a price suggested by the supplier. It is also called *list price*. It is universally accepted to be the price that, in general, the consumer pays for any goods purchased from business entities. It is important to bring up at the beginning, since it is related to pricing terms from the supplier to the interior designer.

In our example at the beginning of this section, two different terms are used to indicate the price to the interior designer for the goods she must order. What were those terms? In practice, there are three different terms that are commonly used to represent the price that the designer must pay to the supplier for goods—net, wholesale, and cost. The example used the term net price. *Net price* represent a 50 percent reduction (or discount) from the suggested retail price (or list price). Some vendors and designers use the term wholesale price to represent net price, meaning net and wholesale mean the same thing. *Wholesale price* can also be defined as a special price given to a designer by a supplier, which is lower than what it would cost the consumer.

The third term used in the example is cost price. *Cost price* is the price that the designer must pay for the goods; it is not always the same as the net or wholesale price. Not all designers have the privilege of purchasing goods at a 50 percent discount from all suppliers. In our example, the designer only received a 20 percent discount from suggested retail from the chair supplier. These smaller discounts often occur because an interior designer only occasionally buys items from a certain supplier. A designer who frequently purchases from the same vendor would be given the full 50 percent discount. A major reason why designers are not permitted the 50 percent discount from retail is because they do not have a quantity purchasing agreement. It should be noted that pricing from the supplier to the designer is governed by federal law. This point will be discussed at the end of this chapter.

Pricing from the Interior Designer to the Client

A few more points must be mentioned about one of the common price terms to clients, suggested retail price. Suggested retail price is the price suggested by the manufacturer for use by the seller. Sometimes the price might be shown by the acronym MSRP, which stands for *manufacturer's suggested retail price*. It is the price that any consumer generally pays for any type of product in a store, from a loaf of bread to shoes, jewelry, gift items, and so on. It can also be the price that the interior designer quotes to a client, since the designer may choose to use this price for many goods.

A second price term that designers use to quote prices to clients is list price. *List price* is generally accepted as being the same as suggested retail price. As with suggested retail price, the list price is the price to the ultimate consumer of the goods, who is called the *end user*. When you purchase an electronic product like a DVD player at a store, you are most likely paying the suggested retail or list price.

Selling price is a term many designers use to refer to the actual price at which they sell goods to the client. In our example, Marjorie's selling price is $36,140 plus tax and delivery. Since some designers sell goods at a discount (a price lower than suggested retail) and others may occasionally sell goods at a price that is higher than suggested retail, selling price is not always the same thing as suggested retail price and list price. The selling price to the end user may be different from the list or suggested retail price, because designers may sell merchandise to the end user at any price they wish. They are not obligated to sell goods at the suggested retail price. In fact, federal laws prohibit manufacturers from requiring merchants to sell goods to the end user at a set price. Manufacturers requiring sellers to sell the same goods to all retail buyers at the same exact price can be considered price fixing. This is discussed at the end of the chapter.

As was discussed in Chapter 23, the meaning of the term "retail" has changed in recent years. Since the price to the consumer can be any price that the seller wishes to quote, it is actually legal for "retail" to be higher than MSRP when a seller sells goods to the end user. This will be discussed at the end of this chapter. In this chapter, retail is considered to be a suggested retail price and is calculated as a 100 percent markup from net.

We have used the term "retail price" several times in this section. *Retail price* is a term that is commonly used in retailing. *Retailing* involves businesses that sell goods to the consumer, or end user, such as department stores and specialty stores. In retailing, retail price generally is not a price suggested by the manufacturer but, rather, a price determined by the retailer. So, in fact, although the price term for the selling of the DVD player mentioned earlier could be the suggested retail price, it might actually be a retail price.

Who knows where all this confusion originated. It is part of the long history of sales transactions over the centuries. Perhaps it is due in part to sellers' desires to keep the price they pay secret from the buyers or manufacturers who are trying to control who can sell their products.

In our discussions in this chapter, we will use the term selling price to mean the price quoted to the client and cost price to mean the price the designer must pay for the goods. However, the other terms are also used in the discussion but are carefully differentiated to prevent confusion.

CATALOG PRICING

New catalogs from suppliers come with a separate price list. A never-ending chore is making sure that the existing catalogs and price lists from suppliers are up-to-date. Someone from the design staff or, occasionally, sales representatives from vendors will need to verify that the price lists on file are accurate.

Many manufacturers send a price list based on suggested retail or list prices—remember that these two terms mean the same thing. When this occurs, the designer must then negotiate with the manufacturer's representative for the discount percentage that the design firm may expect to receive. This may be as small as 10 percent or as much as 50 percent or possibly more for a substantially large order. The manufacturer may offer variable discounts to different design firms, as long as these decisions are soundly based. Such things as purchasing an amount of goods over some specific time period or whether or not the designer will inventory goods are two possible factors that affect discount percentages. The cost price to the designer results from determining the price after the discount percentage has been subtracted from the suggested retail or list price.

The designer must be very careful in understanding what price list he or she is reading. If the designer receives a price list that is not clearly marked "suggested retail," "list," "retail," "net," or "wholesale," the designer should contact the representative or the factory to determine what the price list represents. Since many suppliers offer varying discounts based on the volume of purchases, suppliers more frequently send price lists in terms of list price rather than net price. This is particularly true of furniture items. Architectural finishes and textiles are generally priced the same to all designers and the price lists for these types of goods are generally net prices.

Care must be taken when looking at price lists, since some manufacturers send net price lists, while others send one based on suggested retail. If a designer is sent a net price list, this means that the designer can purchase the goods at the price listed in the catalog. This net price list, of course, is the designer's cost price. No further discount should be taken on this price. A selling price determined by quoting or discounting a net price list means that the designer has sold the goods to the client for the same price that the designer has purchased the goods from the supplier.

DISCOUNTS

We have already used the term "discount" to indicate a decrease in a price. A *discount* is a reduction, usually stated as a percentage, from the suggested retail price. A designer receives a discount from a supplier for ordering goods. Some designers give clients discounts when the clients purchase goods. This is perfectly reasonable and ethical. In the earlier example, we can see that Marjorie received two different amounts of discounts from the two vendors she was utilizing. The full discount price given by most manufacturers is 50 percent from the suggested retail. Remember that this is also called net price and not all designers receive the full discount of 50 percent.

A manufacturer may determine that a 50 percent discount will be given only to those companies that are stocking dealers or that purchase a certain minimal quantity of goods in a given time period. A *stocking dealer* is a vendor that stocks a certain inventory level of goods at all times. Designers who do not carry inventory but may purchase from a particular manufacturer on a regular basis might also earn the large 50 percent discount.

It is not unusual for clients to try to "shop" the price the interior designer gives the client by calling manufacturers and asking for a price on particular items. Clients also shop price by researching on the Internet. For this reason, some manufacturers use code words to protect designers, should clients try to contact suppliers directly to shop the designer's price quotes. One common code word is *keystone*, which means a 50 percent discount. Another price code used by some manufacturers is something like, "your discount is *5/10*." This code might mean that the designer should take $5.00 off the dollar portion of the quoted price and $.10 off the cent portion of the quoted price. For example, if the retail price of the goods is $23.50, the designer's price would be $18.40.

It is essential for designers to know how to calculate a cost price from a stated discount in order to help the designer determine a selling price to the client. The mathematical formula is provided so that you can see how the cost price is determined from a discount on suggested retail. A design firm received a 50 percent discount for purchases made from Martin's Wallcoverings. Wallpaper that has a suggested retail price of $35 per yard would cost the designer $17.50 per yard.

The following formulas might help:

$$\text{Discount in dollars} = \text{Suggested retail price} \times \text{Discount percentage}$$
$$= \$35 \times 0.50 = \$17.50$$
$$\text{Cost} = \text{Suggested retail} - \text{Discount in dollars}$$
$$= \$35 - \$17.50$$
$$\text{Cost} = \$17.50$$

To see the difference in a different discount, another designer receives only a 35 percent discount from suggested retail on the same wall covering:

$$\text{Discount in dollars} = \text{Suggested retail price} \times \text{Discount percentage}$$
$$= \$35 \times 0.35 = \$12.25$$
$$\text{Cost} = \text{Suggested retail} - \text{discount in dollars}$$
$$= \$35 - \$12.25$$
$$\text{Cost} = \$22.75$$

These same formulas are used whenever a designer is calculating discounts to determine cost.

The most common discount used related to pricing goods is the basic discount from suggested retail price. There are several other types of discounts that are also used in the industry. The most common additional types of discounts are quantity, multiple, trade, cash, and seasonal. Two other types of discounts called advertising allowances and deep discounts are specialized discounts utilized by a minority of interior design firms.

Quantity Discounts

Often an interior designer will sell a large quantity of furniture to a particular client or perhaps to several clients. When this happens, they will try to negotiate a larger discount for the order(s). A *quantity discount* is a discount greater than the normal 50 percent discount because a large quantity of merchandise has been purchased at one time. For example, if a designer purchased one chair, the discount would probably be 50 percent, if that is the firm's normal discount. If the designer ordered 500 chairs, the manufacturer would most likely give a larger discount—perhaps 55 percent.

Some manufacturers will offer a quantity discount due to a cumulative number or amount of orders. This means that the special discount is given because of quantity purchases over a given period of time—probably in the previous year or quarter. The discount might increase as the quantity purchases increase. For example, perhaps a designer has more than one project in progress, which includes the specification of plumbing fixtures. The plumbing fixture supplier may give a cumulative discount as an incentive or as an acknowledgment of loyalty to that plumbing fixture supplier. Of course, this type of discount could create cause for ethical concern on the part of the designer. Remember that quantity discounts given by manufacturers to designers are regulated by federal law to prevent price discrimination.

Multiple Discounts

Another type of discount offered for especially large orders is referred to as a multiple discount. *Multiple discounts* are a series of discounts from the suggested retail price. They are not the same thing as a cumulative discount. Multiple discounts are usually only given by manufacturers to designers for very large orders, although occasionally the design firm may offer a multiple discount to the client because of a very large order.

The written notation for such a discount is given as 50/5 or 50/5/2 or some other combination of numbers. This does not mean that the designer takes 55 percent off the retail price in the first example or 57 percent off in the second. Rather, each discount is taken separately. For example, if the manufacturer offers a 50/5/2 discount on a large purchase of $500,000, the cost to the designer would be figured as:

$$\begin{aligned} \text{Total retail price} &= \$500,000 \\ \text{Less 50 percent} &= -250,000 \\ \hline &\$250,000 \\ \text{Less 5 percent} &= -12,500 \\ \hline &= \$237,500 \\ \text{Less 2 percent} &= -4,750 \\ \hline \text{Final Cost} &= \$232,750 \end{aligned}$$

What would the final cost to the designer be if the manufacturer offered a 48/7/3 discount?

Trade Discounts

Many retail stores that sell specialized residential or commercial furnishings products offer trade discounts to interior designers. *Trade discounts* are discounts given as a courtesy by some retailers and vendors to designers and others in the trade. These are usually a small percentage off retail, though they can be as much as 50 percent. For example, if Interior Visions, a retail accessory store, offers designers a 20 percent discount for accessory items purchased from its store for resale, it is offering a trade discount. To calculate what the cost price to the designer would be, use the basic discount formula shown at the beginning of this section. Let us look at an example:

$$\text{Discount in dollars} = \$150 \times 0.20$$
$$= \$30.00$$

$$\text{Cost} = \text{Suggested retail} - \text{Discount in dollars}$$
$$= \$150 - \$30.00$$
$$\text{Cost} = \$120.00$$

Cash Discounts

This next discount term is commonly used in accounting, but one with which the interior designer must be familiar. *Cash discounts* are given by manufacturers and suppliers to those customers who pay their bills promptly. A notation like 2/10 Net 30 must appear on the invoice if a cash discount is allowed. The notation translates into an additional 2 percent deduction from the cost price if the invoice is paid within 10 days of receipt of the invoice. If it is not paid within 10 days, then the cost price is as stated and is due within 30 days. The cash discount is also considered by some to be an expression of credit terms. The notation automatically establishes an interest-free credit of 30 days.

The cash discount is taken after all other discounts have been taken. The following example shows you how to calculate the final amount or cost that the designer must pay to the vendor. The cost to a firm for an order of goods is $5000. The invoice offers a cash discount of 2/10 Net 30. If the firm pays the invoice within 10 days, it only has to pay $4900.

$$\text{Cash discount} = \text{Cost} \times \text{Percentage}$$
$$= \$5000 \times 0.02$$
$$\text{Cash discount} = \$100$$
$$\text{Amount due} = \text{The original invoice amount minus the amount of the cash discount}$$
$$= \$5000 - 100$$
$$\text{Amount due} = \$4900$$

Seasonal Discounts

A discount that will apply more often to an interior design firm that operates a showroom is a seasonal discount. A *seasonal discount* is given to encourage early purchasing of certain goods. This type of discount is to encourage retailers* to purchase certain items that are sold earlier than normal or more frequently during certain seasons of the year. For example, a designer with a showroom that sells accessories might obtain a seasonal discount on holiday accessories, especially in December. It is not something that particularly affects the interior designer, unless he or she has a location that is frequented by walk-in consumer

---

*Any interior design business that has a commercial store location is technically called a retailer, even if it does not actually sell merchandise at retail.

traffic. It most often will be given by a supplier to a designer, though a designer might give a special seasonal discount to sell items such as Christmas decorations during the late summer.

Advertising Allowances

Some suppliers and manufacturers offer an interior designer a special *advertising allowance* if the designer uses their products in promotions and advertising. A small design firm in a Midwestern city might use a carpet company's name in the design firm's advertising, perhaps as a special promotion before the holidays. The carpet company would then give the advertising allowance to the designer to pay for the advertising costs. It is not an extra discount on the purchase of the goods for clients.

Deep Discounting

This last type of discount is a pricing strategy embraced by many manufacturers of commercial furniture in order to obtain very large orders from commercial clients such as a major corporation. *Deep discounting* represents an extremely large discount from the suggested retail price for very large orders. For example, a manufacturer might offer a deep discount of 75 percent off retail for a $5 million order of systems furniture for a large corporate installation. These deep discounts are offered directly to the end user, bypassing an interior design or retailer such as an office furnishings dealer. A designer or dealer might receive a small percentage for servicing the job at the local level.

Deep discounting practices (sometimes called "buying the job") have had a major negative impact on the design industry. These deep discounts, once enjoyed by a customer, will be expected for all purchases from designers and retailers that cannot offer that same price structure. Designers and furniture dealers argue that deep discounts erode profit margins, hurting many firms that sell commercial goods. Other designers state that this pricing policy affects even those designers who sell goods but who rarely do larger jobs. These designers report that they often feel like "order takers" rather than designers.

Manufacturers counter by saying that deep discounts have become a part of the competitive nature of the industry. They state that commercial furniture dealers have forgotten that commercial furnishings products are commodities and that deep discounting is a way of selling that commodity. Many of these representatives feel that deep discounting is a pricing strategy that designers and sellers must understand and learn to accept.

SELLING PRICES

Recall that Marjorie told her client that the price of the products for the real estate office would be $36,140 plus tax and delivery. This amount represents the selling price—another important term related to selling products in interior design—to the client. Design firms operating as retail showrooms that sell merchandise to end-user clients primarily indicate the prices on items at the suggested retail price. Others show prices on merchandise that represent a markup (an increase) on their cost that might be higher than suggested retail. In selling goods to the end user, the designer can sell the merchandise at whatever price he or she determines. This practice can be found in both residential and commercial retail sales. In commercial design, it is more acceptable to use the term selling price rather than the retail price, since the client commonly purchases at a price lower than retail because of the competitive nature of commercial merchandise sales.

Other than using the retail price, the two methods of determining a selling price are discounting from retail and marking up from cost. Both of these methods are used in commercial design. Residential designers who own their own interior design practice but who do not inventory furniture also use either of these two methods depending on their pricing policies.

Discounting from Retail

The designer can offer to the client any discount that he or she wishes when the client is the end user. The selling price based on a discount from retail is calculated in the same way that the discount is calculated to find cost. For example, a designer has prepared a specification of products with a total retail price of $6500. The designer has decided to offer the goods to the client at a 25 percent discount. The selling price would be $4875. This selling price is determined in this way:

$$\text{Discount in dollars} = \text{Retail price} \times \text{Discount percentage}$$
$$= \$6500 \times 0.25$$
$$\text{Discount in dollars} = \$1625$$

$$\text{Selling price} = \text{Retail price} - \text{Discount in dollars}$$
$$= \$6500 - \$1625$$
$$\text{Selling price} = \$4875$$

If the product to be sold had a retail price of $350,000 and the designer offered a multiple discount from retail of 30/5, what would the selling price be for this case?

Markup from Cost

Markup from cost to arrive at a selling price for products sold by interior designers to clients has always been a favored method. It is unlikely that anyone knows with authority why this is the case. A *markup* is a percentage amount that is added to the cost of goods to get the selling price. Suggested retail is usually a 100 percent markup from the net price. The selling price, however, can be any markup percentage or dollar amount that the designer adds to the cost price. Marjorie used a markup from her cost to determine her selling price. Were both items at net?

When the designer knows the cost of the goods, it is necessary for him or her to multiply the cost by the percentage of markup. Let's look at an example other than Marjorie's situation first. An end table costs the designer $250. With a 100 percent markup, the selling price would be $500.

$$\text{Markup in dollars} = \text{Cost price} \times \text{Markup percentage}$$
$$= 250 \times 1.0$$
$$\text{Markup in dollars} = \$250$$

$$\text{Selling price} = \text{Cost} + \text{Markup in dollars}$$
$$= \$250 + \$250$$
$$\text{Selling price} = \$500$$

If the same table were to be sold at only a 50 percent markup, the selling price would be $375.

$$\text{Markup in dollars} = \$250 \times .50$$
$$\text{Markup in dollars} = \$125$$
$$\text{Selling price} = \$250 + \$125$$
$$\text{Selling price} = \$375$$

What numbers from the description of Marjorie's sale would be needed to determine her selling price? What was the amount of markup in dollars? What else does this amount of money represent for Marjorie's company?

There are two ways to find the markup percentage. In one you would find the markup percentage based on the retail price of the product. In the other, you would find the markup percentage based on the cost price of the product. For example, the retail price of a table lamp is $350, the cost price is $175, and the markup in dollars is $175. To find the markup percentage based on the retail price, use the following formula:

$$\text{Markup percentage based on retail price} = \text{Markup in dollars} \div \text{Retail price}$$
$$= \$175 \div \$350$$
$$\text{Markup percentage based on retail price} = 50\%$$

The formula for the markup percentage based on the cost price is as follows:

$$\text{Markup percentage based on cost price} = \text{Markup in dollars} \div \text{Cost price}$$
$$= \$175 \div \$175$$
$$\text{Markup percentage based on cost price} = 100\%$$

In practice, most interior designers use the markup percentage based on the cost price for determining the markup percentage, whereas most retailers use the markup percentage based on the retail price as a method of determining the markup percentage.

Gross Margin

Chapter 16, "Basic Financial Accounting," discussed gross margin as the difference between revenue and cost. The concept of gross margin also is important in terms of pricing merchandise. In this case, it is the difference between selling price and cost. Many design firms use the gross margin or gross margin percentage to determine commission on sales. For firms that do not charge separately for design services, the gross margin on the sale of products must be sufficient to pay all overhead expenses, including the designer's.

This example shows the methodology in terming the gross margin percentage and the gross margin expressed in dollars. Both calculations are important, as it is very useful to know the percentage value of the gross margin as well as the actual dollars. Assume the net price is the designer's cost of $2500 and the designer's selling price of $3375. The gross margin in dollars is $875 and the gross margin percentage would be 26 percent. It is necessary to calculate the gross margin dollars first:

$$\text{Gross margin dollars} = \text{Selling price} - \text{Cost price}$$
$$= \$3375 - \$2500$$
$$\text{Gross margin dollars} = \$875$$

To calculate the gross margin percentage:

$$Gross\ margin\ percentage = Gross\ margin\ in\ dollars \div Selling\ price$$
$$= \$875 \div \$3375$$
$$Gross\ margin\ percentage = 26\ percent$$

To calculate the gross margin in dollars and percentage of the sale that Marjorie made to the real estate office:

$$36{,}140 - 27{,}800 = \$8340$$
$$8340 \div 36{,}140 = 23\%$$

Markdown from Retail

A term that is used in retail when discounts are taken for promotional sales of one kind or another is *markdown*. A markdown is calculated in the same way as a regular discount. Interior designers do not usually refer to the discount from suggested retail price to get their cost or the discount they will give to their clients as a markdown. They may, however, refer to a discount as a markdown if they mark down inventory during a clearance sale.

Prestige Pricing

Products like a Ferrari, diamonds, and antiques, because of their quality, the manufacturer's reputation, or other factors, have obtained a special place in the minds of some consumers. Because of this certain kinds of goods like these can be priced at substantially higher prices than other goods or even some goods of a similar nature. "Prestige pricing involves setting a high price so that status-conscious consumers will be attracted to the product and buy it."[1]

Prestige pricing can affect interior design services fees as well. Interior designers with a special expertise or high reputation charge higher rates for their services based on this same concept. This is discussed in Chapter 23 in the section, "Value-Oriented Method."

Pricing Review

We have discussed several terms related to the price designers pay for goods that they sell to clients. We have also discussed several terms that are used to define the price that designers sell to the clients. How to calculate those prices is an integral part of this discussion. Because of the complexity and importance of this terminology, it is useful to review those terms.

The cost price to the interior designer could be retail, retail less a trade discount, or retail less a full discount that equals the net price or the wholesale price. It could also be retail minus a less than full discount given by the supplier, a cash discount after the cost amount was determined, or an amount after quantity discounts were taken from the retail price.

What Would You Do?

Jeff has been working on an adaptive use project in which a former firehouse is being converted into a bed and breakfast. It is in a very nice older neighborhood, but it is not in a historic district. The guest rooms will be on the second floor, which was previously the living quarters, and the public spaces like the lobby and dining/kitchen will be on the first floor. The client has told Jordan that he will not pay for changes shown on the plan indicating an accessible guest room. Nor will he add an elevator.

The selling price to the client could be retail, suggested retail, list price, retail less a discount, or cost plus a markup. Specialty discounts that apply primarily to the designer from the supplier would include seasonal, advertising allowance, and deep discounts.

DEPOSITS, DOWN PAYMENTS, AND RETAINERS

Alice expects her clients to pay a deposit of 50 percent of the total purchase price for all goods ordered that are not custom-made prior to ordering the goods. David tells his client, Mr. Robinson, that he requires a down payment of $10,000 toward the purchases that David will be making for the Robinson's summer home. The design contract from Miller Interiors to ACD Developers for preparing tenant improvement drawings requires a retainer of one-half the total design fee at the time the contract is signed. These three terms have similar meanings, but actually have different legal definitions. Many designers use these terms interchangeably, although this should not be the case. This section will explain those differences.

The first two terms—deposit and down payment—legally refer to situations where the interior designer sells merchandise to clients. The term retainer is most associated with services. Designers who order from any type of supplier or vendor commonly are required to pay part or all of the price for goods and services up front, at the time the order is placed. This is also called *pro forma credit* (see Chapter 7). Interior designers who have not established credit with suppliers require some prepayment from their clients. This money is then passed along to the suppliers. Interior designers also seek to establish credit with manufacturers and suppliers so that they do not have to pay anything at the time of the order. This gives the design firm more flexibility in its cash management.

Prepayments from clients are an important way for the interior designer to determine if the client is really serious about continuing with the project. Someone who is not really interested in the designer's ideas and concepts will be reluctant to pay a deposit or down payment for goods. Likewise, if they are not serious, they are unlikely to pay a retainer for design services.

The term deposit has several legal definitions. For our purposes, *deposit* means money that is part of the purchase price, prepaid by the buyer as security in contracts for the sale of goods. As our example at the beginning of this section relates, Alice has required a 50 percent deposit before merchandise will be ordered. It is common for designers to request that clients provide a deposit at the time the order is prepared in order to process orders. This is especially true if designers must special-order goods for the client. The deposit is credited toward the full purchase price as the contract is fulfilled and is returned in accordance with the contract. If for some reason the contract is not fulfilled, then the designer must return any remaining funds that the client has paid as a deposit. For example, if the client paid a deposit of $5000 and the merchandise delivered to the client only amounted to $3700, the designer would have to return $1300 if the contract concerning further orders or work was terminated.

Funds collected from clients as deposits generally do not have to be deposited in escrow accounts and do not have to be used solely for the client who has given the deposit. The term deposit must be used in contracts and agreements, and the designer should check with his or her accountant to be sure that this is true in his or her state.

A *down payment* is a portion of the total selling price paid at the time goods are ordered. Like the deposit, designers often use the down payment money as the prepayment that is required by the supplier. As with a deposit, the designer may have to return all or part of the down payment if the client cancels the order.

The term down payment does create a problem for designers in several states. Some states require that money that is collected as a down payment be deposited in a separate escrow account and be used exclusively for the client from whom it has been collected. In other words, David, in our example, must place the down payment of $10,000 in escrow for Mr. Robinson and cannot use those funds to order something for any other client. Check with your tax accountant or attorney to see if your state regulates the use of down payments.

A *retainer* is a payment to a professional to cover future services or advice by that professional. Retainers are not prepayments to be applied to the sale of goods but, rather, are for the contracting or retaining of design services or other professional services. Miller Interiors requires a retainer before it will begin the work for ACD Developers. Interior designers and other design professionals in allied areas usually require that clients pay a retainer to show good faith before work begins.

Designers can also create an open-ended design contract in which the designer is "on retainer" with a client, similar to when someone "retains" his or her attorney or has an attorney on retainer. This means that the designer is more or less on call to the client whenever the client requires design services. The fee for those services already has been negotiated. Additional discussion about retainers for design services contracts was presented in Chapter 24.

Federal Laws and Pricing Practices

The Federal Trade Commission (FTC) was established by the federal government as an independent agency in 1914 through the Federal Trade Commission Act. The purpose of this act and the commission is for consumer protection, and to prevent unfair or deceptive competition or practices between businesses.

The Sherman Antitrust Act dates to 1890. It prohibits practices by which businesses make agreements in restraint of trade or engage in price-fixing to limit competition. An example of *restraint of trade* is when two or more businesses have agreed not to sell in each other's territory or to each other's customers. This agreement limits the consumer's options.

Price-fixing occurs when two or more businesses agree to sell the same goods to the consumer at the same price. This relates directly back to the concept of suggested retail. At one time, certain consumer goods were sold at the same price, no matter where someone went to purchase them. These prices were dictated by the manufacturers. Some people even referred to these goods as "fair trade goods." However, enforcement of the Sherman Act negated these "fair trade" pricing polices. Today, all goods sold to the consumer are sold at whatever price any merchant that carries the goods determines to sell them. This means that a suggested retail price by the manufacturer is just that—suggested. The designer can sell the goods at any price that he or she determines—higher or lower than the suggested retail price. If the manufacturer insists that the designer sell the goods to the consumer at a particular price, then the manufacturer is in violation of the Sherman Act.

You may have noticed that certain items in retail stores are the same price regardless of the store. This same price might be right down to the exact manufacturer and product item number. Although this seems to be a violation of the Sherman Act, a true violation only exists if these two stores made an agreement to price exactly the same or if the manufacturer required that the stores price exactly the same. On the face of this, it would seem that the two stores are probably selling the goods at the "suggested retail price."

One of the most important pieces of legislation that the commission enforces is the Robinson-Patman Act. This legislation makes it illegal for a merchant to charge various merchants different prices for the same goods. Price discrimination "occurs when a seller charges different prices for commodities of like grade and quality."* This price discrimination must effectively lessen competition or create a monopoly. For example, if a manufacturer were selling the same quantity of product to two different design firms, it would have to offer the goods at the same price to both. However, if one firm had a record of purchasing a larger quantity of goods or stocking a quantity of goods, then the manufacturer could sell the goods at different prices to each designer.

Price discrimination only affects sales between merchants. A merchant has the legal right to sell to the consumer at any price that he or she determines. If Wendy Jones Interiors decided to sell a Knoll chair to Mrs. Smith for $1500 and the same chair to Mr. Peters for $100, the designer would not be in violation of any laws, as long as Smith and Peters were the end users.

There are several other pieces of legislation affecting businesses that prevent unlawful business practices; these are related to such things as monopolies, mergers, and labor relations. The ones already discussed, however, have the most relevance to an interior design practice. If you wish to investigate these other pieces of legislation, you might want to start by visiting the Web site of the Federal Trade Commission.

*Emerson, 2004, p. 493.

FREIGHT AND FOB

The predominate amount of goods ordered for any type of client comes from a location away from the office of the interior design firm. Naturally, some custom items are manufactured in the immediate vicinity. However, even these items involve a certain amount of cost to get the goods from the manufacturer or supplier to the designer's office or the job site. *Freight*, also called shipping, is the cost and process involved in the delivery of goods from the manufacturer to the interior designer. Shipping charges can be quite costly for the interior designer, especially those located a great distance from manufacturer's factories. It is very important for the design firm to understand what the shipping policies are for the different manufacturers and suppliers it uses.

Most frequently, freight is handled by trucking companies that are working as a transportation source for the manufacturer. Many manufacturers have their own trucks to handle the freighting of products from the factory to the interior designer's warehouse, but many use independent companies, especially for small orders. Goods are sometimes shipped by train, but this is generally done only for very large loads or when the manufacturer sends one of its trucks "piggyback." *Piggyback* means that the truck's trailer is loaded on a train flatcar and is shipped by train to the general destination. The trailer is removed from the train and is driven to the warehouse or the client's final destination. Small items, like accessories, fabrics, and many wall coverings, are shipped via a parcel delivery service, such as UPS or FedEx.

An important acronym in this industry that is directly related to freight or shipping charges is FOB. If you look in a price list for a desk or other furniture products, you will find this acronym along with either the word "factory" or "destination." These last two terms define which party—the manufacturer or interior designer—is responsible for the freight charges and when ownership of the goods changes hands. According to the Uniform Commercial Code (UCC), *FOB* means "free on board." It also is referred to as "freight on board." Both interpretations mean the same thing. For our purposes, we will use "free on board," since that is the definition used by the UCC.

FOB means that the manufacturer is responsible for the cost of loading the goods onto a freight truck or train. That simply is what FOB means in terms of pricing freight charges, although there is more to freight costs than loading the goods on a truck. There is the actual cost of transporting the goods from the factory to the location designated by the interior designer and the ownership of the goods when the truck leaves the loading dock.

The cost of transporting the goods to the destination is covered in the second part of the notation. If a manufacturer's catalog says *FOB, Factory*, this means that the buyer assumes ownership or title of the goods when they are loaded on the truck at the factory. In this case, the interior designer pays all transportation costs and assumes all risks during transit. If the catalog has the notation *FOB, Destination*, then the manufacturer retains ownership of the goods and assumes all risks until they reach the destination. The cost of transportation is also paid by the manufacturer in this case.

Another notation that is used by some manufacturers is *FOB, factory— freight prepaid*. What this means is that the manufacturer passes ownership of the goods to the buyer as they leave the factory loading dock but the manufacturer will pay the freight charges. This is done as a means of reducing the manufacturer's liability during shipping. It is also a convenience to its customers, since the freight charges are absorbed by the manufacturer. To be clear, the interior designer has ownership and responsibility for damages during transit, but the manufacturer pays the transportation charges to the destination.

Zone pricing is another term found in some catalogs concerning shipping charges. In *zone pricing*, a manufacturer determines two or more shipping zones based on geographic distances from the factory. Anyone within each zone pays the same amount for shipping, each zone having a different rate. Shipping charges for locations within each zone are averaged. When a manufacturer uses zone pricing, the seller pays the actual freight and bills the buyer for the zone average charge. For example, perhaps a desk company that is located in California uses a zone price for shipping. Let us assume the zones have been divided similarly to the way time zones are divided. The cheapest shipping charges will be in the zone that includes California—the point of origin. As the zones progress toward the East, the shipping charges will be higher.

Freight charges are also legitimate charges that the client should pay if the goods are not sent prepaid by the supplier. Most interior designers charge clients *actual freight*, which means that the designer will bill the client whatever the interior design firm is billed for the transportation of the goods to the designer's warehouse or the job site. Some firms add a small service charge to the actual freight charges to cover handling the payment and the necessity of dealing with the freight companies if there are any damages in transit.

Rather than charging actual freight, a firm may determine a freight factor on all items that must be shipped. A *freight factor* is obtained by finding the average and usual freight charges for all the kinds of goods and quantities of goods received FOB, Destination. This factor is added to the selling price or the cost price (as determined by the policies of the firm) of any goods ordered for the client that are shipped to the designer's warehouse.

There are times when some item needs to be rushed from the supplier to the project. The most common "rush" is shipping textiles for a custom upholstery job to the upholsterer or seating manufacturer. Wall coverings are also a common rush item. Naturally, anything can be needed in a hurry requiring express shipments. These express charges are also legitimate extra charges to the client if, in fact, the rush was not caused by a delay by the interior designer.

A clause should be included in the contract to cover the cost in the event an express shipment is needed. A few other terms related to the freight process will be discussed in Chapters 31 and 32.

DELIVERY AND INSTALLATION CHARGES

Another legitimate charge to clients to complete a project is for needed delivery and installation of products at the job site. A discussion about the delivery and installation process as part of contract administration is provided in Chapter 32. This section focuses on terminology and basic procedures concerning charging for these needed services.

Although the two terms may seem like the same thing, in reality they are not. *Delivery* means taking tangible goods to the job site and placing them in their correct location. *Installation* means that some additional services are involved in the delivery process, such as assembly or construction of the products. An area rug is delivered to the site and placed where the interior designer has specified. Wall-to-wall carpet must be installed to complete a job.

The cost of delivering many kinds of goods is often absorbed by the design firm. This is especially true when the client's location is within a limited geographic area of the design studio or warehouse. Beyond this limited geographic area, most firms charge clients for the cost of delivering the merchandise. Due to the extra work involved when something needs to be installed or assembled, installation charges are always added to the price of the actual goods, regardless of the job site location.

Delivery charges can be either a flat rate, determined by how far away the client is from the warehouse, like the zone shipping pricing discussed earlier, or an hourly charge. Hourly charges are often quoted as door-to-door. *Door-to-door* means that the client is charged from the time the delivery truck leaves the designer's warehouse loading dock to the time it leaves the client's location. It should be noted that if the interior designer is using a warehouse service to deliver goods to the client, the contract with the warehouse company should be clear as to who has liability for damages or other loss while the goods are at the warehouse or in transit from the warehouse to the job site.

Delivery services involve more than transporting a sofa or desk, for example, from a local warehouse to the job site, and these services impact the amount of the charges that will accrue whether or not the interior designer charges the client for the delivery service. Trained personnel are needed to check in the merchandise from the freight company truck that has brought the goods from the manufacturer. Receiving the goods involves inspecting the items for damage. (This is discussed further in Chapter 32.) Delivery services continue with the transportation of the merchandise to the client's location. Depending on the items, the goods will be uncartoned at the site, simple assembly may be needed, and the merchandise will be placed in the desired location. Delivery services also include removal of any cartoning or packaging materials, and dusting or slight cleaning of the merchandise. As will be discussed further in Chapter 32, the delivery personnel or the designer should also explain to the client how to care for the merchandise. All of these services represent expense items that can be charged to the client or absorbed by the interior designer. When a warehouse service is used by the designer, the charges are almost always charged to the client.

Other types of products require some sort of installation or assembly. Wallpaper, carpet, drapery, and other architectural finishes need to be installed. A roll of carpet is not finished goods. Until the carpet has been installed, that item is not complete. The tradespeople and craftspeople who do this work charge for their time and materials to complete the installation. As for architectural finishes, all these installation charges are the liability of the client, and the design firm must remember to pass them on in the pricing of the finishes.

Interior design projects often involve remodeling or renovating existing spaces. The charges to install architectural finishes in these circumstances are often higher than for new construction projects. Designers must charge not only for the installation of the new goods but also for the removal of the old materials and for the preparation of the surfaces for the new goods.

Many kinds of furniture items also require installation or specialized assembly. Custom cabinets for the kitchen or a conference room must go through final assembly on-site. A wall-hung bookcase unit in a home needs to be assembled and properly hung on the wall. Open-office systems furniture needs to be assembled by a trained installer. Many desks to house desktop computers require some assembly. Wall-hung accessories are other items that also require installation and possibly assembly.

Exactly what constitutes installation services depends on the products being installed. In general, the goods must be delivered to the job site, and some type of preparation of the surfaces or area is required prior to installation. In addition, specialized supplies are often required, such as tack strips for carpet, adhesives for wall coverings, and wall anchors for wall-hung furniture items. When the items are installed, initial cleaning or dusting will be needed, and, as with the delivery of simpler items, maintenance and care instruction should be provided by the installer or the designer.

These installation services constitute the charges that are required to make a finished product and should be absorbed by the client and not the design firm. The designer must be familiar with the job site so that he or she can explain to the installer prior to the installation what services will be required. Neglecting to tell the carpet installer that the existing carpet is a glue-down installation (which will require removal of the carpet and preparation of the floor) will result in an improperly quoted price on the installation of the new carpet. In many design firms, this error in pricing comes out of the designer's commission or revenue for the company.

When the designer neglects to add charges for delivery and installation to the estimate and final pricing of the job, the client is under no legal obligation to pay for the work. The work must be completed, and this means that the charges will be absorbed by the design firm or possibly the vendor. Thus, care in specification of all architectural finishes, custom cabinets, and any goods requiring installation is very serious.

SALES AND USE TAXES

Developing design solutions and documents for interiors projects involves professional services. As we have already seen, many interior designers or firms also sell merchandise to clients to generate revenue. Some states or municipalities require sales tax be collected for professional services—most do not. Almost all jurisdictions require sales tax be collected on goods sold to clients. Sales taxes that are not collected from the client will be collected by the state or city from the interior design firm. It is very important for the interior designer and the design firm to fully understand the laws relating to the charging of sales tax on the goods and services they provide.

We discussed in Chapter 10 that in order to sell merchandise to clients, the design firm must obtain a resale license from the state sales tax agency as well as municipal or county agencies if they require the collection of sales taxes. Permits also must be obtained if the business is located in other cities or states. The resale tax certificate exempts the designer from paying the sales tax at the time that he or she orders the merchandise for the client. It is then the designer's responsibility to collect the sales tax from the client and report and pay the collected taxes to these revenue agencies.

In many states, the design firm is required to pay a *use tax* on goods purchased by the design business. In other words, if the designer uses, stores, or consumes tangible goods for which tax has not been collected by the seller, the design firm must pay a use tax. Goods that the design firm purchased from out-of-state suppliers for use in the design firm's business would be subject to a use tax if those goods would normally have a sales tax charged against them if they were sold in the state in which the design firm was located. In other words, a use tax takes the place of sales tax on goods used by the operations of the design firm that the firm purchases from out-of-state suppliers. The liability to pay the use tax is on the buyer, not the seller. For example, ABC Interiors has purchased a computer from an out-of-state store for use in its accounting office. Since ABC Interiors is a business, it does not have to pay sales tax on the computer, but it does have to pay use tax. ABC Interiors must report and pay that use tax to the state tax agency. The use tax ensures that the state will receive some tax moneys on the sale of goods used by the business.

There is much differentiation in the tax laws from state to state regarding when sales and use taxes must be collected. Some jurisdictions do not require the collection of sales tax at all. It is therefore very important for the firm to understand all the laws of the state in which they are doing business. What might be taxable for a design firm working out of an office in New York City and selling to a client in New York City might not be taxable in New Jersey. At the time of this writing, only Alaska, Delaware, Montana, New Hampshire and Oregon did not collect sales tax. However, the reader is advised to check with the appropriate state agency where the business is formed and does business to determine if sales and use taxes must be collected. Even these five states or municipalities within the states may have some sort of sales tax requirements depending on the type of goods and/or services provided by a business.

The remainder of this section focuses on the sales tax—not use tax—that must be charged on purchases made by the designer firm's customers. Generally, the following guidelines are applicable anywhere, but in no way are they to be construed as absolutely true for all design practice areas.

Clients (and all of us) buy many kinds of goods that are considered tangible personal property. *Tangible personal property* is any property that is movable, can be touched, or has physical existence. Items that are considered tangible personal property are subject to sales tax collection when sold to the end user. Some examples of personal property are sofas, desks, chairs, and draperies.

Some items that are tangible do not literally become so without some process such as labor to complete the item. Thus, labor, installation, delivery, and freight have various kinds of interpretations as to when sales tax must be collected and when they are exempt. A case in point is draperies. In many states, the labor to make the drapery and hang the finished product in the home is taxable, since it is considered a vital part of completing the item. However, the charges a drapery store might ask to rehang drapery after it has been cleaned are not taxable, since the labor of simply hanging the drapery is considered a service.

Certain kinds of items that are at first considered and are personal property in that they are moved from the factory to the job site are legally considered *fixtures* (sometimes called capital improvements). A fixture is legally defined as "a thing which was once personal property, but has become attached to real property in such a way that it takes on the characteristics of real property and becomes a part of that real property."[2] Items such as wall-to-wall carpeting, wall coverings, and installed mirrors are a few examples.

Sales tax must be charged if the installation of the product becomes part of the building or becomes permanently affixed to the structure in such a way as to make it difficult or impossible to remove it without damaging the structure. When this happens, the product becomes a fixture. Depending on the answer to this analysis and the state laws that prevail, tax may or may not have to be charged. In many instances, sales tax is charged on the material and supplies needed to manufacture the finished goods, but not the labor. In some states, as in the drapery example, if the labor to manufacture and install the capital goods is necessary to make the "finished goods," then sales tax must also be charged on the labor.

In most cases, freight and delivery charges are either considered a service and generally are not taxable or are considered part of doing business and are calculated into the price of the goods. If for some reason a finished good does not exist without these services, sales tax may need to be collected. Most often this happens when freight and delivery charges are calculated into the price of the goods, sales tax *technically* can be calculated and must be paid to the state or city revenue office. For example, a designer does not call out a delivery charge as part of her sales agreement, but she has included the delivery charge in the price of the furniture item. She is thus charging sales tax on delivery, and this sales tax must be paid to the state or other revenue office. It is important, as with all sales tax collection policies, for the design firm to obtain information from the firm's accountant or the state and city revenue departments regarding the requirements for charging sales tax in all situations.

In general, design fees, such as hourly fees or a flat fee that do not relate to specific purchases of goods, are exempt from sales tax because the design fee is compensation for services. If, however, the design fee is added to the selling price of some goods, then the total price is taxable. For example, the designer does not show a fee for design services as a separate item on his invoice. Instead, he added a 25 percent charge for design services to the selling price of $5000 for office furniture. The taxable amount would be $6250—$5000 for the tangible goods and $1250 for the design fee. Is this ethical? If the design fee was a separate line item, then sales tax would only be charged on the tangible goods.

The design firm is responsible for recording sales and use taxes and paying the appropriate amounts to the state tax agency on a quarterly basis. The firm must also keep complete records of items that are exempt from taxes. The burden of knowing which items are taxable and which items are not wherever the design firm does business is on the design firm. State tax auditors have the authority to seize the moneys and/or property of the business if they discover that the business has not submitted the proper amount of sales and use taxes.

THE ROLE OF THE DESIGNER/SPECIFIER

Susan is one of the partners of an interior design firm specializing in hospitality projects. The contracts for these projects include specification of FF&E, but the merchandise is always purchased through the hotel's or restaurant's corporate offices. Susan's firm considers themselves to be designers/specifiers, since they do not sell merchandise but they do prepare the plans and specifications.

An interior designer/specifier can specialize in residential and/or commercial projects. They have made a determination that they do not wish to involve themselves in actually selling merchandise. Interior designers who work in architectural offices are another group of designers who infrequently involve themselves in the direct selling of merchandise to clients. Designer/specifiers, however, are responsible for many of the same activities that those who do sell products are responsible for.

There are many responsibilities related to specifying a project, whether the designer will be directly selling the merchandise or not. Of these activities, three are of special concern to the designer who does not sell merchandise to clients: (1) estimating a project budget, (2) preparing the purchasing specifications, and (3) assisting the client in evaluating and selecting suppliers.

Item 25-1 on the CD provides a sample worksheet that can be used to estimate the costs of product specification.

Estimating a Project Budget

Even though the designer/specifier is not selling merchandise to the client, the client naturally needs to have some idea of what the project will cost. However, the actual cost of the project cannot be known until the client either begins purchasing from suppliers or the bid process has been completed. Designer/specifiers who work with residential clients often budget or price a project based on the retail prices of the specified goods. Since it is possible for the client to obtain some of the specified goods "on sale" or at a discount from a seller, the budgeted price will almost always be slightly higher than what the client actually pays for the completed project. Of course, if the client delays purchasing any of the items, the prices may be higher than the budgeted amounts.

When a designer/specifier works with a commercial client, the project will probably go out for competitive bidding. *Competitive bidding* is a process whereby several, perhaps dozens of, vendors provide prices for the project to the client. The final cost of the project to the client is not known until the bidding process is over. This results in a more difficult budgeting situation for the designer/specifier and the client. The designer cannot guarantee a firm price but can budget based on methods such as: (1) a retail basis with estimates as to potential discounts, (2) a cost price plus percentage markup, or (3) a cost price plus a predetermined high-low negotiated markup. The first two are self-explanatory. The third budgeting option needs a bit of explanation.

Occasionally, a bid is set up so that the sellers who are providing prices must agree to only a specified markup on their cost. This condition is clearly indicated in the bid documents that the sellers obtain at the onset of the bid. Sellers must carefully consider if this negotiated or set markup is sufficient to justify providing a bid on the project. The budget is then closer to the actual purchase price, since the costs of the products are fairly well known by the designer.

Preparing Purchasing Specifications

Purchasing specifications can be as simple as what many designers call an equipment list or as complex as formal competitive bidding documents. A comprehensive equipment list provides quantities, descriptions, manufacturers' names, and a budgeted unit price (see Figure 25-1). This equipment list is then used by the client when he or she is shopping in order to purchase the necessary goods. Along with the equipment list, the designer might also provide the names and addresses of recommended sellers, installers, and craftspeople who can meet the demands of the designer and the client in completing the project.

Specification list for:
Ralph Smithson
Job Number 20547

Quantity	Manufacturer	Prod. No.	Description	Unit price	Extend price
2	B&B Italia	D277B	Diesis Sofa Fabric: COM Maharam 451801090 Mohair Color: 090 Magenta	$6500	$13,000
2	Cartwright	20/123	Club chair Fabric: Black Leather Finish: Ebony	3165	6330
2	Bernhardt	2BB 36/914	End table Finish: Frame—Black Top: Maple	2009	4018
1	Excel Custom		Custom Coffee Table 60" × 60" × 18" Per drawings Finish: Marble	4500	4500
2	Atherton	L9968	Table Lamp Finish: Coffee	1295	2590
1	Amazing Custom Cabinets		Custom Entertainment Unit Built to drawings (see attached) Finish: Maple and Ebony per drawings	27,300	27,300
		Total for Product			$57,738
		Freight and Delivery			4,619
		Sales Tax			3,975
		Total			$66,332

FIGURE 25-1.

A comprehensive equipment list that is used to prepare a project specification.

When a formal bid is used to purchase goods and services, the designer is responsible for preparing the specifications for all of the FF&E. Along with these specifications, additional documentation is included that clarifies the responsibilities of the sellers, installers, and tradespeople who are awarded the bids, along with information about many other aspects concerning the completion of the project by the winning bidders. An explanation of the bid process and the documentation that must be included in a formal bid are discussed in Chapter 30.

Assisting the Client with the Evaluation and Selection of Sellers

KD Interiors has been hired to design and specify a 50,000-square-foot office complex for a county government agency. Because it is a government agency, the FF&E must go out for a competitive bid. There are at least ten vendors who have met the requirements for bidders and are expected to bid. Another 45 vendors have obtained the bid documents and are interested in bidding. The client has just informed the project manager at KD Interiors that the county wants the firm to help evaluate the bids even though this was not expected when the design contract was negotiated.

When the designer prepares a simple equipment list, he or she commonly makes recommendations as to potential sellers and suppliers of the merchandise and/or installation of products. One might argue that the responsibility of assisting the client with evaluating and selecting sellers is more critical if formal bid documents are necessary. The bidding process allows any seller who feels that he or she is capable of supplying the specified merchandise to provide a bid to the client. But not all sellers are really able to fulfill the coordination and requirements of bids, especially for major projects. For example, although J. D. Furniture Store, which is a small retailer, may wish to bid on a project like a major hotel installation, the designer and client must determine whether or not J. D. Furniture Store really is capable of ordering, delivering, and installing the merchandise called for in the bid. This is the kind of service that KD Interiors will be helping the county with in the opening example.

In some bids, the exact specification of merchandise is left a little vague, so the client and the designer must evaluate alternative merchandise. Frequently, multiple sellers of office systems furniture are involved in providing bids. The designer must assist the client in determining if the products from several different manufacturers are sufficiently the same as the product named in the bid specification. Although the example is for office systems, the designer may have to provide this same type of assistance for every single product specified.

One of the major concerns of the designer who does not sell merchandise to clients is that clients may purchase different merchandise from what has been specified. The designer is concerned about proper quality and suitability for the intended purpose when the client purchases on his or her own. To limit liability, the designer must include clauses in the design contract and the purchase specification regarding this issue. This was discussed more fully in Chapter 24.

SUMMARY

One of the tasks of the interior designer is to budget and price merchandise for the client. This happens whether or not the interior designer is expecting or has contracted to sell the merchandise to the client. For those that sell merchandise, the competition of the marketplace and the demands of the consumer—whether residential or commercial—force designers to review their pricing policies and strategies to be sure they are competitive. The days of selling every item at more than 100 percent markup are gone for all but a small number of designers. Deep discounting practices have certainly cut into personal commissions and business revenues, forcing many designers and design firms out of the industry.

It is very important for interior designers to understand the many ways in which goods can be priced. The pricing terminology discussed in this chapter covers the more commonly used terms for the sale and cost price of the goods that the designer might sell or use for budgeting. Other important topics in this chapter were down payments and deposits, shipping and delivery charges, and the applicability of sales and use taxes.

The next chapter in this part discusses the Uniform Commercial Code (UCC). The UCC deals with laws pertaining to the sale of goods and other commercial transactions. These issues are of critical importance to the buying and selling of merchandise by an interior designer.

REFERENCES

1. Berkowitz et al., 1994, p. 379.

2. Clarkson, 1983, p. 1203. Copyright West Publishing Co.

CHAPTER 26

The Sale of Goods and the Uniform Commercial Code

Key Terms and Concepts

These key terms and concepts are important to material in this chapter. Many of these terms will be utilized in other chapters as well. Be sure you understand these items as you read this chapter.

Terms and Concepts

Uniform Commercial Code (UCC)	Electronic signature
Goods	Firm offer
Sale	Title
Seller	Shipment contract
Buyer	Destination contract
Merchant	Risk
Price	Sales on approval
End user	Restocking charge
Statute of Frauds	Conforming goods
Open-terms	Nonconforming goods
Click-on agreement	72-hour right of refusal

Critical Issues

After completing this chapter you should be able to:

- Explain the purpose of the Uniform Commercial Code and how it impacts the practice of interior design.
- Compare an interior designer as a merchant and a seller.
- Discuss how the Statute of Frauds affects an interior designer.
- Explain if and when an oral agreement for the sale of goods remains a valid contract.
- Explain the differences in a sales agreement for the sale of goods and for services.

- Describe what happens—according to the UCC—if the designer fails to include the price and/or quantity of goods on a purchase order.
- Explain acceptance as is regulated by the sale of goods.
- Discuss when an electronic order of goods is and is not a valid contract.
- Compare a shipment contract to a destination contract.
- Describe the rights the seller has when buying goods.
- Explain the buyer's rights when a consumer purchases goods from an interior designer.

When you buy goods from a store, do you know what your rights are as a purchaser of those goods should you have a problem with one of them? What if you bought an item at a yard sale? Perhaps you ordered merchandise online. As an interior designer, are you aware of the laws that affect your purchases from suppliers and manufacturers? Do you have any idea of what the law states about the ability of your client to refuse delivery of goods or to cancel an order? These questions and hundreds of others are regulated by common law, along with a uniform set of regulations concerning the law of sales called the Uniform Commercial Code (UCC).

Article 2 of the UCC is concerned with the sale of goods, including the transfer of the title for goods from one party to another. The offer to sell goods and the acceptance to buy those goods creates a contract. The nature of a sales contract has many differences from a contract for services and from many other contracts. The UCC is the primary authority that governs the transfer of title when goods are sold. This transfer of title is covered within the law of sales. The law of sales, as represented by Article 2 of the UCC, governs the sale of goods. Article 2 *does not* cover the sales of services, real estate, or intangible property such as stocks. Should a dispute arise over the sale of goods, the UCC provisions prevail, whereas a dispute over the sale of services would be governed by common law. These laws affect sales between merchants, between merchants and consumers, and between consumers and consumers—in other words, all sales transactions *involving goods*.

For the majority of the members of the interior design profession, selling and ordering goods for clients is an everyday occurrence, yet few have ever heard of the Uniform Commercial Code. It seems that most designers learn about the intricacies of selling and buying goods from experience. This may be fine if you are purchasing a loaf of bread from the grocery store. However, designers who own an interior design practice and make the sale of merchandise their major source of income need more knowledge about the rights and responsibilities involved in ordering and selling goods.

The section of the UCC that deals with sales is quite extensive. We will, however, attempt to provide some basic understanding regarding how the UCC affects the daily work of the interior designer who engages in the sale of goods.

This chapter is not meant to be an in-depth discussion of the UCC, nor should it be considered legal advice. Readers are advised to verify application of the UCC to their jurisdiction. States amend the UCC, and interpretations mentioned in this chapter may differ in a specific state. The reader is encouraged to investigate the specific interpretations of the UCC by going to the Web site for the National Conference of Commissionaires on Uniform State Laws or the state attorney general's office.

HISTORIC OVERVIEW

Most laws related to commercial business activity, including interior design, originate from the individual states. During the early years of this country, this fact often resulted in the passage of confusing and conflicting laws. As the nation's commercial business activity became more complex, the problems became more acute.

In the late 1800s, the National Conference of Commissioners on Uniform State Laws (NCCUSL) was established to create uniform statutes related to business activities. These statutes, revised over the next 55 years, helped to illuminate many of the problems of commercial business. Yet there remained instances in which these uniform statutes overlapped. Work was begun in 1945 to revise all the statutes into one uniform document. In 1957, after much work, the Uniform Commercial Code (UCC) was completed.[1]

The code consists of nine articles dealing with many aspects of commercial transactions. The article (or section) that is specifically concerned with the normal practices or activities of interior designers is Article 2: Sales. The UCC has been adopted by all states except Louisiana. This state has only adopted certain sections of the code and has state laws to cover other issues. The article concerning sales is the primary part of the UCC that Louisiana has not adopted, but it uses its own laws to cover the sales of goods. However, according to legal texts, for practical purposes, the reader may assume that all states have adopted these laws. The UCC is periodically updated by the NCCUSL to reflect current commercial transactions and customs. You can go to the Web site of the NCCUSL (www.nccusl.com) to research changes and specific information on the UCC.

The purpose of the UCC is to help "state legal relationships of the parties in modern commercial transactions. The Code is designed to help determine the intentions of the parties to a commercial contract and to give force and effect to their agreement."[2]

DEFINITIONS

The UCC can be thought of in a way as the model building code. Each state may interpret the statutes in Article 2 and other sections of the UCC related to their individual legislative needs. Many of these interpretations related to whether the buyer of goods is an end user (consumer) or a merchant. It is therefore necessary to define some common terms as they relate to the code. Although there are many definitions in the code, the main ones that we wish to look at here are those for goods, sale, seller, merchant, buyer, and price.

Goods (Section 2–105) are any items that are tangible, that is, have physical existence and can be moved and would include custom-made goods. Furniture and accessories are tangible goods. The sale of tangible goods is covered by the UCC. Items such as carpet, wall coverings, and window treatments are goods, because they have physical existence. When these items are permanently attached to a home or a building, they are generally considered real property. Or are they? The sale of the merchandise itself from the supplier to the designer and the designer to the client would be covered by the UCC, since the goods do not become real property until they are "permanently" attached to the home or office. If the client later wants to remove these goods from his or her home or office and sell them, or even sell the building with the merchandise intact, the sale would be governed by real estate law.

A *sale* (Section 2–106) occurs when the seller transfers title or ownership of the goods to a buyer and the buyer has provided some consideration to the seller. For example, Marcia purchased a sofa from Gail, an interior designer. Marcia paid Gail $4000 for that sofa by check. The sofa was delivered to Marcia, and Marcia paid the subsequent invoice sent by Gail for delivery charges after the delivery of the sofa. Whenever the designer agrees in good faith to sell a piece of furniture to a client for some amount of money and the client takes delivery of the furniture and sends the designer a check for the agreed-upon price, a sale has occurred. There are, however, some special considerations with regard to when "ownership" actually occurs. This will be discussed later in the chapter.

In the preceding example, Gail provided goods to her client, Marcia; thus, Gail is a seller. To be clear, a *seller* (Section 2–103) is anyone who sells goods or contracts to sell goods. A manufacturer who sells goods to an interior designer also is considered a seller. When someone holds a garage sale, technically that homeowner is a seller. However, both the interior designer and the manufacturer are also considered "merchants." Special conditions affect the sale of goods between merchants.

A *merchant* (Section 2–104) is anyone who is involved with the buying and/ or selling of the kinds of goods with which he or she is dealing. Someone who "holds himself or herself out as having knowledge and skill unique to the practices or goods involved in the transaction"[3] is also considered a merchant. Thus, although the interior designer who sells a personally owned stereo to a friend is a seller, if he or she sells a chair to that same friend and that sale occurs through the business, the designer is now considered a merchant. Naturally, manufacturers and suppliers of goods to the interior designer are also considered merchants, as would any retailer selling goods to the consumer.

Many interior designers who sell goods never have a showroom, warehouse, or installation crew who are employees of the firm. Any interior designer, however, who purchases goods, whether or not through a firm's inventory account, and resells them to a client so that the purchase and the resale "pass through" the design firm's books is a merchant.

A person becomes a *buyer* (Section 2–103) when he or she contracts to purchase or purchases some good. Marcia, the client in the example above, is a buyer. A buyer also is someone who buys from someone who is in the business of selling goods; thus, Gail the interior designer is also a buyer. The designer is protected by the same rights as the end user, as long as the purchase is from a seller whose business it is to sell the sofa.

The term *price* (Section 2–304) can be any kind of payment from a buyer to a seller, including money, goods, services, or real property. Therefore, it is possible, for example, for a client to offer to trade his or her own professional services as the price of a sofa.

A term used frequently in this chapter and others in this book is *end user*. It is not officially part of the UCC but is a term that is commonly understood to mean the person who ultimately owns and uses goods. It is defined in this chapter in order to clarify the term.

STATUTE OF FRAUDS

State legislatures provide specific requirements for when certain types of contracts must be in writing to be enforceable. The common terminology for this statue is the *Statute of Frauds*. When goods are sold, this statute clarifies requirements and conditions of when these contracts actually exist and their terms. A base condition of the statute is that a contract for the sale of goods over $500 must be in writing to be enforceable. Although the base dollar amount is generally considered to be $500, an amendment to the statute in the UCC in 2003 changed the amount to $5000.[4] The practitioner should contact the attorney general's office within his or her state to clarify this base amount. Although a written contract for the sale of goods does not mean that the designer will force the client to take the goods, it does give the designer the legal right to sue for payment, if he or she so chooses. Other situations when the statute affects other types of contracts was discussed in Chapter 24. The Statute of Frauds can be found in Section 2–201(1) of the UCC as it applies to the sale of goods.

The form of the writing for the sale of goods does not have to be a formal single document along the lines of that described in Chapter 24. Often, orders for goods are a combination of faxes and sales slips or purchase orders. If something is ordered verbally, it should always be followed up by a written sales confirmation. The order should name the parties involved, provide a description of what is to be ordered, and indicate the quantity and price. It should also be signed by the person to be charged. For the ordering of goods, the critical elements are the quantity of what is to be ordered and signature.

There are also specific exceptions to when an agreement must be in writing. First, between merchants, an oral agreement is valid if one party sends the other party a signed confirmation outlining the details of the agreement. The receiving merchant has ten days to respond in writing to any conditions or content of the offer to which he or she does not agree. Failure to respond within the ten days forms a valid contract.

Second, in some states an oral contract for the special manufacture of goods that are not suitable for anyone else and whose manufacture has substantially been started forms a contract. For example, Mary Jones Designs places a telephone order to Smith's Drapery Company for the manufacture of ten different-sized arched mini blinds at a price of over $1800. A month later, after production has been started but not finished, the client cancels the order and Jones calls to cancel the order. If it is unlikely that the blinds can be sold to another client of Smith's Drapery Company, Mary Jones Designs is liable. It is for this reason that designers include in the terms of their confirmations a statement that a restocking charge, say at least 25 to 50 percent, is charged for any order the client cancels.

Third, in some states if one party to the contract admits in court or in legal proceedings that a contract does exist, then an oral contract is binding for what was admitted. For example, Robert Class places a telephone order for 50 yards of Wilton weave carpet from an English mill. The value of the carpet is $6000. The mill ships 500 yards. Class refuses the shipment, and the mill sues. Class admits in court that he ordered 50 yards of carpet. Since Class admits that an oral contract did exist, he would be liable to pay for the 50 yards of carpet but not the extra yardage.

Finally, an oral agreement is enforceable up to the amount of payment made and accepted or the amount of goods delivered and accepted. For example, if a designer makes a verbal contract to order mini blinds for a client and the client provides the designer with a deposit, the client is liable to pay for and accept the quantity of blinds that the deposit covers. If the designer delivers a portion of the order for the blinds, the client is also liable for the value of the blinds that are delivered.

Interior designers should not agree to sell goods to clients and/or order goods for clients without a written contract, more commonly referred to as a sales order or sales confirmation. Written agreements and follow-up agreements to verbal orders to suppliers is not only good practices but protects the interior designer. The designer who places orders for clients without having the client sign a confirmation may not have legal recourse if the client later refuses delivery. If the designer fails to send a confirming order to the manufacturer, the manufacturer may not be bound to a sale. And the designer who fails to read an acknowledgment for an oral agreement is obliged to accept whatever was orally agreed to.

THE SALES CONTRACT

Chapter 24 discussed design contracts for services, providing an overview of the basic elements of a contract. The statutes related to the sale of goods as covered by the UCC generally follow the principles of contract law, although there are exceptions because the nature of selling and purchasing agreements varies. This is especially true when the selling occurs between merchants. This section will look at how "offer," "acceptance," and "consideration" occur in sales law.

The buying and selling of goods occurs in person, over the phone, by mail, by fax and via the Internet. The form of the agreement to buy and sell can thus also take many forms. Section 2–204 states, "A contract for the sale of goods may be made in any manner sufficient to show agreement, including conduct by both parties which recognizes the existence of such a contract."[5] The date of the agreement, description of what is being sold, price, and signature by the person being charged—items discussed in Chapter 24 on contracts for services—are handled somewhat differently from a contract for the sale of goods. Those differences are discussed throughout this chapter.

Offer (Sections 2–204, 2–205, 2–206, 2–305, 2–308, and 2–311)

Normally, a contract exists when an offer is followed by an acceptance. In sales law, however, the nature of offers and acceptances renders the point at which a contract exists more inexact. Because offers and acceptances in sales contracts are exchanged verbally, through the mail, electronically by e-mail and faxes, and by the behavior of the buyer and seller, it is more difficult to determine exactly when a contract exists. To assist with this problem, the UCC in Section 2–204 states that a contract exists when there is sufficient agreement to an offer so that a contract has been formed. This agreement may be verbal, written, or by the actions of the parties. For example, the price for a sofa in a catalog is an offer. When the designer sends a purchase order for this sofa to the manufacturer, a contract is formed.

In contract law, the terms of the offer and the acceptance must be clearly stated before the contract can be effective. Because of the unusual circumstances that surround offers and acceptances in sales law, the UCC allows for the offer to be valid even if one or more terms of the agreement are not stated, provided that the parties intend to go through with the contract and the courts can agree that a contract is intended and can determine a remedy for breach of contract.

Open-Terms Provisions—An Introduction

If the designer forgets to put all pertinent information on the purchase order that will be sent to a supplier, in most situations the contract will still be effective. When items are left off of the purchase order, that act provides a definition of the term *open-terms*. Provisions within the UCC allow the contract to be valid even when some of the terms of the contract are indefinite. Terms include quantity, description, part number, delivery location, payment, and price.

In general, if the terms are incomplete, it is likely that the contract will be valid, as long as it can be shown that both parties intend to fulfill the contract. However, the more terms there are that are left incomplete, the more difficult it will be for the courts to determine if the contract is valid. For example, should a designer order some tables and all the terms needed in the purchase order are present except the finish of the wood, the order would still be valid. However, if the quantity is missing, the order is usually considered invalid, since the courts cannot determine the full value of the contract in order to establish a remedy. If the parties intend for a contract to exist, then one does exist, even if some of the information is missing.

Sally prepared a purchase order for four items from the same manufacturer for her client. She was in a hurry and left out the description of the sofa but included the catalog number, and also forgot the finish code for the coffee table and end tables. Her price for the end tables was also missing. Assuming only the information given above was on her preprinted purchase order, what other information seems to be missing?

Open-Price Term

If the price is missing, the other party can cancel the offer or determine a reasonable price. The question here is whether the two parties intend to conclude an agreement in "good faith," which would mean an honest and fair price. For example, should ABC Design Company agree to furnish drapery tiebacks for a client but forget to provide a price for those tiebacks, the client can either set a reasonable price for the items or cancel the order for the tiebacks. It is, obviously, not a good idea to leave the price off a purchase order to a supplier or to the client.

The reasonable price concept most often is only reasonable to the person who is setting the price. The interior designer should always be the person who sets the price to the client. Naturally, the interior designer should know what the price will be from the supplier before quoting prices to a client and placing an actual order. Any form or manner in which the interior designer gets a quotation from a supplier should clearly indicate it is just that—a request for quotation and not an order. In this way, the designer is prevented from inadvertently ordering goods at a price that is higher than what the client is willing to pay before the client agrees to even purchase the goods.

Open-Payment Term

Another open term that is related to offers is an open-payment term. A payment term means the way it can be paid—cash or check, for example—and when it is due. If a payment due date for the goods has not been specified, the UCC stipulates that payment is due upon delivery to the buyer or at the time of "receipt of goods." The buyer receives the goods when he or she takes physical possession of the goods. Additionally, if payment terms have not been specified, the payment must be in cash, check, or agreed-upon credit. When the designer (or supplier) has included a phrase such as, "Payment due within 10 days of receipt of invoice," the designer has effectively given the buyer ten days of credit at no cost.

For the client, receipt of goods takes place when the goods are delivered to his or her home or office or when the client leaves the designer's place of business with the goods. According to subsections 2–310 (b and c), receipt of goods shipped from a manufacturer to the designer occurs when the goods are placed in the hands of the carrier. This is the reason that invoices often arrive prior to the goods. However, this means that payment is due before the goods can be inspected. All buyers have the right to inspect the goods before they make payment. These same subsections provide for that right of inspection, but the inspection must be done promptly. If the goods are not as ordered, the seller must be notified immediately if the buyer does not want to be bound to pay.

Open-Delivery Term

If the location for the delivery has been omitted, it is customary that delivery be made at the seller's business location. Neglecting to specify that the goods are to be delivered to the designer's warehouse service facility could result in a freight truck arriving at the designer's home office or wherever his or her place of business is located. In another situation, the goods might remain at the supplier's location, requiring the designer to pick up those goods rather than the supplier delivering them to a warehouse. In either case, this omission could be quite costly to the designer. It is unlikely that major manufacturers of goods would not call to check with the designer as to a delivery location. However, the manufacturer is not obligated to do so if the delivery location has been omitted from the order.

Interior designers must also be very clear in circumstances where very large shipments or deliveries are made from a supplier. Manufacturers want to ship out goods as soon as they are ready even if that means more than one shipment. The UCC gives them that right if agreement as to full or partial shipments was not made in the original order. Section 2–307 states that delivery and payment are due at one time for all the items being sold, unless provisions in the agreement or "circumstances" allow for delivery and payment in lots—meaning partial shipments. The designer should have a term on the purchase order that informs the supplier as to whether shipment of less than the full order is acceptable.

The designer needs to protect him- or herself concerning partial deliveries to the client as well. For large-sized projects involving multiple items, it is not unusual for the client to want the goods delivered as soon as they arrive. The designer usually prefers to deliver the goods to the client promptly in order to keep cash flow operating smoothly. However, in order to receive payments for goods delivered in lots rather than as a whole, a term in the sales contract must be provided that would notify the buyer of this fact. When several deliveries are made to the client to complete one order, without a written term in the contract, payment is not required until the entire order has been delivered. It should also be noted that making multiple deliveries to the same client is expensive, as the warehouse service will charge for each trip from the warehouse to the job site.

Open-Quantity Term

It is critical for the interior designer to include the quantity of each item that is being ordered from a supplier and subsequently in the client's invoice. It is difficult if not impossible for a court to determine what to do when the quantity of goods has not been specified. Not only does it make it impossible to know if a sufficient "number" of items was delivered, but it is also impossible for the courts to determine what the charges for the items should be.

The Firm Offer

Normally, in contract law, an offer to sell or buy goods has a time limit. That time limit can be set by the offeror (seller). If the offer is not in writing or is not accompanied with payment by the offeree (buyer), the offer can be revoked by the seller at any time before the buyer can accept. However, in sales law, special provisions are made when the seller is a merchant, and they apply whether the buyer is a merchant or an end user. If the merchant makes an offer in writing, whether or not consideration has been given by the buyer, or a time limit to the offer has been set, the merchant cannot revoke the offer either during the time limit or for a reasonable length of time. This is referred to as a *firm offer*. It is critical to point out that a firm offer must be in writing and signed by the offeror. This provision protects the buyer— whether that buyer is an interior designer buying from a supplier or a client buying from the interior designer—from quoting one price and then raising the price. For example, Mary Smith signs a written contract to sell $30,000 of furniture to Susan Rose, but Rose does not sign the agreement and does not provide any deposit. Ten days later, Smith realizes that she made an error in her calculations. If Rose accepts the contract within a reasonable length of time, Smith will lose $2000, since she used a net price list to discount some of the goods. Legally, Smith cannot revoke the offer, since it was a "firm offer" in writing and was signed by her.

The points in this discussion are important to the interior design practice. They show the value of good preparation of paperwork of the specification list, the contract for the client, and purchase orders. Designer omissions can cost time and money. They can even result in lawsuits against the designer.

Acceptance: Sections 2–206 and 2–207

Suppliers and manufacturers generally articulate their terms of sales through catalogs and price lists. Of course, some suppliers for custom goods, for example, discuss terms of sales with designers and prepare a proposal that then outlines the terms of sale. Ordering is based on the terms established in a price list or on a proposal from a supplier. The designer must also be careful to see if a time limit is involved in the offer and order process as price changes can intercede and cause the designer to lose money.

When the designer orders from a manufacturer or supplier, if acceptance is not made in the manner specified by the seller, the acceptance can be rejected or considered a counteroffer. However, the law generally allows the acceptance to be valid if it is received within the time limit set, even if it is by a different method of acceptance. Usually the seller wants an oral acceptance, followed by a signed acceptance of the sales proposal. When the supplier sends or otherwise indicates an acceptance to the merchant to buy (receipt of the designer's purchase order), a sales contract has been formed. In general, the acceptance should mirror the offer; that is, if the offer was made via a purchase order sent through the mail, the acceptance should be mailed. If the order was placed via fax, the acceptance should be faxed, and so on.

Although interior designers should only place orders with suppliers after a written purchase order is provided or accompanies a purchase, some designers do not avail themselves of this type of documentation 100 percent of the time. The excuse of being in a rush to order and too busy to follow up is poor practice. For example, Ralph Brown telephoned in an order for mini blinds and did not follow up with a written confirmation. When the blinds were ready for installation, Brown found that they were the wrong size. The size of the length had been made the size of the width, and vice versa. Brown claimed that the blinds company had made the mistake. The blinds company played a tape recording of the telephone order. It was clear that Brown had given the dimensions incorrectly. He had to pay for the blinds and reorder them, using the correct sizes.

Interior designers establish their terms of sale through their sales agreements and proposals to clients, and acceptance of those agreements is represented by the client's signature on the sales agreement. In the designer/end-user relationship, there are usually few problems or questions related to the existence of the contract. This is because, in everyday practice, the designer prepares a confirmation proposal that states who is being charged; lists the quantities, descriptions, and prices of the items being sold; lists the terms of sale, such as when payment is due; and requires the signature of the client on the confirmation. Assuming price is not an issue, rarely does the client make acceptance in any way other than by signing the confirmation.

A key to the agreement between designer and client is the time limit of the offer and whether or not the client has signed the agreement. If the designer's proposal states that the offer is good only for ten days (or some other time limit), the client must respond within that ten-day period; if he or she does not, the designer does not legally have to honor the original offer. If there is no time limit stated, the client has a "reasonable length of time" to respond. For example, a month after receiving the proposal, the client signs and returns the confirmation. However, the price of the goods to the designer has increased during that time. The designer may very well be expected to sell the goods at the quoted price, thus lowering his or her profit margin. Thus, it is important that all offers to sell goods to clients have stated on the confirmation a time limit for acceptance.

In contract law, a contract exists only if all the terms of the offer are exactly matched by the acceptance. Any differences constitute a counteroffer. In sales law, it is not uncommon for sales between merchants for the terms on the purchase order and the terms of the acknowledgment to contain some differences. In interior design practices, the quantity, description, and price commonly match. Terms such as ship date and general terms of the sale often vary. The UCC allows for a contract to be formed when the conditions of the purchase order and the acknowledgment are different, as long as the offeree's response indicates a definite acceptance of the original terms of the offer and there are no conditional terms in the offer or acceptance. For example, designer A sends a purchase order to manufacturer B for some custom-made bedspreads. The purchase order is prepared following the instructions in the catalog. The acknowledgment comes back from B with the statement, "On condition that a 50 percent deposit be submitted within ten days of receipt of acknowledgment. No work will be started until deposit is received." If this term is not stated in the catalog, no contract exists, unless the buyer agrees, because the seller has added a condition to the terms of the offer.

When the differences in terms are minor and neither party objects to the differences, a contract has been formed. If the offer and acceptance are made over the phone, the printed confirmation and acknowledgments are proposals to the oral contract and, again, a contract has been formed, as long as no objections are made, no conditions have been placed on the order or acceptance after the original offer has been made, and the differences are minor.

What all this means to the designer is that he or she not only must carefully prepare the terms of sale on his or her purchase order used to order from suppliers but also must be familiar with the terms and conditions of sale from all the suppliers. What is ordered is usually not the problem in interior design orders. The price, ship dates, warranties, and payment terms are more often the issue. Chapter 31 contains an example of the terms and conditions on the back of a firm's sales order—the document that should be used to clarify what is ordered for each client (see Figure 31-3).

Should the acknowledgment from the supplier contain discrepancies with regard to quantities, descriptions, and so on, it is important for the designer to make prompt written notification of the errors to the supplier. There are literally only a few days to generally a maximum of ten days to catch and correct any changes in an order. Failure to do so means acceptance of the acknowledgment, hence a contract, and the designer then "owns" the merchandise, even if the error has been made by the supplier.

If there are material differences between the designer's purchase order terms and a supplier's acknowledgment terms, the designer may be protected by the UCC constraints against material differences. A material difference means that there are substantial or essential changes to the original. However, to be protected, the designer is encouraged to object in writing to any terms that are different from his or her own.

Consideration: Section 2–304

Recall from Chapter 24 that consideration is the price one pays to another party for fulfilling a contract. Consideration is usually monetary payment in cash, check, or credit payment. In general, the UCC does not differ with the general contract law precept that consideration must be part of the acceptance. Between designer and client, the consideration is primarily a deposit that is paid when the agreement, which states that the client will pay full value at a later time, is signed. Between designer and supplier, consideration is generally the good faith credit that the supplier affords to the designer, knowing that the designer will pay the supplier in full after the goods have been shipped.

There are strict rules governing consideration when the buyer or seller attempts to modify the contract. One of the most problematic areas of this issue is for price increases. For example, after the designer sends the purchase order to the supplier and the supplier acknowledges the order to the designer but merchandise has not been shipped yet, the supplier informs the designer that the price will go up 10 percent as a result of an increase in materials price. The designer subsequently notifies the supplier that he or she accepts the increase. Later, the designer changes his or her mind and says that he or she will only pay the original price. Whether or not the designer accepts the increase orally or in writing, he or she is bound by the new price. This is true as long as it can be shown by the supplier that the change in price is due to a reason such as a change in availability of materials to manufacture the finished goods, causing an increase in price for the finished goods. If the supplier makes a mistake in his or her pricing, the modification of the contract is invalid.

Once the terms and conditions are agreed to by the designer and the supplier, later modifications agreed to are binding, if they are reasonable as a result of something that is beyond the control of the party who is asking for the modifications. If the supplier later tells the designer that the price will be higher and the designer does not agree, the contract is revoked. If the original or modified contract must meet the Statute of Frauds or has a condition that changes must be in writing, these changes must be in writing to be valid.

ELECTRONIC AGREEMENTS AND SIGNATURES

Electronic agreements have become widespread in interior design, as merchandise is ordered from suppliers via facsimile machines and the Internet. Interior designers frequently use facsimile (faxed) electronic processes to purchase goods and services for clients. The UCC accepts this method of creating a contract for goods, assuming the designer receives a mirrored faxed acknowledgment from the supplier. There are two cautions when faxes are used for ordering. The first is that the designer should set his or her fax machine to print a report that shows that the fax was received by the vendor. A report of this kind is especially important when time is of the essence for an order. For the small design firm, this report helps the owner know that the supplier has received the fax and that it has not gone to a wrong party or is in cyberspace somewhere. A sample of this type of report is shown in Chapter 31 (Figure 31-3).

For a fax, the normal terms and conditions of sale, which are generally on the back of the sales order to a client or perhaps on the back of the acknowledgment from the supplier, are generally not faxed. A statement to the effect, "The product is sold subject to the terms and conditions of sale of goods by 'the design firm,' which are available for review upon request,"[6] is necessary to protect the designer and suppliers who use faxes for acknowledgment of orders. It is the seller's responsibility to make sure that the buyer knows the terms and conditions of the sale, whether these terms are printed in a price list, on the sales agreement, or on an acknowledgment, or are covered by a clause such as the above for a fax.

Businesses' use of the Internet is not foreign to most readers, who may themselves have purchased many kinds of goods online. Of course, online purchasing also impacts when interior designers purchase from vendors or clients purchasing from interior designers. Buyers need to be sure that they look over the terms of sale shown on a Web site of the seller so that the buyer understands his or her rights concerning nonconforming goods, returns, damages, and the like. Online buyers also need to understand how goods are to be paid for and refund policies, if any. From the seller's point of view, these same items need to be carefully and clearly stated on the Web site.

It is very important for buyers to realize that many online selling situations create a *click-on agreement*, where the buyer clicks a box that says something like "I agree" or "Accept." The moment the buyer clicks, that creates the legal acceptance needed to form a contract and for the buyer to be bound by the terms of sale—even if the buyer didn't bother to read the terms.

Online purchasing also brings questions about *electronic signatures* (or e-signatures). Recall that contracts generally cannot be enforced unless signed by the party to be charged—the buyer (interior designer or client) for most of the situations in interior design. A signature can be created digitally using special keys or codes within the system. Another way of attaching a signature to a contract is by use of a digitizer pad. A signature is digitized into the computer using a stylus. Readers are no doubt familiar with this method, since most credit card purchases today use it. A contract or agreement can be signified by the party to be charged by the party signing the document and then electronically sending the signed document via e-mail or fax.

For the most part, when a disagreement occurs concerning an online sale, courts generally interpret existing contract law and the UCC principles for a determination. E-contract law is still being created, so the judgments and determination about any particular case in any specific jurisdiction can vary greatly. Questions concerning online contracts should be directed to the reader's state/provincial attorney general's office, since e-signature laws vary from state to state.

In the United States, the Electronic Signatures in Global and National Commerce Act (E-SIGN Act) was passed in 2000 to "provide that no contract, record, or signature may be 'denied legal effect' solely because it is in an electronic form."[7] This makes electronic signatures as valid as on-paper signatures in the United States. An earlier federal law, the Uniform Electronic Transactions Act (UETA), passed in 1999, clarifies that an e-signature is valid whether it is digitally recorded, is the name at the end of an e-mail, or is a click-on located in a Web site.[8]

What Would You Do?

Reston Carpet, Inc. is a supplier of carpet for use in homes and offices. Over the telephone, a sales representative for Reston offers to sell Diane Smith of Smith Anderson Interiors 325 yards of Magnum plush carpet at a price of $21 a square yard. The Reston sales representative also verbally agreed to keep the offer open for 21 days and hold the stock for that time. Smith told him that the offer appears to be fine and that Smith will let Reston know of Smith's acceptance within the next week after she confirms the price with her client. Five days later, the Reston rep sends Smith an e-mail that Reston has withdrawn the offer. Smith immediately telephones the Reston rep and accepts the $21-per-square-yard price for the 325 yards of carpet she needs for her project. The Reston factory claims that there never was a sales contract formed between Reston and Smith and refuses to sell the carpet to Smith at that price.

TITLE

Peter has ordered several furniture items for the client opening a small office, the client having paid a 50 percent deposit. The furniture items have been delivered by the supplier to Peter's warehouse service and are being held pending delivery to the client's office. Peter has not yet paid the supplier for the items in full. The items were shipped to the warehouse FOB, Factory. Who has title to the furniture as defined by the UCC?

In legal terms, ownership of goods is called *title*. When goods are bought and sold, ownership of those goods changes hands from the seller to the buyer. For a sale to take place, goods must exist and must be identified in the contract. Section 2–401 of the UCC clarifies the law related to the title of goods. Unless otherwise specified and agreed, title passes when possession changes from the seller to the buyer.

The most common way title passes is at the time and place that the physical delivery of the goods is made by the seller to the buyer. This is clear-cut when the sale occurs between the designer and a client. The designer should use a sales confirmation describing what has been sold. If the goods are delivered to the client's home or job site, a delivery ticket or other evidence of what has been delivered and accepted should be used. The delivery ticket also should be dated and signed by the client. This provides clear evidence of what has been delivered and that the title has passed to the buyer. The description of the goods on the delivery ticket should mirror what has been written on the sales confirmation, signed by the client prior to ordering (or turning over) the goods. A signature accepting delivery is very important in case the client does not pay for the goods for any reason. A signed delivery ticket shows acceptance of the delivery and title transfer, and thus responsibility for payment.

When the designer buys from a manufacturer, title often passes by use of a shipment or a destination contract. A *shipment contract* means that the title to the goods passes to the buyer when the manufacturer (seller) places the merchandise into the hands of the shipper. In the previous chapter, the term FOB, Factory was also defined as title passes when the goods are placed by the supplier into the hands of a shipper. Recall that FOB is an abbreviation for "free on board." A price list does not have to specifically say "factory." A shipment contract means from the place the goods are originally shipped. Since title has passed to the buyer once the goods are on a shipping vehicle, the buyer is also responsible for the risk. This is discussed in the next section. This is the most common way title changes hands unless otherwise noted in the price list, catalog, acknowledgment, or other documentation from the seller.

When the seller uses a *destination contract*, the manufacturer retains title of the goods until they arrive at the buyer's delivery address—the destination of the shipment. Ownership of the goods and subsequent responsibility of risk is retained by the manufacturer until the goods are delivered. The manufacturer often places "FOB, Destination" in the catalog to indicate this ownership matter. If the purchase order does not designate a destination, the supplier will instruct the shipper to deliver the goods to the designer's place of business listed on the purchase order.

The reader may be familiar with another term of shipment, called COD (cash on delivery). Shipments sent COD require that the buyer pay cash (or other approved payment) at the time the merchandise is delivered to the buyer's location.

Some buyers do not require shipping or delivery and take the merchandise right from the studio or showroom. When no delivery is required, the title passes to the buyer when the contract is made. If the buyer refuses delivery or wants to otherwise return the goods, title reverts to the seller.

RISK

Since title can change at differing times, the UCC must address who is liable for the risk of loss during the shipping of the goods. Shipping of goods is governed by the UCC in Sections 2–319 through 2–323.

FOB and the subsequent notation following it indicates who assumes the risk of loss should the goods be damaged in transit. In a shipping contract, the risk for loss is transferred to the buyer when goods are passed to the carrier. If the goods have been damaged before they arrive at the buyer's location, it is the buyer's responsibility to recover damages from the carrier. For example, Darby & Smith Designs was waiting for a large shipment of furniture for a radio station in Chicago. The truck was in an accident on the freeway, damaging all the furniture. Darby & Smith Designs will have to deal with the shipping company concerning claims for damages.

In destination contracts, the risk for loss is transferred to the buyer at the buyer's destination. If the goods have been damaged in transit, it is the seller's responsibility to recover the damages from the carrier. In the example, the manufacturer, not Darby & Smith Designs, must deal with the shipping company concerning claims for the damaged furniture, since the manufacturer retains title in this case.

When there is no delivery required, risk passes in different ways, depending on whether or not the seller is a merchant. If the seller is a merchant, then risk passes when the buyer receives the goods. If the seller is not a merchant, then risk passes when the seller gives the merchandise to the buyer. This very subtle difference is there only to show that a merchant selling goods has more responsibility concerning the damage of undelivered goods than a nonmerchant seller. Additional discussions concerning FOB and shipping can be found in Chapters 25 and 31.

SALES ON APPROVAL

A common special sale situation in the interior design profession is the *sale on approval*. In this situation the client is not sure about a product and takes it to his or her home or business location in order to see if it is appropriate. If the client subsequently keeps the product, he or she pays for it; otherwise, he or she is obligated to return the product. As with any kind of sale, it is best practice to have the client sign an appropriate document indicating that the item is on approval and the length of time the item can remain in the client's possession.

There is a normal condition to the sale on approval regulated by the UCC that is explained by the following example. Jane Miller finds a sofa on a showroom floor but is not sure that it will go with her decor. She asks if she can try it "on approval." The store allows her five days to decide. If she calls and says that she will keep the sofa before the five days are up or fails to call before the five days and makes no attempt to return the sofa, the store considers the sofa as sold and sends her a bill. If Miller damages the sofa before the five days are up and before she approves of the sale, the loss is Miller's. If it is damaged in transit or in some way but through no fault of Miller, the loss is the seller's (Sections 2–326 and 2–327).

THE SELLER'S RIGHTS AND OBLIGATIONS

Many laws have been passed to protect consumers from unscrupulous sellers. Although the concept of "buyer beware" is still a reasonable caution, the seller also has rights as well as obligations. A key issue for many designers is the concern that the buyer will cancel the order or want to change the order after it has been placed with a supplier. Designers as sellers should protect themselves from these problems by including clauses in the sales agreement that stipulate under what conditions an order can be canceled or changed. Many designers indicate that restocking charges will be assessed if the client cancels an order. This *restocking charge* is considered a fee to cover the paperwork costs that have already been accumulated, as well as a small penalty for taking back merchandise that the client does not want. In almost all cases, a manufacturer will charge the designer a restocking charge for canceling an order as well. The buyer's right to cancel a contract is discussed in the next section, "The Buyer's Rights and Obligations."

The seller has other rights when the buyer refuses to accept the goods or in some other way breaches the sales contract. In general, when the buyer breaches the sales contract, the seller is allowed to withhold delivery of the goods. One situation involves partial deliveries to clients. For example, Sarah Randolph ordered new dining room and living room furniture from Smyth's Interiors. Smyth's delivered the living room furniture, but the dining room items were not in yet. Since the goods had been delivered, Smyth's billed Randolph for the partial delivery. Randolph refused to pay the bill. It must be clearly stated in the terms and conditions on the sales contract from Smyth's Interiors that partial deliveries would be billed separately. As long as this is the case, then Randolph would be in breach of contract. Smyth's could withhold delivery of the other furniture items until Randolph paid for the previous delivery.

Another frequent problem for designers occurs when a client claims that the items delivered are not those specified in the sales agreement. Most frequently, this concerns a color of fabric. Let us say that New Age Foods ordered 50 forest green upholstered chairs. When the chairs were delivered, New Age Foods claimed that the chairs were not the right color green and refused to accept and pay for the goods. If the designer can show that the fabric was substantially the correct color (barring anything greater than a dye lot variation), the buyer would be in breach of contract to refuse acceptance of the order. The designer, on written notification, would have a right to cancel the order and could sue the client for breach of contract. However, if the designer was not justified in canceling the order, the buyer could sue the designer for breach of contract.

In some situations the seller may resort to canceling the contract with the buyer when the buyer has breached the contract (UCC 2–703[f]). A breach may mean that the client has refused to pay for the goods or wrongly refuses delivery of the goods. Canceling the contract requires notification to the client that he or she is in breach and that the client is still obligated to pay for any goods already delivered. A cancellation clause is again important in the sales agreement in the first place to better protect the designer should this situation occur. It is advisable to negotiate with the client over the issues rather than resort quickly to canceling future deliveries, however.

If a client becomes insolvent while he or she has taken delivery but has not yet paid for the goods, the designer has the right to demand the return of the goods. This must be done quickly, however. The written demand for the return of the goods usually must be done within ten days of delivery of the goods.

It is unfortunate that one of the common problems interior designers face with clients is disagreements concerning what was ordered versus what was delivered. Often this is caused by the designer using vague descriptions of goods in sales agreements. The seller has an obligation to deliver the goods described in the sales agreement within a specified time period. In most situations, any discrepancy in what was delivered versus what was ordered is the responsibility of the seller. Designers must protect themselves from the potentiality of a buyer trying to cancel an order, refuse an order, or refuse to pay for goods. This can be done by being very careful in writing up the descriptions of the goods on the sales order, getting the buyer's signature on the sales order, carefully preparing the purchase order, and checking on the progress of orders.

To mitigate the problem of a client saying that the fabric (or other finish) color is not correct, designers order a cutting or sample from current stock that is sufficient to fulfill the order. The designer does not actually place the order for the goods until the sample has been received and approved by the designer and client. If the delivered goods are as described, the buyer knows what will be ordered, and the buyer knows the terms and conditions of the sale, the buyer has no choice but to pay for the goods. Table 26-1 lists some hints on how to avoid problems in selling goods.

THE BUYER'S RIGHTS AND OBLIGATIONS

Special-order and custom goods ordered for a client often create challenges for the interior designer. Because of long lead times for delivery, clients might forget what the product that they approved three months ago looks like. They may remember that the fabric was a different color. Details in design might now be foggy to them, since many special orders and customs are ordered from photographs and drawings rather than after seeing an actual item. These examples are only a few of the challenges the designer faces. These challenges also relate to buyer's rights and obligations related to the sale of goods. Although the discussion and examples focus on the client as a buyer, these buyer's rights and obligations also apply to the interior designer in his or her relationship with vendors and suppliers.

If the seller has delivered the goods that are described in the sales contract, the buyer has an obligation to pay for those goods. Because of this obligation, it is important for the interior designer to describe what is to be ordered on the sales agreement in sufficient detail so that the client clearly understands what he or she is purchasing. If the sales agreement states, "one 30 by 60 desk," there is a

TABLE 26-1.

Tips That May Help the Designer Avoid Problems When Selling Goods.

- Fully describe on the sales agreement the goods to be ordered and sold. Include dimensions, finish selection, and/or fabric name and color number for furniture items. Include similar information for other products.
- Do not process any purchase orders until the client has signed the sales agreement and has provided the required prepayment.
- Be sure to go over the terms and conditions on your sales agreement with each new client and whenever a client orders goods from the firm.
- Obtain credit reports on all new clients.
- Request textile cuttings of current stock to ensure color matches are correct before finalizing the purchase with the supplier.
- If you use faxes or e-mails to order goods, make sure that you receive a report copy of the fax that the supplier has received the purchase order and/or that you print a hard copy of all e-mails that you send or receive concerning purchases, acknowledgments, and quotes.
- Obtain client signatures or initials, approving all goods that might be questioned, such as upholstered furniture items.
- Make sure that your terms and conditions concerning the client's right to cancel an order are clear and protect the design firm. Be certain that you also explain the client's legal rights to cancel an order.
- Work only with manufacturers and suppliers who provide reputable service and goods. Understand the terms and conditions of sale from every supplier with whom the firm does business.
- Keep the client informed of the progress of all special orders.
- Inspect all merchandise at the time of delivery to the firm's warehouse. Make sure this is done prior to paying the supplier in full.
- Insist that the client signs off on all delivered goods. Take care of any discrepancies immediately so that the client has little room to argue for nonpayment.

lot of room for argument on both sides as to whether the right desk actually has been delivered. However, if the sales order states, "one Stowe-Davis, Number 3060DP, 30 by 60, double-pedestal desk; finish, walnut; trim, polished chrome," there is very little disagreement as to what was to be ordered and what was delivered.

Any modification in what has been delivered versus what is described gives the buyer the right to refuse the delivery. If the delivered goods are as described in the sales agreement, they are referred to as *conforming goods*. If the goods are somehow different, they are nonconforming goods. *Nonconforming goods* are simply any goods that are not as described in an order.

The buyer is also obligated to make payment for the delivered conforming goods in accordance with the terms in the sales agreement. For example, if the terms are cash payment upon delivery, the designer expects the client to pay in cash or at least with a check. If the terms are a credit purchase, the buyer is expected to make payment within the time frame indicated in the sales agreement. COD shipments are valid only if COD shipment has been agreed to in the sales contract (Section 2–601).

The buyer also has a right to inspect the goods prior to paying for them. When the designer sells goods to the client, the client has the right to inspect the items to be sure that the delivered goods are those specified in the sales agreement. The buyer may refuse the goods if in any respect they do not conform to what is described in the sales agreement. He or she may also accept any part of the order or reject the nonconforming goods, or even accept the goods even if they are nonconforming.

If they are nonconforming goods, the buyer (designer or client) has the right to refuse the goods (or any part of the order that is nonconforming) and to not pay for the nonconforming goods. Designers purchasing goods for the client also have the right to inspect the goods prior to paying the supplier. Even though it is common for the manufacturer to send a bill for goods prior to the designer receiving the goods, the designer has a right to inspect and verify that the order is correct prior to being obligated to pay for the goods. According to the UCC, this right is absolute for all buyers, except for COD orders (Section 2[606a]). This is just one reason that it is very important for the designer to check all deliveries from manufacturers and suppliers.

If the buyer rejects the goods as nonconforming, the buyer must promptly notify the seller of the same. A telephone call is notice, but the written notice is more binding, since it is tangible evidence. Written notification with a full description of what the problems are is the best way to provide notification. If the buyer does not provide notice and retains the goods, the seller expects the buyer to pay for those goods.

The longer the goods are in the hands of the buyer, the more likely it is that the buyer will be obligated to pay for the goods, even if they are nonconforming: "Inaction results in acceptance."[9] The buyer's failure to inspect and reject the goods within a stated or reasonable time period constitutes acceptance. If the buyer rejects some or all of the goods as nonconforming but uses the goods without prior agreement from the seller, the buyer is taking ownership of the goods and the seller by law expects the buyer to pay for the goods.

State laws generally allow buyers a *72-hour right of refusal* concerning any contract signed in the home or other location, not the seller's place of business. In some states, this is called a three-day right of cancellation. This means that even if the goods are as ordered, the buyer has 72 hours in which to return the goods and receive full repayment. In many states, this right of refusal only applies to contracts signed in the buyer's residence. The right of refusal allowance for contracts signed in a residence was developed to protect buyers from feeling pressured into purchasing from a seller who has come to the residence. The exact conditions of the right of refusal vary by state and can be researched by visiting the Web sites for the office of the state attorney general.

Although many companies have the philosophy that "the customer is always right," according to sales law, this is not necessarily true. Designers who buy and sell goods need to understand not only their rights as a seller but also the rights of buyers.

SUMMARY

Many interior designers buy and sell goods almost every day of their practice. Many find that selling goods to clients is often a profitable way of producing revenues for the interior design practice. But the buying and selling of goods also has many legal considerations and constraints. Although it is easy for a designer to write a purchase order for goods, there are many regulations that govern legally how that order can be placed, how ownership of the goods can change hands, and what responsibility the seller has to the buyer concerning defects or injury that might be caused by the goods.

In this chapter, I have tried to explain the basic concepts of the law of sales, as regulated by the Uniform Commercial Code. I have defined basic terms related to sales and selling, and we have discussed how a sales contract is made and noted how a sales contract is different from a normal contract. We have also briefly discussed the Statute of Frauds. Also included was a revised section on electronic agreements and signatures, as well as explanations of when title and risk passes from the seller to the buyer and the responsibility of the seller and buyer in selling goods.

Although the UCC standardizes most of the laws related to the sale of goods, the designer must still check with the firm's attorney to know which part of the code is valid in his or her state and if there are any state or city regulations that supersede the UCC.

REFERENCES

1. Stone, 1975, p. 2.
2. Clarkson et al., 1983, p. 9.
3. Miller, Jentz, 2006, p. 331.
4. National Conference of Commissioners on Uniform State Laws, 2003 Amendments UCC Article 2, summary p. 2. Available on Web site, www.nccusl.org.
5. Quinn, 1999, p. 2/201.
6. Quinn, 1999, p. 2/201.
7. Miller, Jentz, 2006, p. 314.
8. Miller, Jentz, 2006, p. 316.
9. Quinn, 1999, p. 2/201.

CHAPTER 27

Warranties and Product Liability

Key Terms and Concepts

These key terms and concepts are important to material in this chapter. Many of these terms will be utilized in other chapters as well. Be sure you understand these items as you read this chapter.

Terms and Concepts

Warranty

Warranty of title

Express warranty

Implied warranty of merchantability

Implied warranty of fitness for a particular purpose

As is

Products liability

Strict liability

Critical Issues

After completing this chapter you should be able to:

- Discuss the intent of product warranties.
- Compare the warranty of title to the express warranty.
- Differentiate a statement of express warranty from puffing.
- Explain the implied warranty of merchantability.
- Explain why it is critical for interior designers to be cautious in how they describe the suitability of products for any particular client project.
- Explain why or why not an interior designer is liable if a client is injured because of the failure of a product specified by the interior designer.
- Discuss the difference between a full and limited warranty.
- Discuss product liability and professional negligence.
- List the elements that a litigant must prove to show negligence in a strict liability cause of action.

"I know you are concerned about traffic paths showing because of the traffic with your four children using the family room and play room. This plush carpet will not show traffic paths because it is thicker and denser," the interior designer told the client. "The color will also help with this concern," the designer continued. Finally convinced by what the designer said, Mrs. Jones instructed the interior designer to go ahead and order the carpet. Six months after installation and when the client cleaned the carpet, she called the designer complaining about the fact that traffic paths did remain after cleaning. She demanded that the carpet be replaced at no cost to her.

Today's litigious society means that interior designers must fully understand the implications of warranties and product liability. Specifying and selling furniture and other goods to clients creates a legal responsibility. Whether the designer sells furniture, fixtures, and equipment for a small residential studio or specifies large quantities of products for a commercial project, the client expects to receive properly specified goods. Many are concerned about the wear and tear and maintenance of the items specified, whether in a home or commercial facility, because maintenance costs time and money.

A designer specializing in assisted-living facilities and senior-living apartments specified tables and chairs for the dining room of an assisted-living facility. From the catalog literature, the designer is convinced that the chairs would be appropriate for the ambulatory residents who sit in the assisted-living area of the facility. After all, the manufacturer is one of the many that specialized in furnishings for health-care facilities. Would it be fair for your firm to be held responsible if any of the chairs, within a reasonable time frame, broke, causing harm to one of the residents? This is the type of question that this chapter will address.

Designers are liable for the performance of the products that are specified in any project. They can also be held accountable for what they say about products and how the product might perform for the client's situation. Products must meet the expectations of reasonable use and fitness for the situation in which they will be used. The first part of the chapter on warranties is directly related to these concepts.

Product liability is directly related to the designer's specification of goods and products, since many of these items can, if improperly made or installed, cause physical harm or damage to the client's property. The designer is responsible for making sure that the products are specified and installed in such a way as not to cause injury to the people who will use the products or cause damage to the space in which the products will be installed. The second half of the chapter discusses these issues.

Product liability is based on warranty as well as negligence. The reader is advised to return to Chapter 4 and review the section on negligence in order to fully appreciate the information in this chapter.

WARRANTIES

Interior designers and their clients often rely on the word or deeds of others based on some fact or assurance. In contract and sales law, a warranty is "a promise that something in furtherance of the contract is guaranteed by one of the contractor, especially the seller's promise that the thing being sold is as promised or represented."[1] Buyers regularly ask questions about warranties—or written guarantees—on many of the products that they purchase. The days when the phrase "buyer beware" was standard for consumers has long since past. Consumers are protected by a large number of regulations and laws that place much of the burden on the marketplace to provide safe products rather than on the buyer to be wary. Other regulations and laws help to satisfy the customer so that what he or she purchases meets correct standards of design, manufacturing, and use. Warranties are one way that the buyer is protected.

Warranties place a burden on the seller that the goods he or she sells meet certain standards. Four important kinds of warranties are governed by the UCC when commercial sales occur:

1. Warranty of title (Section 2-312)
2. Express warranty (Section 2-313)
3. Implied warranty of merchantability (Section 2-314)
4. Implied warranty of fitness for a particular purpose (Section 2-315)

When a designer or a design firm offers a warranty on a product, failure to honor that warranty is a breach of contract duty and gives the client the right to sue. The seller's breach also allows the customer to cancel the order.

Warranty of Title

The first aspect of warranty of title is that the seller has title to the goods and can legally sell them to others. Title signifies legal ownership of the goods, and this warranty routinely exists when goods are sold, since only the legal owner can legally sell the goods. Basically, this means that the seller, knowingly or not, is not selling stolen goods or goods that he or she does not have authorization to sell. For example, Jason had a chair in his studio for almost a year on approval from a vendor. Jason sold the chair to a client who liked it. If Jason did not subsequently pay the vendor for the chair, he had no warranty of title to sell the chair. Here is another example. If an interior design firm does not have authority to buy and sell Steelcase systems from Steelcase because it does not have an agreement as a Steelcase dealer, the firm would not be able to tell the client that it could purchase the goods from Steelcase and sell the products to the client. Since the design firm cannot take title to the goods from Steelcase, it cannot pass the title on to the client.

A second aspect of warranty of title is that the buyer is protected from loss if he or she unknowingly buys goods with a lien attached. A *lien* means that someone other than the person who has ownership or possession of the goods has a security interest in the goods. In the example with Jason, the vendor who actually owned the chair had a security interest in the goods and could have filed a lien against Jason for selling the chair. The buyer of the chair probably did not know that Jason did not actually have title, thus he or she would be protected and would be entitled to recover the cost of the chair if the vendor actually filed a lien. If the buyer buys the goods knowing that there is a lien, he or she will not be able to collect from the seller.

A third aspect of warranty of title concerns infringement. This means that the goods do not have any patent, copyright, or trademark claimed by anyone. For example, a designer creates a logo for a client of the design firm in which he works, and the copyright is registered by the design firm. However, the client was not shown the design at that time. Six months later, the designer starts a design practice and contacts the former client about possible work.

The client hires the designer to produce a logo and is shown the logo that the designer has designed for his previous employer. The client has bought that design and has incorporated it into all of the client's letterhead. The original design firm can sue both the client and the designer for infringement.

Express Warranty

Nora's client was very concerned that the wall covering that was to be used in the locker room of a country club would hold up to moisture. Nora told the client that the grass cloth was specially treated to resist moisture; thus the client gave the go-ahead to order and install the grass cloth. Unfortunately, the claim was untrue. Promises, claims, descriptions, or affirmations made about a product's performance, quality, or condition that form the "basis of the bargain" is an *express warranty*. In effect, the *basis of the bargain* means that the information provided is what primarily influences the decision of the buyer. Interior designers and salespeople, in the course of their discussions with clients about a product's viability, often make statements about what the product can or cannot do. When are these statements covered under express warranty and when are they not? It depends on the words used or circumstances surrounding the sales interaction.

The seller does not need to use words such as *warranty* or *guarantee* in the sales presentation, nor does he or she even need to intend to make such a warranty. How precise these statements have to be and how strongly they must be worded is not clear in the UCC, so care must be taken to say exactly what is meant to avoid misunderstandings. Nora's comment that the grass cloth was specially treated created an express warranty. Goods that are sold based on a sample are also creating express warranties. For example, many designers sell merchandise from a catalog, with the client never seeing the piece before purchase and delivery. The goods delivered must conform to what was displayed in the catalog. Designers who sell goods in this way need to be sure they clarify fabric choices, wood or metal finishes, and so forth on sales orders so that what is ordered is clear to the client.

When statements made by the seller are only the seller's opinion or relate only to the worth of the product generally, no express warranty is made. For example, Jim Jones says to a client, "This is the best open-office system on the market." It is an expression of opinion, not based on statements of fact. This kind of salesmanship is called *puffing*. On the other hand, such a statement from Jim Jones as "This wood flooring is care-free" is a promise that can be interpreted by the customer as meaning that he or she will not have to wax the floor. In this situation, an express warranty very likely is being made by Jones. It is very likely an express warranty because, like so much in the law, different judges can interpret the words and intention behind the words in many ways. Therefore, care should always be taken when using words that express quality.

If the salesperson is believed to be an expert concerning the goods being sold, the statements of opinion are more likely to constitute express warranties. Although opinions expressed by an interior designer who specifies but does not sell products about a manufacturer's product would probably be considered puffing, the statements made by a manufacturer's representative who has worked for that company for many years could be considered express warranties. Since the UCC does not make it clear what puffing is and what an expression of warranty is, it is important to be careful when making statements about quality and performance of a product. If the statement is reasonable and a reasonable person believes the statement, a warranty may be created.

Implied Warranty of Merchantability

The implied warranty of merchantability affects sales made by merchants. When a client purchases goods from an interior designer, the designer is considered a merchant by the UCC. It is implied that when a merchant sells goods, the seller understands the characteristics of the goods he or she is selling and can thus specify them for proper use. Implied warranties exist as operations of law. In its simplest form, the UCC says that the goods must be "fit for the ordinary purposes for which such goods are used."[2] As long as the merchant is a merchant of the kind of goods in consideration, he or she is held liable. Thus, a desk sold by an interior designer to the owner of a real estate office automatically has an implied warranty of merchantability associated with the desk.

Under this section of the UCC, goods sold must be of fair to average quality and must be comparable in quality to other similar goods. They must be fit for the normal purpose of the good. They must be packaged and labeled adequately, and must conform to the statements made on the packaging or labels. For example, strippable wallpaper must be strippable; fire-retardant fabric must not ignite or burn within the limits stated on the binder; a solid brass headboard must be made of solid brass.

This section of the UCC makes an implied warranty of merchantability applicable to every sale by a merchant. Liability does not disappear even if the merchant is unaware of any defect in the product. The interior designer most likely will be liable, along with the manufacturer, when a product fails or causes some injury to a person or property.

Implied Warranty of Fitness for a Particular Purpose

Implied warranty of fitness for a particular purpose affects the goods that any seller—merchant or not—sells to another. When the seller knows the intended purpose for the goods and the buyer must rely on the seller's knowledge to select or recommend goods for the purpose, an implied warranty of fitness for a particular purpose exists.

The seller does not need to know the exact purpose of the purchase. If he or she has a general idea of the purpose and if the buyer has relied on the seller's knowledge or skill in selecting the goods, an implied warranty of fitness also has been created. For example, Mrs. Damon hires John Simmons to redecorate her home. As part of the services offered, Simmons sells to Damon the wall coverings for the kitchen and the bathrooms. Damon makes it clear to Simmons that the wallpaper in the bathroom must be able to withstand a lot of steam and dampness, since her husband takes long, hot showers. A few weeks after installation, the wallpaper begins to peel away. Since Simmons knew the purpose of the goods and Damon relied on the professional knowledge of Simmons, a breach of an implied warranty of fitness exists. Of course, the paperhanger, if he or she also knew the purpose of the purchase, is also liable for breach.

Magnuson-Moss Warranty Act

The Federal Trade Commission (FTC) enforces the Magnuson-Moss Warranty Act. This legislation was enacted to make it easier for the consumer to understand what is being warranted in any product sold to end users. Warranties between merchants are regulated by the UCC rules.

The act does not require that sellers provide a written warranty for goods sold to consumers. If the cost of the consumer goods is more than $10 and a seller chooses to make an express written warranty, the warranty must be labeled as "full" or "limited." In addition, if the goods have a value of over $15, the Magnuson-Moss Warranty Act requires that a written warranty be provided to the potential consumer.[3] In this case, who warrants the goods, what is covered, any limitations, the legal rights of the consumer, and how enforcement is made must all be spelled out.

Full warranties require repair or replacement at no charge to the buyer should goods be defective. There cannot be a time limit for the replacement. If there is, it is not a full warranty but, rather, a limited warranty. When repairs cannot be made in a reasonable time, the product must be replaced or a refund must be given the consumer. Limited warranties must be clearly stated as to what is warranted and the time limit of the warranty.

Disclaimers of Warranty

An express warranty can be disclaimed if the manufacturer or seller does not make any express promises or statements of fact relating to or describing the goods. Designers must always be careful about what they say concerning the performance, suitability, or other factual statements about products they specify and/or sell. This is true whether the statements are written or verbal. Saying "We guarantee that this fabric will not show wear for five years" constitutes an express warranty. A disclaimer to that statement might be this: "We provide no warranty beyond that of the manufacturer, and their tests under normal use in a home indicate the fabric will show no significant wear for five years."

An implied warranty of merchantability can be verbal, but it must be specific as to disclaiming merchantability and must use the term *merchantability* in the oral or written disclaimer. For example, Michael Cobb of Cobb Designs sells Mr. Smith a budget-priced guest chair to be used as a desk chair based on the needs described by Smith. Cobb verbally informs Smith that he does not warrant merchantability of the chair, since it is not fit for use as a desk chair. Cobb also attaches a note, making the same disclaimer to the sales agreement. The chair does not hold up, and Smith wants Cobb to replace it. Since it was disclaimed as to merchantability, Cobb is not liable to replace the chair on those grounds.

An implied warranty-of-fitness disclaimer must be in writing and displayed prominently. Using the term *warranty of fitness* in the disclaimer is strongly suggested, though the term *fitness* is not required. For example, a designer sells a client a kitchen stool with a cane seat, which will be used at a kitchen counter. The confirmation says something like, "ABS Designs provides no warranty of fitness beyond that of the manufacturer's for normal, reasonable use." A few weeks after purchase, the client uses the stool to stand on and the cane breaks, resulting in injury to the client. The designer is not liable, since the client was using the stool in a manner that was not normal and reasonable for the product.

Disclaimers of fitness are also written with such words as *as is*. It is common to see retailers label used furniture "as is" to protect themselves against claims on used or damaged goods. According to the UCC, however, even new merchandise is sold "as is" to imply that no warranty other than what the manufacturer has provided exists.

If a client refuses to inspect goods before signing a delivery ticket, there is no implied warranty concerning defects. This is because the client has refused, for whatever reason, to inspect the goods prior to acceptance. If the seller does not ask the buyer to inspect the goods and the goods are damaged or defective, the seller is liable.

What Would You Do?

Shelly's job responsibilities included interior design services as well as selling furniture and accessories. Her income was partially dependent upon commission on the sales of furniture, although that commission was not a very high percent on the sale.

Mr. Robinson had talked to Shelly two previous times about the layout of his restaurant, and now they were discussing specific products for the interior. "Well, I keep saying that this chair will not hold up for use in a restaurant, even with vinyl fabric for the upholstery. It is just too flimsy. I think you need to move up in price to this chair, which has better quality construction and nicer fabrics," said Shelly to Mr. Robinson.

"Well, I don't know. This whole thing is beginning to cost me way more than what I figured and what you estimated when we first sat down to talk about the project. You keep trying to upgrade me on the products. I've checked on the Internet about the less costly chair, and it is supposed to be a commercial-grade chair," replied Mr. Robinson.

"Look, Mr. Robinson, if you insist on buying the cheaper chair, we will not be responsible if it doesn't hold up," retorted Shelly.

PRODUCTS LIABILITY

As consumers, we expect the products we purchase to be safe and not cause harm. When interior designers purchase products for clients from a manufacturer, the designer expects the same safety of design and manufacture. There is an expectation that the products will meet certain minimal standards of materials, workmanship, and design for its intended use. If the products fail, certain express or implied warranties may have been breached. Manufacturers and sellers of products may be liable to end users, bystanders, and other merchants if individuals are physically harmed or if property damage occurs. This is called *products liability*. Products liability includes the areas of tort law related to negligence and strict liability and contract law related to warranty.

Products Liability and Negligence

In Chapter 4, we defined negligence as a failure to use the care that is expected of a reasonable person, and this failure to use care results in injury to another person or his or her property. Manufacturers of products must use this same care in the design, materials selection, production, and testing of their products so that they will be safe when they are used as intended.

Mr. and Mrs. Franklin purchased a dining room suite, including eight chairs, for their new home from interior designer May Jefferson. Jefferson knew that the manufacturer was a reputable company and had used the company's products numerous times. The Franklins liked the style of chair and relied upon Jefferson's expertise in design when they approved the chairs. The Franklins gave a dinner party a short time after the chairs had been delivered. One of the guests leaned back on the chair, causing the chair to tilt up and rock on its back legs. One leg cracked, causing the chair to collapse, and, consequently, the arm of the guest was broken. The guest attempted to sue the manufacturer and the designer.

In a tort case, the person that was in some way harmed or injured is also referred to as the plaintiff. In situations concerning product liability, the plaintiff must show that the manufacturer did not use due care and that the defective product caused an injury. The plaintiff must also show that he or she used the product as designed and knew the risk of using the product incorrectly. In the example about the Franklins, the injured guest's products liability lawsuit would only succeed if he could prove that the chair had been manufactured improperly, that the chair had been sold in a defective condition, and that he had been using the chair for its intended purpose. Although the designer did not specify the chairs for "rocking," Jefferson would be involved in the lawsuit because she had specified the chair. The example tries to show that, regardless of what the intended purpose of a product, clients might use their purchases in ways that could cause them harm and could leave the designer open to legal problems.

Designers must take the time to be sure that they specify products that are suitable for a client's use and that the client has been warned if the designer feels the client is demanding a product that is unsuitable for the client's use. If the designer believes the client wants an unsuitable product, the designer should be willing to refuse the order—after diplomatically suggesting more suitable alternatives. Should this just not be possible, written disclaimers, indicating that warnings have been given and that the designer accepts no responsibility for misuse, should be given to the client, and a copy should be kept on file. This procedure may not eliminate all liability, but it would show the court that a conscientious effort to warn the client has been made.

Strict Liability

Strict liability means that "a seller is liable for any and all defective or hazardous products which unduly threaten a consumer's personal safety."[4] It is also a legal doctrine related to negligence regardless of fault. Strict liability specifically related to products exists to protect the consumer from harm as a result of products sold to any consumer. This is true in spite of the seller's intentions or care; however, "the principal consideration under the doctrine of strict liability is the safety of the product, not the conduct of the manufacturer or supplier of the goods."[5]

Whenever the interior designer specifies a product, if the product fails, causing injury, the designer is almost always named in the lawsuit along with the manufacturer. The designer is included in the suite because tort law related to product liability allows that anyone involved in the distribution of products can be held liable. It should be remembered that product liability usually is concerned only with reasonable, normal use of a product. If the client uses a product in a way in which it was not designed for use, the interior designer is not held liable.

Strict liability is sometimes called liability without fault. Generally considered a negligence tort, liability without fault involves some act that has departed from the use of reasonable care. For the designer, this may result from putting incorrect information in drawings, documents, and/or specifications that causes injury. For example, if the designer incorrectly labels a material in a construction drawing and the structure later fails, causing injury, the designer is responsible, based on this premise.

For strict liability to be applied to a products liability case, the plaintiff must prove the following:

1. The goods were defective when purchased.
2. The seller or manufacturer was in the business of selling the product.
3. The defective goods would be unreasonably dangerous to any user.
4. Physical injury occurred to the plaintiff or to his or her property.
5. At the time of the injury, the goods were substantially in the same condition as when they had been purchased.

For example, Mr. Shasta of Shasta Commercial Interiors orders fabric from a textile company that is described as fire retardant for use on restaurant booths. A few months after the fabric has been installed, a dropped cigarette smolders and ignites it, causing extensive damage to the restaurant. A strict liability case is brought against the textile company and (probably) the designer, if it can be shown that the goods were defective at the time of purchase. Further, it has to be shown that injury was caused to the premises, that the untreated fabric was dangerous in its use, and that the fabric was in a basically unchanged condition since purchase. Although most of the liability in this case rests on the manufacturer of the fabric, there is nothing in tort law or in the UCC to prevent the unknowing designer from also being held liable.

Liability without Fault for Design Defects

Interior designers create many design elements and custom products. Designers also specify and sell products that primarily have been designed and manufactured by someone else. In both cases, the designer may be liable if the design of the specified product causes injury due to defective design. For example, Mary Nixon designed and produced the drawings for a custom table desk. The table desk was manufactured according to the specifications and drawings provided by Nixon. Three months after delivery, the client was propped on the front edge of the table desk (but he was not actually sitting on the desk). The desk leg nearest where the client was propped split at the joint, causing the client to fall on his left side and break his left arm. It would appear that there was a design defect in the way the joint between the top of the table leg and the table desktop was designed. The specifications and drawings provided by Nixon appear to have been inadequate for safely using the desk for its intended purpose. It could be argued that the design was adequate as a desk. Had the client been actually sitting on the desk, Nixon would less likely have been held liable, since a desk is generally not designed to be sat upon.

Interior designers must be careful that the custom treatments and products that they design are properly designed and meet performance standards relating to the structural integrity of the design. Those who are unfamiliar with product design should either refrain from creating custom designs themselves or retain the services of product designers, craftspeople, or other appropriate experts to help in the design of custom goods. Designers also need to be constantly vigilant that the goods that are specified from manufacturers are designed safely and have no history of liability from design defects.

Warranty Law and Products Liability

Warranty law and products liability is the only portion of products liability related to the UCC. All other law related to products liability is found in tort and contract law. Warranty responsibility and product liability are based on the areas of warranties that have been discussed in the previous sections. They are mentioned here in relation to an injury to a third party.

In contract law, the only parties that have regress for injuries are the parties to the contract. However, much of what is governed by the UCC easily affects third parties who are not a part of the original contract. The UCC provides regulations that make the manufacturers and/or sellers liable to injuries to parties who are not a part of the original contract. For example, Mrs. Johnson hires an interior design company to redecorate her home. Through this company, she has some wall-hung shelves installed in the living room. One day, a bracket pulls out of the wall so that a shelf strikes a guest of Johnson. The guest sustains a head injury. If it were not for UCC Section 2-318, the guest would not be able to sue the installer for an implied warranty of merchantability—only Johnson could.

However, the UCC is not clear as to how responsible sellers and manufacturers are. It was written with three alternatives, which give different levels of responsibility. Alternative A is limited to household members and their guests who use or are injured by the goods. Alternative B is broader, not limiting injury to family members or guests, and alternative C is the broadest, protecting anyone who is injured by the defective product. Thus, should someone who is using a product sustain some injury if the product fails, though he or she did not purchase the product, the person has grounds for filing a lawsuit.

SUMMARY

Whether the interior designer specifies goods for projects or specifies and sells goods to the client, the designer has many legal responsibilities related to those professional tasks. It matters very little whether an interior designer primarily does residential spaces or commercial spaces. The public and the profession expect that anyone who is engaged in the practice of interior design will accept the legal responsibility of his or her practice activities. Far too many consumers choose not to accept responsibility and blame others for their problems or misfortunes. Thus, it becomes even more necessary for the interior designer to understand and accept his or her legal responsibilities.

The legal responsibilities that were described in this chapter should be of concern to any size or type of design practice. Of course, the size and complexity of many commercial projects makes the commercial interior designer more exposed to liability, especially as concerns warranties and products liability.

Specifying and selling goods and materials to consumers as part of one's interior design business comes with legal responsibilities and sometimes consequences. Constant care is very important. The designer (1) should not get involved in design projects that may be out of his or her area of expertise, (2) must understand the needs of the client so that he or she can create proper specifications that go beyond aesthetic decisions, (3) must take care to specify products that he or she is familiar with or has researched, and (4) must maintain accurate records to limit his or her liability.

REFERENCES

1. *Oxford American College Dictionary*, 2002, p. 1594.
2. Quinn, 1991, p. 2.
3. Miller and Jentz, 2006, p. 394.
4. Black, 1990, p. 1422.
5. Brown and Sukys, 1997, p. 263.

*A*s a healthcare designer, I look forward to greater understanding about the effect of the built environment on healing and to healthcare providers having an appreciation of the factors that play a role in the physical, emotional, and spiritual well-being of patients, their families, and staff. At the new millennium, interior designers have much to celebrate in the level of professionalism that has been achieved in a relatively brief period and in the number of projects of outstanding merit.

Jain Malkin is President and founder of a San Diego, California interior architecture firm that specializes in healthcare facilities. Her pioneering efforts to create life-enhancing hospital interiors have won her international acclaim and several first-place design awards. Malkin has lectured widely and written numerous articles on the psychological effects of healthcare environments. Through her publications she has been recognized for her research-based approach to the design of healing environments. She is the author of *Hospital Interior Architecture* and *Medical and Dental Space Planning: A Comprehensive Guide to Design, Equipment, and Clinical Procedures* and her new book *A Visual Reference to Evidence-based Design*.

Courtesy Jain Malkin Inc.
www.JainMalkin.com
Photographer: Steve McClelland

Photographer: Gary McGuire

Project Management

32. Contract Administration: Delivery and Project Closeout

Delivery and Installation
Project Closeout
Postoccupancy and Follow-up

CHAPTER 28

The Project Management Process

Key Terms and Concepts

These key terms and concepts are important to material in this chapter. Many of these terms will be utilized in other chapters as well. Be sure you understand these items as you read this chapter.

Terms and Concepts

Project management	Transmittal letter
Project manager	Stakeholders
Design process	Single source of contact
Programming	Owner's representative
Schematic design	Milestone chart
Design development	Bar chart
Contract documents	Gantt chart
Contract administration	Critical path method (CPM)
Work plan	Time management
Deliverables	80/20 rule
Competitive bidding	Time records
Walk-through	Project file
Punch list	Value engineering

Critical Issues

After completing this chapter you should be able to:

- Discuss why project management is an important responsibility of an interior designer.
- List and discuss at least six key tasks of a project manager.
- Discuss typical tasks of the phases of a design project and how these tasks are impacted by the responsibilities of a project manager.
- List and explain deliverables that are common to a residential project and a commercial project.

■ Explain the interaction responsibilities between a project manager and clients, and between a project manager and consultants for the project.

■ Describe the differences between a milestone chart, a bar chart, and a CPM chart for scheduling a design project.

■ Discuss methods of project budgeting.

■ Explain the importance of time management and time recording for interior designers.

■ List and discuss the types of items that are important to retain in a project job file.

■ Discuss how value engineering can help satisfy a client's need for budget control.

It does not matter if the newest project a firm has obtained is a new casino hotel or the remodeling of a second home. Other than the context of size, the project process and phases are essentially the same. All projects must be managed so that the required work is done quickly, correctly, and with as few problems as possible—all the while remaining on track to also bring the design firm a reasonable profit. This is not an easy task. Projects rarely progress without an assortment of challenges, worries, and delays.

All of the graphic documents and specifications that the student finds familiar in the completion of studio projects is only part of the process of completing a project. Rarely do they have the opportunity to sit in on one of the many meetings between a designer and the client or the designer and any of the other stakeholders who are likely involved in the design, construction, and installation of an interiors project. Rarely do they see the detailed record keeping that must be undertaken as the project progresses from the moment the design contract is signed to when the final walk-through at the completion of the installation occurs.

This chapter offers a very complete, though brief, discussion of the project management process. It begins by providing a brief overview of what project management is and the role of the project manager. A section in which the phases of a complete design project are discussed is followed by an overview of the working relationships with the various stakeholders that are part of the overall project.

The chapter continues by explaining scheduling methods that help the designer and design manager keep track of activities for each project. Other controls or project management techniques included are project budgeting, time record keeping, time management, and project files or job books. The chapter concludes with a brief discussion on value engineering—a process borrowed from architecture that has found its way into interior design.

WHAT IS PROJECT MANAGEMENT?

It really does not matter if the project is residential or commercial. Projects today can easily involve dozens of trades and certainly hundreds of types of products that must be procured, received, installed (or built), and integrated into the final interior. Thus, one of the key reasons that clients hire interior designers is for their project management skills. Certainly, interior designers are hired for their creative skills and ability to translate client needs into aesthetically pleasing and functional interiors. However, the complex nature of designing interiors today requires quality project management as well as creative design skills.

Project management is the process of organizing and controlling all the tasks and resources for an interior design project from beginning to end to satisfactorily solve the client's problems and provide a reasonable profit to the design firm. A project solution that does not solve the client's problems might be an aesthetic interior, but if it does not function or meet other needs, it will likely be considered an unsatisfactory solution. Projects must also provide a reasonable profit for the design firm regardless of the method of compensation.

Project management skills are important because of the speed with which decisions must be made and information transmitted. Clients complain if the interior designer does not get back to them within a few hours, if not a few minutes. Every client feels that his or her problem or question has priority. "It is getting difficult to project-manage today because there is so much to manage!" could be said by many interior designers today.

Effective project management begins with a detailed understanding of the client's goals and a comprehensive scope of services that defines what the design firm must do for the project. As was discussed in Chapter 24 on design contracts, the scope of services describes what must be done in essentially sequential order. The sequence of tasks should also follow the generally accepted tasks of the design process of programming, schematic design, design development, contract documents preparation and contract administration.

Project management also involves relationship management. Even when only one interior designer is responsible for the project, he or she must exercise and maintain working relationships with the client, vendors, installers, contractors, and anyone else involved. A design team can grow to dozens of individuals working for the same firm or joint ventures of design firms on mega projects. And these interior designers and project managers again must maintain effective working relationships with perhaps dozens of other stakeholders.

It is rare that a design firm is only working on one project at a time. Even a sole proprietor has to have more than one project in process. Scheduling becomes another critical task in project management. New projects are accepted after a determination of how they will fit into the schedule of existing work is resolved. Office and project schedules must be refined and managed. The designer or team members responsible for the project are all likely working on phases of different projects. Thus, everyone must become skilled at multitasking and time management.

In order to be a successfully managed project, the *project manager* (also referred to as a PM), who most often is the interior designer in charge of the project, must use both the creative and analytical sides of the brain. The client is looking for a creative solution, yet in many cases, the client is looking for a solution that solves his or her problem, whether or not it is a creative solution. The client is also looking to the interior designer to manage all the details and installation of the project. Successful project management requires many things. Key tasks of the project manager are listed in Table 28-1.

In some firms, the project manager is not an interior designer involved in the actual design solution but a specialized staff member. However, the PM's role remains to coordinate with the design team and the client and other stakeholders for the completion of the project. The hundreds if not thousands of details that can be involved from the initial meeting to the completion of the project must be controlled and coordinated by the project manager.

As for the project interior designer, he or she certainly wishes to provide a creative solution, for that is why most designers go into the interior design profession in the first place. As a businessperson, the interior designer must also execute all of his or her responsibilities so that the firm can earn a reasonable profit. Engaging in work that will not generate a reasonable profit should be left

TABLE 28-1.

Key Tasks of a Project Manager.

- Prepare the proposal and contract.
- Establish and oversee the project schedule.
- Select a project team.
- Serve as primary client contact.
- Supervise the design team.
- Establish and oversee the budget.
- Coordinate with consultants.
- Oversee the project files.
- Supervise quality control.
- Provide design input.
- Utilize good communication skills.
- Prepare and distribute project status reports.

to those times the interior designer engages in community service work. These goals are not in opposition to each other, for they require planning, communication, management, and business skills that all function together. Few designers can be successful without carefully managing their projects.

The skills used to perform project management tasks are acquired as the designer works alongside experienced interior designers. The designer learns about scheduling, for example, by first learning how long it takes for common tasks to be achieved and then by being responsible for scheduling. Learning the various management skills plays a critical part in the designer's success so that he or she can control the project instead of letting the project control the designer.

What Would You Do?

A client, Susan Brown, arrived for her appointment with Rita Jones of Master's Office Furniture carrying her laptop computer and some sample boards. After some pleasantries, Ms. Brown set up her computer in order to show her some drawings.

Susan Brown explained, "We are planning to build six urgent-care centers in the immediate vicinity and two to four more in other parts of the state. They will all have the footprint shown in these drawings. We want your firm to provide a minimal amount of design time to specify upholstery fabric and wall accessories to fit into the environment of this state. Naturally, we will be buying all the furniture and finish materials from your firm except the floor coverings. Those will be provided by the contractor."

Rita looked closely at the drawings on the laptop and noticed a design title block from a design firm in another state. The sample boards looked like a label that had been glued to the board had been removed.

"Why aren't you having the design firm that created the drawings do this work for you?" asked Rita.

"Oh, we've paid them their fee and don't want to pay them for travel to this state," replied Ms. Brown.

PHASES OF AN INTERIOR DESIGN PROJECT

Project management is best understood when the parameters of a project are defined. Those parameters are defined using the scope of services, which should follow the phases of an interiors project. These phases mirror project phases in architecture, and most generally fall into these five phases: (1) programming, (2) schematic design, (3) design development, (4) preparation of contract documents, and (5) contract administration. Numerous tasks are performed in each phase; some distinctly different from other phases and other tasks that seem similar from phase to phase. A client's needs might not require an interior designer to perform all the tasks of each phase for each project. An overview of typical tasks in each phase is discussed in this section, with typical tasks listed in Table 24-3 related to the development of the scope of services in a design contract. This section will not attempt to describe how these phases or how a project should be done. There are many other books the reader might use for this purpose. Note that the discussion of the phases of an interior design project follows the definition of the phases (or performance domains) as researched by the NCIDQ for the examination.

A critical part of project management is the interrelation of the scope of services to the whole of the management process. The preprogramming and planning of a project that occurs when the scope of services is developed for the design contract often results in a document called a work plan. The *work plan* "defines all the tasks or scope of work that is needed and includes clarification of deliverables, schedule, the needed resources and budget to take the project from inception to completion."[1] A work plan helps the designer clarify everything that has to be done and the correct order of tasks so that the project schedule can be more easily determined. *Deliverables* are documents and presentation materials that must be prepared to explain the design concepts and eventually allow the project to be built and installed. Examples are floor plans, sample boards, models, construction documents, and bid documents. They are called deliverables because they must be "delivered" (or provided) to the client.

Programming Phase

The *programming phase* is the information-gathering portion of an interior design project. The designer seeks as much information as possible on such things as client expectations, functional needs, aesthetics, and factors concerning the interior space itself. Client interviews are conducted to determine the client's goals and objectives, visits are made to the job site, or floor plans are obtained from the client or architect in order to understand any physical limitations of the project spaces. An inventory and an analysis of existing furnishings and equipment are conducted to help in later determination of product specification. In addition, interviews with employees might be conducted. If architectural drawings do not exist, designers may be required to field-measure the site. A review of applicable codes is critical to be sure that any legal restraints are taken into consideration. The designer will investigate with the client the extent that sustainable and environmental design issues can impact the overall design. Much time must be spent and careful notes must be taken in order for the interior designer to successfully design and prepare the documents required for completing the project. These comments describe only some of the activities in this very important first phase of the design project.

Designers are helped through this process by utilizing a variety of specialized forms such as Figure 28-1. This form is also included on the CD as Item 28-1.

Client interview forms help firms define the client's needs that are related to space requirements and furnishings and equipment requirements. For large commercial office projects, designers might find that using employee questionnaires is a more efficient use of time. When the client feels that he or she needs to use existing equipment, the designer can use a special form to analyze and inventory the furniture and equipment that the client already owns. These are

Design firm name and address

Designer: _____   Date of interview _____ Job # _____

Client: _____   **Project location:**

Address: _____   Address: _____

_____

_____

_____

Phone: _____   Site: _____

Cell phone: _____   _____

Email: _____   _____

☐ Existing clients   ☐ New clients

Estimated budget: **Desired completion date:**_____

Construction: _____   Custom: _____

Furniture: _____   Accessories: _____

Project area:

Scope of services:

Deliverables:

Consultants:

FIGURE 28-1.

The type of form that designers use to take notes at an initial meeting with a client. It can later assist in the development of a contract or for project specification research.

Special considerations:

Health issues:

Pets:

Entertaining:

Style preferences:

Color preferences:

Bank reference:

Credit check

Credit application

Reimbursable expenses:
    Travel
    Printing/Copying documents
    Express

    Per diem
    Long distance

Notes:

FIGURE 28-1.

(*Continued*)

just a few examples of the special forms that designers create to help obtain the information they will need about the client's requirements and the interior space to be designed.

Schematic Design Phase

The *schematic design phase* involves the execution of preliminary design decisions through the development of written design concepts, bubble diagrams, adjacency matrices, block plans, preliminary floor plans, and any appropriate design sketches. In addition, the initial selection of furniture, materials, finishes, and equipment are made during this phase. Naturally, the interior designer also applies applicable codes, accessibility guidelines, other regulations, and environmental standards required for the project to preliminary documents and selections. The designer is working with estimating forms for the architectural finishes, furniture specifications, construction estimates from contractors, and budgets. Estimating forms such as the one shown in Figure 28-2 help designers in this phase of the project.

With the review and approval of the selections and graphic documents, the designer is ready to move on to the next phase of the project. It is very important for the designer to obtain client signatures or at least the initialing of plans, drawings, and specification sheets prior to moving to the next phase. Obtaining client sign-off during the schematic phase provides the designer with assurance of proper reimbursement for any changes that the client makes while the designer is preparing finalized drawings and documents.

Design Development Phase

The *design development phase* of a project involves the preparation of all final furniture plans; presentation graphics, such as perspectives or axonometric drawings; sample boards, if they are to be used; and specifications for all the FF&E. Depending on the designer's contract, he or she may also prepare construction specifications, at least at the preliminary level. Since this is the final design stage of the project before contract documents are prepared, it is critical that the interior designer conduct final consultations with any technical consultants to review any changes that might have been made after presentation of the schematic drawings to the client.

Along with these graphic documents, the designer prepares a more complete project budget, which is necessary at this stage. Figure 28-3 shows an example of a form that the designer can use to develop a budget estimate for a project that will not be put out for competitive bidding. Depending on the project and the actual design responsibilities, the client will receive either the actual pricing and equipment lists for FF&E or an estimate with broader specifications pending formal bidding. Once again these documents are reviewed with the client as a final presentation before the contract documents are prepared. At the conclusion of the presentation, the designer should have obtained written client approvals of all drawings and specifications before moving the project on to the contract documents stage.

Contract Documents Phase

The *contract documents phase* of the design projects involves the final preparation of all construction or working drawings (which in part create the contract documents and are sometimes referred to as CDs), schedules, and specifications that are required to build and install the design project. These plans, drawings,

G. S. Hinsen Company
2133 Bandywood Drive
Nashville, Tennessee 37215
Phone: (615) 383-6440
Fax: (615) 269-5130

QUOTE REQUEST
WINDOW TREATMENTS

Workroom:_____

DATE:_____   CLIENT:_____   ROOM:_____

DATE QUOTE
REQUESTED:_____

NUMBER OF
WINDOWS:_____

SIZE OF
WINDOWS:_____

FABRIC(S) to be used: TYPE/CONTENT   WIDTH   REPEATS

(1)_____   _____   _____   _____

(2)_____   _____   _____   _____

(3)_____   _____   _____   _____

(4)_____   _____   _____   _____

SPECIFICATIONS:

LINING:_____

BLACKOUT LINING:_____

INNER LINING:_____

PLEAT STYLE:_____

HANDSEWN (circle):   yes   no

TRIM TYPE:_____

TRIM APPLICATION:_____

HARDWARE: SUPPLIED BY:_____

	DIMENSIONS	QUANTITY	FINISH
RODS:_____	_____	_____	_____
BRACKETS:_____	_____	_____	_____
FINIALS:_____	_____	_____	_____
RINGS:_____	_____	_____	_____

NOTES:

_____

_____

_____

*PLEASE QUOTE YARDAGE/MATERIALS NEEDED SEPARATE FOR EACH PIECE WINDOW.

FIGURE 28-2.

An estimating form that helps the designer establish the window treatments needed for a project. Similar forms can be created for estimating other parts of a project. (Reproduced with permission, Grei Hinsen, G.S. Hinsen Company, Nashville, TN)

Proposal : P3029
Terms : C.O.D.

337 East Indiantown Road
Showroom D-6
Jupiter, Florida 33477
(561) 745-4146
Fax (5610 745-0361

Date : 1/30/07
TeamPartner : Michael A. Thomas
Page: 1

FL IB #0864

Bill To: Ship To:

PROJECT or AREA : Office Cabinet						
QTY	ITEM NO.	DESCRIPTION	PRICE	PLUS	EXTENDED	TX.
1	Custom	Material and labor to fabricate and install custom laminate cabinetry for office. Counter top to be Leatherlam	$6,800.00	(40%)	$9,520.00	X
1	Glass / Mirror	Pensinsula glass top to be 1/2" thick x overall 78" long x 32" wide with a 16" radius curve at one end.	$275.00	(40%)	$385.00	X
7	Hardware	Cabinet hardware: Modern Objects #2482 Finish: Antique pewter	$11.50	(40%)	$112.70	X
1	Hardware	Leg for support of glass top	$85.00	(40%)	$119.00	X

Special Info : Deposit Required $5,400.00. Please sign and return a copy with your deposit to above address.	SubTotal	$10,136.70
	Sales Tax	$658.89
	Proposed Totals	$10,795.59

Proposal Approved	Deposit Paid
_____ Date _____	

FIGURE 28-3.

A proposal/estimate form showing items that would be ordered for the client's project. (Reproduced with permissions, Michael Thomas, FASID, CAPS, Design Collective Group, Jupiter, FL) and other documents are described in Chapter 30. They are technical construction drawings, not furniture floor plans or other presentation drawings like perspectives. Care in the preparation of these drawings is very important, since serious liability issues are at stake if errors are made in the construction drawings. Of course, interior designers can only prepare the construction drawings to the extent that the law in their jurisdiction allows. If they are not allowed to develop construction drawings in their jurisdiction, they will consult with an architect, engineers, or other licensed individuals to be sure the drawings produced by licensed consultants meet client approvals.

For projects that will be procured through the competitive bid process, detailed specifications concerning the FF&E are prepared along with the construction specifications. The designer who is responsible for also managing the competitive bid assembles several other documents that are necessary for the competitive bid process to occur in an orderly, fair, and appropriate manner. The competitive bid process will be discussed in Chapter 30.

Many residential projects and small commercial projects do not require a competitive bid. In these cases, project management at this stage includes preparing lists of recommended vendors or contractors in the name of the client or that are recommended to the client.

Contract Administration Phase

The *contract administration phase* is the portion of the project that involves the competitive bid process or the placing of orders for all the furniture and equipment, as well as the actual construction and installation work. The project management responsibility for the interior designer at this stage centers on the finalizing of bid documents and assisting or supervising the bid process with regard to all the work that is the responsibility of the interior designer. Depending on the interior designer's contract with the client, the designer might become involved in negotiation concerning any disputes in the bid documents. An important responsibility during contract administration is the review of shop drawings and submittals from vendors as well as on-site supervision of construction and installation of FF&E to the extent permitted by jurisdictional regulations.

To the designer, on-site supervision generally means making occasional trips to the job site as needed to be sure that all furniture and furnishings are being installed properly. If the designer has the proper license, it can also include supervision of certain aspects of the construction of the space or installation of products. Certain phases of the project require that the designer be on the job site for substantial periods of time. Other phases require only a short visit once a day or every few days. The client, however, often feels that on-site supervision means that the designer will be on the site all day, every day, seeing to every detail of the construction and installation. For most projects, this is, of course, impossible and impractical. How much supervision and what kind of supervision—even who in the office or representing the office is to supervise—should be clearly spelled out in the scope of services and discussed with the client.

Work supervision, along with the ordering of merchandise or letting construction contracts, occurs during this phase. Coordination and cooperation with the architect, general contractor, and subcontractors is necessary to ensure that the handling of the overall project is accomplished smoothly. Interior designers are traditionally responsible for the installation supervision of the architectural finishes and furnishings that they have specified for the project. Today, interior designers in many jurisdictions must hold the proper license to legally perform installation supervision or must be willing to relinquish this responsibility to a licensed contractor. You are advised to learn what the law requires in your jurisdiction.

All postinstallation or postoccupancy activities are an acknowledged part of the contract administration phase. This includes a final site inspection called a *walk-through*, where the designer, with the client, determines if there are any omissions or damages. Notations are made on a form, commonly called a *punch list*. Final payment to the designer is often withheld until all items on the punch list are taken care of. Larger design firms often prepare postoccupancy evaluations a short time after the client has moved in. A detailed discussion of the contract administration tasks is in Chapters 31 and 32.

One form that is used by design firms throughout the phases of the project is the transmittal letter (see Figure 28-4), The *transmittal letter* is a form letter that can be used for many purposes. It can be used to send information to the client, consulting architects and/or engineers, subcontractors, leasing agents, manufacturers, or anyone who is involved with the project. Another version of a transmittal letter has been included on the CD as Item 28-2.

The transmittal letter is designed to eliminate the need to write a separate letter or memo in order to transmit or ask for information. The fill-in-the-blank format makes it easy to use for a variety of purposes and is most commonly sent with materials or drawings of any kind. As can be seen by the example, it provides space to tell the receiver what is being sent and for what purpose, and it also gives instructions to the receiver for resubmittal or any action that the sender requires. It is an invaluable aid to speedy correspondence. Usually it is a two-part form: the original goes with the material being sent, and the copy is placed in the job file. Of course, a transmittal can also be sent via e-mail as an attachment.

Design-Build

A type of design and construction process that has received a growing amount of attention is design-build. In a design-build project, "a single contract is given to a single entity for both the design of the facility as well as the construction of the building."[*]

Most projects have been created with more than one entity or company involved in the process. Normally, an architect or designer creates the design and plans for a client. These are handed off to a contractor who hires subcontractors to complete the project. The design-build concept not only involves a single source for all the work but helps to fast-track the project.

The project is fast-tracked in part because the negotiation for the design and construction is done at one time. The sometimes protracted bidding process is nearly eliminated. Of course, for a design-build project to work as it should, the single source must have the appropriate design, construction contracting, and supervision personnel either as part of the firm or as a legal joint venture.

Clients can achieve effective cost control when using design-build. Everything is negotiated up front, as a fixed price can be determined for all phases of the project. If something goes wrong, the single source firm cannot simply up-charge the client for changes. Another advantage to the client is that he or she has one firm to deal with rather than what can be dozens in a normal construction and FF&E project.

For the design-build firm, there is more liability and risk, since it takes on risks that are more often left to others. However, the potential revenue benefits have led many firms to bring on these extra services to their design firm in order to offer more to potential clients. A very good reference on design-build is *Design-Build* by Jeffrey Beard, Michael Loulakis, and Edward Wundram.

*Piotrowski and Rogers, 2007, p. 10.

JAIN MALKIN INC.
5070 Santa Fe Street
Suite C
San Diego CA 92109
858/ 454-3377
858/ 272-6199 Fax
www.jainmalkin.com

L E T T E R   O F   T R A N S M I T T A L

To: Date:

_____

                                                            Re:

_____

                                                            Job No:

_____

                                                            Sent Via: **Mail**

_____

Purpose of Transmittal: ☐ For Review and Comment   ☐ For Approval   ☐ As Requested
                           ☐ Correct and Resubmit   ☐ For Your Use

Date	No. of Copies	Dwgs	Prints	Specs	Other	Description

Comments:

By: Copies:

_____   _____

FIGURE 28-4.

A typical transmittal letter which often accompanies other documents. (Reproduced with permission, courtesy Jain Malkin Inc., San Diego, CA)

STAKEHOLDERS

A project may seem to be an adventure that is embarked upon only by the client and the interior designer. But they happen to be only the main players on the team. Anyone who is involved in the project and somehow has an interest in the project is commonly referred to as a *stakeholder*.

An interior design project may have numerous stakeholders when the project is large and complex. The stakeholders might simply consist of the client, the interior designer, and the vendors who will eventually be hired to complete the installation on many smaller projects.

The project manager (or project designer) is responsible for ensuring that the members of this sometimes widely diverse group of stakeholders know what all the members of the team are supposed to do and when and how they are supposed to do their tasks. The project manager also checks to be sure that they have accomplished their tasks. As any interior designer, from the sole practitioner to the senior project designer at the largest interior design firm, would agree, this is hardly ever an easy task. Managing the working relationships of the different stakeholders is always a challenge and a key task of the project designer/manager.

The first stakeholder is the most important—the client. Clients expect the PM will keep them informed of the progress of the project. In some cases, the client will be satisfied with an occasional phone call telling him or her that all is well and on schedule. Other clients require monthly, even weekly, meetings. Clients sometimes require this constant communication because they want to feel "in control" of the project, and having the project manager constantly report to them makes them feel in control. Others need the information to ensure that they will be prepared for the eventual move into the new facility. A residential client may be selling one home to move into another; a business that is moving from one location to another has a burdensome task. A move, as the reader no doubt understands, is a time-consuming, stressful period for some clients.

Good client communication is an especially important key to ending a project with a satisfied client. They have, after all, decided to spend a great deal of money on your services and to accept your advice. That does not mean they will give you carte blanche with those funds or without keeping them informed and involved. Promptly returning phone calls and e-mails, sending them update memos, and holding an appropriate number of face-to-face conferences alleviates their stress and their questions.

For that communication to run smoothly in a commercial project, the PM will want the client to designate someone as the single source of contact. A *single source of contact* is one particular individual who has the authority to make decisions regarding the project and to whom all communication is to be directed. The project manager for the design firm will be that contact for the client. The designer must know very early who the contact will be for the client. For large projects, it is not uncommon for the single source of contact for the client also to have the title of project manager.

Clients sometimes refer to that single source as the *owner's representative*. This term has become more common in recent years as the contact between the design firm and the client. This individual might be an employee of the firm or a consultant hired by the client. The owner's representative may be the only person the designer or project manager meets with after the design concepts are completed and approved at the end of the design development phase of the project. The owner's representative keeps the client informed from the information passed by the project manager. Using the term single source of contact or owner's representative is more often a part of a commercial project than a residential one, since it is much more obvious who the contact is for a residence. Residential clients sometimes use the services of an owner's representative or a facilitator to serve the same purpose.

For a residential project, using the concept of a single source of contact helps residential interior designers who find themselves with extra challenges that happen when both home owners make decisions. For example, it is not unusual for the wife to approve a furniture item that the husband later does not like. One way the residential interior designer can protect him- or herself from problems of disagreement between the spouses is for both to be asked to sign off on all paperwork and selections. Although it may feel clumsy to the designer at first, it can truly save the designer from legal litigation or ethics complaints.

Some clients want to know how the activities of the project will be undertaken. Others assume you will do what is required without constant detailed explanations. It is the responsibility of the project manager to explain how the project will proceed through its phases and what will happen during each phase. By setting up the scope of services in the design contract in the logical order of the design process, clients get a preview of the work activities to be expected. A commercial project RFP may require detailed scope descriptions that are reviewed and updated on a regular basis. Clients who have not worked with an interior designer before often require more education on the process, and the project manager must be ready to provide that feedback.

Clients enjoy visiting the job site and seeing the progress that is (hopefully) being made once construction or installation begins. Sometimes these visits cause the project manager, designer, and contractors problems. It is important that the client be cautioned about refraining from directly instructing workers on the job site. Construction workers, in particular, are not required to be diplomatic and to respond to the instructions of clients. Be sure the client understands that he or she should direct questions and changes to the proper foreman, to the project manager, or to the designer. For example, on one residential construction project, the owner, being retired, spent most of every day on the site. He kept questioning and interrupting the workers until one day the framer said, "I was hired to do this job according to the plans. If you want to do the work, here's a hammer. I'll go home."

There are other potential stakeholders associated with the client. Publicly funded projects often include individuals who are interested in the completion of the project. In some cases, they may even have a financial stake in the project, as evidenced by a patron providing major funding of a museum. Publicly funded projects might also have community leaders or community staff members on a project committee that will regularly meet with the design team. Privately funded projects that are large in scale also have potential stakeholders who are members of the corporation's board of directors or executive officers.

Another group of stakeholders who may have input into design decisions are the staff members that will work in the facility or in some other way use the facility. An example of the latter would be a church building committee composed of members of the congregation. Even a residential project has stakeholders beyond the owners. The first that comes to mind are the children, but other relatives might indirectly impose their ideas. All of these example stakeholders might not be at all the meetings, but the lead designer and project manager must keep them in mind when communicating to the source of contact and the group who will be making the decisions.

On our hypothetical project, another stakeholder group is the design staff. The lead designer, who may or may not also be the project manager, has need of one or more other designers who will help gather information, produce all the design documents, and keep the project manager informed about the progress of the project. To make this relationship work, proper communication between the project manager and the design team and adequate delegation of responsibilities are necessary. The team members must know what must be done and how and when it must be done, and they must be given the trust and responsibility to get the work done in a professional and appropriate manner to meet the expectations of the designer and the client. The lead designer must trust the team members if they are to carry through with their responsibilities. The project manager—if different from the lead designer—must properly delegate work to the team members.

Many large projects involve the use of one or more technical consultants. The project manager first must determine which technical consultants, such as architects, engineers, or specialty designers like a lighting designer, are required. He or she may hire these individuals as part of the design firm's contract or may recommend certain ones to the client. These stakeholders work with the interior design team and provide expertise that might not be available in the project designer's office. If these consultants are hired directly by the client, then the interiors project manager must communicate with the consultant to ensure a smoothly designed project.

As the design team begins to specify products for the job, another important working relationship with other stakeholders is between the designer and various trade sources. Suppliers provide product information and pricing, obtain samples for the designer, and give other assistance that might be needed. This relationship is complex, since the designer might require information from dozens of suppliers and craftspeople. It is also important that the relationship be kept neutral so that no unprofessional or unethical promises are made between the vendors and the design team.

If we assume that demolition or construction work occurs as part of the project, another group of stakeholders will be the general contractor and subcontractors. Clear communication between the designer and the general contractor and subcontractors is necessary. Instructions to the general contractor and through that firm to the subcontractors must come from only a single source at the design firm—that is, of course, the project manager. Changes during construction that were not part of the original documents are costly no matter how small that change. Scheduling is also very important to ensure that the scheduling and work of the tradespeople is kept on track and does not negatively affect the progress of the project.

It certainly helps when all of these working relationships run smoothly. Additional information about the people with whom the designer coordinates all of the tasks on an interior design project will be discussed in the next chapter.

PROJECT SCHEDULES

Scheduling of the design team's activities and the work that needs to be completed to construct and/or install the project is a very important project management responsibility. Project schedules are prepared during programming as part of the revised work plan, are refined during schematics, and are updated throughout the project. The project manager/designer carefully monitors the schedule, informing the client of any changes that can impact the due dates of upcoming activities and the completion of the overall project. Project schedules help the designer maintain control of the project. Breaking down a large task into manageable units helps the designer get the task done on time.

Project schedules can take many forms, depending on who is using the information. Designers might use a schedule set up on a daily basis or use week-by-week descriptions of what must be done to reach the target completion date. For the project manager or design director, a week-by-week or monthly schedule is needed to aid in accepting, estimating, and assigning new work.

Computer software is available to assist with project scheduling. Very sophisticated systems used by large design firms make scheduling for complex projects faster. Simpler programs for smaller firms are also available to help with scheduling. Depending on the complexity of the software, the program can produce numerous reports once data about time lines, activities, and due dates have been entered. A design firm that will be involved in projects for large commercial corporations, public agencies, and the government will want to use a project management software program that is compatible with any used by the client. Simple project scheduling software for smaller design firms is available from several sources. Although the author does not endorse any particular software brands, a popular scheduling software in the industry is Microsoft Project®.

It is important that the scheduling software or other manual scheduling method used by a design firm provide adequate visual displays of the work tasks and sequence of the tasks. The three most common methods used for visualizing the project schedule are the milestone, the bar chart (also called a Gantt chart; named for Henry Gantt), and the critical path method.

Milestone charts may be the easiest method of scheduling a project. In this method, the designer outlines the activities required for the project and then establishes target dates for their completion (see Figure 28-5). Space can be included to indicate who is responsible for each activity. The actual date of completion should be noted, as this will aid in future estimating. The biggest advantage in using the milestone chart for scheduling is that it is so easy to use. It is a very good method for controlling the schedule of small projects that are not very complex. No specialized software is required, since it can be set up using common word-processing software; however, it may also be an option on specialized project management software.

A more graphic method of showing the scheduling of a project is by use of a bar chart. Figure 28-6 provides an example. *Bar charts* consist of a description of tasks required in the left-hand side and horizontal bars on the right-hand side,

Project: Weldone Residence
Designer: Maryanne

Task Name	Days	Earliest Start	Earliest Finish	Latest Start	Latest Finish	Actual Finish
Interview Client	3	9/23/0X	9/26/0X	10/3/0X	10/8/0X	9/23/0X
Obtain Floor Plan	1	9/24/0X	9/25/0X	10/7/0X	10/8/0X	9/24/0X
Inventory Existing Furniture	1	9/25/0X	9/25/0X	10/7/0X	10/8/0X	10/5/0X
Sketch Preliminary Plan	7	9/26/0X	10/7/0X	10/8/0X	10/17/0X	10/6/0X
Make Preliminary Selections	5	9/26/0X	10/3/0X	10/10/0X	10/17/0X	10/7/0X
Prepare Preliminary Budget	2	10/6/0X	10/7/0X	10/15/0X	10/20/0X	10/8/0X
Meet with Client	1	10/7/0X	10/8/0X	10/17/0X	10/20/0X	10/8/0X
Revise Preliminary Plan	5	10/8/0X	10/15/0X	10/20/0X	10/27/0X	10/14/0X
Revise Selections	3	10/7/0X	10/20/0X	10/27/0X	10/30/0X	10/17/0X
Prepare Final Budget	1	10/20/0X	10/20/0X	10/29/0X	11/3/0X	10/23/0X
Make Final Presentation to Client	2	10/20/0X	10/22/0X	10/30/0X	11/3/0X	10/24/0X

FIGURE 28-5.

A sample milestone chart. The chart indicates the activities to be performed, the estimated days for completion, and the target dates for starting and stopping each activity.

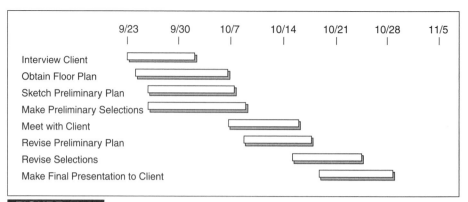

	9/23	9/30	10/7	10/14	10/21	10/28	11/5

Interview Client
Obtain Floor Plan
Sketch Preliminary Plan
Make Preliminary Selections
Meet with Client
Revise Preliminary Plan
Revise Selections
Make Final Presentation to Client

FIGURE 28-6.

A bar chart that graphically shows the time span required to complete designated project activities.

showing the time in days, weeks, or months that is required to complete the task. As a management tool, designers can use this chart on a daily or weekly basis to show their responsibility if they are working on more than one project. To assist with overall project management, the project manager can prepare a monthly chart for each designer to help the design manager determine whether he or she is available for additional work.

A disadvantage of using the bar chart in the interior design profession is that it does not necessarily show how one activity affects another activity or which is the most important activity needed to complete the project on time. As the reader knows, many tasks in completing an interiors project overlap—with one task moving to completion when another must begin. Analysis of the most important activities can be developed with more careful project analysis and a more complex color-coded bar chart. It works well for most small to somewhat complex projects, although it is not particularly appropriate for large or very complex projects. It can be done manually; some firms put bar charts up on a wall to show the project's or firm's progress on the work being done in-house. Computer software is also available for creating bar charts.

If the design project is quite complex so that the interrelationships of the required tasks are critical, the third method of scheduling may be called for, the *critical path method* (CPM). This scheduling method is dependent upon the interrelationships of activities and the detailed tasks of each activity. Any one activity in a sequence cannot be completed unless the previous tasks and related activities have been completed. Generally, only the larger interior design firms find CPM appropriate for project scheduling when they are involved in large projects. CPM is commonly used by architects and the construction industry to maintain control of the interrelated construction process, however. This method would be very difficult to manage manually, so the project manager should obtain some type of computer project management software.

Briefly, CPM scheduling starts by identifying the interrelationships of the tasks to be performed. This analysis shows the project manager which tasks must be done before the next or other tasks can be performed, thus establishing the critical path (see Figure 28-7). A simple critical path in an interior design project occurs when the designer obtains the client's needs, prepares floor plans, obtains the client's approval, orders products, and installs and/or delivers products. It is clear that it is impossible, as well as unwise, to try to do any one of these tasks prior to completing the one directly preceding it. As the interrelationships are entered into the computer, along with due dates and the duration of each task, the computer automatically makes the calculations to adjust for changes in the schedule. Then

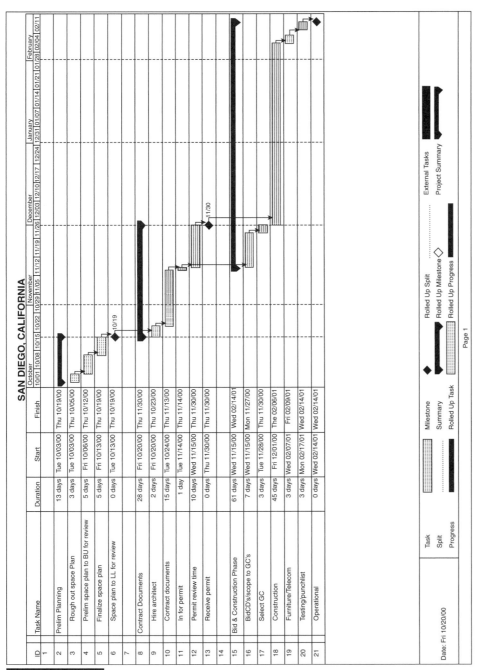

FIGURE 28-7.

Critical path method chart. (Reprinted with permission, Allyson Grenier, Phoenix, AZ)

new charts are produced, which can be given in different formats to the interior design team members, the client, and other stakeholders.

PROJECT BUDGETING

Regardless of the type of project, establishing and sticking to the budget is a critical issue for both the client and the interior designer. Specifying a project that comes in significantly over the client's budget can lead to a potential lawsuit and ethics charges. These reasons alone make accurate project budgeting a concern for designers. Clients rarely grant designers free rein with an unlimited budget. In fact, the budget that the client has in mind is almost always smaller than can reasonably be accomplished. Many clients do not reveal the full nature of the budget, fearing that the designer will spend that much and not less; by keeping it a secret, they think that perhaps the project will come in below what he or she wanted to spend.

Many interior designers are hired after other budget decisions for construction and structural elements of the project already have been made. It then becomes more of a challenge for the interior designer to effect the same creative and exciting ideas that he or she would want if he or she had been involved in the project at an earlier stage. It is never an easy task to convince the client to upgrade finishes, modify structural elements, or purchase higher-quality furnishings after these kinds of decisions are established.

Project budgeting for the interiors will involve estimating the costs of furniture, architectural finishes, accessories, and perhaps non-load-bearing construction of such things as partitions, lighting, cabinets or other built-ins, and the like. For example, depending on its size, a new kitchen with all new cabinets, counters, wall and floor finishes, ceilings, and lighting can start at $20,000 for something modest and can reach $75,000 and more quite easily—before appliances are included. The furniture alone for an office of around 175 square feet can start at about $25,000 (retail). How does the less experienced designer go about determining a budget?

One method that can be used concerns developing quality ranges. Design firms can develop three or four quality ranges from among the manufacturers with which they commonly do business. In a way, it would be like using the grade ranges of fabric for upholstered goods. The lowest grade or group of manufacturers would be those with budget lines. A second group would be those that provided medium-quality goods—goods that would be serviceable and would provide several years of satisfactory use. A third group would be many of the high-end manufacturers, whose products are known for their high quality. The last group would be those manufacturers that could supply custom goods or that are known to carry the very best quality items. Some design firms find it useful to develop a checklist that describes these ranges. These checklists are discussed with the client to clarify the differences in the product groups. The furniture representatives or the manufacturers' literature can be helpful sources of information to develop these quality ranges.

A second budgeting technique is the use of "typicals." Commercial interior designers who have a significant amount of experience with certain kinds of spaces develop layouts of typical spaces, for example, offices or a doctor's exam room, or even a hotel guest room. At its simplest, this technique starts with an average or typical furniture arrangement. There can even be more than one typical arrangement for a similar space—something that is commonly done for hotel guest rooms. Adding a quality level to the typical space provides a budget idea that the designer can discuss with the client. Residential designers also find this method useful as a starting point when they are helping a client understand the potential overall cost of furnishing a portion of the home.

It is also possible to do product budgeting based on a square-foot factor. In this case, the designer utilizes historical data that he or she has collected on a variety of project types and conditions. As preliminary discussions of project feasibility and budget are conducted, the designer can use these factors to clarify potential costs to the client. For example, a residential design firm can use this information to give a "ballpark" budget of all furniture and finishes for a high-end house based on the livable square footage of the house. A commercial designer may use historical square-foot factors to provide information to a client who is considering furnishing a law partner's office. The designer can even show the client that a contemporary style office might cost X dollars per square foot, while a traditional style will cost some other factor per square foot.

Of course, the designer can also estimate each item by using standard materials cost and labor charges for individual items such as window treatments, carpeting, tile, and so on. Materials estimates can also be obtained by the designer's use of reference books. Designers often prefer this method, as the design of a residence and many types of commercial properties can be very customized and difficult to budget in a ballpark fashion.

There are, of course, a few built-in problems in using any of these techniques for budgeting. Clients may make decisions based on price rather than on the quality required. This may back the designer into a corner, and he or she may be forced to use products or design concepts that do not provide for the best finished project. Another problem is that the client may assume that the budget is the designer's final price and may go elsewhere in order to find a less expensive solution. This is why most designers commonly quote budget ranges rather than single numbers. Ranges give the designer flexibility in the specification of products without appearing to be always over the budget when the actual prices are determined.

MANAGING AND RECORDING YOUR TIME

In Chapter 23 we reviewed many different ways that an interior designer can be compensated for services. Everyone, however, is restrained by time. There are only 24 hours in a day, and most do not want to work that many hours a day! Whether one charges based on time or some other method, managing and recording your time accurately does impact the bottom line. If an interior designer is too busy to keep track of his or her time, how can he or she know if the fixed-fee or markup method or whatever fee method a designer uses is fairly compensating him or her? Revenue from product sales may still work as a reasonable compensation method, but who is to say whether one day the client will purchase product on his or her own through the Internet or sources that become open to the public? Effective time management and faithful time recording are critical skills and tasks for the professional interior designer.

Time Management

As workloads continue to increase and the client continually demands that turnaround time on information be faster, time management is not a task or skill that can be ignored. The Internet has brought us the opportunity (or problem) of working 24/7/365. Clients want answers now, not in a few days. We barely have time for our personal lives amid all our other responsibilities. There never seems to be enough time to get everything done. Getting into a habit of using good time management can help the designer do all that is needed to be done, on time and with a lowered level of stress. Table 28-2 suggests ten common time wasters.

To an interior designer, one of the absolute truths is that time equals money. Whether the designer is paid by the hour or receives compensation in some other way, the efficient, productive use of time has a direct bearing on the designer's yearly income. It is therefore very important for the interior designer to make the best use of his or her time while on the job.

Typical Reasons People Waste Time on the Job.

- Inadequate planning
- Telephone interruptions
- Procrastination
- Personal disorganization
- Unrealistic time estimates
- Attempting too much
- Inability to say no
- Crisis management
- Socializing
- Making mistakes

Time management and organization problems have existed for many years. The first book I found on the subject was *How to Get Control of Your Time and Your Life* by Alan Lakin, published in 1972. It remains a useful treatment of the subject even though you might find one of the other dozens of books on time management more effective for you. A few good references have been included for your further reading.

These theories were not developed to make a person a slave to his or her job but, rather, to help the person organize his or her time to be as productive as possible. That does not mean that one's time is planned so rigidly that there is no room for flexibility to meet emergencies. In interior design, it sometimes seems that every day is filled with emergencies. Its purpose is not to control time but to control the *use* of time. The basic premise is based on creating to-do lists, prioritizing those lists, and keeping a calendar and a notebook handy; preferably all in the same notebook or electronic device. Figure 28-8 shows an example of a computer-based to-do list.

Time management is simple and is based on the common basic management responsibilities of planning, decision making, and control. A designer plans the day (or week or month) by making decisions about what will be done and will not be done, hopefully, during any one time period. These plans and decisions then help the designer better control what he or she does with time

Alan Lakin and other time management experts discuss the 80/20 rule. As it relates to time management, the *80/20 rule* maintains that when activities are arranged in order of importance, 80 percent of a person's time will be spent performing 20 percent of the activities. What this means is that in a list of ten items, if a person accomplishes the two most important items, he or she has achieved 80 percent of the total value of time spent. Most companies can look at sales records and see that approximately 80 percent of the sales were generated by 20 percent of the sales staff. The main thrust of the 80/20 rule is that one should concentrate one's efforts on the few items on the list with the highest priority to generate the greatest value or return.

A key effective time management tactic is to keep the to-do list handy, along with a daily appointment calendar. Designers use several sizes of notebook organizers in configurations of calendars, note pads, phone numbers, and so forth to meet personal needs. Others use handheld electronic organizers that can be downloaded back and forth to their computer. Still others use organizer software or contact software on their computer and print out daily and weekly calendars to carry in their attaché case. Regardless of the system used, it is best to have a monthly calendar, a day-to-day calendar divided by hours, pages for a

ITEM	ABC	DAILY TASK LIST	TIME EST.
		Check and respond to emails	:30
		Call Sally James: carpet pricing for Smith	:15
		Call Ned for Lunch ?? Thursday	
		Verify RFP pickup for Hospice Center	:15
		Discuss Hospice center proposal with Jim	:45
		Review Allegro plans with Tom	
		12:00 Lunch with Barbara W at Green Gables	1:30
		Finish Allegro plans review	1:00
		Check and respond to emails	:30
		4:00 Conference call with DKD	:45
		Time sheets	
		Specs for MicroAge 3rd Floor	

FIGURE 28-8.

A prioritized to-do list showing activities and time estimates for the completion of each task.

to-do list, memo paper, and address pages. You might want to experiment with different systems to find the one that provides you the best method of recording your calendar appointments and due dates and to-do lists. Figure 28-9 is an example of a computer-based time management record.

Another important tactic that is very useful but often difficult to achieve is handling papers once. That is, reading the paper, mail, memo, and so forth, then filing it or discarding the paper rather than creating stacks of paper all over the office. This can easily be accomplished by setting aside a certain amount of time each day as part of your to-do lists for handling mail and filing. Forgetting to go through the mail consistently can lead to missing checks from clients and not paying bills in a timely fashion.

E-mail is another task that has taken a large part of everyone's time each day. One can get dozens of e-mails each day, each wanting some sort of response. The first strategy is to allow a certain time each day to open e-mails and decide

Thu Oct 26, 2000

Po To-Do's	
think about artafactual furniture	2-18-00
call barry for lunch	10-16-00
Proposals due on TSG Call C	10-26-00
verify FFE deliv sched on Credit union	10-26-00

7

8 8:00a - 9:00a meet w K French re: PCC

9

10 10:00a - 2:00p OSW Des Dev

11

12

1

2 2:00p - 3:00p Az Biz conf call

3

4 4:00p - 5:00p ASSCU weekly jobsite meeting

5

6

7

Printed 8:43a 10/20/00

FIGURE 28-9.

A computer-based time record system sheet. (Reprinted with permission, Fred Messner, IIDA, Phoenix Design One, Tempe, AZ)

what must be done with each. Start with good spam software to separate all the junk that will come into the system. Don't open such e-mails, as most will then just send you even more spam. Set up special in-boxes for current projects so that you do not lose important e-mails.

Of course, there is a lot more to time management than these simple strategies concerning to-do lists and prioritizing tasks. Time management also involves confident decision making, becoming organized, and learning how to deal with procrastination. It also involves learning how to handle interruptions, how to delegate effectively, and even how to say NO, which sometimes can be very difficult. Time management also requires that you learn to reward yourself when you meet goals and, on the other hand, not beat yourself up when you are not making the progress that you would like.

Time management works, but it takes a certain amount of discipline to get into the habit of creating to-do lists and prioritizing them every day, and learning all the other techniques that will help you become a more effective employee or owner. Even though new habits are difficult to establish, it is necessary to keep at it in order to become a designer who rapidly earns promotions and responsibility.

Time Records

Getting into the habit of good time management will make recording time the designer works on any project much easier. Being "too busy to keep track of my time"—an excuse many designers use when I've asked them about time recording—does not justify refusing to use time management practices. Being too busy to keep track of his or her time might really mean that the designer is doing work that should be assigned to someone else, or that they are a poor delegator and even with an assistant feel they must do everything themselves. It is crucial that the designer keep accurate time records for all professional services, even if the designer does not actually charge the client by the hour.

Keeping time records is not a difficult task. It does, however, take discipline to record the different activities and times involved as accurately as possible on projects and/or other company business. It is easy for most people to keep track of a day's activities on one sheet of paper and then transfer the time related to individual projects and nonbillable time to the appropriate sheet for that project. A manual system such as this can utilize a simple form such as that shown in Figure 28-10. Each record includes the client's name or the project's name, the designer's name, a description of the work performed, and the hours of work per description. This form can record all the work done for the day or week and then be transferred to a form for individual projects. It could also be modified to be used only for the project. Note that this form has been included on the CD as Item 28-4.

Many designers use some type of computer-based daily planner to keep track of appointments, so recording of time becomes quicker and less of a hassle. The records can be kept on a daily basis and, depending on the needs of the firm, can be compiled on a weekly or a monthly basis. Figure 28-8 and 28-9 show a page from two different computer-based contact systems. The computer system allows for a great deal of additional information to be included in the database. The computer system also can be interactive so that each staff member can check on the appointments of other designers if necessary.

Time records are only as accurate as the design firm owner and employees keep them. How exact the records need to be is a function of management control. For most companies, it is practical to keep track of time to the quarter hour; that is, the designer reports work on any project or house time that is related to 15-minute intervals. (Keeping track to the exact minute is micromanaging and will only annoy most designers.) Designers record the activities of a normal workday plus any overtime.

Utilizing time management and time recording can lead to more effective use of time and prevent the loss of billable time. Clients demand your undivided

Time Record

Designer: _____   Week of: _____

Page: _____ of _____

Date	Project Code	Task		Billing		
		Description/Notes		**Time**	**Fee Rate**	**Bill Amount**
				Totals		

FIGURE 28-10.

A sample form for keeping track of all billable hours worked by a design staff employee.

attention even though they know this is not practical. Time management helps you keep the promises you make. Accurate time recording helps ensure that you bill for all the time you have spent on a project, helping improve your profitability. Additional tips on time management have been added to the CD as Item 28-3.

Reasons to Make Time Record Keeping a Habit

Time equals money in interior design whether the designer charges by the hour or in some other manner. Keeping track of time while working on projects helps the designer understand if a type of project is profitable for the time invested. Recording nonbillable time is also important, as it can help a practice owner more carefully realize what kind of assistance is needed with administrative tasks.

Here are several specific reasons to make time record keeping a habit:

1. Accurate time records are necessary for billing if the design firm is charging by the hour for professional services. Some clients wish to see time records before paying the bill.

2. Time records help the designer or firm owner check on the progress of current jobs. This is necessary in order to determine if too much time is being used. If the project is running over the estimated time, the reasons need to be analyzed. Does the client change his or her mind often? Is the designer nonproductive? Was there an error in the requirements or plans? Has enough time been budgeted?

3. Keeping accurate time records helps a designer or the design firm determine what kinds of projects are actually profit making. When a firm is working with many clients who require a lot of hand-holding or the firm's time for activities like specification writing and drafting, certain fee methods provide more potential revenue (and profit margin) than others. This cannot be determined accurately if time records are not kept.

4. A record of time worked on previous projects helps the design firm determine budget and fees for new projects. For example, if the firm knows that a 3000-square-foot model home can be completely designed in X hours, that information saves the firm time and errors in writing new contracts.

5. Historical time records can also help a firm decide if it even wants to take on certain kinds of projects, since they may be very time-consuming while returning a very small profit margin.

6. Time records can be of assistance to managers when they are arranging performance reviews of employees. Interior designers in many firms are looking for the majority of the designer's time to be billable. Time records help the firm determine if designers are productive for the firm. Depending on how important this is to the design firm, those designers who are billing closest to their goals are more likely to receive salary increases or to be rewarded in other ways.

7. Time records and historical utilization records assist the firm's owner in making overall budget and planning decisions that are necessary for the continued future health and growth of the design firm.

8. A wide variety of management control reports can be generated from time sheets. Some of these reports were discussed in Chapter 17.

PROJECT FILES OR JOB BOOKS

Five years after the Brooks project was completed, Mary received a call from Mrs. Brooks asking for help replacing a furniture item. Their new puppy chewed up two pillows on the sofa and ruined the fabric. Mary was able to find the fabric pattern and supplier in her job book files. After contacting the supplier and obtaining a sample of the current fabric, it was determined that fabric was still available.

Keeping all the records and documents concerning a particular project so that the project designer—or anyone else in the office—can quickly track the answers to questions is a very important task for the project manager. Whether it is to answer a question on a project in process or to help a client out on an older project, creating a *project file* or project job book is the mechanism used for this type of control. The project file usually consists of file folders or notebooks in which the designer keeps all the pertinent data and paperwork related to the work in progress. It might be supplemented with boxes or other binders containing swatches and samples of materials. The project file serves as a complete record of all the designer's efforts to organize a project and can be used to create the installation manual.

Keeping a project file up-to-date and organized requires discipline, just as time management does. But it is immensely useful to the designer, to the design firm, and to the client. All the information the designer needs about the project is in one place. As questions arise or changes are made, the designer has a complete reference to use when talking to a client, vendors, or personnel in the design firm. The well-organized project file makes an impressive statement to the client about how the designer and the design firm keep control of projects. Having all the information in one place saves valuable time when questions arise. There should be no need to scour the office for information or to answer questions.

If the designer in charge of the project is absent for any reason, the project file allows other members of the firm to seek out answers to clients' and vendors' questions. Even if the lead designer leaves the firm, another designer should be able to pick up the project file and complete the project successfully.

As was the case for the Brooks, the project file also is invaluable as a future reference tool. If the client wants to replace items or is in need of repair of items specified, it is easy to check the project file for exact product information. If legal problems arise during or after the project, the project file will serve as a thorough reference tool for the firm. In addition, a project file is helpful as a sales tool in marketing efforts. Clients may wish to see how the firm expects to control their project, so displaying a well-organized project file, with all its various parts, may be the answer.

Although projects are all different, many have similar qualities. Project files help the firm with projects that are similar in many ways. For example, project files can help determine the following:

1. Why the design time estimate was or was not accurate
2. Whether or not products performed as specified and if vendors were a problem
3. If taking additional work from the same client would be inadvisable, perhaps because an inordinate number of changes were made by the client

The project file should have the following categories of information: meeting notes, correspondence, samples, and floor plans.

Meeting Notes

Interior designers often work on several projects at the same time. Keeping all the information on each project straight without taking notes is a recipe for disaster. Most people do take notes, but some choose to trust their memories rather than put notes in writing. Perhaps they feel that by taking notes they are not giving their undivided attention to their client. However, memory is not always perfect. Meeting notes can become important in court if any type of legal challenge has been raised.

Meeting notes should include the notes taken during the initial interview, which are used to develop the design contract and all subsequent interview notes or forms obtained concerning client needs. Include the date and time of the meeting and the names of those in attendance. They do not have to be verbatim to be useful but should contain the salient details of the discussions. It is a good idea to retain the original notes taken during the various meetings that the designer may have attended. Many designers send transcribed copies of meeting notes back to the client or other interested parties to be sure that there are no misunderstandings as a result of the meeting. Telephone notes to any of these parties should also be kept in this section.

Preprinted forms that are specially designed for recording the meeting notes can be used. Some designers use electronic organizers for quick notes, but these still seem impractical when interviewing clients. Other designers use a laptop computer for taking notes, since this negates the necessity of transcribing the notes later. Most designers simply take notes.

Always take notes. Take a lot of notes. Do not trust your memory. In fact, although students are used to taking notes in class, it is a useful habit to enlarge this habit by dating all notes and drawings—even rough sketches—to get into the habit and to see a progression of design solutions.

Correspondence

The meeting notes described above are only one type of correspondence that should be retained in a project file. Another type is what is considered general correspondence. Copies of all correspondence sent to or received from the client should be kept in the project file. First among this group is a copy of the signed design contract. Many firms find it best to retain the original, signed design contract in a separate file, held by the design director or the owner of the design firm. Project designers use a copy that can be marked up and file the original to protect it from loss or damage. Insert any other letters or memos sent to or received from the client as well. This includes any e-mail messages. A hard copy should be printed out of your e-mail messages to a client and any responses from the client. Hard copies are important even if you have a separate in-box on your computer for each client and project. There is always the chance that the server will be down when you most need to review e-mails in these computer-based files.

Other correspondence to and from factories and representatives, architects, and construction contractors also must be retained. Correspondence to and from factories and representatives include letters concerning pricing, special treatments or fabrics, custom work, availability for shipping, freight charges, and so on. When the design project involves construction activities, the file includes correspondence to and from the general contractor or subcontractors. Again, all e-mails concerning the project should also be printed and placed in the project file.

Everything that goes into the file should be accurately dated. Do not throw away any of the preliminary work sheets, even when finalized sheets have replaced them. Sometimes a client signature for approvals is noted on a preliminary drawing and later disputed on the final drawings. Pricing information or brief notes might be on preliminary sheets that may be needed to clarify or defend some action or decision. Leave cleaning out the files until after the project has been installed and all moneys have been collected. A backup copy of the computer-based correspondence and notes produced by the design firm should be stored in a fireproof file.

A large number of original or, in some cases, photocopies of project documents should also be in this section of the project file. Table 28-3 lists some of these documents. In-depth discussions of many of these forms are contained in other chapters.

TABLE 28-3.

Typical Documents Included in a Project File.

☐ **Correspondence**
  Signed design contract
  Memos and transmittals from vendors and suppliers
  Meeting minutes and subsequent replies from client and vendors
  Other correspondence related to the project

☐ **Project-Programming Documents**
  Client interview questionnaires
  Job site analysis
  Space-programming questionnaires
  Employee work area summaries
  Existing furniture inventories

☐ **Project Specifications and Budgets**
  Furniture specification sheets
  Estimates for architectural finishes and window treatments
  Other budgeting forms
  Samples and approved cuttings

☐ **Drawings**
  Preliminary plans drawn from site measures
  Preliminary sketches, especially those approved by the client
  Contract documents
  Shop drawings
  As-built documents

☐ **Bidding and Procurement**
  Bid specifications
  Purchase orders
  Acknowledgments
  Invoices
  Shipping documents
  Change orders
  Punch lists
  Site inspection reports

☐ **Miscellaneous**
  Warranties
  Maintenance documentation
  Postoccupancy evaluations
  Internal post-project documentation
  Anything else pertinent to the project for future reference

Samples

All types of projects will include the specification of many types of textiles and other materials. Retaining a small sample of these items is important to retain as part of the project file. Samples should not be stuffed into a box or a folder with no identification. These must be accompanied by a full description, including the manufacturer, the product name and/or number, the color name or number, and a code for determining what furniture item (for upholstery) or room name/ number (for window treatments, wall treatments, and floor finishes) goes with which sample.

Samples may be organized piece by piece or room by room. Using a form such as the one shown in Figure 22-1 or perhaps a smaller form printed on card stock can help the firm keep track of all the materials that are specified for a project. The control sheet is ideal for setting up an installation manual so that the installation of furniture items will go more smoothly.

Storage systems for filing samples vary widely depending on the type of project. Residential designers find it convenient to maintain samples in boxes. Sturdy, solid-faced magazine storage boxes, clear-plastic boxes (that can hold shoes), or other appropriate-sized storage tubs can be used. Residential designers use storage boxes when fabric samples must be obtained in larger memo samples to appropriately show patterns to the client. Commercial designers generally use a notebook or expandable, closed file folders to store samples. However, for some projects, they would also use other storage boxes.

Floor Plans

The project file should have a copy of the final floor plan(s). If the project is very large, it might be convenient to have the large floor plans reduced on smaller sheets and include room-by-room plans. The copy of the signed, approved floor plans should also be included in the project file. Of course, backup copies of the CAD file should be maintained in a fireproof file.

Preliminary plans also should be maintained until all moneys have been collected and the project has been fully installed and approved. Disputes at the time of installation often can be mitigated by referring back to approved preliminary drawings and plans. In addition, maintaining these earlier plans and sketches allows the designer more leverage when charging clients for changes at the very end of the project.

The design firm should develop a system of coding the plans to the control sheets, as previously discussed, and to the written specifications. This makes it easy to identify specific items on the floor plan and is a key in the development of installation manuals. An example of this is shown in Figure 30-1.

Other Items

Some projects have additional items that should be placed in the project file. The smaller-sized design firm will often maintain copies of many forms that normally would be in the bookkeeping area, in the warehouse, or in the hands of the managers. These items might include a copy of the formal bid specifications, equipment lists, invoices from manufacturers, time records, and freight information. Follow-up notes, if done by management, concerning profitability, marketing information, problems, or successes may also be kept in the file.

VALUE ENGINEERING

Every client is looking for the very best value for the dollars spent on an interiors project. Few designers have had a client say that "money is no object." A strategy borrowed from architecture and engineering practice that can help bring greater value for dollars spent is through a process of *value engineering*. Value engineering is a method of analyzing and specifying products and design solutions based on cost-effectiveness. The key concept in this strategy is to find acceptable substitutions to higher-cost design concepts in order to provide quality outcomes at lower cost. Value engineering is best applied at the early stages of a project before many design decisions have been made but can be applied to many phases of a design project. For the interior design of facilities, it can be very effective applied to the specification of products or materials. When this method is utilized at the beginning of a project, it saves the designer time in analyzing various options against the known budget.

At times designers have referred to value engineering as "making a silk purse out of a sow's ear." Of course, many designers feel that this is just not possible. A more positive approach to value engineering is that it involves doing the very best design job possible at the lowest cost to the client. Sometimes this can be relatively simple, such as substituting a rayon blend fabric for silk for an upholstered item or using a textured vinyl wall covering rather than natural-grass cloth.

Clients, however, may use the method as a pure cost-cutting mechanism, especially at the end of a project. This can create a wide range of difficulties for the interior designer. The best way to prevent cost cutting at the end of the project is to have frank and complete budget discussions with clients at the beginning of the project. Residential and commercial clients appreciate interior designers who show them up-front estimates for design projects. Residential clients, who may lose track of how expensive it is to design or remodel a home, appreciate budget estimates.

Value engineering can be another useful tool for interior designers to use when they are showing clients how they offer value and knowledge in design. In addition, applying value engineering in appropriate ways can be useful when the designer is trying to show how he or she may be different from competitors.

SUMMARY

In recent years, a key criterion for clients when deciding to hire an interior designer has been the designer's ability to manage the project. Interior design projects have continually become more complex regardless of the type of space under consideration. Designers often handle many projects at one time, creating the need to control the large volume of details for all the work in progress. Project management is a very important part of a satisfactory design experience. With so many firms vying for design dollars, customer service via good project management means the difference between a healthy firm and one that may go out of business.

It is vital for the interior designer to be able to manage his or her time and the time of the firm's employees. It is also important for the designer to keep the projects under control. This means that the designer must develop the discipline and skills of time management. Poor time management and lax time recording can mean significant losses of revenue due to unbilled billable project time. The firm must develop a satisfactory means of project management and of scheduling the various projects that come into the office.

Part of managing the details is record keeping of documents, drawings, samples, and correspondence. Effective record keeping assists the designer in quick and accurate communications with any of the stakeholders. Designers have found that a well-planned methodology of project file retention is the best way to control details of the project. Classic time management and time recording techniques are essential parts of project management for any size interior design firm.

In this chapter, we have looked at the basic concepts of project management, work relationships, different scheduling method, budgeting, time records, time management, and the value of the project file. All of these project management systems help the designer and the firm manage the project effectively.

REFERENCE

1. Piotrowski, C., and Rogers, E. 2006, Designing Commercial Interoris, 2E., supplemental materials.

CHAPTER 29

Trade Sources

Key Terms and Concepts

These key terms and concepts are important to material in this chapter. Many of these terms will be utilized in other chapters as well. Be sure you understand these items as you read this chapter.

Terms and Concepts

Trade sources	Mart
Vendor	Trade building
FF&E	Showroom
Jobbers	Manufacturer's dealer
Representatives	Turnkey design
Reps	Tradespeople
Independent reps	Craftspeople
Factory reps	General contractor (GC)
Trunk show	Construction manager
Market	Subcontractors (subs)
Market center	Secondary subcontractors

Critical Issues

After completing this chapter you should be able to:

▩ Discuss the importance of trade sources for interior designers.

▩ Differentiate how the various trade sources work with interior designers.

▩ Explain what kind of information manufacturers representatives can provide.

▩ Explain the importance of attending major trade shows.

▩ Discuss why trade showrooms are open only to the trade.

▩ Discuss the difference between the responsibilities of a general contractor and subcontractors.

▩ Explain the benefits of online trade libraries and sources.

Sometimes there are too many choices and not enough time to research all the product options possible for a client's project. Projects with very tight budgets often present the opposite problem of not enough choices. Yet if you consider all the variations on products, colors of textiles, and the other permutations of products, the number of choices most designers have for specifying their interiors projects is almost incalculable. The opportunity to seek out the best products to specify for a residence or a commercial project provides a creative expression for many professionals that got them into interior design in the first place.

Those products and services related to the products come from a wide variety of sources, many of whom only work with people in the industry or trade such as interior designers. The manufacturers, suppliers, and tradespeople who provide the various goods and services a designer uses to complete a project are called *trade sources*. The majority of trade sources comprise the manufacturers of different furniture and furnishings products. Others are the suppliers and tradespeople who supply a custom product or install a product.

The designer finds these trade sources in many locations. A trade source may be a manufacturer across the country from the designer or in some other part of the world. It might be a resource at a local trade-only showroom or at a major trade mart in New York City, Chicago, Los Angeles, or many other cities. A trade source is also the cabinetmaker who is depended upon for custom millwork or furniture items and the artisan who makes beautiful blown glass accessories. The local installer of tile, wall coverings, carpet, lighting fixtures, and many other items needed in the interior are other examples of trade sources. These examples are merely a few of the many sources that are utilized by the interior designer.

Vendor, a term used often in this chapter and subsequent chapters, encompasses all the listed sources and even the interior designer. More precisely, a vendor is someone who sells products or services either to the end user or to some other person, like the designer. Commercial clients are used to working with vendors, whom they classify as anyone from whom they purchase any product or service. Residential clients, on the other hand, are used to working with salespeople or designers and may not be familiar with the term vendor.

For the student, understanding who all the trade sources are and what they offer is a big task. This chapter tries to help the reader sort out the different places designers can go to obtain products and services. The various trade sources not only represent the manufacturers and/or suppliers of the goods and services but also provide information to help the designer make choices and even to help the designer's clients make choices.

It is essential for the designer to find the trade sources that complement his or her business ideals. In this chapter, we will look at the different kinds of trade sources utilized by interior designers.

MANUFACTURERS

In the 2006 *Interior Design* magazine "A to Z Index" within the "Buyers Guide," there were 104 pages that listed (in small print) manufacturers of various kinds of furniture. There were 280 companies listed as manufacturing seating alone, 103 manufacturers of carpet, and 163 manufacturers of lighting fixtures. These do not likely hit upon the smaller local manufacturers that exist in every market that do not end up in the Buyers Guide listing. Perhaps you get the picture—the manufacturing of furniture and furnishings products is big business in the twenty-first century.

Most of the goods that a designer specifies and/or sells to clients come directly from the manufacturers of all the different types of FF&E products needed for residential and commercial interior finishing. Manufacturers also provide specification information, manufacturing criteria, and maintenance information on their goods. They provide product catalogs, price books, tear sheets, samples of textiles and finishes such as woods for desks, and even sample products. In addition, manufacturers help the interior designer obtain special products or semi-custom-designed products when the standards in the catalogs are insufficient.

Other sources related to manufacturers are *jobbers*. These trade sources are wholesalers who purchase smaller quantities of goods from manufacturers—usually a specific category of goods—and resell them to the trade. Textiles, accessories, and even furniture can be obtained from jobbers. Since some manufacturers will only sell large quantities, designers can still obtain goods from a jobber in the smaller quantity required. The designer might have to pay a higher price for the goods than if he or she could order directly from the factory.

Manufacturers' sales representatives (discussed in the section that follows) provide information, catalogs, samples, and pricing to the designer. These individuals make appointments with the designer to discuss the products, show new items, and provide other appropriate specification assistance. Of course, the interior designer might obtain this information by visiting a local or regional showroom.

The terms and conditions of ordering and selling for each manufacturer differs, and the designer needs to be sure that he or she understands those terms. Finding out, for example, that a company charges a 25 percent fee for using a COM (customer's own material) on seating after the fabric and the seating have been ordered and delivered is poor business practice. The product catalog and sales representatives provide information on how to order and the conditions of sale. Specific questions are directed primarily to a sales representative, although, of course, the designer can contact the factory directly.

A design firm must establish credit with each manufacturer with which it wishes to deal. It is not unusual for many manufacturers to never allow some design firms to order on credit and thus be required to pay for the goods in full at the time of ordering. The smaller design firm has the hardest time establishing credit and must be prepared to make substantial prepayments when ordering from many manufacturers for the first time. Other information about working with trade sources and getting orders placed correctly will be covered in Chapter 31.

SALES REPRESENTATIVES

It is most common for interior designers to work with a local or regional representative of manufacturers. That is not to say that there are not times that the designer must contact someone directly at the factory concerning an order or product specifications. *Representatives*, or *reps*, are terms used to refer to the men and women who either work for the manufacturer or represent the manufacturer to the architecture and design (A&D) community.

There are two kinds of reps: independent representatives and factory representatives. *Independent reps* work for themselves or a sales group. Many handle several manufacturers' products. These products may be related (e.g., all are from lighting manufacturers) or, as is more often the case, may be a combination of furniture and other products. *Factory reps* work for one particular manufacturer as employees of the company. They only represent that manufacturer's products or possibly only a segment of the manufacturer's product line. Both kinds of representatives are extremely helpful to the interior designer, and most small firms would not survive without their valuable assistance.

Representatives quote prices, give product information, and can make special product presentations to the client. They can also arrange for samples to be sent to the designer, provide the designer with information needed to write specifications, and distribute catalogs to the designer and, in some cases, to the end user. Some reps bring information and even samples of new merchandise to the attention of designers by having a trunk show. A *trunk show* occurs when a manufacturer's rep invites one or more interior designers to view a small selection of new merchandise. The term is also associated with the garment industry and retail, in general. The trunk show could take place at the designer's studio, or the rep may invite more than one designer to a hotel conference area. The trunk show refers to the traveling salesmen's traditional use of a trunk to transport the selection of goods that the salesman wishes to show retailers at the retailer's store. Sales representatives today often conduct these product showings by use of a laptop computer and CD-ROM discs at the designer's office or other location.

Manufacturers' sales representatives also have a role in generating sales independently of a designer or a dealer. For products generally used in commercial design, reps make calls on potential clients. Leads are generally turned over to dealers or are referred to designers. Sometimes, of course, the representatives sell directly to the client, bypassing the designer or vendor.

MARKET CENTERS, MARTS, AND SHOWROOMS

An enjoyable professional activity for many interior designers is attending one or more of the market shows around the country. *Market* is a term that many interior designers use to mean that they are going to visit one of the annual shows. These annual shows give manufacturers an opportunity to showcase new products and educate various members of the built-environment industry about their products. Trade shows are primarily held at major market centers and marts. *Market centers* are concentrations of trade sources in one area of a city. A *mart* is a building in which many firms have separate showrooms or share showroom space. A smaller-sized building consisting of predominately trade showrooms might be called a *trade building*. A *showroom* is the leased or owned space that a manufacturer uses at a market center or other location to display merchandise to the trade. Visiting marts and showrooms allows the designer the opportunity to see samples of the products that he or she is specifying. Designers often bring clients to the mart or showroom so that the client can see the items that are being specified.

The largest marts are located in the major urban areas of cities such as Chicago, New York, Toronto, Dallas, High Point, North Carolina, San Francisco, and Los Angeles. There are a large number of regional marts and trade buildings located in many other cities in the United States and Canada. The Merchandise Mart in Chicago is still the largest single mart in the United States and holds the largest national contract market. As one would expect, the number of marts and trade buildings fluctuates annually.

Marts and trade buildings have building access policies that limit admittance to the building and its many showrooms to the trade only. Trade showrooms also have similar access limitations. Often special passes—obtained by trade members from the mart's leasing agent or other mart officials—are needed to gain entrance to many of the floors in the mart. Showrooms generally admit individuals without passes if they have proper credentials that identify them as members of the trade. Proper credentials might include a business license, a tax license, business checking account information, an association membership card, or other documentation beyond a business card that establishes the individual as a representative of a design business. Admittance to a showroom does not automatically allow the individual to purchase products from the manufacturer.

Student members of ASID and IIDA or other professional organizations are able to get into most of the showrooms by showing their student membership card. Showrooms, however, have their own policies, and some do not admit anyone unless he or she has an official building pass.

Merchandise, if it is priced in the showroom, is often tagged with a suggested retail price or a price code. This is done to protect the designer's profit policies as he or she shows clients the products specified for the project. Occasionally, showrooms have sales in which discontinued items or slightly damaged floor samples are sold to the trade at very good prices.

Trade shows or "markets" are scheduled at many of the larger marts. Manufacturers use these shows to introduce their new products. These shows often include seminars, workshops, and continuing-education classes. The combination of educational programs and the opportunity to inspect a great number of products is an important updating tool for designers. Recall from Chapter 1 that furniture shows began in the nineteenth century!

Probably the largest furniture show in the United States is held at the NeoCon World's Trade Show in Chicago, primarily at the Merchandise Mart. Frequently, more than 50,000 interior designers, architects, facility planners, and related professionals travel to Chicago in June to see the new products. Although contract furniture is highlighted at NeoCon, many residential products, as well as floor coverings, wall coverings, lighting, and accessories, are displayed. Numerous seminars offering continuing-education unit and other learning unit credits are also offered for attendees.

Other large furniture shows are held in other parts of the country. The International Home Furnishings Market is held in April in High Point, North Carolina. This show targets the residential interior design industry. The annual January "Buyers Guide" issue of *Interior Design* magazine, as well as the buyer's guides in other trade magazines, have an extensive calendar of industry events helping designers plan their market trips. Specialty shows are also held at these same marts either just prior to the major market shows or at other times of the year. Other specialty shows are held in various cities during the year. Actual dates and locations of furniture and specialty shows, as well as of the many conferences for interior designers, are published in the trade magazines. Most of the smaller regional marts also have shows. These generally attract the local design community. Item 29-1 on the CD lists information on the largest trade shows generally held during the year.

Market shows like NeoCon Chicago are exciting, energizing events, especially for students who are attending them for the first time. Even professionals approach markets as an endurance contest, hoping their feet will hold up to all the walking! There is so much going on that it is difficult for designers to decide what to do each day. There is a tendency for first timers to overload themselves with brochures and catalogs. Professionals have learned to bring an abundance of business cards and request materials so that manufacturers can mail their catalogs to the designer. Owners of small design firms who have had problems with getting mailings may want to bring their business license or resale license as well.

When students enter a trade showroom, they should be respectful of the employees who work there and should be courteous enough to listen to the sales presentations. They can ask the rep questions but should pay attention to their answers. Designers and students who attend markets with serious intent find new product lines and helpful reps who can add immeasurably to their future business.

Students should be cautioned to not grab for every sample, catalog, or brochure. It is true that some reps do not like to talk to students, but students who act and dress professionally, ask intelligent questions, and request that information be sent to them often earn respect and gather much information from representatives. The major shows generally include presentations and events planned for students.

What Would You Do?

Judy Smith has been working with a client, Mr. and Mrs. Stevenson, on their home for the last five years. Little by little, they have worked on the remodeling and finishing of the 4500-square-foot house in a small resort community. The house is a three-story Victorian on a quiet wooded lot in a residential area that has been rezoned for commercial use as well as residential.

Six months ago Mr. Stevenson informed Judy that they were going to convert the house into a bed and breakfast, now that he has retired from his job as a school principal. They hired Judy to continue to work with them on any additional remodeling that must be done in order to "cost-effectively" (as Mr. Stevenson remarked) get the property ready to accept its first guests as quickly as possible.

Judy is a registered interior designer in her state but has never obtained a contractor's license. The Stevensons were told by the city that in order to convert the house to a bed and breakfast, they would have to bring the electrical and other mechanical systems up to code. Other mechanical and structural changes were needed in the kitchen and second-floor bedroom spaces that would be for guests. Judy has also made some additional suggestions to change finish materials and space usage for the first floor to accommodate the greeting of guests and their use of the living room as a "lobby" living room. However, the Stevenson's are reluctant to proceed with the changes the city and Judy have recently stipulated.

LOCAL SHOWROOMS

Many manufacturers locate regional showrooms or showroom/sales offices in cities like Boston, Phoenix, Minneapolis, Denver, and Miami, to name just a few. Some of these are for major furniture manufacturers, like Herman Miller and Knoll International, or various suppliers of fabrics, wall coverings, carpet, and floor materials. Local showrooms generally are restricted to the trade and have similar policies for admittance, pricing, and purchasing as showrooms in the marts. Local trade buildings and showrooms increase the opportunity for designers to view more actual products when the designer's office is too far from the major marts.

Designers can often place orders directly from small, local showrooms. The usual establishment of credit, prepayment, and other terms of sale exist when working with small, local showrooms as with buying directly from manufacturers.

In some cities, several manufacturers may locate within a local trade building, creating a small mart. It is not unusual for these local trade building tenants to organize special events like speakers, provide space for professional association offices, and admit students to view products.

RETAIL SPECIALTY STORES

Retail stores that sell lighting fixtures, accessories, art objects, and furniture pieces can be a convenient resource for the interior designer. They are generally not owned or franchised by any of the manufacturers whose products are displayed. Many designers in smaller firms often frequent retail specialty stores to purchase items that they need in a hurry.

A retail specialty store by tradition is open to the public as well as the trade. In fact, these stores generate the majority of their revenue from retail sales directly to the consumer. A trade showroom generates its revenue from sales to interior designers and others in the trade.

Retail specialty stores often give trade discounts to interior designers. These trade discounts are reduced prices given to trade members so that designers can then resell them to their clients. The reader may wish to refer back to Chapter 25 for more information on trade discounts.

MANUFACTURER'S DEALERS

Manufacturer's dealers (or just dealers) are generally not owned or franchised back to the manufacturer but are privately owned businesses. They are usually retail furniture stores, as opposed to specialty shops, that have made special arrangements with one or more manufacturers of furniture to feature selling those products at a higher volume than other products. They frequently stock inventory of considerable size of those specific products. However, they sell a wide variety of products—not just ones from one or two manufacturers.

A full-service dealership offers design, selling, and installation services. It may also provide other services such as installation of flooring and wall coverings. Thus, it can help a client through the entire design process, from programming to completion. This sometimes is referred to as *turnkey design*. In architecture, turnkey projects commonly include financing assistance, perhaps even property acquisition, as well as design services. Dealers often become involved in bidding on projects specified by other dealers or outside interior design and architectural firms. Smaller dealerships may operate a bit more like a retail store.

The term manufacturer's dealer is most associated with office furnishings dealers. However, there are many residential furniture retail stores that actually serve as dealers. Dealerships often offer a trade discount to independent designers. In some geographic areas, some of the products sold at a dealership are only available through that dealer.

TECHNOLOGY AND TRADE SOURCES

Interior designers have increasingly looked to the Internet for information and ordering of products. Thousands of sources are available online or offer CD-ROM substitutes for printed catalogs. The computer and other electronic means of procuring goods for projects is a necessary resource for interior designers regardless of specialty or size of firm. Of course, the Web is not the only way designers use technology for ordering. It is very common for designers to use fax machines to place orders and receive faxed acknowledgments. Some companies utilize e-mail or other online methods for orders and acknowledgments.

Computer technology opens the world to the designer. One can search catalogs and other information directly from manufacturer's Web sites. Internet catalog libraries have been created so that designers have access to the catalogs of numerous vendors and manufacturers. In addition, there are many auction sites and thousands of very small-business tradespeople and craftspeople who sell specialty items via their own Web sites. Once an item is found, the picture and information can be downloaded and printed for later reference. The availability of pricing online varies greatly. Some companies that seek out the end user will have pricing available on their Web sites. Companies that deal more exclusively with the trade might require a special code from the designer in order to access the price list. Otherwise, prices must be obtained from representatives, printed price lists, or from dealers. Most online sites and product libraries are for reference only, although some sites provide purchasing capabilities.

A manufacturer's Web site—such as Herman Miller, Baker Furniture, Collins & Aikman Floorcoverings, Nevermar (laminates), and Thomasville Furniture, to name just a few—are open to anyone who has access to the World Wide Web. Online libraries are to the trade only. A designer has to subscribe to the library in order to receive a password that will give the designer access to the information (see Figure 29-1). This serves the same purpose as a closed showroom; it gives the interior designer access to product information and pricing that are not available to the general public. The information in these online libraries gives the small practitioner access to products from hundreds of manufacturers around the world. These resources add more suppliers to their libraries every day and have product listings for both commercial and residential needs. Some companies may also have chat rooms to exchange information and may provide online newsletters, planning tips and assistance, industry news, and other features.

Other kinds of information can be obtained from the World Wide Web as well. The *Sweets Catalog Files* published by McGraw-Hill for construction, architecture, and interiors products is just one free reference available online. The professional associations have Web sites providing information for members and nonmembers. A designer can also search for almost any kind of information needed on business operations, marketing, or financing topics or any other topic of interest. The types of information that can be obtained from online sources is unlimited.

Web addresses for many companies are listed in the buyer's guides and source guides of the many trade magazines. As a product resource, company

FIGURE 29-1.

Home page for designeresources.com Web site. This site is one of many that provides product information by subscription to interior designers. (Reproduced with permission, designeresources.com, Greenville, SC)

Web pages and online libraries have revolutionized product source research for the interior designer.

TRADESPEOPLE AND CRAFTSPEOPLE

Interior designers are always looking for individuals and companies that can provide installation services of architectural finishes and/or build and create specialty items of all kinds. *Tradespeople* and *craftspeople* are these resources for goods and services to the design community and the general public. Cabinetmakers, painters, carpet and floor-covering installers, and wallpaper installers are a few examples. Drapery workrooms primarily manufacture for designers and retail specialty stores and do not generally market directly to the end user. There are also craftspeople who make custom products of various kinds, especially furniture items, and who work with interior designers and may somehow market to end users.

It is important for designers to work with quality craftspeople who are dependable and trustworthy. New craftspeople and tradespeople should be investigated by the designer. This investigation should include obtaining references from their clients and inspecting their work by visiting previous job sites. Some tradespeople, such as painters and carpet installers, must be licensed contractors and hold bonds insuring their work. Individuals who are involved in structural work or installation of architectural finishes are often required to be licensed by their state. Hiring unlicensed contractors in states that require licensing can leave the designer open to lawsuits.

When beginning to work with new tradespeople, the designer should be sure that he or she understands how the tradespeople work, not just what they make and the quality of their work. Will the cabinetmaker prepare working drawings of the custom furniture from just a plan and elevation, or is the designer expected to prepare all of the working drawings? If materials must be sent to the tradespeople, for example, fabric to an antique refinisher, how will freight charges be handled? Will the installer accept delivery of goods (such as carpet) in the designer's name, or will the designer have to receive the goods and have the installer pick up the carpet from the designer? These are just a few questions that the designer must ask of potential tradespeople.

CONSTRUCTION CONTRACTORS

Rachel's client has hired her to remodel the kitchen and family room. The client has indicated that he wants to replace the cabinets and appliances, and add a gas-burning fireplace in the family room. It is also likely that he will want an island with the range in the island and the client prefers that to be a gas range. Rachel realizes that she will need some guidance from consultants.

Perhaps it is easy for the reader to see that Rachel's project is just one example of design projects involving structural work that necessitates the use of one or more construction contractors. *General contractors* (often called GCs) are contractors that hold a license that allows them to contract and supervise all phases of a construction project. Commercial designers regularly work with general contractors or construction management companies that oversee the entire project. A *construction manager* is an individual who oversees the construction project as an agent for either the general contractor or the owner.

General contractors often hire *subcontractors* (also called subs) to do the specialized work. There are specialized subcontractors who do concrete work; plumbing; electrical work; framing; sheet metal; heating, ventilation, and air conditioning (HVAC); painting; roofing; carpet installation; ceramic tile; landscaping; and many other specialized trades and crafts involved in the construction and finishing of commercial and residential buildings. There can even be *secondary subcontractors* who are hired because the project may require special skills or equipment that the subcontractor does not have. For example, in construction, when a cinder block stem wall is required, it is usually filled with a special cement mixture to strengthen the wall. The masonry subcontractor may hire a secondary subcontractor to take care of this job, since it requires a special piece of equipment.

In some states, designers must hold either a contractor's license or a specialty license to give instructions and supervisory information to subcontractors and installers—even carpet and wallpaper installers. An interior designer whose license is related to interior design practice (through a title or practice act) might not automatically be able to do the supervision granted by a contractor's license. The designer should know the law in his or her jurisdiction. Thus, designers must be careful about giving instructions to subs on the job. Designers should always request changes through the supervisor of the tradespeople involved or through the general contractor.

Select contractors and subs after thoroughly researching the company. They need to have the proper licenses and bonds to execute the needed work. Ask to visit projects they have worked on. Also ask for references from designers and architects who may have used the contractor. Contractors and subs that will not provide references or copies of licenses should not be hired.

It is common that the designer obtains two or three quotes from different contractors. It is just good sense to let the contractor know you are getting other quotes. Naturally, the work should not proceed until a contract between the designer and the contractor that details what will be done and the price quoted for the job is finalized. Remember that when you recommend contractors to the client, you could also be liable for problems even when the client pays the contractor directly for the work.

It is the responsibility of the interior designer to instruct the client, who may never have had a custom home constructed or experienced a remodeling or renovation project on a home or a commercial space, on the process that will take place. The designer should clarify the chain of command and how the various decisions and communications will take place right from the beginning of the project to its completion.

The men and women who work in the trades professionally do the work as it is drawn, specified, and contracted. Directions provided by the interior designer or the client counter to those documents are often ignored unless the subcontractor is clear that someone other than his or her foreman can provide that direction. This is why working drawings have to be done correctly, or the work might be stopped if corrections are required. Of course, a contractor or a subcontractor who sees errors in the drawings and specifications that could be dangerous or that violate codes will call this to the attention of the designer.

Making changes in a job after the contract is let (awarded) requires a change order. *Change orders* are documents that describe any modification in construction projects or interiors furnishing projects after the contract has been awarded. Change orders usually result in higher prices for the project, because something extra had to be done that was not called for in the original drawings and specifications. Change orders are also discussed in Chapter 30.

It is important for the client to understand that he or she should not try to give directions or in any way supervise the subcontractors, unless, of course, the client is his or her own general contractor. Fights have been known to break out when subs refuse to make a change that is requested—or demanded—by the client. If the client or the designer has a question or wants to make a change, the change should be discussed with the general contract or contractor and a change order needs to be issued by the designer to the general contractor, who will then direct the work to the subcontractor after a change order has been prepared.

SELECTING TRADE SOURCES

It is obvious from the previous discussions that there is a vast array of suppliers and sources of products and service providers that can be utilized to complete any type of interior design project. Designers are constantly searching for high-quality tradespeople and subcontractors as well as unusual products for their projects. When the economy is good and building booms, it becomes difficult to locate any kind of tradespeople who can work in a timely fashion. Lead times can be quite long for many quality workers in the field, and the designer must explain that issue to clients at the inception of the project.

Managing a firm's resources and selecting resources are important tasks in an interior design practice. That is the first important part of selecting trade sources—determining what kinds of materials and catalogs will be necessary in the studio. An interior designer's library can easily become clogged with sample books, catalogs, flyers, and price lists. When catalogs and sample books were complimentary, interior designers thought nothing of collecting every book and sample sent to the office. Today more manufacturers are charging for their catalogs and especially samples, requiring designers to think carefully about what materials they will place in their library. Of course, today, many product catalogs are virtual catalogs—available on CD-ROMs or able to be viewed on the Internet. This helps, but the designer still requires information on the products and how to get the information that he or she needs about these items.

Establishing Vendor Accounts

Interior designers who sell merchandise to clients generally have to special-order the items, as only the biggest firms have a showroom with inventory of sellable merchandise. Designers prefer to establish credit with the various vendors and suppliers they work with rather than paying up front when the order is placed. As with any consumer, the interior designer must establish a good credit relationship with a vendor in order to be able to pay on credit.

Most suppliers expect payment in full before the order is put into production. This payment in full might be in cash (checks really) by the designer or when the designer has an open account with the vendor. Designers who must pay up front require clients to pay up front as well. Interior designers frequently require a 100 percent payment by the client before the order is placed. Naturally, not all clients are willing to pay in full for something that may take several months to obtain. Thus, designers might need to have flexible prepayment terms.

To establish an account with a vendor or supplier (also called an *open account*), the designer or firm must first fill out a credit application. The information required on the credit application is similar to that which the designer may request of clients wishing to purchase on credit (and not using a credit card). Table 31-1 in Chapter 31 provides an outline of what information will be required of the designer. Be sure you understand what the credit limit will be so that you are not embarrassed by needing more credit than your limits allow. That definitely will mean late delivery of goods.

Open accounts are only given to designers who have a good credit history. In addition to having a good credit history, some are only given an open account when they order a specified dollar amount of goods from the supplier over some time period, which could be anywhere from one year to three years' duration.

A good credit history is the key to obtaining an open account with a vendor. Designers and firms must be very vigilant in paying all bills on time. Late payments and nonpayments with one vendor will negatively impact the designer's ability to purchase from other vendors. Good credit history is why many interior design firms carefully watch their finances on a monthly basis. It is also why many sole practitioners do not take much in the way of a salary from the business so that they have plenty of funds in their accounts to take care of those vendor orders that have not given them an open account. Destroying a credit history with a vendor can lead to very serious consequences for the designer who wishes to sell merchandise to clients.

Members of ASID and IIDA have an added benefit of membership in that many companies are industry partners to the associations. These partnerships provide a wide range of information and product availability from hundreds of resources for members. Industry partners respect their membership with ASID and IIDA and are eager to assist practitioner members. Of course, other associations also have industry partners who can provide valuable assistance to designers in other professional organizations.

The firm's business plan gives management guidelines on what to keep as resources. If the firm is not doing residential design, there is little need for residential-grade carpet samples. Design firms that are lucky enough to work with high-end clients have little use for budget furniture catalogs. But then, these comments only state the obvious. How does a design firm really find and maintain the best sources? Some suggestions follow.

1. *Clarify the business plan.* The focus of the practice is a primary determining factor in what types of resources are needed in the studio or office. This will show the firm who its client groups are and the kinds of design services the firm is prepared to offer. It will help direct the firm to the kinds of trade sources that are needed. Part of this process should include a review of project files and purchase order files in order to determine which major vendors have been the most successful for the design firm. It should consider eliminating suppliers that have given the firm poor service, regardless of the products the suppliers offer.

2. *Review current resource materials on a regular basis.* The design firm should clean out its current library and resource materials at least once a year. Catalogs with five-year-old price lists may need to be discarded, especially if no one in the office can remember buying from the source recently. Old price lists could get the firm in trouble if discontinued goods are specified. The librarian can request new tear sheets or even entire catalogs from manufacturers that are used frequently. Manufacturer's representatives can be called and asked to update the firm's catalogs and samples. It is, after all, part of the service that the rep provides. The firm should obtain CD-ROM catalogs for products that it uses frequently. It can set up bookmarks on the Internet for the most frequently used Web-based catalogs. With the appropriate direction, students or interns can be hired to purge the library.

3. *Carefully review new sources.* The design firm should keep only those new items that fit the design firm's product and jobs profile. It should return or discard those items that do not add to the firm's library. The firm should also get to know the representatives or the craftspeople from the resources the firm maintains. Questions on pricing, delivery schedules, exclusivity, customs, warranties, quality, and manufacturing and

terms of sale are important to have clear before ordering from a new source.

4. *Visit factories and workshops.* A great way to learn about a supplier's products is by arranging a tour of the factory or workshop. Tours are relatively easy to arrange for small suppliers, such as upholsterers and cabinet shops. Special arrangements must be made to visit large manufacturers' factories. Be sure you know what you want to ask the tour guide/owner about the company. If possible, arrange time to also talk to the order processing department.

5. *Try to work with sources on the firm's terms.* Small design firms need to find sources that will take lower prepayments with orders whenever possible. Establishing good credit with every source is the best way to improve terms. Smaller firms might also have to work with suppliers that are closer to the design firm geographically, so that goods can be drop-shipped directly to the client. This method also reduces the cost of the project, because freight charges are somewhat reduced.

6. *Establish policies for representative's visits.* First of all, the designer needs to know the contacts are for his or her area. A representative might live locally or live out of state and only visit the area occasionally. It is also a good idea to have a contact at factories and suppliers that the designer uses frequently. Unless designers enjoy constant interruptions, they should require reps to make appointments to show new items. Many larger firms require reps to meet with the design staff during lunch hours, and the reps provide the meal. This works well, and reps do not complain about the cost, unless very few of the design staff show up.

7. *Clarify payment and credit policies.* The smaller the design firm, the more likely the supplier will require payment in full at the time of ordering. This is because most manufacturers and suppliers only grant credit terms to designers who order frequently or in large quantities.

8. *Designers must do their job.* Designers sometimes try to pass the buck when they make a mistake or create a problem, and try to pass it on to the trade source. A professional, responsible, and ethical interior designer who does his or her job does not to have to worry about passing the buck because of liability issues.

9. *Develop loyalty to sources.* Although it is not unusual for designers to use more than one company for painting, custom cabinets, and several sources for various goods, working with a quality supplier and providing a substantial amount of business to that company each year will reap benefits to the design firm. One obvious benefit is granting of better credit terms. Another is that loyal sources will bend over backward to help out loyal designers.

10. *Do not demand or expect specification fees.* Reps and suppliers complain about designers who demand specification fees (an activity that is considered unethical by the professional associations). Specification fees must be revealed to clients even when freely granted by the supplier.

By now, the reader has an understanding of the vast amount of responsibility that an interior designer has in the execution of a design project. It is critical that the designer only take on projects for which the designer is qualified. Many things can go wrong, including providing incorrect information to vendors, making mistakes on drawings, and forgetting to tell tradespeople about site conditions or perhaps peculiarities of the client. He or she must do the necessary research to understand the proper specification of any product that goes into the project. The designer must carefully prepare the documents needed for the job. Above all, the interior designer should take care of problems that arise as quickly and professionally as possible.

SUMMARY

An interesting exercise for the reader is to investigate through the local yellow pages the number of trade and retail sources of goods that are available. This small snapshot of research will help the reader see that the sources that the design firm uses or maintains information about are many and varied. Those chosen regularly by the design firm should complement the firm's work. Trips to market shows give designers a very good opportunity to review sources and to talk to sales representatives or factory salespeople. Because of the wealth of products available to designers, it is important for designers to carefully select the products, representatives, and other trade sources that fit into the firm's type of business. The Internet has brought a new dimension to finding just the right product for a client. Online libraries, Web sites of major manufacturers, and Web sites of specialty craftspeople help make sources known to potential clients.

A very important part of utilizing various trade sources is researching the source and determining how or if the source can be of benefit to the designer. Not all of the thousands of sources are appropriate for each design firm. Some will have purchasing policies that make working with a particular company prohibitive. Others might not offer the quality of workmanship that the designer requires. The chapter has provided brief discussions of these issues, with other information to follow in Chapter 31, "Contract Administration."

The discussion of trade sources in this chapter that are utilized by the interior designer provides some information about where designers can find the products and services that they will use for their clients. Professionals can easily become familiar with the sources available in the geographic areas in which they plan to conduct business that may be available from manufacturers, suppliers, or craftspeople throughout the world. Students can learn about manufacturers and suppliers by reading trade magazines, going on the Internet and searching out products, visiting local trade showrooms, visiting one of the market shows, or visiting local design offices.

CHAPTER 30

Contract Documents and Specifications

Key Terms and Concepts

These key terms and concepts are important to material in this chapter. Many of these terms will be utilized in other chapters as well. Be sure you understand these items as you read this chapter.

Terms and Concepts

FF&E projects

Contract documents (CDs)

Construction documents

Construction drawings

Working drawings

Movable equipment

Schedules

Specification (specs)

Closed specification

Open specification

Or equal

Proprietary specification

Base bid (specification)

Descriptive specification

Performance specification

Reference specification

Construction Specifications Institute (CSI)

MasterFormat™

MASTERSPEC®

Competitive bidding

Single-source purchasing

Bid documents

Best and final offer (BAFO)

General conditions

Invitation to bid

Open competitive selection

Closed competitive selection

Bid list

Prequalified

Instructions to bidders

Exclusions

Bid form (tender form)

Base bid (actual bid)

Alternate bid

Bond forms

Bid bond

Performance bond

Labor and materials payment bond

Mechanic's lien

Bid opening

Modifications

Addenda

Change orders

Submittal

Critical Issues

After completing this chapter you should be able to:

- Compare the purpose and types of materials in a set of contract documents to a set of construction documents.
- Describe what kinds of schedules are included in a set of construction documents.
- Explain why it is better to use generic or trade names to identify products on construction drawings rather than actual product names.
- Discuss the differences between an open and closed specification and provide an example of each.
- Provide key characteristics and uses of the proprietary, descriptive, performance, and reference specifications.
- Discuss the advantages and disadvantages of using proprietary specifications for a commercial project.
- Discuss why it is important for specifications to be written in a clear concise manner—in accordance to the type of specification used.
- Explain the purpose of the competitive bid process.
- Explain why the competitive bid process is less often used for a residential interiors project.
- List and explain the documents needed for a competitive bid.
- Compare the purposes of the bid bond, performance bond, and the labor and materials payment bond.
- Compare the purposes of addenda, change orders, and submittals.

Interior designers create the plans and lists of furniture and other items needed to complete the project for the client. In many cases, these documents are used by the interior designer and the vendors who deliver furniture and subcontractors that are hired to install architectural finishes or other interior products. Projects that have minimal or no construction work involved are often referred to as *FF&E projects*. That acronym stands for furniture, fixtures, and equipment.

Many other projects require contract documents consisting of construction drawings—which mostly consist of drawings for partitions and other non-load-bearing features for an interiors project—specifications, and schedules. Contract documents are needed for many types of residential and commercial projects when it is necessary for the client to obtain competitive bids, or prices, for the completion of an interiors project.

There are many industry standards that impact the production of the complete set of contract documents. An understanding of what constitutes contract documents is necessary for any practitioner regardless of specialty. A residential designer might become involved in a project where he or she prepares construction drawings and specifications for remodeling and additions to a home. This is, of course, only if local laws allow for those tasks to be performed by an interior design professional. Commercial interior designers frequently are involved in developing parts of the contract documents, since many private entities, such as a hotel, a corporate office center, or department store, as well as government agencies, utility companies, and schools, or any of many other types of commercial facilities require competitive bidding for the build-out and furnishing of commercial facilities.

Depending on whether a project is FF&E, construction and FF&E, public, or private, certain processes in the preparation of construction documents and specifications will be different. This chapter primarily discusses the documents that are associated with projects that must be competitively bid, with emphasis placed on formal bid specifications. It also includes a discussion of the bid process and the documents that are added to the construction drawings and specifications to complete the contract documents package.

CONTRACT DOCUMENTS

Jennifer was working with Henry to review the dimensioned floor plans and elevations for the Cannon Group Consulting firm project offices. Grace was completing the specifications for the furniture, and others in the firm either had completed reviews or were working on other sheets in the drawings set. They were completing the contract documents so that bids could be obtained for the interior construction and furnishings. Jennifer found some errors in the drawings, and Henry said to ignore them, as the firm could send out an addendum once the drawings were issued.

The fourth phase of a project is referred to as the contract documents phase. It is in this phase of a project that all the documents needed to build and bid (or purchase) the project are completed. *Contract documents* consist of all the construction drawings, specifications, and contracts or agreements between the designer and the project owner and others that might be involved in the construction of the project. A complete set of contract documents (also called CDs) include architectural drawings, schedules, specifications, modifications, and contracts related to the actual build-out of the project. *Construction documents* are thought of as the drawings and specifications portion of the contract documents.

This package of documents and drawings are a legal document, constituting a contract, and thus ensures that the project will be executed according to the design concepts and wishes of the interior designer and the client. Technically, to vary from the construction documents without approval constitutes breach of contract. Contract documents must be prepared carefully and accurately. Errors in the drawings or other documents will result in liability issues as well as potential lost revenue for the interior designer. Legal disputes can harm the designer's reputation and even result in penalties imposed by a court. Errors in contract documents can also lead to ethics complaints and potentially disciplinary measures by the designer's professional association.

This section of the chapter will briefly discuss construction drawings and schedules. Specifications, documents for the competitive bidding process, and modifications will be covered separately. Table 30-1 lists the most common documents that are usually involved in the construction documents phase of a project.

Construction Drawings

Although the construction drawings are discussed separately from specifications, it is important to begin by saying that the two items are used collectively to complete a project. Together they are the instructions on how to complete the project. The drawings show what is to be done visually, while the specifications explain how the work is to be done and the quality of work required.

The *construction drawings* portion of contract documents typically consists of all plans, elevations, and details required for building the structure or the

TABLE 30-1.

Contract Documents.

> **Contract Documents**
>
> Agreement between owner and contractor
> Conditions of the contract
> Construction documents
> Modifications: addenda and change orders
>
> **Construction Documents**
>
> Drawings
> Specifications
> Schedules
>
> **Bid Documents**
>
> Invitation to bid
> Instructions to bidders
> Bid form
> Bid requirements
> Construction drawings

interior. Many in the industry call these drawings the *working drawings*. For an interiors project, a set of CDs would include dimensioned partition drawings; section drawings; mechanical drawings, including electrical and telephone location plans; reflected ceiling plans; plumbing plans; HVAC plans; other mechanical plans (such as for sprinklers in a commercial building); interior construction elevations; and construction details. Additional specialized drawings, such as plans from lighting designers, commercial kitchen and foodservice designers, health-care system designers, and others, might also be included. Preparation of additional drawings would be done by the person who designed the exterior structure.

Many interior and architectural firms also include equipment plans or furniture plans in the working drawings. Equipment plans show the location of, and identify by code, the movable equipment in the project. By *movable equipment*, we mean furniture and other equipment, such as refrigerators, that can be easily moved and are not part of the structure. Movable equipment is rarely bid with the construction of the walls. In most projects, furniture and equipment drawings are provided to the general contractor for information only. They are obviously necessary for the furniture bid.

Interior designers prepare many furniture or equipment plans using a variety of techniques. Some are very detailed and in fact look a lot like a detailed rendered floor plan. Others are very simple, giving the bare essentials of shapes and sizes along with notes. The equipment or furniture plan must also relate to written specifications. Regardless of technique, it must communicate to various stakeholders what goes where without the interior designer needing to be on the job site.

The equipment plan for bidding purposes must be very clear and understandable. When projects are to be bid, it is common for interior designers to prepare a separate equipment or furniture floor plan for information and use in installation. Some designers use codes that correspond to information in the written specifications to clarify each furniture item in the bid. Codes may be simple numbers or letters, accompanied by a furniture schedule describing these items of furniture (see Figure 30-1), or more complicated multinumber codes. Codes are used to indicate generic types of furniture and furnishings, not

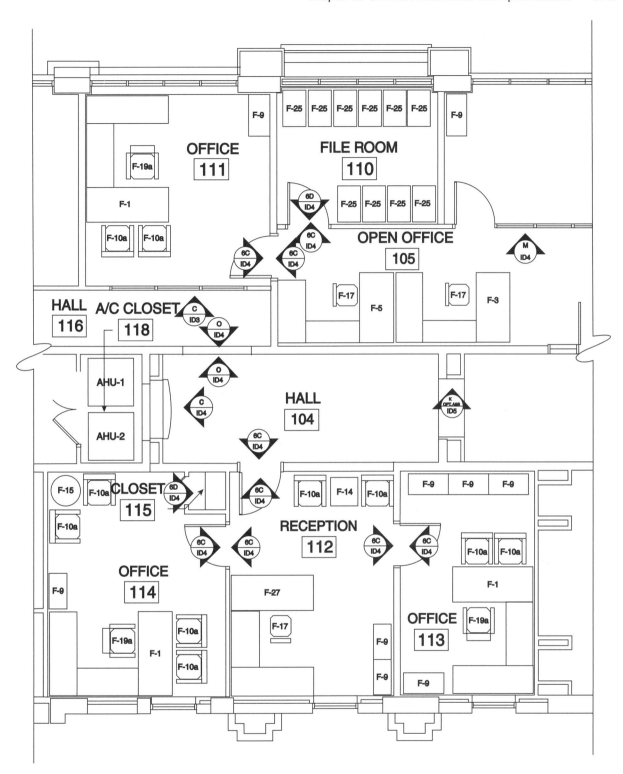

FIGURE 30-1.

Coded furniture schedule—partial floor plan. (Reproduced with permission, Sally Thompson, ASID, Personal Interiors by Sally Thompson, Inc. Gainesville, FL)

specific product information, just as generic information is often used in notations on construction drawings. These codes then need to be further explained in the specifications.

The exact format and coordination between plans and specifications must be clear enough for the vendor to know what he or she is bidding on. They must also be easy enough for the design firm to produce and also to make any required changes to the plans. However, the design firm should individualize the formats, since they are, in part, a marketing tool.

Trade names and product numbers should not be used on the equipment plans, since errors can occur. Trade names and product numbers, if used, should be limited to the written specifications. All information in schedules or code keys should be generic descriptions. This is because it is easy to transpose numbers on plans. If the designer must write product names and numbers many times, it would be easy to make this kind of error, resulting in an incorrect bid. If it becomes necessary to change or substitute a different product, forgetting to make the changes in product numbers on the plans can cause incorrect bidding or the wrong product being ordered.

Although it is better to use generic names for furniture, furnishings, and room names, generic descriptions can lead to misinterpretations if the terms used are not clarified. For example, *chair* can mean guest chair, armchair, posture chair, club chair, dining chair, stool, occasional chair, or executive chair. *Table* can mean dining table, coffee table, end table, cocktail table, occasional table, conference table, table desk, or Parsons table. And *rest room* can mean the women's, room, men's room, powder room, lavatory, bathroom, or lounge.

Many other examples of generic furniture, furnishings, and room terminology exist. Although it is important for designers to use generic terms, it is equally important for terms to be consistent, clear, and defined within the specifications. To aid in defining all generic terms, a key needs to be placed either in the specifications or on one of the sheets of equipment plans.

Any number of books can further clarify how to prepare a set of construction drawings and equipment plans in detail. Several are mentioned in the references.

Schedules

Schedules are an important part of the instructions concerning how a project is to be completed. In this situation, a *schedule* is usually a tabular chart or graphic used to clarify project items that cannot easily and completely be distinguished from representations on floor plans and other construction drawings. Schedules are commonly prepared for doors, windows, and interior room finishes. Interior room finish schedules include information for walls, floor treatments, and ceiling heights and treatments. Schedules for other specific items, such as lighting fixtures and furniture, are also used by designers. Finish schedules are commonly prepared in tabular form, while door and window schedules are commonly prepared in graphic form. The format of these schedules varies greatly from office to office. Tabular schedules are often computerized by using word-processing or spreadsheet programs or as part of the CAD software used by the firm.

For the same reasons given for equipment plans, the information provided in the schedules included in the working drawings should be generic. Trade or manufacturer's names are to be supplied in the written specifications. For interiors projects that are not very large or complicated, some designers include a materials key with the finish schedule. The materials key is similar in format to the finish schedule. This materials key does name manufacturers. If it is used, it should be used in the specifications. It would not be appropriate to use a materials key if a performance or descriptive specification were used.

SPECIFICATIONS

Even the most detailed construction drawings alone do not provide enough information for contractors to build or supply what is needed for an interiors or construction project. In fact, in court cases, the written word supersedes disputes over drawings. The *specifications* portion of the contract documents is the written instructions to the general contractors and vendors. Specifications (simply referred to as "specs" by many in the industry) are prepared in a technical fashion and provide information about descriptions of the materials or products required, qualities and workmanship, installation requirements, responsibilities of bidders, and the like. They are needed for structural materials and designs as well as for the FF&E required for the interior. This section discusses the types of specifications used for the FF&E. If the reader is in need of information on the preparation of specifications for structural work, he or she should refer to the references for suggested books.

Small interior design firms that work directly with the client for specification and subsequent purchase of the products will likely use a simple, though detailed, specification list to clarify what is to be provided for the project. Of course, it is necessary for the designer to clarify the quantities, description, and perhaps pricing on these simple specifications. Figure 25-1 showed an example of this type of simple equipment list. If a custom item or an attachment such as a mirror is part of the project, the interior designer may prepare notes concerning the quality and installation procedures required for those items as part of the equipment list or separately. Many of the documents discussed later in this chapter are not utilized when simpler equipment lists are used rather than competitive bid specifications, because the terms and conditions concerning ordering the merchandise previously have been agreed to by the designer and the client.

When the whole or part of the construction and/or procurement of the goods is to be procured by competitive bid, a different type of specification is required. Written specifications for a project can be quite complex. There are many opportunities for mistakes if the firm preparing the specifications is careless. As mentioned at the beginning of this section, discrepancies occur between what is shown on the drawings and what is stated in the written instructions. Since it is easier for people to interpret the written word than drawings, when there are discrepancies between the two, the courts often base judgments on the specifications. It is therefore essential for the designer to prepare the specifications clearly, without any ambiguity, errors, or omissions.

It is important to realize that the specifications should complement the drawings, not duplicate them. Specifications should describe what is needed, along with quality standards. In addition, the drawings should show dimensional and location information. Drawings can also indicate quantities, sizes, generic identification of materials, and interrelationships of space, materials, and equipment. Some designers also provide quantities of the goods required in the written specifications. Although this is very helpful to the vendors who are bidding, vendors commonly are required to be responsible for the quantities.

When a specification is written for a product such that no other product can be substituted for it, it is commonly called a *closed specification*. Closed specifications require that only an exact match of the specification be provided by the vendor. Substitutions are not allowed.

An *open specification* is one in which the owner is willing to consider substitutions to what was originally specified. This type of specification usually has the words "or equal" incorporated into the specifications. *Or equal* means that products that are the same as, or very closely similar to, what has been specified will be considered.

There are four customary kinds of formal specifications. These four types of specifications identify the goods and/or materials needed in different ways. This is done so that the designer and the client can have better control over what is actually bid by vendors. Concern for control of the bidding process is desired by both the interior designer and the client. The four types of specifications are (1) proprietary, (2) descriptive, (3) performance, and (4) reference.

Proprietary Specification

Anna's client is a private entity that requires competitive bids for furniture and equipment that will exceed $5000. The project budget for the accounting department has been estimated at $36,000. The client wants particular manufacturer's products as specified by Anna's firm. She plans to use a proprietary specification format for the bids, since there are at least five vendors who can provide a competitive bid on the furniture specification. If there was only one vendor, Anna would need to change the specifications in order for the client to still obtain the desired products.

A *proprietary specification* names the products and materials by manufacturer's name, model number, or part number. With a proprietary specification, there is no doubt about what the designer and client wish to have bid (see Table 30-2). The basic proprietary specification is a closed specification, since it does not allow for any substitutions. If the specifications allow for no substitutions or do not have an "or equal" clause (which would allow for a substitution), then the proprietary bid might be called a base bid. "The term *base bid* means that all people who wish to provide materials for the project must base their bid on the product named in the specification."[1] The term base bid has another meaning related directly to the actual bidding process discussed later in the chapter. The proprietary specification that allows for substitutions is considered an open bid or open specification, because it allows for many products to be substituted for the item being specified. If only a single source is named, it is considered a closed bid or closed specification.

The advantages of the proprietary specification are as follows:

1. It is the easiest specification to write. In many cases, the designer only needs to provide the basic descriptive information of manufacturer, product number, and finishes/fabrics to complete the specifications.

TABLE 30-2.

Sample of a Very Simple Proprietary Specification.

Reception Area				
Item	Quantity	Description	Unit	Total
LC-5	4	Knoll 250LS Barcelona Chair Leather: Black		
T-3	1	Knoll 56T-MIN Mercer Coffee Table 44½″×44½″ Finish: Nero-Black Marble		

When more detail is needed, manufacturers often provide information to the designer that can be reproduced in the specifications.

2. It is easier to use for preparing drawings. With known product sizes, drawings are more accurate. The designer does not have to make allowances in the drawings for possible larger or smaller sizes of a product that might be bid.

3. The designer has maximum product control over the project. The carefully worked out design concept can be realized, since the products used to develop the design concept will be the ones purchased.

4. The time element from invitation announcement to order entry is faster, since alternate products do not have to be evaluated by the client. Since everyone is bidding on exactly the same products, the competitive bid concept is more fully realized.

There is an important disadvantage to using proprietary specifications. This type of specification can limit competition in some markets. Most private businesses and public agencies go through a bid process to obtain more than one price for a project. Sometimes there are not sufficient numbers of bidders in a given market area that can provide the products. When this is the case, it is often necessary to have an "or equal" clause in the specifications.

When the specifications must include an "or equal" clause, extra time is required for the designer and/or client to evaluate the bids and the substitutions. Design control can be lost, since the client may choose a product that is similar in appearance but lower in price than the original specification. What is equal in this situation is open to subjective judgment on the part of the client, the designer, and the bidders.

Another problem with a proprietary specification is that government agencies generally require that more than one product be specified. This allows for competition for government contracts. A proprietary specification can work in this case only if an "or equal" clause is allowed. If more than one product is specified, technically it is no longer a proprietary specification.

To protect all the parties concerned when they have to deal with an "or equal" clause, definitions of what procedures will be followed concerning the submittal of alternates must be included in the specifications. A common practice recommended by the Construction Specifications Institute (CSI) is to submit requests related to substitutions prior to the close of the bid. These requests might include detailed descriptions of the substituted product. In some cases, clients ask that a sample product be submitted prior to the close of the bid for evaluation. Some firms require that vendors pay for the time the interior designer must spend in evaluation of substitutions, especially if substitutions are not allowed as originally stated in the specifications.

Descriptive Specification

A *descriptive specification* does not use a manufacturer's name or trade name for the goods being specified. Rather, it describes, often in elaborate detail, the materials, workmanship, fabrication methods, and installation of the required goods. The descriptive specification is considered an open-bid specification.

There are two advantages to the descriptive specification. First, it allows the designer to prescribe exactly what he or she wishes to specify for the project while not using a proprietary form of specification. When there are many similar products that have subtle differences, such as happens with floor coverings, a descriptive specification helps to ensure that what is bid is actually equal to what is being specified, even if the goods come from different manufacturers. There are also situations in which the client wants a certain product for the project but may have a difficult time obtaining sufficient numbers of competitive bids on that product if he or she is using a proprietary specification. A descriptive specification helps to narrow the "or equal" alternates so that the client can get what he or she wants.

Second, the descriptive specification allows for some performance criteria to be used in the situations for which a complete performance specification is not appropriate. With floor coverings again, many manufacturers have carpets that can meet the simple descriptive specification of such things as fiber, pitch, stitches per inch, and pile height. This may not be enough to be sure that the carpet or carpet quality required of the project is bid. Performance criteria related to such factors as static electricity, delamination, and crocking can be included in the specification for these kinds of goods. Other goods, such as furniture, which may not have such stringent requirements, can be written as descriptive specifications (see Table 30-3).

There are a number of disadvantages to using descriptive specifications. First, it requires time to produce them, and they can be quite lengthy. Second, it requires more precise descriptions of the products. The descriptive specification of an open-office system work surface would have to read something like "A cantilevered hanging work surface, 64 inches wide by 30 inches deep by 1 inch thick. The finished top surface shall be a light ash, wood grain laminate, and the edge shall match. Support finishes shall be black." The same description in a proprietary specification would read as follows: "Herman Miller, A2310.3064LALABU."

Another important disadvantage of the descriptive specification is that the volume of information needed to prepare one can lead to errors and loopholes, which allows for products being bid that were not intended. In the previous example, if the designer did not write in "a light ash, wood grain plastic laminate" but only wrote "plastic laminate," the client would not get what he or she desired—the light ash wood finish—but would probably get a plain or neutral finish.

Finally, the descriptive specification, unless it is written very carefully, can result in the designer losing control of the product and design concept. As this discussion shows, an omission in the specification can result in the wrong finish being specified for the job. The bidder would have the right—after the contract was awarded—to ask for additional moneys to change the product finish to the intended light ash. The omission and resulting cost to the client could also lead to the client's being able to sue the designer.

Performance Specification

Another type of open-bid specification is a performance specification, also written without trade names. The *performance specification* establishes the product requirements based on exact performance criteria. Any product that meets the performance criteria can be used. The performance of the goods is based on the end product, and thus performance criteria are based on the accomplishment of that end. Performance specification criteria for carpeting is shown in Table 30-4. Performance results of a product are often the key to this type of specification.

Performance specifications are based on qualitative or measurable statements. It is common for specifications to require that certain tests and methods of testing be done. Bidders must submit test data with their bids. This information is available from the manufacturers for the designer's use in

TABLE 30-3.

Sample Descriptive Specification for Open-Office Systems Work Surfaces.

12.7 Work Surface

A. General

1. Work surfaces shall suspend from architectural walls or freestanding panels. Components attached to the work surface shall be removable by hand or with the use of a minimum of tools.
2. Vertical support elements (VSE 1-12) shall support hanging components on 1-inch intervals and shall easily allow for vertical height adjustment of the work surface.

B. Component

1. Work surfaces shall be made of warp-resistant materials and have squared corners and edges.
2. Work surfaces shall be finished using high-pressure plastic laminates that are scratch and heat resistant (up to 250°) available in a variety of colors. Edges shall be finished with a matching vinyl material.
3. All work surfaces must be provided with cantilever-type support brackets that allow for easy installation and removal from panels and wall-hanger strips with a minimum of tools.
4. Work surface tops shall be capable of having various under-counter drawers, storage units, or other accessories suspended below, installed with a minimal use of tools.
5. Cantilevered work surfaces shall be able to support up to 200 pounds when weight is located at the front edge of work surface. (Test data must be provided.)
6. Work surfaces shall be available in the following nominal sizes:

WST-1:	24 inches deep by 30 inches wide
WST-2:	24 inches deep by 36 inches wide
WST-3:	24 inches deep by 42 inches wide
WST-4:	24 inches deep by 48 inches wide
WST-5:	24 inches deep by 54 inches wide
WST-6:	24 inches deep by 60 inches wide
WST-7:	24 inches deep by 66 inches wide
WST-8:	24 inches deep by 72 inches wide
WST-9:	30 inches deep by 30 inches wide
WST-10:	30 inches deep by 36 inches wide
WST-11:	30 inches deep by 42 inches wide
WST-12:	30 inches deep by 48 inches wide
WST-13:	30 inches deep by 60 inches wide
WST-14:	30 inches deep by 66 inches wide
WST-15:	30 inches deep by 72 inches wide

---

writing the specifications. Manufacturers can provide testing information to the bidders.

When data from the manufacturer is not available or appears inconclusive, it may be necessary for the bidder to supply a sample of the product for testing, as is often the case with various textiles. For example, if the designer wished to use a carpet material on the wall, it would be necessary for the designer to specify some kind of performance criteria for that textile and for the manufacturer to either supply data for its use or to supply a sample that could be tested.

Some designers prefer this type of specification, because it allows for flexibility in what can be bid. Other designers feel that this is a major problem with a performance specification. Ambiguities and confusion can sometimes occur, resulting in inappropriate products being bid. Advantages are the same as for the descriptive specification: full control when it is not appropriate to use proprietary specifications. Disadvantages are also the same: extra preparation

TABLE 30-4.

Performance specification for carpeting. (Reproduced with permission, Wade
Carter, Interior Surfaces Guild, Scottsdale, AZ).

SPECIFICATIONS	
PILE FIBER CONTENTS	100% Advanced Generation Nylon
CONSTRUCTION	Dense Cut Pile Graphic
GAUGE	1/10
PILE HEIGHT	.250
PILE WEIGHT	30 Oz.
PRIMARY BACK	Polypropylene
SECONDARY BACK	ActionBac
YARN SIZE	
PLY	2 Ply Heat Set
DYE METHOD	Beck Dyed
TOTAL WEIGHT	60 Oz.
STITCHES PER INCH	8.3
PATTERN REPEAT	
TESTING	
RADIANT PANEL (ASTM E-648)	Class 1
SMOKE DENSITY NBS (ASTM E-662)	Less than 450
FHA-HUD	
DOC FF-1-70	Passes
STATIC PROPENSITY	Built-in Antistatic Control

Notes Specifications listed above are subject to normal manufacturing tolerances.
Chair pads are necessary under office chairs, with roller casters to prevent premature or
accelerated wear and to preserve appearance.
Color may vary from dye lot to dye lot.

and evaluation time, possible errors, possible loss of design concept, and loss
of product control.

Reference Specification

A *reference specification* utilizes an established standard, such as the standards of
the American Society for Testing and Materials (ASTM) and the American
National Standards Institute (ANSI), rather than written, detailed descriptions
or performance criteria for required products. These established standards
generally provide minimal acceptable standards of performance for various
kinds of products. Because of this, the reference specification is considered an
open bid.

The designer must check these standards to be sure that these minimums
are satisfactory for the needs of the project. If the standard is too low, the
reference specification cannot be used. It is also necessary for the designer to
be fully familiar with the standards, because the standards sometimes provide
options for materials or workmanship. The designer must be sure that he or
she specifies the standard or level of standard required for the project. If this is
not done, the bidder then has the option of using a lower standard than the one
the designer may have intended to use. Reference specifications are more
widely used in construction. They may be utilized by the interior designer for
such things as wall and floor products and installation.

As the reader might expect, there are advantages and disadvantages to the
reference specification. One advantage to using a reference specification is that it
saves time, because only the standard must be stated; there is no need to write a
long, descriptive specification or performance specification. Another advantage

is that a reference specification also can be used to help explain a complex performance specification or descriptive specification for specialized products or installations. The disadvantage is that if the designer is not fully aware of the up-to-date standard, the designer may allow for products and workmanship that do not meet the desired requirements.

SPECIFICATION ORGANIZATION

When the FF&E for a project is put out for a competitive bid, it is standard practice to utilize a formalized organization to the specifications. The complexity of many projects can make it very difficult for true competitive analysis of bids unless a standardized format is used to locate information in an orderly fashion. As legal documents, specifications should not be written in obscure language or with information omitted. Even with the use of computer applications in the preparation of specifications, this document requires a great deal of time, thought, and accuracy.

Following a standardized organization allows for greater speed and accuracy by the vendors who will be providing bids. The furniture vendor is only interested in what furniture and furnishing items are required. The framer, electrician, plumber, and all the other trades are likewise only interested in what they are being asked to provide.

The organizational format most frequently used in the design and construction professions was developed by the Construction Specifications Institute. The CSI is a nonprofit organization whose purpose is to improve professional documentation, especially specifications. With its membership spanning the full range of the construction professions, CSI has been able to develop a common language of construction and a standardized format for the preparation of specifications. The Web address for CSI is listed in the Internet Resources.

MasterFormat™, published by CSI, is the most widely accepted method of organizing specifications. Figure 30-2 shows a portion of the CSI system. The detailed numbering system, organized by materials, trades, functions, and space relationships, reduces the chances of omitting important information. It also makes it much easier for the designer to make changes while the specs are being written.

The design firm can establish its own version of standardized specification language. All the popular word-processing software products provide sufficient flexibility for the designer to develop template sections that are needed in a furniture and finishes specification. Software is available from CSI to assist firms in computerizing their specification tasks.

A design firm frequently needing to use detailed specification formats may be interested in obtaining one of the standard text systems. Standard text systems on computer discs are available from trade associations, manufacturers, and some of the professional organizations. These standard text systems have a fill-in-the-blank format. However, these standard text systems require that the user have a thorough understanding of the construction process in order to know what to leave in and what to take out of the specification.

Another standardized specification is the ARCOM AIA *MASTERSPEC*® *Interior Design*. This program has short-form master specifications, which follow the CSI format. MASTERSPEC® has specification information for interior construction, finish, and equipment items for several types of commercial facilities. It also has reference materials and provides background information on the various materials. This system was the first set of specification standards for interior materials and products. It simplifies interior product specifications, since it is a user-friendly system that is used to complete intricate interior specifications.

MASTERFORMAT™

DIVISION NUMBERS AND TITLES
DIVISION 0—PROCUREMENT AND CONTRACTING REQUIREMENTS
DIVISION 1—GENERAL REQUIREMENTS
DIVISION 2—EXISTING CONDITIONS
DIVISION 3—CONCRETE
DIVISION 4—MASONRY
DIVISION 5—METALS
DIVISION 6—WOOD, PLASTICS AND COMPOSITES
DIVISION 7—THERMAL AND MOISTURE PROTECTION
DIVISION 8—OPENINGS
DIVISION 9—FINISHES
DIVISION 10—SPECIALTIES
DIVISION 11—EQUIPMENT
DIVISION 12—FURNISHINGS
    120513—FABRICS
    121000—ART
    122000—WINDOW TREATMENTS
    123000—CASEWORK
    124000—FURNISHINGS AND ACCESSORIES
    125000—FURNITURE
    126000—MULTIPLE SEATING
    129000—OTHER FURNISHINGS
DIVISION 13—SPECIAL CONSTRUCTION
DIVISION 14—CONVEYING EQUIPMENT
DIVISION 21—FIRE SUPPRESSION
DIVISION 22—PLUMBING
DIVISION 23—HEATING, VENTILATION, AND AIR CONDITIONING
DIVISION 25—INTEGRATED AUTOMATION

DIVISION 26—ELECTRICAL
DIVISION 27—COMMUNICATIONS
DIVISION 28—ELECTRONIC SAFETY AND SECURITY

©2004 *MasterFormat*™ copyright is held in the U.S. by The Construction Specifications Institute (CSI) and in Canada by Construction Specifications Canada (CSC). For more information: www.csinet.org

FIGURE 30-2.

A partial listing of the Construction Specifications Institute (CSI) MasterFormat™ Division Numbers and Titles, 2004 edition. (Available on the internet at www.csinet.org/masterformat)

Figure 30-3 shows a sample page for wood flooring. Materials in this specification system are periodically reviewed and updated. Contact ARCOM to be sure you are working with the most current version.

Whatever format the firm chooses to use, specification language should be kept clear and direct. In the field of interior design, sentence structure traditionally uses the indicative mood. For example, "The vendor shall remove all cartoning and packaging materials." Another alternative recommended by specification writing professionals is the use of the imperative mood. In this case, instructions do not use the phrase "the vendor shall" or the "contractor will." Words such as "shall" and "will" are omitted, creating an imperative mood. In the preceding example, in the imperative mood, the sentence would read, "Remove all cartoning and packaging materials."

Language must be used carefully, as words can have a double meaning.[2]

Shall and Will   Often used incorrectly. "Shall" is used to designate a command; "will" implies a choice.

All   "The Contractor shall assume the responsibility for All unacceptable work." This sentence leaves no Doubt about the contractor's responsibility.

MASTERSPEC — EVALUATIONS 5/97
© 1997 The American Institute of Architects

The Hardwood Plywood and Veneer Association (HPVA) publishes ANSI/HPVA LF, *Laminated Wood Flooring*. This standard establishes requirements for grade of plies, moisture content, machining, bond line (delamination resistance), construction (ply assembly), formaldehyde emissions for products made with ureaformaldehyde or melamine-formaldehyde adhesives or surface coatings, and finish of engineered-wood flooring. Veneers for the face ply can be of one or more species. Common species used include pecan, hard maple, red oak, white oak, birch, ash, beech, black walnut, southern pine, and black cherry. Face Grades established by the standard are Prime (practically clear with minor imperfections) and Character (sound wood variations and a greater allowable level of imperfections than Prime). Veneers are rotary cut, sliced, or sawed from a log, bolt, or flitch. Sawed veneers are the most durable and look the most like traditional solid-wood flooring products.

APPLICATION CONSIDERATIONS

Controlling the moisture content of wood is critical both before and after installation. Wood is hygroscopic, meaning it changes dimensionally with the absorption or release of moisture. Swelling and shrinking varies with the wood species, cut, and type of flooring. Because engineered products' cross-ply construction adds dimensional stability, moisture control for engineered-wood flooring is less critical than for solid-wood flooring.

Manufacturers kiln-dry wood flooring so it will behave predictably. During transit, delivery, and storage, it must be protected from moisture. Before installation, wood flooring must stabilize at (acclimatize to) the temperature and relative humidity of space in which it will be installed. After installation, and even after finishing, fluctuations in environmental conditions cause shrinking and swelling.

Wood flooring installations must accommodate movement. An expansion space is required at the perimeter of the installation. For larger installations, more expansion provisions may be required.

Concrete slab substrates must be dry and protected from subsurface moisture by appropriate grading and drainage, a capillary water barrier of porous drainage materials, and a membrane vapor barrier. Temperature, relative humidity, and ventilation affect concrete drying time. A slab allowed to dry from only one side generally takes 30 days for every 1 inch (25.4 mm) of thickness to dry adequately.

For adhesive attachment to concrete, slabs must be clean and free of curing compounds, sealers, hardeners, and other materials that may interfere with an adhesive bond.

Spaces below wood flooring must be dry and well ventilated. Cross-ventilate crawl spaces and cover the ground with a polyethylene vapor retarder. If solid-wood flooring is installed over wood sleepers on a concrete slab, NOFMA recommends covering the sleepers with a polyethylene vapor retarder and making provisions for ventilating the airspaces between sleepers.

TROPICAL WOODS

Tropical moist forests, including rainforests and seasonal or monsoon forests, provide the hardwoods generally called *tropical woods*. The destruction of rainforests is an important environmental issue. More than half the plant and animal species on Earth are found in tropical rainforests concentrated mainly in the South American Amazon Basin, Africa's Congo Basin, and Southeast Asia.

Land-use changes, not the timber industry, are the major cause of rainforest destruction according to most reports. Some organizations assert that boycotting the use of tropical woods may accelerate the destruction of rainforests because it devalues the timber as a resource and encourages changes in land use to those uses that immediately profit the local human population. Organizations concerned with preserving rainforests generally also have social agendas. They encourage responsible, sustainable forestry-management practices and timber production as a means of providing for a region's human population. If desired, verify that

WOOD FLOORING 09640 – E6

FIGURE 30-3.

Sample specifications page from MASTERSPEC Section 09640—Wood Flooring Evaluation. (Used by permission of ARCOM Master Systems, publishers of MASTERSPEC for the American Institute of Architects)

Writing technical specifications and preparing the remaining documents needed for a bid are time-consuming activities. In truth, neither is an activity that many designers enjoy. Small firms that infrequently produce formal contract documents and bid specifications may wish to hire specification-writing consultants. Independent practitioners provide consulting services to design professionals who do not feel qualified or who do not have the time to prepare construction and/or detailed interiors specification for bids. Larger firms may assign a staff member to be responsible for the preparation of all specifications issued by the firm. These specialists need to be experienced in interior design and/or architecture, and should have an eye for and interest in detail and a thorough knowledge of such things as materials, products, construction methods, and building codes. CSI has developed a certification process for qualified specifiers, who are entitled to refer to themselves as certified construction specifiers (CCS). Information about this program is available from the CSI Web site.

What Would You Do?

Sam is the project manager and primary designer on a large medical office building for a major health-care provider. His firm also has a subsidiary company that procures furniture for clients if the client approves. The client didn't realize that the design firm also had a sales division, since it was not located in the same office building. The fact that they had the sales division was revealed during the initial presentation for the design contract.

The client company was very clear to Sam that the product specifications had to be put out to bid. They also told him that company policy required at least ten vendor bids be obtained. This project was budgeted at $176,000 at net.

There were two items in the specifications that the client was very interested in having in the specification package, as they had standardized on the items at other locations. One was an ergonomically designed desk chair, and the other was a small side chair used in the waiting room.

Sam prepared the specifications so that the minimum number of bidders could easily be achieved. When he was checking on fabric options for the ergonomic chair—he wanted to specify a COM fabric—Sam was offered an extra 10 percent discount on the ergonomic desk chairs below what other bidders would be able to purchase the chair. He mentioned this to his boss, who promptly contacted the sales manager at the subsidiary company.

COMPETITIVE BIDDING

Many clients require that prices be obtained for the furniture from more than one source. Single-source purchasing is rare with these clients, since the dollar amounts of the projects are so large. Millions of dollars could be spent on the furniture and equipment for a hotel, hospital, or large corporate office complex. The contract for the construction and/or procurement of furniture from a single source is done through negotiation rather than bidding.

Competitive bidding is a process whereby the client has the opportunity to obtain comparative prices from a number of contractors and/or vendors for the construction or supply of the project. The documents needed for the bid process are prepared by a design professional such as the interior designer. The actual bid process takes place after all the construction drawings, specifications, and schedules have been completed.

Competitive bids almost always are required by law for projects involving federal, state, and local agencies, as well as for public businesses, like utilities. Most private businesses also require competitive bids on construction projects and large furniture or equipment orders. A residential project might involve the use of competitive bidding for the construction of the house but rarely for the interior FF&E.

Of course, many clients do not use the competitive bid process. Depending on the size of the project and the client's policies concerning project procurement, the client can purchase goods directly from a vendor of the purchasing department's choosing. This can be thought of as *single-source purchasing*, and the pricing is essentially negotiated. Entities that generally require a competitive bid for purchasing may have policies that allow small-dollar-value purchases to be obtained from a single source. Over that policy value, then the purchase must be bid. That can mean anything over as small an amount as $550 must be bid if the ceiling for a single-source purchase is $500. Clients—unless restricted by law such as government agencies—can directly negotiate with a particular vendor because of some unique quality of the product, project, or circumstance. For example, if the client has a large inventory of Haworth office systems, the client may be able to negotiate directly for additional purchases, regardless of the size of the purchase.

The idea of the bid process is that it allows the client to purchase the products and services required for the project at a price that is as low as possible while maintaining the quality and intentions of the original design concept. This assumption is valid as long as the goods or services being bid on are either the same or can objectively be compared as equal. This, however, is not always possible. When substitutions are allowed, it becomes difficult for the interior designer and client to evaluate the differences in the various products being bid on objectively. Questions then arise about possible compromises in order to maintain the quality and/or design intentions of the specifications. When there are sufficient bidders of a like product, then competitive bids based on the original idea are possible. When a project is designed and/or specified in such a way that few bidders can supply the same product at a fair price, then the bid process is suspect.

Clients who are ready to purchase large quantities of a product and are required to use the bid process often are under pressure to accept the lowest bid. For the designer, this can mean the loss of the original design concept for the project, since a product that does not have the same aesthetic appearance as the original one might be purchased. For example, picture the specification of Knoll Barcelona chairs for a reception area. A bidder may offer a knockoff (an imitation) of the Brno chair instead—two different designs, as the reader is well aware. The appearance and quality are far different from what has been specified. For the client, it can mean that he or she will now own a product that does not meet the performance criteria of the original design. In this example, it is unlikely that the knockoff Brno Tubular chair will hold up as well as the Knoll Barcelona chair.

Competitive bidding may, in some ways, be more expensive than it would for other purchasing methods. There is a greater amount of preparation time of complicated contract documents and specifications for the goods and services. Also, additional documentation related to the bid procedure, general conditions for performance of the bid contract, and other conditions related to the bid and subsequent work must be prepared. When similar but unequal products are bid or products are bid based on performance, the client and designer will be involved in time-consuming evaluations either before the bid submittal or before the awarding of contracts. Additionally, there is a potential for claims and lawsuits related to the bid award if one or more bidders feel that the award was improper.

The bid process continues to exist for most major commercial and governmental projects. The interior designer must include the services for monitoring and coordinating the bid phase in his or her contract. This will help the designer

TABLE 30-5.

Sample List of the Most Common Bidding Documents.

Contract documents
   Contract requirement forms
      Owner/contractor agreement
      Addenda and modifications that have become part of the contract
      Performance bond
      Payment bond
      Insurance certificates
   Conditions of the contract
      General and supplemental conditions of the contract
   Construction drawings
      Specifications
      Drawings
      Schedules

Bidding documents
   Invitation to bid
   Instructions to bidders
   Bid forms
   Bonds
   Addenda and Modifications
   Add to the bidding documents will be all the contract documents

keep control of the design concepts and aesthetic intent of the project. Architects have done this for years. Interior designers, regardless of the size of their practice, must do the same.

In addition to the contract documents, four bid documents must be produced in order to complete a bid. They are (1) the general conditions, (2) the invitation to bid, (3) instructions to bidders, and (4) the bid form. Bond forms—other forms associated with the bid process—are also briefly discussed. Table 30-5 provides a list of the forms or other documents generally used during the competitive bidding process.

General Conditions

There are many conditions and information that establish the basic rules covering the bid and the bid process. The document included in the bid documents that express these rules is a section of general conditions. These *general conditions* set forth the legal responsibilities, procedures, rights, and duties of each party to the contract. A standardized set of general conditions used by many designers and private business owners is the AIA form, AIA document A201™-1997. It is commonly used because it has stood the test of time; however, the standardized form is quite long and cumbersome. Many designers and clients modify the conditions of the document for their particular situation.

Items covered in the general conditions include definitions, the names of the designer and owner, ownership of documents, the responsibilities of the designer and the owner, definitions and responsibilities of the contractors and subcontractors, clauses concerning payments, the time period of project, claims, insurance, change orders, dispute resolution considerations, and other definitions or statements related to the contractual relationship of the parties.

For bids that concern only furniture, AIA document A275™ID-2003, *General Conditions of the Contract for Furniture, Furnishings, and Equipment*, can be used. The general conditions in this document are similar in scope to the ones in document A201 but are related to interior furniture and furnishings rather than construction.

Since both of these forms are lengthy, generalized legal forms, it is necessary for the designer to prepare supplemental conditions for the projects. The supplemental conditions spell out any conditions that are related to the specific project. A supplemental condition that must be stated if the designer uses either of these forms is that the words *designer* or *interior designer* should be substituted wherever the word *architect* is used.

Several kinds of documents may be available from interior design professional association headquarters. Copyright law should be respected when using documents belonging to the AIA, ASID, and IIDA. It is necessary for the designer to obtain permission from the association in order to make copies or to modify the documents in any way. Should the designer/specifier wish to prepare his or her own set of general conditions, these should be reviewed by the design firm's attorney before being submitted to the client. Copies of the AIA forms can be ordered from local AIA chapter offices or by contacting the AIA national office (see the appendix). Sample documents from ASID must be ordered from the association national office.

The Invitation to Bid

One task in the bid process is to determine who can provide a bid for the project. This process is tightly controlled by the client and might essentially be managed by the client or in conjunction with the design firm. The most common way to obtain bidders for a project is to prepare an invitation to bidders (also called an advertisement for bids). The *invitation to bid* notifies potential bidders of the existence of a project. It might be a letter sent to a list of contractors and/or vendors or an actual advertisement placed in the appropriate section of a newspaper. The invitation to bid will include instructions as to where the bid documents can be obtained. The information shown in Table 30-6 is common to an invitation to bid. A sample invitation to bid from a private company is included on the CD as Item 30-1.

Government and public agencies most likely will advertise a bid in newspapers. This process is called *open competitive selection*. In this case, anyone interested in the project who meets the qualifications that are spelled out in the invitation to bid may submit a bid. Private businesses rarely advertise a bid, though they may do so for a very large project. Some private organizations, through careful legal preparation, may have an acceptable *bid list* of potential designers and vendors who would receive the notifications. This selection process is called *closed competitive selection*, since it limits who will be allowed to bid on the project. In this situation, the client contacts several designers/ vendors to make them aware of the project. Only those invited to bid in this manner are allowed to bid on the project.

The advantage of a bid list is that bidders are *prequalified* by the client so that those bidders who have experience with the particular kind of project for which the bid list has been prepared, proven personnel, capital to procure the goods, and so on are the only designers and vendors with whom the client will deal. This also allows the client to maintain a reasonable number of bids, rather

TABLE 30-6.

Items Commonly Included in an Invitation to Bid.

- Identification of the client
- Identification of the architect and interior designer
- Project location
- Description of the scope of work of the project
- When and where bid documents can be obtained
- Prequalification standards, if any
- Description of any bonds or deposits that are required
- Place, day, and time where bids are to be received
- Statements concerning the client's right to reject any and all bids
- Description of any laws or regulations affecting the bid
- Identification of the company or organization responsible for issuing the bid

than a very large number of bids that would require additional evaluation to eliminate unqualified bidders.

One disadvantage of closed competitive selection is that there might be too few bidders, resulting in possibly a higher price for the project. There is also the probability that less experienced, yet qualified, designers and vendors will be prohibited from entering the bid process. Yet, if it is possible to get a sufficient (by the client's estimation) number of qualified bidders through a prequalification bid list system, it is a satisfactory and legal method of obtaining competitive bids.

The invitation to bid provides a summary of the project, the bid process, and other brief pertinent procedures for the project. It informs potential bidders of the project, its scope, and ways in which they can obtain further information. The invitation also states whether a security bond is required, how much it will be, and how long it will be held. The size or length of time for which the bond will be held may discourage some designers and vendors from bidding.

Instructions to Bidders

The *instructions to bidders* document informs bidders how to prepare their bid documents for submittal so that all submittals are in the same form. This helps make it easier to compare bids from multiple vendors and makes the bid process fair to all who wish to participate. It is common for some bidders not to bid on portions of the project if this is allowed by the client. When this occurs, the items not bid on are called *exclusions*. Thus, it is not always easy to start with absolutely comparable bids.

It is important to understand that the instructions to bidders are not a contract offering, but information regarding the project bid. Many firms with client approval schedule a pre-bid meeting for all interested bidders and possibly tour the site. This pre-bid meeting gives all the bidders the chance to hear the same responses at the same time rather than requiring the design firm to potentially having to constantly send out memorandum to all the bidders. Of course, other questions will occur after this meeting, and as necessary, the design firm will issue addendum in response.

Information in the instructions should only tell how to prepare and submit the bids. Instructions to bidders commonly provide (1) information on what form and format to use; (2) information on how, where, and when bids are due;

(3) statements related to site visitations and familiarization responsibilities; (4) statements related to resolution of interpretation of any discrepancies in the documents; (5) information on how bids can be withdrawn; (6) the procedure for awarding the bid; conditions for rejecting bids; and (7) any other pertinent instructions that may be required by the client. Form A701™-1997 from the AIA provides an example document that can be modified to meet the needs of an interiors project. Much of the information that is in the invitation to bid is repeated in the instructions to bid.

Important parts of the instructions are the portions of the bid documents that are usually referred to as the "drawings and specifications." These consist of working drawings and/or equipment plans and the written specifications related to products, materials, and construction methods. The instructions to bidders should only mention where and how these documents can be obtained, how they are to be used by the bidder, and if substitutions or exclusions are allowed (and how they are to be submitted). The actual drawings and specifications do not appear in this portion of the documents.

The Bid Form

To ensure fairness, the actual bid by all contractors or vendors must be submitted in the same way. The *bid form* (also sometimes called a tender form) is a document prepared by the designer or the client and provided to the bidders. The bid form is the document that the vendor uses to inform the client of the bid price. The format generally is set up as a form letter from the bidder to the client. The bid form has blank space in appropriate places to be filled in by the bidder. Figure 30-4 shows a sample bid form. This sample document has also been included on the CD as Item 30-2. If no substitutions or exclusions are allowed in the instructions, a statement reinforcing disqualification of a bidder who submits a substitution or exclusion should be provided here.

Although it is common that the whole of what has been specified in the construction documents an specifications are to be included in the bid, it often happens that clients have asked for some things that will cost more than might fit into their budget. If a client has anticipated that he or she may have a problem in meeting the budget with everything that has been designed, the client may provide a bid package that includes a specification for a base bid and alternate bids. The term *base bid* in this case means the amount of the project the vendor is prepared to supply that is the basic minimum specified without consideration for alternatives. *Alternate bids* are amounts added to or subtracted from the base bid should the client add or subtract parts of the specified project. The concepts of base bid and alternate bids allow the client to be more assured the project will remain with the project budget.

Bond Forms

Submitting a bid for a project is only one part of the documents required of vendors and contractors. *Bond forms* are legal documents used to bind the designer or vendor to the contract as assurance that the designer or vendor will perform the requirements of the contract as agreed upon. They are required for the client's protection. There are three bond forms commonly used in the bidding process: (1) the bid bond, (2) the performance bond, and (3) the labor and materials payment bond.

The *bid bond* is required to ensure that the designer or vendor awarded the contract will sign the contract and execute the project. Proof of a bid bond is submitted with the bid. It is, in effect, a sort of insurance that those who are

---

BID FORM FOR FURNISHINGS CONTRACT

CONTRACT NUMBER: _____

PROJECT: _____

BID OF: _____
(name of bidder)

- a Corporation organized under the laws of the State of _____
- a Partnership, with the following individuals as partners:

_____

- a Limited Liability Company with the following member as General Manager:

_____

- a Sole proprietor.

Present Bid To:

_____

At: Hunter / Noble Inc.
3114 N. 38th St.
Phoenix, AZ

The Undersigned acknowledges receipt and review of the Project Documents, consisting of _____ pages of drawings and _____ pages of written specifications, and addenda No. _____ through _____, and hereby proposes to furnish all materials, labor, and miscellany necessary to provide and install the furniture and furnishings as specified in the aforementioned documents.

The Undersigned further agrees to hold his/her Bid open for thirty (30) days after the receipt of bids. Should the bidder be awarded the contract, he/she shall furnish a Performance Bond and a Labor and Materials Payment Bond in accordance the General Conditions of the Bid, to the owner within ten days after award of bid.

No substitutions or exclusions to what was specified shall be allowed. Any bidder not bidding on all items as specified shall be disqualified.

The undersigned agrees to supply and perform, in accordance with the specifications, all of the materials, labor, and miscellany as specified for:

_____Dollars ($_____).

The Bid Bond and all other required documentation is attached by the undersigned bidder.

It is understood that the owner reserves the right to reject any or all bids, to withhold the award of bid for any reason, and reserves the right to hold all bids for thirty (30) days after the date of opening.

Date of Bid: _____

Name of Bidder: _____

Address of Bidder: _____

Authorized Officer: _____

FIGURE 30-4.

Sample bid form.

bidding are really going to provide what they have bid at the prices they have quoted. The bid bond is obtained by a vendor from a bonding or surety service for the construction, architecture, and interiors industry.

Most firms that submit a bid expect to go through with the contract. However, some firms submit bids only to find out how the competition is pricing services or products. If a firm has made an error in its bid, it may want to withdraw even after the bid has been awarded. The bid bond thus acts as insurance that all who bid are actually interested in going through with the contract. The bid bond may be a lump sum or a percentage amount of the bid. This security amount may be given by using a bond, cash, a certified check, or another method approved by the project owner.* The bid bond of the successful bidder is usually held by the client for some time after the contract has been signed and other bid securities have been obtained. For unsuccessful bidders, the bid bond is returned promptly.

The *performance bond* is required from the winning bidder as a guarantee that the designer or vendor will complete the work as specified. A surety company agreeable to the client and the design firm obtains the bond and would then be liable to pay should the vendor or contractor fail to perform. It protects the client from any loss up to the amount of the bond as a result of the failure of the designer or vendor to perform according to the contract. It is customary for the performance bond to be an amount equal to 100 percent of the value of the bid contract. The premium paid to a surety company is a smaller percentage for the bond insurance. This actual amount varies, based on the actual project conditions and the surety company. The performance bond is returned after completion of the project.

A *labor and materials payment bond* is required of the winning bidder to guarantee that the designer or vendor will be responsible for paying for all the materials and labor that have been contracted for in the event that the designer or vendor defaults on the project. This is to prevent the client from being held responsible to subcontractors for goods not delivered by the winning bidder. This bond is also customarily an amount equal to 100 percent of the contract price. It also is returned after completion of the project.

A legal recourse that is related to the labor and materials payment bond is the *mechanic's lien*. This lien is an action filed by the contractor, subcontractor, or possibly the designer with the county clerk to prevent the owner of the property from giving or conveying title or a deed of trust to the named property until the mechanic who has filed the lien has been paid. In this situation, a mechanic is one who is an employee, subcontractor, or vendor who has been hired to do work by the client or a general contractor.

More simply stated, contractors, subcontractors, their vendors, and, in some states, architects and interior designers may find it necessary to file a lien against the property in order to ensure that the owner of the property will pay the designer or contractor any moneys due. A properly filed lien prevents the owner of the property from selling or conveying title of the property until the lien has been settled. Not all states have provisions that fully allow for a mechanic's lien. The designer should check with the attorney general or registrar of contractors of his or her state to clarify how liens might affect the workings of the designer.

Bid Opening

Vendors that decide they will proceed with a bid on a project must verify that the way they submit the bid meets the requirements spelled out in the instructions to

---

*During construction, the "project owner" can be either the client who will occupy the space or the contractor who has responsibility to build out the project. In the latter case, the contractor relinquishes ownership to the client.

bidders. The first part of the submittal requirements is that the bid proposal bid form is to be sent to the client or designer in a sealed envelope. The instructions to bidders will specify the exact labeling of the envelope, where it is to be delivered, to whom, and by what day and time. Failing to meet these requirements can lead to disqualification of the bid.

There are several reasons a bid can be disqualified if it is improperly submitted to the client or designer. If a bid is delivered after the day and time specified in the instructions, it will be left unopened and rejected. Any bid received that does not conform to the instructions can be rejected. It is also customary that bids cannot be withdrawn after the closing date and time for the receipt of bids, even if the bid opening has not yet taken place. However, the instructions may stipulate the conditions under which a bid can be withdrawn, especially if there are errors in it that would create a hardship for the bidder. In almost all situations, bidders should not be allowed to modify or alter a bid once it has been received and opened.

Once the bids are all received, there may be a public or private *bid opening* where the bids are actually opened. Bids for governmental agencies or public companies, such as utilities, are required to have the bid opening at an open public meeting. The place and time is noted in the invitation to bidders. At that meeting, the client or person charged with administering the bid announces each bidder and his or her bid price. The client usually does not award the bid at that time. The invitation to bid should have informed bidders about the length of time that the client will take to evaluate the bids and to make the decision as to who will be awarded the contract. Although most public agencies most likely take the lowest bid, they are not bound to do so if there are legitimate reasons for rejecting the lowest bid. Care must be taken by the client, therefore, not to announce that firm X is the lowest bidder at the bid opening, since this announcement could later bind the agency, even if it wanted to reject the bid.

For private companies, the bid opening is not required by law to be open to the public. This means that each bidder might not have the opportunity to know what the competition has bid, if his or her own bid is low in comparison to all the others, or if the bidder made an error in reporting his or her prices. According to Justin Sweet,[3] the courts expect the client who uses a closed bid opening to act in good faith with the bidders if a bid comes in substantially lower than all other bids and not penalize the bidder who makes a legitimate mistake.

It remains possible that the bidding process will still involve negotiations. This might occur only with the winning bidder as small changes to the project are negotiated. If larger changes are needed that affect the price, it might be feasible to negotiate with the winning bidder or it might be necessary to reject all bids and rebid the project. When a project involves government or public agencies, a negotiation may include a concept of the *best and final offer* (BAFO). These types of clients may have more flexibility in the selection and negotiation of contracts with one or more of those that propose a bid amount. What could happen is that after the first submission of bids is reviewed, the client would potentially select some number of those bidders and ask them for their BAFO—another bid in essence.

Depending on the provisions in the contract between the interior designer and the client, the designer will assist the client in evaluating the bids. This service can help a client interpret appropriateness of substitutions or any conditions that bidders may have included in their bid document. After a reasonable length of time, the contractor or client will award the bid based on the bid values, negotiate further (assuming there are small changes that need to be made) with the winning bidder, or reject all bids and consider rebidding the project.

Bid Award Notification

After the bids have been evaluated and a decision has been made as to who the successful bidder is, each bidder must be notified of the result. A simple form letter is usually sent to each one of the unsuccessful bidders, thanking each one. It is not legally necessary to inform them as to who the successful bidder is or the amount of the bid. It is often a good idea to include a comment that the bids of the unsuccessful bidders will be held for a certain length of time, as stated in the invitation to bid, in the event that the successful bidder does withdraw. This means that the bids of unsuccessful bidders remain valid offers until the end of the holding period.

Should the owner wish to speed up the actual ordering and/or construction process, a letter of intent is sent to the winning bidder. This letter is a signal to the supplier or contractors to begin work on the project. This can be a form letter when the designer or client frequently issues this type of document or a letter that sets forth the client's intention to go forward with a particular project or portion of a project. Other documents that are used concerning the winning bidder and the continuation of the project are discussed in Chapter 31.

MODIFICATIONS

No matter how hard designers try, nobody is perfect. Errors occur in preparation of the contract documents, and for many reasons, changes need to be made in the plans or specifications once the work begins. *Modifications* are changes in the construction documents. If the changes are made before the contract has been awarded, they would be made by an addendum. Changes made after the contract has been awarded are made by issuing a change order.

Addenda

Shelly found an error in the specifications for a courthouse project. Checking the equipment plans against the furniture specifications, the quantities of a certain chair did not match. She counted the item three times to be sure of her counts. Her boss told her to call the project interior designer for clarification. What needs to happen next?

David was embarrassed and upset when he found three notation errors in the construction drawings he had prepared for a retail store. The bid documents had yesterday been released to prospective vendors. He decided to let the error go and not tell his boss because he had made mistakes before and he was afraid he would lose his job.

Addenda are additions or changes made to the contract documents once they are in the hands of contractors and vendors and as they determine their prices for the project. Contracts for the construction work or FF&E purchasing have not yet been issued. This modification document is only issued during the bidding stage, not after the contracts have been awarded. Any change in the project by use of an addenda become part of the contract documents.

A change in the project may result because the client wants to alter some part of the project, even at this late time. Clarifications also may be needed because of a question from one or more of the bidders or because of errors or technical requirements regarding the documents that are discovered during the bid process. Addenda are used to clarify these changes in relationship to the previously prepared contract and/or construction documents.

Each addendum must be in writing and sent to all bidders. Corrections or clarifications should not be made or accepted orally. All addenda should be prepared as quickly and as clearly as possible. They should come from the person who is responsible for creating the documents. If an allied professional or other design team member finds a questionable item, it should be called to the attention of the specification writer and/or preparer of the construction drawings, and that person should prepare and send the addendum. When addenda are mailed to bidders, there must be sufficient time for bidders to react to the addenda prior to the close of bid. Recall that notification begins upon receipt of the notification, not at the time of mailing. Addenda supersede and supplement the appropriate part or parts of the construction documents or bidding documents. A sample addendum letter is included on the CD as Item 30-3.

According to Harold J. Rosen, addenda are used to provide any of the following kinds of information to bidders:[4]

1. Correct errors and omissions.
2. Clarify ambiguities.
3. Add to or reduce the scope of the work.
4. Provide additional information that can affect the bid prices.
5. Change the time and place for receipt of bids.
6. Change the quality of the work.
7. Issue additional names of qualified "or equal" products.

Of course, other conditions or situations may occur that would require a change in the documents prior to awarding of the contract.

Note that an addendum can also be used to issue instructions after the awarding of the contract has occurred. However, when this term for a change is used at this time, it is only with regard to a change order to the winning bidder or contractor.

Change Orders

Mrs. Brown had visited a model home show and noticed an interesting design of niches surrounding the fireplace in one model. She took a photo of the wall and gave it to her designer and said she wanted a similar design in her house, which was under construction. Fortunately, that part of the house had been framed, but the wall board had not been installed.

Change orders are written permissions or instructions concerning any aspect of the project that modify design concepts, construction designs, or product specifications. A change or modification made after the contract is awarded is documented with a change order. Change orders accepted and signed by the appropriate parties also becomes a part of the contract documents (see Figure 30-5).

Changes may be needed during the course of the project, and change orders are needed to clarify these changes. Perhaps the client wants a window moved to a new location. Maybe the paint color for the doctor's suite must be different. A lighting fixture specified in the restaurant dining room might not be available by the time the project is under way. Any of these examples and many more can occur during the actual construction, ordering, and installation of the project. The use of change orders is also discussed in Chapter 31. Figure 30-5 has also been included on the CD. It is Item 30-4.

Interior designers should not allow any change to occur without a written change order being issued to all necessary parties. Of course, sometimes it is not within the interior designer's authority to issue a change order. Many designers

Change Order

Project Name _____   Change Order #: _____

Project #: _____

Date Prepared _____   Phone: _____

Project Designer/Manager: _____

Change Requested by:

Description of Change to Project or Contract:

Cost Estimate for Change (Attach Additional Paperwork if Necessary)

This is an Authorization to proceed with the change as detailed in **Change Order** _____.

_____   _____   _____   _____

Authorized Agent   *Date*   *Authorized Agent*   *Date*
(Client)   *(Design Firm)*

Only valid if signed by *both* Agents

These changes will impact Final Completion Due Date until: _____. (No Change)

FIGURE 30-5.

A sample change order form.

and contractors allow changes to occur without giving written authorization or notification to the various parties. Clients have been known to tell the contractor to make a change and then forget to inform the interior designer. A seemingly simple change can, in fact, be quite a big deal. If the change is major, such as moving a window, it can affect other trades, schedules, space layouts, and product specifications, to name the most obvious. A good working relationship between the designer and the client and other stakeholders, as well as professional project management by the interior designer, can prevent changes being made without proper authorization and notification.

Changes made after the contract has been awarded also can result in additional charges. Just as the interior designer wants to be compensated to replan a space once the client has given approval, a contractor or vendor will want to be compensated for making changes after the contract is in process. Changes made at this point usually cost the client much more than if the issue had been addressed and changes had been made prior to the issuing of contracts. For example, if the client approved a certain flooring material as part of the bid and then for some reason (not the fault of the vendor or designer) decided to change the material, the new product could be significantly higher in price, even if essentially the same grade of material as the original is used. If the original product has already been ordered, the vendor is under no obligation to refund any part of payments made on the product and also under no obligation to restock the original product.

SUBMITTALS

Nancy requested a sample of the wood finish on the desks ordered for a law office. The client wanted to match wood paneling to the desk stain. Sometimes at the beginning of the contract administration or perhaps during the course of this phase, materials, drawings, or documents may need to be provided by the vendor for approval. As a group, these are referred to as *submittals*. For example, the vendor may have to submit items such as finish samples of certain light fixtures, literature from manufacturers, or test results or certificates related to life safety code requirements. Submittals of shop drawings and finish samples for custom pieces or special installations also may be required of the vendor.

Vendors may have to provide other types of submittals. One would be updates to the designer and owner about construction or delivery schedules. In some cases, the bid documents and instructions to bidders may require that mock-ups be provided by the vendor. A *mock-up* is a full-scale representation of products or construction features. Examples include a full-scale wall with moldings, painted or otherwise finished to specifications so that the client and designer can check the colors, texture, pattern, and so on; setups of systems furniture so that the client can see the actual arrangement of the furniture; even the construction of a full-scale room, such as a patient room in a hospital, with all furniture, finishes, and equipment shown.

Finally it becomes time for contracts or other agreements to be issued to begin the process of ordering the furniture, furnishings, and equipment. The process and documents associated with ordering products is discussed in Chapter 31. Of course, this process is very similar for projects that are not bid. Project finalization and post-ordering issues and forms are covered in Chapter 32.

SUMMARY

Not all projects can be specified by simply creating an equipment list of products and a furniture layout floor plan. There are many projects that the interior designer will be involved in that will include some amount of construction of partition walls, custom cabinets, and other essentially non-load-bearing and/or constructed elements. When this occurs, it is likely the interior designer will be responsible for the preparation of construction drawings.

Formal bid specifications and documents as part of a complete package of contract documents are also often necessary. It is important for interior designers whose practices involve any structural design work or formal bid specifications to be familiar with contract documents and the bidding process. Commercial designers normally are familiar with them, but residential designers must also understand how to prepare contract documents if they become involved in remodeling projects or custom manufacturing of products. There is a substantial amount of terminology associated with contract documents, and the student and professional should be familiar with this terminology.

Floor plans and other working drawings, equipment plans keyed to equipment lists or formal specifications, and various schedules are all part of the contract documents. Most familiar to designers are the formal specifications needed when the client requires competitive bids. Four different kinds of bids are discussed in this chapter: proprietary, descriptive, performance, and reference. For designers who are not commonly associated with the bid process, this chapter also discusses how this important method operates.

Most professionals agree and the NCIDQ defines that once the bids have been received and the contract for the products and construction has been awarded, the project moves into the contract administration phase. This is the phase when the actual construction, ordering of products, and eventual installation of the FF&E occur. Information related to these activities will be covered in the next two chapters.

REFERENCES

1. Reznikoff, 1979, p. 231.
2. Reznikoff, 1989, p. 251.
3. Sweet, 1985, p. 469.
4. Rosen, 1981, p. 177.

CHAPTER 31

Contract Administration

Key Terms and Concepts

These key terms and concepts are important to material in this chapter. Many of these terms will be utilized in other chapters as well. Be sure you understand these items as you read this chapter.

Terms and Concepts

Procurement	Expeditor
Building permit	Terms and conditions
Permitting privileges	"Tag for"
Plan check	Cutting for approval (CFA)
"Red line"	Customer's own material (COM)
Building inspectors	Drop-ship
Move management	Line item number
Progress reports	Back order
Capital construction	Concealed damage
Capital improvements	Box burns
Movable equipment	Expediting

Purchasing Forms

Credit application	Invoice
Confirmation of purchase	Bill of lading
Sales agreement	Packing list
Purchase order (PO)	Freight bill
Acknowledgment	

Critical Issues

After completing this chapter you should be able to:

- Describe the essential business activities that occur during the construction and procurement phase of the project.
- Discuss the role of the interior designer during contract administration should she or he *not* be involved in the procurement of goods for the project.
- Explain the importance of keeping the client informed as the procurement of merchandise is in progress.
- Explain the purpose of each of the project purchasing forms discussed.
- Discuss each item that is needed on a purchase order and the importance of that information.
- Discuss why multiple copies of the purchase order are necessary.
- Explain why the client should be asked to sign the confirmation of purchase.
- Complete mock purchase orders.
- Analyze the information on a purchase orders, acknowledgments, and invoices.
- Explain what should be done when merchandise arrives damaged in transit.

It is difficult to define when one phase of the project ends and the next begins. Yet it is generally agreed that once the bids have been received and the contracts have been awarded for the primary work, the last phase of the project begins. Ordering and procuring merchandise for clients is discussed as part of contract administration based on the defined skills areas and project phases established by the National Council for Interior Design Qualification.

Perhaps an interior designer has prepared the interior design plans and bid documents for a hospital. The furniture, as required by the client, was put out to bid so that the hospital could get the very best price on the furniture. The bids have been returned and the client has determined which bidder will be responsible for ordering, delivering, and installing the furniture. The project is in the contract administration stage. In another case, perhaps that same interior design firm has prepared drawings and plans for a medical office suite. The doctors who own the suite have agreed to purchase directly from the designer who did the design. The interior design firm will now process orders and be appropriately involved when it comes time to deliver and install the goods for the medical suite. The project is in the contract administration phase.

In contract administration, activity centers on the actual construction, placing of orders, and completion of the project. At this critical point in the project, all the other work that has been performed by the interior designer and others come together to make design concepts become reality. All of the activities and responsibilities discussed in this chapter and the next require that the designer take utmost care in the execution of tasks, responsibilities, and paperwork and their supervision, all of which are part of project management.

Most of the time, the interior designer is indirectly involved in the construction of the building or interior. As the reader knows, the interior designer is very limited in what he or she can do concerning load-bearing construction. But this does not mean that the interior designer should be ignorant of the tasks and the paperwork that are necessary during this phase of the project.

This chapter begins with a brief discussion of the paperwork associated with contract administration related to construction that might be part of the designer's responsibilities. Because so many interior designers sell merchandise, the chapter provides a more detailed explanation of the paperwork involved in procuring merchandise for the client.

CONSTRUCTION AND PROCUREMENT ADMINISTRATION

Exactly what role the interior designer plays during contract administration depends on the laws and regulations within the jurisdiction of the project and the scope of services specified in the contract. The interior designer's role can be as uncomplicated as the ordering of merchandise and the checking to be sure that it has been delivered and placed properly. It can be very complex and involve activities such as obtaining permits, coordinating the procurement, and supervising the installation of the FF&E, supervising the installation or construction work of subcontractors, conducting site inspections, and issuing documents related to the conclusion of the project work. Or it can be anything in between.

New construction, major remodeling, and additions to structures are all examples of work where interior designers will in some way find themselves working with the architect and owner on a project. Of course, the interior designer's responsibilities are focused on the interior. With the exception of the installation of architectural finishes and the delivery of furniture, most construction or remodeling that is done on either residential or commercial sites requires a building permit. A *building permit* is an authorization from the city (or other jurisdiction) so that the plans and specifications submitted for construction meet local codes and regulations. It allows the construction work to proceed.

In order for a building permit to be obtained, sets of construction documents along with a permit application are submitted to the building department within the jurisdiction of the project. Laws do not universally allow an interior designer to submit plans to the building department of a jurisdiction to obtain a building permit. When this authority is granted to a designer, it is said that the designer has *permitting privileges*. In the event that the interior designer does not have permitting privileges, the construction documents submitted to obtain a building permit must be prepared and stamped by an architect.

The jurisdiction's building department reviews the plans (or performs a *plan check*) to ensure that the documents meet local building, fire safety, accessibility, and other codes that may apply to the particular project. Remember, the plans must meet the codes that apply in the jurisdiction of the actual project site, not that of the interior designer's office location. In some cases, the plans may be reviewed by the local fire marshal, the public works department, and/or the state (or provincial) health department depending on the project. Plan checkers may find problems with the drawings and will red line the plans. *Red lining* traditionally refers to the fact that plan checkers use a red pencil to make notations and comments on the plans, indicating problem areas. A meeting then occurs with the building officials and the client's agent (such as the interior designer or architect), to go over the plans. Clients sometimes attend these meetings as well. Depending on the quality of the drawings at this stage, a permit may be issued or the plans may have to be redone and reviewed again before a permit can be issued.

The interior designer may have been retained to work with the client in selecting contractors and initiating the construction contracts. The interior designer can only issue construction contracts if he or she is a licensed contractor. This is not the same as a licensed interior designer. (See Chapter 10.) Throughout the construction process, *building inspectors* will inspect the work. They will check to see that the project is built according to the plans, specifications, and appropriate methods. The interior designer (or general contractor) also will inspect the project. If an interior designer is not allowed to give direct supervisory instructions to subcontractors, he or she will provide memos and change orders to either the client or the general contractor on discrepancies or changes that are needed.

Prior to when the project is ready to begin, it is very important that the client understand the potential for disruption in the family or work environment. Remodeling a home cannot be done without some mess and inconvenience to the family. Major remodeling or additions might make it necessary for the family to move to other quarters for several months during the project. For commercial remodeling projects, few businesses can survive if they must totally shut down, even if the project involves only installing new carpet. If the client is moving into a new facility, the interior designer may include move management in his or her scope of services. *Move management* can include a wide range of services to help the client schedule packing and moving furniture and belongings into the new home or commercial site. For example, when a move is involved, additional scheduling must be planned so that employees can pack up their belongings that are in desks and file cabinets or inventory and mark items that need to be moved to the new location. Obviously, this would be true of a family as well.

The construction and/or remodeling of many types of commercial projects must be scheduled outside normal business hours. This means that the interior designer needs to include any extra charges for after-hours or overtime work done by delivery and installation personnel in the estimates and final pricing of the project. Special permits for the construction and even delivery and/or installation of furniture may be required. Many times these types of moves are made on the weekends; the move begins at the end of business on Friday, and the employees move back in on Monday morning. It can be a Herculean effort to schedule all that must be done, but it is an effort that is part of the interior designer's responsibilities.

It is very important for the interior designer to spend time with the client explaining how the project will proceed, prior to initiating orders and starting the construction process. Clients become very nervous during a project. They see the changes taking place, but the changes always seem to happen too slowly. The designer needs to go over the schedule with the client at the very beginning of the project so that the client has a chance to question the designer and gain an understanding of how and when the construction and interior finishing, delivery, and installation will take place.

It is very important that the client understand the scheduling of a project. The designer should spend a lot of time showing the client how each part of the construction and finishing of the project will be done and approximately when each phase will occur. There are reasons that projects often only have one or two tradespeople working on the job site at one time. The designer and tradespeople understand the problems that can occur when multiple tradespeople are on the job site at the same time. However, clients generally do not understand that problems can occur in this situation. For example, rough plumbing and rough wiring are done when the building is in the same condition, but it is not a good idea for the designer to schedule both tradespeople to do their work on the same day. The plumbers will need to be where the electricians are, and vice versa. General contractors and job foremen have had to break up fights when electricians have unintentionally dropped wiring on the heads of plumbers. An entire project has been known to shut down because nonunion furniture installers were on a job site while union workers were still working.

The designer needs to schedule regular meetings with the contractor as well as make regular visits to the construction site. In this way, the designer will know what is going on and can easily keep the client informed of the progress of the project in relation to the interior designer's contract responsibilities. Designers issue *progress reports* to the client so that the client knows what is going on. This is especially helpful in those cases in which the client wishes to be very involved in the project. For out-of-town projects, the designer must include the expenses of traveling to the project site in the contract and have these visits approved by the client prior to the visit. Design decisions regarding any necessary changes in the plans or the orders that are being placed for goods are far more effectively made with this kind of coordination.

Clients can become quite frustrated and stressed over the myriad decisions that they must make during the course of the project or during construction. The designer needs constantly to assure the client that everything is under control and to clarify where the project is on or off schedule. This, of course, means that the designer must be fully informed of the progress of the project so that the progress reports that are given either verbally or in writing to the client are accurate. Holding weekly meetings with the client is not always necessary, but having periodic meetings with the client to discuss the schedule and what will be happening next are important to keeping the client comfortable with the progress of the project. Many large design firms have found that assigning an installation supervisor, in addition to a design project manager, is a very good investment for efficient project administration.

If problems occur that affect the timely completion of the project, it is critical that the designer inform the client immediately. The concept of thinking that "what the client doesn't know won't hurt him or her" might sound good, but clients do need to know when things are going awry. As long as the designer or the firm is working on a solution to the problem, the client most likely will not become unduly nervous when problems occur. If the designer has a solution to the problem prior to calling the client, the client will feel that the designer has already taken care of things.

Changes or corrections made because of errors and omissions that have occurred during the construction need to be brought to the attention of the interior designer. Changes can easily impact the aesthetic and functional goals of the project. Too often, the designer gets cut out of many of these decisions as the contractors and the client rush to complete the project. The interior designer needs to emphasize the importance that he or she is copied any *change order*s issued during construction by other stakeholders. Changes should only be done when a change order—see Figure 30-1 in Chapter 30—has been issued.

The interior designer should also inform the client to be cautious about making arbitrary changes to the plans once the contracts have been let. Contractors often bid projects very low, and changes during the course of construction can be charged at far higher prices than the original bid. "It sure would be nice to have a window on that wall of the bedroom," says the client to the contractor. "Yes, I suppose it would. But that window will now cost you about $700, since the wall already has been framed. It would have cost only about $200 if you had thought of it sooner." By the way, it is unlikely the contractor would tell the client that the window would have been $200 originally unless this was required of the contract.

If the designer has a minor role in the construction process, his or her energies will shift to the administration of the ordering of the goods. At an appropriate time, the FF&E for the project will be ordered. The ordering of architectural finishes is often included in the general construction contract rather than in the interiors contract, although this varies. The reader will recall from Chapter 25 that anything that has to do with the actual building of the structure or that becomes physically attached to the structure is considered real property. In construction, this is often referred to as *capital construction* or *capital improvements*. The furniture, fixtures, and any equipment that is movable is generally not purchased as part of the capital construction. These various furniture items are considered *movable equipment* in construction terms.

When it is time for the designer to order movable equipment, the designer will either do so directly or will coordinate with vendors who will do so. For a commercial project this does not happen until after the bids have been awarded to vendors. Now let us look at the paperwork and process involved in the ordering of goods for a client.

What Would You Do?

Marge Johnson designed a portion of a dentist's office and was paid a fee of $15,000 for the design services. Dr. Green also ordered the chairs for the waiting area and a custom desk, credenza, and bookcases for his office. The manufacturer of the custom furniture had quoted a ten-week delivery because of the special finish and custom details specified by Johnson. These changes were approved by Dr. Green, and he also approved the delivery time.

Two weeks after the scheduled delivery of the office furniture, the manufacturer finally returned repeated inquiries by Johnson informing her that they needed another four weeks to complete the pieces. They were having trouble getting the right quality of wood for the veneer in order for the special finish to work. The manufacturer also now wanted the remainder of the price of the furniture paid in full immediately. Johnson told the client about the problem, and Dr. Green said he could make do with his old desk for awhile.

Just before the expected delivery of the desk, credenza, and bookcase, Johnson read in the paper that the furniture manufacturer had filed for bankruptcy a week earlier. Her calls to the manufacturer went to an answering machine.

ORDER PROCESSING

Interior design firms that procure furniture and other FF&E as well as architectural finishes for clients must be adept at processing a great deal of paperwork. The ideal situation is to have an *expediter*—an individual who is familiar with the company's paperwork system and the requirements of the many manufacturers—be responsible for this order processing and subsequent tracking function. Other roles of an expediter will be discussed later in the chapter. In most firms, order processing is the responsibility of the designer who has been put in charge of the project, although an office manager or an assistant office manager might also have this responsibility. In some cases, a vendor such as an office furnishing dealer will be responsible for the product procurement paperwork should a vendor win a competitive bid for the furnishings. Suppliers are also part of the paperwork management function, since they will be sending paperwork back to the designer related to the order. The interior design firm responsible for purchasing and delivering merchandise is required to order, track, and deliver perhaps several hundred—even thousands—of pieces of furniture, fixtures, and equipment.

Order processing must be done very carefully, as many things can and often do go wrong when interior designers order merchandise. Product numbers can be transposed on a purchase order resulting in the wrong merchandise being shipped. Sometimes the manufacturer can put the wrong item in the box so that the label is correct on the box but the wrong item is inside. Merchandise might be damaged in transit. Sometimes the ship date is weeks after the move-in date. Designers can be faced with the client not paying his or her bill, perhaps claiming that the merchandise delivered is not the merchandise specified. These and many other problems can easily and commonly happen to designers who sell merchandise.

Clear policies and procedures for the ordering of any merchandise and handling the paperwork involved must be set up by all design firms—even the sole practitioner. This is no time for sloppy handwriting, oral agreements, procrastination in reviewing paperwork, or even the lack of careful consideration of a client's credit worthiness. Profit margins on merchandise are too small and competition is too keen for any firm, large or small, to allow itself to be careless in conducting order processing.

There are several paperwork items that are common in order processing. This section describes documents generally used in the process, from the ordering of merchandise to when it is delivered to the job site. Special attention is paid to the purchase order, acknowledgment, and invoice, since these are key items in ordering merchandise.

Credit Application

Alice had worked with the Jones family off and on for three years, designing two homes and a small office for Mrs. Jones. Mr. and Mrs. Jones hired Alice six months ago to design a summer home in a resort area. The Joneses had convinced Alice to begin work even though a contract was not signed. They also said things like, "Oh, we have known each other for so long, is it really necessary for us to sign every piece of paper before you order things?" Alice relented and ordered $75,000 of furniture and finish products without one signature of the client. She just heard that Mr. Jones's business was in receivership and that it was likely that the Joneses would have to declare bankruptcy.

James was very excited about obtaining a contract to redesign a restaurant and a second location for an up-and-coming entrepreneur who had been receiving lots of press on his restaurant in the local press. Part of his contract with the client was to provide the furniture, booths, and custom millwork for the bar. The client told James that the furniture for the existing space and the new location should be ordered as soon as possible, as he wanted the remodeling to be done very quickly and not interfere with business. James agreed to order the chairs—which the client picked out of a catalog—before other design work was under way. The client did give James a check for 50 percent of the price of the seating. For the past two weeks, James has been trying to get in touch with the client to go over plans and to obtain further payment on the chairs, as the manufacturer has demanded a 100 percent payment for the order. The client has not returned James's calls.

Interior designers specify and sell thousands of dollars worth of products to their residential and/or commercial clients. Unfortunately, some of these clients turn out to be bad credit risks. Firms that display items on a showroom floor or in inventory may find it impractical to require a credit check for small purchases, since many sales may be "cash and carry," paid by a credit card. On the other hand, before processing special orders or beginning extensive design services for clients unknown to the design firm, interior designers need to have policies about investigating the credit worthiness of clients. Management may decide, with the advice of the firm's accountant, that special-order purchases or design fees over some specific dollar amount require that a credit check be conducted by the design firm or a credit application be completed by the prospective client.

Part of the credit policy of the interior design firm will be policies concerning deposits and retainers and payment terms. It has become routine for consumers to pay deposits or make payments to service providers before services are rendered. The reader is probably familiar with insurance co-pays required before medical services are rendered or advance payments (applied to the resulting fees) required by attorneys or accountants.

A credit application form should be easy for the client to fill out. After it has been completed, the form should be turned over to the design firm's financial institution or a credit agency for review and recommendation. The designer can check the credit of a residential client by requesting information from a credit reporting agency. Table 31-1 suggests several items that should be included on the credit application. Other items may be suggested by the design firm's accountant or banker. Although the firm should take the opinion of the financial institution or credit agency very seriously, the final decision as to whether or not to extend credit to the potential client should be that of the owner or the appropriate manager. When the designer is working with a commercial client, it is possible for the design firm to also obtain credit information on the business by contacting Dun & Bradstreet directly. A fee is charged by the bank, credit agency, or the on-line credit reporting by D&B for these services.

A credit application never provides 100 percent assurance as to the credit worthiness or good intentions of a client. However, the procedure gives the design firm a greater opportunity to work with clients who will honor their financial obligations. A sample credit application has been included on the CD. It is Item 31-1.

Confirmation of Purchase

Many firms proceed with ordering merchandise on the basis of a verbal agreement given by the client. As the reader will recall from Chapter 26, a verbal contract for the sale of goods whose value is over $5000 with a base amount of

TABLE 31-1.

Items to Include in a Credit Application.

Note that this list includes information that should be obtained for a commercial client. Information on credit worthiness of residential clients can be obtained by means other than a credit application.

Purchaser's name

Purchaser's address, phone, fax, and e-mail

Contact person

Date business established

Bank references including account numbers

Company name and DBA of commercial clients

Type of business (sole proprietorship, partnership, etc.) of business clients

Trade payment references of commercial clients

Federal tax ID or Social Security number

Amount of credit needed

Number of employees

General terms and conditions of extending credit are explained

Other items that can be recommended by the firm's accountant and/or attorney

$500 in some jurisdictions* is not legally binding on the client. For this reason, many firms require that a *confirmation of purchase*—also called a *sales agreement, a purchase agreement*, or a contract proposal—be completed and signed by the client. This form legally requires the client to fulfill his or her financial responsibility to the designer concerning the purchase of merchandise. Company policy should be clear that no furniture or furnishings should be ordered or begun until signed purchase agreements have been obtained from the client.

The design firm should use a form of at least two pages so that the design firm and the client will have a record of the sale (see Figure 31-1). The forms are numbered so that it is easier to track each form to the specific project. When it is signed by the client, the confirmation becomes a legal contract for selling the described merchandise. Do not forget to have the client sign the confirmation. Ordering merchandise without obtaining the client's signature is risky because without a signed confirmation document the firm has no concrete evidence that the client has agreed to purchase the goods. The sales agreement is also legally binding on the designer, as he or she/the firm must sell the described merchandise at the prices quoted and the client must pay for that same merchandise. To be legally binding, the form must contain quantities, descriptions, and prices. It is impractical for a firm to use a series of these forms for a large volume of items. In such cases, a statement such as "The undersigned agrees to purchase the items described per the attached list" will suffice.

The *terms and conditions* of the sale must be stated on the confirmation of purchase, and the client must be made aware of the terms (see Figure 31-2). Terms and conditions might relate to partial deliveries, changes in the job site, warehousing when the client is not ready to accept delivery, and warranties. The terms do not have to be as complex as those in the example; however, they should be complete enough to protect the interior design firm and inform the client of terms concerning the sale of goods. These terms and conditions should be prepared with the advice of the firm's attorney. A sample sales agreement with a slightly different format has been included on the CD. It is Item 31-2.

Many small design firms, especially sole practitioners, use the purchase order (discussed in the next section) as a confirmation of purchase. The argument is that some clients do not like to sign a lot of documents during the design process. Making this judgment call is up to the owner. A purchase order may have proprietary information, such as pricing, that the designer may wish to include on the purchase order but not necessarily reveal to the client unless the client is paying cost-plus for the merchandise. It is better business practice to separate the two ordering tasks by the use of a sales confirmation that has been signed by the client before ordering goods.

It should be noted that a designer who is engaged in commercial design will also receive purchase orders from clients. In some ways, these can be considered a confirmation of purchase, although since they come from the client, they are really a purchase order that signifies the buying relationship. Businesses are used to issuing a purchase order to proceed with a furniture order. It may also be faxed or e-mailed. As clients become more and more comfortable with purchasing goods over the Internet or by fax, even the smaller design firm must become familiar with these methods of confirming and ordering merchandise for interior design projects.

---

*National Conference of Commissioners on Uniform State Laws, 2003 Amendments, Uniform Commercial Code: UCC Article 2—Sales. Summary, p. 2. Available on Web site, www.nccusl.org.

112699

CUNNINGHAMS INTERIORS
BETTY J. UPTON, OWNER

2221 EAST SEVENTH AVENUE • FLAGSTAFF, ARIZONA 86004 • 520-526-0633

SALES AGREEMENT

Date of Order_____19____

Purchaser_____Phone_____

Address_____
                    Street   City   State   Zip

Install at: Name_____Phone_____

Address_____
                    Street   City   State   Zip

SPECIAL INSTRUCTIONS:_____

_____

_____

MATERIALS AND SPECIFICATIONS	Price Each	TOTAL

Additional charges may be incurred for undisclosed defects or conditions that was not identified as part of the estimate.

☐ Subject to final billing for floor preparation
☐ Subject to final measurements
☐ The buyer has provided own measurements and is therefore responsible for all amounts herein
☐ The buyer is responsible for protection of his articles when floor or wall preparations are done.

TOTAL MATERIALS $_____

Labor _____

Sub Total _____

Tax _____

Read the back of this page before signing. The provisions on the back side of this page are part of this agreement.

Total _____

Deposit Due_____   Deposit Paid _____

Sales Representative _____ CK# _____   Balance Due $_____

Purchaser_____

FIGURE 31-1.

A sales agreement (or confirmation of purchase) used as the contract for the sale of merchandise. (Reproduced with permission, Betty Upton, Cunninghams Interiors, Flagstaff, AZ)

FACILITEC
INTERIORS FOR
BUSINESS

4501 EAST MCDOWELL RD.

PHOENIX, AZ 85008

PHONE 602/275-0101

FAX 602/275-0202

TERMS AND CONDITIONS

Applicant (hereafter referred to as **Customer**) agrees that the extension of credit by **Facilitec, Inc.** (hereafter referred to as **Facilitec**) shall be subject to and in consideration of the following Terms and Conditions:

1. Payment is due net 30 days from the invoice date. The **Customer** warrants and affirms that it is financially able to meet the commitments made to **Facilitec** and will pay promptly when due any invoice rendered by **Facilitec** on or before the due date set forth on each invoice. Any deposits required by the manufacturers will be billed to **Customer** and are due upon receipt.

2. The **Customer** should understand that **Facilitec** invoices for product as it is received at the **Facilitec** warehouse or at the job site. **Facilitec** cannot control the schedules of the manufacturers, therefore, multiple invoices can occur on a proposal. It is the **Customer's** responsibility to match the invoices to the corresponding **Facilitec** proposal. If the **Customer** requires a deviation from **Facilitec's** normal billing procedures, additional charges may be applicable.

3. **Customer** agrees to pay a finance charge of 1.5% per month (annual percentage rate of 18%) on all past due balances. Balances are past due after thirty (30) days from the invoice date.

4. At any time, any invoice is delinquent, the **Customer** understands that **Facilitec** may, at it's sole option, suspend credit terms to the **Customer**. If any legal action is required to collect monies due to **Facilitec**, the **Customer** promises to pay, in addition to finance charge, all costs of collection, including attorney's fees.

5. Partial shipments: **Facilitec** agrees to make every effort to deliver and install all products as quickly as possible. However, due to manufacturers shipping schedules and methods, **Facilitec** may only be able to deliver and install portions of the job at a time. **Customer** agrees to pay 90% of invoice amounts and may withhold 10% until completion of the job.

6. Storage: If **Customer** is unable or unwilling to accept installation or delivery of the *products according to the specified schedule,* the product may be stored at the **Customer's** request in the **Facilitec** warehouse, solely as a convenience to the **Customer**. **Customer** shall pay 90% of the invoice amount within thirty (30) days of the invoice date. In addition, **Customer** shall pay a warehouse charge of 1% per month of the invoice amount of such products so warehoused, payable monthly.

7. If **Customer** cancels an order with **Facilitec,** cancellation fees may be applicable.

Company Name

Company Address

Date

Authorized Signature

Print Authorized Signature

Phone Number

FIGURE 31-2.

Typical terms and conditions on the back side of a confirmation of purchase. (Reproduced with permission, Facilitec Interiors, Inc., Phoenix, AZ)

Purchase Orders

Unless an interior designer goes to a retail showroom or store and purchases merchandise for a client with cash or a company check, practically nothing should be purchased for clients without a *purchase order*. Often referred to as a PO, the purchase order is one of the most important forms of paperwork used in the contract administration phase. The interior designer uses the purchase order to initiate orders for merchandise and services from manufacturers, tradespeople and craftspeople, and other vendors. Additionally, many interior designers use purchase orders to initiate orders for supplies or other items that are used by the design firm.

The purchase order is a critically important legal document, since it is another contract that the designer uses. It must be designed so that all the information that the vendor or supplier needs to complete the order quickly and correctly can be easily found. This information is central to establishing a contract for the sale of goods, as discussed in Chapter 26. Considering the scope of projects and the number of different clients that a design firm may be dealing with at any one time, it becomes apparent that the format must be standardized and must complement the recording methods of the remaining paperwork and accounting systems used by the firm.

All firms, regardless of their size, should have a policy prohibiting telephone orders. It is even scarier to think of designers placing orders over their cell phones while they are in their car! It is perfectly acceptable to call a vendor to follow up on orders, but placing an order by phone can be problematic. Many manufacturers do not honor telephone orders until the written order has been received. Telephone orders for any kind of product or service can lead to making mistakes in interpreting verbal instructions or in a duplication of orders and can leave the design firm responsible for paying for unwanted products. Designers also use the telephone to find out about product availability or to request that yardages of fabrics be held pending a confirming purchase order, but they should not let the telephone substitute for proper paperwork.

Another very good procedure used by many smaller firms is to request a *cutting for approval* (CFA) from fabric suppliers before the order actually has been placed. This notation can go on the purchase order if time is of the essence, or a separate form can be faxed to the fabric supplier so that the sample will be received in a timely fashion. When the sample has been received and approved, a notice can go to the supplier to proceed with the order. Of course, this same CFA procedure can be applied to wall coverings, floorings, and specialty finishes of many kinds. What this procedure does is help to ensure that the color of current stock will work with all the other materials that will be used.

Electronic orders via fax or possibly e-mail is commonplace in this industry. When orders are placed via fax, the purchase orders are prepared and faxed to appropriate vendors. When the designer faxes a purchase order, it is a good idea for the designer to have the fax machine set so that a transmission report will be printed for each order and page (see Figure 31-3). This provides a record that the fax was actually sent to the correct party. Vendors often fax back an acknowledgment showing the receipt and confirming the order.

Many suppliers are able to accommodate online order entry. The design firm would need to establish an appropriate online capability with a supplier to order online. In most situations, the designer would not follow up the online order with a paper purchase order, since the order could be duplicated. However, including a purchase order number on the online order or otherwise reference a PO number to the online order is necessary for the designer's record keeping.

Fax Call Report

PERCEPTIONS
480-951 6120
Jan-16-2007 10:04AM

Job	Date	Time	Type	Identification	Duration	Pages	Result
153	1/16/2007	10:03:05AM	Send		1:07	1	OK

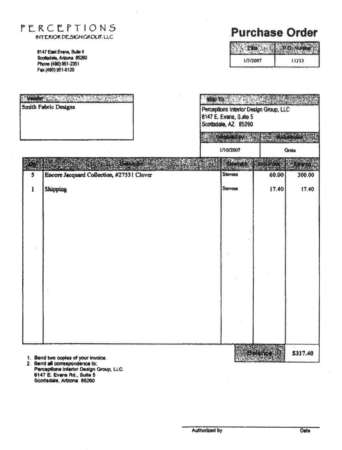

Example of a fax transmission reply, showing that the fax was sent and what was sent. This type of report helps serve as a record of transmitted faxes. (Reproduced with permission, Greta Guelich, ASID, Perceptions Interior Design Group, LLC, Scottsdale, AZ)

It is possible to order via e-mail as well, sending a PO as an attachment. The designer should check to be sure the supplier is able to receive a standard document, say, a Microsoft Word form, as an attachment without problems in compatibility. Otherwise, the attachment should be sent in ASCII type or as a text file so that the vendor is assured of being able to read the attachment.

TABLE 31-2.

Purposes of a purchase order.

1. Serves as the means of obtaining the needed goods and services in the client's interests.
2. Acts as a record of all outstanding orders. Needed for income tax calculations and loan applications.
3. Used to verify information on acknowledgments to be sure correct items were ordered.
4. Acts as a control mechanism for billing clients.
5. Can be used for checking the correct pricing of various suppliers.
6. Used to purchase items for the operations of the design firm.
7. A hard copy of a digital purchase order helps maintain accurate records.

Whether the order is placed by mail, fax, or online, purchase orders play an important role for the design firm that sells merchandise to their clients. The purposes of purchase orders are highlighted in Table 31-2.

The exact content and format of the purchase order should be established with regard to the needs of the individual firm and its accounting practices. The following information should be a part of the purchase order, either as preprinted information or left as blank spaces:

1. *Preprinted sequenced numbers.* Using numerically sequenced purchase orders allows the firm to keep track of each purchase order, whether it is used or thrown out.

2. *The firm's name and billing address, telephone number, fax number, and e-mail address of an appropriate party.* Preprinted forms look more professional, negate mailing or shipping errors resulting from illegible handwriting, and save time.

3. *Space for the supplier's/vendor's name and address.*

4. *Space for the "ship to" location.* This is very important if the design firm does not have the merchandise shipped to the design firm's office location. On occasion, designers require that orders be delivered to some location other than the designer's office. This is referred to as *drop-ship.* It usually means that the shipment will be made to the client's address or job site.

5. *Preprinted boxes or space for additional shipping instructions.* These instructions relate to expected ship date, the preferred freight company, and collected or prepaid charges.

6. *Space for the "tag for" information.* The *tag for information* (or "special info?" box as shown in Figure 31-4) can be placed at the bottom or the top of the purchase order. The client's name or a project number is usually written in this space as a further means of identifying the client who ordered the merchandise or service. Some design firms use project numbers rather than the client's name on all paperwork that travels out of the office. This is done to maintain client confidentiality. Firms also put other brief instructions on the purchase order that will help the receiving party clearly identify where the items are to be located at the job site. Note that the term "tag for" is most commonly used on purchase orders.

The
DESIGN
Collective Group, Inc.
2129 South U.S. Highway One
Jupiter, Florida 33477
IB# 0864

Voice: (561) 745-4146
Fax: (561) 745-0361

Purchase Order

•IMPORTANT NOTICE : Within 5 Days of Receipt, Vendor Must Provide Our Firm With An Acknowledgement, Confirm Costs And Provide Firm Delivery Schedule. We Reserve All Rights To Cancel If Vendor Fails To Provide This Information .

Our Reference # ☐ - ☐ - ☐

Today's Date _____

Vendor _____

Address _____

City, ST, Zip _____

Sidemark _____

Must Complete By _____

Ship Via _____

Ship To _____

_____

Address _____

City, ST, Zip _____

Terms _____
• This Order may be canceled without penalty if Vendor is not able to ship by date specified or fails to notify of any delay.
• No changes nor any substitutions without prior approval.
• Acknowledgements, Shipments & Invoices must be clearly marked with Our Reference Number and Complete Sidemark.
• Any Additional Costs Must be Approved Prior to Proceeding.
• Vendor agrees that acceptance of this order and the terms outlined supercede any other terms and conditions set forth.

Quantity	Specification	Cover, Color, Finish	Each	Total

Special Info?

Subtotal	
Other Charges?	
Freight	
TOTAL	

Authorization To Proceed With This Order Subject To Terms Above :
By _____ Date _____

White - Vendor   Yellow - Client Binder   Pink - Billing   Gold - Receiving

FIGURE 31-4.

A purchase order form. (Reproduced with permission, Michael Thomas, FASID, CAPS, The Design Collective Group, Jupiter, FL)

Figure 31-4 shows an example of a typical purchase order. The body of the purchase order should have space for the following information:

1. *Quantity.* This is not only needed by the supplier, but also it is required by the UCC to create a sales contract.

2. *Catalog number.* This should exactly reflect the sequence of numbers and/or letters that the supplier uses to call out the products from his or her catalog. Reversing one number can lead to the wrong product being shipped.

3. *Description.* The method that the supplier uses in the catalog should be followed. This helps prevent having the wrong item shipped. However, it should be remembered that many suppliers process orders by the catalog number on the purchase order, not the description. The description acts as a check against the catalog number. There is no guarantee that the supplier's order input person will read the description.

4. *Net price.* Including the expected net price on the purchase order works as an additional accuracy check, especially when the designer orders only occasionally from a supplier. Of course, best practice is to know what the net price or price to the designer will be before the purchase order is prepared! Net pricing on the purchase order can also help the firm utilize a cost accounting method for managerial control. Note that the net price should not be included on the purchase order if a copy of the form will be given to the client.

5. *Line item number.* Many firms use *line item numbers* as another method of controlling an order. Each item on the sale order is given a line item number. This number is cross-referenced in the appropriate column on the purchase order. Problems and questions about orders can more easily be tracked with this number. Goods also can be tagged with the line item number. Note that multiples of the same item for the same order are considered one line item.

The bottom of the form should provide space for the authorizing signature. This signature will be either that of the firm's owner or of an authorized manager. Additional information that the design firm wishes the supplier to be aware of can be added in appropriate places—for example, instructions asking the supplier to acknowledge receipt of the purchase order and to provide an expected shipping date.

Each supplier involved in a project receives a separate purchase order. Multiple items to the same supplier for the same client can, of course, be sent on the same purchase order. If the designer is placing orders for multiple items to the same supplier but for two or more *different* clients, a different purchase order should be prepared for each client. Even though some firms place two or more customer orders to the same manufacturer on the same purchase order, better control is maintained by initiating separate purchase orders for each customer.

If two suppliers are involved in the completion of one finished product, such as a sofa that will receive fabric from another vendor, the designer must prepare two different purchase orders. *Customer's own material* (COM) indicates that the designer is not using a fabric available from the chair or sofa manufacturer. One purchase order is written to the sofa supplier, referencing (according to the supplier's requirements printed in the supplier's catalog) the COM fabric. A second purchase order is written to the fabric supplier, referencing the information required by the sofa supplier. This information is often written as an expanded "tag for" block of information in the body of the purchase order, rather than in the normal "tag for" space. Most furniture manufacturers require

ACKNOWLEDGEMENT

Purchase Order #   10007598

Page 1 of 1

BILL TO: **Business One**
100 Circle Drive
Phoenix, AZ 85018
602-555-0000

SHIP TO: **Furniture Install Corp.**
2222 Main Street
Phoenix, AZ 85253

HBF SALES REP: Jane Smith

HBF DUNS #: 255555

CUSTOMER CONTACT:
NAME: John Jones c/o Cool Restaurant 6
PHONE: 602-555-0001
EMAIL: jjones@aol.com

SHIPPING INFORMATION:
CALL BEFORE DELIVERY
John Jones 602-555-0001

ACCOUNT INFORMATION:
ACCOUNT #: 545454
ORDER DATE: 01/01/07
ORDER ENTERED: 01/02/07

TERMS: Net 30
ORDER TAGGING: Cool Restaurant 6
ORDER RECEIVED: 01/01/07

HBF CONTACT:

T: 888-555-5555
F: 888-555-0000
E: hbf@furniture.com

LINE	QTY	STYLE	DESCRIPTION	GRADE FABRIC	NET	EXT
Prod Line:						
1	16	5018-30	Westwood Lounge Chair Armless 27"OW x 36"OD x 30-1/2"OH Finish: 11-Amazon Dark On Maple	F-HBF Nubby #807-44	$980.16	$15,681.60
2	3	5020-30	Westwood Sofa Finish: 11-Amazon Dark On Maple 84"OW x 39"OD x 30-1/2"OH	Grade 1 HBF Leather Vivace/Nero #703-90	$1,838	$5,514

FREIGHT/HANDLING $2,010
SALES TAX $1059.78

ORDER TOTAL	$24,265.38

IMPORTANT NOTICE
No Cancellation will be taken on this order if covers have been cut. This acknowledges your order as it
will be shipped. If incorrect please notify us immediately, in as much as upholstering fabrics are not guaranteed
by the mill. HBF will not be held responsible for wear or fading of any covering materials.
THIS IS IMPORTANT AND SHOULD NOT BE NEGLECTED.

Hickory Business
Furniture, Inc.
900 12th Street Dr. NW
Hickory, NC 28601
TEL 828.328.2064
FAX 828.328.8816

FIGURE 31-6.

A different format of an acknowledgment from a supplier. (Reproduced with permission, Hickory Business Furniture & HBF Textiles, Hickory, NC)

Although acknowledgments vary in format to suit the needs of specific suppliers, it is likely that the following kinds of information will be provided on them:

1. An order number assigned by the supplier.
2. The design firm's purchase order number.
3. The date on which the acknowledgment was prepared.
4. A scheduled shipping date. The order will be shipped some time during that week, not necessarily on that day.
5. What the expected shipping situation will be (e.g., "Collect—Roadway" means that the design firm will have to pay the shipping charges and that the merchandise will come from the Roadway shipping company).
6. Notations as to who ordered the merchandise, the billing address, and the shipping address.
7. The "tag for" instructions.
8. A restatement of quantity, catalog number, description, and pricing information. Many manufacturers put the net price on the acknowledgment. However, others still quote retail prices. If the retail price has been quoted, the acknowledgment will often also quote the discount that the designer will receive for that order.
9. Other information related to billing and shipping.

Each acknowledgment must be checked against the purchase order. Comparing the acknowledgment information against the purchase order must be done so that any discrepancies between the two forms can be found. There is generally very little time for the designer or the client to make changes in the order. Major suppliers often give only ten days and certainly no more than three weeks "from receipt of order" to make any changes in the order. Any discrepancies, but especially those in quantity, catalog number, description, and price, should be discussed with the manufacturer immediately. Delays in calling attention to errors often result in the design firm's receiving the wrong merchandise. Discrepancies regarding the expected shipping date or other shipping information also should be checked to see how they may affect the project's completion. In smaller design firms, the person responsible for checking the acknowledgments is the designer, an assistant, or the bookkeeper. Checking acknowledgments is usually the responsibility of the expediter in larger design firms. Discrepancies must be brought to the attention of the project designer so that he or she can determine how to deal with the problem and discuss possible alternatives with the client.

The supplier may send the design firm an original copy, a fax, or possibly an e-mail version of the acknowledgment. Faxed or e-mailed acknowledgments should also contain similar information. E-mailed acknowledgments need to be downloaded into the designer's order system, or hard copies should be printed so that the designer will have a record of the transaction. The acknowledgment should be attached to the corresponding purchase order in the open purchase order file. A copy may be added to the active project file for reference purposes.

Someone must be responsible for checking all outstanding orders. Many design firms use a "tickler file" keyed to the days of the month. This file is checked daily (in very large firms) or weekly to make sure that goods have been received within the expected ship dates. Checking can be done immediately on orders that are about to be shipped or that have not yet been received, although the ship date has passed. Again, computer programs are useful tools in such situations.

Invoices

An *invoice* is simply a bill. The interior design firm sends out invoices to clients for services performed and/or goods purchased in the client's name. Suppliers send invoices to the designer for the goods or services that the interior design firm has ordered.

Invoices from suppliers are commonly sent at the same time that the merchandise is shipped. The invoice generally arrives at the office a few days before the merchandise. Many suppliers have invoices that look very similar to their acknowledgments; the only difference may be the label. Care in checking the mail is necessary, since invoices must be paid while acknowledgments are for information. The invoice needs to correspond to what was ordered and should be checked against the purchase order and acknowledgment. Since the invoice often arrives a few days before the merchandise, it also should be checked against what is received. Figure 31-7 shows an invoice from a supplier to a designer. In this case, the invoice is for the item shown on the acknowledgement in Figure 31-6.

The invoice may include special pricing such as an extra cash discount for prompt payment. The reader can refer back to our discussion on cash discounts in Chapter 25. These discounts can amount to substantial savings for a design firm that can afford to pay the invoice within the specified time period. Not all suppliers offer this special discount to all designers.

In a small design firm, it is easy for practitioners to forget to send invoices to clients or at least to delay this task. Best practices should include invoicing clients as quickly as possible in order to keep receivables very low and good cash flow into the design firm. Figure 31-8 shows a sample invoice from a designer to a client. The reader must understand that the manufacturers expect prompt payment from the interior designer. Thus, the designer should also be sending out invoices to receive payment from the client.

Goods should be billed within ten days after the goods have been delivered and accepted by the client. Services should be billed once services have been completed for short-duration projects, on a monthly basis for larger projects, or on whatever billing basis for services was agreed to in the contract. Poor cash management through slow billing can be a serious problem for any sized interior design firm. Delays in billing can also lead to a few unscrupulous clients not paying for goods or services at all.

To help the design firm have at least some legal basis for preventing late payment or no payment, the original contract for services or goods should contain such language as "billing upon delivery" or "payment due ten days after receipt of invoice." Some firms try to use item-by-item billing on large projects. This, of course, means that if the project has 20 items that are to be delivered and only two arrive, the firm delivers the two items and bills only for those two items. The next time one or more items arrive, those are also delivered and billed. Although this may help the firm's cash flow, it can cause many costs and headaches to the firm. There is a cost attached each time the delivery truck delivers goods to the client. There is also a cost associated with the preparation and mailing of invoices. Many commercial clients will not pay for goods delivered one at a time, but only upon completion of the work. It is suggested that, whenever possible, deliveries be done in lots or only when the job has been completed. This will reduce delivery and bookkeeping costs for multiple

Send check to:
HBF & HBF Textiles
P.O. Box 60571
Charlotte, NC 28260-0571
Freight Charges NET - Shipments FOB Hickory
No anticipation allowed

PROFORMA #

Purchase Order # 10007598

Page 1 of 1

BILL TO: **Business One**
100 Circle Drive
Phoenix, AZ 85018
602-555-0000

SHIP TO: **Furniture Install Corp.**
2222 Main Street
Phoenix, AZ 85253

HBF SALES REP: Jane Smith

HBF DUNS #: 255555

CUSTOMER CONTACT:
NAME: John Jones c/o Cool Restaurant 6
PHONE: 602-555-0001
EMAIL: jjones@aol.com

SHIPPING INFORMATION:
CALL BEFORE DELIVERY
John Jones 602-555-0001

ACCOUNT INFORMATION:
ACCOUNT #: 545454
ORDER DATE: 01/01/07
ORDER ENTERED: 01/02/07

TERMS: Net 30
ORDER TAGGING: Cool Restaurant 6
ORDER RECEIVED: 01/01/07
SHIP DATE: 03/06/07

HBF CONTACT:

T: 888-555-5555
F: 888-555-5555
E: hbf@furniture.com

LINE	QTY	STYLE	DESCRIPTION	GRADE FABRIC	NET	EXT
1	16	5018-30	Westwood Lounge Chair Armless Finish: 11-Amazon Dark	F-HBF Nubby #807-44	$980.16	$15,681.60
2	3	5020-30	Westwood Sofa Finish: 11-Amazon Dark	COL Leather 1/black	$1,838	$5,514

FREIGHT/HANDLING $2,010
SALES TAX $1,059.78

ORDER TOTAL   **$24,265.38**

IMPORTANT NOTICE
Total amount due.
THIS IS IMPORTANT AND SHOULD NOT BE NEGLECTED.

1/24/07 11:45 am

Hickory Business
Furniture, Inc.
900 12th Street Dr. NW
Hickory, NC 28601
TEL 828.328.2064
FAX 828.328.8816

FIGURE 31-7.

This proforma invoice corresponds to the acknowledgement shown in Figure 31-6. (Reproduced with permission, Hickory Business Furniture & HBF Textiles, Hickory, NC)

PERCEPTIONS
INTERIOR DESIGN GROUP, LLC

8147 East Evans, Suite 5
Scottsdale, Arizona 85260
Phone (480) 951-2351
Fax (480) 951-6120

Invoice

Date	Invoice #
1/2/2007	99796

Bill To

Quantity	Description	Each	Price
1	Lorts Nightstand #9649; Finish: Rirenze; Standard Distress, No wax Match to finish sample enclosed	1,160.85	1,160.85T

The designer acts as the client's agent for all products and services described above. The designer makes no guarentees beyond those of the supplier, if any. Fabrics and leathers are not guarenteed for color match, wearing or fading.

Terms: 80 percent payment required at the time of signing this invoice. Balance is due when products are ready for delivery or when services are completed. All prices are subject to additional charges for storage and freight.

Subtotal	$1,160.85
Tax (7.95%)	$92.28
Total	**$1,253.13**
80% Deposit	$1,002.50
Balance Due	$250.63

ACCEPTED _____

FIGURE 31-8.

A sample invoice prepared by a design firm and sent to a client. (Reproduced with permission, Greta Guelich, ASID, Perceptions Interior Design Group, LLC, Scottsdale, AZ) deliveries. Another sample format for an invoice a designer might use is included on the CD as Item 31-4.

SHIPPING AND FREIGHT

Unless a product for a job is manufactured or otherwise available locally, the interior designer will need to add charges for shipping the goods to the designer's warehouse or job site. Locally available items will also be required to have additional charges for delivery. These topics are discussed in other locations related to specific application. Chapter 25 contains a discussion of how freight and delivery charges affect the price of the goods, Chapter 26 reviews freight concepts as regulated by the UCC, and Chapter 32 discusses delivery charges. In this chapter, we will look at the forms that are specifically related to shipping and freight services.

There are various freight matters that result in additional paperwork management for the designer. The first is the bill of lading. Large sales-oriented firms that consistently expect large orders of goods from suppliers will obtain bill of lading documents for their files. The *bill of lading* is the form that the supplier provides to the truck driver to show what is being shipped and who has title to the goods. The driver carries this form with him or her in the truck; the contents of the truck must match what is on the form. The bill of lading does not mirror a purchase order and may actual relate to several purchase orders to the same design firm or even multiple firms. The bill of lading is not a detailed list, but rather a total quantity of items. If the entire shipment is to one firm, the designer or the warehouse must check the number of items that are delivered to the firm against the number on the bill of lading. Discrepancies in quantity should be noted on the bill, as well as any notations regarding damages to merchandise. It should be noted that most small interior design firms never see a bill of lading, as the size of their orders from a supplier are too small.

Another form that accompanies the delivery is a packing list. The *packing list* is commonly in a plastic envelope attached to the outside of one of the items being delivered. The packing list details by quantity and description what is being shipped from a manufacturer or supplier to the warehouse at a specific time. The designer should check the packing list against all items taken from the truck and against the number on the bill of lading. Again, discrepancies should be noted on the bill of lading if a bill of lading is provided to the designer.

The actual *freight bill* is another use of the term "invoice." It is usually sent a few days after the shipment leaves the manufacturer. The freight bill comes from the shipping company, not the manufacturer, and is the bill for the shipping service.

It is important for the designer or a representative of the design firm (the warehousing service) to inspect all the items as they arrive at the designer's warehouse or job site. Many one-person design firms allow merchandise to be delivered to the client without the designer being available at the time of delivery to inspect the goods. This can be very costly if merchandise has been damaged. Inspection prior to delivery allows damages or errors to be caught, eliminating client dissatisfaction.

Damaged cartons should be immediately opened and inspected as they are removed from the shipper's truck. Whenever practical, all items should be unwrapped or uncartoned so that they may be inspected for *concealed damage*—damage that may exist even though the carton or wrapping appears intact. One type of concealed damage that can occur on wood furniture shipped in a box is called *box burns*. When this happens the carton has rubbed against the wood and that contact has marred the finish. Concealed damage must be reported to the carrier as soon as possible. As the time from acceptance of shipment or the discovery of damages lengthens, successful claims become less probable.

Any damage to cartons, packing, and merchandise should be shown to the driver. Notations about damaged merchandise must be made on the bill of lading or copy of the packing list in order for the design firm to make successful claims. Many designers also take pictures of damaged merchandise. This can greatly help the firm in the filing of claims.

Since the filing of freight claims and disposition of the claims are very time-consuming, many larger firms forgo filing claims on minor damage and make repairs themselves. These charges are costed as overhead expenses. Merchandise that has sustained substantial damage in transit should be refused. However, a freight claim must still be filed, and records such as photographs, showing the extent of the damage, must be kept.

Certain documentation is generally required when the firm is filing a freight claim:

1. The bill of lading
2. The paid freight bill
3. The manufacturer's invoice for the item
4. The inspection report prepared by the freight carrier
5. Documentation of repair costs
6. Documentation of additional freight costs (if any) resulting from the damage
7. Other written or photographic documentation that attests to the damage occurring before delivery to the job site or to the designer's warehouse

Because a shipment has been damaged or is otherwise incorrect does not mean that the designer can demand the shipper automatically return it to the vendor. Most manufacturers will not accept merchandise for return once it has been delivered to the purchasing firm or the design firm has accepted it. Therefore, the firm must get written permission to return damaged (or incorrectly shipped) merchandise. The firm should not simply send the merchandise back to the manufacturer. Each manufacturer has its own policy concerning returns, and these policies must be adhered to in order for the firm to receive proper credit.

When the design firm contacts the freight carrier concerning a shipping question, it should have the bill of lading number, the supplier's name and location, the date of shipment, the description and number of items shipped, and the delivery location. If the information needed is not on the manufacturer's invoice, this information, along with other needed information, can be obtained from the manufacturer.

EXPEDITING

This chapter has mentioned many times that someone from the firm must check all the paperwork going out and coming in to be sure that items are ordered correctly, that the item requested is what will be shipped, and that the items received are the items ordered. Sole practitioners must do all this work themselves. Larger firms are able to use someone who has these responsibilities as the key tasks in their job description. The term associated with the person who is primarily responsible for the ordering and managing of these product orders is the expediter. He or she is an individual who is familiar with the design firm's paperwork system and the various ordering and shipping requirements of manufacturers. In firms that are large enough to have a person responsible for this specific job function, the expediter is a person who constantly monitors all orders *after* the purchase orders have been sent and the acknowledgments have been received. He or she is responsible for the speedy processing of orders. Expeditors might also be responsible for preparing purchase orders, but that would be an operational decision of the owner. In the following discussion, the expeditor does not have the responsibility for preparing purchase orders.

The first activity of the expediter is to check the acknowledgment from the manufacturer against the purchase order. This is a vital step to ensure that all the information matches the two forms and confirms that the correct products and/ or services are being supplied. Discrepancies must be taken care of immediately.

Once all the product information has been checked, the expediter will look closely at the expected ship date. He or she must check to be sure that the products are going to ship within the time specified on the purchase order and that they will arrive when they were promised. If the ship date is not what is expected, the expediter should inform the designer so that the proper action can be taken. Delays in shipping can especially be complicated by items that have one item dependent upon another. A common example is the fabric for seating. If the fabric is delayed, the seating items are also delayed. Depending on the length of the delay, the designer may need to discuss with the client the necessity of reselecting the fabric. Sometimes the expeditor will contact the client or vendor with a facsimile so that a hard copy exists of the contact. A sample facsimile cover form is included on the CD. It is Item 31-5.

On the other hand, merchandise may be coming sooner than expected. Merchandise shipped earlier than desired may have to be warehoused until the job site is ready. If this is the case, the designer must negotiate with the client as to who will be responsible for the charges and where the merchandise should be shipped. At the time of order, it is relatively easy for the design firm to request that the merchandise not be shipped until a date beyond the normal shipping date. There may be an extra charge if the manufacturer must warehouse the finished goods when the designer requests that the shipment be delayed.

More often the ship date is shown to be later than expected. The designer must contact the client to let him or her know about the delay. Short-term delays may be inconvenient but are seldom critical. Delays of three or more weeks may necessitate canceling the original order and finding alternate products.

The expediter is also responsible for tracking shipments once they have left the manufacturer. A very good practice is to have a tickler file by date for the acknowledgments. The expediter can then check weekly on the disposition of any order. He or she can then alert the delivery people of the impending shipment and where it is to be delivered by the trucking company.

It is particularly important to know the disposition of merchandise that is to be drop-shipped to a job site. Someone representing the design firm (or the design firm's warehouse service company) must be at the site to unload, inspect, and deliver the goods to the client. Truck drivers generally are not responsible for unloading the merchandise from the truck, unpacking it, and delivering it to the client. In some firms, the expediter may also be responsible for filing return permissions as well as freight claims. However, a warehouse service may be able to provide these last two services for the design firm.

Once shipments leave the manufacturer, the expediter and designer track them by the bill of lading number, not the purchase order number. The firm receives from the freight company information as to what this number is. The bill of lading number, along with the name and address of the design firm, the name and address of the delivery site, the name of the shipping company, the name and address of the original shipping location, a description and the number of pieces in the order, and the weight of the order must be available for tracking delayed shipments.

SUMMARY

Most of the responsibilities of the interior designer may or may not be over when the project enters the contract administration phase. The extent of a designer's involvement rests on the scope of services and the laws affecting work that can be done by the interior designer related to construction supervision.

This chapter discusses the various kinds of paperwork that are involved once the project reaches the contract administration phase and it is time to order goods or actually begin construction. A brief discussion concerning the permits and other paperwork that are a part of the structural work that occurs in most interior design projects begins the chapter.

Emphasis has been placed on the paperwork connected to ordering merchandise or invoicing of services. The differences between the paperwork management for residential and commercial projects is very subtle. The purpose of the forms themselves are the same. Design firms that function as designer/specifiers and do not sell merchandise to the end user save themselves a considerable amount of paperwork. Those that wish to sell merchandise as well as perform the design service must be prepared to understand and handle the multitude of forms and paperwork involved. We also looked at the paperwork involved in freight or shipping of merchandise to the delivery location and the delivery responsibility.

Designers who are unable to manage the paperwork should hire someone who is skilled in this area. The next chapter covers the tasks of the final portions of the contract administration phase—the delivery of merchandise and the project's closeout.

CHAPTER 32

Contract Administration: Delivery and Project Closeout

Key Terms and Concepts

These key terms and concepts are important to material in this chapter. Many of these terms will be utilized in other chapters as well. Be sure you understand these items as you read this chapter.

Terms and Concepts

Delivery	Certificate of substantial completion
Installation	Record drawings
Project closeout	As-built drawings
Walk-through	Certificate of payment
Punch list	Retainage
Site inspection report	Postoccupancy evaluation
Certificate of occupancy	

Critical Issues

After completing this chapter you should be able to:

- Compare and contrast the delivery process from the installation process.
- Explain why it is important for the client to sign for items delivered to the job site.
- Compare an as-built floor plan to an original construction drawing.
- Describe why a "white gloves" approach to the delivery and installation process is so important.
- Explain what occurs during project closeout and any documents that are utilized.
- Discuss "retainage" and who it most commonly affects.
- Compare a postoccupancy evaluation for clients to one done solely for the design firm.

The previous chapter dealt with the paperwork and tasks in contract administration up to the time that FF&E products are shipped to the job site. Of course, the project is not complete until all the merchandise has been delivered and accepted by the client. In this chapter, we will look at the final activities that occur in contract administration once the orders have been processed and are ready to be delivered to the client. These activities include delivery and installation, project closeout, and postoccupancy reviews.

In small design firms, these activities are customarily administered by the designer, with assistance from others only at the delivery stage. In larger design firms, many of these activities are handled by other employees whose specialized job responsibility revolves around completing the project. The responsibilities of an expediter—discussed in the previous chapter—might include resolving delivery and installation issues.

Whether these activities are done by the project designer him- or herself or are the responsibility of others, the project designer always retains ultimate responsibility for the completion of the project. It is an important part of being a professional interior designer.

DELIVERY AND INSTALLATION

Many activities remain after any construction work is completed and all the structural and mechanical systems are completed. Architectural finishes are needed for walls, floors, and possibly the ceilings. Window treatments will be installed after the walls are finished, and custom cabinets might still need to be added if they were not part of the primary construction contract. Of course, the largest part of the project at this stage is the delivery and installation of all the furniture, accessories, and equipment that are part of the designer's contract, as well as the existing furnishings that must be placed in the spaces.

The delivery process itself can be very stressful for clients (as well as exciting) as they finally see the design concepts and ideas that they have waited for unfold before their eyes. Thus, a week or two prior to the delivery and installation of the furnishings, the designer must schedule a detailed pre-move-in meeting with the client or client's representative concerning delivery and installation. A key task of this meeting is to review the furniture/equipment plans. This is done to be sure that the client has not changed his or her mind about the placement of any of the items. If items are to be moved, revised plans need to be prepared so that the delivery and installation workers are not forced to place the items more than once. The larger the project, the more important this becomes, since clients—especially many commercial project clients—might need to make changes in furniture and equipment locations.

An extra service that the designer may wish to discuss and include in the contract is move management. Depending on the project, the client may be moving from one location to the new project location. The designer can help obtain a moving company to pack and move the client's existing home or office furniture and possessions that are to be used in the new location. For a business, this move must be carefully orchestrated, as the business cannot be shut down for any appreciable time or it will lose business during the move. Pre-move activities such as packing up confidential files or important documents, possibly having key individuals located in temporary space for business to continue during the move, and in general being sure the spaces are ready for occupancy are important parts of the move.

Instructions are given on the purchase order regarding where to ship the goods. As discussed in the previous chapter, most designers have goods shipped to a warehouse before they are ultimately delivered to the job site. *Delivery* includes the activities concerned with moving furniture, furnishings, and equipment from the warehouse or showroom to the job site and placing them in their correct locations. Delivery involves no special activities of assembly, construction, or physical attachment of the products to the building. *Installation* involves assembly, construction, or physical attachment of products to the building. Let us look at delivery services first.

Even if the designer is not part of the pre-move preparation, it is a stressful time for the designer as well. Delivery trucks have been known to have accidents, room to maneuver large trucks suddenly is not available, or elevators are not available for access; such problems can affect the delivery even with excellent planning for the move-in. It is important that the interior designer carefully plan delivery supervision time into the design fee, since the designer will either be expected or want to be present to handle problems that might occur.

The designer should prepare a delivery plan showing locations for all the furniture and other items for the job to let the delivery people know exactly where each piece should be located. These delivery plans must be updated to include any changes in locations of furniture items discussed at the pre-move-in meeting (see Figure 30-1). This is essential for the smooth completion of the project. A floor plan keyed to the purchase order number and line item number is one way to do this if the project is small and does not involve many items. For larger projects, and especially in commercial design, other methods are used. Furniture items on the floor plan are keyed to the purchase order to facilitate delivery.

Design firms that do not have a showroom depend on independent delivery service companies for delivery to the client's home or office. Merchandise is also often shipped to that delivery service's warehouse to await actual delivery. Products such as wall coverings and flooring are shipped to the company that will do the installation of those products. Firms with a showroom might have a delivery staff with company-owned trucks.

Regardless of how the goods reach the job site, delivery crews must be trained in the "white gloves" procedures that lead to satisfied customers. Firms depending on delivery service providers must select this company carefully and monitor the performance of the delivery service to ensure that the company can represent the quality of service the designer wishes for his or her clients. Especially when furniture and accessory items are delivered, clean uniforms, clean hands, polite and respectful behavior, as well as respectful treatment of the client's property should be mandatory. These are just some factors that help a firm continue high-level customer service.

A delivery for a large commercial project often requires that parking lots or even parts of streets be closed to allow delivery trucks easy access to the building. If it is necessary to close a street, the client, designer, or contractor must arrange with the city police to obtain the proper permits for the closure. In a multistory building, the client, designer, or contractor will also have to arrange for access to freight elevators or one of the regular service elevators. Even the installation of furniture at a new home can mean that neighbors may get upset about the number of delivery trucks or tradespeople's trucks that are constantly seen in the neighborhood.

Clients often expect the designer to be present at all times during the delivery and installation of merchandise. This may seem to be an impractical use of the designer's time, but it can be key for maintaining good public relations. The designer should allow for spending a reasonable amount of time on the job site during delivery and installation. This time should be estimated at the beginning of the project and included in the fees for the project. If the designer is at the job site during this crucial time, he or she can reassure an anxious client who may not be sure about finishes and products as they are being installed and/or delivered.

The designer who is present during the delivery and installation of merchandise can speed up the inspection process and, when questions arise, help answer them. How much time the designer spends at the job site during this time will depend on the client, the contract, the particular complexity of the job, and the designer's availability.

From a practical point of view, it is important for the client to sign documentation that indicates what he or she has received during the delivery (or installation) portion of the project. This signifies acceptance and transfer of title, and thereby requires that the client pay for what was delivered. If a copy of the purchase order was sent to the warehouse service or to the designer's warehouse, the client can sign off on this form. Some firms have a separate delivery ticket that accompanies the merchandise. This ticket, shown in Figure 32-1, is at least a three-part form. The parts are as follows:

1. The top or original copy goes to the client.
2. A second copy is sent to the billing office.
3. The third copy is retained by the warehouse whenever a back order, which is a partial shipment, occurs.

Any notations regarding damages or discrepancies between what was delivered and what was ordered should be noted on the delivery paperwork. This helps clarify which damages are the responsibility of the design firm and which damages are the responsibility of the client.

Delivery service should include dusting and vacuuming of the merchandise, carefully inspecting it for any scratches or other damage, and removal of all cartons and packaging materials. It may also be the delivery team's responsibility to show the client how to operate certain items, such as adjustable office chairs. However, this is often the responsibility of the designer.

Installation and assembly is the part of the delivery process that involves assembly or construction of merchandise, or installing physical attachments to the building. Installation includes attaching wall-hung bookcases, other storage units, and mirrors, and assembling open-office furniture. Specialized sets of drawings are often necessary for installations of furniture such as open office systems and some architectural finish specifications. With open-office systems, for example, commercial firms prepare one or more sheets of drawings that aid in the assembly. Plans that show panel configurations and finishes, electrical and telephone service, and either plans or elevations for the location of hanging components are examples.

Routine architectural finish schedules, as part of the construction documents, provide the information needed for designers to specify the locations of these finishes. Wall graphics or designs in flooring materials are examples of drawings that might be needed for architectural finishes and included in the construction drawings. Graphic schedules or interior elevations inform the contractor of the locations of such items as mirrors, complex wall treatments, and various wall-hung units.

Although it does take time to prepare delivery and installation drawings, it is the easiest and simplest way for the designer to guarantee that all the specified goods will be delivered and installed in their proper location. Preparation of these documents provides the designer the assurance that he or she will not be needed on the job site at all times. Showing the client that these kinds of documents have helped on projects in the past will also indicate to the client

DELIVERY TICKET **SO36959**
Job
Proposal PR0028850
Print Date 01/10/07

Customer PO
SalesPerson

Contract Office Group, Inc.
931 Cadillac Court
Milpitas, CA 95035
PHONE: 408-262-6400
FAX: 408-262-1193

Sold To: **Ship To:**   **Install At:**
JOHN DOE   Contract Office Group   JOHN DOE
     931 Cadillac Court
     Milpitas, CA 95035

Line Seq. No.	Description	Quantity
1 SZT-20-721MA1	ZODY TASK CHAIR,FABRIC SEAT/MESH BACK	1
	(721MA1) 4D,PAL BK,PNU/BS,FW/ADJ,ST/HRD	
	.1X- CHR FAB - GAUGE GRADE A	
	005 DEPTH	
	,MA- ZODY MESH	
	001 SUPPORT	
	,TR- SURFACE 3	
	00F BLACK	
	,TR- SURFACE 4	
	00F BLACK	
2 5G90012RG	KEYBOARD TRAY, 19"W X 10 5/8"D	1
	W/SWIVEL MOUSE - 10" SWIVEL RIGHT	
	STANDARD PLATFORM	
	19" GEL WITH SYNTHETIC LEATHER COVER	
3 MPGEL10	10" MOUSE PAD W.GEL PALM	1
	***** PROCESS ORDER AS QUICK-SHIP ****	
4 SV-LABOR-A	COG TO DELIVER & INSTALL CHAIR & KEYBOARD TRAY.	1

Client Signature_____ **Date**_____

Delivered By Signature_____ **Date** _____

FIGURE 32-1.

This type of form can be used to accompany merchandise for delivery and/or installation. (Reproduced with permission, Contract Office Group, Milipitas, CA) that the firm can deliver and install the products without the designer being there at all times.

It is also important for the installation crew to take care of dusting, vacuuming, and removal of trash. Since some companies do not perform such tasks as a routine part of their service, the design firm should be sure that these tasks are included in its contract with the installer. If they are not included, the designer or client will be charged for the extra work.

A final issue concerning delivery installation concerns confidentiality. Throughout the project, the interior designer has learned many private, proprietary issues about the client or client's business. Designers are often given keys to homes and free access to many business properties during the project. This is a significant trust given to the designer. During delivery and installation, vendors and staff also are exposed to the client's private affairs in much the same way. A responsibility of the designer is to carefully select these vendors and staff with consideration for trust and confidentiality. It is unfortunate that occasionally a client will find a personal item missing after a delivery. Interior designers help prevent this from happening by checking on the bonding and insurance of the delivery company prior to hiring them for a job.

What Would You Do?

An interior designer had been hired by a client to specify the furniture for a cabin in a resort community. The designer was also hired to act as an owner's representative concerning the construction and interior finishing by the builder. The designer did have the proper licenses to do the work as an owner's representative.

One of the many items the builder installed was the flooring materials and all wall treatments as specified by the interior designer and approved by the client. The cost of these materials was part of the construction contract. There was an availability problem with the floor tile used throughout the first floor. The builder replaced the original item with one that was more expensive but that was in stock after he told the interior designer about the problem. The builder told the designer it was the only way to get the project done on time. He assumed the designer had informed the client of the upcharge on the tile and installed the more expensive tile, although he did not have a change order from the interior designer.

On a visit to the job site (the client lived out of state), the husband noticed that the tile was different from the sample he thought he remembered. The designer said, "I sent you an e-mail about the tile. Your wife approved the change in material."

"I don't remember receiving an e-mail or letter about the flooring," said the wife.

"This whole project is way over budget. You claimed if we hired you as our agent, you could help keep costs down. You can pay for that mistake yourself!" said the husband.

PROJECT CLOSEOUT

As the last of the products are being delivered and/or installed, the project reaches what is referred to as *project closeout*. This term, which is borrowed from architecture and the construction industry, means that the interior design project has reached the time for final inspections, providing any necessary documents such as warranties to the client, and approval of payments to subcontractors and/or vendors. A list of documents that might be included in the final project closeout phase is shown in Table 32-1. The first task that the designer must perform to close out a project is to make a final inspection, referred to as a walk-through.

TABLE 32-1.

Project Closeout Document Records for FF&E Projects.

Note: Not all items will be a part of all projects.	
Copies of contract documents	Installation floor plans
Copies of construction drawings	Maintenance and use instructions for appropriate FF&E items
Copies of specifications or equipment lists of FF&E	As-built floor plans and other as-built documents
Purchase orders	Invoices to client for goods and other FF&E delivered to project
Acknowledgments	Invoices to client for design fees
Invoices from suppliers	Punch lists
Payment records for invoices from suppliers	Records of repairs or requests for reorder of damaged goods
Bill of lading	Designer's time sheets
Packing list from shipments	Project closeout report
Freight/shipping bills	Invoices for final payments to suppliers
Payment records of shipping bills	Invoices to client for final payment for goods and services
Delivery tickets or records	Archive copies of CAD drawings

Walk-Through

A *walk-through* is a final inspection of the job site to be sure that everything that has been ordered is present and that any omissions as well as any damages are noted. The walk-through inspection is conducted when all the furniture and furnishings have been delivered and installed. This task is conducted by the designer, client, and perhaps contractor. Each area of the project is inspected, and a list of these omissions and damages are made. This inspection list is most commonly called a *punch list* and details everything that must still be taken care of in order for the project installation to be completed. Some firms call the punch list the *site inspection report*.

A punch list should be carefully prepared by room or area so that it will be easier for the delivery and repair people to find and complete the omissions or repairs. A copy of the punch list should be given to the client after it is signed by the client and designer. Another copy can be used by the design firm to prepare work orders, repair tickets, and memos in order to expedite missing goods. For firms that charge design fees on a phased basis, the billing of the final part of the fee cannot be made until after the walk-through is done. Many clients will not make final payments until all the items on the punch list are taken care of. It is to the designer's benefit to take care of these items as quickly as possible. A sample punch list form has been added to the CD. It is Item 32-1.

The walk-through is also a good time for the designer to fine-tune the project. Designers realize that it can result in some additional specification or sale of merchandise. Commercial clients especially have a difficult time budgeting for accessories at the beginning of the project. But when the installation is winding down, they often see the need for wall hangings, desk accessories, plants, and other items that can complete the project. Residential clients as well may be interested in buying merchandise that was originally specified but was deleted for budgetary purposes once the furniture was delivered.

Complaints and Repairs

Regrettably, this is the stage at which many designers lose interest in the project. It is critical for good client relations and possible future referrals that complaints, repairs, omissions, and replacement of damaged items should be taken care of as soon as possible. It is always more difficult for the designer to take care of nagging problems with an ongoing project than to be designing a new project. Unresolved problems cause bad feelings and can result in poor recommendations from clients. Small, unresolved problems can also mean serious problems with the firm's cash flow, as uncollected receivables can mount. The design firm should have available for the repair work highly qualified furniture repair people who are experienced with all kinds of wood and metal furniture.

As much as possible, the firm's aim should be to handle complaints and repairs before the client is even aware of them. When custom items are being manufactured, the interior designer should, if at all practicable, visit the workroom or shop to inspect the products before they are finished and prior to delivery. This helps catch problems that may occur during the custom item's manufacture. A competent warehouse service that inspects and repairs furniture can eliminate minor damages before furniture has been delivered to the client. Delivery personnel that handle the merchandise as if it were their own also avoid potential problems. The firm should hire only competent, experienced installers. The delivery and installation people must be required to clean up the job site. And delivering all the goods at one time helps to solve a lot of complaints.

Final Documentation

As the project nears completion, several additional documents or permits are provided to the client. The first of these is the *certificate of occupancy*. The certificate of occupancy is issued by the local building department usually directly to the client and certifies that the building or space has been inspected, meets codes, and is approved for occupancy. This certificate applies to the structure, not to the interior movable furniture products. Generally, the owner may not move in or deliver/install products or finishes that were not part of the construction contract and part of the building permit until the certificate of occupancy is issued.

The designer or architect issues another form after the final inspection and punch list have been completed. The *certificate of substantial completion* clarifies everything that has been done and indicates if something is missing. As part of issuing this certificate or notice, the designer also should make sure that any extra materials, such as extra carpeting, ceramic tile, and wall coverings, are left at the job site and that suppliers have cleaned the areas for which they are responsible. If doing so is applicable to the designer's responsibility, the interior designer may also obtain a certificate of occupancy.

For a construction project, the contractor is required to maintain a set of drawings at the job site. If any changes are made, they must be added to these *record drawings* so that a complete record of the construction work exists. These drawings are often referred to as *as-built drawings*, since they reflect how the interior or building was actually built rather than what was shown in the original construction drawings. Sometimes a firm will be requested by the client to prepare a "clean" set of as-built drawings, meaning that changes are incorporated into the drawing rather than added to the set of prints. However, the record drawings created during construction must also be retained. Of course, a copy of the specifications and of all the addenda and change orders are also kept with the record drawings set. When the project has been completed, the record drawings are turned over to the interior designer or the architect from the contractor. A print or copy of the as-built drawings, the specifications, and addenda are then given to the client.

Depending on the responsibility of the interior designer, contractors will invoice either the interior designer or the architect for work that has been completed. If the designer feels that the work has been done satisfactorily, he or she will issue a *certificate for payment*. This form tells the client that the supplier or contractor has completed parts of or most of the work and has sent an invoice for that work, and that the interior designer recommends that the client pay the supplier for that work. Certificates for payment can be issued during the course of the project, since some subcontractors will complete all their work, have it inspected and approved significantly prior to the end of the project. The term *retainage* (this can also be referred to as a holdback) is associated with the certificate for payment. Depending on the contract, the client may retain a certain amount—commonly 5 to 10 percent—to ensure that all the work, omissions, and problems are taken care of.

Warranties and maintenance information on all equipment and products delivered as part of the project comprise another set of documents provided to the client at the end of the project. These documents are provided by the appropriate vendors who have supplied and installed the merchandise. In addition to the documents, instructions may be required on how to operate equipment. These instructions also are provided by the vendors. If the interior designer has sold the goods to the client, then he or she should be prepared to transfer the warranties and instructions, and provide appropriate training to the client.

Commercial clients frequently request that the designer prepare maintenance schedules. In general, maintenance schedules inform the physical plant workers how to clean, wax, vacuum, remove stains from, and otherwise maintain the furniture, fabrics, and architectural finishes. Such a schedule can be made up from the information provided by the manufacturers. The preparation of a formal maintenance schedule is often a separate design service, though it is sometimes included and charged for in the design contract.

When everything has been completed or otherwise is in accordance with the interior designer's contract, the final payment to the interior designer should be made.

POSTOCCUPANCY AND FOLLOW-UP

The project is complete. The furniture, accessories, and all the other items in the specifications or bids have finally been delivered. Every item on the punch list has been taken care of, repaired, delivered, or replaced. The client has even paid the design firm for all outstanding invoices. This is a happy time for interior designers! "We don't have to think about the Ross project anymore," the project designer announces. Perhaps this should not be the case, however.

Many professionals have learned that good customer service and an excellent reputation with clients comes from the activities the designer conducts after the client has moved in and paid all the bills, just as with the creative design and execution of the project in the first place. Merely because everything that was supposed to get done has been done should not signal to the designer that he or she can forget about the project. The designer who would rather move on forgets that repeat business or referrals can come from satisfied clients. If the designer forgets his or her clients, the chance for subsequent work is likely to vanish.

An excellent way for the designer and client to review the success of a project is to make a postoccupancy evaluation. A *postoccupancy evaluation* (POE) is a thorough review of the project and site visit that is conducted from both the designer's and the client's point of view perhaps a month or more after the project is completed. The goal of the POE is to determine the success of the project solution and project management process and whether or not the client is satisfied. The rationale is twofold: (1) to understand client satisfaction or, more importantly, dissatisfaction with the project solutions if problems exist before they become critical issues that might hurt the design firm and (2) to improve the project processes used by the interior design firm so that even better results can occur on all future projects.

Frankly, many firms do not get involved in postoccupancy evaluations of a project because the designer is afraid of hearing criticism or because they have already moved on to the next project. It is shortsighted for the design firm or the designer not to seek comments on client dissatisfaction. If problems exist, the designer needs to find out and take care of them before they fester and become crises. For example, an employee who is dissatisfied with a new office may not truly be dissatisfied with the office design, aesthetics, or furniture but really only needs someone to tell him or her how to adjust the desk chair, or that employee may simply need another file cabinet. If these kinds of problems go undiscovered, then criticisms made by employees can give the client the impression that the project was unsuccessful.

Formal postoccupancy evaluations that involve questionnaires or on-site surveys, resulting in reports, can be included in the design contract or sold to the client as a separate service. Commercial designers most frequently use the formal POE, though many of them do not. An informal postoccupancy evaluation, in which the interior designer interviews the client to determine his or her satisfaction with the project, can be done by any firm for free or can be included for a nominal fee in the design contract's scope of services.

 A postoccupancy evaluation can best be conducted by means of some sort of questionnaire. Figure 32-2 shows a sample questionnaire. This form is also included on the CD. It is Item 32-2.

Of course, the design firm can make up its own questionnaire, consisting of any number of questions needed for the formality or informality of the survey. In either situation, the questionnaire should be structured to gather information on user satisfaction concerning the installation, aesthetics, and functional planning, or any other information that the individual designer and client may seek to obtain.

An in-house evaluation of the project—which is called by many a post-project evaluation—is also good practice procedure. Soon after the project has been completed, this evaluation should cover a time analysis to see if the project was completed within the time estimate. It should identify any problems related to the project, the client, the manufacturers and suppliers, the delivery process, and so forth. The design director may also do a profitability analysis to evaluate whether or not the project itself was profitable. This evaluation will help the design firm determine whether it should seek this kind of project in the future. A sample form that can be used for this task is included on the CD as Item 32-3.

Of course, the interior design firm or project manager should send a thank-you letter or postcard to the client at the conclusion of the project. Many designers drop off a small gift as part of the thank you. For a residential client, the thank-you gift might be a gift certificate to his or her favorite restaurant.

Post Occupancy Evaluation---an Office Project

Project Area/Department_____ Date _____

The purpose of this evaluation is to help your company and the design firm asses the planning and design of your work area and the spaces of the department in the recent design project. Your answers are anonymous so please answer with complete candor.

Rate the following items using this rating scale:

Very Satisfied	Satisfied	Dissatisfied	Very Dissatisfied	Not Applicable To Me
4	3	2	1	0

Rating

1. Work space allowance for office/work station _____
2. Layout of space and furniture meets functional work needs _____
3. Guest seating is adequate _____
4. Desk top space for paper work is adequate _____
5. Desk top space for equipment needs is adequate _____
6. Location/adjustability of my computer area _____
7. Adequate file drawer space for the next 6 months _____
8. Adequate shelves for reference materials in my office _____
9. Adequate non-file drawers for supplies in my office _____
10. Provision for security of work area and documents _____
11. Adjustability of my desk chair provides comfort _____
12. The light levels in my work area are comfortable _____
13. Task lights are adequate _____
14. My computer screen is free of glare _____
15. Acoustical privacy is adequate _____
16. Overall noise levels _____
17. The printer I use is conveniently located _____
18. The copy machine I use is conveniently located _____
19. Team areas or conference rooms are nearby _____
20. Adequate space for team sessions _____
21. Overall satisfaction with new office/work station _____
22. My work space is aesthetically pleasing _____

In this space provide comments you would like to include. Use the back of this sheet if you need to.

Thank you for your time in completing this evaluation, your candid ratings and comments!

FIGURE 32-2.

A simple postoccupancy evaluation (POE) form that can be used to evaluate an office design project. A POE document can take many formats designed to meet the needs of the design firm and client.

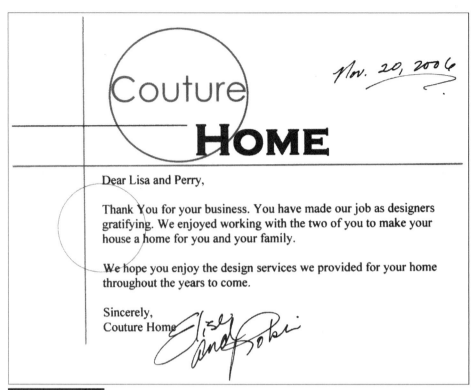

Dear Lisa and Perry,

Thank You for your business. You have made our job as designers gratifying. We enjoyed working with the two of you to make your house a home for you and your family.

We hope you enjoy the design services we provided for your home throughout the years to come.

Sincerely,
Couture Home

FIGURE 32-3.

A sample note card thanking clients for their business. It is an imortant follow-up for good business practies. (Reproduced with permission, Robin Wagner, Wagner Somerset, Clifton, VA)

A commercial client might not be able to accept a gift; however, a floral arrangement or plant for the open house is generally acceptable. A sincere thank-you note is most effective when it is a handwritten note, even if it is really a "form letter." It shows an added measure of concern for the client and appreciation of his or her business (see Figure 32-3).

If a postoccupancy evaluation or meeting is not conducted, the design firm should solicit comments on the handling of the project from the client. Designers who are committed to providing their clients with excellent customer service carefully evaluate their clients' comments. They use the in-house evaluation and their clients' comments, obtained from follow-up mailings, to improve any phase of the service of the project that has been determined to be substandard. Poor customer service is unacceptable in a professional interior design practice.

SUMMARY

Unlike projects in the classroom, professional work does not end with the completion of floor plans, sample boards, and other documents required by the instructor. Professional work does not end when FF&E has been ordered as well. The FF&E must be delivered and installed at the site, and many documents must be prepared to close out the project. This chapter has discussed the many final tasks of the contract administration phase. Many designers do not enjoy taking care of the paperwork or following up on the orders for the merchandise that they specify. Yet this is a very important part of project management.

This chapter concludes the overall discussion of project management. The professional designer is constantly dealing with administrative activities and paperwork. These activities, along with the creative processes of the actual design projects, are the heart of the interior design profession.

The twenty-first century has opened with low unemployment driving heightened competition for employees, expansion of global employment, and segregation of economies respondent to available workforces. Taken together, these tumultuous times have brought forward "quality of life" as a driving force in homes and workplaces across America—and that bodes well for design industries.

A commercial interior designer by background, Marilyn Farrow, FIIDA has served the Institute of Business Designers as National President and the International Design Association as International President. Farrow's writings, speeches, television appearances, and consulting on the professional practice of interior design, client needs, and workplace trends have been featured internationally. She is currently self-employed, providing consulting services to corporate and design firm clients nationwide.

PART VIII

Looking Ahead

CHAPTER 33

Getting the Next—or First—Job

Key Terms and Concepts

These key terms and concepts are important to material in this chapter. Many of these terms will be utilized in other chapters as well. Be sure you understand these items as you read this chapter.

Terms and Concepts

Job search	Functional resumé
Informational interview	Combination resumé
Executive search firms	Cover letter
Headhunter	Enclosure
Resumé	Portfolio
Career summary	Digital portfolio
Career objective	HTML
Chronological resumé	

Critical Issues

After completing this chapter you should be able to:

- Explain the importance of an organized job search.
- Discuss the purpose of the resumé.
- Explain the characteristics of the different types of resumés and when each can be used.
- Draft your resumé with emphasis on a career objective or career summary.
- Explain the purpose of a cover letter and what it should contain.
- Outline the types of items that are most often included in a portfolio.
- Explain why a portfolio is never finished.
- Discuss how you can tailor your portfolio to a job interview at a residential versus a commercial firm.
- Compare and contrast an electronic resumé to a paper resumé.
- Discuss benefits and disadvantages of creating an electronic version of your portfolio.

The ease with which you may find the next—or first—job fluctuates wildly in direct relationship to the economy. In good times there are plenty of jobs available at all levels. When the economy becomes tight, even seasoned professionals have a hard time finding new employment opportunities. The roller-coaster ride of finding an interior design position can change at any time. Because the interior design profession does ebb and flow with the economy, students and design professionals must be thorough in their approach to their career efforts. When they are ready to make a move or to start the job search process, they must do so with careful thought and planning.

The job search can be a time-consuming and stress-producing period. The number of books on how to write a resumé or a cover letter, how to have a successful interview, and so on grows every month. However, going to a bookstore to look for a guide to aid in the job search for a specific career in interior design can be frustrating.

This last section of this text provides two chapters that divide the job search into topics concerning the search for potential openings and preparation for the actual encounter with a prospective employer. This chapter discusses the job search, the resumé and cover letter, and the portfolio. It also includes a consolidated discussion of these topics in relation to electronic communication. The next chapter focuses attention on the interview and follow-up. It also includes the popular section for students to discuss the transition from student to professional and provides some comments about job changing for professionals who are looking to make a major career change.

THE JOB SEARCH

The job search can be a quick process, or it can seem to take forever. In good times graduates have their choice of jobs. Professionals can sometimes write their own ticket in a booming market location. But, naturally, this is not always the case. Searching for a position that suits the graduate or experienced professional requires thought and planning—just like any interior design project. You must manage this process right from the beginning, keeping a record of all correspondence, keeping copies of each letter and resumé that is sent out, and recording phone calls and other contacts. Taking notes during phone calls and preparing follow-up notes after interviews are also useful techniques. Look at each negative response as an opportunity to learn how to make future inquiries positive. And, most important, don't give up!

Whether the market for interior design jobs is good or poor, for the student, the job search begins long before graduation. The student must evaluate what part of the profession holds the most interest for him or her. Is it doing residential or commercial design? Is the student afraid to make presentations and therefore does not want to be a salesperson? Does the student find making technical working drawings boring but working with colors exciting? These kinds of questions, coupled with questions related to lifestyle choices, geographic preferences, and many others, need to be asked so that the student can determine where to seek employment and what kind of employment to seek. Sometimes using a book such as Richard Nelson Bolles's *What Color Is Your Parachute?* is a help in determining career goals more precisely.

Information about the specialties of the interior design field, responsibilities within different work environments, and potential employers is available from many sources. College advisors and career counselors can be helpful sources of information regarding different design companies. Students can join student chapters of professional associations. If your school does not have a chapter, you should make an effort to attend the professional chapter meetings at the local level. Students are always welcome at professional association meetings. The book *Becoming an Interior Designer* by this author provides insights and input from interior designers in numerous specialties from all over the country. Students can also talk to relatives who might have worked with designers or who know someone in the industry. If you are looking to move to a new city, perhaps your professors can make suggestions. Obviously, the Internet can be a great help in this situation.

One of the best ways to understand what the interior design field is all about is to schedule an informational interview with an interior designer working in the type of situation in which you might have an interest. Who better to tell the student about what it is like to work in residential design than someone who is actively doing just that kind of work?

An *informational interview* is a way in which the student can get a better picture of what it is like to work in a certain interior design specialty or type of interior design firm. In this case, you are doing the interviewing rather than the designer. The first step is to plan several questions that you want to ask the designer. Assume that you will take only 15 to 30 minutes of the designer's time, so be precise about what you want to know. Next, choose a few designers whom you want to interview and then call and ask for that 15 to 30 minutes of their time. The designer will most likely want to talk to you at his or her office. When it is time for the encounter, be prompt, be pleasant, and do not try to turn it into a job interview. You will turn off the designer if this is your ploy. Dress professionally and be respectful. Don't overstay your time unless the designer seems to let the clock continue to run. Send him or her a thank-you card within a few days after the interview.

University career placement offices have information about many corporate employers. Unfortunately, most interior design businesses are closed corporations, so information about them probably will not be listed in the resources of the placement office. The placement office might have alternatives if you are not looking for a strictly "on-the-boards" type of design position. Some examples include department stores, print media, and the federal government. It is necessary to be more creative in your research.

Reliable standbys for gathering information on design firms include yellow pages ads, local publications, and classified ads. Yellow pages ads do not always provide the name of the owner or the manager of a design firm, but they can give some information related to the company. A small interior design practice is usually listed under the owner's name. The name of larger firms may include several names or may have been invented, like Excellent Design Inc. Firms that sell a lot of merchandise often list in their ads the product lines that the firm carries. These product lines will help the student determine if the firm is primarily a residential or a commercial interior design firm. Don't just look under "interior design," as many companies will have larger ads listed under "furniture" and "office furniture."

Local home and business magazines sometimes have advertisements of many different interior designers. Perhaps once a year these magazines focus on interior design or on one of the associations so that companies will advertise in them. Also, some cities have a "promotional" magazine that covers cultural, home, business, and social events. Many design firms also advertise in these magazines.

The Sunday classified section of the newspaper is a possible place to find interior design and trade-related job notifications. These classified ads, however, often only provide the barest amount of information about a position. Sometimes the firm does not even publish its name but asks the respondents to mail resumés to a box number. The job seeker should respond to anything that sounds remotely possible and interesting. A student should not be discouraged about applying if the ad states that only applicants with X years of experience should apply.

Professionals who are looking for new positions usually hear about job openings by word of mouth. Others discreetly put out the word to allied associates, such as sales reps, that they are looking for a new position. Quite a lot of job searching and interviewing occurs during trade shows, like NeoCon in Chicago. This is especially true for designers and others who are interested in sales positions. However, design firms may also advertise that they will be interviewing during one of the NeoCon shows.

Employed professionals who are looking for another position must be discreet. The search has to go on while still completing current responsibilities. Disregarding your current work responsibilities in order to go out on interviews is a very bad idea. Understandably, employers do not like their employees looking for another job while they are still working. Yet, of course, not everyone can afford to quit a current job in order to look for a new job. And almost all books on searching for a job advise readers not to quit the current job before they have obtained a new job.

Here are a few hints for the professional who is seeking a new job while presently employed. Do not use company time, company telephones, or company supplies for the job search. It is acceptable to schedule appointments during the lunch hour, but it is not acceptable to fake appointments in order to go on interviews. If it is necessary for you to take an extended period of time for an interview, use vacation time; do not call in sick. Schedule as many interviews during that extended day or period as you possibly can. Remember, the employee owes loyalty to the employer as long as the employee is on the payroll. Abusing the employer by making interview appointments or long-distance phone calls at the present employer's expense is not only unprofessional but also could be grounds for termination. Employment-at-will doctrines mean that you should give some notice when you are ready to leave. Someone has to be prepared to take over any projects that you are leaving behind.

Executive Search Firms

Another source of potential positions is through the use of professional employment agencies or an executive search firm. Don't let the title confuse you into thinking that it is only for the very experienced. Of course, some are, and they will not take on a recent graduate or someone with only a few years of experience. If you wish to use this method of locating a job, you need to do some homework about the companies before you sign on with one.

These professional employment agencies are sometimes called *headhunters*. It refers to those companies that search out and essentially "steal" an executive or an employee from one firm in order to place that employee in another firm. The term is commonly used today to refer to any executive search firm.

Professional designers often work with executive search companies when they seek management positions. An executive search firm works on a commission that generally is paid by the hiring employer. Because of this, the search firm is interested in helping the employer, not you. The job of the search firm is to fill contracts with employers. These firms are usually looking for the senior-level designer or manager-level positions in the design firm, and it may only be willing to help place you only if you exactly meet the qualifications desired by the employer. A contingency firm looks for a wider range of types and salary levels of positions. This type of agency might be a better opportunity for the less experienced designer.

If you decide to use an executive search firm, investigate it thoroughly to be sure that it deals with the interior design and architecture industries. Names of firms that specialize in interior design and architecture positions can sometimes be found in the classified sections of trade magazines. If you are going to use an executive search firm, know what you are looking for before you approach one. If the job seeker uses an agency to obtain leads, he or she should understand all the restrictions and fees involved. This could mean that you will waste a lot of time waiting for the firm to find you something if you don't fit its profile. If you are interested in working with an agency, you may want to check *The Directory of Executive Recruiters* at a local library to find recruiters in your area and field.

Some executive recruiting companies may want you to sign an exclusive agreement with them. Employment experts suggest that you do not sign an exclusive agreement. It is not appropriate for them to want to do this. It also limits your possibilities.

RESUMÉS

Whether you are a student embarking on your first position in the profession or an experienced professional wanting to move on to new challenges, one of the most important tools you will use to obtain a position is a resumé. A *resumé* is a summary of a person's qualifications and often plays a significant part in whether an applicant will obtain an interview. In some companies, a resumé is also important in reviews for promotions.

The resumé must instantly communicate fundamental information related to your work experience, education, personal information, special skills related to the desired position, and career objectives. The length of a resumé for a student rarely should exceed one page. The professional who has several years' experience will by necessity have a longer resumé. However, few professionals need a resumé that is longer than about three or four pages. A resumé is always accompanied by a cover letter, if it is mailed or faxed. If the resumé is e-mailed, it is more courteous to send a short note along with the resumé. A worksheet to help you develop your resumé has been included on the CD. Look for Item 33-1.

Physical Appearance of a Resumé

"The resumé and letter came in handwritten, on lined notebook paper. It wasn't even on letter-size paper! It sure got my attention—that is, I promptly put it in the do not call file!" claimed a design director.

This true comment shows that the appearance of the resumé can, by itself, make a good or bad impression. Of course, trying to create something to get attention can work, but for most firm owners and managers, fancy, creative resumés and cover letters can just be an inconvenience. They are interested in the content, not fancy types, designs, or origami folding. It is rare that odd-colored paper and creative designs on resumés really help applicants get an interview. Remember that the resumé will be filed in a standard letter-sized manila folder. If the resumé is a strange size or shape, it might get lost or filed in the "round file."

It might seem boring, but using white, buff, or maybe a light gray paper with perhaps a minimal attention-getting design is best. Pastels are also acceptable, but the darker colors can make it difficult to read. The text should reproduce as a dark black image. You should coordinate paper color, fonts, and possibly designs with the cover letter. The resumé must have perfect spelling and good grammar. Contact information should be easy to find and easy to read. Using a different font in the contact information is acceptable, as long as it is legible.

For the body of the resumé, headings should be bold so that they stand out and attract attention. Single-space the resumé, with double-spacing between major sections. Do not forget to leave sufficient side margins so that the prospective employer may write notes in the margins. Remember to keep your length reasonable, considering your experience.

Letter-quality laser printers produce the best printout—do not photocopy them. Copy centers provide laser printing service if you do not have access to your own laser printer. Do not use a current employer's equipment to prepare a resumé or other job search tools!

Finally, before you print your copies, proofread your resumé two or three times over a period of time or have someone else also proofread the resumé. Spell checkers do not always spell words correctly. You could have a wrong word spelled correctly that you or the spell checker do not catch (for example, manger for manager).

Certain kinds of information are expected in all resumés. How this information is presented will vary somewhat with the format used by the applicant, as discussed later in the chapter. Table 33-1 provides a list of active verbs that can be used in resumés and cover letters. Let us look at the common items that are included in resumés first.

Contact Information

Contact information generally heads up a resumé. This is simply your name, address, telephone number, cell phone number, e-mail address, and perhaps a fax number. Students should consider including both a permanent address and an address at school. Do not use a fax or e-mail address at work as part of your contact information!

Although these items are common and the employer needs some way to get in touch with you, privacy issues have become more prevalent in recent years.

TABLE 33-1.

A Partial List of Active Verbs That Can Be Used in Resumés and Cover Letters.

Accomplished	Executed
Achieved	Formalized
Arranged	Gathered
Assisted	Improved
Collected	Initiated
Communicated	Introduced
Composed	Managed
Conceptualized	Negotiated
Conducted	Organized
Contributed	Performed
Coordinated	Prepared
Created	Presented
Demonstrated	Reviewed
Designed	Scheduled
Developed	Selected
Directed	Supervised
Established	Trained
	Wrote

You may wish to set up a separate e-mail account for the job search and only use a cell phone number rather than home number for the contact number. Never put a Social Security number or other personal numbers of that type on the resumé!

Career Summary and Career Objective

The *career summary*, in a few brief sentences, provides a significant statement concerning your ability to handle the job for which you are applying. It usually contains brief snapshot information about skills and accomplishments. Specifics will be further discussed in the "Work Experiences" section.

Here is an example for a professional who is seeking a position as a representative with a manufacturer: "Ten years' sales experience for office furnishings dealers, specializing in Herman Miller and Steelcase open-office systems. Exceeded sales goals 11 out of 15 years." A career summary for an experienced interior designer might read, "Senior project manager with 11 years' experience in hospitality design with one of the top design firms in the country. Experienced in all aspects of the design process, certified in AutoCAD 2007, and recipient of numerous awards for creative work."

For the student who is beginning a career, a *career objective* is often more appropriate. A career objective statement alone or in combination with a career summary is also effective for a professional who is making a major job shift, A career objective talks about what you want to do rather than what you have already accomplished; for example, "Energetic recent graduate seeking employment with a creative residential design firm that also includes opportunities to design assisted-living facilities."

When you are using a career objective, it is important that it not be so narrow as to limit other possibilities—assuming you are open to other possibilities—or so broad that it seems that you have no direction or objective. Consider this objective: "A position as an interior designer." It is too vague and indicates to the employer that you have not given much thought to your future.

Education

For the recent graduate, a most important block of information on a resumé will summarize his or her education. This section follows the career objective for students, since it is the primary "experience" a student has had up to this point. A professional commonly includes educational experience farther down on the resumé, since work experience is more important.

It is best to begin this section with academic training first. Supplemental courses and seminar attendance should be listed after academic degrees. Begin first with the highest degree you have earned. Included should be the name of the institution and its location, the kind of degree earned and the year granted, major, minor, and any academic or career-related activities. Students should only list their grade point average if it was exceptionally high. About a year after graduation, you should drop the grade point average from the resumé. Students do not need to list high school education, unless it was a prestigious school or a foreign educational institution.

For professionals, employers are not as interested in grade point average or academic activities. Professionals should also include professional continuing-education units (CEU) and any other formal educational training in this section. However, if the professional has taken a large number of CEU classes, he or she should list only the most recent and any others that show updating related to the job being sought.

Professional Accomplishments

Professional should include information on certifications, licensing, and awards. A subheading can be used under "Education" or a separate section such as "Certifications and Awards" or "Professional Accomplishments" can be included. Involvement in professional associations should be listed with the proper acronym. Listing numerous committees may make your resumé too long, so only highlight when you have been an officer or chair of a committee. If your list of awards and involvement is long, you can always prepare a supplement that details this information and provide it if requested by the employer.

Work Experience

Depending on which format you choose for your resumé, the work experience portion will be written differently. Traditionally, the work experience section lists the name and location of the company, the years worked for each, and the title of the position held. This is followed by one or more brief narrative statements about skills developed, responsibilities, and/or accomplishments in each position. Students will want to place the internship first in the work experience section, followed by summaries of part-time jobs held.

Professionals need to list projects for which they have been responsible. The organization of this information varies with the job objective. It is not necessary to list every single project in which you have worked. If you have extensive experience, highlight the key projects that might be of interest to the prospective employer. For example, it would make more of an impression to note that you were the project designer for a restaurant in the Belagio Hotel than to include an unrelated list of small projects on which you worked three years ago. Be selective about your project list so that your resumé does not become too long. Also, ethics are involved here, so you must be careful about how you take credit for work in which you might have been a team member but not the project designer.

Personal Information

The most important personal information on a resumé will be contact information. Anything else is left up to the individual. Some applicants feel they must include marital information, names of children, service records, height, weight, and health conditions. It is not necessary to put this information on the resumé. The employer cannot legally ask for any of this information, except within the bounds discussed in the next chapter. Volunteering this information could prejudice a decision, and the applicant would not have any grounds for challenging the prejudiced decision. That is also true of certain community activities in which you may have participated. Unfortunately, these can also unwittingly cause a prospective employer to discriminate against you. There would be nothing you could do, since you volunteered the information.

Skills and Key Words

Technology has increased the importance of being sure that you include reference terms that identify skills in interior design. Skills terms and key words are especially important in an electronic version of your resumé. In that context, an employer can scan resumés for an assortment of key words. Any resumé that contains those words will be in the "save" pile, while those that do not have those terms will likely be ignored. This scanning process is probably only used by larger firms; however, the smaller firms are likely to also manually scan for skills as well.

An interior design firm is going to look for terms and words such as AutoCAD, CAD, project management, Microsoft Project, LEED® specialist, building codes, and other terms that key into skill sets, knowledge areas, and design tasks that are critical to the staff. Including the terms of the profession in your resumé—whether you are sending it out electronically or by snail mail—will help get your resumé noticed.

Do not forget to include knowledge of languages. Fluency in any foreign language will be an important skill for large firms doing global business. Fluency, by the way, means that you can speak, write, and read the language as well as a native. Conversational skill means you can speak it but might not be able to read and write it very well. Language skills are also important to many small firms in many markets.

Another approach for experienced professionals is to include a section highlighting core competencies or areas of expertise. This emphasizes that you know how to apply knowledge in the field, and it indicates skill attainment at an advanced level. A few examples are bid specification coordination, accessibility evaluation, and sustainability problem solving.

References

It is not necessary to list references on a resumé or even to provide them without a request from the prospective employer. Most references are not checked until after the interview and before an offer has been made. Most employers assume that the work and education history are the starting point for your references. These are the people whom they will likely first want to contact. Unless the employer asks for a copy of a list of references or references are required in any employment application that must be filled out, most of the discussion of references will occur during the interview.

A professional who is seeking a job while he or she is still working may not want the current employer to know that he or she is looking for a job elsewhere. If this knowledge gets back to the current employer, the professional could be instantly terminated. You can clarify why you do not want the prospective employer to contact a current employer during the job interview. If you are concerned that a previous employer may give a bad reference, ask that the employer not be contacted. It is necessary that you provide a brief explanation of the circumstances surrounding this request to the prospective employer, however. It is interesting to note that many employers no longer give a reference—good or bad—to a former employee. This extends, in some cases, to student interns as well. Employers are concerned about the possibility of being sued by former employees if it can be shown that the bad reference is the reason the employee did not get the job. Thus, the applications from some employers are written containing language that releases former employers from liability from what is said in a reference.

Students can also use the services of college career placement offices to maintain references. This is a convenience for those who are asked to provide personal references, since they only have to write the reference once, and then it is kept on file at the placement office. Prospective employers then request a copy of the reference from the placement office. It is common courtesy to ask an individual such as a professor, personal acquaintances, perhaps a designer at some other firm, or a sales representative prior to giving his or her name as a reference.

What Would You Do?

Mary was very excited about the opportunity to work with a local television celebrity. Four months ago, Mary had planned and specified furniture for the very large living room and dining spaces. The items specified for the living room included two custom-made end tables and a matching coffee table, which were all oversized. The materials and finishes of these items matched custom cabinets designed for the dining room. The custom tables and cabinets were nearly ready for delivery. Most of the other furniture had already been delivered.

Yesterday Mary received a call from the celebrity's assistant. The message was that the rest of the furniture not already delivered was canceled. "She won't need any of those other items, as she has just accepted a position with a station in San Francisco and will not need those items anymore. Since she will not be taking them, she also wants her deposit back on those items."

RESUMÉ FORMAT

The three most common resumé formats are the chronological, the functional, and the combination. No one format works best in all cases. Which of the basic formats you should use depends on the intended audience and the purpose of the resumé. The experienced designer who is attempting to make a career change from "on-the-boards designer" to salesperson will need a different format from the technician who is trying to obtain a position of total project responsibility. A student's resumé will be formatted differently from that of an individual who has been out of work for some reason for a number of years.

By far the most commonly used format is the chronological resumé, which lists all experience in reverse chronological order. Functional resumés do not give specific employment history and are sometimes used by individuals who have been out of work for some time. The combination format generally combines the chronological and functional resumé to help elevate the negative issues that a functional resumé may raise. Information about how to structure an electronic resumé is also included later in this section.

Chronological Resumé

The style of resumé that remains the most common is the one that provides information in reverse order. It is called a chronological resumé and states educational and work experiences exactly when they occurred. This type of resumé is easy to follow and clearly shows the work history of the individual. For an individual with several years of experience, this information is very important to employers. Many employers prefer this traditional format for resumés. It is not recommended, however, if the job seeker has a spotty work record, is seeking to make a significant change in his or her career, or has been out of the workforce for some time.

Experienced professionals should provide work history in reverse chronological order, followed by educational experience. If the experienced (and older) designer places education first, it can draw attention to age, which, unfortunately, can lead to discrimination. Work history is more important than educational experience for the experienced professional anyway. Students should place educational experience first, since that is the most recent activity.

When you are listing your educational experience, you would commonly list the school and the degree information. It is not necessary to list the year you

---

Mary Anderson

| 1234 Granite Avenue | Circle City, Arizona | 602-555-9782 | E-Mail: mary@xxx.com |

OBJECTIVE: Entry-level design position with a commercial interior design firm specializing in health care and hospitality. Particularly interested in a challenging position which will increase my experience and involvement in interior design.

EDUCATION: Northern Arizona University, Flagstaff, AZ. 1998.
B.S., Major: Interior Design.
Minor: Marketing.
GPA 3.8/4.0.

EXPERIENCE:

Summer, 1998   **Design One, Phoenix, AZ.**
Intern.

Commercial and residential firm specializing in hospitality.
Space planning and design documents for a bed and breakfast and two other projects.
Client meetings, interaction, and project presentations.
Meetings with manufacturer's representatives.

Summer, 1996–97   **Desert Construction Co, Mesa, AZ.**
Draftsperson.

Assisted in the preparation of working drawings for custom home builder.

COMPUTER SKILLS

• AutoCAD 13 and 14
• Microsoft Office Word and Excel for documents and
   spreadsheets
• Microsoft PowerPoint for presentations

HONORS/ACTIVITIES

American Society of Interior Designers
Student Chapter, 1996–1998
   Chapter Treasurer, 1997
   Volunteer for the Showhouse (Phoenix chapter) 1997
Phi Kappa Phi Honor Society,
   Northern Arizona Chapter

FIGURE 33-1.

Chronological resumé prepared by a student who is seeking a first job.

obtained your degree. For an older professional, this is voluntarily providing information that could be used to discriminate against the applicant. Include academic honors if they apply. Figures 33-1 and 33-2 are examples of chronological resumés and show examples of how to list work experience. Figure 33-1 shows how a student could list education.

Functional Resumé

The *functional resumé* presents information in order to emphasize qualifications and skills, rather than the order in which they were obtained. Emphasizing overall qualifications is done to quickly interest the employer with your

Sandra A. Mathews
200 Mocking Bird Lane
Richmond, Virginia 23375
Phone (314) 555-2000
E-mail sandram@xxx.net

KEY WORD SUMMARY

Ten years' experience in health care, hospitality, and corporate office design. Project Manager, Senior Designer. AutoCAD 2000, PowerPoint, Microsoft Project. Marketing responsibility, team management, NCIDQ certified, ASID chapter leadership, BS Interior Design.

DESIGN EXPERIENCE

Carson Jefferies, Inc. Richmond, VA.

1994 to present. Project Designer
1991–1994 Senior Designer
Direct design teams of 3–8 professionals in design of hospitality and health care projects.
Space plan and design corporate offices. Familiar with Haworth and Herman Miller systems.
Responsible for obtaining contracts of over $230,000 in fees in past two years.
Hired and scheduled subcontractors and supervised installations.
Developed two presentations using PowerPoint, which have become templates for company.

Associated Interior Architects. Del Mar, CA.

1989–1991. Designer
Space plan and design executive offices, law offices and banking facilities.
Assisted senior designers with drafting, product research and specification writing.
Assisted in space planning two open-office systems projects of over 25,000 square feet each.

EDUCATION

U.C. San Diego
Part-time, 1990–1991. Classes in Marketing.
Arizona State University
1989 Bachelor of Design Science. Major: Contract Interior Design

PROFESSIONAL AFFILIATIONS

International Interior Design Association, Professional member
Chapter Publicity Committee
American Society of Interior Designers, Professional member
American Institute of Architects, Affiliate member
NCIDQ Certificate # 55555

FIGURE 33-2.

Chronological resumé prepared by a professional, shown in a format that is acceptable for electronic transmission or scanning.

qualifications and possibly overlook a spotty work record. Many employers do not like the functional resumé, since they are concerned with a prospective employee's work history, so this tactic often does not work. However, it is still an option for many job applicants. If an applicant presents a functional resumé, it would not be uncommon for the prospective employer to ask for a chronological work history to be provided as well.

For an experienced professional perhaps looking for freelance contract work, a functional resumé can help focus on the experiences in design that are probably going to be needed for that type of work situation. For example,

---

WILLIAM C. BLAKE

| 9700 N. 19th Street | Tallahassee, FL 32000 | (P) 850.555.9876 | blake@xxx.com |

SUMMARY

Highly motivated individual seeking an entry-level position in interior design. Previous work experience provides superior work ethic and demonstrated ability to successfully work with others. Negotiated contracts in public relations areas.

MAJOR WORK EXPERIENCES

Interior Design

Part-time design assistant for a residential design firm. Select finishes and products, develop sample boards, prepare furniture floor plans under direction of design firm owner.

Technical Writer

Three years' experience in large architectural firm. Responsible for developing proposals and other marketing materials. Collaborated with the firm's PR consultant on many projects.

Event Planner

Two years working as an assistant to a major event planner in Nashville, TN. Obtained pricing information, developed schedules, supervised small party set-ups.

Public Relations

Ten years' public relations experience in private sector. Excellent print media placement record. Good writer and researcher. Skilled in organizing special events. Worked with several interior design and architecture firms. Involved in contract negotiations for events.

EDUCATION

Florida State University 200x. Bachelor of Arts: Interior Design
O'More College of Design. Intermittent. Took design classes part-time.
University of Michigan 1984 Bachelor of Science Major: Journalism/Public Relations

AFFILIATIONS

American Society of Interior Designers, Student Member
Publishers Publicity Association
Public Relations Society of America

FIGURE 33-3.

Functional résumé prepared by an individual who has made a career change.

someone wishing to freelance CAD work will want to focus job experience and skills with CAD (see Figure 33-3).

Combination Résumé

A *combination résumé* utilizes characteristics of both the chronological and the functional résumé and combines them into one. Usually, this results in a résumé in which functional skills are described, as in the normal functional résumé, followed by a brief chronological listing of educational and work experiences. A combination résumé highlights skills that are related to the job being sought and deemphasizes either a limited or a spotty work history. This kind of format can work very well for students whose skills learned in school and internships will be of greater interest to a prospective employer than work history that consists of a series of part-time jobs. Figure 33-4 is an example of a résumé using the combination format.

Jennifer Alvarado
1875 Wacker Drive
Chicago, Illinois
312-555-3000

SUMMARY
- Four years' commercial sales experience for an office furnishings dealer
- Experienced in marketing interior design services
- Design project team manager
- Seven years commercial interior design: government and corporate
- Three years residential interior design
- Computer skills: Microsoft Office, Project, and Act!

SALES AND MARKETING SKILLS
Maintained numerous commercial accounts with last employer. Developed many new accounts with government agencies and corporate. Generated over seven million dollars in sales last year (second highest total for ten sales people). Equaled or exceeded sales goals each year.

Developed successful marketing strategies for two interior design firms and two contractors.

SUPERVISION SKILLS
Hired, trained and supervised two sales assistants to help manage my accounts. First sales assistant recently began working as sales representative. Also supervised design assistants when working as a project team manager. Overall project manager for several large government agency projects.

DESIGN SKILLS
Experienced in commercial space planning and interior design. Familiar with open-office systems products, and various qualities of commercial and residential furniture and furnishings products. Some experience in residential design/sales.

WORK HISTORY
1998 to present.	Account Representative	Quality Office Furnishings, Inc.	Chicago, IL.
1996–1998	Interior Designer	Smyth Design Consultants	Evanston, IL.
1991–1996	Interior Designer	Best Interiors, Inc.	Chicago, IL.
1988–1991	Design Associate	Regal Home Furnishings	Oak Park, IL.

EDUCATION
Southern Illinois University. 1988. Bachelor of Science. Major: Interior Design.

PROFESSIONAL MEMBERSHIP
American Society of Interior Designers, Professional member since 1994.
NCIDQ certified. Certificate # 55555

FIGURE 33-4.

A combination resumé style for a professional seeking new responsibilities in his or her career as a sales representative.

THE COVER LETTER

You should never send out a resumé without a *cover letter*. Think of it as a marketing tool as important as any of those discussed in Chapters 19 and 20. It is an opportunity for you to personally introduce yourself in such a way that the employer, hopefully, will have no alternative but to read your resumé and call you for an interview immediately. Those items in a nutshell are the purposes for always including a cover letter.

Just as the design firm targets its marketing efforts, you must target potential employers. Tailoring the cover letter to each company accomplishes this objective. Each letter must sound as if it were written only for that company, even if it contains primarily "stock" paragraphs used in practically every letter you send. Cover letters can be created for different purposes. Some are in response to an advertisement that you saw in a newspaper. Another can be the result of a personal contact with the employer, perhaps someone you met at an association meeting. Others are sent based on a recommendation by a professor or an interior designer. Professional designers may also send cover letters to executive or professional search companies. Then, of course, there are the broadcast letters that you might send to perhaps dozens of employers, hoping that one will interest an employer enough to call you to set up an interview.

Content

With the purpose of the cover letter in mind, as always, start by doing some homework. If the letter is in response to an advertisement, look up the company in the yellow pages or check to see if it has a Web site. If you are a member of one of the professional associations, you might get some information about the company by calling the local chapter office. Be sure you know how to spell the name of the person who gave you a referral, if you use the name of a personal contact. This may sound simple, but you will lose a few points if you misspell the name of the person who gave you the referral in your letter. Most likely, your professor will be able to tell you something about the company that he or she mentions to you. If you are writing to an executive search company, remember that it helps companies find employees. It does not help the employee or an applicant find a job. With a broadcast letter, do as much research on each firm as you can, as if you were responding to an ad.

The cover letter should only be one page in length. Longer letters, even those from experienced professionals, may not get read by busy design directors or personnel managers. It is important for the letter to get the reader's attention quickly and to make him or her want to read your resumé and then call you for an interview. Positive attention is gained by using good business-writing techniques, professional language, and perfect spelling.

Standard business letters include the sender's contact information in a simple format or appropriate letterhead design (see Figure 33-5). Do not use the stationery of the company where you are currently working or interning! The letter must be dated, of course. The prospective employer's address should be preceded by the name of the person to whom the letter is being directed. Your research should tell you who this is by name and job title. Letters addressed to "To Whom It May Concern" or "Personnel Office" or that use other generic salutations usually end up in the trash.

It is generally recommended by business writing consultants and employment counselors that the cover letter contain about four paragraphs, each with a particular purpose. The first paragraph should attract attention by stating the purpose of your letter in concise words. Write with enthusiasm and interest. Let the prospective employer know that you know something about the company and why you want to work there. This is also where you begin to target your letter by stating why you are contacting this company. For example, if the letter is in response to an advertisement, this paragraph should give the name and date of the announcement. If it is a letter of inquiry, this should be clearly stated (see Figure 33-6).

Applicant's name
Address
Area code and phone number

Date

Name and title of employer
Name of company
Address
City, State, Zip Code

Dear Mr. (Mrs. or Ms.) Smith:

The first paragraph should state the reason for the letter. Give the employer information about the specific position for which you are applying. If you are responding to an advertisement or have gotten the contact through someone the employer will know, state that information.

The second and third paragraphs are where you can provide some specific information about yourself and why you are interested in working for the firm. Include statements that explain how previous academic training or work experience qualifies you for the position. Relate your skills and experiences to the company's needs or the job requirements.

For professionals with several years of experience, the third paragraph will probably be necessary to complete the basic information you wish to tell the employer. Whether you are a student or professional, do not simply repeat what the employer can read in the resumé—expand or clarify upon what you have stated in your resumé.

A final paragraph thanks the reader for his or her time and indicates your desire for a personal interview. Be concise. If you are going to be in the city at a particular time, mention that you will be calling to set up an interview at that time. If you intend to get back to the employer rather than wait for him or her to call you, indicate that. Or say something like, "I look forward to hearing from you soon." Remember to say thank you "for your consideration" or use other appropriate wording.

Add a closing greeting such as "Sincerely,"

(leave four lines for your signature)

Type your full name

Enclosure (or Enc.). This is used to indicate you are sending something with the letter, in this case, your resumé.

FIGURE 33-5.

A sample cover letter that shows what should go into each section of the letter.

The second and third paragraphs should contain specific information about the applicant's skills and interests in the position in order to keep the reader interested. Tell the prospective employer how your skills relate to the job that was advertised or that you heard about, or otherwise meets his or her needs. Focus your attention on the employer's known or probable needs, not on your needs. A major impression will be made when the employer sees that you have done some homework about the company. If you do not respond to the specific needs mentioned in the ad, the letter, again, could end up in the trash. Statements about your personal goals and interests as they relate to the particular position and company can also be placed in these paragraphs.

Although there is no set order in which this information should be presented, it is most frequently presented in terms of its importance to the position as the applicant understands it. Mention two or three skills or accomplishments

Julie Adams
8090 S. Willamette Street
Philadelphia, Pennsylvania
215-555-1448
E-mail jadams@xxx.com

October 26, 200x

Mr. Timothy O'Niel
AAD, Inc.
1237 N. 17th Street, N.W.
Washington, D.C.
202-555-1400

Dear Mr. O'Niel:

Over an eight-year period, I have worked as a Designer and most recently a Senior Designer at a highly respected commercial design firm in Philadelphia. At this point in my career, I seek an opportunity to apply my design and supervisory skills in a management position.

During the last few years I have been personally responsible for obtaining and designing many of the largest projects ever undertaken at my company. As a Senior Designer I am responsible for supervising design teams in the execution of projects.

It is not difficult to hear flattering comments about the quality design work produced at AAD, Inc. I believe the negotiation and design skills that I have refined at Design Three will further add to the success of your firm. In addition, I grew up in Baltimore and have a strong association with the Washington, DC and Baltimore markets.

As you will see from the enclosed resumé, I have broad commercial experience in health care, hospitality, corporate offices, and university facilities.

Over the past four years, I have been preparing myself for management by enrolling in courses in pursuit of a master's degree in business.

I have considerable talent, enthusiasm and interest to offer as a design manager to AAD, Inc. and would appreciate the opportunity to meet with you personally to discuss such a position. I will call you next week to confirm a convenient time for a personal interview.

Sincerely yours,

Julie Adams

Enc.

FIGURE 33-6.

A cover letter in which an individual is inquiring about a possible position at a firm. Note how the applicant starts the letter.

that directly relate to the position. For example, if you have CAD skills, state what version software you have experience in. Professionals should describe not only skills but also other accomplishments, such as sales records and management experience (see Figure 33-7). For students, this section should deal primarily with course work. Students should point out the skills in which they are particularly proficient. Students would also want to describe responsibilities they had during internships or other interior design or trade-related work that they did while in school.

Sally Johanson
7654 W. Main St.
Boise, Idaho
208-555-1000
E-mail: sjones@xxx.com

August 18, 200x

Mr. Roger Smith, Director of Design
Myer's Interior Design
82 W. Willow Lane
Denver, CO

Dear Mr. Smith:

I found your recent advertisement on the World Wide Web too interesting to resist! I remember visiting your showroom many times with my parents when I was growing up in Boulder. The opportunity to move back to Denver and work for your excellent company is very exciting.

At university, I specialized in residential interior design—which is my passion. My training was quite complete, covering all phases of design development, production, presentation and business practices. From project evaluations, I can state that I have strong skills in space planning, color coordination, drafting, presentation skills and rendering.

My internship was completed at Beverly Miller's Interiors in Boise, where I have remained for the last six months. My responsibilities include color coordination, preparation of presentation boards, drafting, rendering and order processing. This experience has taught me about the excitement and complexity of residential interior design.

I am anxious to meet you personally so as to present my portfolio to you. My experience at Beverly Miller's Interiors has been wonderful; however, I have decided to return to the Denver area permanently. I will be calling your office on August 27 to confirm an interview appointment. I have enclosed my current resumé for your review.

Thank you for your time, and I look forward to meeting you next month.

Sincerely,

Sally Johanson

Enclosure

FIGURE 33-7.

A cover letter that an individual has prepared in response to a listing posted on the World Wide Web.

One caution about these middle paragraphs. Do not try to use this space to repeat all the information in the resumé. You are trying to get the employer interested in reading your resumé by highlighting key information.

The last paragraph should tell the prospective employer what you want—most likely an interview. You want the employer to call you, but do not wait for the employer to respond. Many job seekers will plan to be in the city where the letter was sent for only a few days. If this is the case, it should be mentioned in the closing paragraph so that the prospective employer knows when the applicant will be available. The last paragraph should include a reference to the enclosed resumé as well as the availability of the portfolio for review. Of course, you should also thank the employer for taking the time to review the letter and resumé.

If you state in that last paragraph that you will be calling the employer concerning making an appointment at a convenient time, check your calendar

TABLE 33-2.

Tips for Preparing a Cover Letter.

- Address the letter by the employer's name—never "To Whom it May Concern."
- When you can drop names, do so: "I was referred to your company by John Jones, the owner of Jones Thompson Flooring."
- Discuss accomplishments and results. This goes for the resumé as well.
- Be brief and concise. Use good grammar and correct spelling.
- It is okay to use industry jargon and buzzwords. You better know what you mean if you use any jargon you put in your letter, however.
- Do not include negative information such as "I left ABC Interiors because of a disagreement with the owner." However, this might come up in the interview.
- Do not make your letter sound like you are begging for a job.
- Always say thank you at the end.

before you mention specific dates. Do not bother to call the employer on Mondays and Fridays if you can help it. Most design managers are in meetings on Mondays or otherwise are catching up after the weekend; some are lucky enough to leave early on Friday. And do not expect to be asked for even an informational interview if your letter arrives only a few days before you!

Use a simple ending, such as those shown in Figures 33-6 and 33-7. Leave four spaces for your signature, with your name spelled out below. Since you are including a resumé, the word *Enclosure* or the abbreviation *Enc.* should be placed below the signature. Table 33-2 provides some additional tips on preparing cover letters.

Physical Appearance

The appearance of the cover letter can quite easily attract attention—positive or negative. I remember receiving, in response to a newspaper advertisement for an experienced interior designer, a handwritten letter on ruled paper. It certainly made an impression. Many interior designers try to make the letter as creative looking as possible, using fancy type styles, funny folds, logo-style designs, and pastel colors. These techniques do attract attention, but they also often get in the way of the content and businesslike attitude for which the employer may be looking. You may use a logo, design element, or graphic, but use discretion. Unless you are applying for a job as a graphic designer, your graphic should not be more interesting than your text.

Use quality bond paper and business size envelopes (referred to as number 10) or use a large flat envelope that is 9 inches by 12 inches. Black ink on white, gray, or ivory paper is the most businesslike combination, though light, pastel colors are not a problem for many prospective employers. The exact job opening and the kind of design firm will dictate whether these creative techniques are a help or a hindrance to the effectiveness of the cover letter. Serif fonts (they have little "feet"), such as Times Roman and New Century Schoolbook, are easier to read than san serif fonts. Specialty fonts can be used in the letterhead and the contact information on resumés. It is very common to coordinate the paper, fonts, and general style of the cover letter and the resumé.

Use letter-writing techniques that personnel managers and owners will appreciate. Do your very best to make even a broadcast letter sound like it was written just for the reader. Perfect spelling along with good grammar is mandatory. Have someone else read the letter, perhaps a professor if you are a student. A professional who still does not feel comfortable writing may want to hire a freelance writer or resumé writer to help with preparing the cover letter. Do not photocopy letters and then change the address. Personally address each one.

PORTFOLIOS

Portfolios are of critical importance to an interior designer at any level of practice. This visual field requires visual "proofs" of one's ability to design interiors. Simply stated, a *portfolio* is a visual presentation of what you can do as an interior designer that shows your best work. The term portfolio is also used to refer to the binder in which the visual items are placed. At first it will be filled with projects from classes and then replaced by drawings and project photos of professional work. Although your portfolio may contain numerous items, not all of them will be used when you interview for jobs. When this is the case, it should contain design work that relates to the design position that you are seeking and the needs of the prospective employer. Keep these two thoughts in mind as we discuss the interior design portfolio.

Before we get deeper into the discussion of what should go into a portfolio, it is important to emphasize to the reader that there is an ethics issue concerning portfolios. Recall that the work product of an employee belongs to the design firm, not the employee. When you decide to look for another job, association codes of conduct specifically state that you cannot take drawings or other documents without permission.

Your portfolio is never really "finished," as it must be constantly updated and refined to meet current or expected needs in the job search process. For the experienced professional, the portfolio must show a range of work, with emphasis on the present. For the student who is seeking that all-important first job, the portfolio must exhibit the very best work that the student can do and also must present the breadth of the student's abilities so as not to limit the prospective employee from any reasonable, possible opportunity.

Whether the portfolio is for the professional or the student, the portfolio must show the very best work that the individual can execute. Students make the mistake of including something from all the studio classes they take. The employer is not really interested in the work you did your first year, nor are many interested in seeing that work in order to see a progression of your talents. They assume you improve your skills over time and want to know what you can do for them right now.

The images or drawings you include should also show that you have the skills to perform the duties of the job for which you are interviewing. If you are interviewing for a job in a residential studio, emphasize work in that specialty. A portfolio that shows multiple examples of sample boards but does not show drafting skills wastes both the employer's and the job seeker's time. It also shows the prospective employer that the job seeker has not done any homework about the design firm or its needs.

In addition, portfolios should be self-explanatory. Many times it is necessary for the designer to send his or her portfolio to a prospective employer for a review before an interview will be granted. That means that you will need to use good, clear writing skills to explain items in the portfolio. Explain what you really need to explain without a lot of extra details. A mistake students and professionals often make in writing concept statements or other statements about their design work is that they explain what can be seen in the drawings and neglect to include information that might explain reasons for direction and choices. When the designer is not there to explain his or her involvement, the parameters of the project, and how the designer arrived at the solution, the prospective employer expects the portfolio to be able to answer these questions. If it does not, then all that the prospective employer can review is the individual's technical competence in the preparation of drawings and boards.

A portfolio should also be well organized so that it clearly tells your story. A logical order is needed to help when you present the portfolio. Remember that a portfolio tells a visual story about you. It must be neat and well organized to help provide a favorable impression of you. If it is sloppy and appears to have been thrown together haphazardly, it will likely lead to a short interview. You will be nervous, so having items in disarray will only make you more nervous. If you have done your homework and know something about the firm and its present needs, you will know how to organize the portfolio so that each piece that you include demonstrates how you can help the prospective employer. Of course, this means that you will want to make some slight adjustments to the contents of your portfolio for each job interview.

Ideas on format, general contents, and processes to produce the portfolio can be quite similar for the professional and the student. A professional's portfolio will be more extensive than a student's and will likely only show drawings or photographs of completed projects. A professional's portfolio will not contain many items from school, unless the job change is happening within only a year or two of graduation or the professional has recently gone to graduate school. Thus, the remaining discussion of a portfolio will be a generalized discussion on what to include, the format, the media, and it will include some ideas about making a portfolio presentation using electronic as well as written materials.

What to Include

Even though the portfolio is a visual tool, it also should contain certain written documents. Include one or two clean copies of your resumé and references list even if you have already mailed these to the employer. If you sent your portfolio to an employer—which sometimes happens when you are interested in a firm at a distance from your residence—enclose a cover letter. The contents of the cover letter will be similar to one that accompanies your mailed resumé but also can be modified to focus attention on your portfolio. Each of these written items should be placed in plastic sleeves within the portfolio, with the cover letter first and the resumé second. A table of contents is a nice touch if it is an extensive portfolio. To have a complete visual package, consider coordinating the paper color of your enclosed cover letter and resumé to the overall theme you have used in the portfolio.

Each section of the portfolio should be labeled. Pieces that are not self-explanatory should have brief, written descriptions of the design project or the piece. This is particularly important when you are not there to explain the items in the portfolio. They also help you remember key concepts that you want to cover, since you might be nervous. Since hand lettering is considered an important skill by many design firms, written materials could be hand lettered. However, word-processed documents are certainly acceptable. Avoid using a large variety of fonts.

It is important that the portfolio include examples of all the skills of which you are capable. Table 33-3 suggests many of the items that should be included if at all possible. The items selected should be your best work. Professors can help guide you on this choice. Professionals will want to lead with a

TABLE 33-3.

Items Commonly Included in a Portfolio.

- Sketches that show the decision-making process
- Furniture floor plans
- CAD drawings
- Color boards
- Working drawings
- Freehand sketches
- Perspectives, elevations, and/or isometric drawings
- Examples of lettering skills
- Technical renderings in any media in which the designer is competent
- For professionals, slides, photographs, or publication reprints showing completed projects for which the designer was primarily responsible
- For students, at least one completed project

recent award-winning project and even include a copy of the award certificate. Additional comments on what to include in your portfolio is included on the CD as Item 33-2.

It is generally acceptable for students to rework (if possible) earlier project solutions once they have been graded. However, any "reworked" projects should still reflect what you are capable of doing. Depending on what kinds of projects you have done in school, you might need to develop new documents such as cabinet drawings, construction drawings in CAD, and rendered perspectives to have a breadth of work that is needed for a specific design studio. It should end with another quality piece to serve as a "last impression" of what you can do. Do not include poor-quality work or work you feel you have to apologize for—if it is not very good, either rework it or leave it out.

The next suggestion is to show the employer that you have an understanding of the issues involved in designing the types of interiors that the firm undertakes by showing work that relates to the specific job and firm. Obviously, a student's portfolio will not necessarily have an extensive selection of either residential or commercial projects, so a student must show a variety of items that will help demonstrate his or her skills in the techniques and processes of interior design. The professional may find it easier to emphasize certain types of work, but he or she may also have to show the breadth of his or her experiences in designing projects when making a job change.

Since you may only have 30 to 60 minutes for the entire interview, you need to limit the number of items in your portfolio. Twenty-five to 30 items or pages should be sufficient, especially if they directly demonstrate the skills needed for the position. You probably will not want to have more than about 45 items in the portfolio, or it will either bore the reviewer or decrease the time available for the interviewer to ask you questions. Besides, having too much to show or taking too much of the reviewer's time at some point becomes disrespectful of his or her busy schedule.

In order to present a high-quality portfolio, you should photograph sample and project boards as soon as possible after having completed them. You need to store projects, drawings, models, and so on carefully so that they do not become damaged. A former student of mine lost all her original work when her apartment roof leaked. She had no photos of any of her work. If you take photographs, take more than one image or have multiple copies made, so that you will have back-up copies. Standard film and good-quality digital photography, even though it may be of amateur quality, can be useful.

Since professionals generally are not allowed to take drawings and documents that you have made while employed at a design firm, you may have to spend the time and money to photograph finished projects. However, be sure you obtain the client's permission to photograph the interiors and that you have permission to duplicate work done at your place of employment. The rights clause in a design contract that relates to photographs does not cover a designer's personal use of photos.

Students (and even professionals who have just a few years of work experience) should also retain at least some preliminary work. Employers like to see the thought process behind design solutions, and sketches do this. Although most of the examples are commonly parts of projects, it is important to show at least one complete project presentation. This complete project should include the verbal explanation of the design problem, floor plans, color boards, renderings, and any other written or graphic documents that were a part of the project's requirements.

Media for Portfolios

Students often have large documents and boards for their portfolios, since large boards and drawings are common presentation media in school. Transporting large items can be a problem for applicants that seek job opportunities in other cities. Many professionals also have some items in a large format. However, portfolios can be presented using several different types of media. The specific use of digital media is presented in another section of this chapter. This section briefly discusses some other choices.

Color-slide transparencies (35 mm) are easy to transport, relatively inexpensive to produce, and if taken correctly, produce long-lasting true color images. A disadvantage of using slides is that you need to carry along a slide viewer, since the prospective employer might not have a slide projector available. A good choice is to use a handheld viewer that is easy to operate and reliable. Try not to get stuck in a situation in which the prospective employer must hold up sheets of slides and look at them by means of the light of a ceiling fixture.

It is easy to take slides of flat work with a small amount of equipment. All that is needed is a 35-mm camera, a tripod, and if daylight film is used, an area with good, consistent natural light. If natural light is not available, the proper combination of film and photo floodlights must be used. Your photo shop can advise you on film. Using the camera's flash unit can produce glare, hot spots, and inconsistent results.

Photographic prints are easier to present but are more expensive than slides. Photographic prints from film should be at least 5 inches by 7 inches. Prints 8 inches by 10 inches are even better, yet each 8 by 10 print can cost several dollars to have made from a slide negative. Everyone is used to printing his or her own digital prints. Not all cameras can begin with a good-quality image that can be reproduced as a large-format print. The digital camera creating the original image must have high megapixels counts to create good-quality 5-by-7-inch or 8-by-10-inch prints. The best prints are also made from images that are TIFF GJPE. prints will not be as crisp as a TIFF.

Professionals may want to purchase prints or slides of photos taken of projects they designed. Many firms use the services of a professional architectural photographer to take photos of high-quality or of unusual projects. If the design firm has paid for the originals, it may be necessary for the designer to obtain permission from the owner of the design firm to obtain duplicate images. The designer should pay for his or her own copies wanted for a personal portfolio.

A medium still used by designers is the photo mechanical transfer (PMT). As mentioned in Chapter 19, a PMT is a high-contrast positive print. This is an exceptionally good medium to use when you want to reduce working drawings and floor plans that have not been originally drawn using CAD. Design items that you want produced as PMTs must be crisp, black-and-white technical work. Color work cannot be made into PMTs.

Format of the Portfolio

A key decision that you will make as you create the portfolio relates to the format. You will be carrying your portfolio in taxicabs, automobiles, trains, buses, and airplanes. Items will be laid out on conference tables and desks, and possibly even be mailed across the country. Although a common format size for boards and drawings in academia is 20 inches by 30 inches, portfolios are actually becoming smaller in size. The 8-by-10-inch, 11-by-14-inch, and 14-by-17-inch formats are easier to present and transport. Many schools are requiring one or more projects to be presented using electronic media presentation techniques. Photography allows for reducing the 20-by-30-inch traditional size to smaller formats.

The larger-size formats make it easy to present original work, yet the smaller-size formats are easier to handle. Frankly, some employers still like to see 1/4-inch-scale drawings and full-sized sample boards. Therefore, you might want to have both large- and small-sized format items available. When you are finalizing the schedule for an interview, you can inquire about any preferences that the prospective employer may have.

Whatever format you decide upon, it is important as much as possible for you to present all the examples consistently in either a vertical or a horizontal manner. This will aid you during the interview because you will not have to keep flipping the items in the portfolio around. If you have used both horizontal and vertical presentation formats, you will have to give more thought as to how the portfolio will be organized and presented, and if items need to be redone (if possible) or possibly eliminated from the portfolio. An option is to group horizontal items separately from vertical format items.

There are different methods of binding pages, so choose one that will allow you flexibility. The most common include plastic pages (available in different sizes) that are held in place with nylon or metal screws. Depending on the brand, you can add and subtract pages easily. Many items, such as sketches, renderings, and plans, can be mounted on paper that matches mat board or black photographic paper and can be inserted into plastic notebook sleeves. Remember that each side of the plastic sleeve is a "page." Use this to your advantage as you organize drawings and written statements. For written items, try to stick to one type font. Multiple type fonts can accidentally make the portfolio look messy. You have to be careful about reducing a large original. CAD drawings are generally not a problem, but hand-drafted items may be difficult to read, and details may be difficult to discern. Larger sheets can be neatly folded.

Another type of portfolio is essential: a case large enough to accommodate sample boards and prints of architectural drawings. These are usually the large-sized binders that have been common for decades. They are more difficult for you to handle during a presentation and transport if you are traveling out of state. This type of binder will have to be checked as baggage, since it cannot fit into an overhead bin on an airplane.

The physical binder itself should be of good quality and look very professional. Drawings rolled up in a tube may be convenient for carrying, but they do not communicate the right level of professionalism, nor do the cardboard portfolios that many students use during college. It is not, however, necessary to spend a lot of money on leather-bound books. When you ship the portfolio, also arrange to pay for the shipping costs when the prospective employer sends it back to you so that the employer will not have to pay these charges.

GOING ELECTRONIC

Technology affects nearly every aspect of the interior design profession. The fact that it impacts the development of a resumé and the job search process should not, of course, be a surprise. Increasing numbers of resumés of interior designers are being posted on job search sites.

Few readers are unfamiliar with using electronic media and the Internet to find information and transfer information from one location to another. During the development of this edition, it was decided that consolidating all the information related to seeking a position in interior design via electronic methods into one location would be helpful. This section briefly discusses using the Internet for job searches, structuring a resumé for transmittal via the Internet, and constructing a portfolio on a CD or DVD format.

Electronic Job Search

The Internet is another place for you to search out job possibilities. The Internet has become popular for job posting because it is cheap, offers the opportunity of sending a large number of applications, and is fast.

For interior designers, the first way to use the Internet for a job search is to take advantage of job banks available on association Web sites. You need to be a member to use this service, and it is one benefit of becoming a member of an association. Keep in mind, however, that in certain associations this member benefit might not be available to students.

Another online way of finding employment is to search the Web sites of interior design firms. Many have links on their Web sites for a candidate to obtain information about possible openings and how to apply for those positions. If the firm does not have a link for application, the site provides information about the firm that can help a candidate determine if that is the type of firm he or she might want to work for. One can always contact the firm via e-mail links or in another manner.

There are other search locations that can be used as well. One of the best known is monster.com. At these sites you can post your resumé, look for posted jobs, get job hunting tips, and much more. Numerous job search sites on the Web can be found by entering "interior design + jobs" into a search engine. The author does not endorse any one site as best or better than another.

Commercial sites aid both the applicant and the employer. Fees are generally required by either party to use the online services, although some do not charge. You must sign up with one of these sites and can then post a resumé or post a job opening.

Electronic Resumés and Cover Letters

Design firms receive resumés by fax and e-mail—sometimes in greater numbers than by regular mail. Preparing a resumé for fax transmission has no special needs. Posting a resumé by e-mail, anticipating that it might be scanned by the employer via computer, or otherwise posting on an Internet job site requires the candidate to use some special techniques (see Figure 33-8).

Michael Smith

From: "Michael Smith" <msmith33@xxx.net>
To: "Albert Jones" <ajones@jonesarchitecture.xxx>
Sent: Monday July 17, 200x 9:27 AM
Subject: employment request

Dear Mr. Jones
jones architecture and design

I am very interested in talking to you about the job opening your firm advertised in the Sunday newspaper. I believe I would be a perfect fit for your firm. Allow me to tell you why.

* I have a bachelor's degree in interior design from a FIDER accredited school with a 3.9 GPA.
* The internship I completed last summer was at a design firm very similar to yours. I received high praise from the intern supervisor.
* I have worked part time through school and understand what "work" means.
* My language skills include fluency in Spanish and some German.
* I have taken extra AutoCAD classes to improve my skills.
* My family lives in your city now.

You will see by my resume that I am the person you are looking for to join your firm. I can send you a partial electronic portfolio when we discuss an appointment to meet you in person.

I appreciate your time very much. I know you are very busy.
Michael Smith

Mike Smith
Ravenswood Street
Anywhere, USA
Phone (111) 555-4567
E-mail msmith33@xxx.net

OBJECTIVE: Entry-level design position with a commercial interior design firm associated with an architect. Want a challenging position which will help me grow as a professional in commercial design and contribute to a high-quality design firm.

EDUCATION: University of Florida
        Bachelor of Design, Major Interior Design
        GPA 3.9/4.0.

EXPERIENCE
        Summer 200x and Fall 200x
        Gainesville Design Services
        Intern: Commercial firm specializing in offices and retail.

FIGURE 33-8.

An example of a resumé sent via e-mail preceded by a cover letter.

Produced drawings for senior designers, prepared specification selections.
Attended client meetings and office meetings with representatives.

Summer, 200x.
Alliance Construction Co. Atlanta, GA.
Draftsperson.
Assisted in the preparation of working drawings for custom home builder.

COMPUTER SKILLS
    AutoCAD 200x
    Microsoft Office Word
    Microsoft PowerPoint

LANGUAGE SKILLS
    Spanish. Can speak and write fluently.
    German. Can speak some.

HONORS/ACTIVITIES
    American Society of Interior Designers
    Student Chapter President 200x
    Student Chapter Treasurer 200x

FIGURE 33-8.

(*Continued*)

For the most part, your electronic resumé or cover letter will be very similar to printed versions. Your cover letter will use the same content suggestions made previously. The resumé must include the same categories of information: contact data, a career summary or objective, education, experience, and any optional information you might like to include. The differences are more in terms of how to present the information.

Let's review a few points about paper resumés that might be scanned by employers. Larger employers scan resumés using an OCR (optical character recognition) scanner to help speed up the process of eliminating those that do not meet their specific needs. The computer scans for key words so that the employer can narrow the number of resumés even further. We talked about how important it has become to include key words in the previous section on resumés. However, some additional information may be useful. When you describe your experiences, use terminology that shows you know what the industry is about. The use of key words as well as industry jargon in resumés is important in order to have your resumé "found" by a prospective employer. The employer uses a similar concept when going to a resumé posting site on the Web. He or she would punch in a small string of key words that would help narrow the field, just as you do when you are searching for any information on the Web. Some of these key words and terms in interior design include "AutoCAD" and names of other software programs, certifications such as "NCIDQ," a state license, a degree, job titles, professional affiliations, and terms like "interior design," "hospitality industry" (or other specialties), and "project manager." Table 33-4 provides several other tips concerning scanned resumés and cover letters.

Sending document via e-mail is another frequently used method of electronic job hunting. In fact, some design firms prefer e-mailed contacts, since the

TABLE 33-4.

Tips for Scanned Resumés and Cover Letters.

The version of your resumé you think might be scanned needs to follow some very specific guidelines. Scanners are sensitive and will eliminate those that it cannot read properly.

- Print on white paper only with little texture.
- Do not use bullets, underlining, boldface type, boxes, other graphics, or italics.
- Use quotation marks ("") to call attention to special words.
- Do not use fanciful fonts. Use simple fonts such as Times Roman, Courier, Helvetica, or Ariel.
- Use a type size of 12 or 14 points.
- Some acronyms will be recognized depending on the key words that are entered by the employer. If you are not sure, spell them out.
- Print using a laser printer for the best-quality image.
- Send the letter and resumé in a large, flat envelope. Folds can confuse the scanner.
- Do not bracket your phone number. Use a period such as 123.456.7890.

employer can handle them much faster. A downside is that when it is sent to a specific person, that person might not see the e-mail for a few days. If it is sent to the firm's general "contact us" link, it might not get to the right person for even longer. However, using e-mail instead of snail mail can be effective.

Some job seekers use e-mail to send their resumé as an attachment. If you choose to do this, be sure you have a short and clear cover "letter." It takes more time, but employers appreciate having this introduction as they would a cover letter with a mailed resumé. Your subject line is also important so that your e-mail is not discarded as spam. If you send your resumé as an attachment, only do so when you are absolutely sure that your computer has no viruses that can harm the recipient's computer. As the reader probably knows, attachments are where viruses often exist. Remember that attachments can become garbled and unreadable. This seems to happen less today, but it still can affect some computers.

To save time, some job seekers incorporate their resumé within the body of an e-mail. Although you are not sending a true cover, you can begin your e-mail with a short cover note that precedes the resumé. This will help the employer understand where you heard about the firm, what type of job you are seeking, and why you are interested in this company just as if you sent the package by regular mail. It is also a good idea to make the opening cover look like a letter by using the standard "Dear Mr. Jones:" at the beginning and ending it with "Sincerely" and your full name. Then separate the cover from the body of your resumé with a line of asterisks (*) to show where the letter stops and the resumé begins.

As with a document that might be scanned, the first rule to follow when you e-mail a resumé is not to use any fancy formatting as extra tabs, boldface or italics on fonts, or anything else that is nonstandard. The other important rule is to always save your text as an ASCII file. Both these issues are important, since different servers will read (or not read) your e-mail. You might also try sending your e-mail version resumé to some friends that use a different server to see if any changes need to be made. Another way to check how it looks is to e-mail it to yourself. That way you can see what the format looks like and then make adjustments.

Only e-mail a resumé if you have been asked to do so. When you e-mail your resumé, in the cover remind the prospective employer about your earlier conversation. Keep this resumé to a reasonable length, though it is not necessary to keep it to one page. The page length for e-mails (and HTML) is somewhat difficult to pin down, so you can make it longer than your print version. Remember that the longer the resumé is, the longer it will take to download. One last point is to be sure to print out copies of the e-mailed resumés you send out for your job hunt file.

Another alternative is to post your resumé on the Web. We have already discussed this as part of the job search section above, but a few more specific comments related to resumés are in order. Posting your resumé on the Internet can give you more flexibility with content and design than sending either an e-mail or a regular printed version. You are able to use boldface, italics, colors, different font sizes, and even graphics to call attention to your information: "This on-line presence . . . demonstrates to employers your awareness of technology and may be a little extra that puts you ahead of the competition."[1] Here are a few other hints for using a Web resumé:

- Avoid photographs of yourself
- Do not use too many links—you may lose the employer
- Watch the contrast of colors of fonts against that of the background—it needs to be readable
- Use simple graphics that will not take too long to download

You may want to check the references for books that can help further if you wish to prepare an electronic resumé.

Electronic Portfolios

Of course, today there are many electronic media that can be used for the portfolio. An easy and reasonably economical way of using electronic media is by transferring portfolio items to the computer. Digital photographs can be taken of boards and photographs of job sites by the applicant. Project photos for professionals should be done by professional photographers, who will have better-quality digital cameras than most do-it-yourself photographers. Small items can be scanned into the computer, and line drawings are easy to utilize. Digital photos and scanned items can be manipulated to your format and even, in some cases, to repair small errors. The images can then be printed on a high-resolution laser printer for multiple copies. Color copies are also feasible and less expensive than photographic prints if a photo printer is not available.

A more sophisticated use of electronic media is by transferring work to CD-ROM discs, DVD discs, or even the Web. A DVD disc provides more storage space, which might be needed to include numerous graphic images.

It is easy to transfer almost all portfolio items to a writable disc. CAD files can be copied directly to the disc. Other drawings can be scanned with a flatbed scanner. Digital photographs can be taken of sample boards, models, and other three-dimensional items. Digital photos of actual installations can also be transferred to the CD-ROM disc.

What is the advantage of going to the extra expense of transferring work to a media CD? Flexibility with layout, ease of transport, and excellent quality of images. Using a CD also shows the prospective employer that you are on the cutting edge of the industry. Of course, you have almost instantaneous communication over the Web.

With CD media, you have a preprogrammed presentation where the viewer experiences your portfolio as you want him or her to, without interruption.

You are then getting the viewer's undivided attention during the presentation. You can integrate animation, voice-overs, and music to make it even more personalized. In addition, you control the timing, sequence, and pace of the information in your presentation.

A CD-ROM also can be created to be more interactive with the viewer; that is, the viewer can follow the sequence from beginning to end as in a preprogrammed presentation, or the viewer can have options (links) that allow him or her to move from one section to another of the material. When the presentation is controlled by the viewer, he or she can focus upon areas of interest and skip others. For example, if the company is looking for someone for its hospitality department, the design director can skip work related to other types of facilities and concentrate on the quality of solutions and technical work in hospitality.

These presentations can also be programmed into a personal Web site. You may be able to link your Web site with one of the job search sites or bring your laptop along and let the interviewer look at your Web site during the interview. The one caution with Web site portfolios is that you must be careful about image file size and the number of images you include. As the reader probably well knows, the more graphics you include on a Web site, the longer it takes for them to load. Employers may become impatient waiting for a complex portfolio to download. If the portfolio is sent as an e-mail, large attachments with a lot of graphics can crash the receiver's system. A portfolio on a Web site will need to be revised and updated. The designer must either be able to program with *HTML*—which is a Web site design language—or pay someone to update the site.

Students may be able to receive assistance in setting up an electronic portfolio from departmental or university computer centers. There are also many software programs that can help the professional do the work themselves. Professionals can also get help from commercial copy centers, or they can hire a graphic designer or a Web site designer. There are also several books out now on how to use the computer to create a digital portfolio. Some of these titles are listed in the references.

We all use e-mail, and e-mail has become a common way for individuals to inquire about or apply for a job. Creative and individualized e-mail addresses that are provocative may be fun among friends, but they have no place in the job search. You don't need to eliminate your favorite e-mail address if you don't want to, but during the job search and on the job, realize that suggestive, provocative, and downright rude e-mail addresses will not be accepted.

SUMMARY

Each of us grows in our own way as we seek fulfillment in our careers. As the professional gains experience in the field, he or she seeks greater levels of responsibility and challenges in the workplace. Often it is necessary to seek new responsibility in another firm, even in another city. For the student, the first job is an important first step in establishing a successful and satisfying career in the interior design profession. Obtaining a position does not come easily to most of us.

At one time or another, each person who reads this book will need to prepare portfolios and resumés and embark on the job search and the stressful interview process. It is hoped that the information in this chapter will help each one of you find that perfect position.

REFERENCE

1. Nemich and Jandt, 1999, p. 75.

CHAPTER 34

Landing the Job

Key Terms and Concepts

These key terms and concepts are important to material in this chapter. Many of these terms will be utilized in other chapters as well. Be sure you understand these items as you read this chapter.

Terms and Concepts

First impressions	Illegal questions
Interview styles	Burn out

Critical Issues

After completing this chapter you should be able to:

- Appreciate some of the factors that employers use to evaluate a resumé, and utilize this information to develop a better resumé and handle an interview successfully.

- Discuss the necessity of preparing for a job interview, including the importance of doing "homework" about the firm where the applicant is about to be interviewed.

- Explain the importance of projecting the right image for the job interview through dress and etiquette.

- Explain diplomatic responses to illegal or improper questions posed during the job interview.

- Draft a generic thank-you letter that might be used following job interviews.

- Discuss why it is important for a new hire to make a good impression the first few weeks on the job.

Looking for a job is serious work. You have already spent a great deal of time determining what kind of job in the interior design industry is of interest to you and preparing your resumé, portfolio, and cover letters. All that effort has been followed up with letter writing and phone calls in order to get an interview.

Now you have one—congratulations!

The next step is to be sure you are prepared for the interview so that you can put your best foot forward and, if you also like the company, find that the interviewer likes you well enough to offer you a position.

Interviewing for a job is not to be taken lightly. You do need to prepare yourself for each one of these important presentations and negotiation sessions. They are that, please remember. You are presenting yourself to a potential employer who needs to be impressed by your skills but also your personality and professionalism. And you are negotiating as you discover more about the company and "negotiate" to become a part of the company.

Becoming a part of an interior design firm for the first time is an exciting feeling as you finally get to do the work that you have trained to do. The work you get assigned in the beginning might seem trivial at first, but that is because they need to see you up close and personal to see what you really can do. It gets better; always remember that. Assuming, of course, that you give it your all every day.

This chapter provides the reader with suggestions about how employers review resumés and cover letters. The information may help you in your preparation of these important tools. It continues with an extensive discussion on interviewing, providing tips on negotiating that stress-producing event.

A section of this chapter has been included for the professional who has been working for some time and considering making a move. It does not go into the depth of discussion about this topic but provides some insights for consideration. Making a professional change of jobs is never an easy decision, but sometimes it is necessary to improve responsibility challenges and income opportunities.

HOW EMPLOYERS REVIEW RESUMÉS AND COVER LETTERS

Potential employers receive dozens of resumés by mail, fax, and e-mail every week, whether or not they have an opening. If the employer has placed an ad, he or she will scan the letters for those that match the requirements stated in the ad. They are likely to manually scan for key words throughout the resumé. Those that do not match will be put in a separate pile and may or may not ever be read again. If the company has no current openings, an employer may give the cover letter a glance and determine if they are worth retaining for future reference, noting that the resumé mentions certain skills that are generally needed by the company.

Certain features almost always will automatically eliminate a letter from consideration. Such things as poor spelling, sloppy appearance, a "To Whom It May Concern" salutation, too many pages, or an obvious lack of skills will often mean round-file filing. There are several other items that an employer either looks for or uses to evaluate a resumé:

1. *Relevance to the design firm*. Employers are impressed when an applicant has done some research about the firm. For example, career objective and career summary statements that relate to the work done by the firm to which the individual is applying. If it is clear in the cover letter and resumé career objective that the applicant wishes to do commercial design, it will not receive much notice at a residential design studio. Employers are also looking for any statement in the cover letter that refers to the actual work done by the firm.

2. *Referring to how the applicant heard of the job opening or the firm*. "I was excited about your advertisement in the Sunday *Gazette* for a design assistant." "My senior studio professor at State University suggested I contact you about an internship." These comments show the

prospective employer that you know something about the firm rather than that you have sent a broadcast mailing.

3. *Using key words or phrases to catch the reviewer's attention.* Employers are looking for certain skills, accomplishments, educational background, and other issues that are specifically related to their design specialty. When those key words or phrases are used (e.g., AutoCAD 2007, increased sales, award-winning projects), they will catch the reviewer's eye, and he or she will likely slow down and pay more attention to the letter and resumé.

4. *Clarity of employment history.* Employers want to know what the applicant did and where he or she worked prior to applying for the position. Providing every detail in the resumé is not necessary, but vagueness will get the applicant nowhere. The employment history section naturally tells the prospective employer what you have done in the past and have to offer. Whenever possible, include comments that quantify your experience as these will stand out.

5. *Good communication skills.* Designers do not just communicate in their drawings. Writing skills and verbal skills are equally, if not more, important for some positions. The cover letter and resumé must use proper grammar and perfect spelling. Students, in particular, often write paragraph-long sentences. Revise your letters and resumé. Have someone else make suggestions as well. Finally, don't just trust the spell checker on the computer.

6. *"Creative writing."* Employers become suspicious of resumés filled with more active verbs or claims of accomplishment than seem reasonable for the individual's apparent level of experience. Out-and-out lying is easily discovered and should never be engaged in. Always be truthful in what you include in the resumé and cover letter.

7. *Achievement.* Employers want to hire an individual with a proven level of accomplishment. They are looking for indications of successful project management, profit making, or anything else that indicates the applicant knows how to achieve goals. This is another reason to think about outcomes, quantifying accomplishments, and skill sets as you prepare the sections of your resumé.

8. *Broad interests.* Most employers want to hire individuals who are loyal and dedicated to the interior design profession, but they do not want one-dimensional employees. Indicate involvement in professional associations, community groups, and other outside activities. Be careful not to go overboard, however. You may sound too busy with hobbies and outside interests to have time to work.

9. *Care and thought.* Interior design is a profession in which attention to detail is essential. Careful drafting, proofreading, and execution of a resumé and cover letter are important. Sloppy work, poor grammar, or minimizing statements related to the employer's potential needs will raise doubt as to the individual's concern for a client's project.

10. *Neatness.* This is obvious, but it is worth repeating.

INTERVIEWS

Preparing yourself for interviews through job searching and resumé development is a critical part of landing an interview. For interior designers, developing one's portfolio is a serious part of the process. It is the representation of your skills and the only way you can convince an employer that you can do the job for which you are interviewing. Now all that time has paid off, as you have obtained an interview, and you are ready to make your case to a prospective employer.

This is your chance to make a good impression, to convince the employer that you are the one person in the world who can handle the job. If you are a student, this is the opportunity for which you have been working so hard for so many years. If you are a professional, this could be the start of something new: a new city, new responsibilities, more pay, or whatever has brought you to decide to change your job. In just about every reference book, you will read that the interview is where little things more often than not torpedo a good candidate. The hints and comments in this section, hopefully, will help you as you travel through the interview process to achieve success.

The planning and preparation for your interview is no less important than any other kind of planning and preparation discussed in this text. Once an interview has been obtained, it is necessary for you to do some preparation. You will need to check and modify your portfolio for the interview. Then you will need to prepare yourself with regard to your appearance for the interview. You also must verify details about the location of the interview. And finally, you will want to prepare yourself mentally for one of the most nerve-wracking experiences you will go through.

If the interview is in your hometown, about 24 hours before the scheduled interview, call to check on details. If the interview requires that you travel a long distance, call about 48 hours ahead, if practicable. Find out exactly with whom you will be interviewing and how to pronounce his or her name. The person who will be interviewing you will not necessarily be the person who responded to your letter. Larger design firms will have a personnel manager who is in charge of interviewing prospective employees prior to the design director interviewing them. If more than one person will conduct the interview, ask for their names and job titles. Request an agenda, so that you will know how much time you will be spending with each person.

Double-check the day and time of the interview. No matter how much time has passed from the time you set up the interview, call to confirm the time. If you have any questions about how to get to the studio or office, or you are not sure where to park, ask for directions at this time. In large cities, it is probably safer to take a cab than it is to drive, but check for suggestions about this also. If there is any reason that you cannot keep the interview, call and personally talk to the interviewer to tell him or her. Initial interviews can be as short as 30 minutes or can last 2 hours, though an hour is the average. In either case, plan to spend about 20 minutes showing your portfolio and the rest of the time answering questions.

Now that you know what the situation is, go through your portfolio and be sure that every item is where you want it for the interview. Familiarize yourself with what you are going to show the interviewer, and confirm in your mind the order in which you wish to show it. If something has become damaged, take time to repair it or try to replace it. Place an extra, unfolded copy of your resumé in the portfolio. Also check to be sure that a pen and pencil are in your portfolio, your pocket, or your handbag.

Before the interview, check the outfit that you plan to wear. Make sure it is clean, well pressed, and does not have loose buttons or threads. Be sure your shoes are shined. Think about wearing something on the conservative side, since all employment experts agree that the interview is the time to dress conservatively even in a creative field like interior design. However, this does not mean that you have to wear a black or navy blue suit, unless you know that this is standard at the design firm you will be visiting.

Your mental preparation includes anticipating and thinking about the kinds of questions the interviewer may ask you and that you may want to ask the interviewer about the company. Some common questions are included at the end of this section.

It is never permissible to be late, unless it is due to something totally beyond your control. If you are held up in traffic or miss your plane or connection, call the interviewer as soon as you can. To avoid being late, make a point of arriving at the office or studio at least 10 to 15 minutes early. These few extra minutes will give you a cushion in case you experience a traffic jam or difficulty in finding the office. It also gives you a chance to try to relax and collect yourself before going into the interview. Before you check in with the receptionist, go to the restroom to check your overall appearance.

When you check in with the receptionist, be sure to smile and tell the receptionist who you are, with whom you have an appointment, and what time the appointment is for. Remember to be friendly and cordial but professional to everyone you meet. Most likely you will be told to have a seat. You can mentally prepare yourself by reviewing points you would like to make. But for the most part, it is better to have done that before you arrive and use waiting time to try to relax and think positive about the way you will conduct yourself and the outcome of the interview. Try to use this time to compose yourself by reading a magazine. Try to relax; don't fiddle with your portfolio, briefcase, or handbag.

If by chance you are interviewing out of state, there is a possibility that someone from the office will meet you at the airport. Of course, you will know this ahead of time and your preparation for this is to travel in professional casual dress. If you know you are going right into the interview from the airport, then you should travel in business apparel. It also helps to know what the person looks like or arrange a meeting place so you can easily contact this person. Several additional tips are provided on the CD as Item 34-1.

What to Wear to an Interview

What you wear to the job interview is a part of the overall impression that you will leave with the interviewer. It will not get you the job, but it might lose it for you. Many interior design professionals find it acceptable to be trendy or even casual in their everyday business apparel. However, most interviewers expect more conservative apparel for the interview. If you have researched the company as well as you can, you will have some idea of what normal business attire is like at that design firm. This will be your guide as to how trendy or how conservative you must appear.

Image and Dress on the Job

Individuality is expressed in many ways—sometimes to the detriment of the individual and the consternation of the employer or client. Personal image and appropriate professional dress on the job is something of a hot topic in interior design.

At some point students must switch from wearing casual clothes every day to wearing suits and ties or dresses and jackets. Although a school may not have had the authority to send a student home because of the outfits he or she wears, the employer certainly can. Employers do have the right to establish appropriate dress codes for employees.

Consider that much of what an individual communicates about him- or herself is conveyed by dress and body language. Remember the scene in the movie *Pretty Woman* when Julia Roberts goes shopping for clothing on Rodeo Drive in Beverly Hills? If you are unconvinced, try this experiment. Dress very casually and visit a high-end clothing or jewelry store. Walk around and observe how you are looked at. If a clerk approaches you, what does he or she say? About a week later, dress in a nice business suit and go back to the same store. Now how are you treated? Even in today's more casual world, appearances do make a difference.

Clothing does make the man and the woman in a business environment. What you wear is a reflection of you, your company, and even your perception of your professionalism and worth as an interior designer. The self-image you portray begins with many subtle things. A smile, a handshake, and the tone of your voice give those to whom you come in contact an inkling of what you are like. You might not like the fact that others in the working world will not care for your piercing, tattoos, and very personal hair styles. There is a place for personal expression and it's generally not going to be in the office environment. Modifying or improving your self-image in the working environment is a matter of learning ways to overcome the factors that hold you back from achieving greater success in your career.

The suit remains the most important garment in the business world and the interior design profession as well. Since suits are usually worn by people who help us make important decisions about our lives, such as doctors and attorneys, we are more willing to accept the wearer as an authority figure and important. People who wear suits are usually given more respect than those who do not wear suits. The jacket is as important for a woman as a suit is for a man, although a woman does not have to just wear suits. A woman who wears a jacket is thought of as a serious person who wields authority and power. She can wear a jacket with a dress or trousers and still convey that professional image.

Of course, wearing a suit or a dress and heels to a construction job site is not only impractical but can also be dangerous. It is not necessary for you to dress up, but it is not good to dress too casually either. Remember, you lose authority when you dress down. Foremen and tradespeople must still recognize you as an authority.

Purchasing a new wardrobe for that first job is going to be somewhat expensive, but you don't have to wear an Armani suit to dress professionally. Here are a few tips on shopping for business garments for the first or even perhaps the next job:

- Before you go shopping, review what you already have in your closets so that you can pinpoint your needs.

- When you shop for business apparel, don't wear casual clothes or casual shoes. You will have a more accurate idea of what you will look like wearing clothes similar to what you are buying.

- Shop where you can get in-store tailoring or alterations done. In this way, you can get assistance from a sales clerk who knows how to fit you properly.

- Sales clerks pay more attention to and more quickly help those customers who are dressed up than those who are wearing shorts, T-shirts, and hiking boots—even on a Saturday.

- For women who are on a limited budget, buy separates rather than dresses—but still of the best quality you can afford. Separates allows you to mix and match, which provides more versatility to a limited wardrobe.

- Wool is still preferred for suits, although polyester/wool blends wrinkle less. Even in the summertime, a fine-quality wool suit looks good, does not lose its shape, and wrinkles less. Cotton and linen are more comfortable in the summer, but they wrinkle and hold their wrinkles until they have been cleaned and pressed.

- Fit is very important. Buy what fits, not what you think you will get into if you go on a diet. A poor-fitting, expensive garment will look worse on you than a good-fitting, moderately priced garment.

Wear apparel that is comfortable. Do not use the job interview to break in a new pair of shoes. Business suits with ties for men is standard. Conservative fabrics in solid colors are commonly accepted. Women should also choose conservative suits and dresses with jackets. Sundresses, sleeveless dresses, or low-cut dresses do not project the kind of impression that businesspeople like to see.

Women also should be careful about what kind of accessories they add to their outfit. Refrain from wearing brightly colored or boldly patterned scarves; dangling, noisy bracelets; or oversized earrings—anything that attracts more attention to the accessories than to yourself. Refer back to Chapter 21 for additional suggestions for general business dressing. Now let's get to the heart of the matter of this chapter—the interview.

The Interview—First Impressions

An old advertisement once stated, "You only have one chance to make a first impression." Now is that chance, and it can be very critical to the outcome of your interview. However, you are not concerned, as you have done your homework, know what you want to say, and have even practiced that first encounter. When your interviewer arrives and greets you, be prepared to shake hands. It is not necessary to use a bone-crushing handshake. Just make it sincere. Prepare for this by having your portfolio, handbag, or attaché case positioned so that you can pick them up with your left hand, leaving the right hand free to shake hands. Smile! Say hello, introduce yourself. You want this job, don't you?

When you arrive at the conference room or office where the interview will be held, wait for some indication from the interviewer as to where to sit. If he or she does not make any indication as to where to sit, choose a chair that is either directly across from the interviewer or at a 90-degree angle. These two positions make it easier to show your portfolio and to maintain eye contact.

Remember that the purpose of the interview is for the employer to get to know you personally, ask you questions, and try to evaluate whether or not you would be a good addition to the firm. The interviewer will be looking for information and personal conduct that shows you will be able to do the job and will fit in to the existing team. If the applicant is an experienced professional, the interviewer is also looking for clues that you are even willing to work for the firm.

The interview is also a time for you to evaluate whether this particular firm is really the kind of firm for which you wish to work. Just because a firm has a good reputation does not mean that you will want to work for it. Gather your own internal list of what you want to know about the company through the questions you will ask during the interview.

As you are sitting through the interview, there are several things to keep in mind. Try not to use distracting mannerisms. Don't play with a paper clip or pen, fuss with your hair or accessories, and so on. Let your body language and visual presentation communicate that you are an interested professional. Be sure to listen to the questions the interviewer asks. Do not think of what you want to say so that you do not hear what is being asked. If the interviewer says something you don't understand completely, ask him or her to clarify the point. Think before you speak, and do not interrupt the interviewer. Use eye contact, but do not try to stare the interviewer down. Use body language that is open and receptive to what is being discussed, not defensive. Smile; show interest. If you do not show interest in your work or if you sound bored or defensive as you describe it, you will not be making a favorable impression and you can be guaranteed of not getting an offer.

Interview Styles

Remember that the first "interview" encounter is when you greet the receptionist upon your arrival. When a firm is large enough to have someone at the front desk, he or she knows you are coming and has been told to evaluate this encounter with him or her. That is why arriving early enough to gather your thoughts and yourself before you enter the office or studio is so important.

There are many different styles of interviewing. In some cases, the employer will purposely ask you questions that will put you under even more stress than you are already experiencing. The idea, as far as the employer is concerned, is to find out how you might react under the worst conditions. This probably does not happen in interviews with interior design firms very often, but stress-inducing questions could come up. Stay calm, recognize what the interviewer is doing—it's not a personal attack—and do not become sarcastic or attack. If the interview is conducted in a particularly stressful manner, maybe you would not want to work there anyway.

Another style of interviewing is the situational interview. In this case, the interviewer will ask a lot of questions like, "What would you do if the client vetoed every single design idea you presented at the final presentation?" The interviewer is trying to see how you think on your feet. These kinds of questions are most likely to be asked if you are applying for a management position or perhaps a project manager position rather than a position as a designer. In any case, think about your answers and take these questions seriously.

Some firms use team interviews. This means that you might be questioned by more than one person during the interview or you will be passed from staff member to staff member during the interview. This happens frequently in larger design firms, where an ability to fit into the team and existing company's culture is important. Understand that everyone probably has a preplanned part to play in the interview. One interviewer may be casual, another may be formal, and another may appear not to be interviewing you at all but observing your behavior. Be respectful of everyone, and be prepared for a long interview process.

Most interviews in interior design are not designed to induce stress. In fact, many owners and managers of design firms with whom I have talked insist that they try to make the candidate as comfortable and at ease as possible. They remember what it was like! Stress your qualifications in terms of what you can do for the company. Graduating students need to indicate a willingness to learn. Be enthusiastic in your answers, and stress your positive characteristics. But do not exaggerate your experience or your abilities. It will not take much time for the employer to find out that you are not an expert with CAD if you said you were but are not. And do not try to pass off someone else's work for yours in your portfolio. That, too, will be found out very quickly and will always lead to dismissal.

The Interview—Discussing Qualifications

During your interview, never bring up personal problems, argue, blame others, or beg for the job. Even if you have left your previous job under difficult circumstances, do not blame anyone at the other company for your problems. It tags you as a difficult person and will probably influence the interviewer to pass you over. If you are asked if you were ever fired, you do have to be honest. But it is not necessary to go into a long, detailed discussion of what happened. Make some brief comments about what happened and hope the interviewer moves on.

Perhaps during the interview, you determine that you are not interested in working for the company. It is important that you complete the interview but inform the firm promptly that you are not interested in pursuing the position further. Those of you who are students should not accept an interview if you really have no interest in working for the company. Some students like to go on interviews to "practice" for the job they want. This is poor business etiquette that can come back to haunt you later. An informational interview as discussed in the previous chapter and arranging for an actual interview for "practice" are not the same thing.

Unless the interviewer brings it up, do not ask about salary and benefits until the latter part of the interview. It is considered very bad form if the first question you have is about salary and benefits. You first need to ask questions that will help you understand if you want to work at the company. Questions you might ask include the following:

- How many people work in the company?
- What are the company's plans for growth or expansion?
- What are the job responsibilities of this position?
- Will I be working with only one designer or several (for an entry-level position)?

When you have asked your questions, you might also want to ask, "Are many other people being interviewed?" "When will you be making a decision?" You need to know what will happen next.

If you get an offer, that is the time when you will begin to discuss details about salary, benefits, and responsibilities. Be prepared to give a salary range that you must have, but wait until the employer has indicated what the salary will be. Employers, of course, want to hire you at as low a salary as is reasonable for the position. But do not sell yourself short. If the salary offer is way below what you need to live on or is way below what you understand the competition is paying, say so.

Remember that benefits such as health insurance, reimbursement of professional association dues, and employee discounts are important parts of the compensation package. One company with an excellent health insurance program, a profit-sharing program, and a generous discount for personal purchases but that offers a low salary might offer a better opportunity than another company offering a higher salary but weaker benefits (all other things being equal). Compensation in interior design is notoriously low in comparison to other professions, although it has become competitive within the industry in more recent years. Designers generally agree that they do not go into interior design to become rich. You might want to read the section in Chapter 14 on different compensation methods.

For the most part, if you are offered a position, be prepared either to accept or to reject it at that time. If you are offered a position that is different than the one you expected or you are being offered a lower salary than you were expecting, it is acceptable to ask for time to consider the offer. If you really want the position, say so. If you have another interview that day, do not keep one employer dangling to see if someone else might have a better offer. Many designers now request that offers be put in writing. This does not have to be a formal employment contract, as described in Chapter 15, but it should include key points concerning salary, benefits, and work responsibilities. A written offer of this kind is not generally necessary for students who are interviewing for their first job but is more common for experienced designers, especially those who are shifting into management or quasi-management positions. If you are not made an offer but there is no indication that you have been rejected, ask the interviewer when he or she will be ready with a decision. Do not leave without knowing what the salary range is if you have been given an offer.

One very good clue that the employer is interested in you is if he or she suggests showing you around the studio or office. This is usually only done if the candidate interests the employer and he or she wants to introduce you to staff members. However, if you have not actually been offered the position, don't assume anything. Every once in a while, an employer just tries to be nice and shows off his studio but doesn't offer you a job.

The time of the offer or non-offer is the best clue that the interview is over. Watch for other clues, such as that the interviewer is stacking the job application, your resumé, and his or her notes together, or the interviewer is pushing his or her chair back in preparation for getting up. This is the time to summarize your interest in the position and why you are the best candidate. State this in a few sentences so that you do not overstay your welcome at the end. When the interview is over, get up and leave promptly. If an offer has been made and you have accepted it, be sure that you understand what day you are to start, the time, and anything else that needs to be taken care of by you, either prior to your first day or on your first day on the job. In the excitement, it is not uncommon for the applicant to forget to ask about these issues!

If you don't get an offer, it will probably be disappointing. Be gracious and professional. Thank the interviewer for the time to talk to him or her. It is important to keep a good attitude at this point because needs change in interior design all the time. The firm that doesn't need you today may have work come in that requires hiring additional staff next week. You can ask for feedback and perhaps they will comment on some weak points or otherwise why you don't fit at this point into their staff. It is even okay for you to ask them if they know of other firms that might be looking for someone. They might not suggest anyone, but certainly it shows them your sincerity in obtaining a position in a design firm such as theirs.

Typical Interview Questions

There are many kinds of questions that commonly are asked in interviews. Interviewers will ask questions in order to find out about your personality and demeanor. They want to determine whether or not you will fit in to the existing group. They will ask questions to determine your overall interest in interior design and the specialty area that you are interested in pursuing. If you are a recent graduate, the interviewer probably will ask you about your educational background and the classes you took.

Questions are likely to come up to find out about your ambitions in the field and, to some degree, your future plans with regard to your career. They may even ask questions to find out if you have any "skeletons in the closet," to discover whether you left a prior job under bad circumstances. It is important that you prepare yourself for these questions in advance. The questions shown in Table 34-1 are typical of ones asked in an interior design interview. You may want to think of some others as well.

ILLEGAL QUESTIONS

Kelly was asked during a job interview if she had any small children. "You see, this job requires that the designers be free to travel around the state to meet with clients," said the employer. Kelly hesitated since she had a four-year-old child.

Jose was asked if he was a citizen. He was, in fact, born in Nebraska, but he refused to answer the question.

TABLE 34-1.

Common Interview Questions.

General Questions for Any Candidate
Why do you wish to work for us?
What do you know about our company?
How did you hear about our company?
Have you applied to any other companies?
Tell me about the qualifications you have for this position.
Are you willing to do the traveling out of town that is necessary for this position?
Tell me about yourself.
How long have you lived in this city?
How much compensation are you expecting?
What will you add to our company?
Describe what you consider to be your weaknesses.
How do you plan to overcome those weaknesses?
Could you name a coworker that we could contact that could tell us something about you?
Do you have any objections to taking our entry psychological tests?

Questions Common for Entry-Level Positions
Why did you select the college or school you attended?
Why did you select a major in interior design?
Did you have any leadership experience in college?
How do you think your colleagues in your major would describe you?
How do you view this job in relationship to your long-term goals?
Describe your reactions when your work was criticized.
What are your ambitions for the future?
How long would you expect to stay with our company?
Did you find it comfortable to work in the classroom studio?
How long do you think it will take you to make a meaningful contribution to our firm?

Common Questions for Candidates with Prior Professional Experience
Tell me about your previous experience and how those positions relate to this position.
How do you think you can best contribute to this firm?
Why are you looking for another position?
Are you a leader?
What are your ambitions for the future?
You appear to be overqualified for this position. Why are you applying for this position?
If you are offered a position with this company, tell me what you would do during the first month on the job.
How much are you worth?
How would you describe your supervisory (management) style?
How have you increased sales or profits at your present employer?
How do you think your present boss would describe you?
May we contact your present employer?
Please tell me how many days of work you missed last year.

There are many questions that can no longer be asked in a job interview and can no longer appear on a job application. These questions relate but are not limited to age, sex, religion, marital status, parental status, sexual preference, and ethnic origin. For example, the employer cannot directly ask you how old you are, your date of birth, your religion, or your native tongue. Keep in mind that many questions that do not seem to be sexually discriminatory actually are.

Questions directed at women such as asking whether they are single or married, what their husband does for a living, whether or not they plan to have children are all considered illegal. Sometimes these questions come up in very casual ways such as, "Are you going to be able to work evenings and weekends when needed?" This question could be innocent or actually a ploy to find out if you have children. These discriminatory kinds of questions must not influence the employer's decision as to whether or not to offer a job to an individual. They are most often asked by owners of firms who are generally less experienced at the interview process.

There are ways in which certain discriminatory questions can be asked so as to make them legal. This is especially true if the question has a direct bearing on the ability of the individual to perform the job. Although it is illegal to ask you "How old are you," it is legal to ask "Are you between the ages of 25 and 45?" You may wish to review appropriate sections from the books of Lewin G. Joel III, Fred S. Steingold, and Steven Mitchell Sack listed in the references for specific ways in which questions can and cannot be asked during interviews or on job applications.

When you are asked a question that you believe to be illegal or about which you feel uncomfortable answering, you must be prepared to say something. Many of the job-hunting books suggest that you answer the question, while others suggest not offering personal information. Another way of handling this situation is to say something like, "I do not understand what that has to do with the requirements of the job or my qualifications to do the job." When they respond, comment on how that will not be a problem for you without necessarily detailing personal information.

Some interviewers may not have hired anyone for some time and may not be aware that some questions cannot be legally asked anymore. Making a big issue of such questions, if you honestly feel the person is asking the question innocently, could result in your not getting the job. If the interviewer asks too many of these kinds of questions or ignores your hesitancy in answering them, you always have the right to terminate the interview and to obtain a job somewhere else.

It is sad to say, but discrimination in hiring decisions will occur. However, if you feel you have been denied a job based on discrimination, you have recourse should you choose to pursue it. "You may have a cause of action if you can prove that you were discriminated against in the job application process . . . . If you feel you have a legitimate gripe, the first step is to file a complaint with your state human rights commission or the EEOC."[1] Of course, you can hire a private attorney and file a civil suit if you wish. Only you can decide whether or not you want to work for a firm that appears to discriminate.

FOLLOW-UP

What you do after the interview plays an important part in portraying the professional image you set out in that interview. The first thing you should do is prepare notes detailing what was talked about. As soon after the interview as is practical, write up this information as part of your job search record keeping. This should be done whether you have accepted an offer, rejected an offer, or not even received an offer. Notes related to salary, benefits, expected performance levels, and your general impressions of the firm can be important if you have not made a decision about the company or the company has not made a decision about you. If an offer was not made or you were rejected, these notes will help you understand what may have gone wrong so that you can correct the errors during future interviews. If you were offered a job, this same information will be important in the future so that you will know what the agreed-upon responsibilities are on which you will later be evaluated.

Good business etiquette also calls for you to send a thank-you note or letter to the interviewer immediately after the interview. A short letter or note will indicate to the prospective employer that you are a professional. Even if the firm does not have an opening for you, you will be remembered later. Thank the interviewer for giving you his or her time, restate your interest in the position, if you are still interested, and follow through on any promised information you agreed to supply. Be enthusiastic in whatever you say in the note. You will make the greatest impression by sending a thank-you letter in the first place. Complete that first impression by sending a handwritten note, neatly written with correct spelling. Figure 34-1 provides a suggestion for content only. Some job hunting experts suggest sending an e-mail thank you instead of one by snail mail. Whichever way you choose, simply remember to send a thank you.

A follow-up phone call is also appropriate in place of a note, especially if the interviewer has indicated that a call is appropriate. It might be to set up a second interview or provide some information that for some reason you did not have at the time of the interview.

If you have been offered a position but have asked for time to consider the offer, it is best if you call the interviewer promptly and follow up with a refusal or an acceptance letter. In most situations, the employer is hoping for an immediate response. Depending on the situation, you can ask for 24 to 48 hours. Waiting longer can be a problem and can indicate to the prospective employer that you are not interested. It also can start you out in the job relationship on a sour note, if you decide to accept the offer. By responding within a reasonable time frame, the company knows whether or not you are interested in the position and, in the case of your refusal, has a letter for the company's records.

If you are interested in a position with the firm but you know that the firm is still interviewing others, it is necessary to keep the design firm interested in you. Be sure to add something in your note or letter summarizing your qualifications and stating how you can contribute to the company.

What Would You Do?

Mary was very excited about getting an interview with a particular design firm. Even though she was new to the city, the firm had a great reputation for cutting-edge design and was highly recommended as a place to really learn and move up in the field.

When she arrived for her interview, she had to wait 45 minutes in the lobby. Chad, the design director, finally came out and led her to the conference room. He introduced Mary to Karen and Don, two designers in the firm. After a few minutes of pleasantries, Don asked Mary why she wanted to work at this company. While she was responding, Karen left the room. Then Chad asked her to show them her portfolio. As she was explaining the projects in her book, Karen returned to the conference room along with the owner of the company, Eric.

After she was done with her portfolio, Eric asked her why they should hire her. Mary began to respond, when Eric's cell phone went off and he took that call. Don told her to go ahead and answer anyway, which she did. Eric asked her to repeat what she said, and before she could answer, he asked her if she was married, if she had any kids, and if she planned on having any more kids.

Marilyn Norton
2571 N. Paradise Lane
Sacramento, California
(916) 555-2410

February 18, 200x

Mr. Sandford Hopkins
Hopkins, Dodge, and Russell, Inc.
1849 Grass Valley Avenue
Reno, Nevada

Dear Mr. Hopkins:

Thank you for giving me the opportunity to meet with you yesterday and discussing my joining your firm as a Project Designer.

While you interview the other individuals you are considering, I hope you will take the time to examine my resumé and will decide in my favor. I feel confident in my ability to be a productive contributor to the on-going success of Hopkins, Dodge, and Russell.

I would like to review three important facts that show I am the most qualified candidate for the position of Project Designer. First, I have seven years' experience with a full-service commercial design firm, where my responsibilities involved all areas of a design project from programming through contract administration. Second, my experience and knowledge of AutoCAD 14, 2000, and PowerPoint allow me to contribute immediately to your firm. Third, since I am already NCIDQ certified, you will be hiring a designer who will easily be licensed in Nevada.

Should you need any further information, I will be happy to provide it. I look forward to your positive response to my application at the end of the week, when you conclude your remaining interviews. Thank you again for your time and consideration.

Sincerely,

Marilyn Norton

FIGURE 34-1.

A sample follow-up thank-you letter that would be sent after a job interview.

THE FIRST JOB

The last semester of school can be a nerve-wracking time for students. It is when their classes in their major seem to be the most difficult at the same time that they are busily putting together their portfolios and resumés for jobs or internships. As graduation looms, they realize that friendships nurtured over the past few years will change or fade as they and their friends go in different directions and possibly end up on opposite sides of the country. The transition from student to professional is not easy for most individuals.

A great way to make the transition from student to practitioner is an internship at the end of the senior (or last) year. Almost all interior design curriculums today require or at least recommend that students include an internship as part of their major. Some schools suggest the internship between the junior and senior year; others at the end of the senior year. When to do an internship is a matter of school policy and personal preference. There are advantages for either time. Concerning transitions, the timing of an internship at the end of the course work is great because you are then ready to go to work—something that might happen at the internship location.

These internships help students see how all the course work that they have taken relate to the work done "in the real world." In addition, internships provide students some work experience that they can include on their resumé. Of course, the internship experience is different for everyone. However, the point is to get the most from the internship. You should have had something to do with arranging it, and you should discuss your responsibilities with the employer. The focus should not be on whether you are being paid or not; the focus should be on what you will learn. You must remember that you will only get out of the experience what you are willing to put into it. So, if you sit back and wait for someone to teach you something during your internship, you will probably be very disappointed with your experience. You may even have earned a poor recommendation from the employer.

Your first job is important, because it becomes the groundwork for your career. This is not to say that your first job represents what you will always do in interior design. If you ask any professional who has been working for 15 years or more about his or her career path, you will find that a career in interior design is never a straight path. It zigs and zags and even may throw you a few curves. I once had a student who always finished her commercial projects very quickly in comparison to everyone else in the class. I asked her about it one day, and she said, "I hate doing commercial projects so much, I just want to get it over with." Naturally, her first job was with a residential design firm. About a year later, she was visiting the school, and we got to talking. "Say, do you know of any commercial design firms that are hiring?" she asked. "I hate residential design!"

Your first job is also important for other reasons, for it is where you will learn to work in interior design. You will learn methods of pulling together design projects that you never heard of in school, not because your professors didn't know them, but because each designer and each design firm has different ways of working. You will begin to make business and industry contacts as you socialize with professionals in your area. Attending and participating in professional associations will help, since you will be able to network with designers of all levels of experience. You also will learn how to dress, how to "talk," and how to act like an interior design professional. Most likely, that first job will help you build your confidence as a designer.

Because it is your first job, do not be cavalier about the experience. Most of you will learn very quickly that you must park your egos at the door, because you will be directed, reprimanded, and pushed to learn from bosses, other designers, and even clients. This is not school, and this first job in interior design is probably not like any other job you have ever had. Just because you graduated from a wonderful, accredited school (or anywhere else, for that matter) does not mean that you know more than your boss. I have often told students, much to their chagrin, that now that they are graduating, they will begin to learn about work and how to do interior design. Here are a few truths about that first job:

- They really mean you are to be there at 8:00 A.M. every day.
- One hour for lunch means one hour.
- Talking to friends on the phone is not allowed.
- Many project decisions are made within minutes, not days and weeks.
- Reading magazines because you have "nothing to do" is not a positive task.
- You can't take every Friday off to meet up with friends for a long weekend.
- The boss is always right even when he or she is wrong.
- December 24th is not a holiday.
- You will get criticized in front of others, and it will not feel pleasant.
- The boss will probably not give you positive feedback all the time—get over it.

Of course, the comments above are truthful and maybe a little harsh as well. The work environment is not school, and your time is not your own but the company's. Maybe you will be lucky and have a boss that mentors and congratulates more than criticizes. Those really hard instructors are that way for a reason, because interior design is a demanding, sometimes high-stress, time-sensitive profession whether you are just starting or own the company.

Don't be afraid to ask questions. The only dumb question is the one you don't ask. You are not expected to know everything. Keep your eyes and ears open, ask to be involved, ask questions, and your colleagues will start giving you more responsibility. Table 34-2 lists a few suggestions about how you can prepare yourself for the transition between student and professional. I am sure your professors will have others.

A few years ago when I was on a sabbatical, I spoke to many interior designers about their expectations of the entry-level employee. A few of the comments they made—in no particular order—were as follows: be punctual, reliable, accurate, detail oriented, able to communicate verbally, a team player, well organized, disciplined, and motivated. I also asked these same professionals to describe the ideal employee. Probably the best answer was, "Someone who wants my job." Think like the owner. Consider his or her problems as a designer and a businessperson. Aspire to learn all you can about the business, and there will likely be no end to your success.

MAKING A CAREER CHANGE

Grace had been working in interior design for several years specializing in residential. About six months ago, a relative had been injured in an accident and needed to be in a wheelchair. Grace had assisted this relative in making some modifications to the home, since it was likely he would remain in a wheelchair or need a walker for the rest of his life. Through this experience and since her

TABLE 34-2.

Suggestions to Assist Students as They Make the Transition from Student to Professional.

- Talk to professionals who are doing the work you want to do. People love to talk about what they do and their work. Make appointments and come prepared with about 15 good questions to ask that will help you find out what it is like to work at a particular kind of company or in a particular type of design specialty.
- Examine your motives and establish goals. Set goals that interest you. Think about what you want to do two, five, or ten years from now.
- Get involved with a professional association. Visit chapter meetings of the different organizations in your area. Students are always welcome. When you are sure about which one(s) you want to join, get involved. Volunteer for committees. It is a great way to get to know people in the business.
- Begin to be a professional. One or two days a week—maybe for studio classes—dress professionally, as if you were going to the office. Get used to being dressed up. You will also likely feel more confident on those days.
- Begin to work like a professional. Use a time management system of some kind. Treat the school day as a workday; that is, start the day at 8 and work until 5.
- On your internship:
  Don't play the critic. You are there to learn, not to criticize the company.
  Don't be lazy or blasé. If you want a good recommendation from this company, cheerfully complete all assigned tasks. Look for things to do or to help out as well.
  Ask questions. They expect you to ask questions.
  If you want to work for this company, show that you want to be there by doing all that is asked and then some.
  When you have nothing to do, look for or ask for something to do. Straighten catalogs or review samples and catalogs. There is a lot to learn about current products by cleaning up the library from time to time.

mother was now unhappily in an assisted-living facility, Grace is deciding to focus attention on remodeling and design of residences for individuals who have experienced a traumatic injury, as well as aging-in-place design.

Will has worked in commercial interior design for eight years, mostly at an office furnishings dealership that worked with a lot of hospitals. Although his income has increased over these years, he has become dissatisfied as he sees the sales associates earning large incomes off the work that he designs. Will is considering making a switch from interior design to sales.

At some point, many interior design professionals—like these two examples based on real people—start thinking about making a career change. I have encountered numerous senior designers who have considered leaving a full-time practice in order to enter the teaching field. Other designers seek the possibilities of additional income by obtaining positions as sales reps with manufacturers and vendors. Some have successfully added a retail showroom to their practice, selling accessories and merchandise to walk-in traffic. And, frankly, some leave the profession to do something else.

Interior design, as has been pointed out many times in this text, can be a fun way to make a living. It is also, to many, a stressful type of work. The competitive nature of the profession often sees clients wanting interior designers to work "cheaper, better, faster." Or they see how it is portrayed on television and don't understand why it takes so long and costs so much. What this means is that there will be increasing pressure on design firms to provide a more comprehensive scope of services at a lower fee. There is a great deal of competition today in the interior design industry in most cities, and clients sometimes give no extra consideration to one design firm over another. Too many interior designers have been too busy with work to consider how they should differentiate themselves from the competition—until work suddenly disappears.

Many clients want the work to be done for less money, yet they also expect it to be perfect—no errors, no omissions, no problems, no excuses. There is also a segment of the high-end client group that cares less for what it costs but more for it to also be perfect. This is probably one of the big reasons that CAD and computer project management is used so prevalently—as long as the designer has entered certain data correctly, the drawings and documents will always be correct. If something goes wrong, clients today are more willing to threaten lawsuits, file ethics complaints, or simply not pay for the work.

Finally, interior design work has to be done faster in many cases. Once clients get their funding, they do not want to lose the interest rate on their mortgage, whether it is for a house or a commercial development. "I sent you an e-mail this morning. Why didn't you get back to me right away!" scream clients. Deep down inside, they may realize that you have other clients, but many of them really do not care. They feel that they are the only important clients. With the ability for communication to be instantaneous, clients now have come to believe that interior design solutions and specifications can be done more quickly as well.

What does all this mean in terms of making career changes? Many senior interior designers "burn out" from working 12-hour days, 6 days a week to just keep up. Some wake up one morning realizing they have been doing this work for 15 or 20 years and they haven't really saved enough to have a good retirement. The long hours do take their toll whether you work for someone else or have your own business.

One day you may find that your current job does not suit your needs anymore. "You can come up with a million (untrue) reasons why you can't leave a situation you dislike. But when you deny reality (or the depth of your unhappiness), it has a way of catching up with you."[2] Before you cut the cord and quit your job or close your studio, you best think about what it is you still want to do and why you think you are dissatisfied. Lots of jobs require long hours. Lots of jobs will be stressful. And in lots of jobs you will have to work with (in some way or another) difficult people.

Look at the job you have, and perhaps talk with someone you trust who can help you see if the current situation isn't really awful but needs to be fine-tuned. If you work for someone else, discuss changes in your responsibilities within the company. Think about whether options like a marketing emphasis rather than strictly design solution planning can work in the current job, and then talk to the boss about how you could do this. When it's your own business, make contact with a business coach who can help you find new options for your business efforts.

If you are unhappy and think you want a totally new direction, you may need to go all the way back to books like Robert Bolles' *What Color Is Your Parachute?* in order to clarify interests. Something simple and quick is to answer the questions in Table 34-3. They don't make you investigate the whole of the situation, but they can get you headed in a direction. There are, of course, other books that are addressed to the mid-career individual that might be of help.

Part of the evaluation and decision process is to talk to someone who knows you well and who will keep your confidence as you contemplate making a career change. If it is going to be something dramatic, such as moving from a design/planning position to one in sales, talk to people who already are working in that position, especially those who have been designers before. They can help you understand what it is like to make a transition and problems with making a career change.

When you are sure about your new career path, make sure that you can afford to make the change. For example, senior designers who want to go into full-time teaching careers are often shocked to learn about the salary differentials. They also may not have the academic credentials necessary for seeking a

TABLE 34-3.

Questions When Contemplating a Job or Career Change.

- What is scariest about changing careers?
- List three to five reasons why you want to leave your present job.
- List three to five reasons why you should stay in your present job.
- What was the reason—the last straw—that helped you decide to leave?
- Did you regret leaving a previous job?
- Do you wish that you had left that other job (or this one) sooner?
- Is there a particular circumstance that would convince you to stay?
- If you leave, how will you support yourself during a transition should you be fired during the job search?
- If you leave, are you really acting in your own best interests?
- Why do you think it is time to make a total career change?
- What will you be looking for in a new career that the current one does not provide?
- Are you prepared for a major difference in income if you embark on a totally new career?
- Do you have a plan for your future related to making a career change?

full-time teaching position. Do not burn your bridges. Walking in and quitting one day without giving notice and with projects unfinished will cause a lot of problems for the company and yourself, since the company may not be very willing to give you a recommendation, assuming you may need it.

Remember that finding a new job, especially in a different field, will take time. Figuring out for sure what it is you want to do and where you want to do it is just the start. How might this impact your family? When are you going to find time to obtain credentials, such as a master's degree, if you want to teach? When are you going to be able to interview without the boss finding out?

Once you know what you are going to do, give ample notice, say thank you for the experience of working there, and say good-bye gracefully. And remember, for most of you, Thomas Wolfe was right—you can't go home again. What this means is that it is unlikely you will want to return to your old position and it is also unlikely they will want you back. So think carefully when making a change.

SUMMARY

Landing a job that is challenging and exciting and that pays reasonably is a time-consuming task. Whether you are a student seeking that first position of consequence in the profession or a professional with years of experience looking for some kind of change, going out into the job market is not something that is done cavalierly. Besides, you wouldn't have gone through all the preparation and work of determining what kind of position you want, refining your portfolio, and developing a dynamite resumé if you were only half-heartedly interested in a good position.

It's important to point out that the real point of the job search is to land a job that brings as much satisfaction as possible. It truly is not about money alone, as work in this creative career does not lead to high incomes—well, not for most of us! Even though it has been said numerous times in this book, one more time will not hurt.

Interior design is an exciting and challenging way to work and a career to take pride in being a part. The profession keeps changing, and you will probably find yourself changing along with it. You don't have to settle for less than you can do or less than you are worth, but you might need to be realistic until you have proven yourself to employers and clients. Applying your interests in the profession to the job search, the time you spend during interviews, and the first few weeks, months, and, yes, years on the job will bring fulfillment.

I used to design clothes for paper dolls as a kid. My mother was a dressmaker and my father was a tool and die maker. So I guess that meant that somehow I was destined to be involved in the creative world somehow. I have enjoyed being involved in the interior design profession very much. The profession means a great deal to me. That's why I have spent so many years teaching others about the professional practice of interior design.

REFERENCES

1. Lewin, 1996, p. 46.
2. Hirsch, 1996, p. 149.

NCIDQ DEFINITION OF INTERIOR DESIGN

National Council for
Interior Design Qualification

Interior design is a multifaceted profession in which creative and technical solutions are applied within a structure to achieve a built interior environment. These solutions are functional, enhance the quality of life and culture of the occupants, and are aesthetically attractive. Designs are created in response to and coordinated with the building shell, and acknowledge the physical location and social context of the project. Designs must adhere to code and regulatory requirements, and encourage the principles of environmental sustainability. The interior design process follows a systematic and coordinated methodology, including research, analysis, and integration of knowledge into the creative process, whereby the needs and resources of the client are satisfied to produce an interior space that fulfills the project goals.

Interior design includes a scope of services performed by a professional design practitioner, qualified by means of education, experience, and examination, to protect and enhance the life, health, safety, and welfare of the public. These services may include any or all of the following tasks:

- Research and analysis of the client's goals and requirements; and development of documents, drawings, and diagrams that outline those needs

- Formulation of preliminary space plans and two- and three-dimensional design concept studies and sketches that integrate the client's program needs and are based on knowledge of the principles of interior design and theories of human behavior

- Confirmation that preliminary space plans and design concepts are safe, functional, aesthetically appropriate, and meet all public health, safety, and welfare requirements, including code, accessibility, environmental, and sustainability guidelines

- Selection of colors, materials, and finishes to appropriately convey the design concept, and to meet sociopsychological, functional, maintenance, life cycle performance, environmental, and safety requirements

- Selection and specification of furniture, fixtures, equipment, and millwork, including layout drawings and detailed product description; and provision of contract documentation to facilitate pricing, procurement, and installation of furniture

- Provision of project management services, including preparation of project budgets and schedules
- Preparation of construction documents, consisting of plans, elevations, details, and specifications, to illustrate nonstructural and/or nonseismic partition layouts, power and communications locations, reflected ceiling plans and lighting designs, materials and finishes, and furniture layouts
- Preparation of construction documents to adhere to regional building and fire codes, municipal codes, and any other jurisdictional statutes, regulations, and guidelines applicable to the interior space
- Coordination and collaboration with other allied design professionals who may be retained to provide consulting services, including but not limited to architects, structural, mechanical and electrical engineers, and various specialty consultants
- Confirmation that construction documents for non-structural and/or non-seismic construction are signed and sealed by the responsible interior designer, as applicable to jurisdictional requirements for filing with code enforcement officials; Administration of contract documents, bids, and negotiations as the client's agent
- Observation and reporting on the implementation of projects while in progress and upon completion, as a representative of and on behalf of the client; and conducting post-occupancy evaluation reports

Reprinted with permission from the National Council for Interior Design Qualification.

Acceptance.   In contract law, one person agrees exactly to the conditions in the contract set by the other party.

Accounts.   Financial entries with different names for clarification to show additions (increases) and subtractions (decreases) to the account.

Accounts payable.   Claims from suppliers for goods or services ordered (and possibly delivered) but not yet paid for.

Accounts receivable.   What others owe to the firm as a result of the sale of, or billing for, goods and services.

Accrual accounting.   An accounting method in which revenues and expenses are recognized at the time they are earned (in the case of revenues) or incurred (in the case of expenses), whether the revenue has actually been collected or the expenses actually have been paid.

Accrued expenses.   Expenses owed to others for a given time period but not yet paid; salary owed during an accounting period but not yet paid is an example.

Acknowledgments.   The paperwork forms that a supplier sends to a designer to indicate what the supplier interprets the designer's order to be; sometimes called confirmations.

Addenda or order updates.   Corrections or changes made to contract documents by the issuance of addenda (addendum is the singular form) and written by the person or firm responsible for the original set of contract documents.

Advertising.   Any kind of paid communication in media, such as newspapers, magazines, television, or radio.

Advertising allowance.   A special discount or other incentive given when a designer uses a manufacturer's product in promotions and advertising.

Agency relationship.   The common-law relationship that exists when one person or entity agrees to represent or do business for another person or entity. Today's employer–employee relationship is a reflection of the agency relationship.

Amortize.   Results from the concept that the value of intangible assets, such as copyrights, patents, and trademarks, are reduced; similar to depreciation.

Angel investor.   Entrepreneurs who want to see someone else succeed and may invest in a business such as interior design.

Arbitration.   When a disinterested third party evaluates the arguments of two parties to a contract.

As-built drawings.   Working drawings prepared after a project has been completed. They indicate exactly what has been built rather than what may have been shown in the construction drawings.

As is. Space is rented without any changes to the interior. Applies on many other situations where a good is sold in the condition it exists and not represented as new.

Assets. Any kind of resource—tangible or intangible—that a firm owns or controls and that can be measured in monetary terms.

Assignment. When rights in a contract are transferred to a party that was not originally part of the contract.

Assumption of risk. The plaintiff who knowingly and willingly enters into a risky situation cannot recover damages if harm or injury occurs.

Back orders. Items that a vendor cannot ship with other merchandise or are otherwise not available for some period of time.

Balance sheet. An accounting form that shows the financial position of a firm at a particular moment in time, including a statement of its assets and liabilities; sometimes called a statement of financial position.

Bar charts. A scheduling method consisting of a description of tasks required on the left-hand side and horizontal bars on the right-hand side showing the time in days, weeks, or months that is required to complete each task.

Barrier-free. Codes created and enforced to make public buildings more accessible to the handicapped.

Base bid. Refers to a proprietary specification that contains an "or equal" substitution allowance. All bidders must base their bids on the goods specified by product name.

Basis of the bargain. Information provided by a salesperson that is the primary influence on the buyer's decision to buy a product.

Benefits. Features of a product or a service that relate to the needs of the client.

Best and final offer (BAFO). When a project involves government or public agencies, a negotiation may include the necessity of a best offer.

Bid. An offer for the amount a person will pay to provide the required specified goods and/or services.

Bid bond. Required of all bidders to ensure that the designer or vendor who has been awarded a contract will sign the contract.

Bid form. Document prepared by the designer or the client and provided to the bidders. The bidders submit their prices for the goods or services on this form. Sometimes also called a tender form.

Bid opening. The time that the owner of a project reveals who has bid on the project. In most situations, the bid opening is private, and only the owner and the designer who is responsible for creating the contract documents are present. Governmental agencies and many public utilities are required to have bid openings open to the public. In this case, anyone may attend the bid opening and find out what others have bid for the project.

Billable hours. The number of hours that a designer works on projects under a contract for design fees. The fees can be charged by any method, if the client is actually being charged for the hours that the designer works.

Billing rate. A dollar amount, combining salary, benefits, overhead, and profit, that is used as the basis for charging clients for services; usually expressed as an hourly rate.

Bill of lading. The form that the supplier provides to the truck driver to show what is being shipped and who has title to the goods.

Bond forms. Legal documents used to oblige the designer or vendor to the contract as assurance that the designer or vendor will perform the requirements of the contract as agreed upon. Three common bond forms are the bid bond, the performance bond, and the labor and materials payment bond.

Bonus plan. Method of paying extra compensation based on the employee's producing more than a specified personal quota.

Box burns. Furniture damage caused when a shipping carton rubs against fabric or frame materials.

Breach of contract. Breach simply means "to break." A breach occurs when one of the parties of a contract does not perform his or her duties as spelled out in the terms of the contract.

Branding. The combination of images and encounters the customer perceives, accepts, and experiences with a product. It is not just a logo on a business card.

Break-even point. The point at which revenues equal expenses. At this point, the firm is neither making nor losing money.

Budgeting. Involves annual managerial goals expressed in specific quantitative, usually monetary, terms. Budgeting encourages the manager to plan for the various events affecting the firm rather than to react to them.

Building codes. Regulations that primarily concern structural and mechanical features of buildings.

Build-out. An industry term for the construction process.

Build-out allowance. Landlord provides a dollar amount per square foot to build partitions and to install basic mechanical systems such as lighting fixtures and architectural finishes.

Building permit. A permit granted by local governmental agencies that allows for the construction of a new building or major interior remodeling.

Building standard work letter. This document outlines what quantity and quality of work will be undertaken by the developer in the construction of a tenant's office or other commercial space.

Buyer. A person who contracts to purchase or who does purchase some goods.

Buying a job. A practice in which a firm prices goods or services at an unusually low rate in order to make the sale.

Capital construction. The cost for actually building the structural components; also referred to as capital improvements.

Career objective. A statement that explains what kind of work the job applicant seeks. It generally is used in the resumé and/or cover letter.

Career summary. In a resumé, a significant summary statement of experiences and skills concerning the applicant's ability to handle the job for which the applicant is applying.

Case study. A marketing tool that tells what the design program was for a particular client and discusses some unique features of the project.

Cash. The cash on hand in the firm's bank accounts, checking accounts, cash registers, or petty cash boxes; considered a current asset.

Cash accounting. The accounting method whereby revenue and expense items are recognized in the time period in which the firm actually receives the cash or actually pays the bills.

Cash discount. An accounting term referring to an extra discount given when a designer or design firm pays an invoice promptly. A notation that commonly looks like "2/10 net 30" appears on the invoice to notify the designer or design firm of the cash discount.

Certificate for payment. A form that tells the client that the supplier has completed parts of, or most of, the work and that the supplier has sent an invoice for that work. This certificate recommends that the client pay the supplier for the invoice.

Certificate of occupancy (CO). A certificate provided by the local building department after the construction of a building has been completed, which means that the owner may now legally occupy the building.

Certificate of substantial completion. A form that reports what has been done and indicates if something is missing concerning the construction of the structural elements.

Certification. A term most frequently associated with legislation that defines who may use a certain title. Also might be called registration.

Certified public accountant. An individual who has met educational and testing requirements established by the jurisdiction in the accounting profession.

Chain of command. The formal reporting links that exist between one level of employee and another; this helps everyone in the organization understand what the formal communication patterns are.

Change order. Written permission or instructions concerning any aspect of a project that modify design concepts, construction designs, or product specifications.

Chart of accounts. A list of all the accounts that a firm is using.

Chronological resumé. States educational and work experiences exactly when they occurred, in reverse chronological order.

Close corporation. A corporation whose shares of stock are commonly held by only a few individuals. The stock is not traded on any of the public stock markets; also called family corporation or closely held corporation.

Closed competitive selection. Occurs when an acceptable list of potential bidders receive notifications of impending bids and are allowed to bid on a project.

Closed probe. A sales technique in which the designer asks the client a question that generally results in a closed response from the client such as "yes" or "no."

Closed specification. A bid specification that is written for a product such that another product cannot be substituted for what is being specified.

Closing. The art of knowing when to ask for the sale.

Codes. Systematic bodies of law created by federal, state, and local jurisdictions to ensure the safety of the public.

Cold calling. When a designer contacts potential clients whom he or she has never met before.

Collateral. Money or property that is pledged in case a loan is not paid. The loan giver takes the collateral if the person who takes out the loan defaults.

Collateral materials. Marketing publications such as brochures, flyers, calendars, and inserts that can be used as sales materials.

Combination resumé. Utilizes qualities of both the chronological and the functional resumé and combines them in one resumé.

Commercial interior design. The branch of interior design concerned with the planning and specifying of interior products used in public spaces, such as offices, hotels, airports, hospitals, and so on; sometimes called contract interior design because it involves a contract for services.

Commission. A method by which an agent acting on behalf of the employer is paid; usually a percentage amount paid to the agent (interior designer), calculated on the agent's sale of goods and/or services.

Compensation. The method of paying an employee for work performed.

Compensatory time. Time off given salaried employees during the normal work week to make up for the overtime hours they have worked.

Competitive bidding. A process whereby the client has an opportunity to obtain comparative prices from a number of contractors and/or vendors for the construction or supply of the project.

Concealed damage. Damage to goods that is not obvious because the original packaging is not damaged. Most often occurs when items are shipped in cartons.

Conditions, covenants, and restrictions (CCRs). Specific regulations for condominiums, townhouses, and some other types of residences in planned communities. If a community has CCRs, it might not allow a home-based business to operate in the community.

Confirmation of purchase. The business form that spells out what goods the designer has agreed to order or sell to the client; also called a sales agreement, purchase agreement, or contract proposal.

Conflict of interest. Occurs when a person puts his or her self-interests before his or her public or fiduciary responsibilities.

Conforming goods. The delivered goods as described in the sales agreement.

Consideration. The "price" one pays to another party for fulfilling a contract.

Construction documents. All of the working drawings, schedules, and specifications that describe what is required for the completion of a project.

Construction drawings. The typical plans, elevations, and details required for building a structure or an interior.

Construction manager. An individual who oversees the construction project as an agent for either the general contractor or the owner.

Continuing-education unit (CEU). Short-term course work in a wide variety of topical interest of a professional nature.

Contract administration phase. The fifth phase of a design project, in which the project is actually constructed and orders for goods are issued and installed.

Contract. A promise or agreement made between two or more parties for the performing or not performing of some act. The performance or lack of performance of this act can be enforced by the courts.

Contract administration phase. The portion of a project that involves actual construction work as well as the placing of orders for all the items required; also called the construction and installation phase.

Contract documents. All the drawings and specifications that together describe what is required for a project, along with contracts or agreements between the project owner and the designer and other stakeholders.

Contract documents phase. The fourth phase of the design project; it involves the final preparation of all construction or working drawings (sometimes referred to as CDs), schedules, and specifications that are required to build and install the design project.

Contributory negligence. In this defense of negligence, it must be shown that both sides have been negligent and that injury has resulted.

Contractual capacity. Each party to a contract must have the legal capacity to enter into a contract.

Control function. A management function that requires that a manager monitor the activities of the firm and take any necessary steps to ensure that the plans, policies, and decisions of the manager and the firm are being carried out.

Conversion. When the rightful property of one person is taken by another, a tort has been committed; can also be a crime of theft.

Co-op advertising. When a manufacturer and designer generally share in the cost of the advertising, or the manufacturer provides an incentive to the designer to sell the particular product being advertised.

Copyright. The method of legally protecting, for a specified period of time, written materials and graphic designs.

Copyright notification. In order to begin the legal protection of written materials and graphic designs, the following must appear in a conspicuous place on the work: (1) "Copyright," "COPR," for copyright,or the copyright symbol ©, (2) year of publication, and (3) the name of the copyright claimant.

Corporation. An association of individuals created by statutory requirements, which is a legal entity. The corporation has existence independent of its originators or any other member or stockholder. It can sue and be sued by others, enter into contracts, commit crimes, and be punished. A corporation has powers and duties distinct from any of its members and survives even after the death of any or all of its stockholders.

Cost-of-living adjustment (COLA). An across-the-board compensation increase meant to offset inflation.

Cost of sales. Refers to the costs paid in the direct generation of revenues. Called cost of goods sold in retail sales businesses; in this case, it refers to changes in inventory.

Cost plus percentage markup. A design fee method that allows the design firm to add a specific percentage to the net cost of the merchandise being purchased by a client.

Cost price. The price that the designer must pay for the goods.

Counter offer. An agreement to the offer in which the terms of the offer have been changed.

Credit. In accounting, the right-hand side of an account.

Crime. When a person (or a business, in the case of a corporation) commits a wrong against society that is regulated by statute.

Critical path method (CPM). A scheduling method that begins by identifying the interrelationships of the tasks to be performed. This analysis shows the designer which tasks must be done before the next or other tasks can be performed, thus establishing the critical path.

Current assets. Resources that the firm would normally convert to cash in less than one year.

Customer's own material (COM). When a designer uses a fabric on a specially ordered, upholstered furniture item that is different from one of the fabrics available from the furniture manufacturer.

Cutting for approval (CFA). A request for a sample of a current dye lot of textiles, wall covering, or other finish to be approved by designer before order is finalized.

Debit. In accounting, the left-hand side of an account.

Debt capital. Business loans that come from creditors, such as commercial banks.

Decision making. The act of making reasonable choices between available alternatives; an important part of the management function.

Deep discounting. An extremely large discount from the suggested retail price that is given to a designer or a design firm when placing very large orders.

Defamation. The wrongful harming of a person's good reputation. If the defamation is in writing, it is called libel; if it is oral, it is called slander.

Deferred revenues. Revenues received for services that have not yet been rendered or the sale of goods that have not yet been delivered.

Delegation. When one person gives his or her responsibilities to another.

Deliverables. Documents and presentation materials that must be prepared to explain design concepts that are given to the client.

Delivery. Includes the activities concerned with moving tangible items from the showroom or warehouse to the job site and placing them in their correct locations.

Demising wall. A partition that divides one tenant space from another. Each tenant pays for one-half the thickness of the wall.

Deposit. Money that is part of the purchase price, prepaid by the buyer as security in contracts for the sale of goods or real estate.

Depreciation. Results from the concept that capital equipment has a limited, useful life. It is intended to express the usage of a fixed asset in the firm's pursuit of revenue.

Descriptive specification. Describes, often in elaborate detail, the materials, workmanship, fabrication methods, and installation of the required goods.

Design development phase. Involves final design decisions for plans, specifications, and preparation of final presentation documents.

Destination contract. A manufacturer retains title of goods until they are delivered to the buyer's delivery address; also referred to as FOB destination.

Direct labor. The time employees spend directly involved in the generation of firm revenues.

Direct personnel expense (DPE). A number that includes not only the salary of employees but also any cost of benefits, such as unemployment taxes, medical insurance, and paid holidays.

Discounting. A reduction, usually stated as a percentage, from the suggested retail price. A full or normal discount from suggested retail is 50 percent.

Doing business as (DBA). A filing required when the name of the business is other than the names of the owners.

Domestic corporation. A corporation formed in one state and doing business only in that state. Domestic corporations are also corporations formed within the United States.

Door-to-door. The client is charged from the time the designer or the delivery truck leaves the designer's studio or warehouse loading dock to the time it leaves the client's location.

Double dipping. A slang term sometimes used by clients who earn revenue from the design and specification of the products and also from selling the merchandise.

Double-entry system. An accounting system using information in the accounting journals and ledgers and in which the accounts are based on the entries found in both the income statement and the balance sheet.

Down payment. A portion of the total selling price paid at the time goods are ordered.

Drawings. In accounting, the withdrawals from the profits of a business by owners in proprietorships and partnerships.

Drop ship. When the designer requests that a manufacturer ship goods to an address other than the designer's business location or warehouse.

80/20 Rule. A business rule used in many situations. From a list of ten items arranged in the order of importance, if one accomplishes only the two most important items, one achieves 80 percent of the total value of time spent.

Electronic signature. A signature on an e-mail, faxed letter, of agreement, or other electronic means.

Employee handbook. A concise reference of company policies for all employees.

Employer identification number (EIN). A number that identifies the business to the federal and state government.

Employment at will. The doctrine that an employee, who is not bound by a written contract and who has no written terms of his or her employment spelled out, has the right to quit his or her job without notice but can also be fired by the employer at any time, with no explanation.

Empowerment. Giving employees the opportunity and authority to carry out the activities of the company without prior approval of a supervisor or a manager.

End user. The ultimate consumer of goods or services; can also mean consumer.

Ensembliers. Shopkeepers and shops dealing with interior products; also called ateliers.

Entrepreneur. Someone who starts and manages his or her own business.

Equities. Claims on a balance sheet by outsiders and/or owners against the total assets of the firm.

Equity capital. Business funding that comes from investors, such as stockholders.

Errors and omissions coverage (E&O). Insurance that covers an interior designer in the event that he or she is responsible for errors or omissions for work performed or advice given to a client.

Ethical standards. What is right and wrong in relation to the professional behavior of the members and even the practice of a profession.

Exclusions. Portions of a competitive bid on which a vendor does not bid.

Expediter. An individual who is familiar with the design firm's paperwork system and the various ordering and shipping requirements of manufacturers. The expediter is responsible for the speedy processing of orders.

Expenses. The amount of outflows of resources of a firm as a consequence of the efforts made by the firm to earn revenues.

Express warranties.   Promises, claims, descriptions, or affirmations made about a product's performance, quality, or condition that form the "basis of the bargain."

Factory reps.   Manufacturer's representatives that work only for one particular manufacturer as employees of the company.

Feasibility studies.   In-depth estimates of planning and providing specifications for a project.

Features.   Descriptions of specific aspects or characteristics of a service or a product; used during selling.

FF&E (furniture, furnishings, and equipment).   Acronym for projects that have minimal or no construction work involved.

Fictitious business name.   A filing required when a business is operating under a name other than that of the owner(s).

Fiduciary duties.   An individual acts in a position of trust or confidence for someone else.

Financial accounting.   Concerned with day-to-day and periodic measurement and reporting of accounting information for use by individuals outside or inside the firm.

Financial management.   Act of planning and analyzing all the financial aspects of a firm in order to help owners manage and control the performance of the firm; often called managerial accounting.

Fire safety or life safety codes.   Regulations that provide a reasonable measure of safety in a building from fire, explosions, or other comparable emergencies.

Firm offer.   When a merchant makes an offer for the sale of goods in writing, whether or not any consideration has been given by a buyer.

Fixed assets.   Resources that are also called property, plant, and equipment, which are the long-lived items used by the firm.

Fixed-fee method.   Some dollar value determined by a designer for the performing of all the services required of a project. The client is then charged that amount, whether the project takes a shorter or longer time than the estimate; also called the flat-fee method or lump-sum method.

Fixture.   In tax terms, a product that could be considered personal property that has become affixed to a building, such as a mirror.

FOB, Destination.   When the manufacturer retains ownership of the goods, pays all shipping expense, and assumes all risks until the goods reach the destination.

FOB, Factory.   When the buyer assumes ownership or title of the goods when they are loaded on the truck at the factory. The buyer assumes the transportation expenses and all risks.

FOB, factory—freight prepaid.   The interior designer has ownership and responsibility for damages during transit, but the manufacturer pays the transportation charges to the destination.

Foreign corporation.   A corporation formed in one state but doing business in another state is referred to by the other state as a foreign corporation.

Four Ps of marketing.   The four basic variables (product, place, promotion, and price) that create a firm's marketing mix.

Fraud.   When someone intentionally misrepresents facts to deceive another party for personal gain.

Free on board (FOB).   When the shipper must assume the expense of loading the goods onto the truck as well as the expense and risk for shipping the goods to the FOB destination; also referred to as freight on board.

Freight bill.   The bill from the shipping company for moving goods from the supplier to the designer or the receiving location; it is a type of an invoice.

Fringe benefits.   Direct or indirect additional payments made to the employee for work performed. Benefits may include paid vacations, profit-sharing plans, and group health insurance.

Functional resumé.   Presents information in order to emphasize qualifications and skills of the applicant, rather than the order in which they were obtained.

General conditions.   Documents that set forth the legal responsibilities, procedures, rights, and duties of each party to a construction project; part of the bid documents.

General contractor.   Individual or company that holds a license to contract and supervise all phases of a construction project; often called the GC.

General partnership.   When two or more people join together for the purpose of forming a business; they alone share in the profits and risks of the business.

Goals.   Broad statements, without regard to any time limit, about what a firm wishes to achieve.

Goods.   Tangible items that have physical existence and can be moved.

Graphic image.   The package of materials that the interior design firm uses to identify itself. This includes the company logo, business cards, letterhead and other stationery, business forms, and drawing paper identification.

Gross margin.   The difference between revenues and cost of sales. Represents the amount of revenue available to cover overhead (selling and administrative) expenses.

Gross profit.   Another term for gross margin. Does not represent profit.

Gross revenue.   All the revenue, prior to any deductions, generated by the firm for a given accounting period.

Gross salary.   The amount of employee compensation before any deductions are taken.

Headhunters.   A term associated with professional executive search and employment agencies that will search out an employee from one firm in order to place the employee in another firm.

Hot button.   An issue that has critical importance to the client.

Hourly fee.   The most commonly charged fee; based on the firm's direct personnel expense. For each hour or portion of an hour that a designer works on a project, the client is charged some dollar amount.

Hourly wage.   A compensation method in which an employee is paid some dollar amount per hour for every hour worked.

HTML.   Stands for Hypertext Markup Language. It is the computer language source code used to develop World Wide Web sites.

Implied contract.   A contract formed by the actions of the parties rather than by an expressed written agreement.

Incentive compensation.   Compensation over and above regular compensation.

Income statement.   An accounting report that formally reports all the revenues and expenses of a firm for a stated period of time. The result shows the net income (or loss) for the firm during the period; also called a profit and loss statement.

Incorporate.   To create a corporation.

Incorporation.   The act or process of forming a corporation.

Independent contractor.   Someone who works for himself or herself and is not subject to the control of an employer.

Independent reps.   Manufacturer's representatives who work for themselves or a sales-representing group; they usually handle several manufacturers' products.

Inferior performance.   Work that varies quite considerably from what is required in a contract.

Informational interview.   An informal interview that allows a student to find out something about the work in a particular profession.

Infringement.   Any unauthorized use of copyrighted materials.

In lots.   Products for one order are transported from the manufacturer to the designer in partial shipments.

Installation.   The specialized part of the delivery process that involves assembly, construction, or physical attachments of products to the building.

Instructions to bidders.   A document that informs bidders how to prepare bids for submittal so that all submittals will be in the same form.

Intentional torts.   Torts that have occurred by a plaintiff on purpose and with knowledge that they were wrongful.

Invasion of privacy.   A legal harm against a person's right to freedom from others' prying eyes.

Inventory.   Goods purchased and held by the business for resale to clients.

Invitation to bid.   Summary of the project, the bid process, and other brief pertinent procedures for the project. It informs potential bidders of the project, its scope, and where to obtain further information; also called an advertisement for bids.

Invoice.   A bill that is sent from the manufacturer or supplier to the designer indicating how much the designer must pay. The designer also uses an invoice to bill the client for goods and/or services provided.

Jobbers.   Wholesalers who purchase smaller quantities of goods from manufacturers—usually a specific category of goods—and resell them to the trade.

Job description.   Communicates the qualifications, skills, and responsibilities of each job classification within a design firm.

Joint venture.   A temporary contractual association of two or more persons or firms in which they agree to share in the responsibilities, losses, and profits of a particular project or business venture.

Journal.   In accounting, a chronological record of all accounting transactions for a firm.

JPEG format.   In digital photography, a method of compressing the image. It creates a usable but not suitable for publication version of a photograph. Stands for Joint Photographic Experts Group.

Kinesics.   The scientific study of the meaning of body positions and gestures.

Labor and materials payment bond. Required of the winning bidder to guarantee that, should the designer or vendor default on the project, the designer or vendor would be responsible for paying for all of the materials and labor that have been contracted for.

Ledger. In accounting, the ledger is a group of accounts; often called a general ledger.

Letter of agreement. A simplified form of contract.

Letter of intent. A letter sent to the winning bidder allowing them to begin work on a project.

Letter of interest. A client sometimes requests letters and supplemental information on the qualifications of prospective design firms prior to the client submitting a request for proposal. Also called a request for qualifications (RFQ).

Liabilities. In accounting, amounts that the firm owes to others due to past transactions or events. Liabilities always have first claim on the firm's assets.

Libel. A wrongful harming of a person's good name through a written communication.

Licensing. A term most frequently associated with a state or province whose legislation defines who may practice interior design.

Lien. When someone other than the person who has ownership or possession of goods has a security interest in the goods.

Limited liability company. A type of business formation that is a hybrid of the general partnership and the corporation and that grants limited liability to its members.

Limited partnership. A business formation created according to statutory requirements. A limited partnership is formed with at least one general partner and one or more partners who are designated as limited partners.

Line item number. On a sales order, items are identified in numerical order. This number helps the firm cross-reference merchandise to purchase orders and other documents.

Line of credit. Short-term business loans that last for one year or less.

List price. Generally accepted as being the same as suggested retail price—a price to the consumer.

Logo. A symbolic image of a company or an organization; also called a mark.

Lump sum. A fee that will cover all the work and expenses required in the scope of services knowing that the fee cannot be increased beyond the fixed amount.

Management. The effective direction of staff members and financial resources under a manager's control toward goals and objectives that the owners of the firm have established.

Manufacturer's dealers. Retailers that feature selected products from a particular manufacturer in a showroom that is open to the public.

Manufacturer's suggested retail price (MSRP). A price established by the manufacturer. It is also called simply retail price.

Markdown. A term used in retail to represent discounts taken from the normal selling price.

Market. In reference to designer resources, a term that many interior designers use to mean they are going to visit one of the annual shows held at the marts.

Market centers.   Concentrations of trade sources in one area of a city.

Market growth.   The second stage of a business or product life cycle when sales of the product or business increases substantially, providing increased profits to the company.

Market maturity.   The third phase of business or product life cycle occurs when sales for the originating company fall off as competitors enter the market and siphon off sales.

Market segment.   A group of customers that has a common characteristic.

Marketing.   Includes all the activities of moving goods and services from producers to consumers.

Marketing analysis.   Involves gathering and analyzing data concerning such things as the abilities and interests of the staff, potential clients, the economy, and the competition in order that the owner and managers can make better plans and decisions about the direction of the firm's business efforts.

Marketing mix.   Operational elements that the design firm can control in the process of marketing and selling goods and services.

Markup.   A term used in retail to represent percentage amounts (converted to dollars) added to the net or cost price to the designer.

Mart.   A building in which many firms have separate showrooms or share showroom space.

Mechanic's lien.   A legal recourse related to the labor and materials payment bond. It is an action that prevents the owner of the property from giving or selling the property to anyone until the lien has been satisfied.

Merchant.   Anyone who is involved with the buying and/or selling of the kinds of goods with which he or she is dealing. A person acting in a mercantile capacity.

Merit pay.   An amount added to an individual's basic annual compensation amount, often for the reward of quality work done in the past.

Milestone charts.   An easy scheduling method whereby a designer outlines the activities required by the project and establishes a target date for the completion of each task.

Mirror image rule.   Unequivocal acceptance of the offer in a contractual situation.

Misrepresentation.   The altering of facts to deceive or the use of fraud for personal gain.

Mission statement.   A philosophical statement of what the firm sees as its role in a profession. It contains broad statements of what the firm wishes to achieve during an unspecified time period.

Mock-up.   A full-scale, usually nonfunctional, portion of a design project, such as a hotel guest room.

Modifications.   Additions or changes made to the contract documents (*see also* Addenda and Change order).

Moonlighting.   When an individual holds or engages in work outside his or her main job.

Movable equipment.   Items such as furniture, accessories, and equipment items that are not fixed to a building structure.

Move management.   A process to help a client get ready to move and the actual move from one location to another.

Multiple.   A billing rate based on a calculation of salary rate, expenses, and a profit margin.

Multiple discounts.   A series of discounts from the suggested retail price, given by manufacturers to designers for placing very large orders.

Mutual assent.   The giving of a contractual offer and acceptance of the offer must be done willingly.

Negligence.   A failure by one party to use due care, resulting in injury sustained by another person or a person's property.

Negotiating.   When two parties are trying to reach agreement about some point of discussion.

Net income (or loss).   The amount of income or loss that results when all expenses are subtracted from revenues. If the result is positive, net income represents the dollar amount of profit the firm has made for the given time period. If the result is negative, net loss indicates that expenses have exceeded revenues for the given time period.

Net price.   A price representing a 50 percent discount from suggested retail.

Networking.   Cultivating mutually beneficial relationships for the purpose of marketing oneself or one's design firm.

Niche.   A very specific or unique focus concerning services or products provided by a firm.

Nonconforming goods.   Any goods that are not as described in a sales order or a purchase order.

Not to exceed limit.   A fee "ceiling" in a design contract or predetermined limit to complete the project requirements.

Offer.   In contract law, one party makes an offer to provide something or do something for another party.

Offeree.   The person to whom an offer has been made in a contract negotiation.

Offeror.   The person who makes the offer in a contract negotiation.

Open competitive selection.   When clients, such as government agencies, advertise impending bids so that anyone who is interested in the project who meets the qualifications that are spelled out in the invitation to bid may submit a bid.

Open probe.   A sales technique in which the designer asks the client a question that generally results in an open response so that the client is encouraged to talk.

Open specification.   A bid specification written in such a way that many products can be substituted for the item being specified.

Operating funds.   Funds needed to keep the doors to the firm open and in business.

Ordinances.   Laws created by local governments such as those for zoning, building codes, and traffic issues.

Or equal.   A term in a specification that allows bidders to substitute what they believe to be products of equal quality to that which was specified.

Other assets.   Financial assets such as patents, copyrights, and investment securities in another firm.

Overhead expenses.   Those expenses that are incurred whether the firm produces any revenues or not; also called selling and administrative expenses.

Owner's equity.   The section on the balance sheet showing the amount the owners have invested in the firm.

Owner's representative.   Someone hired by the client to act in his or her behalf with the designer and others involved in a project.

Packing list.   A detailed list by quantity and description of what is being shipped to the designer from a manufacturer or a supplier. It is commonly placed in a plastic envelope attached to the outside of one of the items being shipped.

Pass through.   In accounting, when goods or services that are billed by the interior designer to the client or end user.

Patent.   An exclusive right to make, sell, and use a product for a specific period of time.

Percentage of merchandise and product services method.   A fee method that allows the designer to negotiate a percentage of profit on the cost of the goods and installation that will be involved in the project.

Percentage off retail method.   A fee method in which a percentage is determined and the dollar amount is subtracted from the retail price of the merchandise.

Per diem.   A dollar amount that is charged to the client to cover hotel, meals, and transportation costs when it is necessary for the designer to travel out of town in the interests of the project. It can also represent a day rate for services.

Performance.   In contract law, when each party does or provides what was agreed upon in the contract, performance has occurred. There are three types of performance: (1) complete, (2) substantial, and (3) inferior.

Performance bond.   Required of the winning bidder as a guarantee that the designer or vendor will complete the work as specified and will protect the client from any loss up to the amount of the bond as a result of the failure of the designer or vendor to perform according to the contract.

Performance evaluation.   Systematic evaluation of the positive and negative work efforts of an employee. It is used to review past performance in relation to agreed-upon responsibilities, which then forms the basis for salary increases, promotions, and/or retention.

Performance reports.   Consists primarily of financial or other numerical information to report information that will be of interest to the owners and managers of the design firm.

Performance specification.   A specification establishing product requirements based on exact performance criteria. These criteria must be based on qualitative or measurable statements.

Permitting privileges.   When a designer is allowed to submit plans to the building department of a jurisdiction to obtain a building permit.

Photo portfolio.   A collection of photographs, slides, or other photographic media that represents projects for which the designer was responsible; used as a promotional tool.

Plan check.   The act of a jurisdiction's building department's review of construction documents before issuing a building permit.

Plan review board.   A local governmental agency whose responsibility it is to review construction drawings prior to issuance of building permits.

Planning.   Involves research of capabilities and resources in order to provide direction for the firm.

Portfolio.   A visual presentation of what an individual can do as an interior designer.

Posting.   The transferring of a journal entry to the correct ledger account.

Postoccupancy evaluation (POE).   Site visit and project review that are conducted to evaluate the existence of any problems in the design and installation of a project.

Practice acts.   Guidelines established by legislation concerning what a person can or cannot do in the practice of a profession in a particular state. Individuals whose profession is guided by practice acts must register with a state board and meet exacting requirements.

Premium.   A product that has a logo, slogan, or other words or graphics printed on an object, such as a T-shirt or a coffee mug.

Prepaid expense.   The early payment of expenses in a period prior to their being required. The prepaid expense is an asset, since the value of the prepaid expense, not yet due, still has value to the owner.

Press release.   Information provided by the design firm or its representatives that might be of interest to the news media.

Prestige pricing.   Certain special products can be priced unusually high due to status or special aspects, like exceptional quality or materials, associated with the product.

Price.   Any kind of payment from a buyer to a seller, including money, goods, services, or real property.

Primary sources.   Information that provides specifics and comes from first-hand sources, such as a questionnaire.

Private, or general, corporation.   The most common type of corporation formed for private, profit-making interests.

Probing.   A selling technique for asking questions in order to uncover the needs of a client.

Procurement.   To obtain the goods and/or services needed for a design project.

Professional corporation.   A special form of corporation created by individuals in professions such as law, architecture, and accounting.

Professions.   Occupations with a recognized and accepted knowledge base, skills, and training.

Profit and loss (P&L) statement.   Another name for the income statement.

Pro forma.   Projected financial information, such as the pro forma income statement; it can also mean "in advance" and be associated with credit.

Programming-phase.   The information-gathering portion of an interior design project.

Progress reports.   Correspondence or verbal reports to the client so that the client is kept informed of the progress of the project and any problems.

Project closeout.   The point at which a project has reached the time for final inspection and for providing necessary documents to the client to bring the project to completion.

Project file.   File folders or notebooks in which the designer keeps all the pertinent data and paperwork related to a project in progress.

Project management.   A process of organizing and controlling an interior design project from beginning to end in order to satisfactorily solve a client's problems and provide a reasonable profit to the design firm.

Project manager.   Individual who is responsible for making site visits and telephone calls in order to keep a project on track; also the job title for a designer who has overall responsibility for all phases of a design project.

Promotion.   Providing information about services or products from the seller to the buyer; includes publicity, publishing, advertising, and direct selling.

Proposal.   An overview or other response to a request for a proposal (RFP) from a client. It is not necessarily a contract. Some designers use the term proposal to mean a contract, however.

Proprietary information.   Information, graphics, or other property that belongs to a particular person or firm.

Proprietary specification.   This specification names products by the manufacturer's name, model number, and/or part number.

Prospecting.   The process of locating new clients and obtaining appointments with them.

Prospects.   Potential clients in a firm's business area.

Proximate cause.   A legal term that connects unreasonable conduct of a designer (or others) to harm that is caused by that conduct.

Publication.   When the creator of a copyrightable work has somehow distributed the work to others for review without restricting its use.

Publicity.   A direct form of promotion that is not paid for.

Public corporation.   Those formed by some government agency for the benefit of the public. The U.S. Postal Service is an example of a public corporation.

Public relations.   All the efforts of a firm that go into creating an image of the firm in order to positively affect the public's opinion of the firm.

Puffing.   A salesperson's statements of opinion, not facts, about a product.

Punch list.   A list that records in detail everything that must be taken care of in order for a project's installation to be completed; also called the site inspection report.

Punitive damages.   Compensation in a tort case or breach of contract; given in order to punish the guilty party because the harm is grievous.

Purchase order.   The business form that a designer uses to order goods and/or services for the client or to order supplies needed by the design firm.

Qualifying.   A term associated with determining whether or not a potential client is really worth pursuing as a prospective client.

Quantity discount.   A discount greater than the normal 50 percent discount, given because a large quantity of merchandise has been purchased at one time.

Quid pro quo.   Latin for "something for something." It is associated with the most commonly understood type of sexual harassment.

Record drawings.   The set of drawings kept at the job site on which any changes made to the building are recorded. These later will be used to create the as-built drawings.

Red lining.   Notes or corrections made in red pencil or other media that call attention to problems or errors on drawings that a jurisdiction checks before issuing a building permit.

Reference specification.   An established standard such as the standards of the American Society for Testing and Materials (ASTM) and the American National Standards Institute (ANSI), rather than written, detailed descriptions or performance criteria for required products.

Referral. Occurs when a client (or other party) tells another person who may be looking for interior design services about a particular design firm.

Reimbursable expenses. Costs that are not part of the design contract but that are incurred in the interest of completing the project. Sometimes referred to as disbursements.

Representatives, or reps. The men and women who act as the informational source to the interior designer about various manufacturers' products. Independent reps work for themselves and are usually responsible for many different manufacturers' products. Factory reps work for only one manufacturer as an employee.

Request for proposal (RFP). A document used by clients to obtain specific information about a large number of design firms that may be interested in providing design services for a project.

Request for qualifications (RFQ). A document used by clients to obtain information on the staff and general qualifications of a design firm prior to a request for proposal mailing. It is also called a letter of interest (LOI).

Resale license. A license required by most state and local jurisdictions when a business sells merchandise to the consumer. Also called a seller's permit.

Residential interior design. The plans and/or specifications of interior materials and products that are used in private residences.

Restocking charge. A fee charged by the designer for taking back merchandise that the client has ordered but does not want.

Restrictive covenant. In an employment contract, a provision that does not allow an employee to work for a competitor; also called a noncompete agreement.

Resumé. A summary of a designer's qualifications.

Retail method. A fee method in which the design fee is derived by charging the retail or suggested retail price for goods sold to clients.

Retail price. Generally means the same thing as suggested retail price; the price quoted to the consumer.

Retainage. Money held back by the client to ensure that all the work, omissions, and problems associated with the project are taken care of.

Retained earnings. The claim on the assets arising from the cumulative, undistributed earnings of the corporation for use in the business after dividends are paid to stockholders.

Retainer. Payments to a professional to cover future service or advice by that professional. In interior design, the retainer is customarily paid at the signing of the contractual agreement.

Rentable area. The total amount of space required by the tenant on which the rent dollar amount (usually by the square foot) will be calculated.

Revenue. The amount of inflows from the sale of goods or rendering of services during an accounting period.

Right of refusal. After a contract has been signed, a buyer has 72 hours to refuse the purchase of goods or services; in many jurisdictions the right of refusal only applies to contracts signed in a residence.

S corporation. A special form of corporation that utilizes many of the benefits of a corporation but that pays taxes as a partnership; formally called a subchapter S corporation.

Sale.   Occurs when the seller transfers title or ownership of the goods to a buyer and the buyer has provided some consideration to the seller.

Schedule.   A tabular chart or graphic that is used to clarify sizes, location, finishes, and other information related to certain nonconstruction parts of an interior or structure. Schedules are commonly prepared for doors, windows, and interior room finishes.

Schematic design phase.   The phase of the design project in which preliminary design decisions and documents are prepared.

Scope creep.   Can signify project requirements that become larger than originally intended due to client requests.

Seasonal discount.   A special discount given to retailers to purchase certain goods earlier than normal. The goods are generally associated with a season or a holiday.

Secondary sources.   Information that generally comes from existing materials, such as a magazine or newspaper article.

Secondary subcontractor.   A subcontractor hired by another subcontractor to provide a portion of the work required of the first subcontractor.

Secured loan.   A loan for which collateral is required as protection against nonpayment.

Self-employment tax.   A tax required of self-employed individuals on income earned.

Seller.   Any person who sells or contracts to sell goods to others.

Selling.   Finding out what a client wants through the use of personal communication and then providing it.

Selling price.   Refers to the actual price that is quoted to the client.

Sexual harassment.   Unwelcome sexual advances or requests for sexual favors from a supervisor directed at an employee in order for the employee to be hired or promoted, or to otherwise influence the work performance of the employee.

Shipping contract.   When the title to goods passes to the buyer at the time the goods are placed on the truck, which is located at the manufacturer's factory. Also referred to as FOB, Factory.

Shop right.   The employer holds a nonexclusive license to any creation or invention of tangible products an employee designs that are a part of the employee's normal working duties.

Short list.   A small number of interior designers or design firms that are selected from a larger group and that have been selected by a client for a presentation in order to negotiate a contract for design services.

Single-entry system.   A simple bookkeeping system that is based on the income statement and includes business income and expense accounts.

Single source of contact.   One particular individual who has the authority to make decisions regarding a project for the design firm as well as the client.

Single-source purchasing.   When the client purchases goods from only one vendor. This term is most often used in commercial interior design.

Slander.   The wrongful harming of a person's good reputation through oral communication.

Sole proprietorship.   The simplest and least expensive form of business. The company and individual owner are one and the same.

Specifications.   The written instructions to contractors and vendors concerning the materials and methods of construction or the interior products that are to be bid on a project.

Specific performance.   A type of remedy related to breach of contract that a court requires. The breaching party is ordered to perform the specific, breached terms of the contract.

Square-foot method.   A method of calculating fees whereby the designer determines a rate per square foot and multiplies it by the amount of square footage of the project.

Stakeholders.   All the parties to a project who have a vested interest in the completion of the project, such as the client, interior designer, architect, and vendors.

Statement of cash flow.   An accounting statement reporting, for a specific period, the changes in cash flows from operating, investing, and financing activities.

Statute of frauds.   Statutory requirements that call for written contracts in certain circumstances. For the interior designer, these include a contract for the sale of goods that have a value over $500 to $5000 (depending on the jurisdiction), any contract that will take more than one year to complete, and any sale of real estate.

Statutory law.   Types of laws created by governmental entities such as the U.S. Congress and state legislatures.

Stocking dealer.   A vendor that stocks a certain inventory level of goods at all times. These sellers and designers often receive larger discounts because of the volume of products they carry.

Straight salary.   A fixed amount of salary paid to an employee no matter how many hours in the week he or she works.

Strategic planning.   A process for creating a specific written vision for a firm and for the future of that firm.

Strategies.   Specific actions that are part of a business or marketing plan for which definite time limits within the year have been set for completing them.

Strict liability.   When a seller is held liable for injury to others, resulting from a product's defects, regardless of fault.

Subcontractor.   An individual or company that is licensed to contract and perform specialized work on an interiors or construction project; also called a sub.

Submittals.   Materials, drawings, or documents that may need to be provided by the vendor to the designer or contractor for approval.

Substantial completion.   Contract performance that cannot vary greatly from what has been spelled out in the contract.

Suggested retail price.   A term related to the price, to be used by the seller and suggested by the manufacturer.

SWOT.   A planning analysis technique used by firms to develop many kinds of plans. SWOT stands for strengths, weaknesses, opportunities, and threats.

Tactics.   Highly specific actions needed to accomplish goals and strategies. They are even more specific than strategies and are usually short-term.

Tag for.   Information that a designer requests that a manufacturer affix to the goods and note on the invoice in order to help the designer deliver the goods to the correct client.

Tangible personal property.   Any property that is movable, can be touched, or has physical existence.

Target marketing.   A marketing method that helps a design firm identify one or more groups of potential customers who are most likely to utilize the services of the firm.

Tenant improvements.   Improvements to a commercial space paid for by the tenant; also called leasehold improvements.

Tenant work letter.   A contract that spells out everything that is done to a leased space by the landlord and tenant. Also referred to as a building standard work letter.

Termination for cause.   Protects the employee from being terminated for some capricious reason. Reasons for termination for cause include negligence, incompetence, dishonesty, disloyalty, and failure to follow company policies.

Testimonials.   Statements that the client has made in a letter that he or she sends or gives verbally to the designer concerning his or her satisfaction with the design firm's work.

Third party.   An individual or company somehow involved in the project or relationship but not a party to the original contract between the designer and client.

Third-party testimonials.   When an interior designer uses a statement from a former client as a reference to help sell his or her services and/or merchandise to a new client.

TIFF format.   A method of reproducing digital photos that produces a high-quality image. It is more suitable for publication as well. Stands for Tagged Image File Format.

Title.   In sales law, title refers to the legal ownership of goods. The person who holds title to the goods owns the goods.

Title acts.   Legislative measures concerned with limiting the use of certain professional titles by individuals who meet agreed-upon qualifications and who have registered with a state board.

Tort.   When a person commits a wrong against another and causes injury to the harmed party. Torts are civil matters and therefore are not legislated by statute.

Trade credit.   When a supplier allows a designer to purchase on credit, the designer is working with the supplier's money.

Trade discounts.   Discounts given as a courtesy by some vendors to designers and others in the trade. These are usually a small percentage off retail.

Trade fixtures.   Items attached to the rented space by the tenant. Depending on the lease, they can be removed if no damage is done to the structure.

Trademark.   Legal protection for distinctive names, logos, or symbols.

Trade sources.   Groups of manufacturers, suppliers, and tradespeople who provide the various goods and services that a designer uses to complete an interiors project.

Transaction privilege (sales) tax license.   Allows the interior designer to pass on the state sales tax to the consumer; issued by state and municipal taxing authorities.

Transmittal letter.   A form letter that a designer can use to send information to anyone involved with the project or to anyone from whom information has been requested.

Trunk show. Occurs when a manufacturer's rep invites one or more interior designers to view a small selection of new merchandise.

Turnkey project. In architecture, a project that commonly includes financing assistance, property acquisition, and all the design and specification services associated with architecture or interior design. Also referred to as turnkey design.

Unemployment taxes. Funds provided by the employer to eligible employees in the event that they are laid off from their job; paid to the employee through the state.

Uniform Commercial Code (UCC). The body of law that guides the relationships between the various levels of buyers and sellers in business transactions.

Uniform laws. Types of laws that try to bring consistency to the numerous versions of similar laws passed by individual states.

Unsecured loan. A loan that does not require collateral as a guarantee.

Use tax. A tax on goods that a business purchases from a supplier in another state for use within the state in which the purchasing business is located.

Utilization rates. A factor identifying the amount of time that a designer spends on billable hours versus nonbillable work.

Value engineering. A method of analyzing and specifying products and design solutions based on cost-effectiveness.

Value-oriented fee method. A fee method by which a design firm prices its services based on the value or quality of the services rather than on the cost of doing those services; also called value-based method.

Variance analysis. A managerial technique in which one looks at financial and numerical data in relation to the differences between planned or budgeted amounts and actual amounts.

Vendor. Someone who sells products or services either to the end user or to another merchant, like the designer.

Vignette. A display of furniture and furnishings in a store or a showroom that simulates an actual room.

Walk-through. A final inspection of a job site to be sure that everything ordered is present and that any omissions or damaged goods are noted.

Warranties. A statement or representation made by a seller concerning goods. Warranties are related to quality, fitness of purpose, or title.

Whistle-blowing. Reporting a company's health or safety violations. Employees cannot be fired for whistle-blowing.

Wholesale price. A special price given to a merchant from a merchant at a value lower than what the goods would cost the consumer.

Workers' compensation insurance. An insurance program paid for by the employer that provides funds to the employee to cover the expenses of work-related injuries.

Work in process. Work under way for a client that has not yet been billed.

Work plan. All the tasks that are required to complete an interior design project.

Work product. Drawings, documents, and other products prepared by an employee that are actually owned by the employer.

Wrongful discharge. Firing an employee without good cause.

Zone pricing.   A manufacturer determines two or more shipping zones based on geographic distances from the factory. Each zone has a different price for the product.

Zoning variance.   Issued by a local jurisdiction so that a business can operate in a residentially zoned area. Other zoning variances may apply, depending on the jurisdiction.

The reader should verify the site's reliability and usefulness. The author does not endorse any site other than those of the recognized interior design professional associations. Please note that in some cases, a resource does not have a web site as of the publication of this book. The most recent phone number available for that resource has been listed for your information.

INTERIOR DESIGN PROFESSIONAL ASSOCIATIONS

These organizations are many of those most representing professional interior designers or interior design professional interests. Note that a wide variety of publications and information is available on the practice of interior design at many of the professional association sites. In some cases, that information is only downloadable to members of the association.

American Society of Interior Designers (ASID)
www.asid.org

Association of Registered Interior Designers of Ontario (ARIDO)
www.arido.ca

Association of University Interior Designers
www.auid.org

Council for Interior Design Accreditation (formally FIDER)
www.accredit-id.org

Interior Design Educators Council (IDEC)
www.idec.org

Interior Designers of Canada (IDC)
www.interiordesigncanada.org

Interior Design Society (IDS)
www.interiordesignsociety.org

International Facility Management Association (IFMA)
www.ifma.org

International Interior Design Association (IIDA)
www.iida.com

Institute of Store Planners
www.ispo.org

National Council for Interior Design Qualification (NCIDQ)
www.ncidq.org

ALLIED PROFESSIONAL ORGANIZATIONS, TRADE ASSOCIATIONS, AND RESOURCES

The following is a selected list of organizations and associations affiliated with the interior design and built-environment industry and professions. A great deal of useful information can be downloaded from many of these sites.

American Institute of Architects (AIA)
www.aia.org

American National Standards Institute (ANSI)
www.ansi.org

American Society of Furniture Designers (ASFD)
www.asfd.com

American Society of Landscape Architects
www.asla.org

American Society for Testing and Materials (ASTM)
www.astm.org

ARCOM Master Systems
www.arcomnet.com

Association of Professional Design Firms
www.apdf.org

British Contract Furnishing Association
Business Design Center
www.thebcfa.com

Building Owners & Managers Association (BOMA)
www.boma.org

Business and Institutional Furniture Manufacturer's Association (BIFMA)
www.bifma.com

Color Marketing Group (CMG)
www.colormarketing.org

Construction Management Association of America
www.cmaanet.org

Construction Specifications Institute (CSI)
www.csinet.org

Contract Furniture Dealer Division
Independent Office Products and Furniture Dealers Association
(formerly National Office Products Association)
www.iopfda.org

Harvard Design Magazine
www.gsd.harvard.edu/research/publications/hdm
Back issues of articles are available at the Harvard Graduate School of Design
site.

Home Furnishings International Association
www.hfia.com

Illuminating Engineering Society of North America (IES)
www.iesna.org

Industrial Designers Society of America (IDSA)
www.idsa.org

International Association of Lighting Designers (IALD)
www.iald.org

International Code Council
www.iccsafe.org

International Furnishings and Design Association (IFDA)
www.ifda.com

National Fire Protection Association (NFPA)
www.nfpa.org

National Kitchen and Bath Association (NKBA)
www.nkba.org

National Trust for Historic Preservation
www.nationaltrust.org

NeoCon Trade Shows
Merchandise Mart Properties, Inc.
www.merchandisemart.com

Organization of Black Designers (OBD)
www.core77.com/obd

Quebec Furniture Manufacturers Association
www.qfma.com

Sweets Network—McGraw-Hill Construction
www.construction.com
Home page for the *Sweets Catalog Files*.
www.products.construction.com
Sweets product information site.

U.S. Green Building Council (USGBC)
www.usgbc.org

Other associations can be discovered by searching Google, Yahoo Business, or www.ipl.org/ref/AON. IPL is the Internet Public Library site.

HELPFUL GOVERNMENT AGENCY SITES

USA.gov
www.usa.gov
A portal to all U.S. government Web sites

Americans with Disabilities Act home page
(Department of Justice)
www.ada.gov

Equal Employment Opportunity Commission (EEOC)
www.eeoc.gov

Federal Trade Commission
www.ftc.gov

Library of Congress
www.loc.gov

Minority Business Development Agency
www.mbda.gov

Occupational Safety & Health Administration (OSHA)
(Department of Labor)
www.osha.gov

U.S. Copyright Office
http://www.copyright.gov
Copies of the documents needed to register copyrights are available online.

U. S. Department of Commerce
www.doc.gov

U.S. Department of Justice
www.usdoj.gov

U.S. Department of Labor
Bureau of Labor Statistics
www.bls.gov

U.S. Patent and Trademark Office
www.uspto.gov

U.S. Internal Revenue Service
www.irs.gov
Most of the IRS forms and instruction booklets are available online.

U.S. Small Business Administration
www.sbaonline.sba.gov
A large amount of information for setting up and maintaining a small business is downloadable from the site.

GENERAL LEGAL RESOURCES

You can obtain specific information on legal requirements within your state by going to the home page for your state government (www.<state name>.gov). It will have links to the specific information you need.

Cornell Law School.
www.law.cornell.edu.
A very good site for a wide variety of federal and state laws. Other law school sites also provide legal information to the public.

National Conference of Commissioners on Uniform State Laws (NCCUSL)
www.nccusl.org

Nolo
www.nolo.com
A publisher of legal information on a wide variety of legal and business management topics.

GENERAL BUSINESS SITES

Allied Board of Trade, Inc.
914-273-2333

American Institute of Certified Public Accounts
www.aicpa.org

American Management Association
www.amanet.org

American Society of Appraisers
www.appraisers.org
Some members specialize in business valuations.

American Women's Economic Development Corporation
212-692-9100

Dun & Bradstreet
www.dnb.com

Fuessler Group
www.fuessler.com
Their publicity directory is available from this site for the A/E/C industry

Insurance Information Institute
www.iii.org
Insurance organization that promotes public understanding of insurance. Many insurance agencies and companies can be found on the Internet through searches on any business search engine.

John Wiley & Sons
www.wiley.com
Publisher of hundreds of interior design, architecture, and business topics books.

Lyon Mercantile Group
www.lyoncredit.com

National Society of Accountants
www.nsa.org

National Small Business Association
202-293-8830

Society for Marketing Professional Services
703-549-6117

Standard & Poor's Register of Corporations, Directors, and Executives
www.standardandpoors.com
212-2-8000

Thomson Gale Research Company
www.gale.com
Publishers of e-research and educational publishing for libraries, schools, and businesses, including the *Encyclopedia of Associations*.

Toastmasters International
www.toastmasters.org

Ulrich's International Periodicals Directory
www.ulrichsweb.com.
Extensive database, but not all magazines/periodicals are listed.

U.S. Hispanic Chamber of Commerce
www.ushcc.com

CAREER AND JOB INFORMATION

American Society of Interior Designers
www.asid.org

Career Resource for Interior Design Industry
www.interiordesignjobs.com

Careers in Interior Design
www.careersininteriordesign.com

International Interior Design Association
www.iida.org

Job-Job
www.job-e-job.com
Provides a listing of jobs available in architecture, interior design, and engineering.

Monster
www.monster.com
A popular job recruitment Web site for a wide variety of jobs.

U.S. Department of Labor, Bureau of Labor Statistics
www.bls.gov
Provides information on salary averages.

GENERAL REFERENCES

ARTICLES AND COLLATERAL MATERIALS

The listed articles, brochures, material from Web sites, and other collateral materials represent only a small number of items on the topics in this book.

Abercrombie, Stanley. 1987. "News: Leaders Meet." *Interior Design*. October.

————. 1999. "Design Revolution: 100 Years that Changed our World." *Interior Design*. December. pp. 141–98.

American Society of Interior Designers. 1997. "Clients Are Impressed by Project Management." *ASID Professional Designer*. March/April. p. 17.

————. 1998. "Design Specialties." *ASID Professional Designer*. July/August.

————. 1998. "Design Fees and Profits." *ASID Professional Designer*. September/October.

————. 1998. "Strategic Planning for the Small Design Practice." *ASID Professional Designer*. March/April.

————.1998. *Strategic Mapping Research. Phase III*. June.

————. "Design Fees and Profits." *ASID Professional Designer*. September/October 1998.

————. 1998. *ASID Code of Ethics and Professional Conduct*. Washington, DC: ASID.

————. 1999. "The Road Map to Growth." *ASID ICON*. November.

————. 2000. "Primary Basis of Complaints Being Filed." Information from ASID Ethics Office. August

————. 2006. Web site information.

————. 2000. "Procedures for Filing an Ethics Complaint." ASID Web site. June.

————. 2005. *The History of ASID*.

————. 2005. *Consumer Use of Design Services*. ————. 2005. *Inside Small and Medium Design Firms*.

————. 2005. *Know Your Client*.

————. 2006. Web site information.

Bacskai, Andrew. 2001. "Inside the Big Guys." *ASID ICON*. November. pp. 20–24.

————. 2002. "Body of Evidence." *ASID ICON*. March. pp. 27–30.

Bauer, Natalie. 2004. "Fringe Benefits." *Perspective*. Spring. pp. 24–28.

Bernardo, Stephanie. 1985. "Fire Me . . . and I'll Sue!" *Success!* July/August.

Brandt, Roslyn. 1995. "Can You Manage?" *Contract*. April. pp. 76–77.

Burke, Kimberly. 2002. "The 24–7 Work Week: The New Norm." *ASID ICON*. August. pp. 24–28.

Buschy, Jennifer Thiele. 2000. "Wanted: Architects and Designers for Hire." *Contract*. September. p. 96.

"Buyers Guide." 2000. *Interior Design*. January

"Buyers Guide." 2006. *Interior Design*. April.

Caan, Shashi. 2003. "The Future of Design: Finding the Soul of Our Art." *Perspective*. Winter. pp. 41–43.

Castlelman, Betty. 1987. "How Will Licensing Affect Me?" *Designers West*. June.

Collins, James C., and Jerry I. Porras. 1996. "Building Your Company's Vision." *Harvard Business Review*. September/October. pp. 65–77.

Conlon, Ginger. 2000. "Cashing In." *Sales and Marketing Management*. June. pp. 95–102.

Corlin, Len. 1986. "Marts Accelerate Development." *Contract*. December.

Costello, Katriel. 2005. "All Business?" *Perspective*. Fall. pp. 10–14.

Dahle, Cheryl. 1998. "Fast Start: Your First 60 Days." *Fast Company*. June/July.

Dale, P. Adrianne. 1995. "The Ethics Process: Inside Perspective." *ASID Report*. September.

"Design Revolution: 100 Years That Changed our World." 1999. *Interior Design*. December.

Ebstein, Barbara. 1985. "Licensing: The Design Concern for the Eighties." *ASID Report*. January–March.

Farley, Susan E. "Guarding against Knock Offs." *ASID ICON*. Spring 2005. pp. 42–48.

Fast Company. 2000. "The Internet: What Does It Look Like?" *Fast Company*. March.

Federal Register. 1991. *Nondiscrimination on the Basis of Disability by Public Accommodations and in Commercial Facilities; Final Rule*. vol. 56. no. 144. Washington, DC: Department of Justice.

Finter, Andrea. 1985. "Senior Designers' Average Pay: $37,300." *Contract*. June.

———. 1984. "Designer Salary Poll Links Job Tenure and Compensation." *Contract*. July.

Foti, Ross. 2004. "In Search of Excellence." *Perspective*. Winter. pp. 25–26.

Foundation for Interior Design Education Research. 2006. Web site information.

———. 1993. *FIDER Fact Kit*. February.

Gaulden, Joan. 2000. "The Business Value of the Internet." Seminar handout.

Gerasimo, Pilar. 2000. "25 Ways Your Business Will Change." *ASID ICON*. November. pp. 30–33.

Gerasimo, Pilar. 2001. "Another Satisfied Customer?" *ASID ICON*. March. pp. 11–14.

Gibson, Woody. 1980. "Design Wages Depend on Function," *Contract*. October.

Goldsborough, Reid. 1999. "Changing the Future of Doing Business." *Interiors & Sources*. June. pp. 40–41.

Goldsborough, Reid, and Angela Frucci. 2001. "Working the Web." *ASID ICON*. June. pp. 12–19.

Gueft, Olga. 1980. "The Past as Prologue: The First 50 Years. 1931–1981: An Overview." *American Society of Interior Designers Annual Report*.

Gura, Judith B. Fall. 1999. "Modernism at the Millennium." *Echoes*.

Hammonds, Keith H. 1999. "How We Sell." *Fast Company*. November. pp. 294–306.

Harragan, Betty Lehan. 1986. "Career Advice." *Working Woman*. September.

Henderson, James P. 2003. *Practice Analysis Study for the Profession of Interior Design*. National Council for Interior Design Qualification.

Herman Miller. Inc. 1994. *A Brief History of Herman Miller*.

Hughes, Nina. June 1987. "Interiors Platform." *Interiors*.

Imperato, Gina. 1998. "How to Give Good Feedback." *Fast Company*. September.

Institute of Business Designers. 1993. Membership Information. Brochure.

———.1993. *CEUs and You. A Guide to Developing a Self-Directed Learning Path for the Professional Member*. Brochure. February.

———. 1992. *History of IBD*. Unpublished manuscript.

Institute of Business Designers. 1989. *Code of Professional Conduct*. Brochure.

———. 1980. "Code of Ethics."

Institute of Business Designers. 1980. *Code of Ethics*. Institute of Business Designers. Pamphlet. p. 105.

Interior Design Educators Council. 2006. Web site information.

———. 1994. "Members of Interior Design Organizations Vote on Unification." Press release. May.

———. 1999 and 1992. Membership brochure.

———. 2006. Web site information.

———. 1999. Membership information. Brochure. June.

Internal Revenue Service. 2006. *Publication No. 15-A. Employer's Supplemental Tax Guide*. Department of the Treasury. January.

———. 1999. *Starting a Business and Keeping Records*. Publication No. 583. Department of the Treasury.

———. 1999. *Tax Guide for Small Business*. Publication No. 334. Department of the Treasury.

Interior Designers of Canada. 2006. Web site information.

"Interiors & Sources 2000 Directory and Source Guide." 2000. *Interiors & Sources*. January.

"Interiors & Sources 2006 Directory & Source Guide." 2006. *Interiors & Sources*. International Codes Council. 2000. As reported by ASID Grassroots. Brochure. April

International Society of Interior Designers. 1992. Membership information. Brochure.

———. 1984. *Perspective*. Fall.

International Interior Design Association. 1997. *IIDA Code of Ethics*. ———. 2006. Web site information.

Jensen, Charlotte S. 2001. "Design versus Decoration." *Interiors & Sources*. September. p. 91.

Joiner, Colene. 1998. "Your Code of Ethics: How Can It Help You?" *ASID Professional Designer*. May/June.

Jones, Carol. 1999. "Defining a Profession: Some Things Never Change." *Interiors & Sources*. September.

Kaplinger, Eunice, and Susan Ray-Degges. 1998. "Can Ethics Be Taught or Is It Too Late?" *Journal of Interior Design*. vol. 24. no. 1.

Kettler, Kerwin. 1985. "Is There More to Licensing Than a License?" *Designer Specifier*. May.

Kroelinger, Michael D. Spring. 1992. "Unified Voice Update." *Perspective*. Institute of Business Designers.

———. 1993. *Mission and Benefits of Unification*. Unpublished material.

Kubany, Elizabeth Harrison, and Charles D. Linn. 1999. "Why Architects Don't Charge Enough." *Architectural Record*. October.

———. 1999. "How To Increase Your Fees in a Tough Market." *Architectural Record*. November.

Lande, Kim. 2005. "Entrepreneurial Eyes." *Perspective*. Winter. pp. 44–48.

Leonard, Woody. 2000. "The New Internet Security Threats." *SmartBusiness*. July.

Ligos, Melinda.2000. "Clicks and Misses." *Sales and Marketing Management*. June. pp. 69–76.

Loebelson, Andrew. 1996. "Interior Design Giants." *Interior Design*. January.

———. 1985. "Mart Fever Is Epidemic." *Contract*. December.

Long, Deborah H. 1998. "Why We Need Ethical Decision-Making Skills." *ASID Professional Designer*. May/June.

———. 2000. *Ethics and the Design Profession*. Continuing Education Monograph Series. National Council for Interior Design Qualification.

Marberry, Sara. 2003. "Giving Back to the Design Profession." *Perspective*. Spring. pp. 27–32.

Martin, Caren, and Denise Guerin. 2006. *The Interior Design Profession's Body of Knowledge: 2005 Edition*. Published jointly by American Society of Interior Designers, Council for Interior Design Accreditation (formerly FIDER), Interior Designers of Canada, International Interior Design Association, and National Council for Interior Design Qualification.

Martin, Jane D., and Nancy Knoohuizen. 1997. "Create a 'Bang' with Easy-to-Use Marketing Techniques." *ASID Professional Designer*. July/August. pp. 14–15.

McCarroll, Thomas. 1992. "Entrepreneurs: Starting Over." *Time*. January 6.

McCracken, Laurin, and Ann Carper. 1992. "Designers on Stage." *Contract*. November. pp. 66–67.

McLain-Kark, Joan H., and Ruey-Er Tang. 1986. "Computer Usage and Attitudes toward Computers in the Interior Design Field." *Journal of Interior Design Education and Research*. Fall. vol. 12. pp. 25–32.

Merchandise Mart Properties. 2000. *The Merchandise Mart Buyers Guide*. June.

Merle, Jan S. 1995. "The Internet: Hype or Harbinger of Business, 90s Style?" *ASID Report*. November/December. pp. 16–18.

Milshtein, Amy. 1994. "First Timers." *Contract*. November 1994. p. 84.

Muoio, Anna. 2000. "Should I Go .com?" *Fast Company*. July. pp. 164–72.

National Council for Interior Design Qualification. 2006. Web site information.

———. 1998. *Analysis of the Interior Design Profession*. NCIDQ.

National Conference of Commissioners on Uniform State Laws (NCCUSL). 2003 Amendments UCC Article 2. Available on Web site at www.nccusl.org.

National Institute of Business Management. 1998. *Fire at Will: Terminating Your Employees Legally*. Special Bulletin No. 239A. National Institute of Business Management.

Nolo Web site. 2005. "Corporation Basics." October. Available at www.nolo.com.

———. 2005. "Professional Corporations" October. Available at www.nolo.com.

———. 2005. "S Corporation Facts." October. Available at www.nolo.com.

"Open vs. Closed: The Results Are In." 1992. *Interior Design*. June.

Piotrowski, Christine M. 1998. "Strategic Planning for the Small Design Practice." *ASID Professional Designer*. March/April. pp. 18–21.

Polites, Nicholas. "Arkansas Enacts Tiered Licensing System: Interior Designers Weigh Consequences." *Interior Design*. July 1993.

Ranallo, Anne Brooks. 2005. "Life-Long Learning." *Perspective*. Fall. pp. 36–42.

Rayle, Martha G. 1992. "Unified Voice Task Force (UVTF) Update." Newsletter published by American Society of Interior Designers. April.

Rebholz, Jenny S. 2006. "Power in Numbers: Marketing to Boomers." *ASID ICON*. Spring. pp. 52–56.

———. 2005. "Practice Innovators." *ASID ICON*. Winter. pp. 62–64.

Rosenfeld, Jill. 2000. "Information as if Understanding Mattered." *Fast Company*. March. pp. 203–19.

Ross, Ken L., Jr., and Gail Burns. 2003. "The Role of Mentoring in the Design Profession." *Perspective*. Winter. pp. 17–20.

Ross, Jim. 2002. "The Art of Self Promotion." *ASID ICON*. May. pp. 10–13.

Row, Heath. 1998. "These Cards Mean Business." *Fast Company*. August. p. 62.

Russell, Beverly 1992. "Into the Ninth Decade: A Historic View of Interior Design through the Contribution of Women." *IBD Perspective*. Fall.

———. 1985. "Interiors Business: New Moves toward Interior Design Licensing." *Interiors*. March.

Schonfeld, Erick. 2000. "Corporations of the World, Unite! You Have Nothing to Lose but Your Supply Chains!" *Fast Company*. June. pp. 123–32.

Senn, Jan. 2000. "Motivating Your Staff." *ASID ICON*. November. pp. 8–10.

Siegel, Alan M. 1995. "ASID Code of Ethics and Professional Conduct: A Primer." *ASID Report*. September.

Slavin, Maeve. 1983. "Jobs Are Not What They Used To Be." *Interiors*. September.

Staffelbach, Andre. 1992. "Does the Public Consider You a Professional?" *IBD Perspective*. Summer.

Stern, Linda. 1995. "The Perfect Proposal." *Home Office Computing*. February. pp. 81–86.

Stern, Natalie. 1982. "Top Contract Furniture Sales People Can Boost Earnings 33% with Timed Move." *Contract*. November.

Strogoff, Michael. 2003. "Coping with Success: Growing Pains of Successful Design Firms." *ASID ICON*. November. pp. 20–26.

Sykes, Claire. 2005. "Managing Your Organization with Morals in Mind." *Office Solutions*. May/June. pp. 34–35.

Talarico, Wendy. 1999. "Listening to Computer Experts." *Architectural Record*. August. pp. 74–78.

"The Source Guide 1999–2000." 2000. *Contract*. January.

"The Source Guide 2006." 2006. *Contract*. January.

Tingas, Pauline. "Taking Orders." 2006. *Perspective*. Spring. pp. 44–50.

Tobias, Sheila, and Alma Lantz. 1985. "Performance Appraisal." *Working Woman*. November.

Taute, Michelle. 2005. "Compass vs. Computer." Perspective. Winter. pp. 22–25.

Unified Voice Task Force. 1994. Newsletter sent to IBD members. April.

———. 1993. "Interior Design Organizations Target July 1994 for Unification." Press release. September.

U.S. Small Business Administration. *Developing a Strategic Business Plan*. no. MP21.

———. 1998. *State of Small Business: A Report of the President*.

———. 1991. *State of Small Business: A Report of the President*.

Vollmer, John L., Ph.D. 2000. "Sole Practitioner: Self-Employed or Contingent Worker? Investigating Worker Misclassification and Its Implications to Commercial Interior Design." *Journal of Interior Design*. vol. 26. no. 1. pp. 56–61.

Voss, Judy. 1996. "White Paper on the Recent History of the Open Office." Holland, MI: Haworth.

Wagner, Michael. 1985. "Interiors Business. Salaries and Bonuses Are up for Designers." *Interiors*. September.

Warshaw, Michael. 1998. "Get a Life." *Fast Company*. June/July.

Webber, Alan M. 1998. "Are You a Star at Work?" *Fast Company*. June/July.

Weigand, John. 2006. "Defining Ourselves." *Perspective*. Winter. pp. 26–34.

Whitemyer, David. 2006. "Practice (and Title) Makes Perfect." *Perspective*. Winter. pp. 16–20.

Zeiger, Lisa. 1999. "House Fraus." *Interiors*. September.

BOOKS

Aaker, David A. 1995. *Developing Business Strategies*, 4th ed. New York: John Wiley & Sons.

Aaker, David A., V. Kumar, and George S. Day. 1998. *Marketing Research*. 6th ed. New York: John Wiley & Sons.

Abercrombie, Nicholas, Stephen Hill, and Bryan S. Turner. 1994. *The Penguin Dictionary of Sociology*. New York: Allen Lane Publications (Penguin Books).

Abercrombie, Nicholas Stephen Hill, and Bryan S. Turner. *The Penguin Dictionary of Sociology*. 4th ed. 2000. New York: Penguin Books.

Alderman, Robert L. 1982. *How to Make More Money at Interior Design*. New York: Whitney Communications Corporation.

———. 1997. *How to Prosper as an Interior Designer*. New York: John Wiley & Sons.

Alexander, Roy, and Charles B. Roth. 2004. *Secrets of Closing Sales*. 7th ed. Paramus, NJ: Penguin/Portfolio.

Allen, David. 2003. *Ready for Anything*. New York: Viking/Penguin.

Allen, Jeffrey G. 1997. *The Complete Q & A Job Interview Book*. 2nd ed. New York: John Wiley & Sons.

Allwork, Ronald. 1961. *AID Interior Design and Decoration Manual of Professional Practice*. 2nd ed. New York: American Institute of Interior Designers.

American Heritage Dictionary of the English Language. 2000. 4th ed. Boston: Houghton-Mifflin.

Anthoy, Robert N., and James S. Reece. 1983. *Accounting Text and Cases*. 7th ed. Homewood, IL: Richard D. Irwin.

Applegate, Jane. 1995. *Strategies for Small Business Success*. New York: Plume.

Axtell, Roger E. 1991. *Gestures*. New York: John Wiley & Sons.

Axtell, Roger E. 1997. *Do's and Taboos around the World for Women in Business*. New York: John Wiley & Sons.

Baker, Ronald J. 2006. *Pricing on Purpose*. New York: John Wiley & Sons.

Ball, Victoria. 1982. *Opportunities in Interior Design*. Skokie, IL: VGM Career Horizons.

Baldrige, Letitia. 1993. *Letitia Baldrige's New Complete Guide to Executive Manners*. New York: Rawson Associates.

———. 1985. *Letitia Baldrige's Complete Guide to Executive Manners*. New York: Rawson Associates.

Ballast, David K. 2006. *Interior Design Reference Manual*. 3rd ed. Belmont, CA.: Professional Publications.

———. 2002. *Interior Construction & Detailing*. Belmont, CA: Professional Publications.

Bangs, David H., Jr. 1995. *The Business Planning Guide*. 7th ed. Chicago, IL: Upstart Publishing.

———. 1998. *The Market Planning Guide*. 5th ed. Chicago, IL: Upstart Publishing.

———. 2005. *Business Plans Made Easy*. 3rd ed. Irvine, CA: Entrepreneur Media.

Barnhart, Tod. 1995. *The Five Rituals of Wealth*. New York: HarperCollins.

Barr, Vilma. 1995. *Promotion Strategies for Design and Construction Firms*. New York: Van Nostrand Reinhold.

Beard, Jeffrey L., Michael C. Loulakis, and Edward C. Wundram. 2001. *Design Build*. New York: McGraw-Hill.

Beatty, Richard H. 2000. *The Resume Kit*. 4th ed. New York: John Wiley & Sons.

Beam, Burton T., Jr., and John J. McFadden. 1998. *Employee Benefits*. 5th ed. Homewood, IL: Dearborn Financial Publishing.

Becher, Tony. 1999. *Professional Practices*. New Brunswick, NJ: Transaction.

Beckwith, Harry. 2000. *The Invisible Touch*. New York. Time Warner Books.

Belker, Lorin B., and Gary s. Topchik. 2005. *The First-Time Manager*. 5th ed. New York: American Management Association.

Bender, Peer Urs. 1995. *Secrets of Power Presentations*. Willodale, ON: Firefly Books.

Bennett, Peter D., ed. 1995. *Dictionary of Marketing Terms*. 2nd ed. Chicago, IL: American Marketing Association.

Bennis, Warren. 1994. *On Becoming a Leader*. Reading, MA: Perseus.

Berger, C. Jaye. 1994. *Interior Design Law and Business Practices*. New York: John Wiley & Sons.

Berman, Karen and Joe Knight (with John Case). 2006. *Financial Intelligence*. Cambridge, MA: Harvard Business School Press.

Berkowitz, Eric N., Roger A. Kerin, Steven W. Hartley, and William Rudelius. 1994. *Marketing*. 4th ed. Burr Ridge, IL: Richard D. Irwin.

———. 1997. *Selling the Invisible*. New York: Time Warner Books.

Besson, Taunee S. 1999. *Cover Letters*. National Employment Weekly Career Guides. 3rd ed. New York: John Wiley & Sons.

Birnberg, Howard. 1992. *New Directions in Architectural and Engineering Practice*. New York: McGraw-Hill.

———.1999. *Project Management for Building Designers and Owners*. Boca Raton, FL: CRC Press.

Bixler, Susan. 2005. *Professional Presence*. 2nd ed. New York: Perigee.

Bixler, Susan, and Nancy Nix-Rice. 1997. *The New Professional Image*. Holbrook, MA: Adams Media.

Black, Henry Campbell (with Joseph R. Nolan and Jacqueline M. Nolan-Haley). 1990. *Black's Law Dictionary*. 6th ed. St. Paul, MN: West Publishing.

Blades, William H. 1994. *Selling: The Mother of All Enterprise*. Phoenix: Marketing Methods Press.

Blanchard, Ken (with John P. Carlos and Alan Randolph). 1996. *Empowerment Takes More Than a Minute*. New York: MJF Books.

Blanchard, Ken, Donald Carew, and Eunice Parisi-Carew. 2000. *The One-Minute Manager Builds High-Performing Teams*. New York: William Morrow.

Bliss, Edwin. 1983. *Doing It Now*. New York: Bantam Books.

Bly, Robert W. 1998. *The Lead Generation Handbook*. New York: American Management Association.

———. 1998. *The Six Figure Consultant*. Chicago: Upstart Publishing.

———. 1994. *Business to Business Direct Marketing*. Lincolnwood, IL: NTC Business Books.

———. 1991. *Selling Your Services*. New York: Henry Holt.

Blum, Laurie. 1996. *Free Money from the Federal Government for Small Businesses and Entrepreneurs*. New York: John Wiley & Sons.

Bolles, Richard Nelson. 2007. *What Color Is Your Parachute?* Berkeley, CA: Ten Speed Press.

Bond, William J. 1997. *Going Solo*. New York: McGraw-Hill.

Bossidy, Larry, and Ram Charan. 2004. *Confronting Reality*. New York: Crown Press.

Breighner, Bart. 1995. *Face to Face Selling*. Indianapolis: Park Avenue.

Brown, Gordon W., and Paul A. Sukys. 1997. *Business Law*. 9th ed. New York: Glencoe/McGraw-Hill.

Buhler, Patricia. 2002. *Human Resource Management*. Avon, MA: Adams Media.

Burg, Bob. 2006. *Endless Referrals*. 3rd ed. New York: McGraw-Hill.

Burley-Allen, Madelyn. 1995. *Listening: The Forgotten Skill*. New York: John Wiley & Sons.

Burstein, David, and Frank Stasiowski. 1982. *Project Management for the Design Professional*. New York: Watson-Guptill.

Campbell, Nina, and Caroline Seebohm. 1992. *Elsie de Wolfe: A Decorative Life*. New York: Clarkson N. Potter.

Canfield, Jack, Mark Victor Hansen, and Les Hewitt. 2000. *The Power of Focus*. Deerfield Beach, FL: Health Communications, Inc.

Caplan, Suzanne. 2000. *Finance and Accounting*. Holbrook, MA: Adams Media.

Carmichael, D. R., Steven B. Lilien, and Martin Mellman. 1999. *Accountant's Handbook*. 9th ed. New York: John Wiley & Sons.

Carron, Christian G. 1998. *Grand Rapids Furniture*. Grand Rapids, MI: Public Museum of Grand Rapids.

Casperson, Dana May. 1999. *Power Etiquette*. New York: American Management Association.

Chasteen, Lanny G., Richard E. Flaherty, and Melvin C. O'Connor. 1995. *Intermediate Accounting*. 9th ed. New York: McGraw-Hill.

Clarkson, Kenneth W., Roger LeRoy Miller, and Gaylord A. Jentz. 1983. *West's Business Law, Text and Cases*. 2nd ed. St. Paul, MN: West Publishing.

Cochran, Chuck, and Donna Peerce. 1999. *Heart and Soul Internet Job Search*. Palo Alto, CA: Davies-Block Publishing.

Cohen, Jonathan. 2000. *Communication and Design with the Internet*. New York: W. W. Norton.

Collier's Encyclopedia. 1975. Vol. 15, s.v. "Marketing." New York: Macmillan Educational Corporation.

Collier's Encyclopedia. 1984. "Interior Design and Decoration." Vol. 13. New York: Macmillan.

Collin, Simon. 1997. *Doing Business on the Internet*. London: Kogan, Page.

Concise Oxford American Dictionary. 2006. Oxford, NY: Oxford University Press.

Conry, Edward J., Gerald R. Ferrera, and Karla H. Fox. 1993. *The Legal Environment of Business*. 3rd ed. Boston: Allyn and Bacon.

Cook, Kenneth J. 1994. *AMA Complete Guide to Strategic Planning for Small Business*. Chicago: American Marketing Association.

———. 1995. AMA *Complete Guide to Small Business Marketing*. Lincolnwood, IL: NTC Business Books.

Cook, Marshall. 1999. *Time Management*. Holbrook, MA: Adams Media.

Cooke, Robert A. 1999. *Small Business Formation Handbook*. New York: John Wiley & Sons.

Covey, Stephen R. 1989. *The Seven Habits of Highly Effective People*. New York: Fireside Books.

Covey, Stephen R., A. Roger Merrill, and Rebecca R. Merrill. 1994. *First Things First*. New York: Simon and Schuster.

Cowley, Michael, and Ellen Domb. 1997. *Beyond Strategic Vision*. Boston: Butterworth-Heinemann.

Cramer, James P. 1994. *Design Plus Enterprise*. Washington, DC: AIA Press.

Cramer, James P. and Scott Simpson. 2002. *How Firms Succeed*. Atlanta: Greenway Communications.

Crandall, Rick. 1998. *1001 Ways to Market Your Services*. Lincolnwood, IL: Contemporary Books.

———. 2003. *Marketing Your Services for People Who Hate to Sell*. Revised ed. New York: McGraw-Hill.

Crawford, Tad and Eva Doman Bruck. 2001. *Business and Legal Forms for Interior Designers*. New York: Alworth Press.

Cushman, Robert F., and James C. Dobbs. 1991. *Design Professional's Handbook of Business and Law*. New York: John Wiley & Sons.

Czinkota, Michael R., Masaaki Kotabe, and David Mercer. 1997. *Marketing Management Text and Cases*. Cambridge, MA: Blackwell Publishing.

Daily, Frederick W. and edited by Bethany Laurence. 2005. *Tax Savvy for Small Business*. 9th ed. Berkeley, CA: Nolo Press.

Dale, Paulette. 1999. "Did You Say Something, Susan?" *How Any Woman Can Gain Confidence with Assertive Communication*. Secaucus, NJ: Birch Lane Press.

Davidson, Jeff. 1994. *Marketing on a Shoestring*, 2nd ed. New York: John Wiley & Sons.

Dawson, Roger. 1992. *Secrets of Power Persuasion*. Engelwood Cliffs, NJ: Prentice Hall.

———. 1994. *The 13 Secrets of Power Performance*. Englewood Cliffs, NJ: Prentice Hall.

———. 1999. *Power Negotiating*. 2nd ed. Englewood Cliffs, NJ: Prentice Hall.

Delmar, Ken. 1984. *Winning Moves—The Body Language of Selling*. New York: Time Warner Books.

deWolfe, Elsie. 1913/1975. *The House in Good Taste*. Reprint ed. New York: Arno.

Dible, Donald M. 1974. *Up Your Own Organization*. 2nd ed. Reston, VA: Reston Publishing.

Dienhart, John W., and Jordan Curnutt. 1998. *Business Ethics*. Santa Barbara, CA: ABC-CLIO.

DiFalco, Marcelle, and Jocelyn Greenkey Heiz. 2005. *The Big Sister's Guide to the World of Work*. New York: Fireside Books.

DiResta, Diane. 1998. *Knockout Presentations*. Worcester, MA: Chandler House Press.

Drucker, Peter F. 1995. *Managing in a Time of Great Change*. New York: Truman Talley/Dutton.

———. 1973. *Management: Tasks, Responsibilities, Practices*. New York: Harper & Row.

Dun & Bradstreet. 1999. *D&B Business Rankings*. Bethlehem, PA: Dun & Bradstreet.

Dunung, Sanjyot P. 2006. *Starting and Growing Your Business*. New York: McGraw-Hill.

Edwards, Paul, and Sarah Edwards. 1996. *Secrets of Self-Employment*. Revised ed. New York: Tarcher/Putnam.

———. 1999. *Working from Home*. 5th ed. New York: Tarcher/Putnam.

Edwards, Paul, and Sarah Edwards (with Linda Rohrbough). 1998. *Making Money in Cyberspace*. New York: Tarcher/Putnam.

———. 1998. *Getting Business to Come to You*. 2nd ed. New York: Tarcher/Putnam.

Elias, Stephen. 1999. Patent, *Copyright and Trademark*. 3rd ed. Berkeley, CA: Nolo Press.

Elias, Stephen, and Patricia Gima. 2000. *Domain Names: How to Choose and Protect a Great Name for Your Website*. Berkeley, CA: Nolo Press.

Entrepreneur Magazine. 1999. *Starting a Home-Based Business*. 2nd ed. New York: John Wiley & Sons.

Entrepreneur Media, Inc. 1999. *The Entrepreneur Magazine Small Business Advisor*. 2nd ed. New York: John Wiley & Sons.

Emerson, Robert W. 2004. *Business Law*. 4th ed. Hauppauge, NY: Barron's.

Emery, Vince. 1996. *How to Grow Your Business on the Internet*. Scottsdale, AZ: Coriolis Group.

Epstein, Lee. 1977. *Legal Forms for the Designer*. New York: N & E Hellman.

Eskenazi, Martin, and David Gallen. 1992. *Sexual Harassment. Know Your Rights!* New York: Carroll & Graf.

Eyler, David R. 1994. *The Home Business Bible*. New York: John Wiley & Sons.

Farren, Carol E. 1999. Planning and Managing Interior Projects. 2nd ed. Kingston, MA: R.S. Means.

Fast, Julius. 1970. *Body Language*. New York: Simon & Schuster.

Feather, Frank. 2000. *Future Consumer.com*. Toronto: Warwick.

Finnigan, Dan and Marc Karasu. 2006. *Your Next Move: Success Strategies for Midcareer Professionals*. New York: Sterling Publishing.

Fisher, Lionel L. 1995. *On Your Own*. Englewood Cliffs, NJ: Prentice Hall.

Fisher, Roger, and William Ury. 1981. *Getting to Yes*. New York: Penguin Books.

Fishman, Stephen. 1996. *The Copyright Handbook*. 3rd ed. Berkeley, CA: Nolo Press.

Fishman, Stephen. 2004. *Working for Yourself.* 5th ed. Berkley, CA: Nolo Press.

Fletcher, Tana, and Julia Rocklin. 2000. *Getting Publicity.* North Vancouver, B.C.: Self-Counsel Press.

Foote, Cameron S. 2002. *The Business Side of Creativity.* Revised ed. New York: W.W. Norton.

Forsyth, Patrick. 1999. *Marketing Professional Services.* 2nd ed. London: Kogan/Page.

Frey, Fred L., and Charles R. Stoner. 1995. *Strategic Planning for the New and Small Business.* Chicago, IL: Upstart Publishing.

Friday, Stormy, and David G. Cotts. 1995. *Quality Facility Management.* New York: John Wiley & Sons.

Fridson, Martin S. 1995. *Financial Statement Analysis.* New York: John Wiley & Sons.

Frost, Susan E. 1995. *Blueprint for Marketing,* 2nd ed. Portland, OR: SEF Publications.

Gardella, Robert S. 2000. *The Harvard Business School Guide to Finding Your Next Job.* Boston, MA: Harvard Business Reference.

Garner, Bryan A., ed. 2004. *Black's Law Dictionary.* 8th ed. St. Paul, MN: West Group.

Getz, Lowell. 1986. *Business Management in the Smaller Design Firm.* Newton, MA: Practice Management Associates.

———. 1997. *An Architect's Guide to Financial Management.* Washington, DC: AIA Press.

Getz, Lowell, and Loebelson, Andrew 1983. *How To Profit in Contract Design.* New York: Interior Design Books.

Getz, Lowell, and Frank Stasiowski. 1984. *Financial Management for the Design Professional.* New York: Watson-Guptill.

Gerber, Michael E. 1995. *The E Myth Revisited.* New York: Harper Business.

———. 2005. *E Myth Mastery.* New York: Harper Business.

Gerbert, Philipp, Dirk Schneider, and Alex Birch. 2000. *The Age of E-tail.* Oxford, UK: Capstone Publishers.

Gilbert, Jill. 2004. *The Entrepreneur's Guide to Patents, Copyrights, Trademarks, Trade Secrets, and Licensing.* New York: Berkley Books.

Gitman, Lawrence J., and Carl McDaniel. 2003. *The Best of The Future of Business.* Mason, OH: Thomson.

Gitomer, Jeffrey H. 1994. *The Sales Bible.* New York: William Morrow.

Gladwell, Malcolm. 2000. *The Tipping Point.* New York: Back Bay Press.

———. 2005. *Blink.* New York: Little, Brown.

Gomez-Mejia, Luis R., David B. Balkin and Robert L. Cardy. 2005. *Management.* 2nd ed. New York: McGraw-Hill.

Gordon, Ian H. 1998. *Relationship Marketing.* New York: John Wiley & Sons.

Graham, John W., and Wendy C. Havlick. 1994. *Mission Statements.* New York: Garland.

Gray, John. 1999. *How to Get What You Want and Want What You Have.* New York: HarperCollins.

Greusel, David. 2002. *Architect's Essentials of Presentation Skills.* New York: John Wiley & Sons.

Griessman, B. Eugene. 1994. *Time Tactics of Very Successful People.* New York: McGraw-Hill.

Haldane, Bernarad. 2000. *Haldane's Best Cover Letters for Professionals.* Manassas Park, VA: Impact

Hale Associates, Inc. 1998. *Analysis of the Interior Design Profession.* Washington, DC: National Council for Interior Design Qualification.

Hansen, Jeffrey A. 1998. *Surviving Success.* Grants Pass, OR: Oasis Press.

Harding, Ford. 1998. *Creating Rainmakers.* Holbrook, MA: Adams Media.

———. 1994. *Rain Making.* Holbrook, MA: Adams Media.

Harmon, Sharon Koomen and Katherine E. Kennon. 2005. *The Codes Guidebook for Interiors*. 3rd ed. New York: John Wiley & Sons.

Harris, Cyril M. 2006. *Dictionary of Architecture and Construction*. 4th ed. New York: McGraw-Hill.

Harvard Business Essentials. 2005. *Entrepreneur's Toolkit*. Cambridge, MA: Harvard Business School Press.

———. 2006. *Marketer's Toolkit*. Cambridge, MA: Harvard Business School Press.

Hauser, Barbara R., ed. 1996. *Woman's Legal Guide*. Golden, CO: Fulcrum.

Haviland, David, ed. 1994. *The Architect's Handbook of Professional Practice*. Student Edition. Washington, DC: AIA Press.

Haylock, Christina Ford, and Len Muscarella. 1999. *Net Success*. Holbrook, MA: Adams Media.

Heim, Pat, and Susan K. Golant. 1995. *Smashing the Glass Ceiling*. New York: Fireside Books.

———. 2005. *Hardball for Women*. Revised ed. New York: Plume.

Heinecke, William E. (with Jonathan Marsh). 2000. *The Entrepreneur*. Singapore: John Wiley & Sons.

Helzel, Leo B., and Friends. 1995. *A Goal Is a Dream with a Deadline*. New York: McGraw-Hill.

Hiebing, Roman G., Jr., and Scott W. Cooper. 1999. *The One-Day Marketing Plan*. 2nd ed. Lincolnwood, IL: NTC Business Books.

Hinkelman, Edward G. 1997. *Canada Business*. San Rafael, CA: World Trade Press.

Hinze, Jimmie. 2001. *Construction Contracts*. 2nd ed. New York: McGraw-Hill.

Hirsch, Arlene S. 1996. *Love Your Work and Success Will Follow*. New York: John Wiley & Sons.

Holtz, Herman. 1998. *The Consultant's Guide to Getting Business on the Internet*. New York: John Wiley & Sons.

———. 1998. *Proven Proposal Strategies to Win More Business*. Chicago, IL: Upstart Publishing.

———. 1998. *The Consultant's Guide to Getting Business on the Internet*. New York: John Wiley & Sons.

———. 2000. *Getting Started in Sales Consulting*. New York: John Wiley & Sons.

Hood, Jack B., Benjamin A. Harady, Jr., Harold S. Lewis, Jr. 1999. *Worker's Compensation and Employee Protection Laws*. St. Paul, MN: West Publishing.

Horn, Sam. 2006. *Pop! Stand Out in Any Crowd*. New York: Perigee/Penguin.

Horngren, Charles T., George Foster, and Srikant M. Datar. 2000. *Cost Accounting*. 10th ed. Upper Saddle River, NJ: Prentice Hall.

Hyatt, Carole. 1998. *The Woman's New Selling Game*. New York: McGraw-Hill.

Ittelson, Thomas. 1998. *Financial Statements*. Franklin Lakes, NJ: Career Press.

Ivancevich, John M., Peter Lorenzi, and Steven J. Skinner (with Philip B. Crosby). 1994. *Management*. Burr Ridge, IL: Irwin.

J. K. Lasser Institute. 1994. *How to Run a Small Business*. 7th ed. New York: McGraw-Hill.

Jackson, Barbara J. 2004. *Construction Management Jump Start*. Alameda, CA: Sybex.

Jenkins, Michael D. 1999. *Starting and Operating a Business in the United States*. Palo Alto, CA: Running 'R' Media. (Includes a CD-ROM, with information on all 50 states.)

Jenks, Larry. 1995. *Architectural Office Standards and Practices*. New York: McGraw-Hill.

Jennings, Marianne M. 2006. *Business Ethics*. 5th ed. Mason, Ohio: Thomson.

———. 2006. *The Seven Signs of Ethical Collapse*. New York: St. Martin's Press.

Jentz, Gaylord A., Kenneth W. Clarkson, and Roger LeRoy Miller. 1987. *West's Business Law—Alternate UCC Comprehensive Edition*, 3rd ed. St. Paul, MN: West Publishing.

Joel, Lewin G., III. 1996. *Every Employee's Guide to the Law.* New York: Pantheon Press.

Johnson, Spencer, MD. 1998. *Who Moved My Cheese?* New York: G. P. Putnam.

Johnson, Allan G. 1995. *The Blackwell Dictionary of Sociology.* Cambridge, MA: Blackwell Reference.

Jones, Gerre L. 1983. *How to Market Professional Design Services.* 2nd ed. New York: McGraw-Hill.

————. 1980. *Public Relations for the Design Professional.* New York: McGraw-Hill.

Jones, Katie. 1998. *Time Management.* New York: American Management Association.

Jones, Nancy L., with Phil Philcox. 2000. *The Woman's Guide to Legal Issues.* Los Angeles Renaissance Books.

Kaderlan, Norman. 1991. *Designing Your Practice.* New York: McGraw-Hill.

Kanungo, Rabindra N., and Manuel Mendonca. 1996. *Ethical Dimensions of Leadership.* Thousand Oaks, CA: Sage Publications.

Karlen, Mark. 1993. *Space Planning Basics.* New York: Van Nostrand Reinhold.

Katzenbach, Jon R. 1998. *Teams at the Top.* Boston,: Harvard Business School Press.

Keegan, Warren J., Sandra E. Moriarty, and Thomas R. Duncan. 1995. *Marketing.* 2nd ed. Englewood Cliffs, NJ: Prentice Hall.

Kendall, Dick. 1995. *Nobody Told Me I'd Have to Sell.* New York: Birch Lane Press.

Kendall, Pat. 2000. *Jumpstart Your Online Job Search.* Rocklin, CA: Prima Publishers.

Kennedy, Joyce Lain. 1995. *Hook Up, Get Hired! The Internet Job Search Revolution.* New York: John Wiley & Sons.

Kerzner, Harold. 2003. *Project Management.* 8th ed. New Jersey: John Wiley & Sons.

Kliment, Stephen A. 1998. *Writing for Design Professionals.* New York: W. W. Norton.

————. 1977. *Creative Communications for a Successful Design Practice.* New York: Watson-Guptill.

Knackstedt, Mary. 2005. *The Interior Design Business Handbook.* 4th ed. New York: John Wiley & Sons.

Koren, David. 2005. *Architect's Essentials of Marketing.* New York: John Wiley & Sons.

Kotler, Michael. 2000. *Marketing Management.* Millennium ed. Upper Saddle River, NJ: Prentice Hall.

Kotler, Philip, and Gary Armstrong. 1999. *Principles of Marketing.* 8th ed. Upper Saddle River, NJ: Prentice Hall.

Kotter, John P. 1996. *Leading Change.* Cambridge, MA: Harvard Business School Press.

Krannich, Ronald L., and Caryl Rae Krannich. 1994. *Dynamite Salary Negotiations.* 2nd ed. Manassas Park, VA: Impact Publications.

Kremer, John, and J. Daniel McComas. 1997. *High-Impact Marketing on a Low-Impact Budget.* Rocklin, CA: Rima Publishing.

Landes, William M., and Richard A. Posner. 2003. *Economic Structure of Intellectual Property Law.* Cambridge, MA: Belknap Press.

Laurie, Donald L. 2000. *The Real Work of Leaders.* Cambridge, MA: Perseus Publishing.

Lavington, Camilee (with Stephanie Losee). 1997. *You've Only Got Three Seconds.* New York: Doubleday.

Lawson, Joseph W. R., II. 1998. *How to Develop an Employee Handbook.* 2nd ed. New York: American Management Association.

LeBoeuf, Michael. 1996. *The Perfect Business.* New York: Fireside.

Leider, Richard J. 1997. *The Power of Purpose.* San Francisco: Berrett-Koehler.

Leone, Bruno. 1995. Ethics. San Diego: Greenhaven Press.

Levinson, Jay Conrad. 1998. *Guerrilla Marketing.* 3rd. ed. Boston: Houghton Mifflin.

Levy, Sidney M. 1994. *Project Management in Construction.* 2nd ed. New York: McGraw-Hill.

Lewin, Marsha D. 1995. *The Overnight Consultant.* New York: John Wiley & Sons.

Lewis, James P. 1995. *Project Planning, Scheduling, and Control.* Revised ed. Chicago: Richard D. Irwin.

Liddle, Jeffrey L. 1981. "Malicious Terminations and Abusive Discharges: The Beginning of the End of Employment at Will." *Employee Termination Handbook.* Englewood Cliffs, NJ: Executive Enterprises Publications.

Lientz, Bennet P., and Kathryn P. Rea. 1995. *Project Management for the 21st Century.* San Diego: Academic Press.

Linton, Harold. 2000. *Portfolio Design.* 2nd ed. New York: W. W. Norton.

Lloyd, Joan. 1992. *The Career Decisions Planner.* New York: John Wiley & Sons.

Loebelson, Andrew. 1983. *How to Profit in Contract Design.* New York: Interior Design Books.

Lohmann, William T. 1992. *Construction Specifications. Managing the Review Process.* Boston, MA: Butterworth Architecture.

Lovelock, Christopher H. 1996. *Services Marketing.* 3rd ed. Upper Saddle River, NJ: Prentice Hall.

Low, Robert. 2004. *Accounting and Finance for Small Business Made Easy.* Irvine, CA: Entrepreneur Press.

Lundy, James L. 1994. *Teams.* Chicago: Dartnell Press.

Macdonald, Keith M. 1995. *The Sociology of the Professions.* London: Sage Publications.

MacKay, Harvey. 1997. *Dig Your Well before You're Thirsty.* New York: Currency/Doubleday.

MacKenzie, Alec. 1997. *The Time Trap.* 3rd ed. New York: American Management Association.

Malburg, Christopher R. 1994. *The All-In-One Business Planning Guide.* Holbrook, MA: Bob Adams.

Marconi, Joe. 1999. *The Complete Guide to Publicity.* Lincolnwood, IL: NTC Business Books.

———. 1995. *Marketing Basics for Designers.* New York: John Wiley & Sons.

Mayer, Jeffrey J. 1999. *Success Is a Journey: 7 Steps to Achieving Success in the Business of Life.* New York: McGraw-Hill.

Mancuso, Joseph R. 1985. *How to Write a Winning Business Plan.* Englewood Cliffs, NJ: Prentice Hall.

———. 1993. *How to Prepare and Present a Business Plan.* New York: Fireside Books.

———. 1996. *Mancuso's Small Business Resource Guide.* Naperville, IL: Sourcebooks.

———. 2000. *Nolo's Quick LLC.* Berkeley, CA: Nolo Press.

———. 2000. *Form Your Own Limited Liability Company.* 2nd ed. Berkeley, CA. (The disc that is included with the book contains information for all 50 states.)

Mann, Thorbjoern. 2004. *Time Management for Architects and Designers.* New York: W. W. Norton.

Marshall, Gordon. 1998. *A Dictionary of Sociology.* 2nd ed. New York: Oxford University Press.

Martin, Jane D., and Nancy Knoohuizen. 1995. *Marketing Basics for Designers.* New York: John Wiley & Sons.

Maslow, Abraham H. (edited by Deborah C. Stephens). 2000. *The Maslow Business Reader.* New York: John Wiley & Sons.

Maslow, Abraham H. 1998. *Maslow on Management.* New York: John Wiley & Sons.

Maxwell, John C. 2002. *Your Road Map for Success.* Nashville, TN: Thomas Nelson.

Maxwell, John C., and Jim Dornan. 1997. *Becoming a Person of Influence.* Nashville, TN: Thomas Nelson.

McCarthy, E. Jerome, and William D. Perreault, Jr. 1993. *Basic Marketing*. 11th ed. Homewood, IL: Richard D. Irwin.

McGowan, Maryrose. 1996. *Specifying Interiors*. New York: John Wiley & Sons

McKain, Scott. 2005. *What Customers Really Want*. Nashville, TN: Nelson Business.

McKenzie, Ronald A., and Bruce H. Schoumacher. 1992. *Successful Business Plans for Architects*. New York: McGraw-Hill.

McKinney, Anne. 1996. *Resumes and Cover Letters That Have Worked*. Fayetteville, NC: PREP Publishing.

Means, R. S. 2000. *Means Interior Cost Data 2001*. Kingston, MA: R. S. Means.

Meigs, Robert F., Mary A. Meigs, Mark Battner, and Ray Whittington. 1996. *Accounting: The Basis for Business Decisions*. 10th ed. New York: McGraw-Hill.

Meier, Hans W. 1978. *Construction Specifications Handbook*. 2nd ed. New York: Prentice Hall.

Mendler, Sandra F., and William Odell. 2000. *The HOK Guide to Sustainable Design*. New York: John Wiley & Sons.

Miller, Roger LeRoy, and Gaylord A. Jentz. 2006. *Business Law Today: the Essentials*. 7th ed. Mason, OH: Thomson.

Mintzberg, Henry. 1994. *The Rise and Fall of Strategic Planning*. New York: Free Press.

Mintzberg, Henry, Bruce Ahlstand, and Joseph Lampel. 2005. *Strategy Bites Back*. Upper Saddle River, NJ: Pearson/Prentice Hall.

Mohammed, Rafi. 2005. *The Art of Pricing*. New York: Crown Business.

Mohr, Angie. 2005. *Managing Business Growth: Get a Grip on the Numbers That Count*. Bellingham, WA: Self-Counsel Press.

Molloy, John T. 1996. *The New Woman's Dress for Success Book*. New York: Time Warner Books.

———. 1988. *New Dress for Success*. New York: Time Warner Books.

Morgan, Jim. 1984. *Marketing for the Small Design Firm*. New York: Watson-Guptill.

———. 1998. *Management for the Small Design Firm*. New York: Watson-Guptill.

Morgenstern, Julie. 2004. *Making Work Work*. New York: Fireside Books.

Morrisey, George L. 1996. *Morrisey on Planning: A Guide to Long-Range Planning*. San Francisco: Jossey-Bass.

Morrison, Terri, Wayne A. Conway, and George A. Borden. 2006. *Kiss, Bow, or Shake Hands*, 2nd ed. Avon, MA: Adams Media.

Mose, Arlene K., John Jackson, and Gary Downs. 1997. *Day-to-Day Business Accounting*. Paramus, NJ: Prentice Hall.

Murphy, Tom. 2000. *Web Rules*. Chicago: Dearborn Financial Publishing.

Murray, Katherine. 1997. *Power Point 97*. 3rd ed. San Francisco: Sybex.

Nemnich, Mary B., and Fred E. Jandt. 1999. *Cyberspace Resume Kit*. Indianapolis: JIST Publications.

Newton, Lisa H., and Maureen M. Ford, eds. 1996. *Taking Sides*. 4th ed. Gilford, CT: Dushkin Group.

Nierenberg, Gerard I., and Henry H. Calero. 1993. *How to Read a Person Like a Book*. New York: Barnes & Noble.

Oasis Press. 1997. *Smart Start Your Arizona Business*. Grants Pass, OR: Oasis Press. (Books are available for all 50 states.)

O'Leary, Arthur F. 1992. *Construction Administration in Architectural Practice*. New York: McGraw-Hill.

O'Shea, Tracy, and Jane LaLonde. 1998. *Sexual Harassment*. New York: St. Martin's Griffin.

Oxford American College Dictionary. 2002. New York: Oxford University Press.

Pachter, Barbara, and Marjorie Brody (with Betsy Anderson). 1995. *Complete Business Etiquette Handbook*. Englewood Cliffs, NJ: Prentice Hall.

Pack, Thomas. 1997. *10 Minute Guide to Business Research on the Net*. New York: Que/Macmillan.

Parker, Roger C. 2000. *Relationship Marketing on the Internet*. Holbrook, MA: Adams Media.

Parsons, Patricia J. 2004. *Ethics in Public Relations*. London, England: Kogan Press.

Patterson, Kerry, Joseph Grenny, Ron McMillan, and Al Switzler. 2002. *Crucial Conversations*. New York: McGraw-Hill.

Peters, Tom. *The Brand You 50*. 1999. New York: Knopf.

Petrocelli, William, and Barbara Kate Repa. 1999. *Sexual Harassment on the Job*. 4th ed. Berkeley, CA: Nolo Press.

Phillips, Patricia, and George Mair. 1997. *Know Your Rights: A Legal Handbook for Women Only*. New York: Macmillan.

Pickar, Roger L. 1991. *Marketing for Design Firms in the 1990s*. Washington, DC: American Institute of Architects.

Pile, John. 2005. *A History of Interior Design*. 2nd ed. New York: John Wiley & Sons.

Pinson, Linda. 2004. *Keeping the Books*. 6th ed. Chicago: Dearborn Trade Publishing.

Pinson, Linda, and Jerry Jinnett. 1998. *Keeping the Books*. 4th ed. Lincolnwood, IL: Upstart Publishing.

Pinto, Jeffrey K., and O. P. Kharbanda. 1995. *Successful Project Managers*. New York: Van Nostrand Reinhold.

Piotrowski, Christine M. 2004. *Becoming an Interior Designer*. New York: John Wiley & Sons.

Piotrowski, Christine. 1992. *Interior Design Management*. A Handbook for Owners and Managers. New York: John Wiley & Sons.

Piotrowski, Christine M., and Elizabeth A. Rogers. 2007. *Designing Commercial Interiors*. 2nd ed. New York: John Wiley & Sons.

Pressman, Andrew. 2006. *Professional Practice 101: A Compendium of Business and Management Strategies in Architecture*. New York: John Wiley & Sons.

Pressman, David. 1999. *Patent It Yourself*. 7th ed. Berkeley, CA: Nolo Press.

Plewa, Franklin J., Jr., and George T. Friedlob. 1995. *Understanding Cash Flow*. New York: John Wiley & Sons.

Poage, Waller S. 1987. *Plans, Specs, and Contracts for Building Professionals*. Kingston, MA: RSMeans.

———. 2000. *The Building Professional's Guide to Contract Documents*. 3rd ed. Kingston, MA: RSMeans.

Popyk, Bob. 2000. *Here's My Card*. Los Angeles: Renaissance Books.

Post, Peggy, and Peter Post. 1999. *The Etiquette Advantage in Business*. New York: Harper & Row.

Preiser, Wolfgang F. E., Harvey Z. Rabinowitz, and Edward T. White. 1988. *Post-Occupancy Evaluation*. New York: Van Nostrand Reinhold.

Putman, Anthony O. 1990. *Marketing Your Services*. New York: John Wiley & Sons.

Quinn, Thomas M. 1999. *Quinn's Uniform Commercial Code Commentary and Law Digest*. 2nd ed. St. Paul, MN: West Group.

Quinn, Thomas M. 1999. *Quinn's Uniform Commercial Code Commentary and Law Digest*. Vol. 1991-1:

Rabb, Margaret Y. 1993. *The Presentation Design Book*. 2nd ed. Chapel Hill, NC: Ventana Press.

Rappoport, James E., Robert F. Cushman, and Karen Daroff. 1992. *Office Planning and Design Desk Reference*. New York: John Wiley & Sons.

Reilly, Brian. 1997. *Create Power Point Presentations in a Weekend*. Rocklin, CA: Prima Publishing.

Reznikoff, S. C. 1989. *Specifications for Commercial Interiors*. Revised ed. New York: Watson-Guptill.

Ries, Al, and Jack Trout. 1993. *The 22 Immutable Laws of Marketing*. New York: Harper Business.

Ries, Al and Laura. 2004. *The Origin of Brands*. New York: HarperCollins.

Roane, Susan. 1993. *The Secrets of Savvy Networking*. New York: Time Warner Books.

———. 1988. *How to Work a Room*. New York: Time Warner Books.

Roffer, Robin Fisher. 2002. *Make a Name for Yourself*. New York: Broadway Books.

Rogak, Lisa. 1997. *Smart Guide to Starting a Small Business*. New York: John Wiley & Sons.

Rosen, Harold J. 1981. *Construction Specifications Writing*, 2nd ed. New York: John Wiley & Sons.

Rouse, William B. 1994. *Best Laid Plans*. Englewood Cliffs, NJ: Prentice Hall.

Rubeling, Albert W., Jr. 1994. *How To Start and Operate Your Own Design Firm*. New York: McGraw-Hill.

———. 1986. *Positioning*. New York: Time Warner Books.

Rubin, Harriet. 1999. *Soloing: Realizing Your Life's Ambition*. New York: HarperCollins Business.

Sabath, Anne Marie. 2000. *Beyond Business Casual*. Franklin Lakes, NJ: Career Press.

Sack, Steven Mitchell. 1998. *The Working Woman's Legal Survival Guide*. Paramus, NJ: Prentice Hall.

Sampson, Carol A. 1991. *Techniques for Estimating Materials Costs and Time for Interior Designers*. New York: Watson-Guptill.

Sandler, Corey and Janice Keefe. 2005. *Performance Appraisals That Work*. Avon, MA: Adams Media.

Schlesinger, Eric, and Susan Musich. 2000. *E-Job Hunting*. Indianapolis: Sams/Macmillan.

Schmidt, Jeff. 2000. Disciplined Minds. Lanham, England: Roman & Littlefield Pub.

Schulhofer, Stephen J. 1998. *Unwanted Sex. The Culture of Intimidation and Failure of Law*. Cambridge, MA: Harvard University Press.

Schweich, Thomas A. 1998. *Protect Yourself from Business Lawsuits*. New York: Scribner.

Sheehy, Gail. 1995. *New Passages*. New York: Ballantine.

Sher, Barbara with Barbara Smith. 1994. *I Could Do Anything If I Only Knew What It Was*. New York: Dell Publishing.

Shilling, Dana. 1998. *The Complete Guide to Human Resources and the Law*. Paramus, NJ: Prentice Hall.

Shonka, Mark, and Dan Kosch. 2002. *Beyond Selling Value*. Chicago: Dearborn Trade Publishing.

Siegel, Harry (with Alan Siegel). 1982. *A Guide to Business Principles and Practices for Interior Designers*. Revised ed. New York: Watson-Guptill.

Siegel, Joel G., and Jae K. Shim. 1995. *Accounting Handbook*. 2nd ed. Hauppauge, NY: Barron's.

Silber, Lee. 1998. *Time Management for the Creative Person*. New York: Three Rivers Press.

Silverman, George. 2001. *The Secrets of Word-of-Mouth Marketing*. New York: AMCOM.

Silverstein, Michael J. and Neil Fiske. 2005. *Trading Up*. New York: Penguin Group.

Simmons, H. Leslie. 1985. *The Specifications Writer's Handbook*. New York: John Wiley & Sons.

Siress, Ruth Herrman (with Carolyn Riddle and Deborah Shouse). 1994. *Working Woman's Communications Survival Guide*. Englewood Cliffs, NJ: Prentice Hall.

Siropolis, Nicholas C. 1994. *Small Business Management*. A Guide to Entrepreneurship. 5th ed. Boston, MA: Houghton Mifflin.

Smith, Rob, Mark Speaker, and Mark Thompson. 2000. *The Complete Idiot's Guide to E-Commerce*. Indianapolis: Que/Macmillan.

Snead, G. Lynne, and Joyce Wycoff. 1997. *To Do, Doing, Done*. New York: Fireside Books..

Stanley, Thomas J. 1991. *Selling to the Affluent*. New York: McGraw-Hill.

———. 1993. *Networking with the Affluent*. New York: McGraw-Hill.

Stasiowski, Frank. 1985. *Negotiating Higher Design Fees*. New York: Watson-Guptill.

———. 2001. *Staying Small Successfully*. 2nd ed. New York: John Wiley & Sons.

———. 1993. *Cash Management for the Design Firm*. New York: John Wiley & Sons.

——— 1993. *Value Pricing for the Design Firm*. New York: John Wiley & Sons.

———. 2003. *Architect's Essentials of Winning Proposals*. New York: John Wiley & Sons.

Stasiowski, Frank, and David Burstein. 1994. *Total Quality Project Management for the Design Firm*. New York: John Wiley & Sons

Steelcase, Inc. 1987. *Steelcase the First 75 Years*. Grand Rapids, MI: Steelcase.

Steiner, George. 1997. *A Step-by-Step Guide to Strategic Planning*. New York: Freepress.

Steingold, Fred S. 2005. *Legal Guide for Starting and Running a Small Business*. 8th ed. Berkeley, CA: Nolo Press.

Steingold, Fred S. 2005. *The Employer's Legal Handbook*. 7th ed. Ed. Amy DelPo. Berkeley, CA: Nolo Press.

Stitt, Fred A., ed. 1986. *Design Office Management Handbook*. Santa Monica, CA: Arts and Architecture.

Stone, Brandford. 1975. *Uniform Commercial Code in a Nutshell*. St. Paul, MN: West Publishing.

Stone, Janet, and Jane Bachner. 1994. *Speaking Up*. Revised ed. New York: Carroll & Graf Publishers.

Sweet, Justin. 1985. *Legal Aspects of Architecture, Engineering, and the Construction Process*. 3rd ed. St. Paul, MN: West Publishing.

Talbot, Marianne. 2000. *Make Your Mission Statement Work*. Oxford, UK: How To Books.

Tate, Allen, and C. Ray Smith. 1986. *Interior Design in the 20th Century*. New York: Harper & Row.

Taylor, Jeff (with Doug Hardy). 2004. *Monster Careers*. New York: Penguin Group.

Thompson, Jo Anne Asher, ed. 1992. *ASID Professional Practice Manual*. New York: Watson-Guptill.

Tingley, Judith C., and Lee E. Robert. 1999. *Gender Sell*. New York: Simon & Schuster.

Tracy, Brian. 2003. *Goals!* San Francisco: Berrett-Koehler Publishers, Inc.

———. 1993. *Maximum Achievement*. New York: Fireside Books.

Twitty-Villani, Teri. 1992. *Appearances Speak Louder Than Words*. Portland, OR: Voyager Press.

Underhill, Paco. 1999. *Why We Buy*. New York: Simon & Schuster.

Veitch, Ronald M., Dianne R. Jackman, and Mary K. Dixon. 1990. *Professional Practice*. Winnipeg, MB: Peguis Publishers.

Viscott, David, MD. 1985. *Taking Care of Business. A Psychiatrist's Guide for True Career Success*. New York: William Morrow.

Viscusi, Stephen. 2001. *On the Job*. New York: Three Rivers Press.

Wakita, Osamu A., and Richard M. Linde. 2002. *The Professional Practice of Architectural Working Drawings*. 3rd ed. New York: John Wiley & Sons.

————. 1999. *The Professional Practice of Architectural Detailing*. 3rd ed. New York: John Wiley & Sons.

Walsh, Ciaran. 1996. *Key Management Ratios*. London: F.T. Pitman.

Walters, Dottie, and Lilly Walters. 1997. *Speak and Grow Rich*. Revised ed. Paramus, NJ: Prentice Hall.

Wasserman, Barry, Patrick Sullivan, and Gregory Palermo. 2000. *Ethics and the Practice of Architecture*. New York: John Wiley & Sons.

Weiss, Donald H. 2000. *Fair, Square, and Legal*. 3rd ed. New York: American Management Association.

West Publishing. 1998. *West's Encyclopedia of American Law*. Vol. 8. St. Paul, MN: West Publishing.

Wheatley, Margaret J. 1994. *Leadership and the New Science*. San Francisco: Berrett-Koehler.

Windham, Laurie (with Ken Orton). 2000. *The Soul of the New Consumer*. New York: Allworth Press.

Williams, Jan R. 2000. Miller *GAAP Guide*. San Diego: Harcourt Professional Publications.

Williams, David J. 1996. *Preparing for Project Management*. New York: American Society of Civil Engineers.

Williams, Terrie (with Joe Cooney). 1994. *The Personal Touch*. New York: Time Warner Books.

Wilson, Robert F., and Adele Lewis. 2000. *Barron's Better Résumés for Executives and Professionals*. 4th ed. Hauppauge, NY: Barron's.

Woods, Mary N. 1999. *From Craft to Profession: The Practice of Architecture in Nineteenth-Century America*. Berkeley, CA: University of California Press.

Woodward, Cynthia A. 1990. *Human Resources Management for Design Professionals*. Washington, DC: AIA Press.

World Book Encyclopedia. 2000. Vol. 17. Chicago: World Book.

Yohalem, Kathy C. 1997. *Thinking Out of the Box*. New York: John Wiley & Sons.

Zeithami, Valarie A., and Mary Jo Bitner. 1996. *Services Marketing*. New York: McGraw-Hill.

Zikmund, William G. 1994. *Business Research Methods*. 4th ed. Fort Worth, TX: Dryden Press

Ziglar, Zig. 1991. *Ziglar on Selling*. Nashville, TN: Thomas Nelson.

————. 2003. *Zig Ziglar's Secrets of Closing the Sale*. Updated ed. Grand Rapids, MI: Revell.

INTRODUCTION

This appendix provides you with information on the contents of the CD that accompanies this book. For the latest information, please refer to the ReadMe file located at the root of the CD.

SYSTEM REQUIREMENTS

- A computer with a processor running at 300 Mhz or faster. Windows 98 or later.
- At least 64 MB of total RAM installed on your computer; for best performance, we recommend at least 128 MB
- A CD-ROM drive

NOTE: Many popular word processing programs are capable of reading Microsoft Word files. However, users should be aware that a slight amount of formatting might be lost when using a program other than Microsoft Word.

USING THE CD WITH WINDOWS

To install the items from the CD to your hard drive, follow these steps:
1. Insert the CD into your computer's CD-ROM drive.
2. The CD-ROM interface will appear. The interface provides a simple point-and-click way to explore the contents of the CD.

If the opening screen of the CD-ROM does not appear automatically, follow these steps to access the CD:
1. Click the Start button on the left end of the taskbar and then choose Run from the menu that pops up.
2. In the dialog box that appears, type **d:\start.exe.** (If your CD-ROM drive is not drive d, fill in the appropriate letter in place of *d*.) This brings up the CD Interface described in the preceding set of steps.

WHAT'S ON THE CD

The following sections provide a summary of the software and other materials you'll find on the CD.

Content

This CD-ROM has been developed to accompany the text *Professional Practice for Interior Designers*, 4th edition. The "Content" folder contains over 80 items that are provided to supplement and expand your use of the book. These documents are organized along the book's chapters. They include forms similar to those from design firms taken from the text and revised to use manually; many other forms discussed in the text and designed primarily to be used manually; and brief articles that complement the book. A 180-day trial version of Design Manager software is also included to gain practice in working with professional software programs.

Forms that contain copyright notices must maintain that notice if you use the forms or modify them for your use. For the latest versions of the forms from the United States Internal Revenue Service (Chapter 10 items), visit www.irs.gov.

Documents are presented in Microsoft Word, Microsoft Excel, and Abode Reader. Design Manager is an executable program that must be downloaded and set up to reside on your computer's hard drive.

Applications

The following applications are on the CD:

Design Manager Design Manager is Project Management, Order Tracking, Time Billing and Accounting Software for Interior Designers. This 180-day free trail version is fully functional software that includes all the latest features available in the Design Manager system.

Adobe Reader Adobe Reader is a freeware application for viewing files in the Adobe Portable Document format.

Word Viewer Microsoft Word Viewer is a freeware viewer that allows you to view, but not edit, most Microsoft Word files. Certain features of Microsoft Word documents may not display as expected from within Word Viewer.

Excel Viewer Excel Viewer is a freeware viewer that allows you to view, but not edit, most Microsoft Excel spreadsheets. Certain features of Microsoft Excel documents may not work as expected from within Excel Viewer.

OpenOffice.org OpenOffice.org is a free multi-platform office productivity suite. It is similar to Microsoft Office or Lotus SmartSuite, but OpenOffice.org is absolutely free. It includes word processing, spreadsheet, presentation, and drawing applications that enable you to create professional documents, newsletters, reports, and presentations. It supports most file formats of other office software. You should be able to edit and view any files created with other office solutions.

Shareware programs are fully functional, trial versions of copyrighted programs. If you like particular programs, register with their authors for a nominal fee and receive licenses, enhanced versions, and technical support.

Freeware programs are copyrighted games, applications, and utilities that are free for personal use. Unlike shareware, these programs do not require a fee or provide technical support.

GNU software is governed by its own license, which is included inside the folder of the GNU product. See the GNU license for more details.

Trial, demo, or evaluation versions are usually limited either by time or functionality (such as being unable to save projects). Some trial versions are very sensitive to system date changes. If you alter your computer's date, the programs will "time out" and no longer be functional.

CUSTOMER CARE

If you have trouble with the CD-ROM, please call the Wiley Product Technical Support phone number at (800) 762-2974. Outside the United States, call 1(317) 572-3994. You can also contact Wiley Product Technical Support at **http://support.wiley.com.** John Wiley & Sons will provide technical support only for installation and other general quality control items. For technical support on the applications themselves, consult the program's vendor or author.

To place additional orders or to request information about other Wiley products, please call (877) 762-2974.

CUSTOMER NOTE: IF THIS BOOK IS ACCOMPANIED BY SOFTWARE, PLEASE READ THE FOLLOWING BEFORE OPENING THE PACKAGE.

This software contains files to help you utilize the models described in the accompanying book. By opening the package, you are agreeing to be bound by the following agreement: